Southern Living.

ANNUAL RECIPES
MASTER INDEX

1979-1988

Oxmoor
House.

© 1989 by Oxmoor House, Inc.
Book Division of Southern Progress Corporation
P.O. Box 2463
Birmingham, Alabama 35201

Southern Living® is a federally registered
trademark of Southern Living, Inc.

Library of Congress Catalog Number: 79-88364
ISBN: 0-8487-0675-7
ISSN: 0272-2003

Manufactured in the United States of America
First Printing 1989

Annual Recipes Master Index 1979-1988

Southern Living® Foods Editor: Jean Wickstrom Liles
Editor: Olivia K. Wells
Copy Editor: Mary Ann Laurens
Editorial Assistant: Pam Bullock
Designer: Carol Middleton
Illustrator: Barbara Ball

To find out how you can receive *Southern Living*
magazine, write to *Southern Living*®, P.O. Box C-119,
Birmingham, AL 35283.

Introduction

Along with the ten volumes of *Southern Living Annual Recipes*, this *Annual Recipes Master Index 1979-1988* will be your best helper in the kitchen. This *Master Index* gives you easy access to a decade of the South's most treasured recipes. In a jiffy, you can have any one recipe of the thousands contained in this collection at your fingertips.

This *Master Index* patterns itself after the General Recipe Index of the annual volumes, cross-referencing each recipe by type of dish and major ingredient. And, as in the annual indexes, the page numbers of all microwave recipes are labeled "M."

In addition to listing recipes under both recipe category and major ingredient, this comprehensive index contains categories from the *Southern Living* monthly columns, "Cooking Light" and "Microwave Cookery," as well as categories of wok cooking and food processor recipes.

All of the *Southern Living* recipes from the past ten years are listed in this *Master Index*. As you know, our *Annual Recipes* publishes every recipe appearing in the magazine during the calendar year. Included are those recipes in the bonus articles that are featured in different state issues in different years. To ensure that you find your favorite recipe, the cumulative index gives all of the page references to those recipes that appeared in more than one edition of *Annual Recipes*.

Enjoy your *Master Index*. It will aid you in finding the ideal recipe for every occasion and help you make cooking a little easier and a lot more fun. You'll agree that it's a welcome and helpful addition to your cookbook library.

Jean Wickstrom Liles

Master Index

All recipes are listed by their complete titles under a specific food category and ingredient. The volume is indicated in boldface followed by the page number. All Microwave recipe page numbers are preceded by an "M."

Almonds

Asparagus, Almond, '83 86
Balls, Coconut-Almond, '84 256
Balls, Toasted Almond Chip, '84 240
Bars, Almond-Chocolate, '83 304
Beans Amandine, Green, '79 276; '82 M20
Beans with Almonds, Green, '84 253
Beans with Almonds, Italian Green, '81 207
Bread, Cocoa-Nut Swirl, '80 257
Broccoli with Almonds, Glazed, '80 12
Brownies, Date-and-Almond, '88 217
Brussels Sprouts Amandine, '79 213
Butter, Asparagus with Almond, '84 85
Butter-Nut Strips, '82 167
Cabbage with Almonds, Creamed, '79 4
Cake, Almond-Blueberry Coffee, '85 152
Cake, Almond-Butter, '86 107
Cake, Almond-Butter Wedding, '86 106
Cake, Almond Legend, '82 8
Cake, Almond Whipping Cream, '80 295
Cake Squares, Almond, '79 111
Cake with Cherry Filling,
    Chocolate-Almond, '84 225
Candied Nuts, '81 261
Candy, Almond Brittle, '80 255
Casserole, Almond-Broccoli, '88 62
Catfish Amandine, Mandarin, '84 183
Celery Almondine, '85 116
Celery Amandine, Buttered, '82 98
Cheese, Almond, '88 173
Chicken and Vegetables, Almond, '86 21
Chicken, Spicy Almond, '88 150
Chocolate Almond Velvet, '81 148
Cinnamon Stars, Swiss, '87 293
Cobbler, Blackberry-Almond, '81 132
Coffee, Chocolate-Almond, '84 54
Coffee Delight, Almond-, '84 115
Coleslaw with Grapes and Almonds, '83 59
Combs, Almond, '84 136
Confections, Almond Cream, '87 198
Cookies, Almond, '83 22, 181
Cookies, Almond Butter, '79 52
Cookies, Almond Spritz, '82 306
Cookies, Chocolate-Almond
    Surprise, '88 M45
Cookies, Light Almond, '83 151
Cookies, Swedish Almond, '85 312
Cream, Peach Almond, '82 108
Cream, Peaches 'n' Almond, '86 229
Cream with Fresh Strawberries,
    Almond, '87 93
Crêpes Gelée Amandine, '83 126
Crunch, Almond Butter, '80 301
Curried Almonds, '82 297
Curried Almonds, Cauliflower and Peas
    with, '79 221; '80 82
Custard with Raspberries, Almond
    Creme, '88 174

Danish, Almond, '87 301
Dessert, Chocolate-Almond, '82 306
Dessert, Mocha-Almond, '80 289; '81 62
Drops, Cherry-Almond, '81 20
Drops, Chocolate-Coconut Almond, '87 223
Eggplant with Almonds, '79 179
Filling, Almond, '87 301
Filling, Almond Cream, '85 320
Filling, Ground Almond, '87 14
Fish, Almond Baked, '88 270
Fish Amandine, '85 179
Fish Amandine, Fillet of, '80 M54
Float, Nutmeg-Almond, '84 106
Frosting, Almond-Butter, '86 107
Frosting, Chocolate-Almond, '83 241
Fruit, Almond-Curried, '83 261
Glaze, Honey-Nut, '87 15
Ice Cream Balls, Almond, '86 315
Leaves, Almond Holly, '86 319
Liqueur, Almond-Flavored, '81 287
Meringue Fingers,
    Chocolate-Almond, '84 158

Muffins, Banana-Honey-Nut, '88 62
Muffins, Peachy-Almond, '86 301
Olives, Almond-Stuffed, '88 95
Orange Lake Amandine, '80 99
Pastry, Almond, '85 177
Pastry Cups, Mushroom-Almond, '88 210
Pears, Almond-Stuffed, '83 207
Peas with Almonds, Curried, '88 M294
Phyllo Nests, Nutty, '87 277
Pie Amandine, Chocolate, '83 300
Pie, Creamy Chocolate-Almond, '85 102
Pie, Toasted Almond, '86 163
Pineapple-Almond Delight, '85 96
Pollo Almendrado, '81 193
Potatoes, Almond Fried, '82 25
Potatoes, Broccoli-and-Almond-
    Topped, '83 3
Pudding, Chocolate-Almond, '82 142;
    '88 24
Pudding, Mandarin-Almond, '85 M12
Puffs, Chicken Nut, '81 260
Quiche, Almond-Topped Crab, '79 127
Rice, Almond, '81 195; '85 M112
Rice, Almond Wild, '86 50

Rice with Almonds, Curried, '83 M285
Roca, Almond, '86 49
Rolls, Cherry-Almond, '84 M198
Salad Amandine, Chicken, '81 37
Salad, Cheesy Fruit-'n'-Nut, '87 56
Salad, Chicken-Almond, '81 133
Salad, Cucumber-Almond, '86 147
Salad Dressing, Almond, '81 37
Sandwiches, Chicken-Almond
    Pocket, '81 240; '83 69
Sauce, Almond-Vanilla Custard, '88 M177
Sauce, Cauliflower with Almond, '82 270
Sauce, Chicken in Orange-Almond, '79 219;
    '80 13
Sauce, Mandarin-Almond Cream, '84 183
Sauce, Shrimp-and-Almond, '87 282
Soup, Almond, '79 48
Spread, Almond Cheese, '87 292
Squares, Cream Cheese-Almond, '85 68
Stir-Fry, Almond-Vegetable, '86 222
Syrup, Almond, '82 47
Tarts, Almond Tea, '85 120
Tea, Almond, '85 43; '86 329
Tea, Almond-Lemonade, '86 229
Toast, Almond French, '88 62
Toast Amandine, Baked, '82 47
Toffee Crunch, Almond-, '88 285
Topping, Almond, '85 152; '86 200
Tortoni, Coffee-Almond, '81 30
Truffles, Almond, '83 298
Wafers, Almond-Filled, '88 120

Ambrosia

Anytime Ambrosia, '86 182
Baked Ambrosia, '83 303
Bowl, Ambrosia, '80 138; '84 313
Brunch Ambrosia, '83 57
Cake, Ambrosia, '79 229
Carrot-Marshmallow Ambrosia, '80 5
Chicken Salad Ambrosia, '85 216
Citrus Ambrosia, '82 287
Cookies, Ambrosia, '81 301; '82 110;
    '86 313
Cups, Sherbet Ambrosia, '82 159
Custard Sauce Ambrosia, '84 256
Fruit Ambrosia, Fresh, '88 184
Fruit Ambrosia, Mixed, '83 10
Honey Bee Ambrosia, '83 267
Layered Ambrosia, '88 304
Mold, Ambrosia, '79 241
Mold, Ambrosia Cream Cheese, '79 249
Old-Fashioned Ambrosia, '80 5
Orange Ambrosia Supreme, '79 37
Peach Ambrosia, '83 53
Pie, Ambrosia, '79 284
Pie, Orange Ambrosia, '80 237
Pineapple-Orange Ambrosia, '88 252
Rhubarb Ambrosia, '88 93
Salad, Ambrosia, '83 231
Salad, Carrot-Ambrosia, '81 252
Sherried Ambrosia, '84 324; '86 317
Tropical Ambrosia, '79 74

Anchovies
  Appetizers, Zesty Anchovy, '83 93
  Mayonnaise, Anchovy, '86 179
Appetizers
  Almonds, Curried, '82 297
  Anchovy Appetizers, Zesty, '83 93
  Antipasto Relish, '86 327
  Apple-Phyllo Rolls, '88 213
  Apple Quarters, Honey-Baked, '86 93
  Artichoke Appetizer, Zesty, '80 146
  Artichoke-Caviar Mold, '87 239
  Artichoke-Parmesan Phyllo Bites, '87 54
  Artichokes, Marinated, '87 250
  Artichokes, Spring, '86 62
  Asparagus Croquettes, '85 265
  Asparagus Rolls, '79 296; '80 31
  Asparagus Rollups, '79 63
  Asparagus Roll-Ups, '84 270
  Avocado-Crabmeat Cocktail,
    Sherried, '87 95
  Bacon Appetizers, Hot, '80 248
  Bacon-Chestnut Wraps, '84 M216
  Bacon Rolls, '84 270
  Bacon Rollups, '79 34
  Bacon-Wrapped Pineapple Chunks, '84 25
  Bacon-Wrapped Water Chestnuts, '79 63
  Bagel Crisps, '86 278
  Bean Appetizer, Black, '83 50
  Beef on a Stick, Marinated, '85 234
  Beefy Party Snacks, '80 249
  Beets, Blue Cheese-Stuffed, '88 211
  Broccoli, Cocktail, '80 192
  Broccoli Soup, Mock Cream of, '85 288
  Brussels Sprouts, Marinated, '88 265
  Burgers, Saucy Cocktail, '83 217
  Burritos, Chinese, '87 181
  Canapés, Cheesy Crab, '86 262
  Canapés, Crabmeat, '88 150
  Canapés, Fruit-Topped, '85 80
  Canapés, Green Onion, '84 M216
  Canapés, Hot Crab, '86 70; '87 239
  Canapés, Hot Swiss, '83 259
  Canapés, Lemon-Cheese, '87 93
  Canapés, Mushroom, '80 285
  Canapés, Party, '86 128
  Canapés, Shrimp, '84 116
  Caponata, '87 166
  Caramel Corn, '88 64
  Caramel Corn, Baked, '81 218
  Caramel Good Stuff, Baked, '80 284
  Caraway Wafers, '81 261
  Carrots, Dilled Baby, '84 80
  Carrots, Dill-Spiced, '87 200
  Cauliflower, Crispy Fried, '80 220
  Cauliflower, Dilled, '83 93
  Cauliflower, French-Fried, '86 211
  Cauliflower, Golden Fried, '82 78
  Cauliflower with Cheese Sauce,
    Fried, '87 231
  Caviar Crown, '83 78
  Caviar Mousse, '83 258; '85 86
  Caviar Pie, '79 154
  Caviar Potatoes, '84 80
  Caviar Potatoes, Appetizer, '86 223
  Caviar, Texas, '86 218
  Celery, Creamy Stuffed, '82 102
  Celery, Jalapeño Stuffed, '79 70
  Celery, Stuffed, '82 98
  Celery Trunks, Stuffed, '85 115
  Cereal Nibblers, Great, '82 297
  Cereal Snack, Toasted, '85 215

Ceviche (Marinated Raw Fish), '80 194
Ceviche, Mexican-Style, '88 115
Cheese
  Ball, Blue Cheese, '80 259; '84 221
  Ball, Blue Cheese-Olive, '82 248
  Ball, Bourbon Cheese, '81 57
  Ball, Brandied Blue Cheese, '85 283
  Ball, Carrot-Cheese, '86 325
  Ball, Cheese, '82 161
  Ball, Cheese and Chutney, '87 247
  Ball, Cheese 'n' Beef, '83 230
  Ball, Chicken-Curry Cheese, '85 118
  Ball, Cocktail Cheese, '83 174
  Ball, Curried Shrimp Cheese, '86 135
  Ball, Deviled Pecan, '80 258
  Ball, Festive Cheese, '79 44
  Ball, Holiday Cheese, '79 285
  Ball, Olive Cheese, '80 258
  Ball, Party Cheese, '84 258
  Ball, Party Pecan Cheese, '81 235
  Ball, Peanut Butter-Cheese, '86 136
  Ball, Pecan Cheese, '83 127
  Ball, Peppered Cheese, '79 100
  Ball, Pimiento Cheese, '80 258
  Ball, Pineapple Cheese, '81 160
  Ball, Pineapple-Cheese, '84 26
  Balls, Cheese and Mushroom, '79 63
  Balls, Fried Ham-and-Cheese, '84 221
  Ball, Shrimp-Cheese, '85 208
  Ball, Smoky Salmon Cheese, '82 247
  Balls, Olive-Cheese, '84 206
  Ball, Tangy Cheese, '81 263, 287
  Bars, Bacon-Cheese Toast, '79 36
  Bars, Camembert, '86 58
  Bear Claws, '81 161
  Biscuits, Cheese, '79 296; '80 31
  Biscuits, Cheesy Sausage, '80 78
  Biscuits, Petite Ham and
    Cheese, '79 193
  Biscuits, Tiny Cheese, '80 192
  Bites, Benne Cheese, '80 121
  Bites, Cheesy Pecan, '82 248
  Bites, Curried Swiss, '85 220
  Bites, Fried Cheese, '82 77
  Bit-of-Brie Appetizer, '88 M8
  Bonbons, Cheese, '87 93
  Cracker Nibbles, Cheese, '84 328
  Crackers, Cheddar, '84 236
  Crispies, Cheese-Bacon, '84 270
  Crispies, Pecan-Cheese, '87 168
  Cucumber Slices, Cheesy, '84 80
  Cups, Cottage Cheese-Spinach, '87 190
  Cutouts, Sesame-Cheese, '82 296
  Feta Cheesecakes, Little, '86 277
  Flaming Cheese, '84 187
  Fondue, Cheese, '81 40
  Fried Cheese, Italian-Style, '83 250
  Herb Cheese, Pot-of-, '85 210
  Herbed Cheese, '88 152
  Little Bits, '79 196
  Log, Cheesy Surprise, '82 247
  Log, Garlic Cheese, '85 21
  Logs, East Indian Cheese, '88 173
  Log, Toasted Pecan Cheese, '86 M288
  Meat-and-Cheese Appetizers, '87 7
  Mexicali Appetizer, Cheesy, '82 108
  Mold, Blue Cheese, '85 210
  Mold, Cheese-and-Wine, '84 197
  Mold, Garlic-Chive Cheese, '85 210
  Mousse, Roquefort, '82 71
  Nuggets, Cheesy Ham, '81 290

Olive Appetizers, Cheesy, '85 113
Olive Appetizers, Cheesy-, '87 246
Pasta Bites, Pesto-Cheese, '87 251
Pastries, Cream Cheese, '80 250
Pastries, Date-Filled Cheese, '83 259
Pastry, Brie Wrapped in, '80 241
Pastry, Sausage Balls in
  Cheese, '80 248
Patty, Lemon-Pepper Cheese, '84 117
Peppers, Cheesy Jalapeño, '80 195
Phyllo-Cheese Triangles, '87 246
Phyllo Triangles,
  Cheese-Filled, '83 259
Phyllo Triangles,
  Spinach-Ricotta, '88 212
Pie, Cheesy Hors d'Oeuvre, '88 91
Potato Skins, Cheesy, '82 78
Puffs, Bavarian Cheese, '80 191
Puffs, Cheese, '79 110
Puffs, Cheese-and-Spinach, '87 246
Puffs, Cream Cheese, '84 151
Puffs, Gouda-Shrimp, '79 234
Puffs, Ham-and-Cheese, '86 277
Puffs, Mexican Cheese, '87 8
Puffs, Surprise Cheese, '79 295;
  '80 31
Quiches, Miniature
  Bacon-Cheese, '83 93
Quiches, Miniature Cheese, '80 150
Ring, Cheese, '81 261
Ring, Strawberry-Cheese, '86 14
Roll, Chili-Cheese, '84 114
Roll, Ham-and-Cheese, '79 234
Rollups, Ham-and-Swiss, '85 113
Round, Brie Appetizer, '82 41
Round, Herbed Cheese, '84 300
Rounds, Cheese, '86 262
Rounds, Parmesan, '85 131
Rounds, Parmesan Party, '82 248
Salami-Cheese Snacks, '88 96
Sour Cream Appetizer, Cheesy, '84 51
Squares, Cream
  Cheese-Almond, '85 68
Squares, Green Chile-Cottage
  Cheese, '86 85
Squares, Jalapeño Cheese, '80 195
Squares, Quick Cheese, '84 191
Sticks, Parmesan, '82 297
Sticks, Parmesan Sesame, '81 39
Sticks, Peppery Cheese, '81 M289
Straws, Cheese, '80 150; '82 137;
  '88 77
Tartlets, Cheese, '88 211
Tarts, Blue Cheese
  Appetizer, '85 300; '86 18
Three-Cheese Appetizer, '80 174
Toast Treats, Cheese, '83 100
Twists, Double Cheese, '85 131
Wafers, Cheese, '80 151
Wafers, Pecan-Cheese, '81 119
Wedges, Cheesy Party, '84 84
Wontons with Hot Sauce,
  Cheese, '83 74
Cherries, Stuffed, '85 81
Chicken Bites, Curried, '85 40
Chicken Bites, French-Fried, '85 160
Chicken, Deep-Fried Walnut, '87 175
Chicken Little Fingers, '80 249
Chicken Liver and Bacon Roll-Ups, '80 200;
  '81 57
Chicken Livers, Party, '83 242

Appetizers *(continued)*

Chicken Liver Turnovers, '79 141
Chicken-Mushroom Appetizers, '88 210
Chicken Nuggets, Baked, '81 149
Chicken Nuggets, Lemon-, '87 283
Chicken Nuggets Supreme, '85 160
Chicken Nuggets with Pineapple
  Sauce, '84 236
Chicken Nut Puffs, '81 260
Chicken-Pecan Log, '81 290
Chicken Puffs, Appetizer, '85 72
Chicken Salad, Old-Fashioned, '83 79
Chicken Salad Tarts, '84 257
Chicken Tempura Delight, '85 66
Chicken Terrine, Vegetable-, '83 224
Chicken Wings, Broiled, '80 149
Chicken Wings, Teriyaki, '85 300; '86 18
Chile-Sausage Squares, '86 297
Chiles Rellenos, Bite-Size, '87 246
Chutney Roll, '83 259
Chutney with Cream Cheese,
  Cranberry-Amaretto, '87 244
Cinnamon Wafers, '84 324
Clam Crisps, '80 151
Clams Casino, '81 125
Clams Oreganata, '85 104
Confetti Appetizers, '84 191
Crab Crisps, '79 63
Crab, Devilish Deviled, '85 264
Crabmeat Balls, '88 150
Crab Mold, '85 318
Crab Puffs, '80 20; '84 269
Crab Snacks, '83 93
Crab-Zucchini Bites, '84 M216
Cracker Bread, Sesame, '87 2
Crackers, Easy Bisque, '83 252
Crackers, Fennel-Rye, '87 2
Crackers, Florida, '86 179
Cracker Snackers, '86 229
Crackers, Oatmeal-Wheat Germ, '84 236
Crackers, Olive-Rye Snack, '84 191
Crawfish on Eggplant, Soft-Shell, '88 222
Cucumber Delights, '84 117
Cucumber Fingers, Fried, '86 146
Cucumber Rounds, '88 78
Dates, Apricot-Stuffed, '80 250
Dips
  Apricot Dip, '86 178
  Artichoke Dip, Deluxe, '80 87
  Artichoke Dip, Seasoned
    Mayonnaise, '80 87
  Artichoke-Seafood Dip, Hot, '80 241
  Artichoke Seafood Dip, Hot, '85 M212
  Avocado Dip, '80 285; '81 57, 306
  Avocado Dip, Zippy, '82 9; '83 69
  Bacon Dip, '82 197
  Bacon-Guacamole Dip, '85 25
  Basket, Dips and Dippers in a, '83 171
  Bean Dip, Hotshot, '87 195
  Bean Dip, Prairie Fire, '80 195
  Beau Monde Dip in Rye Bread,
    Party, '83 127
  Beef Dip, Chipped, '88 M8
  Beef Dip, Hot Cheesy, '80 85
  Blue Cheese Dip, '80 285; '83 169
  Braunschweiger-and-Beer Dip, '85 69
  Broccoli Dip, Cheesy, '83 92
  Broccoli-Garlic Dip, '82 59
  Cabbage, Dock Dip in, '86 179
  Cheese-and-Chile Dip, '83 31

Cheese and Crab Dip, Hot, '81 261
Cheese-Bean Dip, '85 208
Cheese Dip, Meaty, '82 59
Cheese Dip, Seaside, '85 284
Cheese Dunk, Deviled, '80 265
Cheese-Garlic Dip, '80 192
Chicken Dip, Hot, '80 86
Chile-Beef Dip, Hot, '83 218
Chile-Cheese Dip, '87 173
Chile con Queso, '80 194; '81 195
Chile con Queso Supreme, '80 265
Chile Dip, Hot, '82 248
Chili con Queso Dip, '86 81
Chili Dip, '82 161; '88 218
Chili Dip, Cheesy, '80 150
Clam Dip, '79 151; '80 265
Clam Dip, Hot, '82 59
Confetti Snack Dip, '79 107
Crab Dip, Creamy, '80 M135
Crab Dip, Oven-Baked, '82 59
Crab Dip, Tangy, '83 5
Cranberry-Horseradish Dip, '85 65
Cream Cheese Dip, Fruited, '88 261
Cream Cheese-Onion Dip, '79 236
Crudité Dip, '86 105
Crudité Platter with Dip, '84 139
Curried Dip, '81 262
Curry Dip, '80 84; '81 9; '85 132;
  '86 184; '87 25
Curry Dip, Creamy, '84 206
Deviled Dip, '87 25
Dill Dip, '80 265
Dilled Garden Dip, '84 324
Egg Dip, Festive, '79 285
Fiesta Dip, '81 206
Fish Dip, Smoked, '84 46
Fruit Dip, Coconut-Honey, '84 171
Fruit Dip, Creamy, '84 51
Fruit Dip, Fresh, '80 265
Fruit Dip, Heavenly, '81 160
Fruit Dip, Marshmallow, '84 171
Grand Marnier Dip, '86 142
Green Goddess Dip, '84 159
Guacamole, '79 185; '80 74; '83 179
Guacamole, Creamy, '79 91; '83 174
Guacamole Dip, '86 4
Guacamole in Shells, '86 74
Herbal Dip, '86 14
Holiday Dip, '83 321; '84 289
Leek Dip, Creamy, '86 77
Mexican Appetizer, Chilled, '87 197
Mint Dip with Fresh Fruit, '87 146
Nacho Dip, '83 239
Nacho Dip, Layered, '81 261
Olive-Relish Dip, '84 205
Onion Dip, Cheesy, '83 145
Onion Dip, Chunky, '84 257
Orange Dip, Creamy, '84 117; '87 247
Orange Dip, Spicy, '85 230
Orange Sour Cream Dip, '79 208
Oyster Dip, Smoked, '79 233
Parsley-Dill Dip with Fresh
  Vegetables, '85 79
Peach Dip, Creole, '80 142
Pea Dip, Black-Eyed, '81 8
Peanut Butter Dip, '86 135
Peanut Butter-Honey Dip, '85 19
Pepper-Cheese Stacks, '87 80
Pineapple Dip, Cheesy, '80 249
Pineapple-Ginger Dip, '86 104
Salsa Cruda, '87 180

Salsa, Fresh Summer, '87 89
Salsa Picante, '84 108
Seafood Dip, '79 3
Seafood Dip, Hot Cheesy, '84 221
Shrimp Dip, '86 84; '88 M261
Shrimp Dip, Hot, '87 190
Shrimp Dip, Quick, '79 153
Shrimp Dip, Zesty, '80 150
Six-Layer Dip, '81 160
Sour Cream Dip, '86 278
South-of-the-Border Dip, '81 235
Spinach con Queso, Easy, '88 101
Spinach Dip, '80 86; '86 159;
  '87 25, 214
Spinach Dip, Cheesy, '82 59
Spinach Dip, Creamy, '88 132
Spinach Dip, Hot, '80 249
Spinach Dip in Cabbage, '82 155
Sugar Snap Dip, '88 91
Tarragon Dip, '83 78
Tofu Dip, '86 109
Tostada Dip, '84 206
Tuna-Curry Dip, '84 31
Tuna Dip, Low-Cal, '87 25

Vegetable Dip, '79 52; '82 161
Vegetable Dip, Creamy, '82 132;
  '83 99, 180
Vegetable Dip,
  Cucumber-Cheese, '83 128
Vegetable Dip, Fresh, '80 249
Vegetable Dip, Starburst, '82 248
Vegetable Dip, Tangy, '87 196
Vegetable Dip, Zippy, '84 256
Vegetable Garden Dip, '85 215
Water Chestnut Dip, '80 86; '86 183
Yogurt Dip, Fruited, '84 171
Yogurt Herring Dip, '80 232
Zesty Party Dip, '83 259
Eggplant Appetizer, '83 187
Eggplant Caviar, '88 262
Eggplant, Fried Parmesan, '87 166
Egg Rolls, '86 81
Egg Rolls, Chiles Rellenos, '86 296
Eggrolls, Shrimp and Pork, '82 240; '83 18
Egg Rolls, Vegetarian, '86 148
Endive Boats, '84 80
Escargots Provençal, '82 238; '83 156
Fast Goodies, '84 206
Fondue, Fruitcake, '84 258
Frankfurter Appetizers, Bourbon, '85 207
Franks, Pickled Party, '83 174
Franks, Saucy Appetizer, '84 M12
Franks, Tipsy, '85 52
Frog Legs, Crispy, '80 99
Fruit and Cheese Tray, '83 171
Fruit Bowl, Sparkling Fresh, '80 146
Fruit Cascade, '86 104
Fruit Cup, Appetizer, '86 131
Fruit Kabobs, '86 181

Fruit Kabobs with Coconut
  Dressing, '87 251
Fruit with Dressing, Chilled, '85 222
Green Onion Teasers, '82 42
Guacamole Mold, '86 184
Ham-Filled Party Puffs, '84 116
Ham Rolls, '79 153
Ham Rolls, Party, '85 318
Ham Turnovers, Chile-, '88 64
Ham Turnovers, Party, '82 39
Ham Twists, Deviled, '82 86
Hawaiian Dream Boats, '86 151
Hot Munch, Oriental, '87 8
Jalapeños, Shrimp-Stuffed, '88 115
June Bugs, '85 11
Meatballs
    Bacon-Wrapped Meatballs, '79 81
    Brandied Meatballs, '83 78
    Burgundy-Bacon Meatballs, '80 283
    Chafing Dish Meatballs, '81 260
    Chestnut Meatballs, '79 110
    Cocktail Meatballs, '79 63, 207
    Flavorful Meatballs, '84 206
    Ham Balls, '86 256
    Ham Balls, Appetizer, '82 39
    Polynesian Meatballs, '80 207
    Saucy Party Meatballs, '80 149
    Sauerkraut Meatballs, '86 257
    Spiced Meatballs, '79 284
    Sweet-and-Sour Meatballs, '82 247
    Sweet-and-Sour Party
        Meatballs, '79 233
    Tamale Meatballs, '80 194
    Venison Sausage Balls, '80 42
    Zesty Meatballs, '80 250
Melon Balls, Minted, '87 162
Melon, Berry-Filled, '86 93
Mints, Party, '81 119
Mix, Granola Snack, '86 229
Mix, Mexicali Snack, '86 230
Mix, Party, '87 257
Mix, Quick Party, '83 92
Mix, Raisin-Nut Party, '83 60
Mix, Snack-Attack Party, '84 328
Mix, Spicy Party, '81 M138
Mousse, Caviar, '82 71; '83 258; '85 86
Mousse, Crab, '79 117
Mousse, Horseradish, '84 126
Mousse, Irresistible Salmon, '79 284
Mousse, Mustard, '84 127; '86 184
Mousse, Oyster, '81 245
Mousse, Salmon, '83 79
Mousse, Salmon Dill, '81 21
Mousse, Shrimp, '87 196, 251
Mousse, Smoked Oyster, '84 320
Mousse, Tuna, '80 275
Mushroom-Almond Pastry Cups, '88 210
Mushroom Appetizers, Stuffed, '88 210
Mushroom Caps, Crab-Stuffed, '84 160
Mushroom Caps, Marinated, '83 128
Mushroom Caps, Vegetable, '81 246
Mushroom Delight, Stuffed, '87 281
Mushroom Logs, '84 206
Mushroom Rollups, '85 318
Mushrooms, Black Olive-Stuffed, '86 258
Mushrooms, Cheese 'n'
  Bacon-Stuffed, '86 258
Mushrooms, Crab-Stuffed, '81 190
Mushrooms, Crawfish-Stuffed, '86 258
Mushrooms, Drunk, '83 174
Mushrooms, Easy Marinated, '86 217

Mushrooms, Elegant Cheese-Stuffed, '81 57
Mushrooms, Flavor-Stuffed, '85 288
Mushrooms, French-Fried, '82 78
Mushrooms, Italian
  Sausage-Stuffed, '83 127
Mushrooms, Marinated, '80 82, 270;
  '86 135
Mushrooms, Marinated Herb, '86 327
Mushrooms, Parmesan Stuffed, '83 115
Mushrooms, Pâté-Stuffed, '85 118
Mushrooms, Pecan-Stuffed, '84 261
Mushrooms, Pesto-Stuffed, '86 150

Mushrooms, Pistachio-Stuffed, '86 141
Mushrooms, Ricotta-Stuffed, '85 20
Mushrooms, Sausage-Stuffed, '80 248
Mushrooms, Seasoned Stuffed, '84 206
Mushrooms, Shrimp-Stuffed, '80 M135
Mushrooms, Spinach-Stuffed, '86 81;
  '88 131, M261
Mushrooms, Stuffed, '79 212; '81 239;
  '83 13, 66, 126, 136
Mushrooms Stuffed with Crab, '82 249
Mushrooms, Tipsy, '84 M216
Mushrooms with Stems, '86 258
Mushrooms with Tartar Sauce,
  French-Fried, '86 233
Mushroom Tarts, '88 161
Mushroom Tarts, Hot Sherried, '83 78
Nachos, Best-Ever, '79 91
Nachos, Chicken, '84 244
Nachos, Easy, '84 30
Nachos, Make-Ahead, '80 M135
Nachos Supreme, '81 306
Nectarine Cocktail, '85 107
Nuts, Hot Chili, '81 254
Nuts, Sherry-Orange, '86 M289
Nuts, Spiced, '84 257
Nuts, Spicy, '82 161
Nuts, Spicy Curried, '82 250
Olive Quiche Appetizers, '86 159
Orange-Berry Appetizer, '85 81
Orange Halves, Broiled, '85 288
Oyster Nachos, Texas, '87 39
Oysters à la Casino, '80 296
Oysters, Barbecued, '82 247
Oysters Buccaneer, '87 40
Oysters in Patty Shells, '85 257
Pâtés
    Braunschweiger Pâté, '83 251
    Cheese Pâté, Layered, '86 105
    Chicken Liver Pâté, '79 153; '81 235;
        '83 108; '84 205; '88 M132
    Chutney-Cheese Pâté, '84 152
    Cognac, Pâté with, '86 159
    Country Pâté, '86 66
    Crab Pâté, '79 233

    Cream Cheese Pâté, '80 154
    Duck Liver Pâté, '79 227
    Duck Pâté, '79 226
    en Croûte, Pâté, '86 65
    Ham Pâté, '85 279
    Liver-Cheese Pâté, '85 276
    Maison, Pâté, '84 222
    Mock Pâté, '87 251
    Pastry, Pâté, '86 65
    Pork Pâté with Spinach and
        Cream, '83 224
    Shrimp Pâté with Dill Sauce, '85 39
    Spread, Quick Pâté, '84 117
    Vegetable-Chicken Pâté, '86 66
Pea Appetizers, Sugar Snap, '86 115
Peanuts, Sugared, '82 249
Pea Pinwheels, Black-Eyed, '85 300;
  '86 18
Pears, Pineapple-Honey, '86 94
Peas and Dip, Crunchy Snow, '86 62
Peas, Crab-Stuffed Snow, '85 288
Peas, Stuffed Snow, '84 80
Peas with Dip, Sugar, '86 170
Pecans, Barbecued, '83 222
Pecans, Buttery Toasted, '88 77
Pecans, Coffee 'n' Spice, '88 256
Pecans, Hot Pepper, '85 4
Pecans, Orange, '87 292
Pecans, Pepper, '87 137
Pecans, Southern Salted, '80 285
Pecans, Spiced, '79 296; '80 31
Pecans, Sugar and Spice, '82 297
Pecans, Sugar-and-Spice, '86 121
Pecans, Toasted, '84 321; '86 229
Pecans, Toasted Chili, '85 154
Pepperoni Rolls, Ground-, '83 244
Pickles, French-Fried, '82 77
Pickles, Fried Dill, '84 206
Pineapple and Strawberries,
  Skewered, '84 251
Pineapple Delight, Fresh, '79 111
Pineapple Spritz, '86 94
Pita Bread Triangles, '88 211
Pizza-Burger Snacks, '84 30
Pizza Party Snacks, '86 262
Pizzas, Cocktail, '79 110
Pizza Slices, '84 269
Pizza Snacks, Tasty Little, '79 248
Pizza Squares, '87 168
Pizzas, Quick Little, '88 227
Pizza Turnovers, Little, '85 327
Pizzettes, Party, '80 192
Popcorn and Peanuts, Candied, '82 295
Popcorn, Bacon-Cheese, '86 74
Popcorn Balls, Nutty, '88 227
Popcorn, Caramel, '79 219; '86 M212
Popcorn, Crispy Caramel, '85 247
Popcorn Crunch, Cinnamon-, '86 136
Popcorn, Garlic, '83 M315
Popcorn, Harvest, '84 300
Popcorn Mix, Curried, '86 326
Popcorn, Nutty, '85 208
Popcorn, Orange, '86 230
Popcorn, Oriental, '86 74
Popcorn, Pizza-Flavored, '85 236
Popcorn, Pretzel, '84 30
Popcorn Scramble, '87 185
Popcorn, Sesame-Cheese, '79 220
Popcorn Snack, Spiced, '87 8
Potatoes, Ham-Stuffed New, '88 211
Potato Skins, Baked, '86 81

Appetizers *(continued)*

Pretzels, Chewy Soft, '87 159
Pretzels, Homemade, '84 159
Pretzels, Soft, '83 18
Puff Nibbles, '84 191
Quiche Squares, '84 222
Quiches, Tarragon Cocktail, '84 127
Relish Tree, Christmas, '84 257
Riblets, Sweet-and-Sour, '85 276
Rice Balls, '81 51
Rice Mix, Crunchy, '85 327
Rumaki, '80 136
Rye Appetizers, Party, '86 262
Salmon Ball, '80 149; '86 262
Salmon, Drizzled Smoked, '88 91
Salmon Log, '81 22
Salmon Party Roll, '83 127
Sandwiches, Asparagus Spear, '84 165
Sandwiches, Bread Basket of, '86 126
Sandwiches, Dainty Cucumber, '81 119
Sandwiches, Stacking, '86 127
Sandwich Wreath, Festive, '86 333
Sausage-Bacon Rollups, '88 51
Sausage Pinwheels, '80 209
Sausage, Sweet-and-Sour, '88 296
Sausages with Mustard Sauce,
    Smoked, '81 56
Scallop Appetizer, '86 155
Scallop Appetizers, Flaky, '86 327
Scallops, Bacon-Wrapped, '87 94
Seafood Appetizer, Layered, '88 2
Seafood Mold, Chilled, '86 70
Seafood Tartlets, '87 247
Sesame Bites, '88 67
Seviche Cocktail, '83 258

Shrimp Bayou, '88 261
Shrimp Cocktail, '87 173
Shrimp, Coconut-Beer, '85 230
Shrimp Conga, Rock, '80 2
Shrimp, Dilled, '88 150
Shrimp Dippers, '84 324
Shrimp, Icy Marinated, '84 215
Shrimp-in-a-Pickle, '86 326
Shrimp Kabobs, '80 150
Shrimp Manale, '86 268
Shrimp Miniquiches, '87 146
Shrimp Mold, '87 94
Shrimp-Pineapple Appetizer, '85 80
Shrimp Rémoulade, '83 173
Shrimp, Spicy Boiled, '84 289
Shrimp Toast, '86 91
Shrimp Tree, '83 320; '84 288; '85 318
Shrimp with Cocktail Sauce, Boiled, '79 151
Shrimp with Herbed Jalapeño
    Cheese, '87 112
Shrimp, Zesty Marinated, '87 173
Snackwiches, '88 172
Soup, Appetizer Tomato, '86 258

Spinach-Filled Phyllo Triangles, '84 52
Spinach Madeleine in Chafing Dish, '85 319
Spinach Quichelets, '87 67
Spinach Quiches, Miniature, '82 38
Spinach Squares, '88 131
Spinach Supreme, Layered, '82 38
Spinach Tarts, '82 249
Spinach Triangles, Phyllo-, '87 53
Spreads and Fillings
    Aloha Spread, '83 93
    Antipasto Spread, '81 25
    Apricot Brie Spread, '86 275
    Apricot-Cream Cheese
        Spread, '82 161; '87 158
    Artichoke-Crab Spread, Hot, '85 81
    Artichoke Hearts with Caviar, '79 142
    Artichoke Spread, Hot, '79 110
    Beef Spread, Hot, '83 50; '84 M216
    Beer Cheese Spread, '81 160
    Beer-Cheese Spread, '85 69
    Braunschweiger-Onion Spread, '79 82
    Broccamoli Curry Spread, '88 55
    Caraway Spread, '85 276
    Caviar-Cream Cheese Spread, '84 256
    Cheese-Horseradish Spread, '84 222
    Cheese-Olive Spread, '79 82
    Cheese Spread, '86 135
    Cheese Spread, Confetti, '84 256
    Cheese Spread, Creamy
        Sweet, '79 264
    Cheese Spread, German, '79 82
    Cheese Spread, Hawaiian, '87 158
    Cheese Spread, Tipsy, '80 150
    Cheese Spread, Zippy, '85 4
    Cheesy Beer Spread, '87 196
    Chicken Salad Party Spread, '88 M8
    Chicken Spread, Festive, '87 158
    Chicken Spread, Tasty, '84 193
    Corned Beef Spread, '87 196
    Crabmeat Spread, '79 81
    Crabmeat Spread, Layered, '83 127
    Crab Soufflé Spread, '85 4
    Crab Spread, Baked, '80 86
    Crab Spread, Superb, '81 235
    Cream Cheese Spread,
        Deviled, '81 235
    Cucumber Spread, '79 295; '80 31
    Edam-Sherry Spread, '84 257
    Egg Mound, Frosted, '79 33
    Egg, Sour Cream, and Caviar
        Spread, '85 279
    Fruit and Cheese Spread, '81 245
    Fruit-and-Cheese Spread,
        Nutty, '87 246
    Fruit Spread, '85 135
    Garden Spread, '86 135
    Garlic Spread, '85 111
    Gruyère-Apple Spread, '81 160
    Ham and Pimiento Spread, '80 285;
        '81 56
    Ham Spread, Cold, '82 248
    Ham Spread, Country, '87 8
    Herb-Cream Cheese Spread, '83 24
    Honey-Nut Spread, '87 157
    Italian Spread, '85 135
    Jalapeño-Cheese Spread, '82 248
    Liver Spread, Sherried, '80 86
    Mushroom Spread, Hot, '81 190
    Olive Spread, Creamy, '81 290
    Olive Spread, Tomatoes with, '85 114
    Party Bread Spread, '82 161

    Pea Spread, Black-Eyed, '86 77
    Pimiento Cheese, Hot, '87 173
    Radish Spread, Fresh, '84 166
    Salmon-and-Horseradish
        Spread, '87 146
    Salmon Spread, '81 149
    Salmon Spread, Smoked, '84 324
    Seafood Spread, '86 M58; '87 146
    Shrimp Spread, '81 306; '85 135;
        '87 111
    Shrimp Spread, Chunky, '85 300;
        '86 18
    Shrimp Spread, Curried, '87 158
    Shrimp Spread, Tempting, '79 57
    Sombrero Spread, '87 111
    Spinach Spread, '88 132
    Spinach Spread, Savory, '82 180
    Sweet 'n' Sour Spread, '86 184
    Tomato-Cheese Spread, '81 157
    Tomato-Cheese Spread, Fiery, '87 196
    Turkey Party Spread, '83 282
    Vegetable Party Spread, '84 166
    Vegetable Sandwich Spread, '85 135
    Watercress Spread, '88 103
Steak-and-Chestnut Appetizers,
    Marinated, '84 323
Steak, Marinated Flank, '83 258; '88 262
Strawberries with Chocolate Cream, '85 81
Strawberries with Walnuts, Stuffed, '85 122
Tabbouleh, '88 211
Taco Appetizer, Layered, '84 206
Tamales, Miniature, '85 154
Tomato Bites, '84 80
Tomatoes, Cucumber-Stuffed
    Cherry, '88 262
Tomatoes, Stuffed Cherry, '84 160;
    '88 95, 212
Tortilla Appetizers, Tex-Mex, '86 297
Tortilla Dippers, Rolled, '86 4
Tostados, Hot Chile Salsa with
    Homemade, '88 115
Tuna Mound, '80 276
Tuna-Pecan Ball, '87 94
Turnovers, Meat, '86 326
Vegetable Appetizer, Tarragon, '83 277
Vegetable Party Tray, Fresh, '82 122
Venison Tenderloin Appetizers, '88 249
Walnuts, Chinese Fried, '81 254
Wings, Hot Buffalo, '87 176
Wings, Satan's, '87 214
Wonton Nibbles, '85 287
Zucchini Caviar, '88 212
Zucchini French Fries, '82 78
Zucchini Hors d'Oeuvres, '80 151
Zucchini Pizzas, '88 212
Zucchini with Cocktail Sauce, French
    Fried, '86 146
Apples
Aspic, Sunshine Apple, '81 73
Baked Alaska, Apple, '80 226
Baked Apple Quarters, Honey-, '86 93
Baked Apples, '79 276; '86 40
Baked Apples, Easy, '82 22, 238
Baked Apples, Honey-, '83 234; '84 244
Baked Apples, Imperial, '82 273
Baked Apples, Maple, '85 232
Baked Apples, Orange-Pecan, '85 45
Baked Apples with Orange Sauce, '84 314
Baked Ham and Apples, '82 M237
Baked Mincemeat-Filled Apples, '80 276
Bake, Squash and Apple, '79 210

Bake, Sweet Potato-Apple, '83 25; '86 282
Bars, Apple Butter, '84 153
Beets and Apples, '80 137; '88 155
Betty, Apple Brown, '83 213
Betty, Pineapple-Apple, '85 46
Brandied Apples, '81 248
Brandied Apples and Cream, '82 M237
Bread, Apple, '79 205; '80 226
Bread, Apple Butter, '84 49; '86 69
Bread, Apple-Nut, '79 12; '85 281
Bread, Apple Pull-Apart, '86 330
Bread, Apple Swirl, '85 4
Bread, Banana-Apple, '85 250
Bread, Fresh Apple-Nut, '87 256
Bread, Zucchini-Apple, '87 255
Brownies, Frosted Apple, '86 216
Burgers, Apple, '86 137
Butter, Apple, '79 200; '81 217
Butter, Half-Hour Apple, '81 203
Cabbage and Apples, Red, '85 32
Cabbage with Apples and Franks, '87 42
Cake, Apple, '83 312; '84 262
Cake, Apple Cider Pound, '84 10
Cake, Apple Coconut, '80 226
Cake, Apple Coffee, '81 249
Cake, Apple-Nut, '87 76
Cake, Apple-Pecan Coffee, '84 242
Cake, Apple Pie, '82 226; '86 301
Cake, Apple Slice, '85 93
Cake, Dried-Apple, '79 13
Cake, Dried Apple Stack, '85 242
Cake, Fresh Apple-Date, '83 300
Cake, Golden Apple-Oatmeal, '86 301
Cake Squares, Apple-Date Dream, '85 10
Cake Squares, Apple-Orange, '84 150
Candied Red Apples, '81 217
Candy Apples, '84 243
Caramel Apples, '79 220
Caramel Apples, Old English, '85 231
Casserole, Apple-Cheese, '84 287
Casserole, Apple-Egg, '85 44
Casserole, Apple Ham, '79 213
Casserole, Cranberry-Apple, '83 311
Casserole, Squash and Apple, '79 209
Cheesecake, Dieter's Apple, '86 318
Chicken, Apple, '85 57
Chutney, Tomato-Apple, '84 180

Cider, Holiday, '82 264
Cider, Hot Mexican, '87 213
Cider, Hot Mulled, '79 205; '84 323
Cider, Hot Spiced Apple, '84 318
Cider Ice, '83 162
Cider Nog, Hot Apple, '84 42

Cider, Red Apple, '80 259
Cider Sauce, '87 224
Cider, Sparkling Apple, '88 276
Cinnamon Apples, Rosy, '87 M37
Cinnamon Apples with Brandied Date
    Conserve, '85 315
Cobbler, Apple-Pecan, '84 M198
Cobbler, Apple Walnut, '79 154
Cobbler, Apple-Walnut, '81 248
Cobbler, Cranberry-and-Apple, '84 306
Cobbler, Easy Apple, '83 174
Cobbler for Two, Apple, '85 261
Conserve, Apple-Cranberry, '82 308
Cookies, Apple Butter Spice, '79 291
Cookies, Apple-Nut, '80 228
Cookies, Apple-Oatmeal, '85 215
Cookies, Fresh Apple, '84 36
Cooler, Minted Apple, '88 169
Crisp, Apple, '84 122
Crisp, Delicious Apple, '82 303
Crisp, Granola Apple, '85 78
Crisp, Orange-Apple, '80 295
Crunch, Apple-Cranberry, '86 300; '87 178
Crunch, Apple-Nut, '82 M238
Cupcakes, Apple-Nut, '82 279
Danish, Deep-Dish Apple, '86 161
Delight, Apple, '80 109
Dessert, Cranberry Apple, '80 253
Dumplings, Apple, '82 273
Dumplings, Old-Fashioned Apple, '84 226
Dumplings with Orange Hard Sauce,
    Apple, '88 224
Fillets, Apple-Carrot Stuffed, '88 M192
Filling, Apple, '85 5
Filling, Apple-Date, '83 301
Filling, Dried Apple, '85 242; '87 229
Flan, Apple, '81 309
Foldovers, Apple, '84 136
Fritter Rings, Apple, '88 44
Fritters, Apple, '81 105; '82 273; '85 14
Fritters, Apple Holiday, '86 314
Glazed Apples, Orange-, '82 51
Golden Apples, '82 254
Ice, Cranberry-Apple, '82 290
Jelly, Apple, '82 149
Jelly, Apple-Mint, '87 134
Jelly, Crabapple, '79 120; '81 217
Juice, Hot Apple, '86 270
Juice, Nectarines in Apple, '83 183
Julep, Apple, '86 103, 215
Kuchen, Apple, '79 24
Loaf, Fresh Apple, '82 206
Loaf, Spiced Apple, '79 215
Marmalade, Apple, '79 120
Melting Apples, '88 19
Muffins, Apple, '83 96; '84 193; '87 23
Muffins, Apple-Bran, '85 M89
Muffins, Fresh Apple, '84 264
Muffins, Spiced Apple, '79 60
Muffins, Spicy Apple-Oat, '86 45
Pancake, Apple-Filled, '86 96
Pancakes with Cider Sauce, Spicy
    Apple, '87 224
Pie, Apple-Cheese, '85 284
Pie, Apple Cider, '84 227
Pie, Apple-Cream Cheese, '81 247
Pie, Apple Custard, '88 236
Pie, Apple-Lemon Chess, '86 220
Pie, Apple-Mincemeat, '85 316
Pie, Apple-Pear, '83 249
Pie, Autumn Apple, '79 205

Pie, Berry-Apple, '88 251
Pie, Blackberry-Apple, '87 130
Pie, Brandy-Apple, '86 301
Pie, Brandy Raisin-Apple, '83 192
Pie, Caramel-Pecan Apple, '85 247
Pie, Cornbread-Sausage-Apple, '87 171
Pie, Cranberry-Apple, '79 264
Pie, Cranberry-Apple Holiday, '81 M269
Pie, Dutch Apple, '81 105; '82 273
Pie, Easy-Crust Apple, '87 11
Pie, Fresh Apple, '84 178
Pie, Grandmother's Apple, '87 212
Pie, Grated Apple, '83 304
Pie, Holiday Apple, '87 260
Pie, Natural Pear-Apple, '88 226
Pie, No-Crust Apple, '88 204
Pie, Old-Fashioned Apple, '82 M299;
    '88 94

Pie, Red Apple, '79 282
Pies, Delicious Fried, '83 84
Pies, Fried Apple, '81 217; '86 302;
    '88 112, 225
Pie, Tart Lemon-Apple, '80 100
Pie, Upside-Down Southern Apple, '88 226
Pie with Hot Cinnamon Sauce,
    Apple, '88 210
Pinwheel, Quick Apple, '85 42
Poached Lemon Apples, Chilled, '86 182
Poppyseed Dressing, Apple Wedges
    with, '86 131
Pork Chops and Apples, Baked, '81 10
Pork Chops, Apple-Crumb Stuffed, '81 234;
    '82 26
Pork Chops, Apple-Glazed, '84 212; '87 35
Pork Chops, Apple-Kraut, '84 50
Pork Chops, Apple-Stuffed, '79 125
Pork Chops, Glazed Apple, '86 300
Pork Chops, Sherry-Apple, '88 40
Pork Chops, Spicy Apple, '87 230
Pork Chops with Crabapple Peaches,
    Broiled, '81 83
Pork Tenderloin, Apple-Ginger, '86 75
Potatoes, Apple-Glazed Sweet, '82 303
Potatoes, Apple-Stuffed Sweet, '88 207
Potatoes Stuffed with Apples,
    Sweet, '82 228
Pot Roast, Spicy Apple, '83 7
Pudding, Apple-Raisin Bread, '88 175
Pudding with Hot Rum Sauce,
    Apple-Nut, '79 86
Punch, Apple-Tea, '85 82
Punch, Hot Apple, '84 324

Apples (continued)

Punch, Hot Spiced, '80 250
Quiche, Crustless Sausage-Apple, '87 70
Relish, Cran-Apple, '84 300
Relish, Spicy Apple, '84 M323
Ribs, Apple Barbecued, '80 111
Rice, Apple-Cinnamon, '86 249
Rings, Apple, '85 232
Rings, Cinnamon Apple, '82 M237
Rings, Cinnamon-Apple, '85 107
Rings, Fried Apple, '81 209
Rings, Honey Apple, '80 243
Roll, Apple, '82 178
Rolls, Apple-Phyllo, '88 213
Rolls, Luscious Apple, '88 225
Salad, Apple, '87 233
Salad, Apple-Apricot, '88 121
Salad, Apple-Carrot, '85 22
Salad, Apple Cider, '83 123
Salad, Apple Crunch, '84 232; '86 331
Salad, Apple-Nut, '80 226
Salad, Apple Snow, '81 224
Salad, Blue Cheese-Pear-Apple, '81 224
Salad, Cheesy Apple, '86 301
Salad, Cherry-Apple, '86 31
Salad, Congealed Apple, '85 252
Salad, Congealed Waldorf, '82 80
Salad, Creamy Waldorf, '87 311
Salad, Crunchy Apple, '80 138
Salad, Curried Apple-Raisin, '80 24
Salad, Deluxe Waldorf, '83 81
Salad, Double Apple, '84 227
Salad, English Pea-and-Apple, '87 24
Salad, Fresh Apple, '81 207
Salad, Frozen Apple-Cream, '82 80
Salad, Frozen Waldorf, '79 126; '82 145
Salad, Ham-and-Apple, '88 139
Salad, Jiffy Waldorf, '88 100
Salad, Lemony Apple-Bran, '86 223
Salad Mold, Apple Cider, '85 54
Salad, Old-Fashioned Waldorf, '81 295
Salad, Peanut-Apple, '80 5
Salad, Spicy Apple, '85 215
Salad, Summer Apple, '80 149
Salad, Swiss-Apple, '84 81
Salad, Triple Apple, '88 122
Salad, Turkey-Apple, '88 123
Salad with Blue Cheese Dressing,
    Apple, '87 103
Sandwiches, Apple, '79 164; '80 130
Sandwiches, Apple-Cinnamon
    Breakfast, '85 298
Sauce, Apple Dessert, '87 M165
Sauce, Apple-Horseradish, '82 229
Sauce, Spicy Apple Dessert, '82 177
Sausage Patties, Apples on, '82 120
Scalloped Apples, '84 70; '87 156
Sesame-Apple Toss, '88 21
Shells, Sweet Potatoes in Apple, '85 206
Shrub, Shenandoah Apple Juice, '79 282
Slaw, Apple-Pineapple, '79 241
Slaw, Fresh Apple, '81 63
Slaw, Nutty Apple, '88 216
Slaw, Red Cabbage-and-Apple, '87 31
Soup, Creamed
    Butternut-and-Apple, '88 228
Spiced Apple Slices, '83 289
Spiced Apples, Skillet, '83 234; '84 244
Spread, Gruyère-Apple, '81 160
Squares, Sour Cream Apple, '82 262

Squash, Apple-and-Pecan-Filled, '88 228
Squash, Apple-Stuffed, '85 206
Squash, Apple-Stuffed Acorn, '83 296;
    '84 285
Squash, Apple-Stuffed Butternut, '81 232
Strudel, Apple, '85 259
Stuffed Apples, Peanutty, '85 25
Stuffing, Apple-Crumb, '81 234; '82 26;
    '83 39
Sundaes, Spicy Apple Ice Cream, '86 M195
Syrup, Spiced Apple, '79 114
Tart, Apple Cream, '84 207
Tart, Deluxe Apple, '84 227
Tarte aux Pommes, La, '80 125
Tarts, Apple-Pecan, '80 282
Tart with Cheese Pastry, Apple, '88 225
Tea, Cranberry-Apple, '88 169
Tea, Hot Apple-Cinnamon, '87 57
Tea, Johnny Appleseed, '85 23
Toast, Apple, '81 278
Topping, Spicy Apple, '87 125
Turnovers, Delicious Apple, '86 25
Turnovers, Fried Apple, '81 161
Turnovers, Puffy Apple, '87 276
Veal Chops, Apple, '87 220

Applesauce

Bread, Applesauce-Honey Nut, '87 300
Bread, Applesauce Nut, '81 305
Bread, Bran-Applesauce, '84 229
Butter, Half-Hour Apple, '81 203
Cake, Applesauce, '80 270
Cake, Applesauce Carrot, '81 202
Cake, Applesauce-Spice, '83 42
Cake, My Favorite Applesauce, '87 263
Cakes, Applesauce Snack, '88 215
Cake Squares, Applesauce, '86 8
Cake with Bourbon Frosting,
    Applesauce, '88 236
Doughnuts, Applesauce, '81 203
Dressing, Apple, '83 181
Fruitcake, Applesauce, '83 258

Loaf, Brandy Applesauce, '81 263
Muffins, Applesauce, '84 284
Muffins, Applesauce Spice, '88 236
Muffins, Bite-Size Applesauce, '82 104
Pancakes, Applesauce, '79 114
Pudding, Applesauce-Graham
    Cracker, '81 34
Ribs, Apple Barbecued, '80 111
Spicy Applesauce, '82 296
Squares, Applesauce-Spice, '86 248

Apricots

Baked Apricots, Delicious, '82 10
Bake, Sweet Potato-Apricot, '85 206
Balls, Apricot, '79 274
Bars, Apricot, '81 247
Bars, Apricot-Oatmeal, '86 216
Bars, Apricot-Raisin, '87 32
Bread, Apricot-Nut, '79 24
Bread, Pineapple-Apricot, '84 7
Bread, Tangy Apricot, '81 249
Breakfast Dish, Sausage-Apricot, '82 10
Butter, Apricot, '82 308
Cake, Apricot Brandy Pound, '83 267
Carrots, Apricot, '84 6
Carrots, Apricot Glazed, '80 89
Chicken Breasts, Apricot, '88 301
Cobble Up, Apricot, '82 138
Cookie Rolls, Apricot, '80 282
Cookies, Frosted Apricot, '81 192
Cooler, Apricot, '81 100
Cornish Hens, Apricot-Glazed, '80 84;
    '87 306
Cornish Hens, Apricot-Stuffed, '84 6
Cream, Peachy-Apricot, '86 163
Dates, Apricot-Stuffed, '80 250
Delight, Apricot, '81 42
Dip, Apricot, '86 178
Divinity, Apricot, '83 297
Dressing, Honeydew Salad with Apricot
    Cream, '84 191
Filling, Apricot, '83 84; '86 107
Freeze, Apricot, '82 10
Frosting, Apricot, '81 192
Frozen Apricot Fluff, '86 242
Glaze, Apricot, '80 280; '82 8; '86 197
Glaze, Apricot-Kirsch, '87 14
Glaze for Ham, Apricot, '85 256
Glaze, Sweet Apricot, '82 304
Ham, Apricot Baked, '84 160
Ice, Apricot Yogurt, '81 177
Jam, Golden Apricot, '80 31
Kolaches, Apricot, '83 84
Loaf, Apricot-Cranberry, '79 235
Loaf, Apricot-Nut, '81 8
Loaf, Tasty Apricot-Nut, '82 10
Mousse, Apricot, '82 72
Nectar, Hot Apricot, '81 265
Nectar, Mulled Apricot, '86 229
Pastries, Apricot, '83 297
Pie, Apricot Surprise, '88 99
Pie, Dried Fruit, '83 249
Pies, Apricot Fried, '86 269
Pie, Yogurt-Apricot, '85 132
Pinwheels, Apricot, '87 276
Pork Chops, Apricot-Sauced, '85 22
Pork Chops, Apricot-Stuffed, '86 76
Potatoes, Apricot-Glazed Sweet, '81 295
Potatoes, Apricot Sweet, '82 228
Pudding, Apricot Bread, '85 24
Punch, Apricot Spiced, '80 269
Salad, Apple-Apricot, '88 121
Salad, Apricot, '81 251; '83 123
Salad, Apricot Fruit, '82 132
Salad, Apricot Nectar, '83 218; '87 236
Salad, Creamy Apricot, '85 263
Salad, Frosted Apricot, '80 248
Sauce, Apricot, '82 212; '87 172
Sauce, Apricot-Walnut Hard, '88 153
Sauce, Fresh Cranberry-Apricot, '87 243
Shake, Apricot, '84 115
Sherbet, Apricot, '81 177

Slush, Apricot-Citrus, **'88** 82
Soufflé, Baked Apricot, **'88** 267
Spread, Apricot Brie, **'86** 275
Spread, Apricot-Cream Cheese, **'82** 161;
   '87 158
Syrup, Apricot Fruit, **'82** 10
Tarts, Apricot, **'79** 282; **'88** 281
Tea, Hot Spiced Apricot, **'88** 248
Turnovers, Fried Apricot, **'86** 24
Wassail, Pineapple-Apricot, **'83** 275

Artichokes
Antipasto Spread, **'81** 25
Appetizer, Zesty Artichoke, **'80** 146
Aspic, Tomato-Artichoke, **'84** 320; **'86** 92
Avocado Acapulco, **'83** 2
Baked Chicken and Artichoke
   Hearts, **'82** 260
Bake, Tomato-and-Artichoke Heart, **'85** 81
Beef with Artichokes, Creamed
   Dried, **'85** 81
Casserole, Asparagus-Artichoke, **'86** 279
Casserole, Italian Green
   Bean-and-Artichoke, **'85** 81
Casserole, Mushroom-Artichoke, **'87** 241
Casserole, Spinach and Artichoke, **'81** 103
Casserole, Spinach-Artichoke, **'88** 252
Caviar, Artichoke Hearts with, **'79** 142
Chicken, Artichoke, **'81** 97
Chicken with Artichoke Hearts, **'88** 54
Chicken with Artichokes,
   Sherried, **'87** 143
Chilled Artichokes with Lemon-Pepper
   Dressing, **'87** 55
Dip, Deluxe Artichoke, **'80** 87
Dip, Hot Artichoke-Seafood, **'80** 241
Dip, Hot Artichoke Seafood, **'85** M212
Dip, Seasoned Mayonnaise
   Artichoke, **'80** 87
Dressing, Artichoke, **'84** 126
Herb-Mayonnaise Dip, Artichokes
   with, **'84** 67
Marinated Artichoke Hearts, **'88** 95
Marinated Artichokes, **'87** 250; **'88** 41
Marinated Cucumbers and
   Artichokes, **'82** 111
Mold, Artichoke-Caviar, **'87** 239
Pasta with Artichoke Hearts, **'86** 209
Phyllo Bites, Artichoke-Parmesan, **'87** 54
Pie, Artichoke, **'79** 25
Pizza with Artichoke and
   Prosciutto, **'87** 182
Salad, Artichoke, **'86** 333
Salad, Artichoke-Rice, **'80** 178; **'81** 41;
   '85 81
Salad, Artichoke-Stuffed Tomato, **'82** 101
Salad, Artichokes with Orzo, **'88** M193
Salad, Artichoke-Tomato, **'82** 239
Salad, Asparagus-Artichoke, **'85** 162
Salad, Italian, **'87** 145
Salad, Marinated Artichoke, **'83** 241
Salad with Artichoke Hearts,
   Rice, **'80** 232
Salad with Artichokes, Chicken, **'86** 186
Soup, Cream of Artichoke, **'82** 232
Spread, Hot Artichoke, **'79** 110
Spread, Hot Artichoke-Crab, **'85** 81
Spring Artichokes, **'86** 62
Steamed Artichokes, **'81** 59
Stuffed Artichokes, **'79** 76; **'82** 92
Stuffed Artichokes, Shrimp-, **'84** 67;
   '87 55

Stuffed with Shrimp and Scallops,
   Artichokes, **'84** 174
Veal with Artichoke Hearts,
   Lemon, **'87** 219
Vinaigrette, Artichokes, **'88** 101

Asparagus
Almond Asparagus, **'83** 86
Almond Butter, Asparagus with, **'84** 85
Basil Butter, Asparagus with, **'85** 40
Basil Sauce, Asparagus with, **'86** 33
Caesar, Asparagus, **'88** 133
Cashew Butter, Asparagus with, **'87** 56
Casserole, Asparagus-and-English
   Pea, **'86** 324
Casserole, Asparagus and Peas, **'80** 152
Casserole, Asparagus-Artichoke, **'86** 279
Casserole, Asparagus-Pea, **'88** M294
Casserole, Asparagus-Spaghetti, **'80** 77
Casserole, Cheesy Asparagus, **'82** 281;
   '83 32

Casserole, Chicken-Asparagus, **'83** 76;
   '84 71
Casserole, Creamy Asparagus, **'80** 76
Casserole, Easy Asparagus, **'83** 255
Casserole, Turkey-Asparagus, **'86** 284
Company Asparagus, **'85** 82
Croquettes, Asparagus, **'85** 265
Cutlets, Asparagus, **'80** 147
Delight, Asparagus, **'82** 269
Delight, Ham-Asparagus, **'86** 48
Dilly Asparagus, **'88** 180
Dinner, Ham-Asparagus, **'80** M10
Eggs à la Asparagus, Creamed, **'81** 201
en Papillote, Shrimp with
   Asparagus, **'86** 145
Fish-Asparagus Divan, **'87** 128
Fried Asparagus, French-, **'79** 66; **'83** 46
Goldenrod, Asparagus, **'79** 66
Holiday Asparagus, **'85** 260
Jeweled Asparagus, **'80** 42
Lemon Butter, Asparagus in, **'80** M123
Lemon Butter, Asparagus with, **'87** M151
Lemon Sauce, Asparagus with, **'86** 62
Loaf, Asparagus-Pimiento, **'84** 86
Marinated Asparagus, **'81** 108; **'83** 46;
   '84 67, 86; **'86** 92; **'87** 74
Marinated Asparagus, Easy, **'81** 148
Marinated Asparagus Spears, **'88** 130
Mayonnaise, Asparagus with Hot
   Wine, **'81** 83
Meringue, Asparagus, **'88** 131
Mold, Asparagus, **'80** 104
Mold, Asparagus-Cucumber, **'85** 252
Mushrooms, Asparagus and, **'85** 108
Mustard Sauce, Chilled Asparagus
   in, **'88** 130
Orange Butter Sauce, Asparagus
   with, **'85** 43
Orange Sauce, Asparagus with, **'83** 46

Pickled Asparagus, **'83** 46
Pilaf, Turkey-Asparagus, **'88** 200
Pork Arlo, **'87** 229
Quiche, Asparagus-Tomato, **'88** 198
Quiche, Springtime, **'83** 122
Rarebit, Uptown Welsh, **'87** 279
Rolls, Asparagus, **'79** 296; **'80** 31
Rolls, Chicken-Asparagus, **'86** M211
Rolls, Ham-Asparagus, **'79** 41
Rollups, Asparagus, **'79** 63
Roll-Ups, Asparagus, **'84** 270
Roulade, Asparagus, **'86** 102
Salad, Asparagus, **'88** 121
Salad, Asparagus-and-Egg, **'86** 305
Salad, Asparagus-and-New Potato, **'86** 69
Salad, Asparagus-Artichoke, **'85** 162
Salad, Asparagus-Horseradish, **'87** 80
Salad, Asparagus Mousse, **'86** 252
Salad, Congealed Asparagus, **'83** 260
Salad Cups, Asparagus, **'83** 47
Salad, Easy Asparagus, **'88** 131
Salad, Marinated Asparagus, **'79** 20
Salad, Peas-and-Asparagus, **'83** 141
Salad, Tart Asparagus, **'81** 203
Salad Vinaigrette, Asparagus, **'88** 56
Salad with Asparagus, Curried
   Chicken, **'81** 36
Salad with Crabmeat-and-Asparagus,
   Congealed, **'84** 86
Sandwiches, Asparagus-and-Ham
   Melt, **'88** M96
Sandwiches, Asparagus Grill, **'79** 164;
   '80 130
Sandwiches, Asparagus Spear, **'84** 165
Sauce, Asparagus White, **'80** 147
Sautéed Asparagus, **'79** 66
Soufflé, Asparagus, **'79** 66; **'83** 265
Soup, Asparagus, **'84** 67
Soup, Asparagus-Potato, **'85** 23
Soup, Cream of Asparagus, **'84** 111
Sour Cream, Asparagus with, **'83** 46
Squares, Asparagus, **'79** 161
Squash Rings, Asparagus in, **'87** 68
Stir-Fried Asparagus, **'87** 52
Supreme, Asparagus, **'80** 77
Supreme, Cauliflower and
   Asparagus, **'79** 287; **'80** 35
Tangy Asparagus, **'84** 86
Tarragon Marinade, Asparagus with, **'83** 47
Tomato Sauce, Asparagus with, **'83** 46
Vinaigrette, Asparagus, **'80** 77
Vinaigrette, Light Asparagus, **'82** 50
Yogurt Dressing, Asparagus with, **'79** 66

Aspic
Apple Aspic, Sunshine, **'81** 73
Basic Aspic for Garnishing, **'84** 189
Chicken Salad, Aspic-Topped, **'88** 88
Coating, White Aspic, **'85** 151
Fish Aspic, **'84** 190
Fish 'n Aspic, **'84** 190
Grapefruit Aspic, **'80** 297; **'82** 112;
   '83 153
Madeira Aspic, **'86** 65
Orange-and-Carrot Aspic, **'86** 199
Shrimp-Coleslaw Aspic, **'79** 88
Shrimp-Cucumber Aspic, **'83** 108
Sunshine Aspic, **'80** 103
Three-Layer Aspic, **'88** 120
Tomato-Artichoke Aspic, **'84** 320; **'86** 92
Tomato Aspic, Bloody Mary-, **'81** 77
Tomato Aspic, Chicken in, **'84** 190

Aspic *(continued)*

Tomato Aspic, Chili Sauce, **'85** 252
Tomato Aspic, Herbed, **'81** 73
Tomato Aspic, Light, **'85** 83
Tomato Aspic, Ranch, **'83** 218
Tomato Aspic, Spicy, **'81** 40
Tomato Aspic, Tangy, **'83** 124
Tomato Aspic with Shrimp, **'79** 241
Tomato-Crab Aspic, **'85** 287
Two, Aspic for, **'83** 209
Vegetable Aspic, Cheesy, **'81** 73
Vegetable Aspic with Horseradish Dressing,
   Crisp, **'87** 152

Avocados

Acapulco, Avocado, **'83** 2
Baked Avocado-and-Crabmeat, **'84** 119
Broiled Crab and Avocado, **'79** 116
Chicken, Orange-Avocado, **'80** 38
Cocktail, Sherried
   Avocado-Crabmeat, **'87** 95
Crabmeat, Avocado with, **'86** 119
Dip, Avocado, **'80** 285; **'81** 57, 306
Dip, Six-Layer, **'81** 160
Dip, Zippy Avocado, **'82** 9; **'83** 69
Dressing, Avocado, **'80** 15
Dressing, Avocado Fruit Salad, **'82** 93
Filled Avocados, Shrimp-, **'83** 2
Guacamole, **'79** 185; **'80** 74; **'83** 179
Guacamole, Creamy, **'79** 91; **'83** 174
Guacamole Dip, **'86** 4
Guacamole Dip, Bacon-, **'85** 25
Guacamole in Shells, **'86** 74
Guacamole Mexican Coleslaw, **'82** 302
Guacamole Mold, **'86** 184
Guacamole Salad, **'80** 14; **'87** 181
Guacamole Sandwiches, **'82** 9; **'83** 68
Guacamole Subs, **'84** 293
Guacamole-Tomato Salad, **'81** 302
Ice, Avocado, **'83** 179
Kabobs, Chicken-Avocado, **'82** 9; **'83** 68
Omelet, Yogurt-Avocado, **'81** 33
Pie, Chili-Tamale, **'83** 68
Pie, Mexican Cheese, **'83** 69
Potatoes, Avocado-Topped, **'83** 3
Relish, Avocado, **'87** 120
Salad, Avocado, **'81** 195; **'82** 9; **'83** 69
Salad, Avocado-Chicken, **'87** 107
Salad, Avocado Fruit, **'87** 41
Salad, Avocado-Garbanzo, **'81** 33
Salad, Avocado-Grapefruit, **'85** 26
Salad, Avocado-Melon, **'82** 164
Salad, Chicken-Avocado, **'80** 139
Salad, Citrus-Avocado, **'82** 265
Salad, Congealed Avocado, **'84** 266

Salad, Congealed Avocado Crunch, **'85** 26
Salad, Crab-Avocado, **'81** 114
Salad, Creamy Avocado and
   Zucchini, **'79** 208
Salad, Dude Ranch, **'80** 15
Salad, Fruited Chicken-Avocado, **'82** 101
Salad, Grapefruit-Avocado, **'83** 316; **'84** 16
Salad, Green Spinach, **'79** 142
Salad in Avocados, Chicken, **'85** 216
Salad in Avocados, Fruited Chicken, **'87** 41
Salad on the Half Shell, Shrimp, **'86** 73
Salad Platter, Chicken-Avocado, **'83** 2
Salads, Congealed Avocado, **'87** 42
Salad, Shrimp and Avocado, **'80** 266
Salad, Spanish Avocado, **'87** 41
Salad Supper, Mexican, **'82** 9; **'83** 68
Salad, Tangy Romaine, **'80** 155
Salad, Tomato-Avocado, **'86** 74
Salad, Tossed Chicken-Avocado, **'80** 4
Sandwiches, Avocado, Bacon, and
   Cheese, **'87** 279
Sandwiches, Avocado-Crabmeat, **'83** 2
Sauce, Avocado, **'80** 198; **'83** 200
Shells, Ceviche in Avocado, **'81** 33
Sherbet, Avocado, **'83** 162
Sherbet, Mexican, **'79** 155
Sorbet, Avocado, **'88** 117
Soup, Avocado, **'88** 160
Soup, Avocado-Banana-Yogurt, **'80** 78
Soup, Chilled Avocado, **'81** 34; **'87** 37
Soup, Creamy Avocado, **'79** 107
Soup, Creamy Avocado-Mushroom, **'85** 25
Soup, Sherried Avocado, **'84** 181
Stuffed Avocados, Crab-, **'86** 73
Stuffed Avocados, Salmon-, **'86** 74
Stuffed Broiled Avocados, **'88** 246
Stuffed with Shrimp Salad,
   Avocado, **'82** 207
Tomatoes, Avocado-Stuffed, **'82** 101
Tostadas, Crispy, **'83** 2
Whip, Avocado, **'79** 107

B

Bacon

Appetizers, Hot Bacon, **'80** 248
Bagels, Meal-in-One, **'88** 159
Bake, Lima-Bacon, **'86** 9
Bars, Bacon-Cheese Toast, **'79** 36
Beans, Bacon-Topped Green, **'80** M123
Biscuits, Bacon-Cheese, **'88** 84
Bread, Bacon-and-Cheese, **'83** 255
Breakfast Bake, **'85** 45
Breakfast Eye-Openers, **'82** 231
Breakfast, Farmer's, **'81** 44
Bundles, Bean, **'80** 246
Burgers, Cheesy Bacon, **'81** 29
Butternut and Bacon, Skillet, **'85** 9
Canadian Bacon, Lima Beans with, **'83** 219;
   '84 245
Canadian-Style Bacon, Glazed, **'82** 197
Carrots with Bacon and Onion,
   Glazed, **'87** 200
Casserole, Bacon and Egg, **'81** 225
Casserole, Egg-and-Bacon, **'85** 248
Champignons au Vin, **'79** 47
Cheesy BLT's, **'85** 92
Chestnuts, Bacon-Wrapped Water, **'79** 63
Chestnut Wraps, Bacon-, **'84** M216

Chicken Bundles with Bacon
   Ribbons, **'87** 68
Coleslaw, Bacon, **'83** 58
Cookies, Take-Along Breakfast, **'84** 59
Cornbread, Cowboy, **'81** 188
Crispies, Cheese-Bacon, **'84** 270
Delight, Bacon-and-Egg, **'85** 143
Dip, Bacon, **'82** 197
Dip, Bacon-Guacamole, **'85** 25
Dressing, Green Beans with
   Bacon, **'85** 147
Dressing, Hot Bacon, **'84** 12
Dressing, Potatoes with Hot
   Bacon, **'88** M294
Eggs, and Hominy, Bacon, **'85** 143
Eggs, Bacon Deviled, **'86** 136
Eggs Benedict, Bacon-and-Tomato,
   '87 195
Franks, Bacon-Wrapped, **'81** 202
Kabobs, Scallop-Bacon, **'81** 111
Linguine Carbonara, **'87** 108
Meatballs, Bacon-Wrapped, **'79** 81

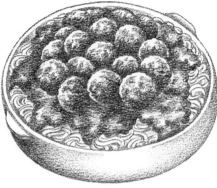

Meatballs, Bacon-Wrapped, **'79** 81
Meatballs, Burgundy-Bacon, **'80** 283
Mushrooms, Cheese 'n'
   Bacon-Stuffed, **'86** 258
Mushrooms with Bacon, Stir-Fried, **'80** 123
Oysters, Bacon-Baked, **'86** 132
Oysters in Bacon, **'83** 211
Pineapple Chunks, Bacon-Wrapped, **'84** 25
Poor Boys, Oyster-and-Bacon, **'87** 40
Popcorn, Bacon-Cheese, **'86** 74
Potatoes, Bacon-Stuffed, **'86** 193
Potatoes, Bacon-Stuffed Sweet, **'86** 224
Potatoes, Bacon-Topped Blue
   Cheese, **'79** 46
Potatoes, Cheesy Bacon-Stuffed, **'81** M61
Quiche, Bacon, **'85** 60
Quiche Lorraine, **'80** M108
Quiche Lorraine, Classic, **'81** 131
Quiche Lorraine, Mushroom-, **'86** 242
Quiche Lorraine, Peppery, **'81** 228
Quiches, Miniature Bacon-Cheese, **'83** 93
Rice, Bacon-Chive, **'83** 129
Rice, Bacon Fried, **'80** 115
Rolls, Bacon, **'84** 270
Rollups, Bacon, **'79** 34
Roll-Ups, Chicken Liver and
   Bacon, **'80** 200; **'81** 57
Rollups, Sausage-Bacon, **'88** 51
Rumaki, **'80** M136
Rutabaga with Bacon, **'83** 243
Salad, Bacon-Topped Potato, **'85** 59
Salad, BLT Chicken, **'87** 144

Salad, Escarole-and-Bacon, '84 85
Salad, Hot Bacon and Black-Eyed, '85 7
Salad, Spinach and Bacon, '81 143
Salad, Wilted Bacon-and-Lettuce, '85 69
Salad with Bacon, Rice, '79 52
Sandwiches, Avocado, Bacon, and
  Cheese, '87 279
Sandwiches, Bacon, Cheese, and
  Tomato, '84 14
Sandwiches, Breakfast, '82 M123
Sandwiches, Grilled Bacon-Cheese, '83 242
Sandwiches, Open-Faced Cheesy
  Bacon, '80 78
Scallops, Bacon-Wrapped, '87 94
Scramble, Bacon-and-Eggs, '80 M267
Soup, Bacon-Beer Cheese, '87 M7
Soup, Bacon-Topped Cheese, '80 M224
Soup, Bean and Bacon, '83 26
Soup, Potato-Bacon, '84 38
Spaghetti, Bacon, '86 213; '87 82
Spoonbread, Corn and Bacon, '81 129
Spread, Bacon-Cheese, '83 241
Squash, Bacon-Flavored, '82 158
Steak, Bacon-Wrapped Flank, '85 59
Supper Supreme, Sunday, '79 76
Tomatoes, Bacon-and-Egg-Stuffed, '80 162
Tomatoes with Bacon, Saucy Fried, '81 210
Vegetable-Bacon Bowl, Marinated, '79 191

Bananas
Alaskas, Banana Split, '87 10
Baked Bananas, '79 103
Baked Bananas, Honey-, '81 268
Baked Bananas with Orange Sauce, '79 115
Bars, Banana Breakfast, '79 124
Berry Flip, Banana-, '88 215
Boats, Banana, '82 50
Bread, Banana, '87 72
Bread, Banana-Apple, '85 250
Bread, Banana-Blueberry, '81 163
Bread, Banana Butterscotch, '79 116
Bread, Banana-Jam, '84 73
Bread, Banana-Nut, '86 8, 70
Bread, Banana-Nut-Raisin, '81 59
Bread, Banana Wheat, '81 14
Bread, Banana-Zucchini, '85 326
Bread, Cranberry-Banana, '80 281
Bread, Hawaiian Banana Nut, '79 235
Bread, Sour Cream-Banana, '79 190
Bread, Whole Wheat Banana, '80 88
Bread, Whole Wheat-Banana Nut, '84 50
Broiled Bananas with Honey, '84 175
Brownies, Chocolate-Banana, '80 160
Cake, Banana, '84 151
Cake, Banana-Blueberry, '86 247
Cake, Banana Coffee, '81 288
Cake, Banana Cream Coffee, '85 46
Cake, Banana-Sour Cream Coffee, '80 186
Cake, Banana Waldorf, '85 118
Cake, Chocolate-Banana, '86 138
Cake, Deluxe Light Banana, '84 314
Cake, Marvelous Banana, '79 115
Cake, Peanut Butter-Banana, '80 87
Candied Bananas, '83 179
Casserole, Sweet Potato-Banana, '86 276
Cookies, Banana Oatmeal, '79 217
Crêpes Flambé, Banana, '84 262
Crush, Banana, '80 88; '83 142
Cupcakes, Banana-Cocoa, '80 130
Curried Bananas, Fillets with Horseradish
  Sauce and, '85 230
Dessert, Banana Cream, '81 180

Doughnuts, Banana, '86 137
Flambé, Banana-Peach, '85 316
Flip, Banana, '83 303
Flip, Orange-Banana, '82 48
Float, Strawberry-Banana, '87 160
Foster, Bananas, '79 18; '83 M114;
  '86 139
Foster, Elegant Bananas, '81 59
Foster for Two, Bananas, '80 115
Foster, Tropical Bananas, '79 231
Fritters, Banana, '79 213
Frost, Banana-Strawberry, '87 199
Frosting, Banana-Nut, '79 115
Ice Cream, Banana Split, '80 176
Ice Cream, Straw-Ba-Nut, '80 177
Ice Cream, Strawberry-Banana-Nut, '88 203
Jam, Banana, '82 296
Jam, Rosy Peach-Banana, '80 142
Kabana, Banana, '86 316
Loaf, Banana-Oat Tea, '87 256
Loaf, Chocolate Chip-Banana, '85 115
Loaf, Hawaiian, '80 225
Milkshake, Banana, '85 47
Milk Shake, Banana-Pineapple, '84 59
Muffins, Banana, '80 88; '84 75
Muffins, Banana Bran, '83 48
Muffins, Banana-Honey-Nut, '88 62
Muffins, Banana-Oat, '87 188
Muffins, Banana-Oatmeal, '84 20
Muffins, Banana-Orange, '84 148
Muffins, Banana Surprise, '82 105
Nog, Banana, '82 290
Nutty Bananas, '79 251
Pancakes, Island, '87 225
Pancakes, Wheat Germ-Banana, '79 114
Pie, Banana Cream, '84 48; '87 207
Pie, Caramel-Banana, '86 M165
Pie, Layered Banana Split, '83 189
Pie, Luscious Caramel Banana, '79 115
Pie, Strawberry-Banana Glazed, '81 181
Pie with Hot Buttered Rum Sauce,
  Banana, '88 204
Pops, Banana, '83 60; '84 44
Pops, Orange-Banana, '82 129
Praline Bananas, '84 313
Pudding, Almost Banana, '88 174

Pudding, Banana, '82 53; '84 94; '85 255;
  '88 16, 32
Pudding, Banana-Mallow, '86 139
Pudding, Basic Banana, '81 59
Pudding, Delicious Banana, '80 9
Pudding, Surprise Banana, '86 7
Regal Bananas, '85 46

Roll, Banana-Nut, '85 112
Salad, Banana, '87 80
Salad, Banana-Mixed Fruit, '79 270
Salad, Frozen Banana, '82 80, 132
Sauce, Banana-Pineapple, '83 48
Sauce, Banana Sundae, '84 275
Sauce, Strawberry-Banana, '81 41
Shake, Pineapple-Banana, '85 215
Sherbet, Banana-Orange, '83 162
Slaw, Banana-Nut, '86 250
Slush, Banana, '83 56
Slush, Banana-Orange, '80 48; '81 155
Smoothie, Banana, '87 160
Smoothie, Strawberry-Banana, '81 59
Smoothie, Tropical, '81 50
Sorbet, Banana-Orange, '88 117
Soufflé, Banana Daiquiri, '84 317
Soup, Avocado-Banana-Yogurt, '80 78
Soup, Strawberry-Banana, '86 161
Splits, Cottage Cheese-Banana, '87 56
Supreme, Banana-Berry, '81 205
Supreme, Bananas, '84 256
Topping, Strawberry-Banana, '87 125
Waffles, Banana-Ginger, '86 96

Barbecue
Backbones, Smoked Country-Style, '82 162
Beans, Barbecued Lima, '82 2
Beans, Barbecued Pork and, '79 100
Beef, Barbecued, '81 18
Beef Brisket, Barbecued, '83 11
Beef Brisket, Denton, Texas,
  Barbecued, '81 55
Beef Brisket with Sauce,
  Barbecued, '86 153
Beef Eye of Round, Grilled, '82 91
Beef Roast Barbecue, '79 159
Beef Roast, Barbecued, '82 96; '83 103
Beef Sandwiches, Barbecued, '81 25;
  '82 31; '83 34
Beef, Saucy Barbecued, '82 156
Beef Short Ribs, Barbecued, '83 178
Beef Shortribs Supreme, '79 14
Bourbon Barbecue, '88 129
Brisket, Barbecued, '86 154; '88 218
Burgers, Barbecued, '82 168
Burgers, Sausage, '83 212
Cabrito, Barbecued, '86 153
Catfish, Barbecued, '80 157
Catfish, Smoked, '84 47
Chicken Bake, Barbecued, '81 97
Chicken, Barbecue, '86 122
Chicken, Barbecued, '82 97, 106; '83 103;
  '85 144; '86 153
Chicken, Barbecued Cranberry, '83 178
Chicken Breasts, Grilled, '84 172
Chicken, Golden Barbecued, '83 136
Chicken, Grilled Barbecued, '81 154
Chicken, Grilled Yogurt-Lemon, '81 111
Chicken, Lemonade, '82 163
Chicken, Marinated Barbecued, '79 90
Chicken, Old South Barbecued, '82 97;
  '83 103
Chicken, Orange Barbecued, '88 123
Chicken, Saucy Barbecued, '83 11
Chicken, Smoky Grilled, '85 160
Chicken, Tangy Barbecued, '86 186
Chicken, Zesty Barbecued, '80 M76
Chicken, Zippy Barbecued, '83 213
Corned Beef Sandwiches,
  Barbecued, '83 130
Cornish Hens, Smoked, '86 142, 154

Barbecue *(continued)*

Corn on the Cob, Barbecued, **'81** 128
Cups, Barbecue, **'79** 129
Dressing, Barbecue Salad, **'80** 74
Fish Fillets, Barbecued, **'86** 182
Flounder Fillets, Grilled, **'83** 213
Frank Barbecue, Tangy, **'79** 63
Frankfurters, Barbecued, **'83** 144
Frankfurters, Oven-Barbecued, **'83** 11
Franks, Barbecued, **'85** 192
Franks, Grilled Stuffed, **'82** 163
Grouper, Grilled, **'86** 185
Hamburgers, Flavorful Grilled, **'81** 110
Ham Slices, Barbecued, **'81** 110
Ham, Smoked, **'86** 92
Home-Style Barbecue, **'88** 145
Kabobs, Barbecued Steak, **'79** 89
Kabobs, Grilled Scallop, **'83** 101
Kabobs, Marinated Sirloin, **'82** 162
Kabobs, Pineapple-Beef, **'83** 212
Kabobs, Sea Scallop, **'82** 162
Lamb, Barbecued, **'79** 58
Lamb Chops, Barbecued, **'79** 89
Liver, Barbecued, **'85** 219
Mackerel, Smoked Salmon or, **'84** 46
Meatballs, Oven Barbecued, **'82** 233
Meat Loaf, Barbecued, **'80** 60; **'81** 275;
  '87 216
Mullet, Smoked, **'84** 47
Outdoor Cooking, **'82** 109
Oysters, Barbecued, **'82** 247
Pork, Barbecued, **'80** 72
Pork Chops, Barbecued, **'81** 10
Pork Chops, Marinated Barbecued, **'79** 90
Pork Chops, Marinated Grilled, **'81** 110
Pork Chops, Oven-Barbecued, **'81** 234;
  '82 26; **'83** 40
Pork Roast Barbecue, **'82** 97; **'83** 104
Pork Roast, Berry Barbecued, **'80** 288
Pork Shoulder, Barbecued, **'81** 111; **'82** 11
Pork Shoulder, Smoked, **'82** 225
Pork, Spicy Barbecued, **'84** 296
Pot Roast, Barbecued, **'79** 17; **'83** 319
Rabbit, Hickory Barbecued, **'82** 216
Ribs, Apple Barbecued, **'80** 111
Ribs, Barbecued, **'80** 111; **'85** 159
Ribs, Country-Style Barbecued, **'79** 42
Ribs, Herbed Barbecued, **'86** 185
Ribs, Oven-Barbecued Pork, **'88** 132
Ribs, Saucy-Sweet, **'81** 166
Ribs, Smoky, **'84** 172
Ribs, Smoky Barbecued, **'80** 111
Ribs, Smoky Oven, **'81** 166
Ribs, Tangy Barbecued, **'83** 160
Roast, Barbecued Rib, **'86** 152
Roast, Grilled Pepper, **'81** 111
Salad, Barbecue Macaroni, **'82** 276
Salmon, Barbecued, **'81** 181
Salmon or Mackerel, Smoked, **'84** 46
Sauces
  Barbecue Sauce, **'84** 172; **'86** 153;
    '88 218
  Barbecue Sauce, Baked Fish
    with, **'84** 92
  Beef Marinade, Tangy, **'86** 113
  Beer Barbecue Sauce, **'84** 173
  Bourbon Barbecue Sauce, **'85** 90
  Brisket with Barbecue Sauce,
    Smoked, **'85** 144
  Dressed-Up Barbecue Sauce, **'84** 173

Eastern-Style Barbecue Sauce, **'88** 145
Easy Barbecue Sauce, **'79** 90; **'82** 178
Lemony Barbecue Sauce, **'88** M177
Mustard Barbecue Sauce, **'84** 173
Orange Barbecue Sauce, Spareribs
  with, **'83** 11
Oven Barbecue Sauce, **'82** 233
Paprika Barbecue Sauce, **'79** 90
Peanut Butter Barbecue
  Sauce, **'81** 233
Piquant Barbecue Sauce, **'79** 159
Savory Barbecue Sauce, **'86** 153
Special Barbecue Sauce, **'82** 177
Sweet-and-Sour Marinade, **'86** 113
Teriyaki Marinade, **'86** 114
Tomato Barbecue Sauce,
  Fresh, **'84** 172
Western-Style Barbecue Sauce, **'88** 145

Sausage, Barbecued, **'86** 153
Sausage, Smoked, **'86** 154
Shrimp, Barbecued, **'82** 74; **'84** 93
Shrimp, Cajun Barbecued, **'87** 95
Shrimp, Grilled, **'85** 103
Spareribs, Barbecued, **'81** 112; **'82** 12;
  '86 232
Spareribs, Barbecued Country-Style, **'80** 73
Spareribs, Easy Barbecued, **'82** 97;
  '83 104
Spareribs, Honey-Glazed, **'82** 163
Spareribs, Orange-Glazed, **'84** 296
Spareribs, Saucy Barbecued, **'79** 14
Spareribs, Southern Barbecued, **'79** 90
Spareribs, Spicy Barbecued, **'84** 93
Spareribs, Tangy Barbecued, **'82** 106
Steak, Barbecued Flank, **'79** 89
Steak, Grilled Black Pepper, **'86** 184
Steak, Grilled Flank, **'80** 152
Steak, Marinated Barbecued Chuck, **'80** 156
Steak, Marinated Flank, **'82** 162
Steak, Saucy Oven-Barbecued, **'83** 10
Steaks with Green Chiles, Grilled, **'85** 144
Steak Teriyaki, Flank, **'81** 110
Steak with Mushroom Sauce, **'83** 212
Trout, Smoked, **'84** 47
Trout with Ginger and Soy Sauce,
  Grilled, **'85** 228
Tuna, Barbecued, **'80** 275
Turkey, Smoked, **'79** 293; **'84** 160
Venison Steaks, Grilled, **'82** 215

Barley

Casserole, Barley, **'84** 281
Rolls, Wine-Sauced
  Beef-and-Barley, **'87** 269

Beans

Bake, Cheesy Beef-and-Bean, **'82** 89
Baked
  Barbecued Pork and Beans, **'79** 100
  Beefy Baked Beans, **'80** 136; **'84** 149;
    '85 142
  Chuckwagon Beans, **'81** 188
  Crowd-Pleasing Baked Beans, **'82** 127
  Easy Baked Beans, **'85** 141
  Favorite Baked Beans, **'86** 210
  Franks, Beans and, **'85** 142
  Franks, Beany Kraut and, **'79** 64
  Franks, Hawaiian Baked Beans
    and, **'80** 136
  Genuine Baked Beans, **'83** 26
  Ham, Baked Beans with, **'80** 136
  Hawaiian-Style Baked Beans, **'86** 210
  Meat Baked Beans, Three-, **'86** 210
  Medley, Baked Bean, **'80** 100
  Mixed Baked Beans, **'87** 92
  Molasses Baked Beans, **'82** 139;
    '84 327; **'86** 20
  Old-Fashioned Baked Beans, **'84** 25
  Picnic Baked Beans, **'83** 143; **'85** 142
  Polynesian Beans-and-Franks, **'84** M11
  Quick Baked Beans, **'80** 136
  Rum-Laced Bean Bake, **'82** 283;
    '83 72
  Smoked Baked Beans, **'79** 150
  Spiced Baked Beans, **'85** 142
  Three-Bean Bake, **'81** 155
Beef-and-Bean Supper, **'82** 2
Beefy Beans, **'82** 59
Black Bean Appetizer, **'83** 50
Black Beans and Cilantro, Southwestern
  Scallop Broth with, **'87** 123
Black Beans and Rice, **'80** 222
Black Beans and Salsa, Poached Chicken
  with, **'87** 217
Black Beans, Cuban, **'88** 196
Black Beans, Spanish, **'84** 327
Black Beans with Yellow Rice, **'82** 2
Black Bean Terrine with Goat
  Cheese, **'87** 120
Black Bean-Tomatillo Relish, **'87** 121
Burritos, Meat-and-Bean, **'81** 194
Casserole, Spicy Mexican Bean, **'84** 114
Casserole, Three-Bean, **'88** 56
Chili and Beans, Ranch, **'79** 270; **'80** 11
Chili Bean Roast, **'87** 268; **'88** 102
Chili Surprise, **'82** 229
Chili, Turkey-Bean, **'88** M213
Chili with Beans, Meaty, **'85** 250
Chimichangas (Fried Burritos), **'81** 196
Chowder, Sausage-Bean, **'83** 20
Creole Beans and Rice, **'80** 223
Dip, Cheese-Bean, **'85** 208
Dip, Hotshot Bean, **'87** 195
Dip, Layered Nacho, **'81** 261
Dip, Prairie Fire Bean, **'80** 195
Dip, South-of-the-Border, **'81** 235
Enchiladas, Spicy Bean, **'88** 18
Franks 'n' Beans, Stove-Top, **'88** 201
Frijoles con Cerveza (Beans with
  Beer), **'81** 66
Garbanzo Dinner, Beef-and-, **'84** 31
Green
  Almonds, Green Beans with, **'84** 253
  Amandine, Green Beans, **'79** 276;
    '82 M20; **'85** 156
  Appalachian Green Beans, **'81** 215

au Gratin, Green Beans, **'80** 116
Bacon Dressing, Green Beans
   with, **'85** 147
Bacon-Topped Green Beans, **'80** M123
Barbecued Green Beans, **'86** 252
Basil Beans and Tomatoes, **'83** 172
Basil, Green Beans with, **'82** 96
Beans, Green, **'80** 126; **'87** M151
Blue Cheese, Green Beans
   with, **'88** 57
Bundles, Bean, **'80** 246; **'83** 67
Bundles, Green Bean, **'83** 180;
   '87 118
Casserole, Chicken-Green
   Bean, **'85** 296
Casserole, Easy Green Bean, **'87** 284
Casserole, Green Bean, **'79** 106;
   '84 145
Casserole, Green
   Bean-and-Corn, **'88** 123
Casserole, Italian Green
   Bean-and-Artichoke, **'85** 81
Celery, Green Beans and
   Braised, **'84** 254
Cheese-Topped Green Beans, **'79** 100
Cheesy Green Beans, **'80** 157
Creamed Green Beans,
   French-Style, **'88** 252
Cumin Green Beans, **'82** 90
Dilled Green Beans, **'82** 106; **'86** 157;
   '88 101
Dilly Green Beans, **'80** 116
French Quarter Green Beans, **'80** 298;
   '81 26
Fresh Green Beans, **'79** 122
Goldenrod Beans, **'83** 111
Herbed Green Beans, **'83** M147, 177;
   '88 M190
Herbs, Green Beans with, **'82** 90
Indian-Style Green Beans, **'88** 265
Italian Green Beans, **'85** 147
Italian, Green Beans, **'87** 10
Italian Green Beans with
   Almonds, **'81** 207
Italiano, Green Beans, **'86** 144
Lemony Green Beans, **'85** 190
Marinated Beets, Green Beans, and
   Carrots, **'88** 162
Marinated Green Beans, **'83** 145
Marinated Italian Beans, **'86** M226
Marinated Vegetables, **'81** 239
Mediterranean-Style Green
   Beans, **'79** 100
Medley, Green Bean, **'85** 108
Minted Green Beans, **'84** 104
Mushrooms, Green Beans with, **'82** 21
Mustard, Green Beans and Tomatoes
   with, **'87** 83
Nutty Green Beans, **'88** M187
Oriental Green Beans, **'88** 43
Pepper Strips, Green Beans
   and, **'86** 170
Pickled Beans, Dressed-Up, **'86** 251
Pole Beans, Old-Fashioned, **'80** 100
Potatoes, Down-Home Beans
   and, **'85** 254
Potatoes, Green Beans with
   New, **'87** 164
Provençal, Green Beans, **'81** 182
Salads. *See* Beans/Salads.
Saucy Green Beans, **'83** 206

Seasoned Green Beans, **'88** 304
Sesame Italian Green Beans, **'82** 174
Snap Beans, **'86** 218
Snap Beans, Simple, **'85** 148
Snap, or Wax Beans, Green, **'85** 105
Sour Cream, Green Beans in, **'80** 116
Sour Cream, Green Beans with, **'82** 90
Southern-Style Green Beans, **'79** 283
Spanish Green Beans, **'80** 116
Spanish-Style Green Beans, **'84** 128
Squash, Beans, and Tomatoes, **'83** 148
Stir-Fried Green Beans, **'85** 148;
   '86 305
Surprise, Green Bean, **'86** 9
Sweet-and-Sour Beans, **'87** 197
Sweet-and-Sour Green Beans, **'79** 184;
   '81 158; **'82** 90
Sweet-and-Sour Green Beans and
   Carrots, **'83** 6
Tangy Green Beans, **'85** M142
Tomatoes, Bean-Stuffed, **'84** 34
Tomatoes, Green Beans with, **'85** 137
Tomatoes, Green Beans with
   Cherry, **'86** 177
Vegetable-Herb Trio, **'83** 172
Zucchini, Green Beans with, **'84** 128
Hot Dogs, Beany, **'82** 190
Lemon-Mint Beans, **'88** 22
Lentil-and-Rice Supper, **'84** 202
Lentil Pilaf, Rice-and-, **'88** 17
Lentil-Rice Stew, **'82** 232
Lentils with Cheese, Baked, **'84** 113
Lentil Tacos, **'88** 197
Lima
   Bake, Lima-Bacon, **'86** 9
   Barbecued Lima Beans, **'82** 2
   Beans, Lima, **'80** 127
   Beef-and-Lima Bean Dinner, **'84** 292
   Canadian Bacon, Lima Beans
     with, **'83** 219; **'84** 245
   Casserole, Ham and Lima, **'79** 192
   Casserole, Lima Bean, **'79** 189;
     '83 313; **'86** 225; **'87** 284
   Casserole, Lima Bean
     Garden, **'83** 218; **'84** 246
   Casserole, Spicy Lima Bean, **'79** 189
   Casserole, Swiss Lima Bean, **'80** 191

Combo, Hot Lima and
   Tomato, **'83** 219
Creole, Lima Beans, **'80** 191;
   '85 137
Deluxe, Lima Beans, **'79** 289; **'80** 26
Fresh Lima Beans and
   Scallions, **'82** 133
Hominy-Sausage Skillet, **'81** 29
Marinated Limas, **'86** 225
Medley, Carrot-Lima-Squash, **'80** 123
Rancho Lima Beans, **'80** 191
Savory Lima Beans, **'83** 219; **'84** 246
Savory Sauce, Lima Beans and Carrots
   with, **'84** 196
Sour Cream, Lima Beans in, **'79** 189;
   '88 41
Spanish-Style Lima Beans, **'83** 25
Succotash, Easy, **'80** 165
Super Lima Beans, **'79** 189
Supper, Sausage-Bean, **'86** 52
Nachos, Best-Ever, **'79** 91
Nachos, Easy, **'84** 30
Nachos, Make-Ahead, **'80** M135
Pinto
   Beef and Bean Supper, **'82** 2
   Chalupa, Bean, **'80** 223
   Chalupas, Bean, **'83** 313
   Chalupas, Pork, **'83** 160
   Chili, Tex-Mex, **'83** 26
   Frijoles Rancheros, **'88** 148
   Pie, Pinto Bean, **'80** 40
   Pinto Beans, **'87** 303
   Ranch Beans, Laredo, **'81** 75
   Razorback Beans, **'84** 328
   Sandwiches, Bean Salad, **'81** 243
   Sausage, Hearty Pintos and, **'88** 296
   Soup, Guadalajara, **'88** 30
   Spicy Hot Pintos, **'83** 26
   Sweet-Hot Pinto Beans, **'86** 114
   Trailride Pinto Beans, **'85** 154
Red Beans and Rice, **'80** 58; **'83** 89;
   '84 37; **'87** 45
Red Beans and Rice, Cajun, **'83** 26
Refried Beans, **'79** 185
Rice, South Texas Beans and, **'85** 252
Salads
   Cannellini Bean Salad,
     Tuna-and-, **'86** 143
   Chilled Bean Salad, **'80** 178
   Cucumber-Bean Salad, **'83** 81
   Five-Bean Salad, Hot, **'81** 149
   Four-Bean Salad, **'79** 20; **'84** 82
   Full o' Beans Salad, **'81** 38
   Garbanzo Salad, **'82** 2
   Garbanzo Salad, Avocado-, **'81** 33
   Garden Medley Salad, **'80** 122
   Green Bean-and-Tomato Salad, **'86** 180
   Green Bean-Peanut Salad, **'86** 117
   Green Bean-Potato Salad, **'83** 80
   Green Bean Salad, **'87** 90
   Green Bean Salad, Cold, **'84** 106
   Green Bean Salad, Crispy, **'82** 239
   Green Bean Salad, Hot, **'86** 298;
     '87 176
   Green Bean Salad, Lettuce and, **'80** 79
   Green Bean Salad, Molded, **'85** 252
   Green Bean Salad, Paprika-, **'86** 191
   Green Bean Salad, Pickled, **'82** 239
   Green Bean Salad, Speedy, **'84** 283
   Green Beans Vinaigrette, **'83** 25
   Hominy-Bean Salad, **'88** 266

Cheese and Limas in Onion
   Shells, **'81** 86
Cheese Limas, Spanish, **'86** 225
Chilly Lima Beans, **'81** 206

Beans, Salads *(continued)*

Kidney Bean-Salami Pasta
Toss, **'85** 165
Layered Salad, **'86** 35
Lima Bean-Tomato Salad, **'85** 137
Marinated Bean-and-Rice
Salad, **'87** 152
Marinated Bean Salad, **'85** 137, 296
Marinated Bean Salad,
Crunchy, **'84** 197
Marinated Combo Salad, **'82** 267
Marinated Corn-Bean Salad, **'87** 9
Mexican Tossed Salad, **'81** 280
Mixed Bean Salad, **'83** 217
Niçoise, Salad, **'86** 35
Overnight Fiesta Salad, **'83** 80
Pinto Salad, **'86** 169
Pole Bean-Potato Salad, Hot, **'79** 74
Pork-'n'-Bean Salad, **'87** 83
Potato-Bean Salad, **'82** 301
Red Bean Slaw, **'79** 247
Rice-and-Bean Salad, **'85** 22
Saucy Bean Salad, **'84** 18
Six-Bean Salad, Colorful, **'87** 82
Southwest Salad, **'81** 113
Sprout Salad, Bean, **'82** 113
Sweet-and-Sour Bean Salad, **'85** 198;
'86 147
Sweet-and-Sour Beans with
Sprouts, **'86** 32
Sweet-and-Sour Vegetable
Salad, **'81** 25
Sauce, Pork-and-Onions with
Bean, **'85** 76
Sausage, Beans, and Rice,
Texas, **'84** 296
Shuck Beans, **'81** 216
Soup, Bean, **'80** 25
Soup, Bean and Bacon, **'83** 26
Soup, Beefy Lentil, **'87** 282
Soup, Black Bean, **'88** 30, 266
Soup, Capitol Hill Bean, **'80** 222
Soup, Chill-Chaser, **'87** 282
Soup, Chunky Navy Bean, **'83** 291
Soup, Cream of Green Bean, **'84** 111
Soup, Drunken Bean, **'87** 283
Soup, Ham-and-Bean, **'84** 4
Soup, Hearty Bean-and-Barley, **'86** 304
Soup, Leafy Bean, **'86** 223
Soup, Lentil, **'83** 292; **'86** 304
Soup, Navy Bean, **'84** 280
Soup, Sausage-Bean, **'85** 88
Soup, Savory Navy Bean, **'87** 282
Soup, Spicy Sausage-Bean, **'83** 229
Soup, Vegetable-Bean, **'83** 317
Soup, White Bean, **'83** 229
White Bean Pot, **'86** 194

Beef

Appetizers, Meat-and-Cheese, **'87** 7
Ball, Cheese 'n' Beef, **'83** 230
Barbecue, Bourbon, **'88** 129
Barbecued Beef, Saucy, **'82** 156
Bouilli, **'80** 58
Bourguignon, Beef, **'79** 104; **'82** 288
Bourguignon, Royal Beef, **'80** 106
Brisket, Barbecued, **'86** 154; **'88** 218
Brisket, Barbecued Beef, **'83** 11
Brisket, Denton, Texas, Barbecued
Beef, **'81** 55
Brisket, Home-Style, **'87** 303

Brisket, Marinated, **'86** 129
Brisket with Barbecue Sauce,
Smoked, **'85** 144
Brisket with Sauce, Barbecued
Beef, **'86** 153
Broccoli with Chive Gravy, Beef
and, **'88** 214
Burgoo, Five-Meat, **'87** 3
Burgoo, Kentucky, **'88** 235
Burgoo, Old-Fashioned, **'87** 3
Burgundy, Beef, **'82** 259; **'83** 125, 281;
'88 25
Burgundy with Pearl Onions, Beef, **'81** 108
Burritos, Cheesy Beef, **'85** 193
Burritos, Meat-and-Bean, **'81** 194
Chalupa, Bean, **'80** 223
Chili, Chuck Wagon, **'81** 282; **'82** 57
Chili, Chunky, **'82** M282; **'86** 3
Chili con Carne, **'82** 310; **'83** 30; **'86** 2
Chili, Cowboy, **'86** 2
Chili, North Texas Red, **'87** 303
Chili, South-of-the-Border, **'83** 283
Chili, Texas Championship, **'81** 54
Chili, Zippy, **'87** 110
Chimichangas (Fried Burritos), **'85** 244;
'86 114
Chinese-Style Beef, **'87** 50
Chipped Beef and Toast, Creamy, **'79** 180
Corned Beef
Brunch Bake, Corned Beef, **'82** 44
Cabbage au Gratin, Corned Beef
and, **'83** 16
Cabbage, Corned Beef and, **'83** 104
Cabbage, Corned Beef Squares
and, **'82** 86
Cabbage, Quick Corned Beef
and, **'79** 54
Dijon Glaze, Corned Beef with, **'87** 54
Dinner, Corned Beef, **'87** 54
Hash, Red Flannel, **'79** 191
Reuben Buns, **'88** 298
Reuben Meat Pie, **'80** 189
Reuben Sandwiches, **'80** M201
Reuben Sandwiches, Broiled, **'81** 240
Reuben Sandwiches, Crispy, **'85** 299
Reuben Sandwiches, Grilled, **'81** 206
Roll, Corned Beef, **'85** 66
Salad, Corned Beef, **'80** 104
Salad, Corned Beef-Cauliflower, **'83** 16
Salad, Corned Beef-Potato, **'85** 213
Salad, Molded Corned Beef, **'82** 86
Salad, Potato-Corned Beef, **'81** 36
Salad, Vegetable-Corned Beef, **'80** 148
Sandwich, Corned Beef and
Cheese, **'79** 214
Sandwiches, Barbecued Corned
Beef, **'83** 130
Sandwiches, Corned Beef, **'83** 291;
'85 242
Sandwiches, Grilled Corned
Beef, **'87** 54
Sandwiches, Meal-in-One, **'80** 218
Soup, Corned Beef, **'83** 16
Soup, French Onion-Beef, **'87** 54
Spread, Corned Beef, **'87** 196
Creamed Beef and Chicken-Topped
Potatoes, **'83** 210
Creamed Dried Beef with
Artichokes, **'85** 81
Cubes in Wine Sauce, Beef, **'79** 264
Curried Beef Dinner, **'83** 4

Dip, Chipped Beef, **'88** M8
Dip, Hot Cheesy Beef, **'80** 85
Élégante, Beef, **'80** 125
en Daube, Beef, **'79** 163
Eye of Round, Grilled Beef, **'82** 91
Fajitas, Beef, **'88** 233
Fajitas, Favorite, **'86** 114
Goulash, Beef, **'83** 231
Goulash, Hungarian, **'81** 227
Gumbo, Texas Ranch-Style, **'82** 226
Jerky, Beef, **'80** 269; **'81** 26
Kabobs, Barbecued Steak, **'79** 89
Kabobs, Beef, **'85** 110
Kabobs Deluxe, Beef, **'82** 182
Kabobs, Marinated Beef, **'82** 105; **'85** 159
Kabobs, Marinated Sirloin, **'82** 162
Kabobs, Marinated Steak, **'80** 184
Kabobs, Pineapple-Beef, **'83** 212
Kabobs, Saucy Beef, **'83** 109
Kabobs, Spirited Beef, **'87** 142
Kabobs, Steak, **'82** 4
Kabobs, Steak-and-Shrimp, **'80** 184
Kabobs, Teriyaki Beef, **'80** 207
Kabobs with Rice, Marinated Beef, **'84** 32
Liver
Creamy Liver and Noodle
Dinner, **'80** 11
Creole Sauce, Liver in, **'87** 33
French-Style Liver, **'80** 10
Gravy, Liver and, **'80** 10
Herbs, Liver with, **'81** 277
Kabobs, Liver, **'80** 185
Patties, Beef Liver, **'81** 277
Saucy Liver, **'81** 277
Sauté, Liver, **'81** 277
Spanish-Style Liver, **'80** 11
Stroganoff, Liver, **'79** 54
Sweet-and-Sour Liver, **'81** 277
Tasty Liver, **'83** 29
Mango-Beef and Rice, **'88** 138
Meatballs, Quick Processor, **'87** 111
Medaillions, Italian Beef, **'87** 305
Medaillions of Beef with Ancho Chile
Sauce, **'87** 122
Mongolian Beef, **'85** 2, 75
Oriental, Beef and Cauliflower, **'80** 220

Oriental Beef and Snow Peas, **'79** 105
Oriental Beef with Pea Pods, **'86** M328
Pastichio, **'85** 194
Peppers, Beef and Green, **'79** 104
Pies, Carry-Along Beef, **'80** 224; **'81** 56
Ribs
Barbecued Beef Short Ribs, **'83** 178
Hearty Beef Shortribs, **'79** 14
Supreme, Beef Shortribs, **'79** 14

Roasts
  Barbecue, Beef Roast, '79 159
  Barbecued Beef Roast, '82 96;
    '83 103
  Beer-and-Onion Sauce, Roast
    in, '80 124
  Brisket Roast, Peppery, '83 319
  Burgundy Roast, Beef, '85 291
  Chili Bean Roast, '87 268; '88 102
  Chuck Roast, Marinated, '80 59
  Chuck Roast, Orange
    Marinated, '85 179
  Cola Roast, '81 298
  Diablo, Beef, '79 17
  Grillades and Grits, '88 126
  Grilled Pepper Roast, '81 110
  Java Roast, '83 319
  Marengo, Beef, '82 284; '83 14
  Marinated Roast, '85 3
  Patio Steak, '87 141
  Pie, Beef Roast Pot, '88 296
  Pot Roast, All-Seasons, '86 89
  Pot Roast, Autumn Gold, '83 7
  Pot Roast, Barbecued, '79 17; '83 319
  Pot Roast, Basic, '81 M208
  Pot Roast, Bavarian-Style, '79 17
  Pot Roast, Bloody Mary, '86 47
  Pot Roast, Cardamom, '79 12
  Pot Roast, Company, '79 162;
    '88 M14
  Pot Roast, Country, '87 216
  Pot Roast, Dillicious, '81 187
  Pot Roast, Easy Oven, '86 52
  Pot Roast, Hawaiian, '81 298
  Pot Roast, Indian, '87 215
  Pot Roast in Red Sauce, '87 215
  Pot Roast in White Wine
    Gravy, '81 299
  Pot Roast, Italian, '81 299; '87 95
  Pot Roast, Marinated, '85 21
  Pot Roast Medley, Vegetable-,
    '83 319
  Pot Roast, Mushroom, '79 17
  Pot Roast, Peppered, '87 215
  Pot Roast, Perfect, '83 7
  Pot Roast, Polynesian, '80 59
  Pot Roast, Regal, '79 17
  Pot Roast, Spicy Apple, '83 7
  Pot Roast, Swedish, '80 59
  Pot Roast, Sweet-and-Sour, '83 8
  Pot Roast with Gravy, '81 298
  Pot Roast with Herbed Red
    Sauce, '88 29
  Pot Roast with Sour Cream
    Gravy, '79 17
  Pot Roast with Spaghetti, '80 59
  Pot Roast with Vegetables, '80 59;
    '81 M208
  Pot Roast with Vegetables,
    Marinated, '88 M52
  Pot Roast, Zesty, '81 206
  Rib-Eye Beef, Spicy, '84 259
  Rib Roast, Barbecued, '86 152
  Rib Roast, Standing, '80 246; '84 187
  Rib Roast with Yorkshire Pudding,
    Standing, '80 252
  Sauerbraten, Quick, '80 139
  Simple Roast, '81 298
  Sirloin Tip Roast with Mustard Cream
    Sauce, Herbed, '88 61
  Supreme, Roast Beef, '83 8

  Vegetables, Company Beef
    and, '88 234
  Wellington, Beef, '83 319
Rolls, Stuffed Sherried Beef, '79 105
Rolls, Wine-Sauced
  Beef-and-Barley, '87 269
Rollups with Rice, Royal Beef, '79 105
Roulades, Beef, '83 47
Roulades, Roquefort Beef, '88 215
Salad, Beef-and-Broccoli, '87 187
Salad, Gingered Beef, '88 61
Salad, Peking Beef, '88 60
Salad, Roast Beef, '80 223; '81 56
Salad, Tangy Beef, '87 M218
Salad, Zesty Beef, '79 56
Sandwiches, Beef and Pork
  Tenderloin, '80 175
Sandwiches, Beef Salad Pocket, '83 267
Sandwiches, Dried Beef Pita, '86 160
Sandwiches, Wake-Up, '84 58
Sandwich, Saucy Beef Pocket, '80 92
Seasoning Blend, Meat, '88 29
Shredded Beef over Rice Noodles, '85 74
Soup, Beefy Lentil, '87 282
Soup, Hearty Vegetable-Beef, '84 102
Soup, Vegetable-Beef, '88 296
Spaghetti, Meaty, '82 19
Spread, Hot Beef, '83 50; '84 M216
Steaks
  Appetizers, Marinated
    Steak-and-Chestnut, '84 323
  au Poivre, Steak, '88 232
  Barbecued Steak, '81 18
  Barbecued Steak, Saucy Oven-, '83 10
  Bean Sprouts, Beef and, '82 281;
    '83 42
  Benedict for Two, Steaks, '85 295
  Blue Cheese Steaks, '84 171
  Braised Steaks, Beer-, '87 96
  Broiled Oriental Steaks, '83 110
  Carpetbagger Steak, '84 87
  Chuck Steak, Marinated
    Barbecued, '80 156
  Continental, Steak, '83 178
  Country-Fried Steak and Cream
    Gravy, '84 8
  Country-Fried Steak, Mock, '87 163
  Curried Beef Steak, '88 60
  Cutlets, Lemon-Flavored, '79 105
  de Burgo, Steak, '84 117
  Diane Flambé, Steak, '79 103
  Diane, Steak, '82 275
  Dianne, Steak, '83 47
  Fajitas, '84 233
  Filet Mignon, Marinated, '84 171
  Fillets au Vin, Beef, '79 137
  Fillets with Horseradish Sauce and
    Curried Bananas, '85 230
  Fingers, Golden Steak, '85 110
  Flank Steak and Mushrooms, '87 61
  Flank Steak, Bacon-Wrapped, '85 59
  Flank Steak, Barbecued, '79 89
  Flank Steak, Beer-Marinated, '87 35
  Flank Steak, Grilled, '80 152
  Flank Steak, Herb-Marinated, '85 275
  Flank Steak, Marinated, '82 162;
    '83 35, 258; '85 86; '88 262
  Flank Steak, Oriental, '83 178
  Flank Steak Pinwheels, '87 141
  Flank Steaks, Delicious
    Marinated, '83 110

  Flank Steak Sukiyaki, '88 233
  Flank Steak, Tangy, '86 184
  Flank Steak, Tenderized, '82 105
  Flank Steak Teriyaki, '81 110
  Flank Steak, Texas, '86 185
  French Quarter Steak, '81 17
  Fried Steaks, Chicken-, '88 110
  Garlic Steak, '84 8
  Greek Pocket Steaks, '81 262
  Grilled Black Pepper Steak, '86 184
  Grilled Steaks, Mesquite-, '85 154
  Grilled Steaks with Green
    Chiles, '85 144
  Grill, Steak Brunch, '82 44
  Ham-and-Mushroom Sauce, Steak
    with, '83 109
  Horseradish Steak, '88 39
  Kabobs, Hot-and-Spicy, '87 193
  Lemon-Butter Steak with Brandy
    Sauce, '85 78

  London Broil, Marinated, '87 32
  London Broil, Peppercorn, '88 60
  Marinated Beef on a Stick, '85 234
  Marinated Steak, '88 233
  Marinated Steak, Mexican, '88 148
  Mexican Steak, '84 76
  Mushroom Sauce, Steak with, '83 212
  Mush, Steak and Gravy with, '81 215
  Oriental Beef, '85 20
  Parmigiana, Beef, '84 8; '85 234
  Pepper-Beef Steak, '85 21
  Pepper Steak, '81 273; '85 57;
    '88 113
  Pepper Steak and Rice, '81 17
  Pepper Steak, Chinese, '82 236
  Pepper Steak, Cracked, '83 109
  Pepper Steak Salad Cups, '86 206
  Pepper Stir-Fry Steak, '81 240
  Pies, Cornish Meat, '84 23
  Pirate Steak, '79 89
  Roulades, Beef, '85 234
  Round Steak, Braised, '87 35
  Round Steak, Parmesan, '80 106
  Round Steak, Red Pepper, '88 214
  Round Steak, Savory Stuffed, '81 18
  Round Steak, Skillet, '83 29
  Round Steak, Tangy, '82 284; '83 14
  Round Steak, Tender Grilled, '85 3
  Saltillo, Beef (Beef with
    Tomatillos), '82 219
  Shrimp, Steak and, '88 123
  Sirloin Steak, Secret, '81 110
  Sirloin Supreme, Shrimp and, '81 131
  Skewered Steak with
    Vegetables, '81 124
  Skillet Steak in Red Wine
    Sauce, '85 21
  Skillet Steak 'n Potatoes, '81 18
  Smothered Beef and Onions, '85 293

Beef, Steaks *(continued)*

Smothered Steak, '79 212
Smothered Steak, Onion-, '87 M189
Stick, Steak on a, '83 109
Stir-Fried Beef, '84 26
Stir-Fried Steak, Fast-and-Easy, '87 50
Stir-Fry, Beef-and-Vegetable, '87 22
Stir-Fry Beef-and-Vegetables, '84 141
Stir-Fry, Steak-and-Vegetable, '84 8
Stuffed Steak, Italian-, '88 232
Stuffed Steak Rolls, '82 135
Stuffed Steaks, Cheese-, '81 17
Sweet-and-Sour Marinated
    Steaks, '83 110
Swiss Steak Cheese Skillet, '80 106
Swiss Steak, Deviled, '80 107
Swiss Steak, Oven, '85 234
Swiss Steak Surprise, '81 17
Swiss Steak with Vegetables, '81 273
Tartare, Steak, '83 78
Teriyaki, Marinated Steak, '84 50
Tournedos Mouton, '83 262
Vegetables, Beef with
    Chinese, '81 211
Vegetables, Beef with
    Oriental, '84 140
Wellingtons, Individual Beef, '82 259

Stew, Bama Brunswick, '87 4
Stew, Beef, '86 51
Stew, Beef-and-Onion, '87 18
Stew, Brown, '85 239
Stew, Burgundy Beef, '88 234
Stew, Company Beef, '83 85
Stew, Mexican, '82 231
Stew Olé, Mexican, '86 296
Stew, Oven Beef, '79 222; '80 64
Stew, Spicy Beef, '86 228
Stew, Sweet-and-Sour Beef and
    Vegetable, '85 87
Stew, White Wine, '82 228
Stew with Drop Dumplings,
    Burgundy, '83 125
Stew with Dumplings, Beef, '84 3
Stew with Noodles, Hungarian, '80 263
Stew with Parsley Dumplings, Beef, '81 76;
    '82 13; '85 M246
Stir-Fried Beef and Vegetables, '88 301
Stir-Fry Beef and Broccoli, '79 47
Stir-Fry Beef and Pea Pods, '80 19

Stir-Fry, Beef and Snow Pea, '82 98
Stir-Fry Beef and Snow Peas, '83 22
Stir-Fry, Beef-and-Vegetable, '81 211
Stir-Fry Broccoli and Beef, '83 110
Stir-Fry, Chinese Beef, '83 151
Stir-Fry, Teriyaki, '83 110
Stroganoff, Beef, '79 163; '81 179
Stroganoff, Beef Burgundy, '85 31
Stroganoff, Light Beef, '86 36
Stroganoff, Liver, '79 54
Stroganoff Sandwiches, Steak, '85 110
Stroganoff, Sirloin, '81 297
Stroganoff with Parslied Noodles,
    Steak, '85 31
Tacos al Carbón, '86 19
Tacos al Carbon, Tailgate, '79 185
Tamales, '80 195
Tempting Twosome, '81 240
Tenderloin Deluxe, Beef, '85 109
Tenderloin, Elegant Beef, '88 244
Tenderloin, Herb Marinated, '83 109
Tenderloin, Lobster-Stuffed Beef, '87 248
Tenderloin, Marinated, '80 146
Tenderloin, Marinated Beef, '81 246;
    '85 302
Tenderloin, Spicy Beef, '88 29
Tenderloin, Spicy Marinated Beef, '83 262
Tenderloin, Stuffed, '86 323; '88 50
Tenderloin with Mushroom Sauce,
    Beef, '88 3
Tenderloin with Mushrooms, Beef, '87 115
Tenderloin with Mushroom-Sherry Sauce,
    Beef, '87 306
Tips and Noodles, Beef, '86 293
Tips on Rice, Beef, '85 87
Tournedos Diables, '87 60
Turnovers, Roast Beef, '88 273
Vegetables in a Noodle Ring, Beef
    and, '85 285
Vegetables, Savory Beef and, '79 163

Beef, Ground
Appetizer, Cheesy Mexicali, '82 108
Barbecue Cups, '79 129
Bean Bake, Cheesy Beef-and-, '82 89
Bean Medley, Baked, '80 100
Beans, Beefy, '82 59
Beans, Beefy Baked, '80 136; '84 149;
    '85 142
Beans, Rancho Lima, '80 191
Beans, Three-Meat Baked, '86 210
Burgoo, Harry Young's, '87 3
Burritos, Chinese, '87 181
Burritos, Fiesta, '86 114
Cabbage-and-Beef Rolls, Easy, '88 49
Cabbage, Italian Stuffed, '84 294
Cabbage Rolls, '83 104
Cabbage Rolls, Beef Stuffed, '81 87; '82 7
Cabbage Rolls, Spicy, '84 2
Cabbage Rolls, Stuffed, '84 217
Cabbage Rollups, Beef-and-, '80 63
Cabbage, Stuffed, '84 282
Casseroles
    Biscuit Casserole, Beef-and-, '83 75
    Cabbage Beef Bake, Zesty, '80 300
    Cheesy Ground Beef Casserole, '79 44
    Cheesy Mexican Casserole, '82 224
    Chili-Rice Casserole, '79 54
    Cornbread Casserole, '81 91
    Cornbread Skillet Casserole, '83 243;
        '84 101
    County Fair Casserole, '79 130

    Creamy Ground Beef
        Casserole, '81 142
    Crusty Beef Casserole, '82 88
    Easy Beef Casserole, '86 M58
    El Dorado Casserole, '81 140
    Enchilada Casserole, '87 287
    Enchilada Casserole,
        Firecracker, '80 260
    Enchilada Casserole, Sour
        Cream, '82 113
    Five-Layer Meal, '81 140
    Italian Cabbage Casserole, '87 42
    Italian Casserole, '80 81
    Layered Beef Casserole, '82 M203
    Layered Grecian Bake, '82 119
    Macaroni Combo, Beef-, '79 194
    Matador Mania, '86 19
    Mexi Casserole, '83 M87
    Moussaka Casserole, '79 179
    Noodle Bake, Hamburger-, '81 140
    Noodles Casserole, Beef-and-, '84 72
    Pastitsio, '87 12; '88 11
    Pizza Casserole, '88 273
    Pizza Casserole, Quick, '83 266
    Sausage Casserole, Ground Beef
        and, '80 260
    Seashell-Provolone Casserole, '80 189
    Sour Cream-Noodle Bake, '79 55
    Spaghetti and Beef Casserole, '79 129
    Spinach and Beef Casserole, '79 192
    Spinach-Beef-Macaroni
        Casserole, '83 313
    Taco Beef-Noodle Bake, '81 141
    Taco Casserole, '80 33
    Vegetable Casserole, Beefy, '79 248
    Vegetable Chow Mein Casserole,
        Beef-and-, '83 313
    Zucchini-Beef Bake, '86 146
Chiles Rellenos Egg Rolls, '86 296

Chili
Basic Chili, '82 M11
Cheese-Topped Chili, '82 M11
Cheesy Chili, '82 310
Chili, '87 17
Company Chili, '82 311; '83 30
con Carne, Beef and Sausage
    Chili, '83 284
con Carne, Chili, '84 72
con Carne, Favorite Chili, '86 293
con Carne, Quick-and-Easy Chili, '86 2
Double-Meat Chili, '79 269; '80 12
Easy Chili, '82 310; '83 30
Friday Night Chili, '86 228
Hominy Bake, Chili, '81 282; '82 58
Hot Texas Chili, '80 222; '81 77
Lunchtime Chili, '81 230
Meaty Chili, '81 282; '82 58

Meaty Chili with Beans, '85 250
Noodles, Chili with, '81 282; '82 57
Potato Chili, Savory, '83 284
Potatoes, Chili-Topped, '83 3
Quick and Simple Chili, '81 282;
    '82 58
Quick Chili, '83 283
Ranch Chili and Beans, '79 270;
    '80 11
Rice, Chili with, '82 M11
Roundup Chili, '79 269; '80 12
Sauce, Chili Meat, '83 4
Sausage-Beef Chili, '86 232
Sausage Chili, Beefy, '82 M11
Simple Chili, '79 269; '80 11
Spiced Chili, Hot, '83 214
Spicy Chili, Old-Fashioned, '79 269;
    '80 11
Texas-Style Chili, '82 311; '83 30
Tex-Mex Chili, '83 26
Tree-Hunt Chili, '87 292
Cornbread, Beefy Jalapeño, '82 142
Cornbread, Cheesy Beef, '81 242
Cornbread Tamale Bake, '79 163
Crêpes, Sherried Beef, '85 M29
Curried Beef and Rice, '88 164
Dinner, Beef-and-Garbanzo, '84 31
Dinner, Beef-and-Lima Bean, '84 292
Dinner, Beef-Cabbage, '81 179
Dinner, Beefy Sausage, '80 M9
Dinner, Black-Eyed Pea Skillet, '86 6
Dinner, Fiesta, '85 110
Dinner, Ground Beef Skillet, '82 60
Dinner, Mexican Beef-and-Rice, '88 199
Dip, Hot Chile-Beef, '83 218
Dip, Meaty Cheese, '82 59
Dip, Tostada, '84 206
Eggplant, Baked Stuffed, '81 133
Eggplant, Beefy Stuffed, '81 204
Eggplant, Cheesy Stuffed, '79 188
Enchiladas, American, '81 170
Enchiladas, Hot and Saucy, '81 141; '82 6
Enchiladas, Skillet, '82 89
Enchiladas, Sour Cream, '87 37
Fiesta, '87 180
Filet Mignon, Mock, '80 81
Filet Mignon Patties, Mock, '82 M68
Fillets, Poor Boy, '82 106
Filling, Beef, '80 81
Flips, Pea, '80 7
Gumbo, Ground Beef, '87 283
Gumbo Joes, '88 158
Hamburgers
    Apple Burgers, '86 137
    au Poivre Blanc, Burgers, '87 186
    Bacon Burgers, Cheesy, '81 29
    Barbecued Burgers, '82 168
    Beefburger on Buns, '84 71
    Beerburgers, '79 129
    Burgundy Burgers, '80 156
    Cheeseburger Biscuits, '79 194
    Cheeseburger Loaves, '86 19
    Cheesy Beef Burgers, '83 217
    Chili Burgers, Open-Face, '81 24;
        '82 31; '83 33
    Cocktail Burgers, Saucy, '83 217
    Deluxe, Burgers, '84 125
    Glorified Hamburgers, '81 73
    Grilled Hamburgers, Flavorful, '81 110
    Hawaiian, Beefburgers, '86 137
    Mexicali Beef Patties, '86 137

    Nutty Burgers, '87 185
    Old-Fashioned Hamburgers, '79 149
    Oven Burgers, '83 130
    Party Burgers, '83 164; '84 39
    Patties, Deviled-Beef, '87 22
    Patties, Hamburger, '82 M172
    Pineapple Burgers, '82 169
    Pizza Burger, '87 185
    Pizza Burgers, '80 M201; '81 73
    Pizza Burgers, Easy, '82 190
    Pizza, Quick Hamburger, '85 243
    Sauce, Hamburgers with
        Tomato, '81 73
    Saucy Burgers, '80 93
    Saucy Hamburgers, Quick, '82 60
    Sausage Burgers, '83 212
    Seasoned Burgers, '85 158
    Seasoned Hamburgers, '84 230
    Seasoned Stuffed Burgers, '86 136
    Sour Cream Burgers, Grilled, '87 287
    Steak-House Burgers, '87 186
    Steaks, Company Hamburger, '82 169
    Steaks with Mustard Sauce,
        Hamburger, '84 230
    Stuffed Burgers, '85 159
    Superburgers, '79 89
    Super Hamburgers, '79 129
    Super Supper Burgers, '82 110
    Surprise Burgers, '82 169
    Tahiti Burgers, '85 179
    Teriyaki Burgers, '81 72
    Vegetable Burgers, Beef-and-,
        '84 125
    Venison Burgers, '87 304
Kheema, Indian, '81 226
Lasagna, '82 119; '83 M6
Lasagna, Beefy, '80 81
Lasagna, Cheesy, '82 224; '88 299
Lasagna, Cheesy Spinach, '83 204
Lasagna for Two, '81 91
Lasagna, Quick, '84 220
Lasagna, Quick 'n Easy, '80 M10
Lasagna, Simple, '81 188
Lasagna, South-of-the-Border, '84 31
Lasagna, Vintage, '79 194
Log, Stuffed Beef, '79 71

Macaroni, Ground Beef and, '85 218
Macaroni, Skillet Beef and, '82 130
Madras, Beef, '87 284
Manicotti, Quick, '79 6
Manicotti, Saucy Stuffed, '83 288
Manicotti, Special, '88 50
Meatballs
    Bacon-Wrapped Meatballs, '79 81
    Barbecued Meatballs, Oven,
        '82 233

Brandied Meatballs, '83 78
Burgundy-Bacon Meatballs, '80 283
Chafing Dish Meatballs, '81 260
Chestnut Meatballs, '79 110
Chinese Meatballs, '83 116; '87 194
Cocktail Meatballs, '79 63, 207
Creole, Meatball-Okra, '83 156
Creole, Meatballs, '82 233
Español, Meatballs, '82 110
Flavorful Meatballs, '84 206
Golden Nugget Meatballs, '82 233
Gravy, Meatballs in, '79 136
Hawaiian Meatballs, '85 86
Hawaiian Meatballs, Tangy, '79 129
Heidelberg, Beef Balls, '83 164;
    '84 39
Paprikash with Rice, Meatballs,
    '85 31
Pizza Meatballs, '85 86
Polynesian Meatballs, '80 207
Red Delicious Meatballs, '85 85
Royal Meatballs, '87 268; '88 102
Saucy Meatballs, '85 68
Saucy Party Meatballs, '80 149
Sauerbraten Meatballs, '85 85
Spaghetti-and-Herb Meatballs, '84 75
Spaghetti with Meatballs, '81 38
Spiced Meatballs, '79 284
Spicy Meatballs and Sausage, '79 163
Stew, Meatball, '79 198
Stroganoff, Meatball, '81 297
Stroganoff, Mushroom-Meatball, '85 85
Swedish Meatballs, '80 80; '86 256
Sweet-and-Sour Meatballs, '82 233;
    '86 240
Sweet-and-Sour Party
    Meatballs, '79 233
Tamale Meatballs, '80 194
Zesty Meatballs, '80 250
Meat Loaf
    Barbecued Meat Loaf, '80 60;
        '81 275; '84 50; '87 216
    Basic Meat Loaf, '88 M14
    Cheeseburger Loaf, '81 236, 276
    Cheesy Meat Roll, '82 136
    Chili Meat Loaf, '81 275
    Corny Meat Loaf, '86 68
    Crunchy Meat Loaf Oriental, '79 212
    Curried Meat Loaf, '86 43
    Easy Meat Loaf, '88 M214
    Fennel Meat Loaf, '88 46
    German Meat Loaf, '87 216
    Glazed Beef Loaf, '86 19
    Hurry-Up Meat Loaf, '82 21
    Hurry-Up Meat Loaves, '88 15
    Individual Meat Loaves, '81 279;
        '82 24; '83 154
    Italian Meat Loaf, '79 187
    Meat Loaf, '81 170
    Mexicali Meat Loaf, '81 275
    Mexican Meat Loaf, '87 217
    Miniature Meat Loaves, '85 24
    Mozzarella-Layered Meat Loaf, '79 71
    Oriental Meat Loaf, '81 M122;
        '83 M194
    Parsleyed Meat Loaf, '83 35
    Parsley Meat Loaf, '87 22
    Pineapple Loaves, Individual,
        '81 M121
    Pizza Meat Loaf, Cheesy, '81 M121
    Roll, Meat Loaf, '79 129

Beef, Ground, Meat Loaf (continued)

Saucy Meat Loaves, **'79** 186
Savory Meat Loaf, **'87** 216
Spicy Meat Loaf, **'79** 71
Sprout Meat Loaf, **'85** 51
Stuffed Beef Log, **'79** 71
Stuffed Meat Loaf, **'79** 187
Stuffed Meat Loaf, Rolled, **'80** 80
Swedish Meat Loaf, **'81** M121
Tasty Meat Loaf, **'83** 213
Triple Meat Loaf, **'79** 186
Vegetable Loaf, Beef-, **'79** 164
Vegetable Meat Loaf, **'85** M29
Wellington, Meat Loaf, **'79** 186;
'87** 284
Mix, Ground Beef, **'84** 71
Moussaka, **'87** 166
Moussaka, Corn, **'87** 190
Mushrooms, Stuffed, **'83** 13
Noodle Dinner, Beefy, **'81** 179
Noodles, Easy Beef and, **'83** 288
Omelet, Beefy Vegetable, **'83** 188
Omelet con Carne, Tex-Mex, **'81** 209
Patties, Foo Yong, **'80** 223
Peppers, Beefed-Up, **'82** 186
Peppers, Beef-Stuffed, **'84** 154;
'85** 146
Peppers, Beefy Stuffed Green, **'81** 86
Peppers for Two, Stuffed, **'80** 84
Peppers, Mexican Green, **'80** 65
Peppers, Stuffed, **'81** 239; **'83** 66
Peppers Stuffed with Beef, **'84** 72
Picadillo (Spicy Beef over Rice), **'80** 193;
'84** 118; **'85** 57
Pie, Broccoli-Beef, **'83** 196
Pie, Cheese-Beef, **'85** 33
Pie, Corn Burger, **'83** 156
Pie, Country, **'83** 155
Pie, Crescent Taco, **'80** 80
Pie, Double-Crust Taco, **'88** 272
Pie, Enchilada, **'83** 155
Pie, Hamburger, **'81** 92; **'84** 13
Pie, Meat-and-Potato, **'84** 23
Pie, Mexicali Meat, **'81** 194
Pie, Mexican Burrito, **'87** 287
Pie, Old-Fashioned Meat, **'82** 110
Pie, Shepherd, **'83** 116
Pies, Individual Taco, **'82** M282
Pies, Natchitoches Meat, **'84** 21
Pie, Sombrero, **'81** 140
Pie, Spaghetti, **'81** 32
Pies, Vegetable-Beef, **'80** 286
Pie, Taco, **'88** 256
Pitas, Curried Beef, **'85** 220
Pizza, Best Ever Homemade, **'80** 233
Pizza-Burger Snacks, **'84** 30
Pizza Cups, **'81** 215
Pizza, Double Cheesy
Beef-and-Sausage, **'86** 77
Pizza, Quick Hamburger, **'85** 243
Pizza Supreme, **'81** 214
Pizza, Tostada, **'81** 16; **'82** 13
Quiche, Green Chile, **'83** 31
Ravioli, Homemade, **'87** 230
Rice, Spanish, **'81** 51
Rice, Spiced Beef and, **'84** 285
Rice, Spicy Beef and, **'83** 231
Rolls, Italian Meat, **'86** 137
Rolls, Spicy Beef, **'85** 110
Roulades, Beef, **'80** 80

Salad Cups, Taco, **'85** M29
Salad, Dude Ranch, **'80** 15
Salad in a Shell, Mexican, **'86** 4
Salad, Mexican, **'81** 36
Salad, Mexican Chef, **'85** 84
Salad, Mexican Olive, **'85** 84
Salad, Mexi-Pea, **'81** 7
Salad, Spicy Chili, **'86** 71
Salad, Spicy Taco, **'87** 287
Salad Supper, Mexican, **'82** 9; **'83** 68
Salad, Taco, **'79** 56; **'83** 145; **'84** 221;
'85** 84
Salisbury Steak Deluxe, **'81** 170
Sandwiches, Barbecued Beef, **'81** 25;
'82** 31; **'83** 34
Sandwiches, Bavarian Pita, **'83** 31
Sandwiches, Beef-Eater, **'86** 72
Sandwiches, Hearty Pocket, **'80** 93

Sandwiches, Hot Pita, **'83** 217; **'87** M6
Sandwiches, Open-Face Pizza, **'82** 3
Sauce, Beer Spaghetti, **'85** 13
Sauce, Herbed Spaghetti, **'85** 13
Sauce, Italian Meat, **'83** 193
Shells, Cheesy Beef-Stuffed, **'83** 217
Skillet, Vegetable-Beef, **'86** 172
Slice, French Beef, **'79** 125
Sloppy Joe Dogs, **'85** 192
Sloppy Joe Pocket Sandwiches, **'81** 200
Sloppy Joes, **'81** 279; **'82** 24; **'83** 153
Sloppy Joes, Easy, **'82** 31, 278; **'83** 34
Sloppy Joes, Pocket, **'85** M328
Sloppy Joes, Simple, **'82** 130
Sloppy Joes, Super, **'83** 130
Snacks, Beefy Party, **'80** 249
Soup, Beefy Black-Eyed, **'85** 6
Soup, Beefy Vegetable, **'79** 113; **'84** M38
Soup, Hamburger, **'80** 263
Soup, Quick Beefy Vegetable, **'80** 25
Soup, Spicy Vegetable-Beef, **'88** 11
Soup, Vegetable-Burger, **'82** 6
Spaghetti, Black-Eyed Pea, **'81** 7
Spaghetti, Easy, **'83** M317; **'84** 72
Spaghetti, Meaty, **'82** 19
Spaghetti, Quick Pepperoni, **'88** 40
Spaghetti, Real Italian, **'81** 233
Spaghetti Sauce, Thick, **'84** 118
Spaghetti, Thick-and-Spicy, **'83** 287
Spaghetti with Mushrooms, Spicy, **'85** 2
Spaghetti with Pizzazz, **'80** 85
Spaghetti, Zucchini, **'83** 160
Squash, Beef-Stuffed, **'83** 134
Squash, Stuffed Acorn, **'83** 15
Steak, Spanish, **'80** 80
Stew, Hamburger Oven, **'84** 4
Stew, Mixed Vegetable, **'84** 13
Stew, Quick Beef, **'86** 302

Stroganoff, Easy Hamburger, **'79** 208
Stroganoff, Ground Beef, **'84** 71
Stroganoff, Hamburger, **'82** 108, 110
Stroganoff, Quickie, **'81** 200
Stromboli, **'87** 283
Supper, Beef-and-Bean, **'82** 2
Supper, Beef-and-Eggplant, **'84** 291
Supper, Oriental Beef, **'79** 192
Supper, Quick Skillet, **'84** 69
Supreme, Beef, **'83** 196
Tacos, **'80** 196
Tacos, Basic, **'83** 199
Tacos, Corn Chip, **'81** 67
Tacos, Jiffy, **'83** M318
Tacos, Microwave, **'88** M213
Texas Straw Hat, **'85** 293
Tostada Compuestas, **'81** 194
Tostadas, Crispy, **'83** 2
Tostadas, Super, **'83** 199
Turnovers, Meat, **'86** 326
Wontons, Tex-Mex, **'87** 196
Zucchini, Beef-Stuffed, **'86** M139

Beets
Apples, Beets and, **'80** 137; **'88** 155
Borscht, Ruby Red, **'83** 176
Cake, Chocolate Beet, **'80** 40
Cake with Almond Topping, Beet, **'86** 200
Chilled Beets and Cauliflower, **'80** 137
Creamy Beets, **'80** 136
Deviled Beets, **'84** 217; **'86** 252
Glazed Beets, Orange-, **'81** 167; **'85** 289;
'86** 187
Glazed Beets, Strawberry-, **'83** 234
Glazed Fresh Beets, **'81** 167
Harvard Beets, **'83** M195
Ivy League Beets, **'84** 122
Marinated Beets, Green Beans, and
Carrots, **'88** 162
Orange-Ginger Beets, **'80** 137
Pickled Beets, **'79** 276; **'81** 216; **'87** 163
Pickled Beets, Easy, **'80** 137
Pickles, Beet, **'81** 210
Pineapple, Beets with, **'79** 249; **'82** 204
Relish, Beet, **'84** 179
Relish, Colorful Beet, **'85** 136
Rice Ring with Beets, **'79** 225
Salad, Beet-Nut, **'79** 74
Salad, Marinated Beet, **'83** 216
Salad Mold, Beet, **'82** 267
Salad, Orange-and-Beet, **'88** 43
Salad, Pickled Beet, **'83** 234
Salad, Tangy Beet, **'86** 199
Soup, Potato-Beet, **'88** 156
Sour Cream Dressing, Beets
with, **'88** M295
Spiced Beets, **'79** 22
Stuffed Beets, **'88** 155
Stuffed Beets, Blue Cheese-, **'88** 211
Stuffed Beets, Potato-, **'83** 234
Sweet-and-Sour Beets, **'81** 167; **'82** 22
Beverages
Alcoholic
Almond-Flavored Liqueur, **'81** 287
Amaretto Breeze, **'83** 172
Banana Flip, **'83** 303
Banana Kabana, **'86** 316
Bellinis, **'88** 77
Bloody Mary, **'80** 221
Bloody Mary, Easy, **'84** 115
Bloody Marys, **'79** 33, 38; **'80** 51
Bloody Marys, Eye-Opener, **'82** 48

Bloody Marys, Overnight, '81 270
Bloody Marys, Pitcher, '81 198
Bloody Marys, Spicy, '87 173
Bourbon Slush, '84 58
Bourbon Slush, Summertime, '81 101
Brandy Cream, '84 312
Burgundy Bowl, Sparkling, '83 276
Café Colombian Royal, '80 M290
Café Cream, '82 312
Café Diablo, '80 259
Café Mocha Cream, '84 54
Café Royal, '80 259
Cappuccino, Flaming, '79 293
Champagne Delight, '83 304
Chocolate, Flaming Brandied, '80 M290
Cider, Hot Mexican, '87 213
Cider, Hot Mulled, '84 323
Cider, Red Apple, '80 259
Coconut Frost, Pink, '79 174; '80 128
Coconut Nog, '83 275
Coconut-Pineapple Drink, '83 172
Coffee, After-Dinner, '81 262
Coffee, Brandied, '81 244
Coffee, Chocolate, '82 43
Coffee Cream, Icy Rum, '83 172
Coffee, Creamy Irish, '79 232
Coffee Delight, Almond-, '84 115
Coffee, Flaming Irish, '79 293
Coffee-Flavored Liqueur, '86 266
Coffee, Mexican, '83 175
Coffee Nog, Brandied, '86 329

Coffee Nog, Irish, '84 258
Coffee, Praline-Flavored, '87 69
Coffee Refresher, Velvet, '79 149
Cranberry Cooler, '86 229
Cranberry-Rum Slush, '84 259
Cranberry Wine Cup, '85 23
Daiquiris, Cranberry, '81 245
Daiquiris, Freezer Lime, '79 141
Daiquiri, Strawberry, '81 156
Daiquiritas, '82 160
Dessert, After Dinner-Drink, '82 100
Dessert Drink, Creamy, '86 131
Dessert Drink, Simply Super, '83 303
Eggnog, Christmas, '87 242
Eggnog, Creamy, '80 259; '83 303
Eggnog Deluxe, Holiday, '79 232
Eggnog, Edenton, '84 251
Eggnog, Thick and Creamy, '80 261
Frosty Sours, '81 156
Fuzz Buzz, '82 160
Ginger Beer, '84 159

Golden Dream, '82 100
Holiday Brew, '81 265
Irish Cream Nog, '82 312
Kahlúa Smoothie, '87 242
Kahlúa Velvet Frosty, '82 244
King Alfonso, '80 259
Lemonade, Hot Buttered, '88 208
Lemon Cooler, '82 48
Lime Fizz, '81 172
Magnolia Blossoms, '87 72
Magnolias, '82 196
Margaritas, Frosted, '84 115
Margaritas, Frosty, '83 172
Margaritas, Pitcher, '83 175
Margaritas Supreme, Frozen, '80 160
Margaritas, Tart, '85 153
Melon Ball Cooler, '86 131
Mimosa Hawaiian, '85 44
Mimosas, '86 91
Minted Delight, '87 107
Mint Juleps, '81 155; '82 41; '85 40
Mocha Deluxe Hot Drink, '82 289
Oklahoma Sunrise, '87 67
Old-Fashioneds, '86 270
Orange Blossom Flips, '80 51
Orange-Champagne Cocktail, '79 39
Orange Liqueur, '81 287
Orange Milk Shake, '84 166
Peach Frosty, '81 156
Peach Smash, '88 161
Peppermint Flip, Hot, '86 329
Piña Coladas, Frosty, '83 176
Piña Coladas, Luscious, '81 134
Plum Slush, '84 139
Punch, Anytime Wine, '79 232
Punch, Bourbon-Tea, '87 57
Punch, Brandy Milk, '85 44; '88 83
Punch, Brandy Slush, '87 72
Punch, Champagne, '85 153, 257;
  '86 101
Punch, Champagne Blossom, '81 50
Punch, Chatham Artillery, '80 121
Punch, Coffee, '88 83
Punch, Coffee-Eggnog, '86 281
Punch, Cranapple-Vodka, '87 72
Punch, Cranberry, '85 90
Punch, Cranberry Percolator, '88 248
Punch, Fruit, '83 52
Punch, Gin, '80 160
Punch, Golden Gin, '79 233
Punch, Golden Spiked, '79 285
Punch, Health-Kick, '80 174
Punch, Hot Cranberry, '84 41
Punch, Hot Molasses-Milk, '86 329
Punch, Hot Pineapple, '82 264
Punch, Hot Wine, '85 265
Punch, Jefferson County, '86 267
Punch, Lime, '84 58
Punch, Milk, '79 38
Punch, New Orleans Milk, '81 50
Punch, Orange-Lime, '82 160
Punch, Party, '81 265
Punch, Perky Rum, '85 116
Punch, Pineapple, '79 174; '80 128
Punch, Raspberry-Rosé, '87 242
Punch, Refreshing Champagne, '84 259
Punch, Rum, '85 265
Punch, Sparkling Champagne, '84 58
Punch, Sparkling Holiday, '81 290
Punch, Spiked Tea, '86 101
Punch, Spirited Fruit, '81 100

Punch, Streetcar Champagne, '88 82
Punch, Tropical Fruit, '83 176
Punch, Vodka, '85 265
Punch, Wedding, '86 107
Raspberry Kir, '86 183
Red Roosters, '87 147
Rum, Hot Buttered, '80 259; '82 244;
  '88 247
Rum Slush, Easy, '79 174; '80 129
Sangría, '79 186; '81 67, 196;
  '82 121; '86 214
Sangría, Easy Citrus, '80 218
Sangría, Orange, '81 237
Sangría, Punchy, '80 160
Sangría, Quick, '81 156
Sangría, Spanish, '83 81
Sangría, Teaberry, '87 147
Sangría, White, '83 180
Screwdrivers, '79 33
Sherry Sour, '87 74
Sipper, Sunshine, '86 179
Slush, Mexican, '83 176
Spritzers, Spiced, '86 229
Strawberry-Banana Smoothie, '81 59
Strawberry Mimosa, Sparkling, '88 169
Syllabub, '81 265; '84 319
Tart Caribbean Cooler, '81 134
Tequila Slush, '83 176
Tequila Sunrise, '83 175
Tomato-Orange Juice Cocktail, '83 169
Vodka Slush, '88 82

Wassail, '83 311
Wassail, Bourbon, '86 270
Whisky Sour Slush, '86 183
Whispers, '86 317
Wine Cooler, '82 41
Wine Cooler, Fruited, '86 176
Wine, Hot Mulled, '83 251
Wine, Hot Spiced, '84 41
Wine Mix, Hot, '81 287
Wine Spice Mix, Mulled, '85 266
Wine Spritzers, '81 94
Wine Welcomer, '81 100
Apple Cider, Sparkling, '88 276
Apple Cooler, Minted, '88 169
Apple Juice, Hot, '86 270
Apple Juice Shrub, Shenandoah, '79 282
Apple Julep, '86 103, 215
Apricot-Citrus Slush, '88 82
Apricot Cooler, '81 100
Apricot Nectar, Hot, '81 265
Apricot Nectar, Mulled, '86 229
Banana-Berry Flip, '88 215
Banana Crush, '80 88; '83 142
Banana Nog, '82 290
Banana-Orange Slush, '80 48; '81 155
Banana Slush, '83 56

Beverages *(continued)*

Banana Smoothie, '87 160
Banana-Strawberry Frost, '87 199
Bloodless Mary, '80 146
Breakfast Eye-Opener, '87 199
Brew, Quilter's, '85 43
Bullshots, '86 91
Café Cappuccino, '82 253
Café Viennese, '82 254
Cappuccino, Chocolate Castle, '84 53
Chocolate, Creole Hot, '80 M290
Chocolate, Favorite Hot, '83 55
Chocolate, French Hot, '86 328
Chocolate Malt, '86 183
Chocolate, Mexican-Style, '81 187
Chocolate Milk, French, '79 38
Chocolate-Mint Smoothie, '84 166
Chocolate Mix, Deluxe Hot, '80 M290
Chocolate Mix, Spicy-Hot, '85 278
Chocolate, Old-Fashioned Hot, '85 23
Chocolate Sipper, '88 83
Chocolate, Special Hot, '82 5
Chocolate, Spiced Hot, '80 50
Chocolate, Spicy Hot, '85 278
Cider, Holiday, '82 264
Cider, Hot Mulled, '79 205
Cider, Hot Spiced, '82 290
Cider, Hot Spiced Apple, '84 318
Cider, Hot Spicy, '84 265
Cider Mix, Beetle, '82 308
Cider Mix, Hot Spiced, '84 42
Cider Nog, Hot Apple, '84 42
Cider, Spiced Apple, '85 256
Cider, Spiced Cranberry, '84 261

Citrus Cooler, '82 160
Cocoa Mix, Hot, '81 287
Cocoa Mix, Hot Mocha-, '82 296
Cocoa Mix, Instant, '86 332
Cocoa, Mocha, '83 318
Cocoa, Quick Hot, '82 5
Coffee, Chocolate-Almond, '84 54
Coffee, Cocoa-, '83 55
Coffee, Creamy, '81 244
Coffee, Frosted, '81 244
Coffee, Mexican, '83 275
Coffee Mix, Fireside, '87 241
Coffee, Mocha, '85 M329
Coffee, Special Spiced, '84 284
Coffee, Viennese Orange, '84 54
Cooler, Spring, '86 214
Cranberry Frappé, '82 263
Cranberry Juice, Sparkling, '88 275
Cranberry-Orange Soda, '79 148

Cranberry Smoothie, '86 183
Eggnog, '83 318
Eggnog, Sparkling, '79 232
Float, Nutmeg-Almond, '84 106
Float, Pineapple Sherbet, '79 148
Floats, Maple-Coffee, '86 195
Float, Sparkling Cranberry, '86 195
Fruit Beverage, Blender, '83 318
Fruit Cooler, Four-, '86 101
Fruit Drink, Three-, '79 38; '80 50;
  '87 199
Fruit Drink, Tropical, '85 43
Fruit Float, Frosty, '87 159
Fruit Juicy, Breakfast, '86 176
Fruit Refresher, Four-, '79 174; '80 129
Fruit Slush, Refreshing, '82 35
Fruit Slushy, '80 146
Grapefruit Cooler, '88 81
Grapefruit-Orange Refresher, '82 174
Grapefruit Refresher, '88 85
Honey-Yogurt Smoothie, Fruited, '88 231
Ice Bowl, '83 152
Ice Cream Ginger Fizz, '83 303
Kona Luscious, '84 54
Lemonade, Fresh Squeezed, '81 172
Lemonade Slush, Pink, '80 151
Lemonade, Strawberry, '80 160
Lemonade with Frozen Tea Cubes, '85 161
Lime Cooler, '87 160
Malt Special, '85 198
Mango Frappé, '86 216
Mango-Orange Smoothie, '86 216
Margaritas, Mock, '88 209
Melon Julep, Rainbow, '80 183
Milkshake, Banana, '85 47
Milkshake, Fresh Strawberry, '82 113
Milkshake, Pineapple, '87 199
Milkshakes, Peanut Butter, '85 198
Mocha Espresso, Italian, '82 254
Mocha, Hot, '84 60
Mocha, Quick Viennese, '79 232
Mocha, Swiss-Style, '82 253
Nog, Speedy Breakfast, '82 47
Orange-Banana Flip, '82 48
Orange Blush, '80 51
Orange Frosty, '86 101
Orange-Lemon Mist, '79 288; '80 35
Orange Pick-Me-Up, '80 232
Orange Slush, '82 49
Orange Spiced Nog, '82 48
Peach Cooler, '85 198
Peaches 'n' Almond Cream, '86 229
Peach Frosty, '83 318
Peach Refresher, '86 103
Peanut Butter Cooler, '84 115
Pineapple Sherbet Float, '79 148
Pineapple Slush, '88 82
Punch. *See also* Beverages/Alcoholic.
  Apple Punch, Hot, '84 324
  Apple-Tea Punch, '85 82
  Apricot Spiced Punch, '80 269
  Autumn Punch, '88 209
  Bubbling Jade Punch, '79 174; '80 129
  Cantaloupe Punch, '81 147
  Children's Punch, '85 322
  Christmas Eve Punch, '86 314
  Christmas Punch, '84 259
  Cider Punch, Spiced, '84 258
  Citrus Party Punch, '83 141
  Citrus Punch, '85 319
  Citrus Punch, Budget, '82 121

Citrus Punch, Fresh, '85 154
Citrus Punch, Party, '84 117
Coffee-and-Cream Punch, '85 116
Coffee Punch, '80 50; '83 275
Coffee Punch, Creamy, '81 50
Coffee Punch,
  Rich-and-Creamy, '82 121
Cranapple Punch, '83 142
Cranberry-Cinnamon Punch, '86 270
Cranberry Punch, '83 275
Cranberry Punch, Holiday, '85 265
Cranberry Punch, Hot, '80 288;
  '84 319; '85 265
Cranberry Punch, Sparkling, '85 277
Cranberry Punch, Tart, '83 318
Eggnog Punch, Holiday, '86 281
False-Kick Punch, '82 121
Frozen Punch Ring, '83 152
Fruit Punch, Golden, '80 299; '83 56
Fruit Punch, Holiday, '79 232
Fruit Punch, Hot, '83 33
Fruit Punch, Party, '82 137
Fruit Punch, Spiced, '88 2
Fruit Punch, Summertime, '80 160
Fruit Punch, Tropical, '80 51
Goblin Punch, '88 228
Golden Punch, '85 207
Grape Punch, Sparkling, '82 48
Holiday Punch, '87 252
Lemonade Punch, Sparkling, '88 276
Lemon Balm Punch, '80 42
Lime-Pineapple Punch, '83 142
Lime Punch, Foamy, '82 264
Merry Christmas Punch, '79 285
Mocha Punch, '84 58, 166; '86 270
Morning Punch, '88 82
Orange Blossom Punch, '83 142

Orange-Mint Punch, '82 121
Orange Punch, Refreshing, '81 39
Orange Sherbet Party Punch, '83 142
Orange Soda Punch, '87 214
Parsonage Punch, '79 148
Party Punch, Special, '81 119
Percolator Punch, Hot, '81 288
Pineapple-Mint Punch, '88 209
Pineapple-Orange Punch, '85 236
Pineapple Punch, '79 174
Pineapple Punch, Spiced, '83 33
Pink Lady Punch, '81 100
Ponche de Piña, '84 58
Raspberry Sparkle Punch, '84 57
Rum Punch, Spiced, '86 179
Sherbet Punch, Double, '79 232
Spiced Punch, Hot, '80 250
Strawberry-Lemonade Punch, '85 116

Strawberry Punch, Creamy, '86 195
Tangy Punch, '83 142
Tea Party Punch, '87 147
Tea Punch, Citrus-, '85 116
Traders' Punch, '87 94
Sangría, Southern, '88 170
Shake, Amazin' Raisin, '86 195
Shake, Apricot, '84 115
Shake, Banana-Pineapple Milk, '84 59
Shake, Cranberry, '83 171
Shake, Frosty Fruit, '87 23
Shake, Peach-Coffee Milk, '84 284
Shake, Peachy Orange, '81 156
Shake, Peanut Butter, '82 48
Shake, Pep, '79 38
Shake, Pineapple-Banana, '85 215
Shake, Strawberry-Orange
  Breakfast, '87 186
Shake, Strawberry-Pineapple, '84 166
Shake, Strawberry-Yogurt, '87 199
Shake, Summer, '82 161
Shake, Sunshine, '79 53
Shake, Tropical, '87 200
Spices, Barclay House Mulling, '86 289
Strawberry-Banana Float, '87 160
Strawberry Cooler, '83 56; '84 51
Strawberry-Mint Cooler, '84 57
Strawberry-Orange Slush, '83 172
Strawberry Slurp, '81 96
Strawberry Smoothie, '86 183
Strawberry Soda, '84 115
Strawberry Soda, Old-Fashioned, '79 49
Syllabub, Plantation, '79 233
Tahitian Flower, '87 159
Tea, Almond, '85 43; '86 329
Tea, Almond-Lemonade, '86 229
Tea, Bubbly Iced, '81 168
Tea, Christmas Fruit, '83 275
Tea Cooler, Spiced, '83 55
Tea, Cranberry-Apple, '88 169
Tea, Frosted Mint, '84 161
Tea, Fruited Mint, '88 79
Tea, Ginger, '81 100
Tea, Hawaiian, '87 57
Tea, Honey, '81 105
Tea, Hot Apple-Cinnamon, '87 57
Tea, Hot Citrus, '83 275
Tea, Hot Spiced, '83 244
Tea, Hot Spiced Apricot, '88 248
Tea, Hot Spiced Fruit, '87 242
Tea, Iced Citrus, '85 162
Tea, Iced Mint, '83 170
Tea, Johnny Appleseed, '85 23
Tea, Lemon, '82 156
Tea, Lemon-Mint, '85 162
Tea, Mint, '87 107
Tea, Minted, '86 101; '88 163
Tea Mix, Deluxe Spiced, '88 257
Tea Mix, Friendship, '83 283
Tea Mix, Spiced, '86 32
Tea, Southern Sun, '81 168
Tea, Spiced Grape, '79 174
Tea, Strawberry, '88 248
Tea, Summer, '85 162
Tea, Summertime, '81 167
Tea, White Grape Juice, '87 57
Tea, Yaupon, '79 31
Toddy, Jolly, '86 229
Toddy, Tasty, '88 82
Tofruitti Breakfast Drink, '88 26
Tomato Bouillon, '83 8

Tomato-Clam Cocktail, '87 252
Tomato Cocktail, '83 M203
Tomato Juice Cocktail, '79 212; '83 230
Tomato Juice Cocktail, Zesty, '83 289
Tomato Juice, Homemade, '81 50
Tomato Juice, Spicy, '85 189
Tomato Refresher, '83 318
Tomato Sipper, Spicy, '86 229
Tropical Cooler, '84 120
Tropical Ice, '79 174; '80 129
Tropical Refresher, '85 198
Tropical Smoothie, '81 50
Vanilla Frosty, French, '79 148
Vegetable Cocktail, Fresh, '82 165
Vegetable Juice Delight, '84 58
Wassail, '84 259, 318; '88 248
Wassail, Cranberry, '88 289
Wassail, Pineapple-Apricot, '83 275

Biscuits
Angel Biscuits, '80 49
Angel Biscuits, Ham-Filled, '80 159
Bacon-Cheese Biscuits, '88 84
Baking Powder Biscuits, '82 195
Beaten Biscuits, '86 54
Benne Seed Biscuits, '79 38
Blue Cheese Biscuits, '88 83
Bran Biscuits, '85 228
Bread, Biscuit, '84 284
Buttermilk Biscuits, '83 208; '85 255, 321
Buttermilk Biscuits, Deluxe, '82 130
Buttermilk Biscuits, Favorite, '81 191
Buttermilk Biscuits, Fluffy, '84 102
Buttermilk Biscuits, Old-Fashioned, '80 77
Buttermilk Biscuits, Quick, '83 311; '88 15
Casserole, Beef-and-Biscuit, '83 75
Casserole, Biscuit-Topped Tuna, '79 113
Cheese Biscuits, '79 296; '80 31; '81 288;
  '83 253; '85 32; '87 78
Cheese Biscuits, Easy, '81 99
Cheese Biscuits, Tiny, '80 192
Cheeseburger Biscuits, '79 194
Cheese Dips, Butter, '80 46
Cheesy Biscuits, Hot, '80 186
Chicken in a Biscuit, '79 263
Cloud Biscuits, '87 15
Cornmeal Biscuits, '85 228
Dressing, Cornbread-Biscuit, '79 296
Feather Biscuits, '80 78
Feather Light Biscuits, '80 246
Flaky Biscuits, '84 228
Grapefruit Juice Biscuits, '83 10
Ham and Cheese Biscuits, Petite, '79 193
Heart Biscuits, Country Ham in, '86 105
Heart Biscuits with Sausage,
  Angel, '87 156
Hearty Biscuits, '83 121
Herbed Biscuits, '85 228
Hot Biscuits, '86 269

Marmalade Biscuits, Carolina, '85 42
Marmalade Biscuit Squares, '79 193
Mile-High Biscuits, '85 41
Nannie's Biscuits, '82 156
One-Step Biscuits, '82 173
Orange Biscuits, '88 85
Orange Puffs, Upside-Down, '83 57
Parker House-Style Biscuits, '79 162
Pepper-Cheese Biscuit Fingers, '88 283
Pepperoni Biscuits, '84 95
Processor Biscuits, Easy, '84 218
Pudding, Biscuit, '79 86
Raised Biscuits, Southern, '82 94
Roquefort Biscuits, Herbed, '84 95
Rye Biscuits, '84 96
Sausage and Biscuits, Southern, '82 43
Sausage Biscuit Bites, '84 95
Sausage Biscuits, Cheesy, '80 78
Scones, Breakfast Drop, '88 83
Scones, Currant, '84 117
Sour Cream Biscuits, '79 128
Sour Cream Biscuits,
  Soft-as-a-Cloud, '86 138
Sourdough Biscuits, '82 201
Sweetened Biscuits, '80 42
Sweet Little Biscuits, '85 305
Sweet Potato Biscuits, '80 287; '84 140
Tomato Biscuits, '86 72
Topping, Biscuit, '86 157, 265
Up-and-Down Biscuits, '88 263
Wheat Bran Biscuits, '81 49
Wheat Germ Biscuits, '86 261
Wheat Quick Biscuits, '85 278
Whipping Cream Biscuits, '80 77
Whole Wheat Biscuits, '83 18; '84 60,
  268; '85 227; '88 83
Yeast Biscuits, '87 71, 301
Yeast Biscuits, Refrigerator, '85 48

Blackberries
Bars, Blackberry, '87 130
Bars, Blackberry-Filled, '79 124
Bars, Blackberry Jam, '82 M185
Cake, Fresh Blackberry, '81 132
Cobbler, Blackberry, '82 139; '83 175
Cobbler, Blackberry-Almond, '81 132
Cobbler, Deep-Dish Blackberry, '80 186
Cobbler, Deluxe Blackberry, '81 132
Cobbler, New-Fashioned
  Blackberry, '87 164
Cobbler, Southern Blackberry, '81 132
Dumplings, Blackberries and, '86 196
Flan, Blackberry, '79 182
Jam, Blackberry, '82 149
Jam, Freezer Blackberry, '84 M181
Jelly, Blackberry, '82 149
Parfait, Blackberries-and-Cream, '87 129
Pie, Berry-Apple, '88 251
Pie, Blackberry, '84 141; '86 152
Pie, Blackberry-Apple, '87 130
Pie, Blackberry Cream, '81 132
Pie, Creamy Blackberry, '88 179
Roll, Blackberry, '82 178
Sauce, Blackberry, '86 152
Sauce, Ducklings with Blackberry, '82 251
Tart, Cherry and Blackberry, '83 225

Blueberries
Appetizer, Orange-Berry, '85 81
Basket, Summer Berry, '84 158
Bread, Banana-Blueberry, '81 163
Bread, Blueberry-Lemon, '85 190
Bread, Blueberry-Oatmeal, '83 139

Blueberries *(continued)*

Bread, Blueberry-Orange, **'87** 140
Bread, Blueberry-Orange Nut, **'84** 141
Bread, Hot Blueberry, **'81** 164
Buckle, Blueberry, **'85** 30
Buns, Deluxe Blueberry, **'81** 164
Cake, Almond-Blueberry Coffee, **'85** 152
Cake, Banana-Blueberry, **'86** 247
Cake, Blueberry Brunch, **'83** 183
Cake, Blueberry Coffee, **'82** 206; **'85** 326;
   '88 263
Cake, Blueberry Streusel Coffee, **'88** 154
Cake, Fresh Blueberry Coffee, **'81** 164
Cheesecake, Blueberries 'n' Cream, **'87** 140
Cheesecake, Blueberry Chiffon, **'87** 76
Cobbler, Blueberry, **'83** 175
Cobbler, Blueberry Pinwheel, **'87** 140
Cobbler, Easy Blueberry, **'83** 183
Cobbler, Fresh Blueberry, **'80** 144
Cobbler, No-Dough
   Blueberry-Peach, **'86** 177
Cobbler, Peachy Blueberry, **'80** 143
Cointreau, Blueberries and, **'82** 100
Compote, Berry-Peach, **'82** 133
Conserve, Blueberry, **'82** 149
Crisp, Blueberry, **'84** 177
Crumble, Blueberry, **'81** 84
Crunch, Fresh Blueberry, **'82** 143
Dessert Squares,
   Chocolate-Blueberry, **'87** 299
Dream, Blueberry, **'88** 94
Fritters, Blueberry, **'85** 152
Glaze, Blueberry, **'83** 143
Huckle-Buckle Blueberry, **'86** 151
Ice Cream, Blueberry, **'88** 203
Jam, Blueberry, **'79** 120; **'85** 130
Kuchen, Blueberry, **'80** 143
Muffins, Blueberry, **'80** 143
Muffins, Blueberry Buttermilk, **'80** 16
Muffins, Blueberry-Cream Cheese, **'86** 14
Muffins, Blueberry Ice Cream, **'82** 143
Muffins, Blueberry-Lemon, **'79** 7
Muffins, Blueberry-Oatmeal, **'87** 24
Muffins, Blueberry Streusel, **'80** 46
Muffins, Easy Blueberry, **'81** 197
Muffins, Golden Blueberry, **'79** 235
Muffins, Old-Fashioned Blueberry, **'86** 161
Muffins with Streusel Topping,
   Blueberry, **'88** 129
Pancakes, Blueberry, **'85** 152
Pancakes, Blueberry Buttermilk, **'79** 114
Pancakes, Sour Cream Blueberry, **'81** 164
Pie, Blueberry Cream, **'84** 142
Pie, Blueberry-Cream Cheese, **'88** 154
Pie, Blueberry-Sour Cream, **'83** 183
Pie, Fresh Blueberry, **'83** 183; **'85** 152
Pie, Fresh Blueberry Cream, **'80** 144
Pinwheels, Blueberry, **'82** 205
Pudding, Blueberry Bread, **'88** 154
Raspberry Custard Sauce, Fresh Berries
   with, **'88** 163
Salad, Layered Berry, **'79** 173
Sauce, Blueberry, **'80** 144; **'86** 248;
   '88 155
Sauce, Cinnamon-Blueberry, **'86** 11
Sauce, Melon Wedges with Berry, **'86** 178
Sauce, Peach-Berry, **'87** M165
Sauce, Peach-Blueberry, **'81** 170
Sauce, Peach-Blueberry Pancake, **'82** 177
Snow, Berries on, **'82** 227

Sorbet, Blueberry-Kirsch, **'83** 120
Squares, Blueberry-Amaretto, **'83** 220
Topping, Blueberry, **'87** 125
Trifle, Lemon-Blueberry, **'88** 210

Bok Choy
Stir-Fry, Bok Choy-Broccoli, **'84** 2

Boysenberries
Cobbler, Boysenberry, **'82** 133
Compote, Berry-Peach, **'82** 133
Cream Mold, Peachy Berry, **'83** 130
Cream Supreme, Boysenberries
   and, **'82** 133
Crisp, Berry, **'83** 130
Pie, Boysenberry, **'82** 133

Bran
Biscuits, Bran, **'85** 228
Biscuits, Wheat Bran, **'81** 49
Bread, Bran-Applesauce, **'84** 229
Bread, Whole Wheat Bran, **'79** 58
Crêpes, Bran, **'83** 70; **'86** 44
Cupcakes, Carrot-Bran, **'82** 16
Eggplant, Ratatouille-Bran Stuffed, **'86** 44
Muffins, Apple-Bran, **'85** M89
Muffins, Banana Bran, **'83** 48
Muffins, Bran, **'84** 53
Muffins, Bran-Buttermilk, **'85** 7
Muffins, Easy Bran, **'83** 55
Muffins, Ever-Ready Bran, **'81** 106
Muffins for Two, Bran, **'84** 211
Muffins, High-Fiber, **'85** 250
Muffins, Honey Bran, **'88** 171
Muffins Made of Bran, **'86** 103
Muffins, Oatmeal Bran, **'81** 236
Muffins, Quick Bran, **'86** 85
Muffins, Refrigerator Bran, **'79** 6
Muffins, Sour Cream-Bran, **'87** 98
Muffins, Spiced Bran, **'84** 229
Muffins, Whole Wheat Bran, **'88** M274
Rolls, Bran, **'85** 145
Rolls, Bran Yeast, **'87** 116
Salad, Lemony Apple-Bran, **'86** 223

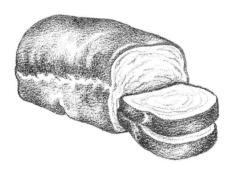

Breads. *See also* specific types.
Apple Bread, **'79** 205; **'80** 226
Apple Butter Bread, **'84** 49; **'86** 69
Apple Loaf, Fresh, **'82** 206
Apple Loaf, Spiced, **'79** 215
Apple-Nut Bread, **'79** 12; **'85** 281
Apple-Nut Bread, Fresh, **'87** 256
Applesauce-Honey Nut Bread, **'87** 300
Applesauce Loaf, Brandy, **'81** 263
Applesauce Nut Bread, **'81** 305
Apricot Bread, Tangy, **'81** 249
Apricot-Cranberry Loaf, **'79** 235
Apricot-Nut Bread, **'79** 24

Apricot-Nut Loaf, **'81** 8
Apricot-Nut Loaf, Tasty, **'82** 10
Asparagus Squares, **'79** 161
Bacon-and-Cheese Bread, **'83** 255
Banana-Apple Bread, **'85** 250
Banana-Blueberry Bread, **'81** 163
Banana Bread, **'87** 72
Banana Bread, Sour Cream-, **'79** 190
Banana Bread, Whole Wheat, **'80** 88
Banana Butterscotch Bread, **'79** 116
Banana-Jam Bread, **'84** 73
Banana-Nut Bread, **'86** 8, 70
Banana Nut Bread, Hawaiian, **'79** 235
Banana Nut Bread, Whole Wheat-, **'84** 50
Banana-Nut-Raisin Bread, **'81** 59
Banana-Nut Roll, **'85** 112
Banana-Oat Tea Loaf, **'87** 256
Banana Wheat Bread, **'81** 14
Banana-Zucchini Bread, **'85** 326
Batter Bread, Soft, **'84** 253
Beer Bread, Easy, **'79** 213; **'84** 160
Biscuit Bread, **'84** 284
Blueberry Bread, Hot, **'81** 164
Blueberry-Lemon Bread, **'85** 190
Blueberry-Oatmeal Bread, **'83** 139
Blueberry-Orange Bread, **'87** 140
Blueberry-Orange Nut Bread, **'84** 141
Bran-Applesauce Bread, **'84** 229
Breakfast Bread, Easy, **'83** 289
Brie Bread, **'87** 143
Brie Cheese Bake, **'87** 117
Brown Bread, **'84** 242; **'88** 63
Brown Bread, Eighteenth-Century, **'79** 72
Brown Bread, Steamed Buttermilk, **'86** 261
Butternut-Raisin Bread, **'79** 25
Carrot Bread, Tasty, **'84** 328
Carrot-Nut Loaf, **'83** 117
Carrot-Pineapple Bread, **'82** 210
Carrot Puffs, **'87** 200
Carrot-Walnut Bread, **'88** 284
Cheddar-Nut Bread, **'85** 41
Cheese Bread, **'82** 174
Cheese Bread, Dilly, **'83** 5
Cheese Bread, Easy, **'82** 74; **'86** 17
Cheese Bread, Quick, **'83** 9
Cheese-Herb Bread, **'85** 283
Cheese Loaf, **'87** 92
Cheese Loaves, Little, **'86** 213
Cheese-Olive Bread, Spicy, **'84** 150
Cheese Puffs, Bavarian, **'80** 191
Cheesy Twists, **'84** 284
Cherry Nut Bread, **'81** 306; **'82** 36
Cherry Nut Bread, Maraschino, **'79** 234
Cherry-Nut Bread, Quick, **'85** 55
Chocolate Date-Nut Bread, **'81** 284
Cinnamon Puffs, **'81** 209
Citrus-Nut Bread, **'83** 294
Coconut Bread, **'83** 140
Cranberry-Banana Bread, **'80** 281
Cranberry Bread, **'79** 242
Cranberry Fruit-Nut Bread, **'79** 275
Cranberry-Orange Bread, **'87** 244
Cranberry-Orange Nut Bread, **'80** 288
Croutons, **'86** M288
Croutons, Celery, **'79** 16
Croutons, Crispy Italian, **'84** 126
Croutons, Garlic-Flavored, **'86** 47
Croutons, Herb, **'81** 150
Croutons, Microwave, **'86** M227
Croutons, Vegetable-Flavored, **'84** 148
Date-Nut Bread, **'85** 306

Date-Nut Loaf, '85 10
Date-Walnut Loaf, Blue Ribbon, '80 15
Easy Bread, '87 168
Eggnog Bread, '83 294
Flatbread, Mexican, '80 197
French Bread, Cheesy, '88 172
French Bread, Herbed, '82 174
French Bread, Herb-Seasoned, '83 198
French Bread, Hot Garlic, '81 83
French Loaf, Herbed, '87 243
Fruit-Nut Bread, Kahlúa, '79 235
Fruit-Nut Twists, '82 253
Fry Bread, '84 140; '85 155
Fry Bread, Indian, '81 56
Garlic Bread, '82 19
Garlic Bread, Cheesy, '84 150
Garlic Breadsticks, '79 70
Gingerbread Loaf, '82 14

Gingerbread, Mocha, '81 207; '82 14
Gingerbread, Molasses, '88 203
Gingerbread, Old English, '79 265
Gingerbread, Old-Fashioned, '81 157, 207;
   '82 14
Gingerbread, Refrigerator, '80 52
Gingerbread, Spicy, '84 263
Gingerbread Squares, '84 16
Gingerbread, Very Moist, '86 261
Ham-and-Cheese Bread, '86 213
Hawaiian Loaf, '80 225
Herb-and-Cheese Pull Aparts, '87 143
Herb Bread, '86 17
Herb Loaf, Toasted, '84 150
Herb Sticks, '83 252
Herb-Vegetable-Cheese Bread, '88 172
Hobo Bread, '86 86
Lemon Bread, '79 275; '87 256
Lemon-Cream Tea Loaf, '84 50
Lemon-Nut Bread, '79 24
Lemon-Pecan Bread, '83 54
Mix, Quick Bread, '81 90; '86 8
Molasses-Nut Bread, '84 24
Monkey Bread, Quick, '81 306; '82 36
Mustard-Rye Ovals, '84 149
Oatmeal Bread, '81 236, 300
Oatmeal Raisin Bread, '81 14
Onion Bread, Easy, '81 162
Onion-Cheese Bread, '79 180; '81 8
Onion-Cheese Supper Bread, '83 112
Onion-Herb Bread, Toasted, '83 266
Onion-Parmesan Bread, '84 284
Orange, Baba au, '86 138
Orange-Cranberry Bread, '85 266
Orange-Cream Cheese Bread, '82 210
Orange-Nut Bread, '82 75
Orange Nut Loaf, '80 226

Orange-Pecan Bread, '79 148
Orange-Pecan Bread, Glazed, '81 250
Orange-Pecan Loaves, '79 215
Orange Puffs, Upside-Down, '83 57
Orange-Pumpkin Bread, '87 300
Orange Tea Bread, '79 234
Papaya Bread, '88 138
Parmesan Herb Bread, '82 235; '83 41
Parmesan Rounds, '79 170
Parmesan Sesame Sticks, '81 39
Parmesan Twists, '83 239
Peach Bread, '82 170
Peach Bread, Georgia, '79 161
Peanut Bread, '87 184
Peanut Butter Bread, '88 64
Pear Bread, '80 218
Pepper Bread, '85 156
Persimmon Bread, '80 228
Persimmon Date-Nut Bread, '82 218
Pineapple-Apricot Bread, '84 7
Pineapple Bread, '83 139
Pineapple-Carrot Bread, '79 106
Pineapple-Nut Bread, '79 215
Pineapple-Pecan Loaf Bread, '87 256
Popover Puffs, Cheese, '85 6
Popover Ring, Cheesy, '80 45
Popovers, Cheddar Cheese, '85 41
Popovers for Two, '81 304
Popovers, Giant Pecan, '83 208
Popovers, Good Old Southern, '79 138
Popovers, Jumbo, '83 225
Popovers, Muffin Tin, '79 138
Popovers, Perfect Blender, '79 53
Popovers, Pimiento, '79 138
Popovers, Seasoned, '86 86
Poppy Seed Bread, '83 140
Poppy Seed Loaf, Quick, '82 75
Prune-Nut Bread, '87 255
Puddings
   Amish Bread Pudding, '80 8
   Apple-Raisin Bread Pudding, '88 175
   Apricot Bread Pudding, '85 24
   Blueberry Bread Pudding, '88 154
   Cheesy Bread Pudding, '83 68
   Chocolate Bread Pudding, '80 8
   French Bread Pudding, '85 231
   Lemon Bread Pudding,
      Old-Fashioned, '88 95
   Old-Fashioned Bread Pudding, '83 213;
      '88 175
   Old-Fashioned Bread Pudding with Rum
      Sauce, '88 32
   Peachy Bread Pudding, '88 175
   Whiskey Sauce, Bread Pudding
      with, '80 58
Pumpkin Bread, '81 8
Pumpkin Bread, Moist, '80 245
Pumpkin Bread with Cream Cheese and
   Preserves, '84 264
Pumpkin-Coconut Bread, '87 255
Pumpkin Loaf, Harvest, '85 232
Pumpkin-Nut Bread, '83 294
Pumpkin-Oatmeal Loaf, '81 49
Pumpkin-Pecan Bread, '87 221
Raisin-Cranberry Bread, '81 305; '82 36
Saffron Tea Bread, '85 26
Sally Lunn, Quick, '87 16
Salt-Rising Bread, '79 145
Sausage-Onion Squares, '83 112
Scones, Breakfast, '88 231
Scones, Currant, '84 117

Scones, Lemon-Raisin, '87 69
Seasoned Breadsticks, '81 84
Sesame Bread Twists, '84 283
Sesame-Cheddar Sticks, '81 150
Sesame Sticks, '83 9
Sesame Wheat Crisps, '81 106
Shortbread, '85 266
Spinach Bread, '83 121; '87 144
Spoonbreads
   Cheddar Spoonbread, '82 196
   Cheese Spoonbread, '86 261
   Corn and Bacon Spoonbread, '81 129
   Corn-Cheese Spoonbread, '88 9
   Garlic Spoonbread, '79 269; '80 14
   Golden Spoonbread, '83 286; '84 17
   Grits Spoonbread, '79 38
   Old Virginia Spoonbread, '84 102
   Spoonbread, '80 43; '81 138
Squash Bread, '79 210
Squash Bread, Spicy, '83 121
Squash Bread, Yellow, '84 140
Stollen, '86 291
Strawberry Bread, '81 250; '83 140;
   '84 49
Strawberry Jam Bread, '79 216
Strawberry-Nut Bread, '79 24

Tacos, Navajo, '84 246
Three-C Bread, '81 284
Toast
   Apple Toast, '81 278
   Bacon-Cheese Toast Bars, '79 36
   Cheese Delights, Toasted, '79 37
   Cinnamon Toast, Buttery
      Skillet, '79 36
   Orange Praline Toast, '79 36
   Shrimp Toast, '86 91
Tomato-Cheese Bread, Herbed, '88 143
Tortillas, Flour, '81 303
Tortillas, Never-Fail Flour, '80 198
Vegetable Bread, Breakaway, '82 74
Wampus Bread, '81 305
Whole Wheat Cardamom Bread, '86 223
Whole Wheat Coffee Can Bread,
   Molasses-, '85 111
Whole Wheat Orange Bread, '85 5
Whole Wheat Quick Bread, '82 65
Wine-Date Nut Bread, '82 253
Yeast
   Almond Danish, '87 301
   Anise-Orange Bread, '83 295
   Apple Pull-Apart Bread, '86 330
   Apple Swirl Bread, '85 4
   Austrian Sweet Bread, '83 294
   Austrian Twists, '80 45
   Bagels, Whole Wheat, '84 20
   Baguettes, '85 70
   Beer Bread, Best-Ever, '82 129

Breads, Yeast (continued)

Beer Bread, Hearty, **'87** 226; **'88** 133
Beignets, **'84** 56
Binning Bread, **'80** 68
Braided Bread, **'88** 76
Braided Loaf, **'82** 17
Braids, Cream Cheese, **'82** 243
Braids, Festive, **'87** 297
Braids, Holiday, **'83** 295
Break-Away Bread, **'86** 56
Brioche, **'81** 122
Brioche Chicken Curry, **'88** 124
Brioche Loaves, Vienna, **'87** 300
Brown Bread, Light-, **'84** 268
Bubble Bread, **'81** 107
Butter-Egg Bread, **'85** 269
Butterhorns, **'84** 267
Cake Bread, Golden, **'84** 269
Caramel Bread, **'82** 75
Caramel-Orange Coffee Ring, **'80** 45
Caraway Puffs, **'82** 174
Caraway Seed Bread, Dark, **'80** 256
Cheese Bread, **'83** 208; **'87** 11
Cheese Bread, Cheddar, **'84** 268
Cheese Bread, Crusty, **'86** 233
Cheese Bread, Pimiento-, **'85** 223;
  '86 166
Cheese Bread, Sour Cream-, **'85** 33
Cheese Bread, Swiss, **'79** 60
Cheese-Caraway Batter Bread, **'85** 33
Cheese Crescents, **'82** 18
Cheese-Dill Bread, Cottage, **'83** 154
Cheese-Herb Bread, **'84** M144
Cheese Loaf, Jalapeño-, **'84** 76
Cheese Loaves, Processor
  Cream, **'85** 48
Cheese-Wine Bread, **'87** 254
Chocolate Loaf Bread, **'88** M188
Chocolate Pinwheel Loaf, **'80** 256
Christmas Bread, **'87** 296; **'88** 288
Christmas Bread, Norwegian, **'79** 234
Christmas Wreath, **'80** 280
Cinnamon Loaf, **'82** 18; **'85** 55
Cinnamon-Nut Bubble Bread, **'80** 22
Cinnamon Raisin Bread, **'80** 22
Cinnamon Swirl Loaf, **'79** 23
Cinnamon Twists, **'83** 53
Cocoa-Nut Swirl Bread, **'80** 257
Coffee Ring, Filled, **'82** 18
Coffee Ring, Sugarplum, **'83** M37
Cracker Bread, Sesame, **'87** 2
Crescents, Festive, **'80** 281
Croissants, **'83** 54; **'84** 188
Croissants, Flaky Butter, **'85** 42
Crust Bread, Country, **'80** 225
Dough, Basic Yeast, **'88** 74
Easter Egg Bread, **'84** 94
Easy Yeast Bread, **'79** 147
Egg Bread, County Fair, **'87** 68
Elephant Ears, **'84** 18
English Muffin Loaf, **'82** 96
English Muffin Loaves, **'85** 42
Figure-8 Bread, **'79** 171
Flat Bread, Italian-Style, **'82** 235;
  '83 41
French Bread, **'79** 158; **'87** 227
French Bread, Easy, **'88** 299
French Bread, Glazed, **'88** 75
French Bread, Herbed, **'85** 222;
  '86 166

French Bread, New Orleans, **'80** 212
French Bread, Whole Wheat, **'88** 63
French Loaves, Crusty, **'85** 37
Fruit-and-Cheese Braid, **'86** 214
Ham Bread with Herb Butter,
  Country, **'86** 255
Herb Bread, **'84** 268
Herb Bread, No-Knead, **'81** 217
Herb-Cheese Bread, **'85** 70
Herb Loaf, Butterflake, **'86** 261
Herb-Sour Cream Bread, **'85** 268
Herman Food, **'82** 200
Holiday Wreath, **'81** 284
Honey-Cinnamon Swirl Bread, **'88** 287
Honey-Granola Bread, **'86** 56
Honey Loaves, Hint o', **'81** 104
Honey Twist, **'79** 80
Honey-Walnut Swirl, **'80** 21
Honey Wheat Bread, **'85** 18, 268
Italian Bread, **'82** 297
Kolecz (Polish Bread), **'80** 29
Lightbread, Coffee Can, **'79** 59
Light Yeast Bread, **'81** 299
Loaf Bread, Hospitality, **'86** 299
Loaf Bread, Old-Fashioned, **'88** 75
Marble Loaf, **'80** 230
Monkey Bread, **'82** 243
Multi-Grain Bread, **'86** 236
Oat Bread, Caraway-Raisin, **'86** 44
Oatmeal Bread, **'81** 300
Oatmeal Bread, Honey, **'80** 60
Oatmeal Bread, Round, **'84** 20
Oatmeal-Raisin Bread, **'83** 59
Oat-Molasses Bread, **'82** 139
Old-Fashioned Yeast Bread, **'79** 284
Onion-Dill Bread, Easy, **'85** 5
Onion Twist Loaves, **'84** 300
Party Bread, **'86** 218
Peanut Butter Bread, **'86** 171
Pizza Batter Bread, **'85** 56
Pocket Bread, **'79** 58
Poppy Seed Loaf, **'83** 254
Portuguese Round Bread, **'83** 295
Potato Bread, **'85** 56
Potato Bread, Old-Fashioned, **'86** 57
Potato Lightbread, **'80** 225
Potato Loaves, **'86** 162
Pretzels, Chewy Soft, **'87** 159
Pretzels, Homemade, **'84** 159
Pretzels, Soft, **'83** 18
Raisin Batter Bread, Salt-Free, **'86** 33
Raisin Bread, Curried Chicken Salad
  on, **'85** 96
Raisin Bread, Homemade, **'87** 300
Refrigerator Bread, No-Knead, **'83** 155
Rounds, Individual Bread, **'83** 159
Rye Bread, **'84** 21
Rye Bread, Swedish Orange-, **'85** 111
Rye Sandwich Bread, **'82** 65
Sally Lunn, **'81** 157; **'88** 163
Sandwiches, Stacking, **'86** 127
Savarin, Holiday, **'80** 280
Soft Breadsticks, **'83** 115
Sopaipillas, **'80** 197
Sour Cream Bread, **'79** 59
Sourdough Bread, **'82** 201
Sourdough Starter, Herman, **'82** 200
Squares, Yeast Bread, **'83** 155
Sugar Plum Bread, **'80** 256
Sweet Christmas Loaf, **'84** 278
Techniques of Breadmaking, **'82** 17

Trinity Feast Bread, **'82** 92; **'83** 83
Wheat Bread, Buttermilk, **'86** 236
Wheat Bread, Pull-Apart
  Maple, **'85** 222; **'86** 166
White Bread, **'79** 275
White Bread, Cardamom, **'82** 236;
  '83 41
White Bread, Old-Fashioned, **'81** 285
White Bread, Special, **'86** 57
Whole Wheat Bran Bread, **'79** 58
Whole Wheat Bread, **'83** 17
Whole Wheat Bread and Rolls,
  Hearty, **'79** 92
Whole Wheat Breadsticks, **'84** 228
Whole Wheat Honey Bread, **'82** 65;
  '83 106
Whole Wheat-Oatmeal Bread, **'87** 85
Whole Wheat-Rye Bread, **'83** M37
Whole Wheat-White Bread, **'82** 130
Zucchini-Apple Bread, **'87** 255
Zucchini Bread, **'85** 111; **'86** 93
Zucchini Bread, Spiced, **'79** 161; **'86** 162
Zucchini Bread, Spicy, **'81** 305; **'82** 36
Zucchini-Carrot Bread, **'83** 190

Broccoli
au Gratin, Broccoli, **'82** M20
au Gratin, Broccoli-and-Eggs, **'85** 289
Bake, Broccoli, **'81** 246
Bake, Cheesy Broccoli, **'83** 255
Bake, Cheesy Italian Broccoli, **'83** 5
Bake, Company Broccoli, **'83** 279
Bake, Potato-Broccoli-Cheese, **'80** 114
Beef and Broccoli with Chive Gravy,
  '88 214
Burritos, Broccoli, **'83** 200
Carnival Broccoli, **'81** 2
Casserole, Almond-Broccoli, **'88** 62
Casserole, Broccoli, **'87** 284;
  '88 M146, 265
Casserole, Broccoli-and-Egg, **'86** 324
Casserole, Broccoli-Blue Cheese, **'85** 260
Casserole, Broccoli-Cheese, **'82** 269; **'84** 9
Casserole, Broccoli-Chicken, **'82** 33
Casserole, Broccoli-Corn, **'83** 313
Casserole, Broccoli-Rice, **'81** 101
Casserole, Broccoli-Swiss Cheese, **'83** 322;
  '85 M211
Casserole, Cheesy Broccoli, **'84** 293
Casserole, Chicken-Broccoli, **'79** 48
Casserole, Chicken Divan, **'82** M203
Casserole, Crabmeat-Broccoli, **'84** 232
Casserole, Ham and Broccoli, **'81** 133
Casserole, Italian Broccoli, **'82** 6, 280;
  '83 32

Casserole, Quick Ham-Broccoli, '82 40
Casserole, Sausage and Broccoli, '80 33
Casserole, Tangy Tuna-Broccoli, '83 75
Casserole, Turkey-and-Broccoli, '86 332
Cauliflower-Broccoli Crunch, '88 216
Cheese Sauce, Broccoli with, '82 107
Chinese Broccoli, '85 M12
Chowder, Broccoli, '79 16
Chowder, Swiss-Broccoli, '80 73
Cocktail Broccoli, '80 192
Crêpes, Royal Brunch, '81 44
Deluxe, Broccoli-Onion, '81 75
Dip, Broccoli-Garlic, '82 59
Dip, Cheesy Broccoli, '83 92
Divan, Chicken, '80 10; '87 M218
Divan, Curried Chicken, '80 83
Divan, Gourmet Chicken, '82 83
Divan, Overnight Chicken, '83 198
Divan Quiche, Chicken, '88 M125
Divan, Sherried Chicken, '80 38
Divan, Turkey, '82 268
Eggs, Broccoli and Creamed, '83 84
Elegant, Broccoli, '81 267
Filling, Broccoli, '81 44
French Sauce, Broccoli with, '81 295
Frittata, Broccoli-Cheese, '81 243
Fritters, Cheesy Broccoli, '79 53
Garden Surprise, '83 112
Glazed Broccoli with Almonds, '80 12
Herbed Broccoli, '88 101
Hollandaise Sauce, Broccoli
  with, '79 244, 276
Hollandaise Sauce, Broccoli with
  Mock, '82 272
Horseradish Sauce, Broccoli with, '81 2;
  '83 206; '84 33
Italian-Style Broccoli, '88 41
Italienne, Broccoli, '82 300
Jade-Green Broccoli, '80 12
Lemon Broccoli, '88 119
Lemon-Broccoli Goldenrod, '84 M89
Lemon Dressing, Chilled Broccoli
  with, '88 270
Lemon Sauce and Pecans, Broccoli
  with, '86 71
Marinated Broccoli, '80 79; '81 40;
  '85 207; '86 157; '88 255
Marinated Broccoli, Tangy, '80 284
Marinated Fresh Broccoli, '81 M139
Medley, Broccoli, '81 206
Medley, Cauliflower-Broccoli, '81 69
Olive-Butter Sauce, Broccoli with, '83 118
Omelet, Broccoli-Mushroom, '85 45
Onions, Broccoli-Stuffed, '84 154
Orange Broccoli, Easy, '85 267
Orange Sauce, Broccoli with, '80 243
Pasta, Broccoli, '84 176
Pasta, Chicken-and-Broccoli, '87 286
Pasta with Broccoli and Sausage, '87 109
Pickled Broccoli, '81 308
Pie, Broccoli-and-Turkey Pasta, '88 269
Pie, Broccoli-Beef, '83 196
Pie, Broccoli-Cheese, '84 235
Pimiento Broccoli, '86 268
Polonaise, Broccoli, '86 55
Potatoes, Broccoli-and-Almond-
  Topped, '83 3
Potatoes, Broccoli-Topped Baked, '86 17
Puff, Broccoli, '81 94; '82 95
Quiche, Broccoli-Rice, '81 228
Quiche, Easy Broccoli, '82 34

Quiche, Italian Broccoli, '85 45
Quick-and-Easy Broccoli, '86 55
Rice, Holiday Broccoli with, '87 252
Rolls, Ham-Broccoli, '86 212; '87 82
Salad, Beef-and-Broccoli, '87 187
Salad, Broccoli, '82 24; '85 249

Salad, Broccoli and Cauliflower, '81 280
Salad, Broccoli and Red Pepper, '83 224
Salad, Broccoli-Cauliflower Pasta, '88 269
Salad, Broccoli-Corn, '87 24
Salad, Cauliflower-Broccoli, '79 20
Salad, Congealed Broccoli, '84 124
Salad, Creamy Broccoli, '79 143
Salad, Creamy Broccoli and
  Cauliflower, '81 23
Salad, Crunchy Broccoli, '83 39
Salad, Curried Broccoli, '86 225
Salad, Fresh Broccoli, '82 34; '87 103
Salad, Hot Broccoli-Potato, '85 23
Salad, Marinated Broccoli, '83 240
Salad, Pepperoni-and-Broccoli, '83 216
Salad Supreme, Broccoli, '83 260
Sautéed Broccoli, '79 246
Savory Broccoli, '79 268; '80 14
Sesame Broccoli, '84 69; '85 8
Sesame, Broccoli with, '80 13
Sesame Seeds, Broccoli with, '82 34
Shrimp Sauce, Broccoli and Cauliflower
  with, '84 248
Soufflé, Broccoli, '81 24
Soufflé, Golden Broccoli, '84 283
Soup, Broccoli, '86 161, M194; '87 288
Soup, Broccoli-Swiss, '86 6
Soup, Cheesy-Broccoli, '86 258
Soup, Creamed Broccoli, '85 24
Soup, Cream of Broccoli, '79 130; '80 188,
  M225; '82 314; '83 66; '86 259
Soup, Cream-of-Broccoli, '88 56
Soup, Creamy Broccoli, '81 75; '82 13;
  '83 99
Soup, Easy Broccoli, '81 307
Soup, Hot Broccoli, '81 235; '83 44
Soup, Mock Cream of Broccoli, '85 288
Sour Cream Sauce, Broccoli with, '87 127
Spears, Saucy Broccoli, '84 35
Spears, Zesty Broccoli, '79 152
Spread, Broccamoli Curry, '88 55
Stack-Ups, Jiffy Tomato, '80 161
Steamed Broccoli, '80 122
Steamed Broccoli with Tangy Chive
  Sauce, '83 101
Stir-Fried Broccoli, '83 227

Stir-Fry Beef and Broccoli, '79 47
Stir-Fry, Bok Choy-Broccoli, '84 2
Stir-Fry Broccoli, '80 19
Stir-Fry Broccoli and Beef, '83 110
Stir-Fry, Chicken-Broccoli, '82 33
Strata, Ham and Broccoli, '80 261
Sunshine Sauce, Broccoli with, '84 248
Supreme, Broccoli, '82 34; '85 68
Supreme, Creamy Broccoli, '82 287
Tomatoes, Broccoli-Stuffed, '83 136
Toss, Broccoli, '86 294
Toss, Cauliflower-Broccoli, '82 54
Toss, Crunchy Broccoli and
  Cauliflower, '83 25
Toss, Italian Cauliflower-Broccoli, '88 269
Vinaigrette, Potato-Broccoli, '85 84
Wine, Broccoli with White, '80 12
Wine Sauce, Broccoli with, '84 187
Brussels Sprouts
  Amandine, Brussels Sprouts, '79 213
  Beer, Brussels Sprouts in, '85 69
  Carrots and Brussels Sprouts, '82 300
  Cashews, Brussels Sprouts with, '81 2
  Casserole of Brussels Sprouts, '86 294
  Celery, Brussels Sprouts and, '79 21
  Cheese Sauce, Brussels Sprouts
    with, '79 246
  Citrus Brussels Sprouts, Calico, '85 303
  Creamed Brussels Sprouts and
    Celery, '83 322
  Creamy Brussels Sprouts, '79 212
  Deviled Brussels Sprouts, '84 248
  Dilled Brussels Sprouts, '88 180
  Fried Brussels Sprouts, '81 308
  Glorified Brussels Sprouts, '86 282
  Lemon Sauce, Brussels Sprouts in, '82 269
  Lemon Sprouts, '85 288
  Lemony Brussels Sprouts with
    Celery, '85 25
  Marinated Brussels Sprouts, '88 265
  Medley, Brussels Sprouts, '79 212;
    '85 267
  Mustard Sauce, Brussels Sprouts
    in, '87 253
  Onion Sauce, Brussels Sprouts in, '81 308
  Orange Brussels Sprouts, '84 34
  Orange Sauce, Brussels Sprouts in, '86 55
  Pierre, Brussels Sprouts, '84 248
  Polonaise, Brussels Sprouts, '85 79
  Rice, Brussels Sprouts and, '79 288;
    '80 26
  Salad, Brussels Sprouts, '87 233
  Salad, Cauliflower-Brussels Sprouts, '83 240
  Sesame Brussels Sprouts, '86 55
  Shallots and Mustard, Brussels Sprouts
    with, '85 258
  Stir-Fry, Brussels Sprouts, '81 308
  Tangy Brussels Sprouts, '88 40
  Tarragon Brussels Sprouts, '83 291
  Wine Butter, Brussels Sprouts in, '86 327
Burritos
  Breakfast Burritos, '84 57
  Broccoli Burritos, '83 200
  Burritos, '80 196
  Cheesy Beef Burritos, '85 193
  Chimichangas (Fried Burritos), '81 196;
    '85 244; '86 114
  Chinese Burritos, '87 181
  Fiesta Burritos, '86 114
  Meat-and-Bean Burritos, '81 194
  Monterey Burritos, '84 292

Burritos (continued)

Pie, Mexican Burrito, '87 287
Vegetable Burritos, '80 197
Vegetable Burritos with Avocado
 Sauce, '83 200

Butter

Apple Butter, '79 200; '81 217
Apple Butter, Half-Hour, '81 203
Apricot Butter, '82 308
Balls, Butter, '82 189
Basil Butter, '87 171
Basil Butter, Asparagus with, '85 40
Cashew Butter, Asparagus with, '87 56
Cheese Butter, '84 114
Chervil Butter, '83 129
Chili Butter, '82 219
Clarified Butter, '81 59
Clarifying Butter, '82 189
Curls, Butter, '82 51, 189
Garlic Butter, '83 193; '84 108
Herb Butter, '86 128, 255, 261, 306
Herb Butter, Cauliflower with, '81 2
Herb Butter, Corn-on-the-Cob
 with, '84 160
Herbed Unsalted Butter, '82 67
Honey-Orange Butter, '79 36; '85 19
Horseradish-Chive Butter, '86 277
Lemon Butter, Asparagus with, '87 M151
Lime Butter, Chicken with, '84 68
Maple-Flavored Butter, Whipped, '79 36
Nectarine Butter, '79 175
Onion Butter, '86 253
Orange Butter, '81 8, 42
Orange-Pecan Butter, '84 75
Peach Butter, '82 308
Pear Butter, '85 130
Pear Butter, Spiced, '80 218
Peppercorn Butter, Green, '88 60
Plum Butter, '88 152
Raisin Butter, '81 272
Sauce, Garlic Buerre Blanc, '88 222
Strawberry Butter, '79 36; '81 286
Tomato Butter, '86 128

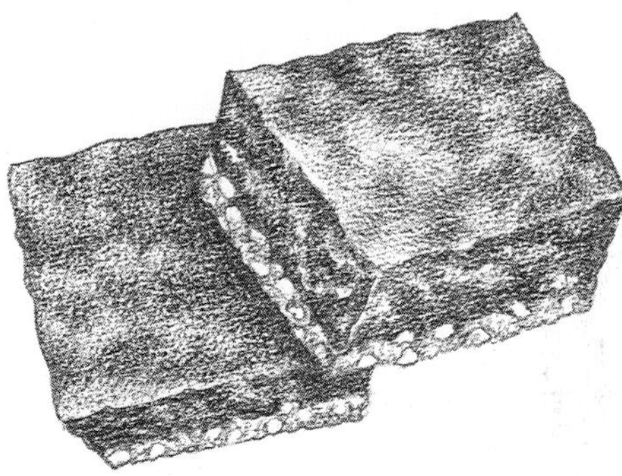

Butterscotch

Bars, Butterscotch, '82 209; '83 297
Bars, Chocolate-Butterscotch, '81 197
Bread, Banana Butterscotch, '79 116
Brownies, Butterscotch, '85 248
Cheesecake, Butterscotch, '86 188
Cookies, Butterscotch, '87 58
Cookies, Butterscotch-Pecan, '84 36
Fantastic, Butterscotch, '83 76
Fudge, Butterscotch Rum, '88 256
Fudge Scotch Ring, '79 273

Pie, Butterscotch Cream, '84 48; '87 207
Pie, Butterscotch Meringue, '83 158
Pralines, Butterscotch, '81 253
Sauce, Butterscotch-Pecan, '82 212

C

Cabbage. *See also* Sauerkraut.

Apples and Franks, Cabbage with, '87 42
au Gratin, Cabbage, '83 279
Bake, Zesty Cabbage Beef, '80 300
Beef-Cabbage Dinner, '81 179
Bubbling Cabbage, '84 2
Caraway Cabbage, '85 32, 289
Casserole, Cheesy Cabbage, '79 4
Casserole, Creamy Cabbage, '80 63
Casserole, Italian Cabbage, '87 42
Casserole, Savory Cabbage, '82 168
Chop Suey, Cabbage, '81 101
Chow-Chow, '82 196
Chowchow, '87 150
Chowder, Hearty Cabbage, '80 25
Corned Beef and Cabbage, '83 104
Corned Beef and Cabbage au Gratin, '83 16
Corned Beef and Cabbage, Quick, '79 54
Corned Beef Squares and Cabbage, '82 86
Country-Style Cabbage, '81 271
Creamed Cabbage with Almonds, '79 4
Creole Cabbage, '87 189
Frankfurter-Cabbage Skillet, '80 166
Hot Cabbage Creole, '87 42
Kielbasa and Cabbage, '85 67
Kielbasa, Cabbage, '87 42
Lemon-Butter Cabbage, '88 156
Medley, Cabbage, '80 64; '83 104
Piccalilli, Kentucky, '81 216
Red Cabbage and Apples, '85 32
Red Cabbage, German-Style, '84 2
Red Cabbage, Pickled, '81 271
Red Cabbage, Sweet-Sour, '79 5
Relish, Cabbage, '83 260
Rolls, Cabbage, '83 104
Rolls, Crunchy Cabbage-Rice, '85 32
Rolls, Easy Cabbage-and-Beef, '88 49
Rolls, Hot-and-Spicy Cabbage, '84 249
Rolls, Spicy Cabbage, '84 2
Rolls, Stuffed Cabbage, '88 18
Rollups, Beef-and-Cabbage, '80 63
Salad, Cabbage, '87 120, 233
Salad, Cabbage and Fruit, '79 286
Salad, Chinese Cabbage, '81 271
Salad, Chinese Green, '88 48
Salad, Garden Cabbage, '81 210
Salad, Nutty Cabbage, '87 42
Salad, Overnight Cabbage, '79 83
Sausage, Cabbage with Polish, '83 104
Sausage-Sauced Cabbage, '81 271
Sausage Surprise, '83 245; '84 42
Scalloped Cabbage, '82 269
Scalloped Cabbage, Cheese, '81 87; '82 7
Skillet, Cabbage-and-Tomato, '86 110
Slaws
　Apple-Pineapple Slaw, '79 241
　Apple Slaw, Fresh, '81 63
　Apple Slaw, Nutty, '88 216
　Aspic, Shrimp-Coleslaw, '79 88
　Bacon Coleslaw, '83 58
　Banana-Nut Slaw, '86 250
　Chicken Coleslaw, '84 2

Chili Coleslaw, '80 178
Coleslaw, '79 152; '82 135
Colorful Coleslaw, '88 166
Corn and Cabbage Slaw, '79 135
Cottage Coleslaw, '80 64
Country-Style Coleslaw, '83 59
Creamy Coleslaw, '83 170
Crunchy Coleslaw, '86 295
Curried Coleslaw, '85 139
Freezer Slaw, '81 279; '82 24;
 '83 154
Fresh Cabbage Slaw, '85 139
Frozen Coleslaw, '82 102
Fruit Coleslaw, Three-, '86 250
Fruited Coleslaw, '83 209; '85 139
Grape-Poppy Seed Slaw, '86 225
Grapes and Almonds, Coleslaw
 with, '83 59
Guacamole Mexican Coleslaw, '82 302
Ham Coleslaw, '84 195
Hot-and-Creamy Dutch Slaw, '87 127
Hot-and-Sour Chinese Slaw, '85 139
Kentucky Coleslaw, '81 216
Layered Coleslaw, '86 180
Make-Ahead Coleslaw, '81 155
Marinated Coleslaw, '79 135
Mexicali Coleslaw, '84 18
Mustard Slaw, Texas, '88 172

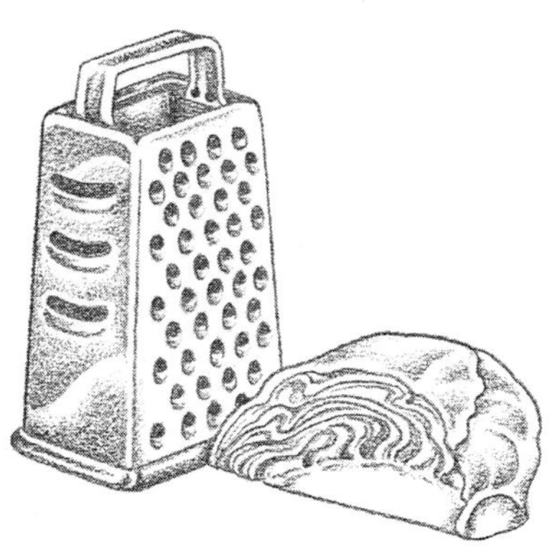

Nutty Cabbage Slaw, '88 218
Old-Fashioned Coleslaw, '80 120;
 '82 225
Old-Fashioned Slaw, '84 149
Orange Slaw, Cabbage-, '79 135
Overnight Cabbage Slaw, '81 88;
 '82 7
Overnight Coleslaw, '79 135
Overnight Slaw, '79 5
Peach Slaw, Party, '86 250
Peanut Slaw, '85 139
Pear Slaw, Peanutty-, '86 250
Pineapple Coleslaw, Curried, '88 172
Pineapple Slaw, Colorful, '86 250
Polka Dot Slaw, '83 59
Red Bean Slaw, '79 247
Red Cabbage-and-Apple Slaw, '87 31
Seafood Slaw, '79 56
Sour Cream Slaw, '87 10
Swedish Slaw, '79 135
Sweet and Crunchy Slaw, '79 104
Sweet-and-Sour Slaw, '81 237
Sweet Cabbage Slaw, '79 76
Tangy Cabbage Salad, '82 55

Tangy Coleslaw, **'83** 59
Tomatoes, Coleslaw with, **'80** 34
Vegetable Slaw, **'81** 280
Zesty Slaw, **'82** 127
Soup, Cabbage, **'83** 291
Spinach Dip in Cabbage, **'82** 155
Stir-Fried Cabbage, **'81** 75, 271; **'85** 109
Stuffed Cabbage, **'84** 282
Stuffed Cabbage, Italian, **'84** 294
Stuffed Cabbage Rolls, **'84** 217
Stuffed Cabbage Rolls, Beef, **'81** 87; **'82** 7
Supreme, Cabbage, **'79** 4; **'83** 206
Sweet-and-Sour Cabbage, **'86** 295; **'87** 189
Tex-Mex Cabbage, **'80** 63
Tomatoes, Cabbage and, **'83** 104
Tomatoes, Tasty Cabbage and, **'86** 72
Wedges, Saucy Cabbage, **'83** 86
Wedges, Smothered Cabbage, **'81** 87; **'82** 7
Wilted Cabbage, **'80** 64; **'88** 229
Cakes. *See also* Breads, Cookies.
Almond-Butter Cake, **'86** 107
Almond-Butter Wedding Cake, **'86** 106
Almond Legend Cake, **'82** 8
Almond Whipping Cream Cake, **'80** 295
Amaretto Cake, Easy, **'85** 79
Ambrosia Cake, **'79** 229
Angel Food
    Chocolate Angel Cake, **'88** 128
    Chocolate Angel Food Cake, **'87** 21
    Chocolate Angel Food Cake with
        Custard Sauce, **'88** 259
    Coconut Angel Cake, Spiked, **'85** 279
    Deluxe Angel Food Cake, **'86** 121
    Ice Cream Angel Cake, **'83** 23
    Lemon Angel Cake, **'80** 147
    Pineapple-Orange Sauce, Angel Cake
        with, **'84** 14
Apple Cake, **'83** 312; **'84** 262
Apple Cake, Dried-, **'79** 13
Apple-Date Cake, Fresh, **'83** 300
Apple-Nut Cake, **'87** 76
Apple-Oatmeal Cake, Golden, **'86** 301
Apple Pie Cake, **'86** 301
Applesauce Cake, **'80** 270
Applesauce Cake, My Favorite, **'87** 263
Applesauce Cake with Bourbon
    Frosting, **'88** 236
Applesauce Snack Cakes, **'88** 215
Applesauce-Spice Cake, **'83** 42
Apple Slice Cake, **'85** 93
Apple Stack Cake, Dried, **'85** 242
Banana-Blueberry Cake, **'86** 247
Banana Cake, **'84** 151
Banana Cake, Deluxe Light, **'84** 314
Banana Cake, Marvelous, **'79** 115
Banana Waldorf Cake, **'85** 118
Bars and Squares
    Almond Cake Squares, **'79** 111
    Apple-Date Dream Cake
        Squares, **'85** 10
    Apple-Orange Cake Squares, **'84** 150
    Applesauce Cake Squares, **'86** 8
    Applesauce-Spice Squares, **'86** 248
    Carrot-Lemon Squares, Golden, **'80** 40
    Carrot Squares, **'79** 256
    Cinnamon Cake Squares, **'87** 222
    Cream Cheese Cake Squares, **'84** 321
    Crumb Cake, Calico, **'87** 261
    Gingerbread Squares, **'84** 16
    Ginger Cake, **'87** 222

Honey-Oatmeal Cake, **'87** 222
Jam Squares, **'81** M289
Orange Cake Squares, **'81** 34
Orange-Pumpkin Cake
    Squares, **'83** 242
Pecan Squares, Easy, **'81** 230
Pumpkin Cake Bars, **'80** 245
Strawberry Shortcake
    Squares, **'85** 122; **'86** 124
Beet Cake with Almond Topping, **'86** 200
Blackberry Cake, Fresh, **'81** 132
Blackberry Flan, **'79** 182
Boston Cream Pie, **'83** 220
Bourbon-Pecan Cake, **'84** 25
Brown Mountain Cake, **'84** 39
Brown Sugar Meringue Cake, **'81** 70
Bûche de Noël, **'84** 304; **'87** 241
Bûche de Noël Cake, **'82** 262
Butter Brickle Cake, **'85** 118
Buttermilk White Cake, **'86** 235
Butter Pecan Cake, **'80** 229
Butter Pecan Cake, Caramel-Filled, **'88** 278
Cajun Cake, **'87** 138
Caramel Layer Cake, Creamy, **'81** 71
Carolina Dream Cake, **'88** 278
Carrot Cake, **'79** 45; **'82** 137; **'84** 315
Carrot Cake, Applesauce, **'81** 202
Carrot Cake, Blue Ribbon, **'81** 70
Carrot Cake, Coconut-Pecan, **'84** 322
Carrot Cake, Easy, **'83** 215
Carrot Cake, Fresh Coconut-, **'80** 299
Carrot Cake, Old-Fashioned, **'83** M232
Carrot Cake, Old-South, **'80** 120
Carrot Cake, Quick-and-Easy, **'84** 150
Carrot Cake, Spiced, **'87** 296
Carrot Cake, Spicy Fruited, **'85** 117
Carrot Pudding Cake, **'83** 24
Carrot Snack Cake, Easy, **'82** 235
Chart, Cake Failure, **'81** 72

Cheesecakes
    Amaretto Cheesecake, **'81** 150
    Apple Cheesecake, Dieter's, **'86** 318
    Black Forest Cheesecake, **'84** 74
    Blueberries 'n' Cream
        Cheesecake, **'87** 140
    Blueberry Chiffon Cheesecake, **'87** 76
    Brownies, Cheesecake, **'85** 249
    Butterscotch Cheesecake, **'86** 188
    Candy Bar Cheesecake, **'85** 298;
        '86 120
    Cherry Cheesecake, **'79** 50
    Cherry-Topped Cheesecake, **'80** 23
    Chocolate-Amaretto
        Cheesecake, **'85** M294
    Chocolate Cheesecake, **'81** 16;
        '82 305

Chocolate Cheesecake,
    German, **'87** 265
Chocolate Cheesecake, Rich, **'84** 74;
    '85 38
Chocolate Cheesecake, White, **'87** 44
Chocolate Chip Cheesecake, **'85** 114
Chocolate Swirl Cheesecake, **'84** 295;
    '85 26
Cottage Cheese Cheesecake, **'80** 24
Cream Cheesecake, Rich, **'83** 270
Crème de Menthe
    Cheesecake, **'82** 263
Daiquiri Chiffon Cheesecake, **'88** 66
Deluxe Cheesecake, **'80** 23
Feta Cheesecakes, Little, **'86** 277
Frozen Cheesecake with Raspberry
    Sauce, **'84** 73
Fruit-Glazed Cheesecake, **'80** 24
Glazed Cheesecake, **'83** 142
Grasshopper Cheesecake, **'80** 191
Individual Cheesecakes, So
    Easy, **'85** 30
Kahlúa Cheesecake, Heavenly, **'83** 48
Lemon Cheesecake, **'86** 194
Lemon Cheesecake with
    Orange-Pineapple Glaze, **'81** 60
Light-and-Easy Cheesecake, **'88** 55
Make-Ahead Cheesecake Pie, **'81** 233
Marbled Cheesecake, **'87** 261
Marble Mint Cheesecake, **'84** 152
Mile-High Cheesecake, **'86** 334
Miniature Cheesecakes, **'82** 305
Mocha-Chocolate Cheesecake, **'88** 258
Mocha Swirl Cheesecake, **'87** 262
Orange Cheesecake, **'81** 84; **'85** 38
Peaches 'n' Cream
    Cheesecake, **'88** 137
Pear-Berry Cheesecake, **'82** M141
Pear-Glazed Cheesecake, **'79** 67
Pecan Cheesecake, **'85** 38
Pecan Cheesecake, Butter, **'86** 61
Petite Cheesecakes, Holiday, **'86** 321
Phyllo Cheesecakes, Little, **'87** 275
Pineapple Cheesecake, **'81** 32
Pineapple Cheesecake, Ultimate, **'85** 38
Praline Cheesecake, **'83** 270
Pumpkin Cheesecake, **'80** 254;
    '85 280
Raspberry Sauce, Cheesecake
    with, **'87** 116
Sour Cream Cheesecake, **'86** 320
Squares, Cheesecake, **'84** 151
Strawberry Cheesecake,
    Almost, **'86** 32
Sweet Potato Cheesecake, **'80** 287
Tarts, Cream Cheese, **'84** 74
Triple Layer Cheesecake,
    Chocolate-Glazed, **'86** 315
White Chocolate Cheesecake, **'88** 267
Yam Cheesecake, **'81** 224
Cherry Bourbon Cake, **'82** 287
Cherry Cake, **'79** 165
Cherry Cake, Quick, **'81** 238
Cherry Torte, Black Forest, **'88** 178
Cherry Upside-Down Cake, **'82** 56
Chocolate
    Almond Cake with Cherry Filling,
        Chocolate-, **'84** 225
    Banana Cake, Chocolate-, **'86** 138
    Banana Loaf, Chocolate Chip-, **'85** 115
    Beet Cake, Chocolate, **'80** 40

Cakes, Chocolate *(continued)*

Black Forest Cake, **'81** 126
Black Forest Cake, Six-Layer, **'85** 125
Black Forest Cherry Cake, **'83** 302
Black Forest Dump Cake, **'85** 13
Brownie Baked Alaska, **'80** 66
Brownie Delight, Chocolate, **'87** 224
Buttermilk Chocolate Cake, **'79** 13
Candy Cake, Chocolate, **'81** 238
Caramel-Nut Cake, Chocolate-, **'83** 23
Cherry Cake, Chocolate-, **'84** 200;
   '86 239
Coconut Cake, Chocolate-, **'83** 23
Custard Cake, Chocolate, **'88** 175
Decadent Chocolate Cake, **'86** 142
Easy Chocolate Cake, **'80** 140
Frosting, Chocolate Cake with
   Double, **'86** 314
Fudge Cake, Best, **'83** 301
Fudge Cake, Brown Sugar, **'86** 316
Fudge Cake, Chocolate, **'80** 279
Fudge Cake for Two, **'81** 205
German Chocolate Cake, **'81** 296;
   '83 M233
German Chocolate Chip Cake, **'86** 247
Kahlúa Chocolate Cake, **'81** 303
Marbled Cake, Cocoa, **'82** 265
Marshmallow Cake, No-Egg
   Chocolate, **'87** M97
Mayonnaise Cake, Chocolate, **'83** 99
Mocha Cake, Belgian, **'84** 316
Mocha Cake, Double, **'84** 311
Mocha-Chocolate Cake, Dark, **'84** 311
Mousse Cake, Chocolate, **'87** 264
Nut Cake, Rich Chocolate-, **'86** 8
Peanut Butter Cake,
   Chocolate-, **'84** 240
Peanut Butter Cake, Fudgy, **'85** 91
Peanut Cluster Cake,
   Chocolate-, **'87** 184
Perfect Chocolate Cake, **'82** 244
Pound Cake. *See* Cakes/Pound.
Pudding, Chocolate Cake, **'81** 99
Pudding Cake, Hot Fudge, **'88** 255
Pudding, Hot Fudge Sundae
   Cake, **'88** 167
Rocky Road Cake, **'81** 178
Roll, Chocolate Cream, **'85** 317
Roll, Chocolate-Frosted Ice
   Cream, **'84** 200
Roll, Chocolate-Mocha Cream, **'84** 304
Roll, Chocolate Mousse, **'83** 290;
   '88 280
Roll, Chocolate-Orange, **'87** 21
Royal, Chocolate Cake, **'86** 239
Rum Cake, Chocolate, **'79** 67
Sachertorte, **'84** 253
Sour Cream Cake, Chocolate-, **'87** 222
Sour Cream Cake, Chocolate
   Chip-, **'85** 115
Sour Cream Chocolate Cake, **'79** 282
Swiss Chocolate Chip Cake, **'87** 85
Torte, Chocolate Praline, **'84** 165
Torte, Chocolate-Strawberry Ice
   Cream, **'79** 7
Torte, Chocolate Velvet, **'86** 316
Torte, Double-Chocolate, **'79** 67
Torte, Mocha Brownie, **'85** 102
Torte Royale, Chocolate, **'82** 263
Triangle Cake, Chocolate, **'85** 126

White Chocolate-Cherry Cake, **'88** 268
Yule Log, **'79** 281; **'82** 289
Zucchini Cake, Chocolate, **'85** 156
Cinnamon Crumb Cake, **'85** 290
Cinnamon Streusel Cake, **'84** 151
Coconut
   Apple Coconut Cake, **'80** 226
   Chocolate-Coconut Cake, **'83** 23
   Chocolate-Coconut Cake,
      White, **'87** 263
   Christmas Coconut Cake, **'82** 262
   Cream Cake, Coconut, **'81** 179
   Creamy Coconut Cake, **'84** 43

   Fresh Coconut Cake, **'80** 289; **'82** 52;
      '85 281
   Layer Cake,
      Coconut-Pineapple, **'80** 140
   Layer Cake, Stately Coconut, **'81** 70
   Lemon-Coconut Cream Cake, **'81** 179
   Lemon-Coconut Sheet Cake, **'85** 117
   Pineapple Cake Roll, Coconut-, **'84** 304
   Pound Cake. *See* Cakes/Pound.
   Regal Coconut Cake, **'83** 299
   Rum-Orange Coconut Cake, **'88** 224
   Spice Cake, Coconut-, **'84** 255;
      '87 296
   Toasted Coconut Cake, **'86** 60
Coffee Cakes
   Almond-Blueberry Coffee
      Cake, **'85** 152
   Apple Coffee Cake, **'81** 249
   Apple Loaf, Spiced, **'79** 215
   Apple-Pecan Coffee Cake, **'84** 242
   Banana Coffee Cake, **'81** 288
   Banana Cream Coffee Cake, **'85** 46
   Banana-Sour Cream Coffee
      Cake, **'80** 186
   Blueberry Brunch Cake, **'83** 183
   Blueberry Coffee Cake, **'82** 206;
      '85 326; **'88** 263
   Blueberry Coffee Cake, Fresh, **'81** 164
   Blueberry Streusel Coffee
      Cake, **'88** 154
   Braid Coffee Cake, Daisy, **'82** 197
   Breakfast Pullapart, **'81** 278
   Butterflake Coffee Ring, **'79** 216
   Buttermilk Crumb Cake, **'79** 72
   Caramel Bread, **'82** 75
   Caramel Breakfast Rolls, **'79** 193
   Caramel-Orange Coffee Ring, **'80** 45
   Caramel Ring, Easy, **'85** M89
   Cardamom Coffee Cake, **'83** 246;
      '84 17
   Cherry Blossom Coffee Cake, **'80** 21
   Chocolate-Chip Coffee Cake, **'79** 249
   Chocolate Chip Coffee Cake, **'83** 231
   Christmas-Tree Coffee Cakes, **'87** 298
   Christmas Wreath, **'80** 280

Cinnamon-Buttermilk Coffee
   Cake, **'80** 45
Cinnamon Coffee Cake, **'83** M203
Cinnamon Crisps, **'81** 113
Cinnamon-Nut Bubble Bread, **'80** 22
Cinnamon-Pecan Coffee Cake, **'87** 69
Cinnamon Twist Coffee Cake, **'84** 322
Cinnamon Upside-Down Coffee
   Cake, **'85** 256
Cranberry Coffee Cake, **'81** 14
Cranberry-Nut Coffee Cake, **'81** 250
Cranberry-Orange Coffee
   Cake, **'82** 283
Cream Cheese Coffee Cake, **'86** 290
Crescent Coffee Cake, **'81** 229
Danish Coffee Ring, **'80** 20
Fig Coffee Cake, Easy, **'80** 116
Holiday Coffee Cake, **'84** 284
Holiday Wreath, **'81** 284
Honey Twist, **'79** 80
Lemon Coffee Cake, Lightly, **'81** 14
Macadamia Ring Coffee Cake, **'85** 326
Maple-Nut Coffee Twist, **'86** 290
Marbled Coffee Cake, **'86** 9
Muffins, Coffee Cake, **'79** 7
Oatmeal-Coconut Coffee Cake,
   '83 312
Orange Breakfast Ring, **'81** 229
Orange Coffee Cake, **'85** M88
Orange Marmalade Swirl Coffee
   Cake, **'81** 107
Orange-Pecan Coffee Cake, **'86** 86
Overnight Coffee Cake, **'80** 52
Peach Flip, **'79** 217
Pecan-Topped Coffee Cake, **'81** 41
Raisin Coffee Cake, Spicy, **'88** 63
Raspberry Coffee Cake, **'83** 112
Ring, Coffee Cake, **'85** M89
Savarin, Holiday, **'80** 280
Snack Cake, Coffee, **'86** 247
Sour Cream Coffee Cake, **'81** 270
Sour Cream-Walnut Coffee
   Cake, **'79** 209
Strawberry Coffee Cake, **'85** 46
Sugar Cake, Moravian, **'87** 228
Sugarplum Coffee Ring, **'79** 235;
   '83 M37
Sweet Roll Dough, **'79** 80
Tropical Coffee Cake, **'80** 232
Whole Wheat Coffee Cake,
   Crunchy-Topped, **'79** 93
Cola Cake, **'81** 238
Cranberry Upside-Down Cake, **'87** 8
Cream Cheese Cake, Regal, **'80** 140
Cream Cheese Loaf Cake, **'84** 151
Crème de Menthe Cake, **'81** 178
Cupcakes
   Apple-Nut Cupcakes, **'82** 279
   Banana-Cocoa Cupcakes, **'80** 130
   Black Bottom Cups, **'82** 279
   Brownie Cupcakes, **'82** 280
   Carrot-Bran Cupcakes, **'82** 16
   Chocolate Chip Cupcakes,
      Marble, **'81** 239
   Chocolate Surprise Cupcakes, **'85** 91
   Cinnamon-Chocolate
      Cupcakes, **'81** M139
   Cream Cheese Party
      Cupcakes, **'82** 279
   Date Cupcakes, **'84** 7
   Happy Day Cupcakes, **'80** 129

Lemon Moist Cupcakes, '82 112;
'83 153
Mocha Cupcakes, '85 250
Pumpkin Cupcakes, '85 121
Self-Filled Cupcakes, '80 129
Vanilla Cupcakes, Golden, '85 121
Yellow Cupcakes, Easy, '83 241
Daffodil Cake, '84 161
Date Nut Cake, '79 176; '80 5
Decorating Techniques, Cake, '83 72, 240;
'84 224
Fig Cake, '79 32
Fig Preserve Cake, '79 140; '84 316
Friendship Cake, '82 250
Fruit-and-Cereal Brunch Cake, '88 263
Fruit-and-Nut Cake, Stately, '84 226
Fruitcakes
Applesauce Fruitcake, '83 258
Aronowitz Fruitcake, '86 285
Bourbon Fruitcake, '85 315
Brandy Fruitcake, '82 261
Burgundy Fruitcake, '85 292
Favorite Fruitcake, Family, '88 284
Fondue, Fruitcake, '84 258
Japanese Fruitcake, '83 268
Jeweled Fruitcake, '88 260
Kentucky Fruitcake, '86 266
Layered Fruitcake, '87 265
Lemon Fruitcake, '83 258
Mom's Fruitcake, '85 321
Old-South Fruitcake, '79 289
Regal Fruitcake, '83 257
Sherry-Nut Fruitcake, '84 266
Spice Cake, Fruit and, '87 M97
White Fruitcake, '80 280; '85 316
Zucchini Fruitcake, '88 284
Funnel Cakes, '83 250
Gingerbread, Old English, '79 265
Gingerbread, Refrigerator, '80 52
Gingerbread, Spicy, '84 263
Graham Cracker Cake, '79 13
Holiday Cake, Favorite, '81 264
Hummingbird Cake, '82 244
Ice Cream Cake, '86 321
Ice Cream Cake for Grown-Ups, '88 M192
Ice Cream Cake, Fruity, '87 110
Ice Cream Yule Log, '83 253
Jellyroll, Easy, '82 176
Jellyroll Layer Cake, '85 125
Jellyroll, Spiced, '82 176
Lane Cake, '80 121; '83 269
Lemon Cake, Easy, '83 24
Lemon Cake, Glazed, '86 70
Lemon Cake Roll, Elegant, '80 70
Lemon-Cheese Cake, Tart, '88 7
Lemon Gold Cake, '83 301
Lemon Layer Cake, Luscious, '86 61
Lemon Layer Cake, Old-Fashioned, '85 191
Lemon-Pineapple Cake, '86 60, 239
Lemon Pudding Cake, '83 106
Lemon Roll, Snow-Capped, '79 68
Lemon Sponge Cups, '83 10
Lime Layer Loaf, '85 96
Mandarin-Rum Cake, '84 150
Mango Cake, '83 150
Maraschino Nut Cake, '83 268
Mincemeat Spice Cake, '79 246
Molasses Snack Cake, '86 20
Neapolitan Cake, '88 168
Nutmeg Feather Cake, '81 238
Oatmeal Cake, Dutch, '83 95

Orange Cake, '86 61
Orange Cake, Fresh, '83 300
Orange Cake, Mandarin, '83 24
Orange Cake, Williamsburg, '81 120; '82 23
Orange Chiffon Cake, Fresh, '88 179
Orange-Cranberry Cake, '85 314
Orange-Lemon Cake, General Robert E.
Lee, '88 92
Orange Liqueur Cake, '87 84
Orange Marmalade Cake, '85 53
Orange Meringue Cake, '86 336; '87 84
Orange-Nut Butter Cake, '80 254
Orange Nut Cake, '80 70
Orange-Pecan Crunch Cake, '83 10
Orange Rum Cake, '79 2
Orange Shortcake, Fresh, '80 100
Orange-Slice Cake, '81 264
Orange Streusel Cake, '88 10
Peach Cake, Fresh, '85 178
Peaches and Cream Cake, '80 142
Peach Upside-Down Cake, '87 8
Peachy Picnic Cake, '79 178
Peanut Butter-and-Jelly Cake, '85 34
Peanut Butter-Banana Cake, '80 87
Peanut Butter Cake, '79 51; '83 M233
Peanut Butter Swirl Cake, '86 109
Peanutty Layer Cake, Super, '83 222
Pear Cake with Caramel Drizzle, '86 247
Pear Preserve Cake, '85 52
Pecan Cake, Kentucky, '84 263
Pecan Cake with Praline Glaze, '82 196
Pecan Roulade, '87 183
Persimmon Cake, '79 205
Petits Fours, '79 117
Petits Fours, Teatime, '85 119
Pineapple Cake, Heavenly, '83 303
Pineapple-Pecan Upside-Down Cake, '84 25
Pineapple Upside-Down Cake, '80 102;
'88 10
Pineapple Upside-Down Cake,
Skillet, '85 242
Pineapple Upside-Down Cake,
Stacked, '86 239
Popcorn-Gumdrop Cake, '87 262
Poppy Seed Cake, Plantation, '79 13
Poppy Seed Loaf Cake, '81 63
Poppy Seed Loaf, Quick, '82 75

Pound
Apple Cider Pound Cake, '84 10
Apricot Brandy Pound Cake, '83 267
Brown Sugar Pound Cake, '82 135
Buttermilk Pound Cake, '79 285;
'85 255

Buttermilk Pound Cake,
Old-Fashioned, '82 52
Buttermilk Pound Cake, Spiced, '84 73
Butter-Nut Pound Cake, '86 235
Caramel Frosting, Pound Cake
with, '87 39
Carrot Pound Cake, '87 41
Chocolate Chip Pound Cake, '86 178
Chocolate Marble Pound Cake, '88 16
Chocolate Pound Cake, '82 88; '84 10
Chocolate Pound Cake with Fudge
Frosting, '87 296
Chocolate-Sour Cream Pound
Cake, '83 239
Coconut-Cream Cheese Pound
Cake, '85 297
Coconut Cream Pound Cake, '84 10
Coconut Pound Cake, '82 87
Cream Cheese Pound Cake, '81 290;
'86 287
Favorite Pound Cake, '81 132
Five-Flavor Pound Cake, '87 264
Fruited Pound Cake, '81 265
I Remember Pound Cake, '86 180
Lemon Pound Cake, '82 88
Lemon-Sour Cream Pound
Cake, '87 38
Loaf, Pound Cake, '85 306
Mini Pound Cakes, '86 148
Old-Fashioned, Buttermilk Pound
Cake, '88 16
Old-Fashioned Pound Cake, '80 279;
'82 88
Orange Pound Cake, '87 84, 221
Pineapple Pound Cake, '79 148
Praline Pound Cake, '82 88
Problems to Avoid Chart, '84 319
Rose-Geranium Pound Cake, Mrs.
Willoughby's, '84 318
Rum Pound Cake, Buttered, '83 220
Sour Cream Pound Cake,
Cinnamon-Topped, '82 43
Sour Cream Pound Cake,
Elegant, '83 79
Sweet Potato Pound Cake, '83 85
Yogurt Pound Cake, '84 10
Praline Cake, '81 162
Praline Ice Cream Cake, '80 84
Prune Cake, '85 223
Prune Cake and Sauce, '85 118
Prune Cake, Spicy, '79 136
Pumpkin Cake, '81 272
Pumpkin Date Cake, '79 251
Pumpkin Kahlúa Cake, '86 292
Pumpkin Layer Cake, '80 245
Pumpkin Roll, '79 206
Queen Bee Cake, '81 237
Raisin Layer Cake, Spicy, '79 230
Savarin, '79 171
Sorghum Cake, '85 239
Sorghum Tea Cakes, '85 239
Spice Cake, '81 162
Spice Cake, Buttermilk, '81 211
Spice Cake, Dark, '82 314; '83 43
Spice Cake, Old South, '84 263
Spice Cake, Sugar 'n, '84 226
Spice Cake with Caramel Frosting, '82 314;
'83 42
Spice Cake with Chocolate-Coffee
Frosting, '88 268
Spice Cake, Yule Log, '85 314

Cakes *(continued)*

Sponge
    Chocolaty Sponge Cake, '86 60
    Coffee Sponge Cake, '83 229
    Coffee Sponge Cake, Two-Day,
      '86 75
    Daffodil Sponge Cake, '79 175; '80 6;
      '84 315
    Strawberries 'n Cream Sponge Cake
      Roll, '81 95
    Yellow Sponge Cake, '80 250
Squash Cake, '86 200
Stack Cake, Favorite, '87 228
Stack Cake, Old-Fashioned, '81 216

Strawberry Cake Roll, '79 49; '83 129;
  '84 305; '85 172
Strawberry Cream Cake, '86 61
Strawberry Crunch Cake, '79 288; '80 35
Strawberry Delight Cake, '85 30
Strawberry Ice Cream Roll, '84 105
Strawberry Meringue Cake, '86 240
Strawberry Roll, '82 120
Strawberry Roll, Heavenly, '82 176
Strawberry Shortcake, '81 96; '83 122
Strawberry Shortcake, A Favorite, '88 136
Strawberry Shortcake, Elegant, '88 37
Strawberry Shortcake Jubilee, '88 209
Strawberry Shortcake Shells, '88 196
Sweet Potato Cake, '79 207
Sweet Potato Loaf Cake, '81 224
Sweet Potato Log Roll, '82 227
Sweet Potato Surprise Cake, '80 287
Tea Cake, Lemon, '82 169
Tea Cakes, Mexican, '81 196
Teacakes, Old-Fashioned, '84 43
Tipsy Squire, '85 41
Torte, Amaretto, '82 303
Torte, Black Forest, '88 209
Torte, Carob-Pecan, '85 218
Torte, Heavenly Pecan, '81 266
Torte, Mocha-Pecan, '86 26
Torte, Strawberry Meringue, '88 136
Torte, Sugar Cookie, '79 68
Torte, Toffee Meringue, '87 118
Upside-Down Sunburst Cake, '87 9
Vanilla Chiffon Cake, '79 266
Walnut Cake, Black, '80 253; '84 316
Walnut Cream Roll, '84 192
White Cake with Strawberries and Chocolate
  Glaze, '87 76
Zucchini Cake, '79 24
Zuppa Inglese, '85 229
Candies
Almond Brittle Candy, '80 255
Almond Butter Crunch, '80 301
Almond Roca, '86 49
Almond-Toffee Crunch, '88 285

Apples, Candied Red, '81 217
Apples, Candy, '84 243
Apricot Balls, '79 274
Balls, No-Cook Candy, '85 14
Bourbon Balls, '81 254; '83 315
Bourbon Balls, Chocolate, '84 298
Brandy Balls, '86 319
Brittle with Crushed Peanuts, '87 184
Buckeyes, '85 321
Butter Creams, '80 302
Buttermilk Candy, '80 302
Caramel Corn Candy, '84 243
Caramel Good Stuff, Baked, '80 284
Caramel-Peanut Squares, '85 247
Chocolate Brittle, '83 315
Chocolate Brittle, Quick, '82 114
Chocolate-Coconut Almond Drops, '87 223
Chocolate-Covered Cherries, '81 286;
  '84 298
Chocolate-Covered Pecan Fritters, '79 205
Chocolate-Covered Pretzels, '82 295
Chocolate Drops, '84 111
Chocolate Greeting Card, '83 40
Chocolate-Nut Log Candy, '86 335
Chocolate-Peanut Butter Balls, '80 87
Chocolate-Peanut Clusters, '81 16
Chocolate Rum Balls, '80 302
Chocolate-Rum Balls, '88 285
Chocolates, Liqueur Cream-Filled, '87 258
Chocolate Spiders, '85 236
Chocolates, Spirited, '86 278
Chocolate Truffles, '85 114
Chocolate Velvets, '84 298
Coconut-Almond Balls, '84 256
Coconut-Black Walnut Bonbons, '82 307
Coconut Candy, '79 272; '80 250
Corn Brittle, Crunchy, '85 208
Crème de Cacao Balls, '86 266
Crystal Candy, '84 299
Date Loaf Candy, '80 302
Date Logs, '79 274
Divinity, Apricot, '83 297
Divinity, Christmas, '81 286
Divinity, Peanut, '85 233; '87 M278
Divinity, Pink, '86 49
Frosting, Chocolate Candy, '81 238
Fruit Balls, '82 296; '84 299
Fudge
    Butterscotch Rum Fudge, '88 256
    Cherry Nut Fudge, '83 315
    Chocolate Fudge, '82 20
    Chocolate-Peanut Butter
      Fudge, '87 257
    Coffee-Chip Fudge, '86 74
    Cream Cheese Fudge, '84 111
    Creamy Dark Fudge, '82 295
    Creamy Fudge, '81 218
    Double-Good Fudge, '79 M263
    Double Good Fudge, '87 M278
    Fast Fudge, '79 274
    Fudge, '86 266
    Mint Fudge, Dinner, '88 285
    Mocha Fudge, Holiday, '84 298
    Nut Fudge, Quick, '83 316
    Nutty White Fudge, '81 253
    Peanut Butter Fudge, '80 302
    Peanut Butter Fudge, Marbled, '88 65
    Peanut Fudge, Double, '85 91
    Pecan Fudge, Creamy, '84 321
    Penuche, '79 272
    Pistachio Fudge, '83 298

Quick-and-Easy Fudge, '88 M190
  Scotch Ring, Fudge, '79 273
    Tiger Butter, '86 48
Kentucky Colonels, '79 273
Lollipops, Colorful Molded, '81 218
Marzipan, '83 306
Millionaires, '79 M262
Mints, Dinner, '88 66
Mints, Easy Holiday, '84 299
Mints, Party, '79 273; '81 119
Mint Twists, '86 106
Molded Candies, '84 40
Nut Clusters, '81 254
Nuts, Candied, '81 261
Orange Peel, Candied, '81 286
Peanut Brittle, '79 M263; '80 87; '84 298
Peanut Brittle, Golden, '83 223
Peanut Brittle, Never-Fail, '79 273
Peanut Brittle, Orange, '80 302
Peanut Butter-Chocolate Balls, '80 269
Peanut Butter-Chocolate Candy
  Squares, '82 56
Peanut Butter Creams, '79 273
Peanut Butter Easter Eggs, '87 86
Peanut Butter Temptations, '84 29
Peanut Butter Yummies, '83 223
Peanut Clusters, '87 184
Peanutty Clusters, '83 143
Pecan Clusters, '81 266

Pecan Clusters, Roasted, '85 233
Pecan-Coconut Clusters, '86 M251
Pecan Pralines, Original, '81 11
Pecan Rolls, '79 285
Pecans, Brown Sugar, '81 266
Pecans, Glazed, '81 254
Pecans, Honeycomb, '84 300
Pecans, Orange, '84 299
Pecans, Spiced, '79 296; '81 286
Pecans, Spicy, '81 289
Pecans, Sugar-and-Honey, '86 319
Peppermint Patties, '86 278
Potato Candy, '79 273
Praline Clusters, Dark, '86 313
Praline Delights, Spicy, '84 299
Pralines, '79 272; '86 M288
Pralines, Butterscotch, '81 253
Pralines, Creamy, '80 198
Pralines, Dark, '83 52
Pralines, Maple-Pecan, '83 222
Pralines, New Orleans-Style, '86 335
Pralines, Plantation Coffee, '86 241
Pralines, Southern, '79 M263
Pralines, Texas-Size, '79 186
Quemada (Burnt-Sugar Candy), '87 38
Raisin Candy, Mixed, '84 111
Rocky Road, '84 298
Taffy, Old-Fashioned, '80 302
Toffee, English, '79 273

Toffee, Nutty, **'79** M263
Truffles, Almond, **'83** 298
Truffles, Amaretto Dessert, **'86** 319
Truffles, White Chocolate, **'87** 45
Canning. *See also* Pickles and Relishes.
Apple Rings, Cinnamon, **'85** 107
Asparagus, Pickled, **'83** 46
Bean Salad, Pickled Green, **'82** 239
Beans, Appalachian Green, **'81** 215
Beans, Green, **'80** 126
Beans, Green, Snap, or Wax, **'85** 105
Beans, Lima, **'80** 127
Beets, Pickled, **'81** 216
Berries (except Strawberries), **'80** 128
Catsup, Homemade, **'85** 188
Catsup, Spicy Tomato, **'83** 182
Chili Sauce, **'81** 175
Chili Sauce, Chunky, **'85** 188
Chow-Chow, **'82** 196
Corn, Cold-Pack, **'81** 216
Corn, Cream-Style, **'80** 127; **'85** 106
Corn, Whole Kernel, **'85** 106
Cranberry Conserve, **'83** 279
Fruit Juices, **'85** 107
Fruit, Unsweetened Mixed, **'83** 182
Nectarines in Apple Juice, **'83** 183
Okra, **'80** 127
Peaches, **'80** 128
Peaches and Pears, **'85** 106
Peaches, Honey-Sweet, **'85** 107
Peas, Black-Eyed, Field, and
    Crowder, **'80** 126
Piccalilli, Kentucky, **'81** 216
Sauerkraut, Homemade, **'81** 216
Squash, Summer, **'80** 127; **'85** 105
Succotash, **'85** 106
Tomatoes, **'80** 128; **'85** 106
Tomatoes, Stewed, **'83** 182
Tomatoes with Okra, **'85** 106
Tomato Juice, Spicy, **'85** 189
Tomato Puree, Seasoned, **'83** 182
Vegetable Soup, **'80** 128; **'85** 106
Cantaloupe. *See* Melons.
Caramel
Apples, Caramel, **'79** 220
Apples, Old English Caramel, **'85** 231
Baked Caramel Good Stuff, **'80** 284
Bars, Oatmeal-Caramel, **'85** 247
Bread, Caramel, **'82** 75
Cake, Caramel-Filled Butter Pecan, **'88** 278
Cake, Chocolate-Caramel-Nut, **'83** 23
Cake, Creamy Caramel Layer, **'81** 71
Candy, Caramel Corn, **'84** 243
Cobbler, Peach-Caramel, **'86** 300; **'87** 178
Corn, Baked Caramel, **'81** 218
Corn, Caramel, **'88** 64
Crème d'Ange, **'83** 91
Drizzle, Caramel, **'86** 247
Filling, Caramel, **'88** 278
Frosting, Caramel, **'81** 278, M289;
    '82 314; **'83** 43; **'84** 39, 263; **'86** 239;
    '87 265
Frosting, Creamy Caramel, **'81** 71
Frosting, Easy Caramel, **'87** 39
Frosting, Favorite Caramel, **'83** 106
Helado, Caramel-Vanilla (Caramel-Vanilla Ice
    Cream), **'81** 67
Millionaires, **'79** M262
Pie, Burnt Caramel, **'82** 53
Pie, Caramel-Banana, **'86** M165
Pie, Caramel Ice Cream, **'82** 181

Pie, Caramel-Peanut, **'86** 259
Pie, Caramel-Pecan, **'88** 282
Pie, Caramel-Pecan Apple, **'85** 247
Pie, Luscious Caramel Banana, **'79** 115
Pies, Coconut-Caramel, **'87** 260
Popcorn, Caramel, **'79** 219; **'86** M212
Popcorn, Crispy Caramel, **'85** 247
Ring, Caramel-Orange Coffee, **'80** 45
Ring, Easy Caramel, **'85** M89
Rolls, Caramel Breakfast, **'79** 193
Rolls, Caramel-Nut, **'86** 312
Sauce, Caramel, **'79** 79
Sauce, Caramel-Raisin, **'88** 127
Sauce, Easy Caramel, **'87** 38
Squares, Caramel-Peanut, **'85** 247
Squares, Chocolate-Caramel Layer, **'79** 83
Surprise, Caramel, **'88** 202
Syrup, Caramel, **'82** 43
Tarts, Caramel, **'82** 43

Carrots

Aloha Carrots, **'85** 261
Ambrosia, Carrot-Marshmallow, **'80** 5
Apricot Carrots, **'84** 6
Aspic, Orange-and-Carrot, **'86** 199
Baby Carrots, Zucchini with, **'88** 24
Bake, Creamy Carrot, **'85** 67
Ball, Carrot-Cheese, **'86** 325
Balls, Carrot, **'79** 178
Bourbonnaise, Baby Carrots, **'85** 89
Braised Carrots and Celery, **'86** 327
Brandied Carrots, **'87** 253
Brandy Sauce, Carrots in, **'83** 86
Bread, Carrot-Pineapple, **'82** 210
Bread, Carrot-Walnut, **'88** 284
Bread, Pineapple-Carrot, **'79** 106
Bread, Tasty Carrot, **'84** 328
Bread, Three-C, **'81** 284
Bread, Zucchini-Carrot, **'83** 190
Brussels Sprouts, Carrots and, **'82** 300
Cake, Applesauce Carrot, **'81** 202
Cake, Blue Ribbon Carrot, **'81** 70
Cake, Carrot, **'79** 45; **'82** 137; **'84** 315
Cake, Carrot Pound, **'87** 41
Cake, Carrot Pudding, **'83** 24
Cake, Coconut-Pecan Carrot, **'84** 322
Cake, Easy Carrot, **'83** 215
Cake, Easy Carrot Snack, **'82** 235
Cake, Fresh Coconut-Carrot, **'80** 299
Cake, Old-Fashioned Carrot, **'83** M232
Cake, Old-South Carrot, **'80** 120
Cake, Quick-and-Easy Carrot, **'84** 150
Cake, Spiced Carrot, **'87** 296
Cake, Spicy Fruited Carrot, **'85** 117
Candied Carrots, **'82** 269; **'83** 225
Caprice, Carrots, **'84** 6
Casserole, Carrot, **'86** 279; **'87** 285
Casserole, Carrot and Zucchini, **'83** 256

Casserole, Cauliflower-and-Carrot, **'83** 280
Casserole, Scrumptious Carrot, **'84** 328
Casserole, Squash-Carrot, **'81** 157
Combo, Carrot, **'79** 45
Cookies, Carrot, **'82** 137
Cookies, Carrot-Orange, **'83** 149
Cookies, Frosted Carrot, **'81** 7
Cornbread, Carrot, **'80** 89; **'81** 163
Cupcakes, Carrot-Bran, **'82** 16
Deviled Carrots, **'83** 322
Dilled Baby Carrots, **'84** 80
Dilled Carrots, **'85** 24
Dill-Spiced Carrots, **'87** 200
Dilly Carrots, **'85** 85
Fillets, Apple-Carrot Stuffed, **'88** M192
Fried Carrot Balls, **'82** 16
Garden Surprise, **'83** 112
Ginger Carrots, **'83** 9; **'85** 139
Gingered Carrots, **'85** 95
Glazed Carrots, **'81** 304; **'83** 117;
    '85 258; **'88** 304
Glazed Carrots and Onions, **'83** 25;
    '87 128
Glazed Carrots, Apricot, **'80** 89
Glazed Carrots, Ginger-, **'87** 68
Glazed Carrots, Honey-, **'80** 115; **'84** 121;
    '85 18
Glazed Carrots, Lemon-, **'84** 16
Glazed Carrots, Orange-, **'79** 12; **'81** M165
Glazed Carrots, Spice-, **'83** M58
Glazed Carrots with Bacon and
    Onion, **'87** 200
Glazed Carrots with Grapes, **'82** 287
Golden Carrots, **'85** 267
Harvard Carrots, **'83** 117
Herbed Carrots and Onions, **'87** 31
Honey-Kissed Carrots, **'84** 122
Horseradish Glaze, Carrots with, **'85** 66
Julienne Carrots, How to Prepare, **'84** 120
Julienne Carrots, Sautéed, **'82** 91
Julienne Carrots with Walnuts, **'84** 188
Julienne, Tarragon Carrots, **'84** 329
Julienne, Turnips and Carrots, **'86** 295
Lemon Carrots, **'82** 300; **'83** 111
Loaf, Carrot-Nut, **'83** 117
Madeira, Carrots, **'80** 125; **'83** 281
Marinated Beets, Green Beans, and
    Carrots, **'88** 162
Marinated Carrots, **'86** 108, 111
Marinated Carrots, Creamy, **'87** 200
Marinated Carrots, Crispy, **'81** 7
Marinated Carrot Strips, **'88** 176
Marmalade, Carrot-Citrus, **'81** 148
Marsala, Carrots, **'83** 56
Medley, Carrot-and-Leek, **'88** 102
Medley, Carrot-Lima-Squash, **'80** 123
Minted Carrots, **'81** 101
Minted Carrots, Saucy, **'82** 252
Muffins, Carrot-and-Raisin, **'87** 24
Muffins, Carrot-Date-Nut, **'86** 262
Muffins, Carrot-Pineapple, **'81** 6
Muffins, Carrot-Wheat, **'88** 9
Orange-Raisin Carrots, **'80** 24
Orange Sauce, Carrots in, **'82** 107
Orange-Spiced Carrots, **'88** 18
Parsleyed Turnips and Carrots, **'79** 253
Patties, Carrot, **'80** 89
Pecans, Carrots and Celery with, **'84** 254
Pie, Carrot, **'83** 117
Pie, Carrot Custard, **'79** 45
Pie, Carrot Ice Cream, **'86** 200

Carrots *(continued)*

Pie, Cauliflower-Carrot, '82 191
Pineapple Carrots, '83 198
Polynesian, Carrots, '79 45
Puff, Carrot, '84 328
Puffs, Carrot, '87 200
Ring, Festive Carrot, '82 16
Ring, Rice-Carrot, '79 246
Salad, Apple-Carrot, '85 22
Salad, Carrot, '82 137
Salad, Carrot-Ambrosia, '81 252
Salad, Carrot-and-Zucchini, '83 240
Salad, Carrot-Raisin, '83 117; '84 174;
    '87 10
Salad, Carrot-Tangerine, '83 316; '84 16
Salad, Creamy Carrot-Nut, '86 331
Salad, Favorite Carrot, '80 33
Salad, Fruity Carrot-and-Seed, '86 223
Salad, Orange-Carrot, '80 89; '84 325
Salad, Shredded Carrot, '80 178
Salad, Simple Carrot, '82 101; '84 152
Salad, Sunshine Carrot, '82 132
Salad, Turkey-Carrot, '86 283
Saucy Carrots, '87 41
Savory Sauce, Lima Beans and Carrots
    with, '84 196
Scalloped Carrots, '81 6
Scalloped Carrots-and-Celery, '84 M112
Soufflé, Carrot, '79 73
Soufflé, Carrots, '83 265
Soup, Carrot, '80 88
Soup, Carrot-Leek, '86 34
Soup, Carrot-Orange, '79 172
Soup, Cheesy Carrot, '81 262
Soup, Cream of Carrot, '81 307; '88 46
Soup, Curried Carrot, '82 157
Soup, Potato-Carrot, '88 297
Soup, Savory Carrot, '84 107
Special Carrots, '81 108; '84 6
Spiced Carrots Polynesian, '88 85
Squares, Carrot, '79 256
Squares, Golden Carrot-Lemon, '80 40
Stuffed Carrots, '86 324; '87 40
Sunshine Carrots, '82 16; '83 25
Sweet-and-Sour Carrots, '82 137
Sweet-and-Sour Green Beans and
    Carrots, '83 6
Tarragon Carrots, '83 173
Tipsy Carrots, '87 40
Toss, Carrot-Fruit, '82 235
Tropical Carrots, '84 34
Veal and Carrots, Company, '85 22
Veal and Carrots in Wine Sauce,
    '86 M139
Wine, Carrots in White, '81 109
Wine Sauce, Carrots in, '80 88
Wine Sauce, Veal and Carrots in, '81 31
Zesty Carrots, '84 5
Zucchini and Carrots, Buttered, '83 252
Zucchini, Carrots and, '84 262

Casseroles

Apple-Cheese Casserole, '84 287
Apple-Egg Casserole, '85 44
Barley Casserole, '84 281
Bean
    Baked Bean Medley, '80 100
    Baked Beans, Hawaiian-Style, '86 210
    Baked Beans, Three-Meat, '86 210
    Baked Beans with Ham, '80 136
    Beef-and-Bean Bake, Cheesy, '82 89

Green Bean and Artichoke Casserole,
    Italian, '85 81
Green Bean-and-Corn
    Casserole, '88 123
Green Bean Casserole, '79 106;
    '84 145
Green Bean Casserole, Easy, '87 284
Green Bean Salad, Hot, '86 298
Green Beans au Gratin, '80 116
Green Beans, French
    Quarter, '80 298; '81 26
Green Beans in Sour Cream, '80 116
Green Beans, Italian, '85 147

Green Beans Italian, '87 10
Green Bean Surprise, '86 9
Green Beans with Sour Cream, '82 90
Lentils with Cheese, Baked, '84 113
Lima-Bacon Bake, '86 9
Lima Bean Casserole, '79 189;
    '83 313; '86 225; '87 284
Lima Bean Casserole, Spicy, '79 189
Lima Bean Casserole, Swiss, '80 191
Lima Bean Garden Casserole, '83 218;
    '84 246
Lima Beans Deluxe, '79 289; '80 26
Lima Beans, Savory, '83 219; '84 246
Lima Beans, Super, '79 189
Lima Beans with Canadian
    Bacon, '83 219; '84 245
Lima Casserole, Ham and, '79 192
Limas, Spanish Cheese, '86 225
Mexican Bean Casserole,
    Spicy, '84 114
Three-Bean Bake, '81 155
Three-Bean Casserole, '88 56
Cheese Bake, Continental, '81 89
Cheese Casserole, Feather-Light, '79 84
Cheesy Breakfast Casserole, '85 247
Chile-Cheese Casserole, '82 90
Chile-Hominy Casserole, '81 29
Chile 'n' Cheese Breakfast
    Casserole, '88 57
Chiles Rellenos Casserole, '79 84
Chili-Rice Casserole, '79 54
Chili-Tamale Pie, '83 68
Cornmeal Puff, '82 42
Cranberry-Apple Casserole, '83 311
Egg-and-Cheese Casserole, '84 293
Egg-and-Cheese Puff, '85 45
Egg and Rice Bake, '83 119
Egg Casserole, '83 311
Egg Casserole, Brunch, '86 329
Egg Casserole, Cheesy, '81 244; '86 15
Egg Casserole, Scrambled, '80 51; '86 241
Egg-Mushroom Casserole, '83 49
Eggs, Bruncheon, '83 83

Eggs, Chile, '88 80
Eggs, Creole, '82 42
Egg Soufflé Casserole, '83 55
Enchilada Casserole, '87 287
Enchilada Casserole, Green, '79 76
Fruit Bake, Hot, '81 270
Fruit Casserole, Sherried, '80 284
Fruit, Gingered Baked, '81 232
Grits, Baked Cheese-and-Garlic, '83 292
Grits Casserole, Cheesy, '81 270
Grits Casserole, Garlic, '81 47
Grits, Garlic-Cheese, '86 180
Grits, Orange, '81 47
Hominy Casserole, Cheesy, '83 170
Hominy-Chili Casserole, '86 255
Hominy, Gold Coast, '83 52
Hominy, Hot Cheese, '84 77
Hominy, Jalapeño, '82 51
Hominy with Chiles and Cheese, '86 78
Huevos Rancheros, '82 197
Kale, Scalloped, '86 224
Macaroni and Cheese,
    Thick-and-Rich, '84 329
Macaroni Casserole, '84 220; '87 154
Macaroni, Glorious, '84 76
Macaroni-Mushroom Bake, Cheesy, '81 243
Meat
    Beef-and-Bean Bake, Cheesy, '82 89
    Beef-and-Biscuit Casserole, '83 75
    Beef-and-Noodles Casserole, '84 72
    Beef-and-Vegetable Chow Mein
        Casserole, '83 313
    Beef Bake, Zesty Cabbage, '80 300
    Beef Bake, Zucchini, '86 146
    Beef Casserole, Crusty, '82 88
    Beef Casserole, Spinach and, '79 192
    Beef-Macaroni Combo, '79 194
    Beef-Noodle Bake, Taco, '81 141
    Beef Supreme, '83 196
    Beefy Vegetable Casserole, '79 248
    Cheesy Mexican Casserole, '82 224
    Chiles Rellenos Casserole, '84 31, 234
    Chili Hominy Bake, '81 282; '82 58
    Cornbread Casserole, '81 91
    Cornbread Skillet Casserole, '83 243;
        '84 101
    Cornbread Tamale Bake, '79 163
    Corned Beef and Cabbage au
        Gratin, '83 16
    Corned Beef Brunch Bake, '82 44
    County Fair Casserole, '79 130
    El Dorado Casserole, '81 140
    Enchilada Casserole,
        Firecracker, '80 260
    Enchilada Casserole, Sour
        Cream, '82 113
    Five-Layer Meal, '81 140
    Frankaroni Potluck Dish, '88 201
    Franks 'n' Beans, Stove-Top, '88 201
    Ground Beef and Sausage
        Casserole, '80 260
    Ground Beef Casserole,
        Cheesy, '79 44
    Ground Beef Casserole,
        Creamy, '81 142
    Hamburger-Noodle Bake, '81 140
    Hamburger Pie, '81 92
    Hot Doggie Casserole, '88 200
    Italian Casserole, '80 81
    Layered Grecian Bake, '82 119
    Matador Mania, '86 19

Moussaka, '87 166
Moussaka Casserole, '79 179
Moussaka, Corn, '87 190
Pastichio, '85 194
Pastitsio, '87 12; '88 11
Pizza Casserole, '88 273
Pizza Casserole, Quick, '83 266
Sour Cream-Noodle Bake, '79 55
Spaghetti and Beef Casserole, '79 129
Spaghetti Casserole, '84 241
Spinach and Beef Casserole, '79 192
Spinach-Beef-Macaroni
   Casserole, '83 313
Taco Beef-Noodle Bake, '81 141
Taco Casserole, '80 33
Veal and Wild Rice Casserole, '79 180
Veal Cutlet Casserole, '79 109
Venison-Vegetable Bake, '87 304
Microwave
   Bacon-and-Eggs Scramble, '80 M267
   Beans-and-Franks, Polynesian, '84 M11
   Beans, Herbed Green, '83 M147
   Beef Casserole, Easy, '86 M58
   Beef Casserole, Layered, '82 M203
   Beefy Sausage Dinner, '80 M9
   Carrots-and-Celery,
      Scalloped, '84 M112
   Chicken Divan, '80 M10
   Chicken Divan Casserole, '82 M203
   Chicken Tetrazzini, Cheesy, '83 M87
   Ham-and-Potato Casserole, '83 M87
   Ham-Asparagus Dinner, '80 M10
   Macaroni-Ham Casserole, '81 M177
   Mexi Casserole, '83 M87
   Okra and Tomatoes, Fresh, '81 M165
   Onion-Potato Bake, '83 M195
   Pineapple, Scalloped, '84 M323
   Pork Casserole, Cheesy, '81 M74
   Potato Casserole, Creamy, '84 M113
   Sausage and Rice Casserole,
      Oriental, '82 M123
   Sausage Casserole, Easy, '87 M189
   Sausage-Egg Casserole, '86 M12
   Sausage Jambalaya
      Casserole, '82 M203
   Spinach Delight, '84 M144
   Squash Bake, Cheddar-, '84 M113
   Squash Casserole, Cheesy, '82 M21
   Squash Medley, Fresh, '81 M165
   Tuna Casserole, Easy, '82 M203
   Zucchini-Egg Casserole, '84 M113
   Zucchini, Italian, '83 M147
Pineapple Bake, '79 251
Pineapple, Baked, '84 287
Pineapple, Scalloped, '79 106
Pork
   Bacon and Egg Casserole, '81 225
   Bacon Casserole, Egg-and-, '85 248
   Brunch Casserole, '82 124
   Brunch for a Bunch, '88 57
   Casserole, Pork, '83 116
   Chop Casserole, Peppered
      Pork, '81 235; '82 25; '83 39
   Chops and Potato Scallop,
      Pork, '82 114
   Chops Italiano, Pork, '80 72
   Fiesta Pork Bake, '79 265
   Frankfurter Casserole, Layered, '79 64
   Franks, Family-Style, '79 54
   Ham and Broccoli Casserole, '81 133
   Ham and Broccoli Strata, '80 261

Ham-and-Cheese Casserole, '87 78
Ham and Egg Casserole,
   Breakfast, '79 253
Ham and Lima Casserole, '79 192
Ham and Noodle Casserole, '80 300
Ham-and-Potato Casserole,
   Cheesy, '84 326
Ham-and-Rice Casserole, '84 75
Ham and Turkey Bake,
   Layered, '79 252
Ham Bake, Harvest, '79 210
Ham-Broccoli Casserole, Quick, '82 40
Ham Casserole, Apple, '79 213
Ham Casserole, Golden, '82 119
Ham Casserole, Macaroni-, '83 283
Ham Casserole, Vegetable-and-, '84 91
Ham Medley, Creamy, '84 90
Ham Pie, Golden, '87 78
Ham-Rice-Tomato Bake, '87 78
Ham Strata, Baked, '83 283
Ham Tetrazzini, '84 241
Salami-Corn Casserole, '80 209
Sausage and Broccoli Casserole, '80 33
Sausage and Noodle Casserole, '82 123
Sausage-and-Rice Bake, Creole, '88 58
Sausage and Wild Rice
   Casserole, '83 196
Sausage Bake, Eggplant, '85 221
Sausage Bake, Hominy-, '88 51
Sausage-Bean Supper, '86 52
Sausage Breakfast Casserole, '81 270
Sausage Brunch, Italian, '88 57
Sausage Casserole, '81 112; '82 12

Sausage Casserole, Cheesy, '82 124
Sausage Casserole, Country, '79 192
Sausage Casserole, Crunchy, '81 288
Sausage Casserole, Eggplant-, '84 215
Sausage Casserole, Grits-, '84 75;
   '86 241
Sausage Casserole, Ground Beef
   and, '80 260
Sausage Casserole, Hawaiian, '85 42
Sausage Casserole, Swiss, '80 209
Sausage-Cheese Bake, '88 58
Sausage-Chile Rellenos
   Casserole, '88 52
Sausage, Country Grits and, '83 54
Sausage Egg Bake, '81 225
Sausage-Egg Bake, Smoked, '85 248
Sausage Grits, '86 92
Sausage-Lasagna Rollups, '80 236
Sausage-Mushroom Breakfast
   Casserole, '86 95
Sausage-Noodle Bake, '81 92
Sausage-Potato Casserole, '86 217
Sausage-Rice Casserole, '82 50;
   '83 75

Sausages, Baked Zucchini and, '80 300
Sausage Strata, '83 243
Sausage, Wild Rice and, '86 268
Sausage-Wild Rice Casserole, '84 250
Spaghetti Bake, Pork, '81 11
Supper Supreme, Sunday, '79 76
Vegetable-Pork Combo, '85 113
Poultry
   Chicken-and-Dressing
      Casserole, '81 263
   Chicken and Green Noodle
      Casserole, '80 32
   Chicken and Rice Casserole, '80 260
   Chicken-Asparagus Casserole, '83 76;
      '84 71
   Chicken Bake, Company, '80 301
   Chicken Bake, Spicy, '85 251
   Chicken-Broccoli Casserole, '79 48
   Chicken Casserole, Broccoli-, '82 33
   Chicken Casserole, Cheesy, '85 34
   Chicken Casserole, Macaroni
      and, '80 260
   Chicken Casserole,
      Make-Ahead, '84 241
   Chicken Casserole, Mexican, '82 143
   Chicken Casserole, Quick, '81 91
   Chicken Casserole, Rice-and-, '87 154
   Chicken Casserole, Sunday, '83 290
   Chicken Divan, Gourmet, '82 83
   Chicken Divan, Overnight, '83 198
   Chicken-Eggplant Parmigiana, '82 212
   Chicken Enchiladas, '80 301
   Chicken Enchiladas, Easy, '82 89
   Chicken, French Herbed, '86 89
   Chicken-Green Bean
      Casserole, '85 296
   Chicken-Macaroni Casserole, '85 219
   Chicken-Rice Casserole, '86 52
   Chicken Salad, Baked, '86 297
   Chicken, Scarborough, '80 38
   Chicken-Spaghetti Casserole, '84 15
   Chicken, Spicy Mexican, '82 89
   Chicken Supreme Casserole, '84 219
   Chicken Supreme, Hot, '81 76
   Chicken Tetrazzini, '79 268
   Chicken Tortilla Bake, '82 89
   Chicken Tortilla Casserole, '81 166
   Chicken-Wild Rice Casserole, '84 241;
      '85 65
   Crêpes Divan, Elegant, '81 91
   Duck and Wild Rice Casserole, '79 224
   Pollo, Chilaquiles con, '81 66
   Rice Casserole, Mexican, '83 31
   Turkey-and-Broccoli Casserole, '86 332
   Turkey-Asparagus Casserole, '86 284
   Turkey Bake, Layered Ham
      and, '79 252
   Turkey Casserole, '84 327
   Turkey Casserole, Golden, '80 271
   Turkey Casserole, Stuffed, '88 246
   Turkey Florentine, '88 264
   Turkey-Olive Casserole, '87 268
   Turkey Parmigiana, '87 193
   Turkey Salad Bake, '79 253
   Turkey Salad, Hot, '86 297
   Turkey-Spinach Casserole, '84 71
   Turkey-Swiss Casserole, '86 283
   Turkey Tetrazzini, Herbed, '86 47
Provolone Casserole, Seashell-, '80 189
Rice and Green Chiles, '83 152
Rice au Gratin Supreme, '86 78

Casseroles *(continued)*

Rice Bake, Green, **'79** 43
Rice Casserole, **'87** 45
Rice Casserole, Brown, **'87** 118
Rice Casserole, Chili-, **'79** 54
Rice Casserole, Colorful, **'82** 199
Rice Casserole, Jalapeño, **'81** 66
Rice Casserole, Spanish, **'79** 192
Rice Casserole, Wild, **'82** 199
Rice Chantilly, **'86** 82
Rice, Fiesta, **'84** 76
Rice Mélange, **'87** 240
Rice, Mexican, **'85** 147
Rice Pilaf, **'86** 82
Rice, Spanish, **'81** 51
Rice, Spicy, **'85** 256
Rotini Romano, **'87** 193

Seafood
Crab-and-Shrimp Casserole, **'84** 71
Crab and Spinach Casserole,
    Creamy, **'80** 3
Crab Bake, Quick, **'87** 192
Crab Casserole, **'79** 228
Crab, Dressed, **'82** 276
Crab-Egg Casserole, **'80** 260
Crab Imperial, **'79** 82, 116
Crab Imperial, Elegant, **'83** 245
Crabmeat-Broccoli Casserole, **'84** 232
Crabmeat Imperial, **'82** 311
Crab Puff, **'79** 116
Fish and Potato Bake,
    Herbed, **'79** 287; **'80** 34
Fish Casserole, Green
    Chile-and-, **'84** 32
Oyster-and-Corn Bake, **'83** 34; **'84** 44
Oyster-and-Spinach Casserole, **'83** 34;
    '84 44
Oyster-and-Wild Rice
    Casserole, **'83** 34; **'84** 44
Oyster Casserole, **'79** 228
Oyster Casserole, Wild Rice-, **'86** 256
Oysters Johnny Reb, **'82** 42
Oysters, Scalloped, **'79** 225; **'84** 213;
    '86 132
Salmon Casserole, **'81** 22
Salmon Florentine, **'83** 43
Scallop Casserole, **'79** 228
Seafood Casserole, **'87** 109
Shrimp and Rice Casserole, **'79** 228
Shrimp au Gratin, **'85** 79
Shrimp Casserole, **'85** 240
Shrimp Casserole, Chayotes
    and, **'80** 230
Shrimp-Crab Puff, **'79** 57

Shrimp Delight, **'79** 192
Tuna and Peas in Wine Sauce,
    Baked, **'83** 196
Tuna-Broccoli Casserole, Tangy, **'83** 75
Tuna Casserole, **'82** 119
Tuna Casserole,
    Biscuit-Topped, **'79** 113
Tuna Casserole, Nippy, **'84** 241
Tuna Casserole with Cheese
    Swirls, **'88** 256
Tuna-Macaroni Treat, **'82** 131
Tuna Vegetable Casserole, **'81** 135
Vegetable. *See also* Casseroles/Bean.
Asparagus-and-English Pea
    Casserole, **'86** 324
Asparagus and Peas Casserole, **'80** 152
Asparagus-Artichoke Casserole, **'86** 279
Asparagus Casserole, Cheesy, **'82** 281;
    '83 32
Asparagus Casserole, Creamy, **'80** 76
Asparagus Casserole, Easy, **'83** 255
Asparagus Delight, **'82** 269
Asparagus, Holiday, **'85** 260
Asparagus-Pea Casserole, **'88** M294
Asparagus-Pimiento Loaf, **'84** 86
Asparagus-Spaghetti Casserole, **'80** 77
Broccoli-and-Egg Casserole, **'86** 324
Broccoli-and-Eggs au Gratin, **'85** 289
Broccoli Bake, **'81** 246
Broccoli Bake, Cheesy, **'83** 255
Broccoli Bake, Cheesy Italian, **'83** 5
Broccoli Bake, Company, **'83** 279
Broccoli-Blue Cheese
    Casserole, **'85** 260
Broccoli Casserole, **'87** 284;
    '88 M146, 265
Broccoli Casserole, Almond-, **'88** 62
Broccoli Casserole, Cheesy, **'84** 293
Broccoli Casserole, Italian, **'82** 6, 280;
    '83 32
Broccoli-Cheese Casserole, **'82** 269;
    '84 9
Broccoli-Corn Casserole, **'83** 313
Broccoli Elegant, **'81** 267
Broccoli-Onion Deluxe, **'81** 75
Broccoli Puff, **'82** 95
Broccoli-Rice Casserole, **'81** 101
Broccoli Supreme, **'82** 34; **'85** 68
Broccoli-Swiss Cheese
    Casserole, **'83** 322; **'85** M211
Broccoli with Rice, Holiday, **'87** 252
Brussels Sprouts, Casserole
    of, **'86** 294
Butternut Casserole, **'83** 280
Butternut Casserole, Sweet, **'83** 256
Cabbage au Gratin, **'83** 279
Cabbage, Caraway, **'85** 32, 289
Cabbage Casserole, Cheesy, **'79** 4
Cabbage Casserole, Creamy, **'80** 63
Cabbage Casserole, Italian, **'87** 42
Cabbage Casserole, Savory, **'82** 168
Cabbage, Cheese Scalloped, **'81** 87;
    '82 7
Cabbage, Scalloped, **'82** 269
Cabbage Wedges, Smothered, **'81** 87;
    '82 7
Cabbage with Apples and
    Franks, **'87** 42
Calabaza Mexicano (Mexican
    Squash), **'81** 196
Carrot and Zucchini Casserole, **'83** 256

Carrot Bake, Creamy, **'85** 67
Carrot Casserole, **'86** 279; **'87** 285
Carrot Casserole, Scrumptious, **'84** 328
Carrot Puff, **'84** 328
Carrots, Scalloped, **'81** 6
Carrots, Zesty, **'84** 5
Cauliflower and Asparagus
    Supreme, **'79** 287; **'80** 35
Cauliflower-and-Carrot
    Casserole, **'83** 280
Cauliflower and Peas with Curried
    Almonds, **'80** 82
Cauliflower Casserole, **'86** 10, 279
Cauliflower Casserole, Easy, **'82** 204

Cauliflower Casserole, Festive, **'87** 232
Cauliflower Casserole, Herbed, **'79** 221
Cauliflower Italiano, Cheesy, **'82** 300
Cauliflower, Main-Dish, **'79** 221;
    '80 83
Cauliflower Medley, **'80** 220
Cauliflower 'n' Chiles
    Casserole, **'87** 285
Cauliflower-Pea Casserole, **'85** 260
Cauliflower Scallop, **'88** 270
Cauliflower, Spanish-Style, **'79** 21
Celery and Cheese Casserole, **'79** 178
Celery au Gratin, **'83** 38
Celery, Baked, **'82** 98
Celery Casserole, **'80** 246
Celery Casserole, Creamy, **'82** 98;
    '83 255
Celery, Creamed, **'79** 247
Celery, Exotic, **'83** 280
Celery Oriental, **'83** 206; **'85** 116
Celery, Saucy, **'83** 39
Chayote-Cheese Bake, **'80** 230
Cheesy Vegetable Casserole, **'81** 103
Chilaquiles, **'82** 220
Corn and Cheese Casserole, **'81** 128
Corn and Tomato Casserole, **'81** 127
Corn-and-Tomato Casserole, **'84** 145
Corn, Baked Scalloped, **'85** 290
Corn Casserole, **'79** 247
Corn Casserole, Chili-, **'88** 266
Corn Casserole, Fresh, **'80** 165
Corn Casserole, Jalapeño-, **'83** 256
Corn, Elegant Scalloped, **'86** 268
Corn Pudding, **'86** 192
Corn, Scalloped, **'80** 164; **'81** 128;
    '86 111; **'88** 218
Corn with Sour Cream, Baked, **'86** 170

Corn-Zucchini Bake, '79 178
Eggplant and Noodle
    Casserole, '82 230
Eggplant and Squash, '83 187
Eggplant-and-Tomato
    Casserole, '83 187
Eggplant and Zucchini,
    Italian-Style, '79 289; '80 26
Eggplant Bake, '80 82
Eggplant Casserole, '81 205; '84 217
Eggplant Casserole, Easy, '80 202
Eggplant Casserole, Elegant, '82 168
Eggplant Casserole, Flavorful, '79 92
Eggplant Casserole, Super, '80 202
Eggplant Creole, '86 110
Eggplant, Italian, '84 216
Eggplant, Lebanese, '81 24
Eggplant, Mexican, '83 187
Eggplant Parmesan, '83 186; '84 215
Eggplant Parmigiana, '81 19
Eggplant, Rolled Stuffed, '80 63
Eggplant Supreme, '79 188; '86 170
Fresh Vegetable Casserole, '82 225
Garden Casserole, '82 168; '88 122
Garden Surprise, '83 112
Green-and-Gold Scallop, '81 159
Greens Dinner Bake, Grits 'n, '84 281
Green Vegetable Medley, '79 287;
    '80 34
Hash Brown Cheese Bake, '82 50
Lentils with Cheese, Baked, '84 113
Medley, Baked Vegetable, '81 75
Medley Bake, Vegetable, '81 268
Mixed Vegetable Casserole, '83 208,
    256; '86 327
Mixed-Vegetable Casserole, '87 154
Mixed Vegetables, Scalloped, '83 5
Mushroom-Artichoke
    Casserole, '87 241
Mushroom Bake, Windsor, '88 132
Mushroom-Cheese Casserole, '83 216
Mushrooms Supreme, '84 214
Okra Casserole, '79 160
Okra-Tomato Bake, '80 298; '81 26
Onion Casserole, Cheesy, '79 101
Pea Casserole, Cheesy
    English, '83 216
Pea Casserole, Curry, '87 154
Pea Casserole, Quick Fresh
    English, '84 145
Pea Casserole, Reunion, '87 11
Pea Casserole Supreme, '82 281;
    '83 32
Pea-Pimiento Casserole,
    English, '83 207
Peas and Rice, '88 97
Peas, Cajun, '88 3
Peas, Chinese-Style Baked, '86 305
Peas, Mexi-, '88 3
Peas, Party, '79 102
Peas, Sweet-and-Sour, '88 3
Peas with Rice, Black-Eyed, '83 12
Potato-Apple Bake, Sweet, '83 25
Potato-Apricot Bake, Sweet, '85 206
Potato Bake, '83 209
Potato Bake, Creamy, '82 201
Potato Bake, Sweet, '80 287
Potato-Banana Casserole,
    Sweet, '86 276
Potato Breakfast Casserole, '80 52
Potato-Broccoli-Cheese Bake, '80 114

Potato Casserole, '87 190
Potato Casserole, Cheesy, '80 244;
    '83 53
Potato Casserole, Easy, '80 114
Potato Casserole, Fluffy, '80 268
Potato Casserole, Hash Brown, '81 40
Potato Casserole, Irish, '81 263
Potato Casserole, Mashed, '85 296
Potato Casserole, Mushroom-, '84 5
Potato Casserole, Pear-Sweet, '86 280
Potato Casserole, Processor, '86 159
Potato Casserole, Saucy, '81 276
Potato Casserole, Sweet, '79 289;
    '80 26; '85 256
Potato-Cheese Casserole, '79 101
Potato Delight, Sweet, '86 335
Potato-Egg Casserole, Cheesy, '84 5
Potato-Eggplant Casserole, '87 166
Potatoes-and-Berries Casserole,
    Sweet, '84 231
Potatoes and Eggs au Gratin, '79 107
Potatoes and Turnips,
    Scalloped, '85 235
Potatoes-and-Zucchini au Gratin, '84 5
Potatoes, Bourbon Sweet, '86 324;
    '87 280
Potatoes, Candied Sweet, '86 111;
    '88 207
Potatoes, Cheesy New, '85 156

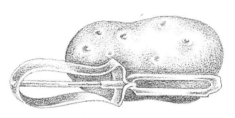

Potatoes, Cheesy Scalloped, '83 82
Potatoes, Christmas, '88 252
Potatoes, Double-Cheese, '86 6
Potatoes, Easy Oven-Baked, '82 202
Potatoes, Fluffy, '84 296; '85 196
Potatoes for Company, Saucy, '82 202
Potatoes, Garlic, '84 296; '85 196
Potatoes Gourmet, '80 114
Potatoes, Gruyère, '83 193
Potatoes, Hot Deviled, '84 296;
    '85 196
Potatoes, Jalapeño, '84 39
Potatoes, Jazzy Mashed, '87 192
Potatoes, Lemon and Nutmeg, '80 36
Potatoes Lorraine, '87 190
Potatoes, Missy, '85 259
Potatoes, Mushroom Scalloped, '87 191
Potatoes, Olive, '80 114
Potatoes, Parmesan, '82 270
Potatoes, Party Scalloped, '87 191
Potatoes, Scalloped, '82 300; '83 211
Potatoes, Sour Cream, '84 39
Potatoes, Special Scalloped, '88 162
Potatoes, Two-Cheese, '80 114
Potatoes, Wayside Scalloped, '79 283
Potatoes with Feta Cheese, '84 295;
    '85 196
Potatoes with Ham Bits,
    Creamy, '87 191

Potatoes with Sherry and Walnuts,
    Sweet, '86 286
Potato-Rum Casserole, Sweet, '84 231
Potato Surprise, Sweet, '81 267
Potato-Tomato Bake, '86 17
Potato-Tomato Casserole,
    Saucy, '79 46
Potato Tuna Bake, Shoestring, '82 211
Pumpkin, Baked, '82 217
Spinach and Artichoke
    Casserole, '81 103
Spinach-and-Celery Casserole, '84 294
Spinach and Egg Casserole, '82 270
Spinach-Artichoke Casserole, '88 252
Spinach Casserole, '79 265
Spinach Casserole, Cheesy, '81 263
Spinach Casserole, Cottage
    Cheese-and-, '84 77
Spinach Casserole, Creamy, '86 111
Spinach-Cheese Bake, '88 10
Spinach-Cheese Casserole, '83 216
Spinach-Cheese Puff, '84 96
Spinach, Cheesy Topped, '84 85
Spinach, Creamy Lemon, '82 302
Spinach, Gourmet Baked, '82 180
Spinach-Parmesan Casserole, '82 281;
    '83 32
Spinach Rice, '85 146
Spinach Supreme, '84 77
Spinach Surprise, '82 42
Spinach with Cheese, Scalloped, '79 8
Squash and Apple Casserole, '79 209
Squash and Egg Casserole, '80 146
Squash, Bacon-Flavored, '82 158
Squash Bake, '82 107
Squash Bake, Cheddar-, '84 128
Squash Bake, Cheesy, '80 183
Squash-Carrot Casserole, '81 157
Squash Casserole, '87 163
Squash Casserole, Baked, '83 149
Squash Casserole, Blender, '81 212
Squash Casserole, Butternut, '79 210
Squash Casserole, Cheesy, '79 123
Squash Casserole, Company, '81 183
Squash Casserole, Crunchy, '84 293
Squash Casserole, Fresh, '82 204
Squash Casserole, Jiffy, '81 M144
Squash Casserole, Summer,
    '81 102, 184
Squash Casserole, Two-, '79 101
Squash Casserole, Yellow, '79 179;
    '85 135; '88 166
Squash Casserole, Zippy, '80 183
Squash, Country Club, '88 M16
Squash, Mexican, '83 31
Squash, Posh, '81 159
Squash Puff, Butternut, '85 205
Squash, Tart Hubbard, '80 214
Tomato-and-Artichoke Heart
    Bake, '85 81
Tomato Casserole, Scalloped, '88 144
Tomatoes, Herbed, '81 102
Tomatoes, Italian-Sauced
    Green, '85 214
Tomatoes, Scalloped, '84 142
Torta, Mexican, '88 149
Turnip Casserole, '83 242; '84 229
Turnip Casserole, Baked, '82 274
Turnips au Gratin, '84 229
Turnips, Scalloped, '79 254
Veggies Casserole, '88 123

Casseroles, Vegetable (continued)

Zucchini and Tomato Bake, '82 158
Zucchini-and-Tomato Casserole, '88 265
Zucchini, Baked, '83 209
Zucchini Casserole, '79 157; '87 154
Zucchini Casserole,
Cheese-Egg-, '84 114
Zucchini Casserole, Cheesy, '82 168;
'84 145
Zucchini Casserole, Italian, '85 59
Zucchini-Jack Casserole, '85 296

Cauliflower
Almond Sauce, Cauliflower with, '82 270
au Gratin, Cauliflower, '82 204
Baked Swiss Cauliflower, '79 100
Beef and Cauliflower Oriental, '80 220
Beets and Cauliflower, Chilled, '80 137
Broccoli Crunch, Cauliflower-, '88 216
Casserole, Cauliflower, '86 10, 279
Casserole, Cauliflower-and-Carrot, '83 280
Casserole, Cauliflower 'n' Chiles, '87 285
Casserole, Cauliflower-Pea, '85 260
Casserole, Easy Cauliflower, '82 204
Casserole, Festive Cauliflower, '87 232
Casserole, Herbed Cauliflower, '79 221
Cheese-Frosted Cauliflower, '85 68
Cheese Sauce, Cauliflower with, '81 101
Cheesy Cauliflower Italiano, '82 300
Chilled Beets and Cauliflower, '80 137
Dilled Cauliflower, '83 93
Festive Cauliflower, '84 34
Fried Cauliflower, '83 5; '84 248
Fried Cauliflower au Gratin,
French-, '79 221; '80 82
Fried Cauliflower, Crispy, '80 220
Fried Cauliflower, French-, '86 211
Fried Cauliflower, Golden, '82 78
Fried Cauliflower with Cheese
Sauce, '87 231
Garden Surprise, '83 112
Goldenrod, Cauliflower, '79 21
Herb Butter, Cauliflower with, '81 2
Lemon Cauliflower, Easy, '83 322
Main-Dish Cauliflower, '79 221; '80 83
Medley, Cauliflower, '80 220
Medley, Cauliflower-Broccoli, '81 69
Medley, Cauliflower-Snow Pea, '87 305
Oriental Cauliflower, '81 75
Peas and Cauliflower, '82 288
Peas with Curried Almonds, Cauliflower
and, '79 221; '80 82
Pie, Cauliflower-Carrot, '82 191
Pimiento Sauce, Cauliflower with, '87 232
Quiche, Cauliflower, '83 86
Salad, Broccoli and Cauliflower, '81 280
Salad, Broccoli-Cauliflower Pasta, '88 269
Salad, Cauliflower, '79 221; '80 83;
'81 225; '84 291; '85 240, 279
Salad, Cauliflower-Broccoli, '79 20
Salad, Cauliflower-Brussels Sprouts, '83 240
Salad, Cauliflower-Lemon, '81 23
Salad, Cauliflower-Pea, '87 231
Salad, Cauliflower-Vegetable, '85 158
Salad, Celery-and-Cauliflower, '83 39
Salad, Corned Beef-Cauliflower, '83 16
Salad, Creamy Broccoli and
Cauliflower, '81 23
Salad, Creamy Cauliflower, '82 102
Salad, Crunchy Cauliflower, '80 4; '82 75
Salad, Layered Cauliflower, '83 240

Salad, Marinated Cauliflower, '82 303;
'84 232
Salad, Orange-Cauliflower, '82 266
Salad, Savory Cauliflower and Pea, '81 280
Salad, Sweet-and-Sour Cauliflower, '81 2
Scallop, Cauliflower, '88 270
Shrimp Sauce, Broccoli and Cauliflower
with, '84 248
Soufflé, Cauliflower, '82 76
Soup, Cauliflower and Caraway, '82 264
Soup, Cream of Cauliflower, '87 M7;
'88 12
Soup, Cream of Cauliflower and
Watercress, '83 126
Soup, Creamy Cauliflower, '82 76
Soup, Fresh Cauliflower, '84 279
Spanish-Style Cauliflower, '79 21
Supreme, Cauliflower and
Asparagus, '79 287; '80 35
Toss, Cauliflower, '85 289
Toss, Cauliflower-Broccoli, '82 54
Toss, Cauliflower-Olive, '85 198; '86 147
Toss, Crunchy Broccoli and
Cauliflower, '83 25
Toss, Italian Cauliflower-Broccoli, '88 269

Caviar
Artichoke Hearts with Caviar, '79 142
Crown, Caviar, '83 78
Eggplant Caviar, '88 262
Mold, Artichoke-Caviar, '87 239
Mousse, Caviar, '82 71; '83 258; '85 86
Pie, Caviar, '79 154
Potatoes, Appetizer Caviar, '86 223
Potatoes, Caviar, '84 80
Spread, Caviar-Cream Cheese, '84 256
Spread, Egg, Sour Cream, and
Caviar, '85 279
Texas Caviar, '86 218
Zucchini Caviar, '88 212

Celery
Almondine, Celery, '85 116
Amandine, Buttered Celery, '82 98
au Gratin, Celery, '83 38
Baked Celery, '82 98
Braised Carrots and Celery, '86 327
Braised Celery, Green Beans and, '84 254
Brussels Sprouts and Celery, '79 21
Brussels Sprouts with Celery,
Lemony, '85 25
Carrots and Celery with Pecans, '84 254
Casserole, Celery, '80 246
Casserole, Celery and Cheese, '79 178
Casserole, Creamy Celery, '82 98; '83 255
Casserole, Spinach-and-Celery, '84 294
Chicken-and-Celery Skillet, '88 6
Creamed Brussels Sprouts and
Celery, '83 322
Creamed Celery, '79 247
Croutons, Celery, '79 16
Curried Corn and Celery, '86 192
Dressing, Celery-Honey, '80 42
Dressing, Watermelon Salad with
Celery-Nut, '80 182
Exotic Celery, '83 280
Orange Sauce, Celery in, '79 70
Oriental, Celery, '83 206; '85 116
Peas and Celery, Deluxe, '81 267
Peas with Celery, Skillet Snow, '84 123
Salad, Celery, '79 70
Salad, Celery-and-Cauliflower, '83 39
Salad, Chicken-Celery, '81 187

Salad, Overnight Alfalfa-Celery, '82 97
Salad, Pear-and-Celery, '87 56
Salad, Pineapple-Celery, '85 95
Sauce, Baked Fillets in
Lemon-Celery, '84 91
Saucy Celery, '83 39
Scalloped Carrots-and-Celery, '84 M112
Soup, Burnet-Celery, '84 107
Soup, Celery-and-Potato, '84 279
Soup, Cream of Celery, '79 71
Soup, Light Cream-of-Celery, '82 279
Soup, Tomato-Celery, '83 M58
Stuffed Celery, '82 98; '86 324
Stuffed Celery, Creamy, '82 102
Stuffed Celery, Jalapeño, '79 70
Stuffed Celery Trunks, '85 115
Toss, Celery-Parmesan, '84 34

Chayotes
Bake, Chayote-Cheese, '80 230
Casserole, Chayotes and Shrimp, '80 230
Fried Chayotes, '80 230

Cheese. See also Appetizers/Cheese.
Almond Cheese, '88 173
Aspic, Cheesy Vegetable, '81 73
Bake, Brie Cheese, '87 117
Bake, Chicken, Ham, and Cheese, '87 217
Bake, Pineapple-Cheese, '79 106
Bake, Spinach-Ricotta, '88 97
Banana Splits, Cottage Cheese-, '87 56
Beans with Blue Cheese, Green, '88 57
Beef Parmigiana, '85 234
Beef Roulades, Roquefort, '88 215
Blintzes, Cheese, '82 146; '83 71
BLT's, Cheesy, '85 92
Blue Cheese, Creamy, '88 173
Breads
Bacon-and-Cheese Bread, '83 255
Batter Bread, Cheese-Caraway,
'85 33
Biscuit Fingers,
Pepper-Cheese, '88 283
Biscuits, Bacon-Cheese, '88 84
Biscuits, Blue Cheese, '88 83
Biscuits, Cheese, '81 288; '83 253;
'85 32; '87 78
Biscuits, Cheeseburger, '79 194
Biscuits, Easy Cheese, '81 99
Biscuits, Herbed Roquefort, '84 95
Biscuits, Hot Cheesy, '80 186
Biscuits, Petite Ham and
Cheese, '79 193
Biscuits, Tiny Cheese, '80 192
Brie Bread, '87 143
Buns, Cheesy Onion, '85 5
Buns, Hurry-Up Cheese, '81 300
Buns, Onion-Cheese, '88 218
Butter Cheese Dips, '80 46
Cheddar Cheese Bread, '84 268
Cheddar-Nut Bread, '85 41
Cheese Bread, '82 174; '83 208;
'87 11
Cornbread, Cheddar, '83 285; '84 17
Cornbread, Cheddar-Jalapeño, '85 3
Cornbread, Cheesy Beef, '81 242
Cornbread, Chile-Cheese, '87 171
Cornbread, Cottage Cheese, '80 90
Cornbread, Swiss Cheese, '79 60
Cottage Cheese-Dill Bread, '83 154
Cream Cheese Braids, '82 243
Cream Cheese Bread,
Orange-, '82 210

Cream Cheese Loaves,
Processor, '85 48
Crescents, Cheese, '82 18
Crusty Cheese Bread, '86 233
Delights, Toasted Cheese-, '79 37
Dilly Cheese Bread, '83 5
Easy Cheese Bread, '82 74; '86 17
French Bread, Cheesy, '88 172
Fruit-and-Cheese Braid, '86 214
Garlic Bread, Cheesy, '84 150
Ham-and-Cheese Bread, '86 213
Herb-and-Cheese Pull Aparts, '87 143
Herb Bread, Cheese-, '84 M144;
'85 283
Herb Bread, Parmesan, '82 235;
'83 41
Herb-Cheese Bread, '85 70
Herb-Vegetable-Cheese Bread, '88 172
Jalapeño-Cheese Loaf, '84 76
Lemon-Cream Tea Loaf, '84 50
Little Cheese Loaves, '86 213
Muffins, Blueberry-Cream
Cheese, '86 14
Muffins, Cheese-and-Pepper, '84 139
Muffins, Cheesy Cornbread, '88 M275
Muffins, Marvelous Cheese, '83 96
Muffins, Sausage-Cheese, '86 213
Muffins, Sesame-Cheese, '86 16
Olive Bread, Spicy Cheese-, '84 150
Onion-Cheese Bread, '79 180; '81 8
Onion-Cheese Supper Bread, '83 112
Onion-Parmesan Bread, '84 284
Parmesan Sesame Sticks, '81 39
Parmesan Twists, '83 239
Pimiento-Cheese Bread, '85 223;
'86 166
Popover Puffs, Cheese, '85 6
Popover Ring, Cheesy, '80 45
Popovers, Cheddar Cheese, '85 41

Quick Cheese Bread, '83 9
Rolls, Cheese, '80 286
Rolls, Cottage Cheese, '81 78
Rolls, Ham-and-Cheese, '82 3
Rolls, Parmesan, '79 181
Rolls, Romano Sesame, '87 144
Sesame-Cheddar Sticks, '81 150
Sour Cream-Cheese Bread, '85 33
Spinach Bread, '87 144
Spoonbread, Cheddar, '82 196
Spoonbread, Cheese, '86 261
Spoonbread, Corn-Cheese, '88 9
Swiss Cheese Bread, '79 60
Toast Bars, Bacon-Cheese, '79 36

Toast, Cottage-Topped French, '85 49
Tomato-Cheese Bread,
Herbed, '88 143
Twists, Cheesy, '84 284
Wine Bread, Cheese-, '87 254
Brownies, Cream Cheese Swirl, '79 51
Brownies, German Cream Cheese, '80 269
Brownies, Walnut-Cream Cheese, '84 240
Buns, Snack, '87 279
Burgers, Cheesy Bacon, '81 29
Burgers, Cheesy Beef, '83 217
Burritos, Cheesy Beef, '85 193
Butter, Cheese, '84 114
Cake, Coconut-Cream Cheese
Pound, '85 297
Cake, Cream Cheese Coffee, '86 290
Cake, Cream Cheese Loaf, '84 151
Cake, Cream Cheese Pound, '81 290;
'86 287
Cake, Regal Cream Cheese, '80 140
Cake Squares, Cream Cheese, '84 321
Cake, Tart Lemon-Cheese, '88 7
Casseroles
Apple-Cheese Casserole, '84 287
Asparagus Casserole, Cheesy, '82 281;
'83 32
Bean Casserole, Swiss Lima, '80 191
Beef-and-Bean Bake, Cheesy, '82 89
Beef Casserole, Cheesy
Ground, '79 44
Breakfast Casserole, Cheesy, '85 247
Broccoli Bake, Cheesy, '83 255
Broccoli-Blue Cheese
Casserole, '85 260
Broccoli Casserole, Cheesy, '84 293
Broccoli-Cheese Casserole, '82 269;
'84 9
Broccoli-Swiss Cheese
Casserole, '83 322; '85 M211
Brunch Casserole, '82 124
Brunch for a Bunch, '88 57
Cabbage au Gratin, '83 279
Cabbage Casserole, Cheesy, '79 4
Celery and Cheese Casserole, '79 178
Celery au Gratin, '83 38
Chayote-Cheese Bake, '80 230
Chicken Casserole, Cheesy, '85 34
Chicken Tetrazzini, Cheesy, '83 M87
Chilaquiles, '82 220
Chile-Cheese Casserole, '82 90
Chile 'n' Cheese Breakfast
Casserole, '88 57
Chiles Rellenos Casserole, '79 84;
'84 31, 234
Continental Cheese Bake, '81 89
Corn and Cheese Casserole, '81 128
Corned Beef and Cabbage au
Gratin, '83 16
Egg-and-Cheese Casserole, '84 293
Egg Casserole, Cheesy, '81 244;
'86 15
Eggplant Parmesan, '83 186; '84 215;
'86 53
Eggplant Parmigiana, '81 19
Feather-Light Cheese
Casserole, '79 84
Grits, Baked Cheese, '80 49, 99;
'83 311; '85 41
Grits, Baked
Cheese-and-Garlic, '83 292; '84 78
Grits Casserole, Cheesy, '81 270

Grits, Cheese, '86 242
Grits, Garlic-Cheese, '80 47; '81 197;
'86 180
Ham-and-Cheese Casserole, '87 78
Hominy Casserole, Cheesy, '83 170
Hominy with Chiles and Cheese, '86 78
Lentils with Cheese, Baked, '84 113
Limas, Spanish Cheese, '86 225
Macaroni-Mushroom Bake,
Cheesy, '81 243
Mexican Casserole, Cheesy, '82 224
Mushroom-Cheese Casserole, '83 216
Mushrooms au Gratin, '81 108
Onion Casserole, Cheesy, '79 101
Pea Casserole, Cheesy
English, '83 216
Pineapple-Cheese Bake, '79 106
Pork Casserole, Cheesy, '81 M74
Potato Casserole, Cheesy, '80 244;
'83 53
Potato-Cheese Casserole, '79 101
Potato-Egg Casserole, Cheesy, '84 5
Potatoes and Eggs au Gratin, '79 107
Potatoes, Cheesy Scalloped, '83 82
Potatoes, Double-Cheese, '86 6
Potatoes Gourmet, '80 114
Potatoes, Gruyère, '83 193
Potatoes, Mushroom Scalloped, '87 191
Potatoes, Scalloped, '83 211
Potatoes, Special Scalloped, '88 162
Provolone Casserole, Seashell-,
'80 189
Rice au Gratin, '83 129
Rice au Gratin Supreme, '86 78
Rice Strata, Cheese-, '81 176
Sausage Brunch, Italian, '88 57
Sausage Casserole, Cheesy, '82 124
Sausage-Cheese Bake, '88 58
Sausage-Chile Rellenos
Casserole, '88 52
Spinach Casserole, Cheesy, '81 263
Spinach Casserole, Cottage
Cheese-and-, '84 77
Spinach-Cheese Bake, '88 10
Spinach-Cheese Casserole, '83 216
Spinach-Parmesan Casserole, '82 281;
'83 32
Spinach Ring au Fromage, '79 8
Squash Bake, Cheddar-, '84 M113, 128
Squash Casserole, Cheesy, '79 123;
'82 M21
Swiss Sausage Casserole, '80 209
Tomato-Cheese Strata, '81 209
Tuna Casserole with Cheese
Swirls, '88 256
Turkey Parmigiana, '87 193
Turkey-Swiss Casserole, '86 283
Vegetable Casserole, Cheesy, '81 103
Zucchini Casserole,
Cheese-Egg-, '84 114
Zucchini Casserole, Cheesy, '82 168;
'84 145
Zucchini-Jack Casserole, '85 296
Catfish Parmesan, '79 184; '86 210
Cheesecake. See Cakes/Cheesecakes.
Chicken, Baked Parmesan, '83 320
Chicken Breasts Gruyère, '80 189
Chicken Breasts Romano, '79 218
Chicken Cordon Bleu, '81 304; '82 83;
'86 37
Chicken, Crispy Parmesan, '80 M76

Cheese *(continued)*

Chicken Fiesta, Breast-of-, **'88** 151
Chicken Monterey, **'82** 275
Chicken, Oven-Fried Parmesan, **'81** 97;
   '82 148
Chicken Parmesan, **'83** 184
Chicken Parmesan, Baked, **'83** 137
Chicken Rollups, Cheesy, **'82** 44
Chicken Skillet, Cheesy, **'80** 115
Chiles Rellenos, **'88** 116
Chili-Cheese Dogs, **'81** M176
Chili, Cheese-Topped, **'82** M11
Chili, Cheesy, **'82** 310
Chunky Cream Cheese, **'85** 306
Coleslaw, Cottage, **'80** 64
Cookies, Cream Cheese, **'80** 282
Corn on the Cob, Parmesan, **'88** M187
Crab Bake, Quick, **'87** 192
Crabmeat au Gratin, **'86** 154
Cream Cheese, Cranberry-Amaretto Chutney
   with, **'87** 244
Cream Cheese Pinches, **'87** 85
Cream Puffs with Chicken Salad,
   Cheesy, **'86** 260
Cream-Style Cheese, **'85** 209
Crêpes, Cheese and Mushroom, **'81** 88
Crêpes, Cheesy Sausage, **'82** 240; **'83** 71
Crêpes, Mushroom-Cheese, **'87** 289;
   '88 135
Crêpes, Spinach-Ricotta, **'81** 52
Crispies, Pecan-Cheese, **'87** 168
Crust, Cheese, **'80** 286; **'86** 264
Crust, Cheesy Crumb, **'88** 86
Crust, Chicken Pot Pie with
   Cheese, **'86** 264
Cupcakes, Cream Cheese Party, **'82** 279
Delight, Strawberry Cheese, **'79** 50
Dessert Cheese, Nutty Date, **'87** 299
Dessert, Creamy Cottage Cheese, **'87** 191
Dessert, Lemon-Cream Cheese, **'84** 95
Dessert, Strawberry-Cream
   Cheese, **'83** 123
Dressing, Blue Cheese, **'79** 69; **'82** 166;
   '86 233
Dressing, Blue Cheese Salad, **'82** 94
Dressing, Creamy Blue Cheese, **'81** 150
Dressing, Creamy Blue Cheese
   Salad, **'86** 123
Dressing, Creamy Roquefort, **'84** 12
Dressing, Garden Salad with Tomato-Cream
   Cheese, **'79** 173
Dressing, Parmesan, **'86** 192
Dressing, Romano, **'80** 174
Dressing, Roquefort, **'79** 85; **'80** 74
Dressing, Special Blue Cheese, **'80** 74
Dressing, Tangy Blue Cheese, **'87** 81
Dressing, Zesty Blue Cheese, **'79** 104
Egg Medley, Cheddary, **'81** M176
Eggs, Cottage, **'85** 44
Eggs, Cottage Cheese Scrambled, **'81** 142
Eggs, Cottage-Scrambled, **'80** 49
Eggs, Cream Cheese Scrambled, **'81** 287
Enchiladas, Cheese, **'81** 194; **'85** 154
Enchiladas, Cheesy Sour Cream, **'79** 25
Enchiladas, Saucy Cheese, **'84** 220
Fillets, Parmesan, **'86** M112
Flounder au Fromage, Baked, **'86** 234
Flounder, Cheesy Broiled, **'84** 69
Fowl, Fancy, **'81** 76
French Toast au Fromage, **'88** 288

Fried Brie, Walnut-, **'86** 244
Frills, Cream Cheese, **'79** 291
Frittata, Broccoli-Cheese, **'81** 243
Fritters, Cheesy Zucchini, **'88** 44
Frosting, Coconut Cream Cheese, **'86** 60
Frosting, Cream Cheese, **'79** 45; **'80** 140,
   253, 299; **'82** 135, 244; **'83** 105, 215,
   M233; **'84** 201, 255, 315, 316; **'85** 118,
   121; **'86** 217, 337; **'87** 58
Frosting, Deluxe Cream Cheese, **'80** 120
Frosting, Fluffy Cream Cheese, **'80** 245
Frosting, Lemon-Cream Cheese, **'81** 157
Frosting, Nutty Cream Cheese, **'85** 117
Frosting, Orange Cream, **'82** 14
Frosting, Orange-Cream Cheese, **'81** 70;
   '82 16
Fruited Cream Cheese, **'85** 306
Fruit with Cheese, Luscious Fresh, **'79** 153
Fudge, Cream Cheese, **'84** 111
Glaze, Cream Cheese, **'84** 150
Grits, Garlic-Cheese, **'88** 126
Grits, Good Morning, **'87** 156
Grits, Gruyère Cheese, **'81** 47
Grits, Jalapeño Cheese, **'85** 43
Grits, Quick Cheese, **'83** M203
Grits, Sliced Cheese, **'84** 75
Ham and Swiss in the Pocket, **'83** 31
Ham-and-Turkey Specials, Cheesy, **'84** 14
Ham-Cheese Chips, **'82** 34
Ham Dinner, Cheesy, **'84** 90
Ham Towers, Cheesy, **'82** M77
Hominy, Hot Cheese, **'84** 77
Kabobs, Swiss-Ham, **'81** 124
Kuchen, Cheese, **'86** 84

Lasagna, Cheesy, **'82** 224; **'88** 299
Lasagna, Cheesy Spinach, **'80** 32; **'83** 204
Lasagna, Cheesy Vegetable, **'79** 84
Lettuce, Cheesy Stuffed, **'79** 175
Little Bits, **'79** 196
Loaf, Cheese, **'87** 92
Loaf, Cheeseburger, **'81** 236, 276
Loaf, Pepperoni and Cheese, **'82** 32
Loaves, Sausage-Cheese, **'88** 235
Macaroni and Cheese, **'83** M7;
   '88 M147, M190
Macaroni and Cheese, Baked, **'82** 199
Macaroni-and-Cheese Deluxe, **'79** 84
Macaroni and Cheese Deluxe, **'80** 236
Macaroni and Cheese Puff, **'79** 5
Macaroni-and-Cheese-Stuffed
   Peppers, **'80** 65
Macaroni and Cheese, Tasty, **'83** 288
Macaroni and Cheese,
   Thick-and-Rich, **'84** 329

Macaroni-and-Cheese with Wine, **'86** 78
Macaroni, Double Cheese, **'82** 224
Manicotti, Cheesy, **'83** 216
Manicotti, Special, **'88** 50
Manicotti, Stuffed, **'83** M6
Mayonnaise, Parmesan, **'86** 79
Meatballs, Golden Nugget, **'82** 233
Meatballs, Mock, **'81** 243
Meat Loaf, Mozzarella-Layered, **'79** 71
Mold, Ambrosia Cream Cheese, **'79** 249
Mold, Cheesy Lemon, **'79** 241
Mold, Creamy Tuna-Cheese, **'81** 135
Molds, Heavenly Dessert Cheese, **'85** 209
Molds, Snowcap Cheese, **'79** 242
Noodles and Mushrooms, Cheesy, **'79** 84
Noodles, Cheesy Parmesan, **'83** M7
Noodles, Ham and Swiss on, **'87** 108
Noodles, Parmesan, **'83** 118
Omelet, Cheddar-Vegetable, **'83** 205
Omelet, Cheesy Picante, **'86** 95
Omelet, Cheesy Vegetable, **'85** 49
Omelet, Ham and Cheese, **'79** 262;
   '80 123
Omelets, George's, **'80** 68
Omelet, Shrimp-and-Cheddar, **'84** 57
Omelet, Spinach-Cheese, **'83** 119
Omelet, Swiss Oven, **'80** 189
Omelet, Zippy Cheese, **'87** 287
Pancakes, Cottage Cheese, **'79** 115
Pasta Stuffed with Five Cheeses, **'88** 197
Pastries, Cream Cheese, **'80** 250
Pastries, Date-Filled Cheese, **'83** 259
Pastries, German, **'86** 78
Pastry, Apple Tart with Cheese, **'88** 225
Pastry, Cheddar, **'86** 206
Pastry, Cheddar Cheese, **'80** 219; **'82** 194
Pastry, Cheese, **'88** 56
Pastry, Cream Cheese, **'82** 39; **'86** 78
Pastry Shell, Cheese, **'85** 284
Pastry Shells, Cream Cheese, **'86** 13
Pastry Shells, Miniature Cream
   Cheese, **'87** 190
Pastry Tart Shells, Cheese, **'85** 216
Pâté, Cream Cheese, **'80** 154
Pâté, Liver-Cheese, **'85** 276
Patty Shells, Cream Cheese, **'81** 266;
   '82 249
Pears, Cheese-Filled, **'81** 268
Pears Stuffed with Cheese, **'82** 290
Pie, Apple-Cheese, **'85** 284
Pie, Apple-Cream Cheese, **'81** 247
Pie, Blueberry-Cream Cheese, **'88** 154
Pie, Breakfast, **'86** 242
Pie, Broccoli-Cheese, **'84** 235
Pie, Cheese-Beef, **'85** 33
Pie, Cheesy Mexican Chicken, **'82** 142
Pie, Chocolate-Cream Cheese, **'80** 69
Pie, Cottage Cheese, **'82** 85
Pie, Green Chile-Cheese, **'84** 234
Pie, Lemon Cheese, **'81** 136; **'82** 146
Pie, Lemon-Cottage Cheese, **'79** 44
Pie, Lemon Cottage Cheese, **'81** 143
Pie, Mexican Cheese, **'82** 9; **'83** 69
Pie, Mincemeat-Cheese, **'80** 253
Pie, Onion-Cheese, **'88** 86
Pie, Quick and Cheesy Corn, **'82** 191
Pie, Tortilla, **'85** M211
Pie, Turkey-Cheese, **'88** 264
Pie, Yogurt-Cheese, **'82** 121
Pie, Zucchini-Ham-Cheese, **'80** 272
Pimiento Cheese, Chunky, **'88** 91

Pizza, Breakfast, '88 288
Pizza, Cheese-and-Mushroom, '83 226
Pizza, Double Cheesy
  Beef-and-Sausage, '86 77
Pizza, Gruyère-Chicken, '87 182
Popcorn, Bacon-Cheese, '86 74
Popcorn, Sesame-Cheese, '79 220
Pork Chops, Cheese-Stuffed, '84 81
Pork Tenderloin with Blue Cheese, '86 76
Preserves, Cream Cheese and
  Peach, '84 264
Pudding, Baked Cheese, '86 78
Pudding, Cheesy Bread, '83 68
Pudding, Corn-Cheese, '80 244
Puff, Egg-and-Cheese, '85 45
Puffs, Bavarian Cheese, '80 191
Puffs, Turkey-Cheese, '87 301

Quiches
    Bacon-Cheese Quiches,
      Miniature, '83 93
    Benedict Quiche, '80 M107
    Blue Cheese Quiche, '84 52
    Cheddar-Leek Quiche, '88 198
    Eggless Quiche, '87 220
    Green Onion Quiche, Cheesy, '83 194;
      '84 42
    Ham-Cheese Quiche, '79 26
    Ham Quiche, Cheesy, '79 127
    Jalapeño Quiche, Cheesy, '84 31
    Lorraine, Perfect Quiche, '79 127
    Lorraine, Quiche, '79 40; '80 M108
    Miniature Cheese Quiches, '80 150
    Sausage-Cheddar Quiche, '79 26
    Sausage Quiche, Spicy, '80 M108
    Spinach Quiche, Cheesy, '81 228
    Squares, Cheesy Hot Quiche, '79 124
    Swiss-Zucchini Quiche, '82 49
    Tasty Quiche, '82 264
    Vegetable Quiche, Cheese-, '81 228
    Zucchini Quiche, Cheesy, '83 312
Ramekins, Three-Cheese, '79 26
Rarebit, Cheese, '86 78
Rarebit, Tangy Welsh, '88 159
Rarebit, Uptown Welsh, '87 279
Rice, Chili-Cheesy, '79 43
Roll, Cheesy Meat, '82 136
Rollups, Date-Cream Cheese, '83 298
Rounds, Parmesan, '79 170
Rounds, Turkey-Mozzarella, '82 3
Salad, Blue Cheese, '88 48
Salad, Blue Cheese-Pear-Apple, '81 224
Salad, Blue Cheese Tossed, '84 195
Salad, Cantaloupe-Cheese, '88 184
Salad, Cheddar-Pea, '84 82
Salad, Cheesy Apple, '86 301
Salad, Cheesy Fruit-'n'-Nut, '87 56

Salad, Cheesy Layered, '81 37
Salad, Cheesy-Vegetable
  Congealed, '86 199
Salad, Cottage Cheese-and-Fruit, '86 16
Salad, Cottage Cheese-Potato, '79 147, 285
Salad, Cottage-Tomato, '85 163
Salad, Cranberry-Cheese Ribbon, '79 241
Salad, Creamy Roquefort, '79 73
Salad, Crunchy-Creamy, '88 100
Salad, Different Cottage Cheese, '85 328;
  '86 22
Salad, Dilled Macaroni-Cheese, '86 208
Salad, Frosted Lime-Cheese, '79 286
Salad, Ham-and-Cheese, '88 138
Salad, Hot Parmesan Potato, '79 78
Salad in Tomatoes, Cottage
  Cheese, '86 208
Salad, Lemon-Cheese, '85 240
Salad, Mexican, '81 36
Salad, Orange-Cottage Cheese, '79 44
Salad, Out-of-This-World Cottage
  Cheese, '79 44
Salad, Party Freeze, '82 145
Salad, Spinach-Blue Cheese, '82 166
Salad, Swiss-Apple, '84 81
Salad, Swiss Tuna, '86 186
Salad, Tomato-Feta, '81 246
Salad, Ziti-Cheddar, '85 165
Sandwich, Corned Beef and
  Cheese, '79 214
Sandwiches, Avocado, Bacon, and
  Cheese, '87 279
Sandwiches, Bacon, Cheese, and
  Tomato, '84 14
Sandwiches, Breakfast, '80 52
Sandwiches, Brown Bread-Cream
  Cheese, '87 M6
Sandwiches, Cheesy Chicken, '82 190
Sandwiches, Creamy Blue
  Cheese-Ham, '87 279
Sandwiches, Gingered Tea, '84 116
Sandwiches, Grilled Bacon-Cheese,
  '83 242
Sandwiches, Grilled Cheese, '82 M172
Sandwiches, Ham-and-Cheese Pita, '87 202;
  '88 44
Sandwiches, Hot Crab-and-Cheese,
  '87 279
Sandwiches, Hot French Cheese, '82 3
Sandwiches, Hot Ham-and-Cheese,
  '85 299
Sandwiches, Open-Faced Cheesy
  Bacon, '80 78
Sandwiches, Open-Faced Cheesy
  Egg, '86 67
Sandwiches, Peanut-Cheese-Raisin,
  '88 140
Sandwiches, Pimiento Cheese, '82 278
Sandwiches, Shrimp-Cheese, '85 242
Sandwiches, Tangy Ham-and-Swiss,
  '85 164
Sandwiches, Tasty Grilled, '84 30
Sandwiches, Toasted
  Chicken-and-Cheese, '85 242
Sandwiches, Yummy, '81 229
Sandwich, Tex-Mex Ham-and-Cheese,
  '86 4
Sauces
    Broccoli with Cheese Sauce, '82 107
    Brussels Sprouts with Cheese
      Sauce, '79 246

Cauliflower with Cheese
  Sauce, '81 101
Cheese Sauce, '79 M156; '81 43, 44,
  225; '82 M123; '83 49, 138, 188;
  '84 57; '85 92; '86 241;
  '88 78, 272
Cottage Cheese Sauce, '87 232
Cream Sauce, Cheesy, '82 79
Devonshire Sauce, Processor, '86 337
Easy Cheese Sauce, '79 22
Garlic-Cheese Sauce, '84 M70
Ham and Eggs on Toast with Cheese
  Sauce, '81 43
Lemony Cheese Sauce, '84 183
Monterey Jack Sauce, '84 293
Mornay Sauce, '80 120; '81 90
Mushroom-Cheese Sauce, '83 190;
  '86 48
Parmesan Cheese Sauce, '79 165;
  '80 162; '85 143
Potatoes with Cheese Sauce,
  Baked, '83 239
Potatoes with Cheese Sauce,
  Stuffed, '87 192
Rich Cheese Sauce, '81 89
Swiss Cheese Sauce, '79 35; '87 289;
  '88 135

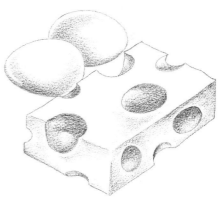

Swiss Sauce, '83 M195
Swiss Sauce, Creamy, '80 M53
Tomatoes with Cheese Sauce over
  Toast, '88 159
Topper, Vegetable-Cheese
  Potato, '86 6
Tuna Salad, Cheese-Sauced, '87 M124
Turnips in Cheese Sauce, '84 229
Vegetable-Cheese Sauce, '85 M152
Scallops, Chip and Cheese, '80 301
Scallops Mornay, '80 164
Schnitzel, Swiss, '80 189
Shell, Rice-Cheese, '82 49
Shells, Cheesy Beef-Stuffed, '83 217
Shells, Cream Cheese, '79 2
Shrimp au Gratin, '85 79
Shrimp, Parmesan-Stuffed, '85 103
Soufflé, Blintz, '88 155
Soufflé, Cheese, '79 72, 261
Soufflé, Cheesy Spinach, '81 53
Soufflé, Corn-and-Cheese, '88 122
Soufflé, Cream Cheese, '88 11
Soufflé Cups, Hot, '85 284
Soufflé for Two, Cheese, '81 226
Soufflé, Rice-Cheese, '79 270
Soufflés, Individual, '80 190

Cheese *(continued)*

Soufflés, Individual Frozen, '80 52
Soufflé, Three-Egg Cheese, '87 234
Soups
   Anytime Soup, Cheesy, '81 307;
      '82 314; '83 66
   Bacon-Beer Cheese Soup, '87 M7
   Bacon-Topped Cheese
      Soup, '80 M224
   Beer-Cheese Soup, '84 246
   Broccoli Soup, Cheesy-, '86 258
   Broccoli-Swiss Soup, '86 6
   Carrot Soup, Cheesy, '81 262
   Cheddar Chowder, Hearty, '79 16
   Corn and Cheese Chowder, '80 228
   Cream of Cheese Soup, '83 99
   Golden Cheese Chowder, '80 73
   Ham 'n Cheese Chowder, '79 199
   Hearty Cheese Soup, '84 4
   Monterey Jack Cheese Soup, '81 112;
      '85 M211
   Onion-Cheese Soup, '87 81
   Onion Soup, Double-Cheese, '85 227
   Onion Soup, Double
      Cheese-Topped, '79 49
   Oyster-Cheese Soup, '84 213
   Roquefort Vichyssoise,
      Velvety, '83 223
   Swiss-Broccoli Chowder, '80 73
   Tomato Soup with Parmesan Cheese,
      Cream of, '86 161
   Vegetable-Cheese Soup,
      Creamy, '81 244
   Vegetable Cheese Soup,
      Creamy, '83 230
   Vegetable Chowder, Cheesy, '80 25;
      '83 20
   Vegetable Soup, Cheesy, '80 73
   Velvet Soup, Cheese, '80 74
Spaghetti, Three-Cheese, '83 105
Spanakópita, '86 58

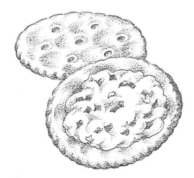

Spreads and Fillings
   Almond Cheese Spread, '87 292
   Aloha Spread, '83 93
   Apricot Brie Spread, '86 275
   Apricot-Cream Cheese
      Spread, '82 161; '87 158
   Bacon-Cheese Spread, '83 241
   Beer Cheese Spread, '81 160; '85 69
   Beer Spread, Cheesy, '87 196
   Caviar-Cream Cheese Spread, '84 256
   Chile-Cheese Spread, '86 297
   Chocolate Cheese Spread, '87 292
   Confetti Cheese Spread, '84 256

Cottage Cheese Spread, '87 107
Cottage-Egg Salad Spread, '82 146
Crabmeat Spread, Layered, '83 127
Crab Spread, Superb, '81 235
Cream Cheese-Olive Spread, '82 35
Cream Cheese Spread,
   Deviled, '81 235
Cucumber and Cream Cheese
   Spread, '82 140
Date Spread, Breakfast, '84 7
Edam-Sherry Spread, '84 257
Fruit and Cheese Spread, '81 245
Fruit-and-Cheese Spread,
   Nutty, '87 246
Garlic Pimiento Cheese Spread, '79 58
German Cheese Spread, '79 82
Gruyère-Apple Spread, '81 160
Ham and Pimiento Spread, '80 285
Hawaiian Cheese Spread, '87 158
Herb-Cream Cheese Spread, '83 24
Herbed Cheese Spread, '87 247
Horseradish Spread, Cheese-, '84 222
Jalapeño-Cheese Spread, '82 248
Lemon-Cheese Filling, '79 68; '88 7
Olive Spread, Cheese-, '79 82
Orange Cheese Spread, '87 292
Pimiento and Three Cheeses, '86 296
Pimiento Cheese, Chunky, '86 295
Pimiento Cheese, Creamy, '86 296
Pimiento Cheese Spread, '82 35;
   '83 93; '86 127
Pimiento Cheese Spread,
   Low-Calorie, '85 215
Pimiento Cheese, West Texas, '84 9
Pineapple-Cheese Spread, '86 126
Pineapple-Cream Cheese
   Spread, '82 35
Ricotta Filling, '80 58
Sandwich Spread, Benedictine, '80 299
Spinach-Ricotta Filling, '81 53
Tomato-Cheese Spread, '81 157
Tomato-Cheese Spread, Fiery, '87 196
Tuna Spread, '83 174
Vegetable Sandwich Spread, '83 174
Waldorf Cheese Spread, '88 173
Zesty Cheese Spread, '82 140
Zippy Cheese Spread, '85 4
Squares, Lemony Cream Cheese, '82 159
Steak Cheese Skillet, Swiss, '80 106
Steak, Parmesan Round, '80 106
Steaks, Blue Cheese, '84 171
Steaks, Cheese-Stuffed, '81 17
Stromboli, '88 272
Supper Supreme, Sunday, '79 76
Tart, Herb-Cheese, '87 98
Tart Milan, '87 70
Tarts, Cranberry-Cream Cheese, '80 154
Tarts, Cream Cheese, '84 74
Tart Shells, Cheese, '88 88
Tarts, Lemon-Cheese, '79 2
Tarts, Sausage 'n' Cheese, '88 51
Terrine with Goat Cheese, Black
   Bean, '87 120
Topping, Cheese, '86 233
Topping, Yogurt-Cheese, '88 55
Tortillas, Cheesy, '81 62
Tortilla Stack, Cheesy Chicken-, '86 3
Toss, Ham and Cheese, '79 55
Trout Florentine, Cheesy, '85 53
Tuna Cheesies, '82 191
Turkey Parmesan, '82 268

Turnovers, Sausage-Cheese, '88 231
Veal Parmigiana, '81 227
Vegetables
   Beans au Gratin, Green, '80 116
   Beans, Cheese-Topped Green, '79 100
   Beans, Cheesy Green, '80 157
   Broccoli-and-Eggs au Gratin, '85 289
   Broccoli au Gratin, '82 M20
   Broccoli Fritters, Cheesy, '79 53
   Cabbage, Cheese Scalloped, '81 87;
      '82 7
   Cauliflower au Gratin, '82 204
   Cauliflower au Gratin,
      French-Fried, '79 221; '80 82
   Cauliflower, Baked Swiss, '79 100
   Cauliflower, Cheese-Frosted, '85 68
   Cauliflower Italiano, Cheesy, '82 300
   Chiles Rellenos (Stuffed
      Chiles), '82 220; '83 150
   Corn, Grilled Parmesan, '82 127
   Eggplant, Cheesy Stuffed, '79 188;
      '82 208
   Eggplant, Fried Parmesan, '87 166
   Eggplant Parmesan, '82 230
   Eggplant, Parmesan Fried, '79 189
   Hash Brown Cheese Bake, '82 50
   Lentils with Cheese, Baked, '84 113
   Limas in Onion Shells, Cheese
      and, '81 86
   Loaf, Pureed
      Vegetable-Cheese, '85 297
   Mushrooms, Parmesan Stuffed, '83 115
   Mushrooms, Ricotta-Stuffed, '85 20
   Okra with Cheese, '80 185

   Onion Bake, Cheese, '82 32
   Onions, Sherried Cheese, '82 32
   Potato-Broccoli-Cheese Bake, '80 114
   Potato Croquettes, Parmesan, '84 210
   Potatoes-and-Zucchini au Gratin, '84 5
   Potatoes, Bacon-Topped Blue
      Cheese, '79 46
   Potatoes, Blue Cheese Stuffed, '81 276
   Potatoes, Cheesy, '82 211
   Potatoes, Cheesy
      Bacon-Stuffed, '81 61
   Potatoes, Cheesy Caraway, '86 17
   Potatoes, Cheesy Chive, '79 46
   Potatoes, Cheesy Crab-Stuffed, '86 17
   Potatoes, Cheesy Frank-Topped, '83 3
   Potatoes, Cheesy New, '85 156
   Potatoes, Chicken-Cheese
      Stuffed, '86 55
   Potatoes, Creamy Cheese, '88 M146
   Potatoes, Parmesan, '82 270
   Potatoes Roquefort, '79 211
   Potatoes, Two-Cheese, '80 114
   Potatoes with Feta Cheese, '84 295;
      '85 196

Potato Fans, Parmesan-, '88 M190
Potato Skins, Cheese, '84 M239
Rice au Gratin, '83 129
Rutabaga au Gratin, '79 254
Spinach-Cheese Puff, '84 96
Spinach, Cheesy Topped, '84 85
Spinach, Savory Parmesan, '85 68
Spinach with Cheese, Scalloped, '79 8
Spinach with Feta, Lemon, '85 190
Squash Bake, Cheesy, '80 183
Squash Boats,
 Parmesan-Stuffed, '79 156
Squash, Cheesy Stuffed, '82 134
Squash Soufflé, Cheesy, '82 146
Squash with Cheese Sauce, Stuffed
 Yellow, '80 162
Tomato Cheese Puffs, '81 48
Tomatoes, Baked Cheddar, '85 43
Tomatoes, Cheese
 Herbed-Topped, '86 108
Tomatoes, Cheese-Topped, '81 160
Tomatoes, Cheesy Cherry, '83 135
Tomatoes, Cheesy Grilled, '79 150
Tomatoes, Cheesy Puff-Top, '86 187
Tomatoes, Cheesy Stuffed, '80 161
Tomatoes, Parmesan, '80 161
Tomatoes, Romano Broiled, '80 42
Turnip au Gratin, '79 289
Turnips au Gratin, '88 229
Zucchini and Tomato au
 Gratin, '82 208
Zucchini, Ham and Cheese
 Stuffed, '79 157
Zucchini Parmesan, '81 108; '82 103
Zucchini, Parmesan, '81 234
Zucchini Pie, Cheesy, '82 103
Vermicelli, Shrimp and Feta Cheese
 on, '87 108
Wafers, Italian, '87 36
Cheesecakes. *See* Cakes/Cheesecakes.
Cherries
 à la Mode, Cherries, '88 202
 Bars, Delightful Cherry, '86 217
 Bread, Cherry Nut, '81 306; '82 36
 Bread, Maraschino Cherry Nut, '79 234
 Bread, Quick Cherry-Nut, '85 55
 Cake, Black Forest Cherry, '83 302
 Cake, Cherry, '79 165
 Cake, Cherry Blossom Coffee, '80 21
 Cake, Cherry Bourbon, '82 287
 Cake, Cherry Upside-Down, '82 56
 Cake, Chocolate-Cherry, '84 200; '86 239
 Cake, Maraschino Nut, '83 268
 Cake, Quick Cherry, '81 238
 Cake, Upside-Down Sunburst, '87 9
 Cake, White Chocolate-Cherry, '88 268
 Cheesecake, Cherry, '79 50
 Cheesecake, Cherry-Topped, '80 23
 Chocolate-Covered Cherries, '81 286;
  '84 298
 Cloud, Cherry-Berry on a, '79 94
 Cobbler, Berry-Cherry, '83 270
 Cobbler, Cherry, '82 91, 139
 Cobbler, Fresh Cherry, '84 178
 Compote, Cherry, '83 139
 Cookies, Cherry Pecan, '82 136
 Cookies, Chocolate-Cherry, '85 324
 Cookies, Christmas Cherry, '88 282
 Cookies, Coconut-Cherry, '79 292
 Cream, Maraschino Russian, '79 231
 Crêpes Flambé, Cherry, '79 18

Dessert, Cherry Cordial, '84 312
Dessert, Holiday Cherry, '80 255
Drops, Cherry-Almond, '81 20
Filling, Cherry, '83 302; '84 225; '88 178
Frosting, Cherry, '86 217
Fudge, Cherry Nut, '83 315
Glaze, Cherry, '83 143
Ice Cream, Black Forest, '88 203
Ice Cream, Cherry, '84 184
Ice Cream, Cherry-Nut, '86 129
Ice Cream, Cherry-Pecan, '88 203
Jubilee, Cherries, '79 18; '83 139
Jubilee, Quick Cherries, '82 M100
Jubilite, Cherries, '86 317
Muffins, Cherry, '82 105
Nuggets, Cherry Nut, '81 286
Pie, Easy Cherry, '82 M299
Pie, Fresh Cherry, '88 178
Pie, Prize-Winning Cherry, '82 57
Pie, Red Cherry, '83 192
Pie, Scrumptious Cherry, '83 250
Pie, Tart Cranberry-Cherry, '87 299
Rolls, Cherry-Almond, '84 M198
Sabayon, Cherries, '88 178
Salad, Best Cherry, '82 302
Salad, Cherry-Apple, '86 31
Salad, Cherry Cola, '80 104
Salad, Cherry Fruit, '87 236
Salad, Cherry-Orange, '79 74; '82 56
Salad, Delicious Frozen Cherry, '81 252
Salad, Elegant Cherry-Wine, '82 56
Salad, Festive Cherry, '84 265
Salad, Fresh Cherry, '83 120
Salad, Frozen Cherry, '79 126
Salad, Port Wine-Cherry, '86 11
Salad with Honey-Lime Dressing,
 Cherry, '83 139
Salad with Sherry Dressing,
 Cherry, '79 165
Sauce, Cherry, '79 91; '83 276; '84 91
Sauce, Chocolate-Cherry, '85 189
Sauce, Chocolate Cherry, '87 M165
Sauce, Elegant Cherry, '79 M156
Sauce, Ham Balls with Spiced
 Cherry, '81 112; '82 12
Sauce, Roast Ducklings with
 Cherry, '86 312
Sauce, Royal Cherry, '85 224; '86 83
Sauce, Spicy Cherry, '83 244
Slump, Cherry, '83 139
Snow, Berries on, '82 227
Squares, Surprise Cherry, '82 57
Stuffed Cherries, '85 81
Syrup, Cherry-Lemonade, '86 214
Tart, Cherry and Blackberry, '83 225
Tarts, Cheery Cherry, '80 238
Topping, Cherry-Pineapple, '87 126
Torte, Black Forest Cherry, '88 178
Chicken
 Acapulco, Chicken, '84 32
 à la King, Chicken, '79 218; '83 137;
  '87 197
 Almond Chicken and Vegetables, '86 21
 Almond Chicken, Spicy, '88 150
 à l'Orange, Chicken, '84 277
 Andalusia, Chicken, '87 103
 Appetizers, Chicken-Mushroom, '88 210
 Apple Chicken, '85 57
 Apricot Chicken Breasts, '88 301
 Ariosto, Shrimp and Chicken, '79 31
 Artichoke Chicken, '81 97

Artichoke Hearts, Chicken with, '88 54
Bag, Chicken in a, '86 M57; '87 23
Bake, Chicken, Ham, and Cheese, '87 217
Bake, Chicken-Tomato, '83 35
Bake, Chicken Tortilla, '82 89
Bake, Company Chicken, '80 301
Bake, Countryside Chicken, '88 39
Bake, Crispy Chicken, '83 115
Baked Chicken and Artichoke
 Hearts, '82 260
Baked Chicken and Dressing, '79 296
Baked Chicken, Breaded, '81 76
Baked Chicken Breasts, Creamy, '83 24
Baked Chicken Breasts, Sherried, '79 83
Baked Chicken Breasts, Wine-, '83 177
Baked Chicken, Citrus Herb, '85 303
Baked Chicken, Fancy, '79 85
Baked Chicken, Herb-, '82 229
Baked Chicken in Wine, '81 109
Baked Chicken, Italian, '82 84
Baked Chicken Parmesan, '83 137
Baked Chicken, Tomato-, '81 281; '82 30
Baked Chicken with Wine-Soaked
 Vegetables, '84 277
Baked Chile Chicken with Salsa, '88 147
Baked Italian Chicken, '83 184
Baked Lemon Chicken, '85 190
Baked Mustard Chicken, '87 10
Baked Parmesan Chicken, '83 320
Bake, Herb Chicken, '82 186
Bake, Pineapple Chicken, '82 120
Bake, Saucy Chicken, '84 220
Bake, Spicy Chicken, '85 251
Ball, Chicken-Curry Cheese, '85 118

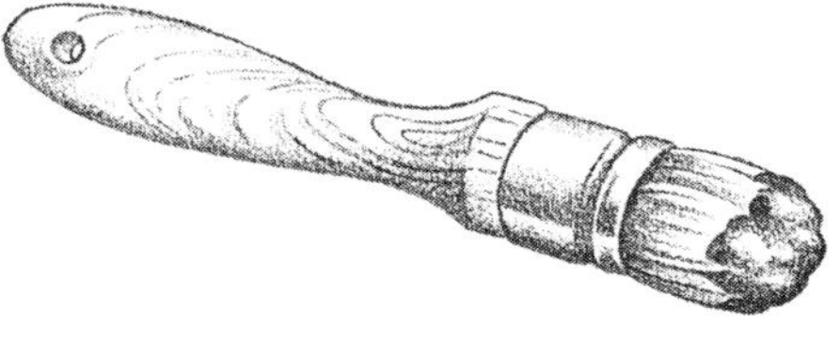

Barbecued
 Bake, Barbecued Chicken, '81 97
 Breasts, Grilled Chicken, '84 172
 Bundles, Chicken-Mushroom, '80 157
 Charcoal Broiled Chicken, '79 90
 Chicken, Barbecue, '86 122
 Chicken, Barbecued, '82 97, 106;
  '83 103; '85 144; '86 153
 Cranberry Chicken, Barbecued, '83 178
 Cumin Chicken, Grilled, '87 142
 Garlic-Grilled Chicken, '87 180
 Golden Barbecued Chicken, '83 136
 Grilled Barbecued Chicken, '81 154
 Lemonade Chicken, '82 163
 Marinated Barbecued Chicken, '79 90
 Old South Barbecued Chicken, '82 97;
  '83 103
 Orange Barbecued Chicken, '88 123
 Saucy Barbecued Chicken, '83 11
 Smoky Grilled Chicken, '85 160
 Tangy Barbecued Chicken, '86 186
 Yogurt-Lemon Chicken,
  Grilled, '81 111
 Zesty Barbecued Chicken, '80 M76
 Zippy Barbecued Chicken, '83 213

Chicken (continued)

Basil Chicken, **'87** 171
Bengalese Chicken, **'79** 12
Bird's-Nest Chicken, **'88** 152
Birds of Paradise, **'82** 224
Biscuit, Chicken in a, **'79** 263; **'80** 30
Bites, Curried Chicken, **'85** 40
Braised Bourbon Chicken, **'86** 51
Brandado, Chicken, **'84** 195
Breast-of-Chicken Fiesta, **'88** 151
Breast of Chicken, Herbed, **'79** 100
Breasts, Island Chicken, **'84** 68
Breasts Lombardy, Chicken, **'82** 242
Breasts, Saucy Chicken, **'83** 184; **'87** 167
Brioche Chicken Curry, **'88** 124
Broiled Chicken, Island, **'84** 288
Bundles, Cheesy Chicken-and-Ham, **'84** 261
Bundles, San Antonio-Style
   Chicken, **'85** 251
Bundles with Bacon Ribbons,
   Chicken, **'87** 68
Burgoo, Five-Meat, **'87** 3
Burgoo, Harry Young's, **'87** 3
Burgoo, Old-Fashioned, **'87** 3
Cacciatore, Chicken, **'80** 39; **'83** 118;
   '84 9; **'86** 42
Cacciatore, Quick Chicken-and-Rice,
   '88 38
Cajun Chicken over Rice, **'87** 268;
   '88 102
Cashew Chicken, **'79** 255; **'80** 8; **'83** 21
Cashew, Chicken, **'88** 38
Cashews, Chicken with, **'79** 207
Casserole, Broccoli-Chicken, **'82** 33
Casserole, Cheesy Chicken, **'85** 34
Casserole, Chicken-and-Dressing, **'81** 263
Casserole, Chicken and Green
   Noodle, **'80** 32
Casserole, Chicken and Rice, **'80** 260
Casserole, Chicken-Asparagus, **'83** 76;
   '84 71
Casserole, Chicken-Broccoli, **'79** 48
Casserole, Chicken-Green Bean, **'85** 296
Casserole, Chicken-Macaroni, **'85** 219
Casserole, Chicken-Rice, **'86** 52
Casserole, Chicken-Spaghetti, **'84** 15
Casserole, Chicken Supreme, **'84** 219
Casserole, Chicken Tortilla, **'81** 166
Casserole, Chicken-Wild Rice, **'84** 241;
   '85 65
Casserole, Macaroni and Chicken, **'80** 260
Casserole, Make-Ahead Chicken, **'84** 241
Casserole, Mexican Chicken, **'82** 143
Casserole, Quick Chicken, **'81** 91
Casserole, Rice-and-Chicken, **'87** 154
Casserole, Sunday Chicken, **'83** 290
Celery Skillet, Chicken-and-, **'88** 6
Chafing Dish Chicken, **'82** 284
Chalupas, Chicken, **'79** 185
Chalupas, Chicken-Olive, **'81** 227
Champagne Chicken, **'85** 251
Champagne Sauce, Chicken Breasts
   with, **'86** 49
Charlemagne, Chicken, **'86** 293
Chilaquiles con Pollo (Tortillas with
   Chicken), **'81** 66
Chinese Chicken and Vegetables, **'81** 212
Chinese Chicken, Lazy Day, **'81** 3
Chinese-Style Dinner, **'84** 26
Chop Suey, Chicken, **'81** 227

Chowder, Chicken, **'83** 20
Chutney Chicken, **'86** 249
Company Chicken, **'80** 39; **'83** 125
Continental, Chicken, **'82** 274
Cordon Bleu, Chicken, **'81** 304; **'82** 83;
   '86 37
Cordon Bleu, Company Chicken, **'82** 274
Cordon Bleu in Mushroom Sauce,
   Chicken, **'86** 198
Country Poulet, **'86** 292
Crabmeat Stuffing, Chicken Breasts
   with, **'85** 302
Creamed Chicken, **'82** 49, 284; **'83** 14
Creamed Chicken, Company, **'82** 84
Creamed Chicken in a Shell, **'79** 138
Creamed Chicken in Patty Shells, **'86** 123
Creamed Chicken over Confetti Rice
   Squares, **'81** 282; **'82** 31
Creamed Chicken over Cornbread, **'86** 231
Creamed Ham and Chicken, **'81** M74
Creole, Chicken, **'86** 231

Crêpes, Chicken, **'80** 39
Crêpes, Chicken-Vegetable, **'83** 70
Crêpes, Creamy Chicken, **'81** 200
Crêpes Divan, Elegant, **'81** 91
Crispy Chicken, **'84** 152
Croquettes, Chicken, **'81** 133
Croquettes, Crispy Chicken, **'88** 206
Curried Chicken, **'86** 43
Curried Chicken, Regal, **'84** 110
Curry, Chicken, **'84** 110; **'85** 220; **'86** 21
Cutlets with Lemon, Chicken, **'85** 8
Dante's Chicken, **'88** 25
Dijon Chicken, **'81** 156
Dilled Chicken Paprika, **'86** 41
Dinner, Chicken-Mushroom, **'81** 3
Dinner, Chicken Peach, **'79** 77
Dinner, Healthful Chicken, **'83** 232
Dip, Hot Chicken, **'80** 86
Divan Casserole, Chicken, **'82** M203
Divan, Chicken, **'80** M10; **'87** M218
Divan, Curried Chicken, **'80** 83
Divan, Gourmet Chicken, **'82** 83
Divan, Overnight Chicken, **'83** 198
Divan, Sherried Chicken, **'80** 38
Dixie Manor, Chicken à la, **'85** 3
Dressing, Chicken and Rice, **'79** 288
Dressing, Tipsy Chicken and, **'88** 151
Drumsticks, Cajun-Style, **'87** 159
Dumplings, Country Chicken and, **'85** 254
Dumplings, Easy Chicken and, **'86** 21
Dumplings, Old-Fashioned Chicken
   and, **'79** 55; **'83** 228
Dumplings with Vegetables, Chicken
   and, **'85** M56
Enchiladas, Chicken, **'80** 301; **'86** 296
Enchiladas, Easy Chicken, **'82** 89; **'86** 231

Enchiladas Terrificas, **'84** 32
Enchiladas with Spicy Sauce,
   Chicken, **'84** 76
English Muffin Delight, **'82** 45
en Papillote, Chicken and
   Vegetables, **'86** 145
Fajitas, Chicken, **'88** 231
Fancy Fowl, **'81** 76; **'82** 13
Fettuccine, Chicken-Pecan, **'86** 52
Fiesta Chicken, Spicy, **'84** 234
Filling, Chicken, **'81** 200
Filling, Chicken Divan, **'81** 91
Filling, Chicken-Olive, **'81** 227
Filling, Curried Chicken, **'88** 125
Filling Luau, Chicken, **'79** 81
Fingers, Chicken Little, **'80** 249
Fingers, Herb-Baked Chicken, **'86** 249
Flautas, **'83** 199
Florentine with Mushroom Sauce,
   Chicken, **'87** 250
Fried
   Beaumont Fried Chicken, **'88** 92
   Bites, French-Fried Chicken, **'85** 160
   Buttermilk Fried Chicken,
      Company, **'86** 177
   Cheese-Stuffed Chicken Thighs,
      Fried, **'88** 206
   Cream Gravy, Fried Chicken
      with, **'85** 241
   Crispy Fried Chicken Breasts,
      '80 155
   Curried Fried Chicken, **'85** 160
   Delicious Fried Chicken, **'86** 156
   Dixie Fried Chicken, **'88** 14
   Drummettes with Horseradish Sauce,
      Fried Chicken, **'88** 207
   Drumsticks, Buttermilk, **'87** 175
   Garlic-Flavored Fried Chicken,
      '79 147
   Garlic Fried Chicken, **'82** 148
   Golden Chicken Nuggets, **'80** 159
   Herbed Fried Chicken, **'87** 91
   Herb-Seasoned Fried Chicken, **'80** 8
   Honey-Butter Sauce, Oven-Fried
      Chicken with, **'85** 18
   Lemon-Fried Chicken, **'79** 77
   Lemon Fried Chicken, **'82** 275
   Mandarin Chicken, Crispy, **'86** 119
   Mexican Fried Chicken, **'81** 166;
      '87 176
   Nuggets, Lemon-Chicken, **'87** 283
   Nutty Oven-Fried Chicken, **'85** 160
   Oven-Fried Chicken, **'84** 118
   Oven-Fried Chicken, Crunchy, **'87** 163
   Oven-Fried Chicken, Crusty, **'79** 77
   Oven-Fried Chicken,
      Golden-Brown, **'86** 21
   Oven-Fried Chicken, Nutty, **'85** 160
   Oven-Fried Chicken, Southern, **'86** 37
   Oven-Fried Parmesan Chicken, **'81** 97;
      '82 148
   Oven-Fried Pecan Chicken, **'84** 288
   Oven-Fried Sesame Chicken, **'79** 77
   Sesame Chicken, **'82** 148
   Special Fried Chicken, **'88** 220
   Spicy Country-Fried Chicken, **'82** 148
   Spicy Fried Chicken, **'83** 5; **'88** 129
   Spinach-Stuffed Chicken Breasts,
      Fried, **'88** 206
   Sunday Dinner Fried Chicken, **'88** 110
   Super Fried Chicken, **'82** 148

Traditional Fried Chicken, **'82** 148
Walnut Chicken, Deep-Fried, **'87** 175
Wings, Hot Buffalo, **'87** 176
Fruited Chicken en Crème, **'83** 264
Garden, Chicken-in-a-, **'80** 18
Ginger Chicken and Cashews, **'85** M11
Glazed Chicken, Fruit-, **'80** 211
Grilled Chicken with Dill Sauce, **'88** 162
Gruyère, Chicken Breasts, **'80** 189
Gumbo, Chicken, **'79** 199
Gumbo, Chicken and Oyster, **'81** 198
Gumbo, Chicken-Ham-Seafood, **'81** 6
Gumbo, Combo, **'81** 198
Gumbo, Easy Chicken, **'83** 156
Gumbo with Smoked Sausage,
    Chicken, **'81** 199
Gumbo Ya Ya, **'87** 210
Hawaiian Chicken, **'82** 274
Hawaiian, Chicken, **'84** 88
Herbed Chicken, French, **'86** 89
Herbed Chicken, Sunny, **'86** 156
Herbed Chicken, Tangy, **'87** M302
Honey Chicken, **'82** 55; **'88** 67
Honey-Curry Chicken, **'87** 36
Honolulu Chicken, **'85** 52
Imperial Chicken, **'81** 238
Italian Chicken, **'86** 122
Jambalaya, Chicken-and-Sausage, **'88** 200
Kabobs, Chicken, **'87** 141
Kabobs, Chicken-Avocado, **'82** 9; **'83** 68
Kabobs, Good-and-Easy Chicken, **'85** 87
Kabobs, Hawaiian, **'85** 157
Kabobs, Marinated Chicken, **'84** M144
Kabobs, Pineapple-Chicken, **'86** M328
Kabobs, Sesame Chicken, **'82** 165
Kabobs, Soy-Chicken, **'86** 156
Kabobs Supreme, Chicken, **'81** 124
Kiev, Chicken, **'80** 39
Kiev, Cranberry Chicken, **'87** 250
Kiev, Oven-Baked Chicken, **'86** 37
Kiev, Oven Chicken, **'82** 83
la France, Chicken, **'86** 248
Lasagna, Chicken, **'87** M302; **'88** 90
Lemon and Wine, Chicken in, **'83** 281
Lemon Chicken, **'81** M138; **'86** 173
Lemon Chicken and Vegetables, **'88** 118
Lemon Chicken, Sweet, **'79** 218
Lemon-Chicken, Sweet, **'84** 69
Lemon-Frosted Chicken, **'88** 170
Lemon-Herb Chicken, **'85** 127
Lime Butter, Chicken with, **'84** 68
Livers
    Bits and Livers, Chicken, **'84** 222
    en Brochette, Chicken Livers, **'84** 222
    Italian Sauce, Chicken Livers
        in, **'83** 117
    Kabobs, Rumaki, **'82** 182
    Mushrooms, Chicken Livers
        with, **'81** 133
    Omelet, Chicken Liver, **'82** 44
    Orange Sauce, Chicken Livers
        in, **'82** 218
    Party Chicken Livers, **'83** 242
    Pâté, Chicken Liver, **'79** 153; **'81** 235;
        '83 108; **'84** 205; **'88** M132
    Pâté Maison, **'84** 222
    Potatoes, Chicken Livers and, **'82** 218
    Rice, Chicken Livers with, **'80** 200;
        '81 58; **'84** 292
    Rice Dish, Chicken Livers and, **'82** 218
    Risotto, Chicken Livers, **'82** 218

Roll-Ups, Chicken Liver and
    Bacon, **'80** 200; **'81** 57
Rumaki, **'80** M136
Sautéed Chicken Livers, **'80** 200;
    '81 57
Scrumptious Chicken Livers, **'84** 230
Spread, Sherried Liver, **'80** 86
Stroganoff, Chicken Livers, **'80** 200;
    '81 57
Supreme, Chicken Livers, **'81** 298
Turnovers, Chicken Liver, **'79** 141
Wine Sauce, Chicken Livers
    in, **'81** 104
Wine Sauce, Chicken Livers with
    Marsala, **'81** 76
Log, Chicken-Pecan, **'81** 290
Luzianne, Poulet, **'86** 197
Manicotti, Creamy Chicken, **'85** 60
Marinara, Chicken, **'86** 77
Marinated Breast of Chicken, **'87** 123
Marinated Chicken, **'87** 61
Marsala, Chicken, **'83** 137
Mexican Chicken, **'80** 124
Mexican Chicken, Spicy, **'82** 89
Milano, Chicken, **'84** 220
Minted Chicken, **'81** 102
Mole, Chicken, **'81** 193
Monterey, Chicken, **'82** 275
Mornay Sauce, Chicken Breasts in, **'81** 273
Mushrooms, Chicken-Stuffed, **'80** 162
Mustard Chicken, **'80** 222; **'86** 293
Nachos, Chicken, **'84** 244
Nuggets, Baked Chicken, **'81** 149
Nuggets, Golden Chicken, **'80** 159; **'81** 237
Nuggets, Lemon-Chicken, **'86** 337
Nuggets Supreme, Chicken, **'85** 160
Nuggets with Pineapple Sauce,
    Chicken, **'84** 236
Onion-Crusted Chicken, **'88** 40
Orange-Almond Sauce, Chicken in, **'79** 219;
    '80 13
Orange-Avocado Chicken, **'80** 38
Orange Chicken, **'83** 278; **'86** M140
Orange Chicken Breasts with Parslied
    Rice, **'87** 242
Orange Sauce, Chicken Breasts
    with, **'79** 77
Orange Sauce, Chicken in, **'83** 8
Oriental Chicken, **'80** 40, 208; **'82** 131
Oriental Chicken with Peanuts, **'82** 236
Oriental Chicken with Pineapple, **'86** 42
Oriental Stuffed Pockets, **'79** 14
Paella, Chicken-Pork-Shrimp, **'82** 245
Paella, Chicken-Seafood, **'88** 68
Paella, Spanish, **'85** 26
Paella Valenciana, **'82** 246
Parmesan, Chicken, **'83** 184
Parmesan Chicken, Crispy, **'80** M76
Parmigiana, Chicken, **'80** 190
Parmigiana, Chicken-Eggplant, **'82** 212
Pasquale, Chicken, **'83** 67
Pasta and Garden Vegetables, **'87** 192
Pasta, Chicken-and-Broccoli, **'87** 286
Pasta Platter, Cold, **'88** 42
Pastry, Chicken in, **'86** 122
Pâté, Vegetable-Chicken, **'86** 66
Peanut Butter-Marmalade Chicken, **'81** 282;
    '82 30
Peas, Chicken with Snow, **'83** 137
Pecan-Rice Dressing, Chicken
    with, **'85** M57

Peppers, Curried Chicken-Stuffed, **'87** 19
Peppers, Devilish Chicken, **'80** 65
Phyllo, Chicken in, **'87** 286
Piccata, Chicken, **'83** 35; **'84** 230
Piccata, Herbed Chicken, **'88** 28
Pie, Biscuit-Topped Chicken, **'86** 157, 264
Pie, Cheesy Mexican Chicken, **'82** 142
Pie, Chicken, **'81** 281; **'82** 31
Pie, Chicken Pot, **'81** 210; **'82** 114;
    '84 21
Pie, Chicken-Vegetable Pot, **'81** 281;
    '82 30
Pie, Deluxe Chicken, **'88** 298
Pie, Double-Crust Chicken, **'87** 111
Pie, Easy Chicken Pot, **'83** 156
Pie, Egg-Stra Special Chicken, **'86** 264
Pie, Montezuma Tortilla, **'83** 199
Pie, Thick 'n' Crusty Chicken Pot, **'87** 267;
    '88 102
Pie with Cheese Crust, Chicken
    Pot, **'86** 264
Pilaf, Chicken, **'82** 246
Piña Colada Chicken, **'86** 21
Pineapple Chicken, **'83** M194; **'85** 3
Pineapple, Chicken and, **'81** 281; **'82** 30
Pineapple Chicken, Oriental, **'84** 288
Piquant Chicken, **'86** 76
Pizza, Gruyère-Chicken, **'87** 182
Plum Sauce, Chicken with, **'82** 236
Poached Chicken Breasts, Wine-, **'85** 58
Poached Chicken with Black Beans and
    Salsa, **'87** 217
Pollo Almendrado (Chicken in Almond
    Sauce), **'81** 193
Pollo con Calabacita (Mexican Chicken with
    Zucchini), **'82** 219
Pollo en Mole de Cacahuate (Chicken with
    Peanut Mole Sauce), **'80** 194
Pollo en Pipián, Mexican, **'88** 31
Potatoes, Chicken-Cheese Stuffed, **'86** 55
Potatoes, Creamed Beef and
    Chicken-Topped, **'83** 210
Potatoes, Sweet-and-Sour-Topped, **'83** 4
Pot, Chicken in a, **'81** 3
Princess Chicken, **'86** 122
Puffs, Appetizer Chicken, **'85** 72
Puffs, Chicken Nut, **'81** 260
Quiche, Chicken Divan, **'88** M125
Quiche Noël, **'82** 310
Rice, Spicy Chicken and, **'88** 200
Roast Chicken and Brown Rice, **'83** 268
Roast Chicken and Vegetables, **'81** 3
Roasted Chicken, Herb-, **'87** 155
Roasted Chicken, Rice-Stuffed, **'88** 38
Rockefeller Chicken, **'79** 219
Rolls, Chicken-Asparagus, **'86** M211
Rolls, Crispy Chicken, **'84** 288
Rolls Élégante, Chicken, **'80** 210
Rolls, Hearty Salad, **'81** 206
Rolls Jubilee, Chicken, **'87** 118
Rollups, Cheesy Chicken, **'82** 44
Rollups, Chicken, **'85** 179; **'88** 38
Rollups, Chicken and Spinach, **'80** 90;
    '82 M68
Rollups, Imperial Chicken, **'80** 217
Rollups in Gravy, Chicken, **'83** 184
Rollups, Sunshine Chicken, **'85** 251
Romano, Chicken alla, **'83** M58
Romano, Chicken Breasts, **'79** 218
Romanoff, Chicken, **'84** 292
Rotelle, Chicken and Tomato with, **'87** 108

Chicken *(continued)*

Salads

Almond Salad, Chicken-, **'81** 133
Aloha Chicken Salad, **'80** 297
Amandine, Chicken Salad, **'81** 37
Ambrosia, Chicken Salad, **'85** 216
Artichokes, Chicken Salad
  with, **'86** 186
Aspic-Topped Chicken Salad, **'88** 88
Avocado-Chicken Salad, **'87** 107
Avocado Salad, Chicken-, **'80** 139
Avocado Salad, Fruited
  Chicken-, **'82** 101
Avocado Salad Platter, Chicken-, **'83** 2
Avocado Salad, Tossed Chicken-, **'80** 4
Avocados, Chicken Salad in, **'85** 216
Baked Chicken Salad, **'86** 297; **'87** 176
BLT Chicken Salad, **'87** 144
Celery Salad, Chicken-, **'81** 187
Chicken Salad, **'86** 232, 261
Chop Suey Salad, **'81** 37
Chutney-Chicken Salad, **'87** 74
Chutney Salad, Chicken, **'82** 108
Coleslaw, Chicken, **'84** 2
Cream Puff Bowl, Chicken Salad
  in, **'86** 232
Crunchy Chicken Salad, **'86** 157, 207
Curried Chicken-and-Orange
  Salad, **'87** 144
Curried Chicken Salad, **'79** 219;
  '84 66; **'85** 96; **'86** 131
Curried Chicken Salad with
  Asparagus, **'81** 36
Exotic Luncheon Salad, **'83** 210

Fancy Chicken Salad, **'79** 55
Filling, Chicken Salad, **'87** 106
Fruit, Chicken Salad with, **'82** 171
Fruited Chicken Salad, **'84** 25, 290;
  '88 88
Fruited Chicken Salad in
  Avocados, **'87** 41
Fruit Salad, Chicken-, **'82** 79
Fruity Chicken Salad, **'83** 157
Grapes, Chicken Salad with, **'86** 117
Green Salad with Chicken,
  Mixed, **'80** 54
Hot Chicken Salad, **'81** 201; **'83** 196
Hot Chicken Salad, Country
  Club-Style, **'86** 10
Hot Chicken Salad, Crunchy, **'80** 138
Hot Chicken Salad Pinwheel, **'80** 139
Macadamia Chicken Salad, **'80** 138
Macaroni-Chicken Salad, **'85** 296;
  '86 302
Mandarin Chicken, Carousel, **'79** 88

Mango, Chicken Salad with, **'86** 215
Marinated Chicken-Grape Salad, **'85** 74
Mexican Chicken Salad, **'85** 84;
  '88 272
Mold, Chicken-Cucumber, **'80** 175
Mold, Chicken Salad, **'83** 80; **'84** 163
Nectarine Chicken Salad, **'79** 175
Old-Fashioned Chicken Salad, **'83** 79
Oriental Chicken Salad, **'85** 216;
  '88 271
Pasta-Chicken Salad, Tarragon, **'87** 155
Pasta Salad, Chicken, **'88** 89
Pea Salad, Chicken-, **'83** 218
Persian Chicken Salad, **'81** 12
Pineapple-Chicken Salad Pie, **'80** 138
Pineapple-Nut Chicken Salad, **'83** 80
Pocket, Chicken Salad in a, **'88** 139
Polynesian Chicken Salad, **'88** 272
Poulet Rémoulade, **'87** 144
Rice Salad, Chicken-, **'81** 203
Rice Salad, Hot Chicken-and-, **'83** 22
Rice Salad, Nutty Chicken-, **'83** 157
Ring Salad, Chicken Jewel, **'83** 282
Sandwiches, Chicken-Salad
  Finger, **'85** 119
Southwestern Chicken Salad, **'88** 88
Special Chicken Salad, **'85** 82;
  '87 183; **'88** M193
Spinach Tossed Salad,
  Chicken-and-, **'83** 157
Spread, Chicken Salad Party, **'88** M8
Stack-Up Salad, Chicken, **'83** 80
Summer Chicken Salad, **'83** 145
Super Chicken Salad, **'82** 174
Supreme, Chicken Salad, **'79** 107, 152
Tahitian Chicken Salad, **'84** 120
Tarts, Chicken Salad, **'84** 257
Tortellini Salad, Chicken, **'87** 288
Tropical Chicken Boats for
  Two, **'82** 186
Tropical Chicken Salad, **'85** 216
Twist, Chicken Salad with a, **'84** 221
Vegetable-Chicken Vinaigrette
  Salad, **'86** 135
Wild Rice-Chicken Salad, **'83** 146
Saltimbocca alla Romana, Chicken, **'80** 212
San Antonio-Style Chicken, **'81** 166
Sandwich, Crispy Chicken, **'81** 114
Sandwiches, Baked Chicken, **'79** 164;
  '80 130; **'84** 165
Sandwiches, Cheesy Chicken, **'82** 190
Sandwiches, Chicken-Almond
  Pocket, **'81** 240; **'83** 69
Sandwiches, Chicken Club, **'86** 160
Sandwiches, Hot Brown, **'80** 202
Sandwiches, Hot Chicken, **'83** 291
Sandwiches, Marinated Chicken, **'86** M45
Sandwiches, Puffed Chicken, **'82** 35
Sandwiches, Toasted
  Chicken-and-Cheese, **'85** 242
Sandwich, Marinated Chicken in a, **'86** 185
Sauce, Creamy Chicken, **'81** 91
Saucy Chick-Wiches, **'81** 25; **'82** 31;
  '83 34
Sautéed Chicken Breasts, **'87** 36
Sauté, Savory Chicken, **'88** 254
Sauté, Sherry-Chicken, **'87** 218
Scallopini with Lemon Sauce,
  Chicken, **'86** 156
Scallopini with Peppers, Chicken, **'85** 78
Scarborough Chicken, **'80** 38

Scotch Cream, Chicken in, **'88** 42
Seasoned Browned Chicken, **'85** 25
Seasoned Chicken, Crunchy, **'87** 217
Seasoning Blend, Poultry, **'88** 28
Sesame Chicken, **'85** 252; **'86** 122
Sesame Chicken, Hawaiian, **'81** 106
Sesame Chicken with Noodles, **'88** M125
Sherried Chicken, **'79** 214
Sherried Chicken with Artichokes, **'87** 143
Sherry Chicken with Rice, **'81** 97
Skillet, Cheesy Chicken, **'80** 115
Skillet Chicken, **'81** 180
Skillet Chicken Dinner, **'86** 249
Skillet Company Chicken, **'82** 60
Soufflé, Chicken-Chestnut, **'79** 107

Soups

Chicken Soup, **'81** 98
Chowder Sauterne, Chicken,
  '84 235
Chunky Chicken-Noodle Soup,
  '88 12
Cream of Chicken Soup, **'85** 243
Curried Chicken Soup, **'86** 34
Enchilada Soup, Chicken, **'86** 22
Ham, and Oyster Soup,
  Chicken, **'79** 198
Homemade Chicken Soup, **'82** 34
Lime Soup, **'88** 31
Mexican Chicken Soup, **'84** 234
Noodle Soup, Chicken, **'80** 264
Quick Chicken Soup, **'86** M72
Rice Soup, Chicken-and-, **'88** 236
Sopa de Lima, **'79** 211
Vegetable Soup, Chicken-, **'88** 18
Soy and Wine, Chicken in, **'84** 26
Spaghetti, Chicken, **'83** 105; **'87** 221
Spiced Chicken, Crunchy, **'85** M57
Spiced Fruited Chicken with Almond
  Rice, **'81** 195
Spicy Chicken Dish, **'87** 267; **'88** 103
Spinach Fettuccine, Easy Chicken
  with, **'88** 89
Spinach Noodles, Chicken and, **'82** 19
Spread, Festive Chicken, **'87** 158
Spread, Low-Fat Chicken, **'82** 290
Spread, Tasty Chicken, **'84** 193
Steamed Dinner, Easy, **'83** M314
Stew and Dumplings, Chicken, **'84** 4
Stew, Bama Brunswick, **'87** 4
Stew, Brunswick, **'80** 264
Stew, Brunswick Chicken, **'87** 4
Stew, Sonny Frye's Brunswick, **'87** 4
Stir-Fried Chicken Curry, **'87** 51
Stir-Fried Chicken, Zesty, **'83** 82
Stir-Fry Chicken à l'Orange, **'83** 82
Stir-Fry, Chicken and Vegetable, **'82** 237

Stir-Fry Chicken-and-Vegetables, '86 68
Stir-Fry Chicken and Vegetables, '86 249
Stir-Fry, Chicken-Broccoli, '82 33
Stir-Fry, Chicken-Vegetable, '83 151;
  '84 13, 141
Stir-Fry, Chicken-Zucchini, '84 50
Stir-Fry, Kyoto Orange-Chicken, '87 96
Stir-Fry, Orange-Chicken, '84 68
Stir-Fry Vegetables with Chicken, '84 195
Strips, Zippy Chicken, '84 205
Stuffed Chicken Breasts, '85 291; '87 36;
  '88 50
Stuffed Chicken Breasts, Peach-, '79 177
Stuffed Chicken Breasts Sardou, '87 269
Stuffed Chicken Breasts, Walnut-, '85 293
Stuffed Chicken Breasts with White Grape
  Sauce, '80 38
Stuffed Chicken, Crab-, '84 101
Stuffed Chicken, Rice-, '81 4
Stuffed Chicken Rolls, Spinach-, '86 248
Stuffed Chicken Thighs, '82 84
Stuffed Chicken, Wild Rice-, '79 219
Sunshiny Chicken, '81 309
Supreme, Hot Chicken, '81 76
Suprêmes de Volaille à Blanc (Chicken
  Breasts in Cream Sauce), '82 83
Sweet-and-Sour Chicken, '79 106; '83 184;
  '84 218; '86 217, 240
Sweet-and-Sour Lemon Chicken, '84 93
Sweet-and-Sour Shrimp and
  Chicken, '87 267; '88 103
Szechwan Chicken, '83 85
Szechwan Chicken with Cashews,
  '81 212
Tahitian Chicken, '84 68
Tamales, Chicken, '88 151
Tangy Chicken, '85 251; '86 292;
  '87 35
Tarragon Chicken, '86 231
Tempura Delight, Chicken, '85 66
Teriyaki, Chicken, '80 M76
Teriyaki Chicken Wings, '85 300; '86 18
Terrine, Chicken-Vegetable, '84 131
Terrine Ring, Chicken, '84 132
Terrine, Vegetable-Chicken, '83 224
Tetrazzini, Cheesy Chicken, '83 M87
Tetrazzini, Chicken, '79 268; '80 M75;
  '83 288
Tomato Aspic, Chicken in, '84 190
Tortilla Stack, Cheesy Chicken-, '86 3
Toss, Quick Chicken, '87 M124
Valencia, Chicken-and-Rice, '85 113
Vegetable Platter, Chicken-and-, '88 M52
Vegetables, Chicken and, '88 165
Vermouth, Chicken and
  Vegetables, '87 M37
Véronique, Chicken, '84 260; '85 302
Waffles, Southern Chicken-Pecan, '82 231
Walnut Chicken, '85 126
Walnut Chicken and Vegetables, '85 194
Wellington, Chicken Breasts, '84 22
Wild Rice, Chicken and, '79 248
Wild Rice, Elegant Chicken
  with, '80 M76
Wild Rice Supreme, Chicken-, '79 77
Wine, Chicken in White, '81 97
Wine Sauce, Chicken and Mushrooms
  in, '81 109
Wine Sauce, Chicken in, '80 8
Wings, Broiled Chicken, '80 149
Wings, Satan's, '87 214

Chili
Bake, Chili Hominy, '81 282; '82 58
Basic Chili, '82 M11
Burgers, Open-Face Chili, '82 31; '83 33
Casserole, Chili-Rice, '79 54
Casserole, Hominy-Chili, '86 255
Cheese-Topped Chili, '82 M11
Cheesy Chili, '82 310
Chili, '87 17
Chuck Wagon Chili, '81 282; '82 57
Chunky Chili, '82 M282; '86 3
Company Chili, '82 311; '83 30
con Carne, Beef and Sausage Chili, '83 284
con Carne, Chili, '82 310; '83 30; '84 72;
  '86 2
con Carne, Favorite Chili, '86 293
con Carne, Quick-and-Easy Chili, '86 2
Cowboy Chili, '86 2
Dip, Cheesy Chili, '80 150
Dip, Chili, '82 161; '88 218
Dogs, Chili-Cheese, '81 M176
Double-Meat Chili, '79 269; '80 12
Easy Chili, '82 310; '83 30
Eggplant Chili, '85 88
Friday Night Chili, '86 228
Hot Spiced Chili, '83 214
Lunchtime Chili, '81 230
Meat Loaf, Chili, '81 275
Meaty Chili, '81 282; '82 58
Meaty Chili with Beans, '85 250
Noodles, Chili with, '81 282; '82 57
Pie, Chili-Tamale, '82 9; '83 68
Potato Chili, Savory, '83 3
Potatoes, Chili-Topped, '83 3
Potatoes, South-of-the-Border
  Stuffed, '86 54
Quick and Simple Chili, '81 282; '82 58
Quick Chili, '83 283
Ranch Chili and Beans, '79 270; '80 11
Red Chili, North Texas, '87 303
Rice, Chili with, '82 M11
Roundup Chili, '79 269; '80 12
Salad, Spicy Chili, '86 71
Sauce, Chili, '81 175
Sauce, Chili Meat, '83 4
Sauce, Chunky Chili, '85 188
Sauce, Spicy Chili, '87 127
Sausage-Beef Chili, '86 232
Sausage Chili, Beefy, '82 M11
Simple Chili, '79 269; '80 11
South-of-the-Border Chili, '83 283
Spaghetti, Herbed Chili-, '84 222
Spicy Chili, Old-Fashioned, '79 269;
  '80 11
Surprise, Chili, '82 229
Texas Championship Chili, '81 54
Texas Chili, Hot, '80 222; '81 77
Texas-Style Chili, '82 311; '83 30
Tex-Mex Chili, '83 26
Topping, Chili, '84 246
Tree-Hunt Chili, '87 292
Turkey-Bean Chili, '88 M213
Vegetarian Chili, '84 280, 327
Venison Chili, '82 216; '86 3; '87 304
Zippy Chili, '87 110
Chocolate
Banana Pops, '84 44
Bars and Cookies
  Almond Chip Balls, Toasted, '84 240
  Almond-Chocolate Bars, '83 304
  Almond Cream Confections, '87 198

Almond Surprise Cookies,
  Chocolate-, '88 M45
Blond Nut Squares, '82 156
Brazil Squares, '82 306
Brownie Alaskas, '83 299
Brownie Bars, Cinnamon, '81 230
Brownie-Mint Dessert, '82 227
Brownie Mix, '82 6
Brownies, Amaretto, '86 246
Brownies, Buttermilk Cake, '87 198
Brownies, Chewy
  Marshmallow, '83 306
Brownies, Chocolate-Banana, '80 160
Brownies, Chocolate Chip, '81 162
Brownies, Chocolate Chip-Peanut
  Butter, '84 73
Brownies, Chocolate-Mint, '85 M294;
  '88 80
Brownies, Chocolate-Nut, '81 129
Brownies, Chocolate-Pecan, '81 64
Brownies,
  Chocolate-Peppermint, '88 262
Brownies, Chocolate Tea, '83 79
Brownies, Choco-Mallow, '87 198

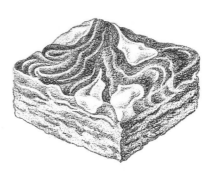

Brownies, Cream Cheese Swirl, '79 51
Brownies, Crème de Menthe, '83 244
Brownies, Crunch-Crust, '87 198
Brownies, Easy, '83 245
Brownies, Favorite, '86 158
Brownies, German Cream
  Cheese, '80 269
Brownies, Heavenly Hash, '83 245
Brownies, Heavenly Honey, '79 83
Brownies, Mocha, '87 93
Brownies, Nutty Blonde, '81 64
Brownies, Nutty Cocoa, '81 64
Brownies, Nutty Fudge, '80 M171
Brownies, Peanut Butter, '87 199
Brownies, Quick, '87 M302
Brownies, Quick and Easy, '82 6
Brownies, Rocky Road, '86 320
Brownies, Walnut-Cream
  Cheese, '84 240
Brownie Waffle Cookies, '86 245
Butter Cookies,
  Chocolate-Tipped, '84 258
Butterscotch Bars, Chocolate-, '81 197
By-Cracky Bars, '84 212
Caramel Layer Squares,
  Chocolate-, '79 83
Cherry Cookies, Chocolate-, '85 324
Chewy Chocolate Cookies, '80 208
Chip Bars, Chocolate, '81 130
Chip Cookies, '84 120

Chocolate, Bars and Cookies (continued)

Chip Cookies, Chocolate, '86 245
Chip Cookies,
    Chocolate-Chocolate, '82 35
Chips Cookies, Loaded-with-, '87 223
Chip Squares, Chocolate, '83 170
Cinnamon Bars, Chocolate, '82 209
Cocoa Drop Cookies, '80 217
Cocoa Kiss Cookies, '85 171
Crème de Menthe Bars,
    Chocolate-, '86 245
Crème de Menthe Bites,
    Chocolate, '88 285
Crispy Cookies, Chocolate, '85 115
Crumble Bars, Choco-, '79 292
Deluxe Chocolate Chip
    Cookies, '79 216
Devil Doggies, '84 37
Different Chocolate Chip
    Cookies, '83 114
Double Chip Cookies, '81 301
Double Chocolate Chip
    Cookies, '79 217
Doubly-Good Chocolate
    Cookies, '82 M185
Dream Bars, Chocolate, '79 256;
    '82 298
Drop Cookies, Chocolate, '84 36
Forget 'em Cookies, '83 256
Fudge Bars, '86 93
Fudge Bars, Yummy, '87 158
Giant Chocolate Chip Cookies, '84 119
Jumbo Chocolate Chip Cookies, '82 110
Light Chocolate Chip Cookies, '86 46
Log Cookies,
    Chocolate-Tipped, '87 294
Macaroon Cookies, Chocolate, '88 217
Macaroons, Chocolate, '83 300; '87 57
Meltaways, Chocolate, '81 302
Melt-Aways, Chocolate Chip, '84 118
Meringue-Chocolate Chip Bars, '84 118
Meringue Kiss Cookies, '86 121
Mint Chip Cookies, Chocolate-, '86 245
Mint Snaps, Chocolate-, '83 103;
    '84 96
Monster Cookies, '84 36
Nugget Cookies, '79 291
Nut Chews, Chocolate-, '81 92
Nut Freezer Cookies,
    Chocolate-, '88 217
Nutty Choco Snacks, '83 305
Nutty Oatmeal-Chocolate Chip
    Cookies, '82 M185
Oatmeal Bars,
    Chocolate-Topped, '86 110
Oatmeal Cookies, Chocolate-, '80 105
Oatmeal Cookies, Chocolate
    Chip-, '84 119
Orange-Chocolate Cookies, '83 113
Peanut Butter-and-Fudge
    Bars, '80 M172
Peanut Butter Bars, '84 243
Peanut Butter-Chocolate Chip Cookies,
    Freezer, '86 230
Peanut Butter-Chocolate Kiss
    Cookies, '86 49
Peanut Butter Cones,
    Chocolate-, '85 14
Peanut Butter Cookies,
    Chocolate-, '85 90

Peanut Butter Cups,
    Chocolate-, '85 14
Peanut Butter Fingers, '79 256
Peanut Butter Squares, Chocolate
    Chip-, '84 118
Peanut Cookies, Chocolate-, '83 223
Peppermint Squares,
    Chocolate-, '81 119
Pinwheel Cookies, Chocolate, '86 245
Sandwich Cookies, Chocolate, '81 192
Sandwich Cookies, Choco-Nut, '84 200
Sandwiches, Chocolate Cookie Ice
    Cream, '87 147
Shortbread Wafers, Cocoa, '88 243
Snappers, Jumbo Chocolate, '81 218
Snowball Cookies, Chocolate, '82 295

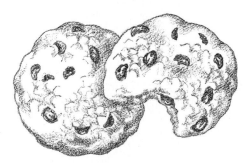

Super Chocolate Chunk
    Cookies, '88 217
Surprise Bonbon Cookies, '88 119
Surprise Cookies, Choco, '80 60
Teasers, Chocolate, '87 44
Whoopie Pies, '86 246
Beverages
    Brandied Chocolate, Flaming, '80 M290
    Café Colombian Royal, '80 M290
    Cappuccino, Chocolate Castle, '84 53
    Cocoa Mix, Instant, '86 332
    Coffee, Chocolate, '82 43
    Coffee, Chocolate-Almond, '84 54
    Coffee, Cocoa-, '83 55
    Coffee, Mexican, '83 175, 275;
        '88 247
    Hot Chocolate, Creole, '80 M290
    Hot Chocolate, Favorite, '83 55
    Hot Chocolate, French, '86 328
    Hot Chocolate Mix, Deluxe, '80 M290
    Hot Chocolate Mix, Spicy, '85 278
    Hot Chocolate, Old-Fashioned, '85 23
    Hot Chocolate, Special, '82 5
    Hot Chocolate, Spiced, '80 50
    Hot Chocolate, Spicy, '85 278
    Hot Cocoa Mix, '81 287
    Hot Cocoa, Quick, '82 5
    Malt, Chocolate, '86 183
    Mexican-Style Chocolate, '81 187
    Milk, French Chocolate, '79 38
    Mocha Cocoa, '83 318
    Mocha-Cocoa Mix, Hot, '82 296
    Mocha Coffee, '85 M329
    Mocha Cream, Café, '84 54
    Mocha Deluxe Hot Drink, '82 289
    Mocha Espresso, Italian, '82 254
    Mocha, Hot, '84 60
    Mocha Punch, '84 58, 166

Mocha, Quick Viennese, '79 232
Sipper, Chocolate, '88 83
Smoothie, Chocolate-Mint, '84 166
Bread, Chocolate Date-Nut, '81 284
Bread, Chocolate Loaf, '88 M188
Bread, Cocoa-Nut Swirl, '80 257
Buns, Chocolate-Cinnamon, '85 5
Buns, Chocolate Sticky, '81 300; '82 124
Cakes and Tortes
    Almond Cake with Cherry Filling,
        Chocolate-, '84 225
    Angel Cake, Chocolate, '88 128
    Angel Food Cake, Chocolate, '87 21
    Angel Food Cake with Custard Sauce,
        Chocolate, '88 259
    Banana Cake, Chocolate-, '86 138
    Banana-Cocoa Cupcakes, '80 130
    Banana Loaf, Chocolate Chip-, '85 115
    Beet Cake, Chocolate, '80 40
    Black Bottom Cups, '82 279
    Black Forest Cake, '81 126
    Black Forest Torte, '88 209
    Brownie Cupcakes, '82 280
    Brownie Delight, Chocolate, '87 224
    Brown Mountain Cake, '84 39
    Bûche de Noël, '84 304; '87 241
    Bûche de Noël Cake, '82 262
    Buttermilk Chocolate Cake, '79 13
    Candy Cake, Chocolate, '81 238
    Caramel-Nut Cake, Chocolate-, '83 23
    Cheesecake, Black Forest, '84 74
    Cheesecake, Candy Bar, '86 120
    Cheesecake, Chocolate, '81 16;
        '82 305
    Cheesecake,
        Chocolate-Amaretto, '85 M294
    Cheesecake, Chocolate Chip, '85 114
    Cheesecake, Chocolate-Glazed Triple
        Layer, '86 315
    Cheesecake, Chocolate Swirl, '84 295;
        '85 26
    Cheesecake, German
        Chocolate, '87 265
    Cheesecake, Marbled, '87 261
    Cheesecake, Marble Mint, '84 152
    Cheesecake, Mocha-Chocolate, '88 258
    Cheesecake, Mocha Swirl, '87 262
    Cheesecake, Rich Chocolate, '84 74;
        '85 38
    Cheesecake, White Chocolate, '87 44;
        '88 267
    Cherry Cake, Chocolate-, '84 200;
        '86 239
    Cinnamon-Chocolate
        Cupcakes, '81 M139
    Coconut Cake, Chocolate-, '83 23
    Coconut Cake, White
        Chocolate-, '87 263
    Coffee Cake, Chocolate-Chip, '79 249
    Coffee Cake, Chocolate Chip, '83 231
    Crumb Cake, Calico, '87 261
    Custard Cake, Chocolate, '88 175
    Decadent Chocolate Cake, '86 142
    Double-Chocolate Torte, '79 67
    Easy Chocolate Cake, '80 140
    Frosting, Chocolate Cake with
        Double, '86 314
    Fudge Cake, Best, '83 301
    Fudge Cake, Brown Sugar, '86 316
    Fudge Cake, Chocolate, '80 279
    Fudge Cake for Two, '81 205

German Chocolate Cake, '81 296;
'83 M233
German Chocolate Chip Cake, '86 247
Kahlúa Chocolate Cake, '81 303
Marble Chocolate Chip
Cupcakes, '81 239
Marbled Cake, Cocoa, '82 265
Marshmallow Cake, No-Egg
Chocolate, '87 M97
Mayonnaise Cake, Chocolate, '83 99
Mocha Brownie Torte, '85 102
Mocha Cake, Belgian, '84 316
Mocha Cake, Double, '84 311
Mocha-Chocolate Cake, Dark, '84 311
Mocha Cream Roll, Chocolate-, '84 304
Mocha Cupcakes, '85 250
Mocha-Pecan Torte, '86 26
Mousse Cake, Chocolate, '87 264
Mousse Roll, Chocolate, '88 280
Nut Cake, Rich Chocolate-, '86 8
Peanut Butter Cake,
Chocolate-, '84 240

Peanut Butter Cake, Fudgy, '85 91
Peanut Cluster Cake,
Chocolate-, '87 184
Perfect Chocolate Cake, '82 244
Pound Cake, Chocolate, '82 88;
'84 10
Pound Cake, Chocolate Chip, '86 178
Pound Cake, Chocolate Marble, '88 16
Pound Cake, Chocolate-Sour
Cream, '83 239
Pound Cake with Fudge Frosting,
Chocolate, '87 296
Praline Torte, Chocolate, '84 165
Pudding Cake, Hot Fudge, '88 255
Pudding, Chocolate Cake, '81 99
Rocky Road Cake, '81 178
Roll, Chocolate Cream, '85 317
Roll, Chocolate-Frosted Ice
Cream, '84 200
Roll, Chocolate Mousse, '83 290
Roll, Chocolate-Orange, '87 21
Royal, Chocolate Cake, '86 239
Royale, Chocolate Torte, '82 263
Rum Cake, Chocolate, '79 67
Sachertorte, '84 253
Self-Filled Cupcakes, '80 129
Sour Cream Cake, Chocolate-, '87 222
Sour Cream Cake, Chocolate
Chip-, '85 115
Sour Cream Chocolate Cake, '79 282
Sponge Cake, Chocolaty, '86 60

Strawberry Ice Cream Torte,
Chocolate-, '79 7
Sugar Cookie Torte, '79 68
Surprise Cupcakes, Chocolate, '85 91
Swiss Chocolate Chip Cake, '87 85
Triangle Cake, Chocolate, '85 126
Velvet Torte, Chocolate, '86 316
White Chocolate-Cherry Cake, '88 268
Yule Log, '79 281; '82 289
Zucchini Cake, Chocolate-, '85 156
Candies
Almond Roca, '86 49
Bourbon Balls, '83 315
Bourbon Balls, Chocolate, '84 298
Brittle, Chocolate, '83 315
Brittle, Quick Chocolate, '82 114
Butter Creams, '80 302
Cherries, Chocolate-Covered, '81 286;
'84 298
Coconut Almond Drops,
Chocolate-, '87 223
Cream-Filled Chocolates,
Liqueur, '87 258
Crème de Cacao Balls, '86 266
Drops, Chocolate, '84 111
Fudge, '86 266
Fudge, Cherry Nut, '83 315
Fudge, Chocolate, '82 20
Fudge, Chocolate-Peanut
Butter, '87 257
Fudge, Coffee-Chip, '86 74
Fudge, Cream Cheese, '84 111
Fudge, Creamy, '81 218
Fudge, Creamy Dark, '82 295
Fudge, Creamy Pecan, '84 321
Fudge, Dinner Mint, '88 285
Fudge, Double-Good, '79 M263
Fudge, Double Good, '87 M278
Fudge, Double Peanut, '85 91
Fudge, Fast, '79 274
Fudge, Holiday Mocha, '84 298
Fudge, Marbled Peanut Butter, '88 65
Fudge, Pistachio, '83 298
Fudge, Quick-and-Easy, '88 M190
Fudge, Quick Nut, '83 316
Fudge Scotch Ring, '79 273
Greeting Card, Chocolate, '83 40
Kentucky Colonels, '79 273
Millionaires, '79 M262
Mints, Dinner, '88 66
Molded Candies, '84 40
Nut Clusters, '81 254
Nut Log Candy, Chocolate-, '86 335
Peanut Butter Balls, Chocolate-, '80 87
Peanut Butter-Chocolate Balls, '80 269
Peanut Butter-Chocolate Candy
Squares, '82 56
Peanut Butter Creams, '79 273
Peanut Clusters, Chocolate-, '81 16
Peanutty Clusters, '83 143
Pecan Fritters,
Chocolate-Covered, '79 205
Pretzels, Chocolate-Covered, '82 295
Rocky Road, '84 298
Rum Balls, Chocolate, '80 302
Rum Balls, Chocolate-, '88 285
Spiders, Chocolate, '85 236
Spirited Chocolates, '86 278
Tiger Butter, '86 48
Toffee, English, '79 273
Toffee, Nutty, '79 M263

Truffles, Almond, '83 298
Truffles, Amaretto Dessert, '86 319
Truffles, Chocolate, '85 114
Truffles, White Chocolate, '87 45
Velvets, Chocolate, '84 298
Cannoli, '80 58
Charlotte Russe, Chocolate, '87 74
Cocoa to Chocolate Equivalents, '84 200
Combo, Strawberry-Chocolate, '85 96
Cream, Heavenly Chocolate, '88 128
Cream, Strawberries with Chocolate, '85 81
Crêpes, Chocolate, '86 164
Crêpes, Chocolate Chantilly, '82 183
Crêpes, Chocolate Dessert, '84 84;
'85 262
Crêpes, Chocolate Dream, '86 164
Crêpes, Chocolate-Orange, '85 263
Crust, Chocolate, '87 264
Crust, Chocolate-Coconut, '87 261
Crust, Chocolate Crumb, '87 261

Cups, Chocolate, '80 207
Cups, Chocolate Lace, '87 133
Cups, Chocolate-Mint, '80 71
Cups, Chocolate-Walnut, '85 213
Cups, Miniature Chocolate, '87 132
Custard, Chocolate, '88 258
Custard, Chocolate-Topped
Amaretto, '87 M37
Date-Nut Delight, Chocolate, '88 168
Dessert, Chilled Chocolate, '83 177
Dessert, Chocolate-Almond, '82 306
Dessert, Chocolate-Coffee Frozen, '85 172
Dessert, Chocolate Dream, '83 198
Dessert, Chocolate Ladyfinger, '86 162
Dessert, Chocolate-Rum, '81 247
Dessert, Chocolate Truffle, '88 281
Dessert, Choco-Maple Frozen, '86 300;
'87 178
Dessert, Cool Chocolate-Mint, '80 109
Dessert, Easy Chocolate, '79 75
Dessert, Frozen Chocolate, '83 76
Dessert, Fudge-Peanut Ice Cream, '88 167
Dessert, Layered Ice Cream, '83 189
Dessert, Peanut-Chocolate, '80 86
Dessert Squares,
Chocolate-Blueberry, '87 299
Doughnuts, Chocolate, '83 95
Doughnuts, Chocolate-Covered, '84 55
Doughnuts, Chocolate-Glazed Potato, '85 6
Frostings, Fillings, and Toppings
Almond Frosting, Chocolate-, '83 241
Buttercream, Chocolate, '84 156
Candy Frosting, Chocolate, '81 238
Chocolate Frosting, '80 M171;
'81 265; '82 262; '83 79, 99,
M233, 253; '84 200; '85 323;
'86 8, 93, 138, 239, 314; '87 M97,
198, 199, 293

Chocolate, Frostings *(continued)*

Cocoa Frosting, **'86** 60
Coconut Chocolate Frosting, **'79** 13
Coffee Frosting, Chocolate-, **'84** 36; **'88** 269
Creamy Chocolate Frosting, **'85** 314; **'86** 316; **'87** 241
Creamy Chocolate Glaze, **'82** 88
Fluffy Chocolate Frosting, **'86** 336; **'87** 58
Fudge Frosting, **'81** 303; **'87** 296
Fudge Frosting, Chocolate, **'83** 105
Fudge Frosting, Quick, **'81** 278
Glaze, Chocolate, **'81** 119; **'83** 220; **'84** 10, 55, 253; **'85** 6; **'86** 315, 316
Glaze, White Cake with Strawberries and Chocolate, **'87** 76
Honey Chocolate Frosting, **'79** 83
Honey Glaze, Chocolate-, **'82** 306
Marshmallow Frosting, Chocolate-, **'83** 245
Mocha Butter Cream Frosting, **'79** 281
Mocha-Buttercream Frosting, **'86** 26
Mocha Cream Filling, **'84** 305
Mocha Frosting, **'83** 301; **'84** 316; **'87** 224
Mocha Frosting, Creamy, **'82** 289; **'84** 311
Nut Frosting, Chocolate, **'80** 140
Peanut Butter Frosting, Chocolate-, **'84** 240; **'87** 222
Peanut Butter-Fudge Frosting, **'87** 184
Peanut Topping, Chocolate-, **'79** 222
Rich Chocolate Filling, **'79** 68
Rich Chocolate Frosting, **'84** 304
Rum Frosting, Chocolate, **'79** 67
Satiny Chocolate Frosting, **'85** 126
Truffle Filling, Chocolate, **'87** 69
White Chocolate Frosting, **'88** 280

Garnishes, Chocolate, **'85** 16
Gâteau Panache, **'83** 269
Granola with Chocolate Morsels, **'86** 69
Ice Cream Balls, Easy, **'84** 106
Ice Cream, Chocolate, **'80** 176; **'86** 129
Ice Cream, Chocolate Chunk-Peanut Butter, **'85** 297; **'86** 120
Ice Cream, Chocolate-Covered Peanut, **'88** 203
Ice Cream, Double-Chocolate, **'88** 203
Ice Cream, Mint-Chocolate Chip, **'88** 202
Ice Cream, Mocha, **'88** 202
Kahlúa Delight, **'83** 67
Leaves, Chocolate, **'88** 281
Loaf, Chocolate Pinwheel, **'80** 256
Meringue Fingers, Chocolate-Almond, **'84** 158

Mexican Fiesta Confection, **'82** 223
Mint Dessert, Chocolate-, **'82** 100
Mint Freeze, Chocolate, **'88** 167
Mocha Alaska Dessert, **'84** 191
Mocha Chiffon, **'86** 75
Mocha Dessert, Frozen, **'84** 311
Mocha Freeze, Royal, **'84** 53
Mocha-Mallow Parfaits, **'80** 219
Mocha Squares, Frozen, **'81** 187
Mousse, Amaretto-Chocolate, **'86** 50
Mousse Baked Alaska, Chocolate, **'85** 195
Mousse, Blender Chocolate, **'82** 71
Mousse, Blender-Quick Chocolate, **'80** 269
Mousse, Brandy-Chocolate, **'85** 102
Mousse, Chocolate, **'88** 280
Mousse, Chocolate-Orange, **'81** 16, 205
Mousse, Chocolate Rum, **'86** 189
Mousse, Creamy Chocolate, **'87** 133
Mousse, Elegant Amaretto-Chocolate, **'86** 337
Mousse, Honeyed Chocolate, **'87** 223
Mousse, Quick Chocolate, **'85** 87
Parfaits, Chocolate-Crème de Menthe, **'85** 161
Parfaits, Chocolate-Peppermint, **'88** 65
Parfaits, Speedy, **'83** 76
Pies and Tarts
Almond Pie, Creamy Chocolate-, **'85** 102
Amandine, Chocolate Pie, **'83** 300
Amaretto Heavenly Tarts, Chocolate-, **'88** 4
Amaretto Mousse Pie, Chocolate-, **'80** 180; **'81** 30
Berry Pie, Heavenly Chocolate-, **'85** 102
Best-Ever Chocolate Pie, **'88** M45
Black Bottom Pie, **'82** 53
Bourbon Pie, Chocolate, **'88** 99
Brownie Pie, Crustless, **'82** 33
Chess Pie, Chocolate, **'81** 161; **'86** 220
Chilled Chocolate Pie, **'88** 99
Chip Pie, Chocolate, **'85** 114
Cream Cheese Pie, Chocolate-, **'80** 69
Cream Pie, Chocolate, **'83** 192; **'84** 49; **'87** 208
Creamy Chocolate Pie, **'85** 298; **'86** 119
Double Chocolate Pie, **'82** M282
Easy Chocolate Pie, **'83** 158
French Silk Pie, **'80** 247
French Silk Tarts, **'79** 236
Frozen Chocolate Pie, **'80** 154
Fudge Pie, **'87** 168
Fudge Pie, Sweetheart, **'86** 316
Heavenly Chocolate Pie, **'87** 260
Ice Cream Pie, Chocolate-, **'87** 224
Kahlúa Pie, **'83** 191
Kentucky Derby Tarts, **'79** 102
Meringue Pie, Chocolate, **'80** 238; **'82** 206; **'83** 158
Meringue Pie, Chocolate-Filled, **'86** 121
Mint Ice Cream Pie, Chocolate-, **'81** 144
Mocha Crunch Pie, Chocolate-, **'81** 136
Mocha Meringue Pie, **'80** 242
Mousse Pie, Chocolate, **'81** 136
Mud Pie, Tipsy, **'80** 255
Peanut Butter Pie, Chocolate-, **'85** 91

Peanut Butter Swirl Pie, Chocolate-, **'87** 262
Pecan Pie, Choco-, **'82** 86
Pecan Pie, Chocolate, **'80** 237; **'83** 12
Praline Pie, Chocolate-, **'86** 259
Silk Pie, Chocolate, **'88** 67
Tin Roof Pie, **'85** 91
Whipped Cream Pie, Chocolate, **'79** 124
Pots de Chocolat, Petits, **'82** 272
Pots de Crème, **'81** 15; **'84** M145
Pots de Crème, Mocha, **'88** M45
Pots de Crème, Rum-Flavored, **'85** 102
Pudding, Brownie, **'79** 265; **'80** 295
Pudding, Chocolate-Almond, **'82** 142; **'88** 24
Pudding, Chocolate Bread, **'80** 8
Pudding, Creamy Chocolate, **'83** 106
Pudding, Hot Fudge, **'81** 208
Pudding, Hot Fudge Sundae Cake, **'88** 167
Pudding with Lemon Meringue, Chocolate, **'88** 258
Roulage, Chocolate-Mocha, **'80** 216
Sauces
Cherry Sauce, Chocolate-, **'85** 189
Cherry Sauce, Chocolate, **'87** M165
Chocolate Sauce, **'83** 189; **'84** 208, 313; **'86** 322
Cinnamon-Fudge Sauce, **'85** 141
Classic Chocolate Sauce, **'85** 207
Creamy Chocolate Sauce, **'88** M177
Double Chocolate Sauce, **'83** 79
Heavenly Chocolate Sauce, **'79** 79; **'82** 167
Hot Fudge Sauce, **'82** 181, 295; **'84** 143
Hot Fudge Sauce, Easy, **'84** 69
Hot Fudge Sauce, Quick, **'82** 212
Kahlúa Chocolate Sauce, **'85** 155
Mint Sauce, Quick Chocolate, **'86** M58
Orange Sauce, Chocolate-, **'86** 165
Peanut Butter Sauce, Chocolate-, **'79** 91, M156
Praline Sauce, Chocolate-, **'85** M295
Supreme, Chocolate Sauce, **'85** 189
Shavings, Chocolate Hearts and, **'86** 26
Shell, Chocolate-Coconut Pie, **'82** 210; **'83** 100
Shell, Chocolate Pastry, **'87** 262
Shells with Kahlúa Cream, Chocolate, **'88** 195
Soufflé, Chocolate, **'84** 317
Soufflé, Chocolate Mint, **'81** 16
Soufflé, Light Chocolate, **'83** 278
Spread, Chocolate Cheese, **'87** 292
Sundae Dessert, Hot Fudge, **'84** 313; **'86** 322
Sundaes, Cocoa-Kahlúa, **'83** M58
Supreme, Chocolate, **'84** 94
Trifle, Chocolate, **'88** 258
Velvet, Chocolate Almond, **'81** 148
Waffles with Strawberry Cream, Chocolate, **'88** 153
Chop Suey
Cabbage Chop Suey, **'81** 101
Chicken Chop Suey, **'81** 227
Salad, Chop Suey, **'81** 37
Chowders
Bluefish Chowder, **'84** 282
Broccoli Chowder, **'79** 16
Cabbage Chowder, Hearty, **'80** 25

Cheddar Chowder, Hearty, **'79** 16
Cheese Chowder, Golden, **'80** 73
Chicken Chowder, **'83** 20
Chicken Chowder Sauterne, **'84** 235
Clam Chowder, **'79** 182; **'81** 32; **'85** 9;
 '86 36
Clam Chowder, New England, **'86** M72
Clam Chowder, Ocracoke, **'79** 31
Clam Chowder, Tomato-, **'84** 251
Corn and Cheese Chowder, **'80** 228
Corn Chowder, **'81** 128; **'83** 20; **'84** M38;
 '85 10
Corn Chowder, Delicious, **'82** 279
Fish Chowder, **'79** 152; **'84** M38
Fish Chowder, Basque, **'86** 36
Fish Chowder, Creamy, **'79** 16
Fish Chowder, Tasty, **'80** 188
Ham and Corn Chowder, **'79** 16
Ham-and-Corn Chowder, **'82** 40
Ham Chowder, Creamy, **'88** M53
Ham 'n Cheese Chowder, **'79** 199
Harvest Chowder, **'83** 317
Mushroom Chowder, **'79** 16
Okra Chowder, Quick, **'80** 185
Oyster Chowder, **'83** 229
Oyster-Corn Chowder, **'83** 211
Sausage-Bean Chowder, **'83** 20
Seafood Chowder, **'85** 9
Seafood Chowder, Southern, **'83** 20
Shrimp and Corn Chowder, **'79** 199
Snapper Chowder, Red, **'85** 217
Swiss-Broccoli Chowder, **'80** 73
Turkey Chowder, **'85** 10
Turkey-Corn Chowder, **'81** 98
Vegetable Chowder, Cheesy, **'80** 25;
 '83 20
Vegetable Chowder, Hearty, **'88** 56

Chow Mein
 Beef-and-Vegetable Chow Mein
  Casserole, **'83** 313
 Noodles, Chow Mein over Crispy, **'85** 286
 Pork Chow Mein, **'80** 208
 Shrimp Chow Mein, **'82** 30

Christmas. *See also* Cookies/Christmas.
 Bread, Christmas, **'87** 296; **'88** 288
 Bread, Norwegian Christmas, **'79** 234
 Cake, Christmas Coconut, **'82** 262
 Cinnamon Ornaments, **'85** 284
 Cœur à la Crème, Christmas, **'86** 278
 Coffee Cakes, Christmas-Tree, **'87** 298
 Cookie Advent Calendar, **'85** 325
 Cookie Cards, Christmas, **'84** 302
 Cookie, Rudolph, **'80** 279, 303
 Cookie, Santa Claus, **'80** 278, 303
 Cookies, Christmas Cherry, **'88** 282
 Cookies, Christmas Date, **'88** 287
 Cookies, Eggnog Christmas, **'79** 255
 Cookie, Sleigh, **'80** 279, 303
 Cookies, Painted, **'86** 322
 Cookies, Spiced Christmas, **'87** 294
 Cookies, Swedish Christmas, **'79** 290
 Cottage, Sugarplum, **'88** 309
 Dessert, White Christmas, **'82** 261
 Divinity, Christmas, **'81** 286
 Fruit Squares, Christmas, **'88** 282
 Jam, Christmas, **'88** 288
 Jam, Christmas Brunch, **'81** 286
 Jelly, Christmas Freezer, **'86** M288
 Lizzies, Christmas, **'87** 257
 Loaf, Sweet Christmas, **'84** 278
 Pie, White Christmas, **'88** 281

Potatoes, Christmas, **'88** 252
Pudding with Brandy Sauce, Baked
 Christmas, **'88** 279
Punch, Christmas, **'84** 259
Punch, Christmas Eve, **'86** 314
Punch, Merry Christmas, **'79** 285
Relish Tree, Christmas, **'84** 257
Salad, Christmas, **'88** 249
Salad, Christmas Snow, **'82** 266
Salad, Cranberry Christmas, **'79** 243
Salad, Eggnog Christmas, **'86** 281
Sandwich Wreath, Festive, **'86** 333
Santa's Whiskers, **'85** 323
Scent, Christmas, **'84** 325
Spices, Barclay House Mulling, **'86** 289
Strawberries, Christmas, **'87** 293
Tea, Christmas Fruit, **'83** 275
Wreath, Christmas, **'80** 280
Wreath, Della Robbia Fruit, **'87** 294

Clams
 Backyard Clambake, **'81** 92
 Bisque, Clam, **'86** 228
 Casino, Clams, **'81** 125
 Chase, Clams, **'79** 85
 Chowder, Clam, **'79** 182; **'81** 32; **'85** 9;
  '86 36
 Chowder, New England Clam, **'86** M72
 Chowder, Ocracoke Clam, **'79** 31
 Chowder, Southern Seafood, **'83** 20
 Chowder, Tomato-Clam, **'84** 251
 Cocktail, Tomato-Clam, **'87** 252
 Crisps, Clam, **'80** 151
 Dip, Clam, **'79** 151; **'80** 265
 Dip, Hot Clam, **'82** 59
 Fritters, Clam, **'79** 151; **'86** 71
 Oreganata, Clams, **'85** 104
 Pizza, Baby Clam, **'87** 182
 Quiche, Clam, **'83** 215
 Sauce, Linguine in Clam, **'81** 83
 Sauce, Linguine with Clam, **'84** 124;
  '88 90
 Sauce, Pasta with Clam, **'84** 291
 Sauce, Vermicelli and Sprouts with Red
  Clam, **'86** 143
 Sauce, Vermicelli with Clam, **'85** 295
 Sauce with Linguine, Clam, **'84** 9
 Shells, Baked Clam, **'87** 94
 Soup, Clam Florentine, **'85** 23

Coconut
 Ambrosia, Anytime, **'86** 182
 Ambrosia, Baked, **'83** 303
 Ambrosia Bowl, **'80** 138; **'84** 313
 Ambrosia, Brunch, **'83** 57
 Ambrosia Cake, **'79** 229
 Ambrosia Cookies, **'86** 313
 Ambrosia Cream Cheese Mold, **'79** 249
 Ambrosia, Custard Sauce, **'84** 256
 Ambrosia, Honey Bee, **'83** 267
 Ambrosia, Mixed Fruit, **'83** 10
 Ambrosia Mold, **'79** 241
 Ambrosia, Old-Fashioned, **'80** 5
 Ambrosia, Peach, **'83** 53
 Ambrosia Pie, **'79** 284
 Ambrosia Salad, **'83** 231
 Ambrosia, Sherried, **'84** 324; **'86** 317
 Ambrosia Supreme, Orange, **'79** 37
 Ambrosia, Tropical, **'79** 74
 Balls, Coconut-Almond, **'84** 256
 Bars, Coconut Granola, **'85** 202
 Bars, Golden, **'84** 255
 Bars, Hawaiian, **'84** 153

Bonbons, Coconut-Black Walnut, **'82** 307
Bread, Coconut, **'83** 140
Bread, Pumpkin-Coconut, **'87** 255
Cake, Apple Coconut, **'80** 226
Cake, Chocolate-Coconut, **'83** 23
Cake, Christmas Coconut, **'82** 262
Cake, Coconut Cream, **'81** 179
Cake, Coconut-Cream Cheese
 Pound, **'85** 297
Cake, Coconut Cream Pound, **'84** 10
Cake, Coconut-Pineapple Layer, **'80** 140
Cake, Coconut Pound, **'82** 87
Cake, Coconut-Spice, **'84** 255; **'87** 296
Cake, Creamy Coconut, **'84** 43
Cake, Fresh Coconut, **'80** 289; **'82** 52;
 '85 281
Cake, Fresh Coconut-Carrot, **'80** 299
Cake, Lemon-Coconut Cream, **'81** 179
Cake, Lemon-Coconut Sheet, **'85** 117
Cake, Oatmeal-Coconut Coffee, **'83** 312
Cake, Regal Coconut, **'83** 299
Cake Roll, Coconut-Pineapple, **'84** 304
Cake, Rum-Orange Coconut, **'88** 224
Cake, Spiked Coconut Angel, **'85** 279
Cake, Stately Coconut Layer, **'81** 70
Cake, Toasted Coconut, **'86** 60
Cake, White Chocolate-Coconut, **'87** 263
Candy, Coconut, **'79** 272; **'80** 250
Cloud, Coconut, **'80** 70
Clusters, Pecan-Coconut, **'86** M251

Cookies, Chocolate Macaroon, **'88** 217
Cookies, Coconut-Cherry, **'79** 292
Cookies, Crinkle Sunflower, **'83** 149
Cookies, Oatmeal-Coconut, **'80** 218
Cookies, Peanut Butter-Coconut, **'83** 113
Cream, Orange-Coconut, **'84** 24
Crust, Chocolate-Coconut, **'87** 261
Custard, Coconut, **'86** 109
Dessert, Chilled Coconut, **'83** 116
Dessert, Macaroon-Sherbet Frozen, **'79** 212
Dip, Coconut-Honey Fruit, **'84** 171
Dressing, Coconut, **'87** 251
Dressing, Orange-Coconut, **'80** 158
Dressing, Tangy Coconut-Fruit, **'84** 171
Drink, Coconut-Pineapple, **'83** 172
Drops, Chocolate-Coconut Almond, **'87** 223
English Cherubs, **'83** 257
Filling, Coconut, **'81** 265
Filling, Coconut Cream, **'84** 200
Frosting, Coconut, **'82** 262
Frosting, Coconut Chocolate, **'79** 13
Frosting, Coconut Cream Cheese, **'86** 60

Coconut *(continued)*

Frosting, Coconut-Pecan, '81 296;
    '83 M233; '84 43, 322
Frosting, Creamy Coconut, '80 287
Frosting, Nutty Coconut, '86 8
Frost, Pink Coconut, '79 174; '80 128
Fruit Bowl, Coconut, '83 111
Ice Cream, Coconut Fried, '85 141
Ice Cream, Fresh Coconut, '79 166
Macaroon Charlotte, '81 296
Macaroons, Chocolate, '83 300
Macaroons, Coconut, '79 52
Macaroon-Stuffed Peaches, '79 178

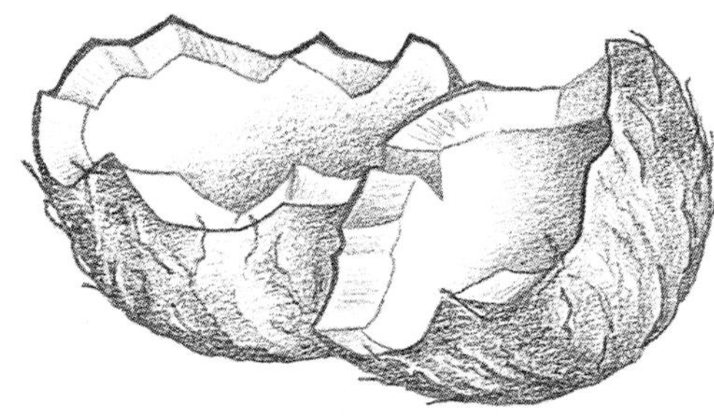

Muffins, Coconut-Molasses, '82 210
Nests, Strawberry Coconut, '88 136
Nog, Coconut, '83 275
Pears, Spicy Coconut, '83 207
Pie, Blender Coconut, '84 236
Pie, Coconut Chess, '86 220
Pie, Coconut Cream, '80 238; '81 136;
    '82 85; '84 49; '87 207
Pie, Coconut Custard, '82 33
Pie, Coconut Macaroon, '88 204
Pie, Coconut Pecan, '81 161
Pie, Coconut-Pecan Chess, '81 248
Pie, Coconut-Pineapple, '84 256
Pie, Fresh Coconut Cream, '80 289
Pie, Magic Coconut, '79 53
Pie, Mock Coconut, '86 200
Pie, Quick Coconut, '83 115
Pies, Coconut-Caramel, '87 260
Pie Shell, Chocolate-Coconut, '82 210;
    '83 100
Potatoes, Coconut-Broiled Sweet, '84 231
Potatoes, Coconut-Orange Sweet, '84 252
Potatoes, Coconut-Stuffed Sweet, '82 204
Puffs, Coconut, '87 277
Salad, Chunky Fruit-and-Coconut, '84 24
Sauce, Coconut-Orange, '85 189
Sauce, Creamy Light Coconut, '82 177
Shrimp, Coconut-Beer, '85 230
Soufflé, Coconut, '79 73; '85 212
Tropical Snow, '86 34

Coffee

After-Dinner Coffee, '81 262
Almond-Coffee Delight, '84 115
Brandied Coffee, '81 244
Cake, Coffee Sponge, '83 229
Cake, Two-Day Coffee Sponge, '86 75
Cappuccino, Café, '82 253
Cappuccino, Chocolate Castle, '84 53
Cappuccino, Flaming, '79 293
Chocolate-Almond Coffee, '84 54
Chocolate Coffee, '82 43

Cocoa-Coffee, '83 55
Colombian Royal, Café, '80 M290
Cream, Café, '82 312
Cream, Icy Rum Coffee, '83 172
Cream Puffs, Java, '81 187
Creamy Coffee, '81 244
Crêpes, Coffee Ice Cream, '84 85
Dessert, Chocolate-Coffee Frozen, '85 172
Dessert, Light Coffee, '88 260
Diablo, Café, '80 259
Floats, Maple-Coffee, '86 195
Frosted Coffee, '81 244
Frosting, Chocolate-Coffee, '84 36; '88 269
Fudge, Coffee-Chip, '86 74
Granita, Coffee-Kahlúa, '88 118
Ice Cream, Coffee, '88 202
Ice Cream Crunch, Coffee, '82 182
Irish Coffee, Creamy, '79 232
Irish Coffee, Flaming, '79 293
Irish Coffee Nog, '84 258
Kahlúa Delight, Make-Ahead, '84 M89
Kona Luscious, '84 54
Liqueur, Coffee-Flavored, '86 266
Mallow, Coffee, '80 109
Mexican Coffee, '83 175, 275; '88 247
Mix, Fireside Coffee, '87 241
Mocha Alaska Dessert, '84 191
Mocha-Almond Dessert, '80 289; '81 62
Mocha Brownies, '87 93
Mocha Brownie Torte, '85 102
Mocha Butter Cream Frosting, '79 281
Mocha-Buttercream Frosting, '86 26
Mocha Cake, Belgian, '84 316
Mocha Cake, Double, '84 311
Mocha Chiffon, '86 75
Mocha-Chocolate Cake, Dark, '84 311
Mocha-Chocolate Cheesecake, '88 258
Mocha Cocoa, '83 318
Mocha-Cocoa Mix, Hot, '82 296
Mocha Coffee, '85 M329
Mocha Cream, Café, '84 54
Mocha Cream Filling, '81 187; '84 305
Mocha Cream Roll, Chocolate, '84 304
Mocha Crunch Pie, Chocolate-, '81 136
Mocha Cupcakes, '85 250
Mocha Deluxe Hot Drink, '82 289
Mocha Dessert, Frozen, '84 311
Mocha Espresso, Italian, '82 254
Mocha Filling, '80 55; '82 262
Mocha Freeze, Royal, '84 53
Mocha Frosting, '83 301; '84 316; '87 224
Mocha Frosting, Creamy, '82 289; '84 311
Mocha Gingerbread, '81 207; '82 14
Mocha, Hot, '84 60
Mocha Ice Cream, '88 202
Mocha-Mallow Parfaits, '80 219
Mocha Meringue Pie, '80 242; '88 163
Mocha Pots de Crème, '88 M45
Mocha Punch, '84 58, 166; '86 270
Mocha, Quick Viennese, '79 232
Mocha Roulage, Chocolate-, '80 216
Mocha Squares, Frozen, '81 187
Mocha Swirl Cheesecake, '87 202
Mocha, Swiss-Style, '82 253
Mousse, Coffee, '84 126
Mousse, Coffee-Nut, '86 319
Mousse, Quick-as-a-Wink, '84 311
Nog, Brandied Coffee, '86 329
Orange Coffee, Viennese, '84 54
Parfaits, Coffee Crunch, '82 159
Pecans, Coffee 'n' Spice, '88 256

Pie, Coffee Ice Cream, '79 231
Pie, Coffee Pecan, '82 74
Praline-Flavored Coffee, '87 69
Pralines, Plantation Coffee, '86 241
Punch, Coffee, '80 50; '83 275; '88 83
Punch, Coffee-and-Cream, '85 116
Punch, Coffee-Eggnog, '86 281
Punch, Creamy Coffee, '81 50
Punch, Rich-and-Creamy Coffee, '82 121
Refresher, Velvet Coffee, '79 149
Royal, Café, '80 259
Spiced Coffee, Special, '84 284
Tortoni, Coffee-Almond, '81 30
Tortoni, Creamy Coffee, '88 268
Viennese, Café, '82 254

Coleslaw. *See* Cabbage or Salads.

Cookies

Almond Butter Cookies, '79 52
Almond Chip Balls, Toasted, '84 240
Almond Cookies, '83 22, 181
Almond Cookies, Light, '83 151
Almond Cookies, Swedish, '85 312
Almond Spritz Cookies, '82 306
Bars and Squares
    Almond Cake Squares, '79 111
    Almond-Chocolate Bars, '83 304
    Almond Cream Confections, '87 198
    Apple Butter Bars, '84 153
    Apple Kuchen, '79 24
    Apricot Bars, '81 247
    Apricot-Oatmeal Bars, '86 216
    Apricot-Raisin Bars, '87 32
    Banana Breakfast Bars, '79 124
    Blackberry Bars, '87 130
    Blackberry-Filled Bars, '79 124
    Blackberry Jam Bars, '82 M185
    Blondie Swirls, '85 248
    Blond Nut Squares, '82 156
    Brazil Squares, '82 306
    Brownie Alaskas, '83 299
    Brownie Bars, Cinnamon, '81 230

    Brownie-Mint Dessert, '82 227
    Brownie Mix, '82 6
    Brownies, Amaretto, '86 246
    Brownies, Buttermilk, '85 249
    Brownies, Buttermilk Cake, '87 198
    Brownies, Butterscotch, '85 248
    Brownies, Cheesecake, '85 249
    Brownies, Chewy
        Marshmallow, '83 306
    Brownies, Chocolate-Banana, '80 160
    Brownies, Chocolate Chip, '81 162
    Brownies, Chocolate Chip-Peanut
        Butter, '84 73
    Brownies, Chocolate-Mint, '85 M294;
        '88 80

Brownies, Chocolate-Nut, '81 129
Brownies, Chocolate-Pecan, '81 64
Brownies,
    Chocolate-Peppermint, '88 262
Brownies, Chocolate Tea, '83 79
Brownies, Choco-Mallow, '87 198
Brownies, Cream Cheese Swirl, '79 51
Brownies, Crème de Menthe, '83 244
Brownies, Crunch-Crust, '87 198
Brownies, Date-and-Almond, '88 217
Brownies, Easy, '83 245
Brownies, Favorite, '86 158
Brownies, Frosted Apple, '86 216
Brownies, German Cream
    Cheese '80 269
Brownies, Heavenly Hash, '83 245
Brownies, Heavenly Honey, '79 83
Brownies, Mocha, '87 93
Brownies, Nutty Blonde, '81 64
Brownies, Nutty Cocoa, '81 64
Brownies, Nutty Fudge, '80 M171
Brownies, Oatmeal, '87 199
Brownies, Peanut Butter, '87 199
Brownies, Quick, '87 M302
Brownies, Quick and Easy, '82 6
Brownies, Rocky Road, '86 320
Brownies, Saucepan Pretzel, '85 171
Brownies, Walnut-Cream
    Cheese, '84 240
Butter Pecan Pie Squares, '81 262
Butterscotch Bars, '82 209; '83 297
By-Cracky Bars, '84 212
Carrot-Lemon Squares, Golden, '80 40
Carrot Squares, '79 256
Cherry Bars, Delightful, '86 217
Cherry Squares, Surprise, '82 57
Choco-Crumble Bars, '79 292
Chocolate-Butterscotch Bars, '81 197
Chocolate-Caramel Layer
    Squares, '79 83
Chocolate Chip Bars, '81 130
Chocolate Chip-Peanut Butter
    Squares, '84 118
Chocolate Chip Squares, '83 170
Chocolate Cinnamon Bars, '82 209
Chocolate-Crème de Menthe
    Bars, '86 245
Chocolate Crème de Menthe
    Bites, '88 285
Chocolate Dream Bars, '79 256;
    '82 298
Chocolate-Peppermint Squares, '81 119
Cinnamon Chews, '84 110
Coconut Granola Bars, '85 202
Coffee Bars, Frosted, '79 256
Date Bars, '84 313
Date Bars, No-Bake, '79 256
Date Bars, Nutty, '84 153
Date-Nut Bars, '80 166
Date-Oat Bars, '80 M172
English Cherubs, '83 257
Fudge Bars, '86 93
Fudge Bars, Yummy, '87 158
Golden Bars, '84 255
Granola Bars, '83 305
Granola Bars, Fruit and Nut, '81 49
Hawaiian Bars, '84 153
Jam-It Bars, '87 159
Jam Squares, '81 M289
Janhagel Cookies, '86 195
Lemon Bars Deluxe, '79 35

Lemon Bars, Tangy, '86 217
Lemon Squares, '81 197
Lemon Yogurt Wheat Bars, '79 93
Lime Squares, '79 2
Marmalade Biscuit Squares, '79 193
Meringue-Chocolate Chip Bars, '84 118
Mincemeat-Spice Bars, '88 231
Nutmeg Logs, Frosted, '85 324
Nutty Choco Snacks, '83 305
Oatmeal Bars,
    Chocolate-Topped, '86 110
Oatmeal-Caramel Bars, '85 247
Oatmeal-Date Bars, Layered, '85 10
Peanut Bars, Chewy, '80 M172
Peanut Butter-and-Fudge
    Bars, '80 M172
Peanut Butter Bars, '84 243
Peanut Butter Fingers, '79 256
Peanut Butter Frosts, '84 153
Peanut Butter Logs, No-Bake, '84 211
Peanut Butter 'n' Jelly Bars, '83 305
Peanut Butter Squares, '83 116
Pecan Bars, '82 209
Pecan Squares, '79 205
Pecan Squares, Easy, '81 230
Pecan Squares, Twice-Baked, '79 291
Pumpkin Bars, '80 40
Pumpkin Nut Bars, '82 217
Raspberry Bars, '82 209; '84 212
Rhubarb Squares, Rosy, '79 111
Strawberry Bars, '81 301
Tropical Bars, '80 284
Wheat Germ Squares, Spicy, '80 44
Zucchini Bars, '85 77
Bonbon Cookies, Surprise, '88 119
Bourbon Balls, '81 254
Bourbon Dunkers, Crunchy, '85 90
Butter Cookies, '85 322
Butter Cookies, Melt-Away, '81 20
Butter-Nut Strips, '82 167
Butter Pecan Cookies, '82 139
Cheesecake Cookies, Chewy, '82 109
Cheese Straws, '88 77
Cherry Nut Nuggets, '81 286
Chocolate Chip Cookies, Giant, '84 119
Chocolate Chip Melt-Aways, '84 118
Chocolate-Mint Snaps, '83 103; '84 96
Chocolate-Peanut Butter Cones, '85 14
Chocolate-Peanut Butter Cookies, '85 90
Chocolate-Peanut Butter Cups, '85 14
Chocolate Snappers, Jumbo, '81 218
Chocolate-Tipped Butter Cookies, '84 258
Chocolate-Tipped Log Cookies, '87 294
Choco-Nut Sandwich Cookies, '84 200
Christmas
    Calendar, Cookie Advent, '85 325
    Cards, Christmas Cookie, '84 302
    Cherry Cookies, Christmas, '88 282
    Date Cookies, Christmas, '88 287
    Eggnog Christmas Cookies, '79 255
    Elf Cookie, '80 279, 303
    Fruit Squares, Christmas, '88 282
    Gingerbread Cookies, '80 278
    Lizzies, Christmas, '87 257
    Mrs. Claus Cookie, '80 279, 303
    Painted Cookies, '86 322
    Rudolph Cookie, '80 279, 303
    Santa Claus Cookie, '80 278, 303
    Santa's Whiskers, '85 323
    Sleigh Cookie, '80 279, 303
    Spiced Christmas Cookies, '87 294

    Strawberries, Christmas, '87 293
    Swedish Christmas Cookies, '79 290
Cinnamon Balls, '79 23
Cinnamon Wafers, '81 192
Cocoa Kiss Cookies, '85 171
Curled Cookies, French, '87 16
Drop
    Ambrosia Cookies, '81 301; '82 110;
        '86 313
    Apple Butter Spice Cookies, '79 291
    Apple Cookies, Fresh, '84 36
    Apple-Nut Cookies, '80 228
    Apple Oatmeal Cookies, '85 215
    Apricot Cookies, Frosted, '81 192
    Banana Oatmeal Cookies, '79 217
    Benne Seed Cookies, '84 318
    Breakfast Cookies, Take-Along, '84 59

    Butterscotch Cookies, '87 58
    Butterscotch-Pecan Cookies, '84 36
    Candy Bit Cookies, '81 192
    Carrot Cookies, '82 137
    Carrot Cookies, Frosted, '81 7
    Carrot-Orange Cookies, '83 149
    Cherry-Almond Drops, '81 20
    Chip Cookies, Double, '81 301
    Chips Cookies, Loaded-with-, '87 223
    Chocolate Chip Cookies, '84 120;
        '86 245
    Chocolate Chip Cookies,
        Deluxe, '79 216
    Chocolate Chip Cookies,
        Different, '83 114
    Chocolate Chip Cookies,
        Double, '79 217
    Chocolate Chip Cookies,
        Jumbo, '82 110
    Chocolate Chip Cookies, Light, '86 46
    Chocolate Chip Cookies, Nutty
        Oatmeal-, '82 M185
    Chocolate Chip-Oatmeal
        Cookies, '84 119
    Chocolate-Chocolate Chip
        Cookies, '82 35
    Chocolate Chunk Cookies,
        Super, '88 217
    Chocolate Cookies,
        Doubly-Good, '82 M185
    Chocolate Crispy Cookies, '85 115
    Chocolate Drop Cookies, '84 36
    Chocolate Macaroon Cookies, '88 217

Cookies, Drop (continued)

Chocolate Macaroons, **'87** 57
Chocolate-Mint Chip Cookies, **'86** 245
Chocolate-Nut Chews, **'81** 92
Chocolate-Oatmeal Cookies, **'80** 105
Chocolate-Peanut Cookies, **'83** 223
Chocolate Sandwich Cookies, **'81** 192
Cocoa Drop Cookies, **'80** 217
Coconut-Cherry Cookies, **'79** 292
Coconut Macaroons, **'79** 52
Cream Cheese Cookies, **'80** 282
Devil Doggies, **'84** 37
Forget 'em Cookies, **'83** 256
Fruitcake Cookies, **'79** 291; **'86** 320;
   '88 286
Fruitcake Cookies, Holiday, **'81** 301
Fruit Cookies, Bourbon, **'86** 334
Fruit Cookies, Spicy Holiday, **'83** 298
Gumdrop Cookies, **'79** 292
Jack-O'-Lantern Cookies, **'87** 214
Lace Cookies, **'86** 8
Lemonade Cookies, **'79** 51
Lemon Yummies, **'81** 301
Macaroons, Chocolate, **'83** 300
Melting Moments, **'85** 191
Meringue Kiss Cookies, **'86** 121
Meringue Surprise Cookies, **'86** 320
Mincemeat Drop Cookies, **'79** 246
Molasses Cookies, Chewy, **'87** 257
Monster Cookies, **'84** 36
Nugget Cookies, **'79** 291
Nutmeg Sugar Cookies, **'79** 136
Oatmeal Cookies, Cinnamon, **'84** 72
Oatmeal Cookies, Crunchy, **'85** 202
Oatmeal Cookies, Easy, **'80** 105
Oatmeal Cookies, Nutty, **'81** 130
Oatmeal Cookies,
   Old-Fashioned, **'80** 106; **'85** 250
Oatmeal Cookies,
   Orange-Glazed, **'80** 60
Oatmeal Cookies, Peanutty, **'80** 106;
   '83 95
Oatmeal Cookies, Spicy, **'81** 197
Oatmeal-Date Cookies, **'82** 109
Oatmeal Krispies, **'85** 115
Oatmeal-Peanut Butter
   Cookies, **'85** 171
Oatmeal-Raisin Cookies, **'87** 221
Oatmeal-Raisin Cookies,
   Frosted, **'79** 290
Oatmeal-Spice Cookies, Giant, **'80** 105
Orange-Chocolate Cookies, **'83** 113
Orange Cookies, Frosted, **'83** 114
Peanut Butter-Oatmeal
   Cookies, **'81** 218
Peanut Cookies, Salted, **'87** 92
Persimmon-Raisin Cookies, **'85** 232
Pineapple Cookies, **'79** 216
Potato Chip Cookies, **'86** 93
Pumpkin Drop Cookies, **'79** 206
Pumpkin-Walnut Cookies,
   Frosted, **'82** 217
Raisin Cookies, Alltime
   Favorite, **'80** 24
Sour Cream Cookies,
   Southern, **'83** 113
Sour Cream-Nutmeg Cookies, **'85** 171
Sunflower Cookies, Crinkle, **'83** 149
Ginger Cookies, **'85** 306
Ginger Crinkles, **'83** 149

Gingersnaps, **'79** 146
Gingersnaps, Best-Ever, **'79** 208
Hazelnut Cookies, **'84** 111
Hazelnut-Lemon Logs, **'84** 117
Heavenly Delights, **'85** 324
Lace Cookies, Florentine, **'88** 120
Lemon Cookies, Sunshine, **'86** 69
Lemon Crinkle Cookies, **'81** 287
Lemon Zephers, **'81** 172
Madeleines, Snow-Capped, **'85** 120
Mailing Cookies, Tips on, **'83** 305
Miracle Cookies, **'83** 149
Oat Cookies, Crispy, **'88** 203
Oatmeal Cookies, Special, **'81** 236
Orange Fingers, **'87** 57
Peanut Butter-Chocolate Kiss
   Cookies, **'86** 49
Peanut Butter-Cinnamon Cookies, **'84** 30
Peanut Butter Cookies, **'82** 56
Peanut Butter Cookies, Quick, **'86** 109
Peanut Butter-Oatmeal Cookies, **'84** 72
Peanut Butter Temptations, **'84** 29
Peanut-Date Balls, **'81** 92

Pecan-Butter Cookies, **'83** 113
Pecan Crescent Cookies, **'85** 324
Peppermint Candy Cookies, **'88** 286
Peppermint Wreaths, Melt-Away, **'85** 324
Pizzelles, **'83** 298
Refrigerator
   Apricot Kolaches, **'83** 84
   Butter Cookies, Valentine, **'81** 20
   Cardamom Cookies, **'79** 12
   Cherry Pecan Cookies, **'82** 136
   Chocolate-Almond Surprise
      Cookies, **'88** M45
   Chocolate-Cherry Cookies, **'85** 324
   Chocolate Meltaways, **'81** 302
   Chocolate-Nut Freezer
      Cookies, **'88** 217
   Chocolate Pinwheel Cookies, **'86** 245
   Chocolate Snowball Cookies, **'82** 295
   Chocolate Teasers, **'87** 44
   Choco Surprise Cookies, **'80** 60
   Crème de Menthe Cookies, **'86** 230
   Crescents, **'85** 321
   Date-Cream Cheese Rollups, **'83** 298
   Date Nut Roll, **'79** 249
   Gingerbread Men, **'84** 299
   Gingerbread Men, Miniature, **'84** 318
   Gingersnaps, Raisin, **'85** 324
   Grandmother's Sandwich
      Cookies, **'82** 306
   Holiday Garland Cookies, **'83** 299
   Holiday Riches, **'83** 257
   Molasses Cookies, **'86** 20
   Oatmeal-Date Sandwich
      Cookies, **'83** 257
   Orange Crispies, **'84** 205

Orange Refrigerator Cookies, **'86** 230
Peanut Butter-Chocolate Chip Cookies,
   Freezer, **'86** 230
Peanut Butter-Coconut
   Cookies, **'83** 113
Peanut Butter Cookies, **'87** 58
Peanut Butter Crisps, **'79** 50
Peanut Butter
   Slice-and-Bakes, **'82** M185
Peanut Butter Snaps, **'81** 237
Pecan-Cheese Wafers, **'81** 119
Pecan Crisps, Sugar, **'86** 230
Raspberry Sandwich Cookies, **'82** 306
Ribbon Cookies, **'87** 293
Sesame-Cheese Cutouts, **'82** 296
Shortbread Cookie Crumbs, **'83** 298
Shortbread Cookies, **'87** 58
Shortbread Cookies, Crispy, **'83** 113
Sour Cream Cookies, Dutch, **'83** 149
Spice Cookies, Slice-of-, **'79** 290
Springerle, **'81** 251
Sugar Cookies, Crisp, **'84** 243
Sugar Cookies, Golden, **'88** 286
Sugar Cookies, Molasses, **'80** 270
Sugar Cookies, Red-, **'81** 21
Sugar Cookies, Valentine, **'82** 20
Sugar 'n Spice Cookies, **'81** 21
Swedish Cookies, **'82** 306
Tea Cookies, **'83** 170
Vanilla Crescents, **'82** 307
Vanilla Slice-and-Bake Cookies, **'85** 171
Wafers, Italian, **'87** 36
Walnut Cookies, **'81** 301
Rolled
   Almond-Filled Wafers, **'88** 120
   Almond Holly Leaves, **'86** 319
   Apricot Cookie Rolls, **'80** 282
   Cheese Straws, **'82** 137
   Chocolate Cookies, Chewy, **'80** 208
   Cinnamon Stars, Swiss, **'87** 293
   Cream Cheese Frills, **'79** 291
   Crème de Menthe Cookies, **'80** 282
   Currant Teacakes, **'80** 88
   Frosted Cutout Cookies, **'85** 236
   Fruit Cookies, Rolled, **'80** 15
   Fruit-Nut Twists, **'82** 253
   Gingerbread Animal Cookies, **'86** 70
   Gingerbread Cookies, **'80** 278
   Gingerbread Man Cookies, **'88** 227
   Gingerbread Men, **'85** 259
   Gingerbread Men Cookies, **'85** 319
   Ginger Cookies, Swedish, **'85** 323
   Grandmother's Cookies, **'85** 319
   Ice Box Filled Cookies, **'79** 112
   Lemon Pecan Dainties, **'80** 208
   Lemony Cutout Cookies, **'85** 323
   Maple Sandwich Cookies, **'85** 322
   Mincemeat Cookies, **'79** 51
   Mincemeat Sweetheart
      Cookies, **'87** 293
   Oat Crispies, **'83** 96
   Oatmeal-Coconut Cookies, **'80** 218
   Oatmeal Cookies, Date-Filled, **'86** 314
   Oatmeal Cookies,
      Slice-and-Bake, **'80** 105
   Oatmeal Nut Crispies, **'80** 208
   Orange-Pecan Cookies, **'88** 119
   Peanut Butter Cookies,
      Double, **'80** 209
   Peanuttiest Cookies, Crisp, **'88** 65
   Pear Mincemeat Cookies, **'84** 264

Pecan Cookies, Easy, '80 208
Scones, Currant, '84 117
Sherry Snaps, '87 94
Shortbread Cookies, Butter
    Pecan, '80 282
Shortbread, Easy Roll-Out, '81 21
Shortbread Sugarplums,
    Pecan-, '83 298
Sorghum Tea Cakes, '85 239
Sugar Cookies, Crescent, '87 294
Sugar Cookies, Molasses, '80 270
Sugar Cookies, Moravian, '85 321
Sugar Cookies, Old-Fashioned, '86 313
Sugar Cookies, Rolled, '79 291
    Teacakes, Old-Fashioned, '84 43
Sandwich Cookies, Viennese, '87 293
Sesame Cookies, Italian, '85 311
Shortbread Cookie, Old-Fashioned, '88 242
Shortbread Cookies, Praline, '88 242
Shortbread Cookies, Spiced, '88 242
Shortbread Madeleines, Orange, '88 242
Shortbread Wafers, Cocoa, '88 243
Snappin' Turtle Cookies, '85 323
Spice Cookies, '87 M278
Sugar Cookies, Cinnamon, '84 73
Sugar Cookies, Molasses, '82 140
Sugar Cookies, Sour Cream, '79 51
Swedish Heirloom Cookies, '81 129
Tea Cakes, Mexican, '81 196
Thumbprint Cookies, Childhood, '85 323
Waffle Cookies, Brownie, '86 245
Wedding Cookies, '82 M185
Whoopie Pies, '86 246

Cooking Light
Appetizers
    Ambrosia, Sherried, '84 324
    Apple-Phyllo Rolls, '88 213
    Artichokes, Marinated, '87 250
    Artichokes with Herb-Mayonnaise
        Dip, '84 67
    Beets, Blue Cheese-Stuffed, '88 211
    Carrot-Cheese Ball, '86 325
    Cheese Tartlets, '88 211
    Chicken-Mushroom Appetizers, '88 210
    Crudité Platter with Dip, '84 139
    Dip, Curry, '87 25
    Dip, Deviled, '87 25
    Dip, Dilled Garden, '84 324
    Dip, Low-Cal Tuna, '87 25
    Dip, Spinach, '87 25
    Dip, Tofu, '86 109
    Dip, Vegetable Garden, '85 215
    Fruit Kabobs with Coconut
        Dressing, '87 251
    Fruit with Lemon Sauce,
        Fresh, '82 290
    Mousse, Shrimp, '87 251
    Mushroom-Almond Pastry
        Cups, '88 210
    Mushroom Appetizers, Stuffed, '88 210
    Nectarine Cocktail, '85 107
    Orange Halves, Broiled, '85 288
    Pasta Bites, Pesto-Cheese, '87 251
    Pâté, Mock, '87 251
    Pears Stuffed with Cheese, '82 290
    Peas, Crab-Stuffed Snow, '85 288
    Pita Bread Triangles, '88 211
    Popcorn Mix, Curried, '86 326
    Potatoes, Ham-Stuffed New, '88 211
    Scallop Appetizer, '86 155
    Shrimp Dippers, '84 324
    Spinach-Ricotta Phyllo
        Triangles, '88 212
    Spread, Broccamoli Curry, '88 55
    Spread, Low-Fat Chicken, '82 290
    Spread, Smoked Salmon, '84 324
    Steak-and-Chestnut Appetizers,
        Marinated, '84 323
    Tabbouleh, '88 211
    Tomatoes, Crab-Stuffed
        Cherry, '82 289
    Tomatoes, Stuffed Cherry, '88 212
    Vegetable Appetizer, Tarragon, '83 277
    Zucchini Caviar, '88 212
    Zucchini Pizzas, '88 212
Apples, Baked, '86 40
Apples with Orange Sauce, Baked, '84 314
Beverages
    Apple Julep, '86 103
    Banana Nog, '82 290
    Cider, Hot Spiced, '82 290
    Cocoa, Mocha, '83 318
    Eggnog, '83 318
    Fruit Beverage, Blender, '83 318
    Fruit Shake, Frosty, '87 23
    Grapefruit Refresher, '88 85
    Mocha, Hot, '84 60
    Orange Slush, '82 49
    Peach Cooler, '86 6
    Peach Frosty, '83 318
    Peach Refresher, '86 103
    Punch, Apple-Tea, '85 82
    Punch, Holiday, '87 252
    Punch, Hot Apple, '84 324
    Punch, Tart Cranberry, '83 318
    Shake, Strawberry-Orange
        Breakfast, '87 186
    Strawberry Cooler, '83 56
    Tea Mix, Spiced, '86 32
    Tofruitti Breakfast Drink, '88 26
    Tomato-Clam Cocktail, '87 252
    Tomato Refresher, '83 318
    Vegetable Cocktail, Fresh, '82 165
Breads
    Banana Bread, '87 72
    Biscuits, Orange, '88 85
    Biscuits, Whole Wheat, '84 60
    Biscuits, Yeast, '87 71
    Cornbread, Dieter's, '87 164
    Garlic Bread, '82 19

    Muffins, Apple, '84 193
    Muffins, Banana-Oat, '87 188
    Muffins, Bran-Buttermilk, '85 7
    Muffins, Honey Bran, '88 171
    Muffins Made of Bran, '86 103
    Muffins, Spicy Apple-Oat, '86 45
    Muffins, Yogurt, '88 55
    Oat Bread, Caraway-Raisin, '86 44
    Pumpkin-Pecan Bread, '87 221
    Rolls, Honey Wheat, '83 278
    Rolls, Vegetable Salad, '82 278
    Toast, Cottage-Topped French, '85 49
    Toast, Slender French, '86 103
    Whole Wheat Cardamom
        Bread, '86 223
Crêpes, Basic, '86 38
Crêpes, Bran, '83 70; '86 44
Crêpes, Ham-and-Egg, '83 204
Crêpes, Light, '86 143
Crêpes, Low-Calorie, '87 77
Crêpes, Plain, '83 70
Crêpes Suzettes, Light, '83 71
Crêpes, Whole Wheat, '83 70

Desserts
    Alaska, Orange, '83 177
    Alaska, Peachy Melba, '88 266
    Ambrosia, Baked, '83 303
    Apples, Melting, '88 19
    Bananas Foster, '88 20
    Bananas with Honey, Broiled, '84 175
    Bars, Apricot-Raisin, '87 32
    Bars, Pineapple-Orange, '82 129
    Bavarian Dessert, Light, '86 6
    Blackberries and Dumplings, '86 196
    Blintzes, Cheese, '83 71
    Blueberry Crisp, '84 177
    Cake, Apple-Nut, '87 76
    Cake, Chocolate Angel Food, '87 21
    Cake, Chocolate Custard, '88 175
    Cake, Deluxe Light Banana, '84 314
    Cake, Heavenly Pineapple, '83 303
    Cake, Orange Pound, '87 221
    Cake with Custard Sauce, Chocolate
        Angel Food, '88 259
    Cake with Pineapple-Orange Sauce,
        Angel, '84 14
    Cake with Strawberries and Chocolate
        Glaze, White, '87 76
    Cheesecake, Almost
        Strawberry, '86 32
    Cheesecake, Blueberry Chiffon, '87 76
    Cheesecake, Dieter's Apple, '86 318
    Cheesecake, Light-and-Easy, '88 55
    Cherries Jubilite, '86 317
    Chocolate Cream Roll, '85 317
    Chocolat, Petits Pots de, '82 272
    Cobbler, Fresh Cherry, '84 178

Cooking Light, Desserts *(continued)*

Cobbler, New-Fashioned
   Blackberry, '87 164
Cobbler, Peach, '84 178
Coffee Dessert, Light, '88 260
Compote, Baked Fruit, '84 314
Compote, Fresh Fruit, '82 272; '84 82
Compote, Melon Ball, '85 157
Cookies, Apple-Oatmeal, '85 215
Cookies, Light Almond, '83 151
Cookies, Light Chocolate Chip, '86 46
Cookies, Oatmeal-Raisin, '87 221
Cream Puffs,
   Strawberry-Lemon, '87 75
Crêpes, Tropical Fruit, '87 77
Crust, Graham Cracker, '86 32;
   '88 55
Custard, Baked Vanilla, '82 129
Custard, Coconut, '86 109
Custard, Light Mexican, '88 149
Custard over Fruit, Stirred, '84 83
Custard, Range-Top Amaretto, '87 77
Custard with Raspberries, Almond
   Creme, '88 174
Flambé, Banana-Peach, '85 316
Fruitcake, Jeweled, '88 260
Fruit Dessert, Caribbean, '84 314
Fruit Dessert, Flaming, '83 302
Fruit Dessert Orange, '84 314
Fruit Dessert, Rainbow, '85 108
Fruit Dessert, Spiced, '82 50
Fruit, Gingered, '83 151
Fruit, Glazed, '85 83
Fruit Medley, Fancy, '84 82
Fruit with Lemon Curd, Fresh, '88 21
Honeydew-Berry Dessert, '83 120
Ice, Cranberry-Apple, '82 290
Ice, Kiwi, '84 315
Ice, Mixed Fruit, '88 85

Ice, Peach-Yogurt, '84 83
Ice, Strawberry, '84 175; '85 108
Ice, Strawberry-Orange, '86 196
Ice, Tangy Cranberry, '87 305
Ice, Tart Cranberry-Orange, '86 317
Kiwi Jubilee, '83 120
Layered Ambrosia, '88 304
Melon Mélange, '84 139
Melon-Mint Julep, '86 196
Meringue Shells, Fruited, '87 32
Meringues, Peach Melba, '87 76
Mousse, Coffee-Nut, '86 319
Mousse, Peach, '85 54
Mousse, Strawberry-Lemon, '82 128
Orange Molded Dessert, '83 302

Oranges and Pineapple,
   Glazed, '86 318
Parfait, Peach, '82 166
Parfait, Pineapple, '84 83
Peach Dessert, Spiced, '83 9
Peaches with Honey-Lime
   Whip, '85 108
Peaches with Nutty Dumplings,
   Spiced, '87 164
Peaches with Strawberry Sauce, '85 8
Peach Halves, Stuffed, '86 196
Pear Fans with Raspberry-Orange
   Sauce, Poached, '88 22
Pears in Custard, Poached, '88 20
Pears in Orange Sauce,
   Poached, '82 19
Pears Poached in Red Wine, '83 302
Pears with Berry Sauce,
   Wine-Poached, '86 144
Pie, Eggnog, '83 205
Pie, Fresh Apple, '84 178
Pineapple, Meringue-Topped, '84 178
Plum Slush, '84 139
Pops, Orange-Banana, '82 129
Prune Bavarian, '86 223
Pudding, Almost Banana, '88 174
Pudding, Apple-Raisin Bread, '88 175
Pudding, Layered Lemon, '82 128
Pudding, Light Plum, '86 318
Pudding, Old-Fashioned Bread, '88 175
Pudding, Orange Custard, '88 174
Pudding, Peachy Bread, '88 175
Pudding, Raisin-Pumpkin, '84 315
Pumpkin Chiffon, '86 223; '88 260
Rice Cream with Mandarin
   Oranges, '85 317
Roll, Chocolate-Orange, '87 21
Sauce, Melba, '87 77
Sherbet, Fresh Mint, '88 23
Sherbet, Instant Fruit, '85 158
Sherbet, Pineapple, '84 83
Sorbet, Blueberry-Kirsch, '83 120
Sorbet, Mango, '86 196
Soufflé, Baked Apricot, '88 267
Soufflé, Light Chocolate, '83 278
Soufflé, Orange Dessert, '83 206
Soufflé, Raspberry-Topped, '85 317
Soufflé, Tart Lemon, '85 82
Strawberries Juliet, '84 82
Strawberries Marsala, '88 171
Strawberry Dessert, Glazed, '84 33
Strawberry Puff, '82 5
Tapioca Fluff, Orange, '87 31
Tart, Fancy Fruit, '82 128
Tart, Fresh Fruit, '84 178
Tart, Green Grape, '87 77
Tart, Kiwifruit-Peach, '88 20
Tart Shell, '87 77; '88 20
Topping, Blueberry, '87 125
Topping, Cherry-Pineapple, '87 126
Topping, Chunky Piña Colada, '87 125
Topping, Raspberry, '85 317
Topping, Raspberry-Peach, '87 126
Topping, Reduced-Calorie
   Whipped, '85 55
Topping, Spicy Apple, '87 125
Topping, Strawberry, '86 32
Topping, Strawberry-Banana, '87 125
Trifle, Raspberry, '88 259
Wafers, Cinnamon, '84 324
Watermelon Frost, '86 196

Yogurt, Lemon-Chiffon Frozen, '85 54
Yogurt, Vanilla Frozen, '87 125
Dressing, Savory Cornbread, '88 303
Eggs and Omelets
   Benedict, Eggs, '85 49
   Cheddar-Vegetable Omelet, '83 205
   Florentine, Eggs, '83 56
   Primavera, Omelet, '87 71
   Roulade with Mushroom Filling,
     Egg, '88 84
   Scrambled Eggs, Mexican-Style, '85 50
   Scrambled Eggs, Spanish, '84 60
   Vegetable Omelet, Cheesy, '85 49
Fettuccine and Spinach, '88 90
Filling, Chicken Salad, '87 106
Filling, Mushroom, '88 84
Filling, Shrimp Salad, '87 106
Fruit Medley, Chilled, '84 60
Fruit Nuggets, Dried, '86 326
Fruit, Warm Spiced, '86 39
Grapefruit, Broiled, '85 7
Linguine with Garlic and Lemon, '88 91

Low Sodium
   Applesauce, Spicy, '82 296
   Asparagus with Basil Sauce, '86 33
   Beans, Minted Green, '84 104
   Beef and Rice, Spicy, '83 231
   Beef Burgundy, '83 281
   Beef Goulash, '83 231
   Biscuits, Flaky, '84 228
   Bread, Bran-Applesauce, '84 229
   Bread, Salt-Free Raisin Batter, '86 33
   Breadsticks, Whole Wheat, '84 228
   Brussels Sprouts, Calico
     Citrus, '85 303
   Butter, Herbed Unsalted, '82 67
   Carrots Madeira, '83 281
   Catsup, Spicy Tomato, '83 182
   Cereal Snack, Toasted, '85 215
   Chicken à l'Orange, '84 277
   Chicken-and-Vegetables,
     Stir-Fry, '86 68
   Chicken, Citrus-Herb Baked, '85 303
   Chicken Dinner, Healthful, '83 232
   Chicken, Herb-Baked, '82 229
   Chicken in Lemon and Wine, '83 281
   Chicken Piccata, '83 35
   Chicken-Tomato Bake, '83 35
   Chicken with Wine-Soaked Vegetables,
     Baked, '84 277
   Chili Surprise, '82 229
   Cookies, Sunshine Lemon, '86 69
   Cornish Hens in Vermouth, '86 33

Cornish Hens, Roasted Rock, '82 66
Dressing, Basil, '88 24
Dressing, Lemon-Herb Salad, '82 67
Dressing, Orange-Yogurt, '85 304
Fish, Curried Baked, '87 5
Flounder Rolls,
   Vegetable-Stuffed, '87 6
Fruit Delight, Hot, '83 281
Fruit Delight, Spiced, '82 229
Fruit, Unsweetened Mixed, '83 182
Ice, Pink Grapefruit, '85 304
Jam, Banana, '82 296
Jam, Freezer Peach, '83 182
Lamb Chops, Dijon, '84 277
Lamb Chops, Orange, '83 35
Linguine with Seafood Sauce, '83 232
Meat Loaf, Corny, '86 68
Meat Loaf, Parsleyed, '83 35
Mocha-Cocoa Mix, Hot, '82 296
Mousse, Orange, '86 69
Muffins, Honey-Oatmeal, '84 229
Muffins, Spiced Bran, '84 229
Mustard, Lower Sodium
   Horseradish, '86 325
Nectarines in Apple Juice, '83 183
Onions, Glazed, '84 104
Orange Scampi, '85 303
Pastry Shell, Sesame, '82 67
Peppers, Corn Stuffed, '84 104
Pie, Nutty Pumpkin, '82 67
Pork, Roast Loin of, '84 276
Potato Bake, Chive-, '82 229
Potatoes, Yogurt-Stuffed, '88 24
Pretzels with Lower Sodium
   Horseradish Mustard, Herb, '86 325
Pudding, Chocolate-Almond, '88 24
Pudding, Lemon Fluff, '85 304
Ratatouille, '84 105
Rice and Shrimp, Curried, '83 231
Rice, Calico Brown, '86 33
Rolls, Low-Sodium Refrigerator, '82 67
Rolls, Low-Sodium Yeast, '84 228
Salad, Asparagus-and-New
   Potato, '86 69
Salad, Citrus Green, '85 304
Salad, Dilled Cucumber, '82 229
Salad Mold, Golden Citrus, '85 303
Salad, Mushroom-and-Pepper, '86 68
Salad, Sesame-Citrus Green, '86 33
Salmon, Poached, '83 35
Salmon Steaks, Marinated, '87 6
Sauce, Apple-Horseradish, '82 229
Sauce, Green Herb, '83 36
Sauce, Seafood, '83 36
Scallops, Sherried, '83 281
Scamp, Tangy Broiled, '87 5
Seasoning Blend, '82 296
Shake, Pineapple-Banana, '85 215
Shrimp Kabobs, Marinated, '84 276
Shrimp, Special Boiled, '83 36
Snapper, Caribbean, '87 5
Snapper, Orangy, '88 23
Soup, Chunky Chicken-Noodle, '88 12
Soup, Chunky Mushroom, '88 12
Soup, Cream of Cauliflower, '88 12
Soup, Spicy Vegetable-Beef, '88 11
Spaghetti, Veal, '84 276
Squash Sauté, '82 67
Squash, Vegetable-Stuffed, '84 104
Steak, Marinated Flank, '83 35
Stew, Cajun-Style Catfish, '88 12

Stew, White Wine, '82 228
Stuffing, Low-Sodium, '82 66
Swordfish, Foil-Baked, '87 5
Tomatoes, Stewed, '83 182
Tomato Puree, Seasoned, '83 182
Tropical Snow, '86 34
Veal, Savory, '83 281
Vegetable Stir-Fry, '84 104
Waffles, Whole Wheat, '84 228
Zucchini, Herbed, '84 104
Zucchini with Baby Carrots, '88 24
Macaroni and Cheese, Baked, '82 199
Main Dishes
   Asparagus Roulade, '86 102
   Beef-and-Barley Rolls,
      Wine-Sauced, '87 269
   Beef-and-Rice Dinner,
      Mexican, '88 199
   Beef and Vegetables,
      Company, '88 234
   Beef-and-Vegetable Stir-Fry, '87 22
   Beef Burgundy, '88 25
   Beef, Chinese-Style, '87 50
   Beef Fajitas, '88 233
   Beef Kabobs, Spirited, '87 142
   Beef Kabobs with Rice,
      Marinated, '84 32
   Beef Medaillions, Italian, '87 305
   Beef Patties, Deviled-, '87 22
   Beef Stir-Fry, Chinese, '83 151
   Beef Stroganoff, Light, '86 36
   Burgers, Seasoned, '85 158
   Burritos, Cheesy Beef, '85 193
   Cabbage Rolls, Stuffed, '88 18
   Catfish, Southern Oven-Fried, '87 163
   Chicken and Rice, Spicy, '88 200
   Chicken-and-Sausage
      Jambalaya, '88 200
   Chicken and Spinach Noodles, '82 19
   Chicken and Vegetables,
      Stir-Fry, '86 249
   Chicken and Vegetables,
      Walnut, '85 194
   Chicken Breasts Sardou,
      Stuffed, '87 269
   Chicken Breasts, Wine-Baked, '83 177
   Chicken Cacciatore, '86 42
   Chicken, Chutney, '86 249
   Chicken Cordon Bleu, '86 37
   Chicken, Creamed, '82 49
   Chicken, Crunchy Oven-Fried, '87 163
   Chicken, Curried, '86 43
   Chicken Curry, Stir-Fried, '87 51
   Chicken Cutlets with Lemon, '85 8
   Chicken, Dante's, '88 25
   Chicken Dinner, Skillet, '86 249
   Chicken Fingers, Herb-Baked, '86 249
   Chicken in a Bag, '87 23
   Chicken in Orange Sauce, '83 8
   Chicken Kabobs, Sesame, '82 165
   Chicken Kiev, Oven-Baked, '86 37
   Chicken la France, '86 248
   Chicken Lasagna, '88 90
   Chicken, Lemon-Frosted, '88 170
   Chicken, Orange, '83 278
   Chicken Paprika, Dilled, '86 41
   Chicken, Pineapple, '83 M194
   Chicken Rolls, Spinach-Stuffed,
      '86 248
   Chicken, Southern Oven-Fried, '86 37
   Chicken Spaghetti, '87 221

   Chicken-Vegetable Stir-Fry, '83 151;
      '84 13
   Chicken with Artichoke Hearts, '88 54
   Chicken with Artichokes,
      Sherried, '87 143
   Chicken with Pineapple,
      Oriental, '86 42
   Chicken with Salsa, Baked
      Chile, '88 147
   Chicken with Spinach Fettuccine,
      Easy, '88 89
   Chile Verde, Light, '88 148
   Cornish Hens, Herbed, '82 271
   Cornish Hens, Orange-Glazed
      Grilled, '86 250
   Crabmeat au Gratin, '86 154
   Crawfish Étouffée, '86 156
   Crêpes, Cannelloni, '86 143
   Crêpes, Chicken-Vegetable, '83 70
   Enchiladas, Spicy Bean, '88 18
   Fillets, Apple-Carrot Stuffed, '88 M192
   Fish Dinner, Skillet, '88 199
   Fish Florentine, '86 35
   Fish Florentine in Parchment, '87 22
   Flounder, Creole-Style, '85 180
   Flounder Rolls with Citrus Sauce,
      Stuffed, '85 180
   Frijoles Rancheros, '88 148
   Grits-and-Ham Pie, Crustless, '86 103
   Haddock Fillets with Zucchini
      Stuffing, '88 M191

   Halibut Steaks Italiano, '88 M191
   Halibut with Swiss Sauce, '83 M195
   Hamburger Pie, '84 13
   Kabobs, Hawaiian, '85 157
   Lamb Chops, Broiled, '85 22
   Lasagna, Cheesy Spinach, '83 204
   Lasagna, Lean, '86 37
   Lasagna, Vegetable, '84 201
   Lasagna, Zucchini, '85 194
   Lentil-and-Rice Supper, '84 202
   Linguine with Clam Sauce, '88 90
   Liver, Creole, '86 108
   Liver in Creole Sauce, '87 33
   Lobster Tails with Spiced Orange
      Sauce, '86 155
   London Broil, Marinated, '87 32
   Manicotti, Spinach, '82 199
   Meat Loaf, Curried, '86 43
   Meat Loaf, Oriental, '83 M194
   Meat Loaf, Parsley, '87 22
   Orange Roughy with Spinach
      Pesto, '88 M192

Cooking Light, Main Dishes (continued)

Pasta Primavera, Almost, '86 38
Pasta Salad, Main-Dish, '82 199
Pasta Verde, '84 201
Pastichio, '85 194
Pear Breakfast Treat, '87 72
Peas and Red Pepper, Sesame
  Snow, '84 175
Pizza, Whole Wheat, '84 33
Pork-and-Noodles Skillet
  Dinner, '88 199
Pork Chop Dinner, '88 25
Pork Chops, Apricot-Sauced, '85 22
Pork, Stir-Fried, '87 51
Pork, Sweet-and-Sour, '85 34, 194
Pork Tenderloin, Marinated, '84 175
Pork Tenderloins,
  Fruit-Stuffed, '87 270
Pot Roast, Marinated, '85 21
Quiche, Eggless, '87 220
Quiches, Individual Spinach, '86 38
Quiche, Swiss-Zucchini, '82 49
Rice-and-Lentil Pilaf, '88 17
Salmon Loaf with Cucumber-Dill
  Sauce, '86 5
Sausage, Dieters' Spicy, '85 49
Scallop Kabobs, Grilled, '83 101
Shrimp, Beer-Broiled, '87 142
Shrimp Skillet, Quick, '87 50
Shrimp, Sweet-and-Sour, '83 278
Snapper à l'Orange, Baked, '85 181
Snapper, Honey-Curried, '85 181
Snapper, Poached, '83 101
Snapper Rolls, Cucumber-Stuffed
  Red, '83 176
Snapper Veracruz, Red, '88 149
Sole Divan, '87 21
Sole Véronique, '85 181
Spaghetti, Meaty, '82 19
Steak au Poivre, '88 232
Steak, Fast-and-Easy Stir-Fried,
  '87 50
Steak in Red Wine Sauce,
  Skillet, '85 21
Steak, Italian-Stuffed, '88 232
Steak Kabobs, '82 4
Steak, Marinated, '88 233
Steak, Mexican Marinated, '88 148
Steak, Mock Country-Fried, '87 163
Steak, Pepper-Beef, '85 21
Steak Sukiyaki, Flank, '88 233
Stew, Burgundy Beef, '88 234
Tofu, Stroganoff, '84 202
Tomato with Tuna Pasta,
  Stuffed, '88 54
Tuna Croquettes with Parsley
  Sauce, '86 108
Turkey-Asparagus Pilaf, '88 200
Turkey Breast and Gravy,
  Roast, '88 303
Turkey Breast, Stuffed, '87 270
Turkey Breast with Special Gravy,
  Roast, '86 282
Turkey Cutlets with Pepper Salsa,
  Spicy, '88 26
Veal and Carrots, Company, '85 22
Veal Picante, '87 31
Veal Picatta with Capers, '87 142
Veal Scallopini, '83 8
Vegetarian Supper, '86 222

Vermicelli and Sprouts with Red Clam
  Sauce, '86 143
Vermicelli, Scallop-Vegetable, '87 143
Zucchini Frittata, '86 103
Oatmeal, Fruited, '88 19
Pancakes, Shredded Wheat, '84 59
Pasta-Basil Toss, '87 33
Pasta, Garden, '82 199
Pasta Provençale, '88 90
Peaches, Spicy Baked, '86 39
Relish, Cranberry, '86 283
Relish, Holiday Cranberry, '88 304
Rice and Mushrooms, Wild, '83 278
Rice, Apple-Cinnamon, '86 249
Rice Casserole, Colorful, '82 199
Rice-Cheese Shell, '82 49
Rice, Lime-Flavored, '84 175
Rice Mix, Fruited Curry-, '86 326
Rice, Orange, '82 200
Rice, Peppered, '82 4
Rice Pilaf, Browned, '87 305
Rice, Seasoned Onion, '82 166
Rice, Spicy Mexican, '88 149
Rice with Tofu, Spanish, '88 26

Salad Dressings
  Blue Cheese Dressing, '82 166
  Coconut Dressing, '87 251
  Cucumber-Mint Dressing, '87 153
  Cucumber Salad Dressing,
    Creamy, '82 79
  Curry Dressing, '82 78
  French Dressing, Miracle, '82 79
  Fruit, Salad Dressing for, '86 40
  Herb Salad Dressing, '86 40
  Horseradish Dressing, '87 152
  Lemon-Yogurt Slaw or Salad
    Dressing, '88 54
  Lime Dressing, '83 120
  Orange-Poppy Seed Dressing, '87 187
  Pineapple-Poppy Seed Dressing, '85 55
  Raspberry Dressing, '87 153
  Soy-Sesame Dressing, '87 153
  Spring Garden Dressing, '85 157
  Stay Trim Dressing, '86 40
  Sweet-and-Sour Dressing, '87 305
  Tangy Dressing, '83 9
  Thousand Island Dressing,
    Special, '82 79

Yogurt Dressing, '85 59, 215; '88 27
Yogurt Dressing, Sweet-Hot, '86 40
Yogurt-Honey Poppy Seed
  Dressing, '83 177
Salads
  Ambrosia, Brunch, '83 57
  Apple-Apricot Salad, '88 121
  Apple-Bran Salad, Lemony, '86 223
  Apple Cider Salad Mold, '85 54
  Apple Salad, Spicy, '85 215
  Apple Salad, Triple, '88 122
  Apple Toss, Sesame-, '88 21
  Asparagus, Marinated, '84 67
  Asparagus Salad, '88 121
  Asparagus Vinaigrette, Light, '82 50
  Aspic, Light Tomato, '85 83
  Aspic, Three-Layer, '88 120
  Aspic, Tomato-Crab, '85 287
  Aspic with Horseradish Dressing, Crisp
    Vegetable, '87 152
  Bean-and-Rice Salad,
    Marinated, '87 152
  Bean Salad, Marinated, '85 137, 296
  Beans with Sprouts,
    Sweet-and-Sour, '86 32
  Bean-Tomato Salad, Lima, '85 137
  Beef-and-Broccoli Salad, '87 187
  Broccoli-Corn Salad, '87 24
  Cantaloupe, Fruit-Filled, '83 120
  Carrot-and-Seed Salad, Fruity, '86 223
  Carrot-Raisin Salad, '84 174
  Cauliflower-Vegetable Salad, '85 158
  Cheesy Italian Salad, '84 33
  Cherry-Apple Salad, '86 31
  Cherry Salad, Fresh, '83 120
  Chicken-Fruit Salad, '82 79
  Chicken Pasta Salad, '88 89
  Chicken Salad, Crunchy, '86 207
  Chicken Salad, Special, '85 82
  Chile-Tomato Salad, Spicy, '88 121
  Coleslaw, Crunchy, '86 295
  Corn Salad, '85 236
  Cottage Cheese Salad in
    Tomatoes, '86 208
  Crab-Wild Rice Salad, '86 207
  Cucumber Mousse, '88 121
  Cucumber-Yogurt Salad, '87 33
  Fruit, Dressed-Up, '82 5
  Fruit Salad, Chef's, '86 35
  Fruit Salad, Curried, '85 107
  Garden-Patch Salad Molds, '86 283
  Garden Salad, Summer, '87 153
  Grapefruit Salad, '88 122
  Grape Salad Mold, '83 120
  Greens, Crimson, '87 153
  Hominy-Bean Salad, '88 266
  Layered Salad, '86 35
  Lettuce, Confetti-Stuffed, '87 24
  Macaroni-Cheese Salad, Dilled, '86 208
  Macaroni-Tuna Salad, Whole
    Wheat, '84 193
  Mandarin Salad Molds, '85 54
  Meal-in-One Salad, '86 43
  Melon Ball Bowl with Cucumber-Mint
    Dressing, '87 153
  Mushroom-Zucchini Salad, '85 8
  Niçoise, Salad, '86 35
  Oriental Salad Bowl, '87 153
  Paella Salad, '86 207
  Pasta Salad, '84 139
  Pasta Salad, Garden, '86 188

Pea-and-Apple Salad, English, '87 24
Peaches in a Garden Nest, '87 154
Potato Salad, New, '84 139
Rice-and-Vegetable Salad, '86 42
Rice-and-Vegetable Salad,
  Brown, '84 202
Shrimp Salad, Fruited, '86 156
Shrimp Salad, Marinated, '85 82
Spinach-Blue Cheese Salad, '82 166
Spinach-Kiwifruit Salad, '87 305
Spinach Salad with Orange
  Dressing, '87 187
Steak Salad Cups, Pepper, '86 206
Tofu Salad, '88 27
Tuna-and-Cannellini Bean
  Salad, '86 143
Tuna Chef Salad, '82 78
Tuna-Mac in Tomatoes, '87 188
Tuna Salad, Curried, '86 208
Turkey Waldorf Salad with Yogurt
  Dressing, '88 53
Turnip Salad, '85 235
Vegetable Salad, Crispy
  Marinated, '84 193
Vegetable Salad, Italian, '82 19
Vegetable Salad, Marinated, '84 13
Vegetable Salad, Minted, '88 23
Vegetable Salad, Tarragon-, '85 288
Vegetable Salad, Winter, '86 42
Vegetables, Zesty Marinated, '82 272
Sandwiches
  Chicken Sandwiches,
    Marinated, '86 M45
  Crab Sandwiches, Open-Faced, '87 106
  Garden Sandwiches,
    Open-Faced, '87 105
  Ham Sandwiches, Open-Face, '85 8
  Lamb Pockets with Dilled Cucumber
    Topping, '87 104
  Open-Face Sandwiches, '84 13
  Pimiento Cheese Sandwiches, '82 278

  Pita Sandwiches, '84 139
  Pizza Sandwiches, Open-Face, '85 22
  Tofu-Veggie Sandwiches,
    Open-Face, '86 5
  Vegetable Pockets, '85 215
  Vegetarian Melt, Open-Faced, '87 106
  Vegetarian Pita Sandwiches, '84 193
Sauces and Gravies
  Apple Dessert Sauce, Spicy, '82 177
  Barbecue Sauce, Easy, '82 178
  Barbecue Sauce, Special, '82 177
  Coconut Sauce, Creamy Light, '82 177
  Cucumber-Dill Sauce, '86 5
  Custard Sauce, '88 259
  Golden Sauce, '88 267
  Gravy, '88 303

  Hard Sauce, Special, '86 318
  Hollandaise Sauce, Mock, '85 49
  Honey-Orange Sauce, '85 108
  Lemon-Chive Sauce, '86 249
  Lemon Sauce, '82 290
  Mandarin Sauce, '84 60
  Mango Sauce, '83 120
  Marinade, Tangy Light, '82 178
  Marinara Sauce, '82 178
  Mushroom Sauce, '83 205
  Mustard-Hollandaise Sauce,
    Mock, '87 269
  Mustard Sauce, '87 22
  Mustard Sauce, Light, '82 178
  Parsley Sauce, '86 108
  Pineapple-Orange Sauce, '84 14
  Pizza Sauce, '84 33
  Rancheros Sauce, '88 148
  Raspberry-Orange Sauce, '88 22
  Raspberry Sauce, '88 267
  Salsa, '88 147
  Salsa Cruda, '88 148
  Salsa, Pepper, '88 26
  Swiss Sauce, '83 M195
  Tarragon Sauce, '83 56
  Tomato Sauce, '85 193, 244
  Tomato Sauce, Spicy, '88 19
  Vegetable-Cheese Potato Topper, '86 6
  White Sauce, Low-Calorie
    Medium, '87 26
  Zippy Sauce, '86 44
Soups and Stews
  Asparagus Soup, '84 67
  Bean Soup, Black, '88 266
  Bean Soup, Leafy, '86 223
  Bean Soup, Navy, '84 280
  Bisque, Squash, '84 280
  Borscht, Ruby Red, '83 176
  Bouillon, Tomato, '83 8
  Broccoli Soup, Mock Cream
    of, '85 288
  Broccoli-Swiss Soup, '86 6
  Cantaloupe Soup, '83 120
  Carrot-Leek Soup, '86 34
  Chicken Soup, Curried, '86 34
  Chicken-Vegetable Soup, '88 18
  Chili, Vegetarian, '84 280
  Chowder, Basque Fish, '86 36
  Chowder, Clam, '86 36
  Crab Soup, Cream of, '88 302
  Cucumber Soup, Cold Minted, '86 34
  Cucumber-Yogurt Soup, '83 205
  Fish-and-Vegetable Stew, '87 220
  Gazpacho, Chilled, '84 138
  Gumbo, Light Seafood-Okra, '86 155
  Minestrone Soup, '86 144
  Peach Soup, '83 120
  Plum Soup, '85 107
  Seafood Stew, '84 280
  Spinach Soup, Oriental, '83 151
  Tomato Soup, Easy, '84 14
  Tomato Soup Plus, '88 170
  Vegetable Soup, '86 187; '88 266
  Vegetable Soup, Light, '84 280
  Vegetable Stew, Mixed, '84 13
Sour Cream, Mock, '83 71, 205
Spread, Cottage Cheese, '87 107
Spread, Hawaiian Ham, '87 106
Spread, Light Strawberry, '85 55
Spread, Low-Calorie Pimiento
  Cheese, '85 215

Spread, Peachy-Raisin, '86 326
Spread, Sugarless Fruit, '84 60
Spread, Tasty Chicken, '84 193
Spread, Vegetable-Egg, '87 106
Topping, Yogurt-Cheese, '88 55
Vegetables
  Artichokes, Shrimp-Stuffed, '84 67
  Artichokes Stuffed with Shrimp and
    Scallops, '84 174
  Asparagus, Company, '85 82
  Asparagus, Stir-Fried, '87 52
  Beans Creole, Lima, '85 137
  Beans, Herbed Green, '83 177
  Beans, Indian-Style Green, '88 265
  Beans Italiano, Green, '86 144
  Beans, Lemon-Mint, '88 22
  Beans, Seasoned Green, '88 304
  Beans with New Potatoes,
    Green, '87 164
  Beans with Tomatoes, Green, '85 137
  Beets, Harvard, '83 M195
  Beets, Orange-Glazed, '86 187
  Beets, Pickled, '87 163
  Broccoli Casserole, '88 265
  Broccoli, Easy Orange, '85 267
  Broccoli, Sesame, '85 8
  Broccoli Toss, '86 294
  Broccoli with Horseradish
    Sauce, '84 33
  Broccoli with Tangy Chive Sauce,
    Steamed, '83 101

  Brussels Sprouts, Casserole
    of, '86 294
  Brussels Sprouts, Glorified, '86 282
  Brussels Sprouts, Marinated, '88 265
  Brussels Sprouts Medley, '85 267
  Butternut-Orange Bake, '86 295
  Cabbage-and-Apple Slaw, Red, '87 31
  Cabbage, Sweet-and-Sour, '86 295
  Carrots and Onions, Herbed, '87 31
  Carrots, Ginger, '83 9
  Carrots, Glazed, '88 304
  Carrots, Golden, '85 267
  Carrots, Marinated, '86 108
  Carrots Marsala, '83 56
  Carrots, Orange-Spiced, '88 18
  Carrots Polynesian, Spiced, '88 85
  Carrots, Tropical, '84 34
  Cauliflower-Snow Pea Medley, '87 305
  Celery-Parmesan Toss, '84 34
  Corn Casserole, Chili-, '88 266
  Crêpes, Vegetable-Filled Bran, '86 44
  Eggplant, Ratatouille-Bran
    Stuffed, '86 44

Cooking Light, Vegetables *(continued)*

Kabobs, Marinated
   Vegetable, **'83** M195
Marinated Vegetables, **'88** 170
Medley, Chinese Vegetable, **'84** 33
Medley, Sautéed Vegetable, **'83** 101
Mixed Vegetables, **'83** M195
Mushrooms, Flavor-Stuffed, **'85** 288
Mushrooms, Savory Fresh, **'85** 268
Onion-Potato Bake, **'83** M195
Onions and Wine, Stuffed, **'85** 268
Onions Stuffed with Peas, **'84** 68
Pea Medley, English, **'85** 236
Peas-and-Corn Medley, **'85** 138
Peas and Ham, Southern, **'85** 138
Peas and Peppers, Stir-Fried, **'87** 51
Peas, Deluxe English, **'84** 68
Peas, Seasoned Black-Eyed, **'85** 138
Peppers, Stuffed, **'84** 202
Potato-Apple Bake, Sweet, **'86** 282
Potatoes and Turnips,
   Scalloped, **'85** 235
Potatoes, Double-Cheese, **'86** 6
Potatoes, Herbed New, **'83** 9
Potatoes,
   Mushroom-Dill-Topped, **'86** 41
Potatoes, Vegetable-Topped
   Stuffed, **'85** 235
Potato Puff, Sweet, **'85** 235
Potato Wedges, Lemon, **'88** 21
Rutabagas, Mashed, **'86** 295
Spinach Quiche, **'85** 49
Spinach Soufflé, **'86** 108
Squash Casserole, **'87** 163
Squash, Fruited Acorn, **'85** 235
Squash with Nutmeg, Acorn, **'85** 267
Stir-Fried Vegetables with
   Curry, **'87** 51
Stir-Fry, Almond-Vegetable, **'86** 222

Tomatoes and Okra, **'87** 164
Tomatoes, Bean-Stuffed, **'84** 34
Tomatoes, Cheese
   Herbed Topped, **'86** 108
Tomatoes, Cheesy Puff-Top, **'86** 187
Tomatoes, Grilled, **'85** 158
Tomatoes, Spinach-Topped, **'88** 265
Torta, Mexican, **'88** 149
Turnips and Carrots Julienne, **'86** 295
Zucchini-and-Tomato Casserole, **'88** 265
Zucchini-Basil Delight, **'85** 267
Zucchini-Basil Scramble, **'87** 34
Zucchini Dressing, **'86** 282

Zucchini, Stuffed, **'86** 187
Zucchini with Pecans, **'87** 31
Yogurt Snack, **'88** 55

Corn

Bake, Corn-Zucchini, **'79** 178
Baked Corn with Sour Cream, **'86** 170
Bake, Oyster-and-Corn, **'83** 34; **'84** 44
Balls, Zesty Corn Dressing, **'82** 307
Bisque, Crab-and-Corn, **'87** 137
Casserole, Broccoli-Corn, **'83** 313
Casserole, Chili-Corn, **'88** 266
Casserole, Corn, **'79** 247
Casserole, Corn and Cheese, **'81** 128
Casserole, Corn and Tomato, **'81** 127
Casserole, Corn-and-Tomato, **'84** 145
Casserole, Fresh Corn, **'80** 165
Casserole, Green Bean-and-Corn, **'88** 123
Casserole, Jalapeño-Corn, **'83** 256
Casserole, Salami-Corn, **'80** 209
Chowder, Corn, **'81** 128; **'83** 20;
   '84 M38; **'85** 10
Chowder, Corn and Cheese, **'80** 228
Chowder, Delicious Corn, **'82** 279
Chowder, Ham and Corn, **'79** 16
Chowder, Ham-and-Corn, **'82** 40
Chowder, Oyster-Corn, **'83** 211
Chowder, Shrimp and Corn, **'79** 199
Chowder, Turkey-Corn, **'81** 98
Cob, Barbecued Corn on the, **'81** 128
Cob, Corn on the, **'79** 122
Cob, Foil-Baked Corn on the, **'81** 128
Cob, Foiled Corn on the, **'80** 165
Cob, Microwaved Corn on the, **'80** M122
Cob, Parmesan Corn on the, **'88** M187
Cob, Seasoned Baked Corn on the, **'82** 134
Cob, Spicy Corn-on-the-, **'84** 149
Cob, Spicy Corn on the, **'87** M151
Cob with Herb Butter,
   Corn-on-the-, **'84** 160
Cold-Pack Corn, **'81** 216
Combo, Zucchini-Corn, **'86** 218
Creamed Corn, Southern-Style, **'81** M165
Creamed Fresh Corn, **'82** 158
Cream-Style Corn, **'80** 127; **'85** 106
Creamy Corn, **'79** 213
Creole Corn, **'81** 128
Creole, Okra-Corn, **'83** 157
Curried Corn and Celery, **'86** 192
Deviled Corn, **'86** 192
Dinner, Corn-and-Ham Skillet, **'83** 190
Escalloped Corn, **'79** 251
Fresh Corn, Seasoned, **'83** M147
Fried Corn, Skillet, **'83** 190
Frittata, Skillet Corn, **'87** 90
Fritters, Corn, **'86** 192
Fritters, Golden Corn, **'80** 165; **'81** 128
Fritters, Skillet-Fried Corn, **'85** 14
Grilled Parmesan Corn, **'82** 127
Herb Butter Sauce, Corn with, **'79** 150
Hush Puppies with Corn, **'83** 286; **'84** 17
Meat Loaf, Corny, **'86** 68
Medley, Okra-Corn-Tomato, **'81** 159
Medley, Peas-and-Corn, **'85** 138
Medley, Skillet Corn, **'86** 192
Medley, Summer Garden, **'84** 158
Medley, Zucchini-and-Corn, **'80** 298; **'81** 25
Mexican Corn, **'80** 157, 165
Mexi-Corn, **'82** M21
Moussaka, Corn, **'87** 190
Okra and Corn in Cream, **'79** 160
Okra, Corn, and Peppers, **'87** M151

Peppers, Corn-Stuffed, **'84** 104
Peppers, Ham-and-Corn Stuffed, **'81** 87
Pie, Quick and Cheesy Corn, **'82** 191
Pudding, Baked Corn, **'83** 314
Pudding, Corn, **'79** 276; **'81** 128; **'86** 192
Pudding, Corn-Cheese, **'80** 244
Pudding, Creamy Corn, **'81** 267
Pudding, Easy Corn, **'83** 280
Pudding, Fresh Corn, **'80** 157, 165

Quiche, Jalapeño-Corn, **'85** 122
Quick Corn Fix-Up, **'81** M4
Relish, Corn, **'81** 129, 175; **'83** 189;
   '84 107; **'85** 136; **'87** 120, 245
Relish Dogs, Corn, **'85** 192
Relish, Easy Corn, **'83** 260
Relish, Virginia Corn, **'79** 283
Salad, Broccoli-Corn, **'87** 24
Salad, Chilled Corn, **'79** 20
Salad, Corn, **'80** 247; **'81** 139; **'85** 236
Salad, Garden Medley, **'80** 122
Salad, Marinated Corn-Bean, **'87** 9
Salad, Shoepeg Corn, **'81** 23
Salad, Tangy Corn, **'88** 176
Salad, Tasty Corn, **'84** 289
Sauté, Corn, **'80** 165
Sautéed Corn and Okra, **'84** 158
Scalloped Corn, **'80** 164; **'81** 128; **'86** 111;
   '88 218
Scalloped Corn, Baked, **'85** 290
Scalloped Corn, Elegant, **'86** 268
Scalloped Corn for Two, **'82** 208
Slaw, Corn and Cabbage, **'79** 135
Smoked Corn, Hickory-, **'85** 145
Soufflé, Corn-and-Cheese, **'88** 122
Soufflé, Zucchini-and-Corn, **'83** 265
Soup, Corn, **'80** 56; **'85** 243; **'87** 156
Soup, Favorite Corn, **'85** 155
Soup, Grilled Corn, **'87** 121
Soup, Shrimp-and-Corn, **'84** 88
Spoonbread, Corn and Bacon, **'81** 129
Spoonbread, Corn-Cheese, **'88** 9
Succotash, Easy, **'80** 165
Tomatoes-and-Corn, Creole-Style, **'84** 142
Tomatoes, Corn-Stuffed, **'82** 270
Tomatoes with Corn, Baked, **'80** 161
Whole Kernel Corn, **'85** 106
Zucchini and Corn, **'86** 177
Zucchini and Corn, Dilled, **'83** 173
Zucchini, Corn and, **'83** 190

Cornbreads

Bake, Cornbread Tamale, **'79** 163
Beef Cornbread, Cheesy, **'81** 242
Bites, Corn Dog, **'85** 245
Buttermilk Cornbread, **'79** 34; **'82** 70

Carrot Cornbread, '80 89; '81 163
Casserole, Cornbread, '81 91
Casserole, Cornbread Skillet, '83 243;
   '84 101
Cheddar Cornbread, '83 285; '84 17
Cheddar-Jalapeño Cornbread, '85 3
Cheese Cornbread, Swiss, '79 60
Chicken over Cornbread, Creamed, '86 231
Chile-Cheese Cornbread, '87 171
Chile Cornbread, '86 254
Chile Cornbread, Green, '82 134
Cornbread, '80 272; '86 231; '87 197
Cottage Cheese Cornbread, '80 90
Cowboy Cornbread, '81 188
Cracklin' Cornbread, Southern, '80 119
Crackling Cornbread, '85 200
Crackling Cowboy Cornbread, '82 114
Crusty Cornbread, '85 255
Dieter's Cornbread, '87 164
Dressing, Cornbread, '86 286; '88 254
Dressing, Cornbread-and-Sausage, '83 213
Dressing, Cornbread-Biscuit, '79 296
Dressing, Cornbread-Sage, '80 262
Dressing, Cornbread-Sausage, '82 307;
   '85 280
Dressing, Fruited Cornbread, '80 262
Dressing, Herb-Seasoned
   Cornbread, '83 315
Dressing, Kentucky Cornbread, '86 281
Dressing, Old-Fashioned
   Cornbread, '84 321
Dressing, Sage-Cornbread, '84 283
Dressing, Savory Cornbread, '88 303
Dressing, Texas Cornbread, '82 243
Dressing, Turkey with
   Sausage-Cornbread, '83 287
Fresh Cornbread, '80 165
Hoecake, Hot Water, '81 56
Hoecakes, Green Onion, '88 112
Honey Cornbread, '83 286; '84 17
Hot Water Cornbread, '88 92
Hush Puppies, '84 102; '87 15
Hush Puppies, Aunt Jenny's, '84 88
Hush Puppies, Cracker, '80 99
Hush Puppies, Easy, '81 191; '85 14
Hush Puppies, Fiery Beer, '86 233
Hush Puppies, Golden, '82 135
Hush Puppies, Onion, '85 14
Hush Puppies, Peppery, '80 221; '88 111
Hush Puppies, Topsail Island, '79 152
Hush Puppies with Corn, '83 286; '84 17
Jalapeño Cornbread, '85 200
Jalapeño Cornbread, Beefy, '82 142
Jalapeño Pepper Bread, '83 121
Lacy Corncakes, '81 242
Lightbread, Corn, '81 137
Light Cornbread, Old Southern, '81 242
Loaf, Cornbread, '85 200
Menfolks' Cornbread, '82 156
Mexican Cornbread, '80 198; '81 137;
   '84 140, 242
Mexican Cornbread, Hot, '83 286; '84 17
Mexican Cornbread, Quick, '81 242
Mexican Flatbread, '80 197
Muffins, Cheesy Cornbread, '88 M275
Muffins, Corn, '82 M282; '84 16
Muffins, Cornmeal, '80 90; '88 92
Muffins, Four-Grain, '80 46
Muffins, Quick Corn, '88 15
Muffins, Sage-Corn, '83 207
Muffins, Southern Cornbread, '85 201

Muffins, Tomato Corn, '81 137
Mush, '81 215
Old-Fashioned Cornbread, '81 242
Onion Cornbread, '88 283
Onion-Topped Cornbread, '84 153
Oysters Casino on Cornbread, '79 34
Pastry, Cornmeal, '81 140
Pie, Cornbread-Sausage-Apple, '87 171
Puff, Cornmeal, '82 42
Quick-and-Easy Cornbread, '83 9
Quick Cornsticks, '81 192
Salad, Cornbread, '87 172
Skillet Cornbread, '81 31; '84 102;
   '85 200
Sour Cream Cornbread, '81 137
Southern Cornbread, '79 123; '81 56;
   '83 12
Southern Corncakes, '88 166
Spoonbread, '81 138
Spoonbread, Cheddar, '82 196
Spoonbread, Golden, '83 286; '84 17
Spoonbread, Old Virginia, '84 102
Spoonbread, Ozark, '85 202
Sticks, Angel Corn, '84 20
Sticks, Blue Ribbon Corn, '84 102
Sticks, Buttermilk Corn, '80 120
Sticks, Corn, '79 275
Sticks, Cornbread, '87 15
Sticks, Favorite Corn, '85 202
Sticks, Firecracker Corn, '85 241
Sticks, Quick Corn, '88 15
Sticks, Southern Corn, '81 242
Toasted Cornbread, '82 174
Ultimate Cornbread, '80 90
Waffles, Cornbread, '79 265
Waffles, Cornmeal, '85 201
Wampus Bread, '81 305; '82 36
Cornish Hens
Brandied Cornish Hens, '81 259
Brown Rice, Cornish Hens with, '82 275
Buttered Cornish Hens, Brandy-, '79 292;
   '80 32
Company Cornish Hens, '83 263
Cranberry Cornish Hens, '86 303
Cranberry-Orange Sauce, Cornish Hens
   with, '86 119
Cranberry Sauce, Cornish Hens
   with, '79 180
Elegant Cornish Hens, '80 227; '81 52
Flambé, Cornish Hens, '80 227; '81 52
Glazed Cornish Hens, Apricot-, '80 84;
   '87 306
Glazed Cornish Hens, Orange-, '83 267
Glazed Stuffed Cornish Hens,
   Orange-, '84 M89
Grilled Cornish Hens, '88 243
Grilled Cornish Hens,
   Orange-Glazed, '86 250
Herbed Cornish Hens, '82 271
Orange Glaze, Cornish Hens with, '79 244
Port and Sour Cream, Cornish Hens
   in, '86 323
Roast Cornish Hens, '86 89
Roasted Cornish Hens, Herb-, '88 29
Roasted Cornish Hens, Lemon, '82 260
Roasted Rock Cornish Hens, '82 66
Smoked Cornish Hens, '86 142, 154;
   '88 168
Stuffed Cornish Hens, '85 261
Stuffed Cornish Hens, Apricot-, '84 6
Stuffed Cornish Hens, Rice-, '82 302

Tarragon, Cornish Hens with, '83 143
Teriyaki Cornish Hens, '86 198
Texas-Style Game Hens, '87 61
Vermouth, Cornish Hens in, '86 33
Wild Rice Stuffing, Cornish Hens
   with, '79 222; '80 64; '82 136
Crab
au Gratin, Crabmeat, '86 154
Avocados, Crab-Stuffed, '86 73
Avocado with Crabmeat, '86 119
Baked Avocado-and-Crabmeat, '84 119
Bake, Quick Crab, '87 192
Balls, Crabmeat, '88 150
Bisque, Crab, '88 251
Bisque, Crab-and-Corn, '87 137
Bites, Crab-Zucchini, '84 M216
Blue Crabs, Festive, '85 103
Broiled Crab and Avocado, '79 116
Cakes, Crab, '81 125
Cakes, Crispy Fried Crab, '80 119
Cakes, Down-East Crab, '79 151

Canapés, Cheesy Crab, '86 262
Canapés, Crabmeat, '88 150
Canapés, Hot Crab, '86 70; '87 239
Casserole, Crab, '79 228
Casserole, Crab-and-Shrimp, '84 71
Casserole, Crab-Egg, '80 260
Casserole, Crabmeat-Broccoli, '84 232
Casserole, Creamy Crab and Spinach, '80 3
Chicken, Crab-Stuffed, '84 101
Cocktail, Sherried
   Avocado-Crabmeat, '87 95
Cornbread, Crab with Chile, '86 254
Crêpes, Crab, '79 165
Crêpes, Sautéed Crab, '84 84
Crisps, Crab, '79 63
Delight, Crab-and-Egg, '84 261
Deviled Crab, '85 104
Deviled Crab, Devilish, '85 264
Dip, Creamy Crab, '80 M135
Dip, Hot Cheese and Crab, '81 261
Dip, Oven-Baked Crab, '82 59
Dip, Tangy Crab, '83 5
Dressed Crab, '82 276
Eggs New Orleans, Crabmeat and, '82 45
Eggs, Shrimp and Crab Scrambled, '79 261
Flounder, Crab-Stuffed, '80 120
Fresh Crab, Preparing, '82 127
Gumbo, Crab and Shrimp, '81 200
Gumbo, Seafood, '83 90
Gumbo with Whole Crabs, Seafood, '85 2
Imperial, Crab, '79 82, 116
Imperial, Crabmeat, '82 311; '83 72
Imperial, Elegant Crab, '83 245
Imperial, Pineapple-Crab, '84 M286
Imperials, Individual Seafood, '84 162
Meunière, Soft-Shell Crab, '80 57

Crab (continued)

Mold, Crab, '85 318
Mousse, Crab, '79 117
Mushroom Caps, Crab-Stuffed, '84 160
Mushrooms, Crab-Stuffed, '81 190
Mushrooms on Toast Points, Crabmeat and, '82 M91
Mushrooms Stuffed with Crab, '82 249
Oysters and Crabmeat, Creamy, '83 211
Pâté, Crab, '79 233
Peas, Crab-Stuffed Snow, '85 288
Pie, Hot Seafood, '80 32
Potatoes, Cheesy Crab-Stuffed, '86 17
Potatoes, Crabmeat-Topped, '83 3
Puff, Crab, '79 116
Puffs, Crab, '80 20; '84 269
Puff, Shrimp-Crab, '79 57
Quiche, Almond-Topped Crab, '79 127
Quiche, Crab, '82 M122, 243
Quiche, Quick Crab, '84 96
Quiche, Sherried Crab, '83 180
Quiche, Simple Crab, '85 207
Ravigote, Crabmeat, '82 250
Salad, Crab and Wild Rice, '79 116
Salad, Crab-Avocado, '81 114
Salad, Crabmeat Luncheon, '82 207
Salad, Crabmeat-Shrimp Pasta, '86 208
Salad, Crab-Stuffed Tomato, '80 148
Salad, Crab-Wild Rice, '86 207
Salad, Delightful Crab, '87 145
Salad, Macaroni-Crabmeat, '81 153
Salad, Super Shrimp, '81 37
Salad with Crabmeat-and-Asparagus, Congealed, '84 86
Sandwiches, Avocado-Crabmeat, '83 2
Sandwiches, Crabmeat, '84 285
Sandwiches, Deluxe Crabmeat, '81 M74
Sandwiches, Hot Crab-and-Cheese, '87 279
Sandwiches, Open-Face Crab Tomato, '81 29
Sandwiches, Open-Faced Crab, '87 106
Sandwiches, Puffy Crab, '83 291
Sauce Piquante, Crab and Shrimp, '83 92
Sauce, Quick Crab Marinara, '85 M151
Sauce, Stone Crab Mustard, '80 3
Sauce, Tangy Stone Crab, '80 3
Sautéed Crabmeat, Roussos, '84 88
Sautéed Seafood Platter, '83 89
Seafood Boil, Low Country, '80 119
Shrimp Bundles, Crab-Stuffed, '81 176
Shrimp, Crab-Stuffed, '84 259
Snacks, Crab, '83 93
Sole in Papillote, '82 22
Soup, Crabmeat, '84 123
Soup, Cream of Crab, '88 302
Soup, Creamy Crab, '80 M224
Soup, Elegant Crab, '80 188
Soup, Quick Crab, '84 279
Soup, Steamboat's Cream of Crab, '81 127
Soup with Marigold, She-Crab, '79 32
Spread, Baked Crab, '80 86
Spread, Crabmeat, '79 81
Spread, Crab Soufflé, '85 4
Spread, Hot Artichoke-Crab, '85 81
Spread, Layered Crabmeat, '83 127
Spread, Superb Crab, '81 235
Steamed Blue Crabs, Spicy, '84 162
Stroganoff, Crab, '79 116
Stuffed Soft-Shell Crabs, '83 91

Stuffed Soft-Shell Crabs, Steamboat's, '81 127
Stuffing, Chicken Breasts with Crabmeat, '85 302
Supreme, Crab, '79 181
Tomatoes, Crab-Stuffed Cherry, '82 289; '88 78
Veal with Crabmeat, New Orleans, '86 94

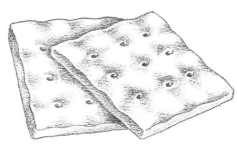

Crackers
Bread, Sesame Cracker, '87 2
Cheddar Crackers, '84 236
Cheese Cracker Nibbles, '84 328
Dessert Crackers, '87 3
Fennel-Rye Crackers, '87 2
Florida Crackers, '86 179
Hush Puppies, Cracker, '80 99
Oatmeal-Wheat Germ Crackers, '84 236
Olive-Rye Snack Crackers, '84 191
Pie, Cracker, '79 113
Snackers, Cracker, '86 229

Cranberries
Brandied Cranberries, '86 269
Bread, Cranberry, '79 242
Bread, Cranberry-Banana, '80 281
Bread, Cranberry Fruit-Nut, '79 275
Bread, Cranberry-Orange, '87 244
Bread, Cranberry-Orange Nut, '80 288
Bread, Orange-Cranberry, '85 266
Bread, Raisin-Cranberry, '81 305; '82 36
Cake, Cranberry Coffee, '81 14
Cake, Cranberry-Nut Coffee, '81 250
Cake, Cranberry-Orange Coffee, '82 283
Cake, Cranberry Upside-Down, '87 8
Cake, Orange-Cranberry, '85 314
Casserole, Cranberry-Apple, '83 311
Casserole, Sweet Potatoes-and-Berries, '84 231
Chicken, Barbecued Cranberry, '83 178
Chicken Kiev, Cranberry, '87 250
Chutney, Cranberry, '80 243; '83 260; '84 265
Chutney, Cranberry-Orange, '79 292
Chutney, Orange-Cranberry, '86 266
Chutney with Cream Cheese, Cranberry-Amaretto, '87 244
Cider, Spiced Cranberry, '84 261
Cobbler, Cranberry, '81 275
Cobbler, Cranberry-and-Apple, '84 306
Cobbler, Easy Cranberry, '86 260
Cobbler Roll, Cranberry, '80 288; '81 248
Compote, Berry, '81 275
Conserve, Apple-Cranberry, '82 308
Conserve, Cranberry, '79 243; '83 279; '85 266
Cooler, Cranberry, '86 229

Cornish Hens, Cranberry, '86 303
Crêpes, Cranberry, '85 262
Crisp, Cranberry-Pear, '83 207
Crunch, Apple-Cranberry, '86 300; '87 178
Cup, Berry Grapefruit, '79 242
Daiquiris, Cranberry, '81 245
Dessert, Cranberry Apple, '80 253
Dessert, Cranberry Surprise, '79 242
Dip, Cranberry-Horseradish, '85 65
Float, Sparkling Cranberry, '86 195
Frappé, Cranberry, '82 263
Frosted Cranberries, '82 280
Glaze, Cranberry, '84 306; '86 171; '88 244
Ham, Cranberry Broiled, '88 301
Ham, Cranberry Glazed, '81 274
Ham, Cranberry-Orange Glazed, '81 295
Ice, Cranberry-Apple, '82 290
Ice, Tangy Cranberry, '87 305
Ice, Tart Cranberry-Orange, '86 317
Jam, Christmas, '88 288
Jam, Christmas Brunch, '81 286
Jelly, Cranberry-Wine, '81 290
Jubilee, Cranberries, '85 312
Jubilee, Tasty Cranberry, '84 305; '85 189
Juice, Sparkling Cranberry, '88 275
Lemonade, Spiced Cranberry, '87 292
Loaf, Apricot-Cranberry, '79 235
Loaf, Cranberry-Ham, '82 M77
Mold, Cranberry, '79 250
Muffins, Cranberry, '81 249
Muffins, Cranberry-Pecan, '84 269
Muffins, Cranberry Streusel Cake, '88 M274
Oriental, Cranberry, '79 126
Pie, Autumn Apple, '79 205
Pie, Berry-Apple, '88 251
Pie, Cranberry-Apple, '79 264
Pie, Cranberry-Apple Holiday, '81 M269
Pie, Cranberry-Raisin, '80 283; '85 316
Pie, Cran-Raspberry, '87 244
Pie, Festive Cranberry Freezer, '84 306
Pie, Frosty Cranberry, '79 249
Pie, Nutty Cranberry, '82 M298
Pie, Peach-Cranberry, '83 249
Pie, Tart Cranberry-Cherry, '87 299
Pie, Walnut-Cranberry, '87 259
Pork Chops, Cranberry, '80 288
Pork Chops, Orange-Cranberry, '86 335; '87 84
Pork Roast, Berry Barbecued, '80 288
Pudding, Cranberry, '84 306
Punch, Cranberry, '83 275; '85 90
Punch, Cranberry-Cinnamon, '86 270
Punch, Cranberry Percolator, '88 248
Punch, Holiday Cranberry, '85 265
Punch, Hot Cranberry, '80 288; '84 41, 319; '85 265
Punch, Hot Spiced, '80 250
Punch, Pink Lady, '81 100
Punch, Sparkling Cranberry, '85 277
Punch, Tart Cranberry, '83 318
Red Roosters, '87 147
Relish, Cran-Apple, '84 300
Relish, Cranberry, '81 275; '83 144; '85 258, 264; '86 283; '87 245
Relish, Cranberry-Nut, '86 275
Relish, Cranberry-Orange, '81 M289; '88 254
Relish, Cranberry-Pear, '85 232
Relish, Holiday Cranberry, '88 304

Relish, Lemony Cranberry, '79 243
Relish, Old-Fashioned Cranberry, '82 297
Ring, Spicy Peach-Cranberry, '85 264
Rolls, Cranberry-Pineapple, '86 275
Salad, Cranberry-Cheese Ribbon, '79 241
Salad, Cranberry Christmas, '79 243
Salad, Cranberry-Topped Green, '87 311
Salad, Cranberry-Whipped Cream, '83 261
Salad, Festive Cranberry, '81 264, 296
Salad, Holiday Cranberry, '82 266, 288
Salad, Holiday Jewel, '81 252
Salad, Jellied Cranberry, '83 279; '85 281
Salad, Layered Cranberry, '84 322;
  '86 325
Salad, Lemon-Cranberry Congealed,
  '87 311

Salad Ring, Cranberry, '80 247
Salad, Tart Cranberry, '79 286
Sauce, Baked Cranberry, '88 257
Sauce, Baked Ham with
  Cranberry-Raisin, '88 244
Sauce, Cornish Hens with
  Cranberry-Orange, '86 119
Sauce, Cranberry, '86 278; '88 280
Sauce, Cranberry Juice, '85 224; '86 83
Sauce, Cranberry Wine, '83 276
Sauce, Fresh Cranberry, '79 283;
  '84 275
Sauce, Fresh Cranberry-Apricot, '87 243
Sauce, Tart Cranberry, '83 261
Shake, Cranberry, '83 171
Sherbet, Cranberry, '88 280
Slush, Cranberry-Rum, '84 259
Smoothie, Cranberry, '86 183
Soda, Cranberry-Orange, '79 148
Sorbet, Cranberry, '82 251
Sorbet, Cranberry Juice, '85 259
Soufflé, Cranberry-Topped Holiday,
  '84 306
Spiced Cranberries, '82 254, 287
Squash, Cranberry-Filled Acorn, '81 M231
Stuffing, Crown Roast of Pork with
  Cranberry-Sausage, '88 49
Supreme, Cranberry, '85 280
Tart, Cranberry-Nut, '84 305
Tartlets, Fresh Cranberry, '87 244
Tarts, Cranberry-Cream Cheese, '80 154
Tarts, Cranberry Holiday, '83 279
Tea, Cranberry-Apple, '88 169
Turkey Loaf, Cranberry-Glazed, '86 171
Wassail, Cranberry, '88 289

Wild Rice, Cranberry-Pear, '83 279
Wine Cup, Cranberry, '85 23

Crawfish
Étouffée, Crawfish, '83 91; '86 156
Mushrooms, Crawfish-Stuffed, '86 258
Salad, Dilled Crawfish, '83 126
Spaghetti, Crawfish, '85 104

Crème Fraîche
Fraîche, Crème, '85 39
Sauce, Crème Fraîche, '79 281

Crêpes
Amandine, Crêpes Gelée, '83 126
Amaretto-and-Orange Crêpes, '86 260
Banana Crêpes Flambé, '84 262
Basic Crêpes, '84 83; '86 38
Beef Crêpes, Sherried, '85 M29
Beef Roulades, '80 80
Bran Crêpes, '83 70; '86 44
Breakfast Crêpes, Country-Style, '79 22
Brunch Crêpes, Nutritious, '80 44
Brunch Crêpes, Royal, '81 44
Cannelloni Crêpes, '86 143
Cheese and Mushroom Crêpes, '81 88
Cheese Blintzes, '82 146; '83 71
Cheesy Party Wedges, '84 84
Cherry Crêpes Flambé, '79 18
Chicken Crêpes, '80 39
Chicken Crêpes, Creamy, '81 200
Chicken-Vegetable Crêpes, '83 70
Chocolate Chantilly Crêpes, '82 183
Chocolate Crêpes, '86 164
Chocolate Dessert Crêpes, '84 84; '85 262
Chocolate Dream Crêpes, '86 164
Chocolate-Orange Crêpes, '85 263
Coffee Ice Cream Crêpes, '84 85
Coquilles St. Jacques Crêpes, '83 13
Crab Crêpes, '79 165
Crab Crêpes, Sautéed, '84 84
Cranberry Crêpes, '85 262
Crêpes, '82 38, 46, 146, 240; '83 13, 71,
  122, 127, 205, 282; '84 186; '86 216;
  '87 126; '88 295
Dessert Crêpes, '84 84; '86 260; '87 290;
  '88 134
Dessert Crêpes, Basic, '82 183; '85 262;
  '86 275
Dessert Crêpes, Dixie, '79 222
Dessert Crêpes, Spicy, '84 262
Divan, Elegant Crêpes, '81 91
Entrée Crêpes, '79 264
Florentine Crêpe Pie, '79 34
Florentine, Crêpes, '80 74
Fruit Crêpes, Tropical, '87 77
Fruit Filling, Crêpes with, '81 96
Ham-and-Egg Crêpes, '83 204
Ham-and-Egg Crêpes with Mushroom
  Sauce, '82 46
Lemon Crêpes with Fruit Filling, '82 46
Light Crêpes, '86 143
Low-Calorie Crêpes, '87 77
Mango-Pineapple Crêpes, '86 216
Mushroom-Cheese Crêpes, '87 289;
  '88 135
Orange Dream Crêpes, '82 183
Peach Crêpes, '82 184
Peach Crêpes, Fresh, '84 186
Plain Crêpes, '83 70
Processor Crêpes, Basic, '87 289; '88 135
Raspberry Crêpes, '87 126
Sausage Crêpes, '88 295
Sausage Crêpes, Cheesy, '82 240; '83 71

Sausage-Filled Crêpes, '79 39
Spinach-Ricotta Crêpes, '81 52
Strawberry Dessert Crêpes, '83 122
Strawberry Ice Cream Crêpes, '87 290;
  '88 135
Suzette, Raspberry Crêpes, '84 84
Suzettes, Light Crêpes, '83 71
Tropical Crêpes, '86 275
Turkey Crêpes, Elegant, '83 282
Virginia Crêpes, '79 264
Whole Wheat Crêpes, '80 44; '83 70
Zucchini Crêpes, '79 157

Croutons
Celery Croutons, '79 16
Crispy Italian Croutons, '84 126
Croutons, '86 M288
Garlic-Flavored Croutons, '86 47
Herb Croutons, '81 150
Microwave Croutons, '86 M227
Vegetable-Flavored Croutons, '84 148

Cucumbers
Aspic, Shrimp-Cucumber, '83 108
Bisque, Shrimp-Cucumber, '79 172
Chips, Cucumber, '85 176
Combo, Cucumber-and-Pepper, '88 176
Cool Cucumbers, '84 152
Cooler, Simple Cucumber, '86 147
Delights, Cucumber, '84 117
Dilled Cucumber on Tomatoes, '84 142
Dills, Lazy Wife, '87 149
Dip, Cucumber-Cheese Vegetable, '83 128
Dressing, Creamy Cucumber Salad, '82 79
Dressing, Cucumber, '80 74
Dressing, Cucumber-Mint, '87 153
Dressing, Tomato, Onion, and Cucumber in
  Italian, '81 83
Fried Cucumber Fingers, '86 146
Marinated Cucumbers and
  Artichokes, '82 111
Marinated Cucumbers and Squash, '86 146
Mold, Asparagus-Cucumber, '85 252
Mold, Chicken-Cucumber, '80 175
Mold, Creamy Cucumber, '84 164
Mold, Lemon-Cucumber, '87 90
Mousse, Cucumber, '79 11; '88 121
Pickles, Cucumber Sandwich, '81 174
Pickles, Dill, '81 174
Pickles, Mixed, '81 174
Pickles, Quick Sweet, '87 149
Pickles, Sour Cucumber, '85 176
Pickles, Sweet Icicle, '85 176
Relish, Cucumber, '85 176
Rounds, Cucumber, '88 78
Salad, Creamy Cucumber, '86 147
Salad, Cucumber-Almond, '86 147
Salad, Cucumber-Bean, '83 81
Salad, Cucumber-Pineapple, '84 124
Salad, Cucumber-Yogurt, '87 33
Salad, Dilled Cucumber, '82 229

Cucumbers *(continued)*

Salad, Dilled Cucumber and
　Tomato, **'81** 153
Salad, Grapefruit-Cucumber, **'80** 100
Salad, Marinated Cucumber, **'82** 111
Salad Mold, Cucumber, **'82** 111;
　'83 81, 253
Salad, Pineapple-Cucumber
　Congealed, **'83** 118
Salad, Tomato-Cucumber, **'86** 218
Salad, Tomato-Cucumber-Onion, **'81** 239
Salad, Yogurt-Cucumber, **'82** 122

Sandwiches, Cucumber, **'88** 159
Sandwiches, Cucumber Pinwheel, **'85** 120
Sandwiches, Dainty Cucumber, **'81** 119
Sauce, Cucumber, **'82** 111; **'84** M286
Sauce, Cucumber-Dill, **'86** 5
Sesame Cucumbers, **'85** 85
Slices, Cheesy Cucumber, **'84** 80
Slices, Fresh Cucumber, **'86** 177
Snapper Rolls, Cucumber-Stuffed
　Red, **'83** 176
Soup, Chilled Cucumber, **'79** 144
Soup, Cold Cucumber, **'79** 130; **'81** 130
Soup, Cold Minted Cucumber, **'86** 34
Soup, Cold Potato-Cucumber, **'88** 160
Soup, Cream of Cucumber, **'81** 98
Soup, Creamy Cucumber, **'80** 171
Soup, Cucumber-Yogurt, **'82** 157; **'83** 205
Sour Cream, Cucumber and Onion
　in, **'81** 69
Sour Cream, Cucumbers in, **'79** 52;
　'80 178
Spread, Cucumber, **'79** 295; **'80** 31
Spread, Cucumber and Cream
　Cheese, **'82** 140
Spread, Shrimp-Cucumber, **'79** 81
Stuffed Cucumbers, **'81** 237
Tomatoes, Cucumber-Stuffed
　Cherry, **'88** 262
Topping, Lamb Pockets with Dilled
　Cucumber, **'87** 104
Tuna Boats, Cucumber, **'83** 136
Vinaigrette Oriental, Cucumber-, **'85** 198;
　'86 147

Currants. *See* Raisins.

Curry

Almonds, Cauliflower and Peas with
　Curried, **'79** 221
Almonds, Curried, **'82** 297
Bananas, Fillets with Horseradish Sauce and
　Curried, **'85** 230
Beef and Rice, Curried, **'88** 164
Beef Dinner, Curried, **'83** 4
Beef Pitas, Curried, **'85** 220
Bites, Curried Swiss, **'85** 220
Casserole, Curry Pea, **'87** 154

Cheese Ball, Chicken-Curry, **'85** 118
Cheese Ball, Curried Shrimp, **'86** 135
Chicken Bites, Curried, **'85** 40
Chicken, Curried, **'86** 43
Chicken, Curried Fried, **'85** 160
Chicken Curry, **'84** 110; **'85** 220; **'86** 21
Chicken Curry, Brioche, **'88** 124
Chicken Curry, Stir-Fried, **'87** 51
Chicken Divan, Curried, **'80** 83
Chicken, Honey-Curry, **'87** 36
Chicken, Regal Curried, **'84** 110
Chicken-Stuffed Peppers, Curried, **'87** 19
Chops, Pineapple-Curry Glazed, **'82** 106
Coleslaw, Curried, **'85** 139
Coleslaw, Curried Pineapple, **'88** 172
Corn and Celery, Curried, **'86** 192
Dip, Curried, **'81** 262
Dip, Curry, **'80** 84; **'81** 9; **'85** 132;
　'86 184; **'87** 25
Dip, Tuna-Curry, **'84** 31
Dressing, Curried, **'84** 115
Dressing, Curry, **'80** 242; **'82** 78
Eggs, Saucy Shrimp-Curried, **'84** 143
Filling, Curried Chicken, **'88** 125
Fish, Curried Baked, **'87** 5
Fruit, Almond-Curried, **'83** 261
Fruit Bake, Curried, **'87** 241
Fruit, Hot Curried, **'79** 225; **'81** 264;
　'84 287
Ham and Peaches, Curried, **'82** 60
Ham Steak, Curried, **'82** 120
Ham with Rice, Curried, **'80** 111
Hurry Curry, **'79** 103
Kheema, Indian, **'81** 226
Lamb Curry with Rice, **'80** 83; **'81** 10
Lamb with Rice Mold, Curried, **'85** 36
Meat Loaf, Curried, **'86** 43
Mushrooms, Curried, **'84** 214
Mushroom Soup, Curried, **'84** M89
Nuts, Spicy Curried, **'82** 250
Peas with Almonds, Curried, **'88** M294
Pie, Crumb-Crust Curried Turkey, **'86** 265
Popcorn Mix, Curried, **'86** 326
Pork Tenderloin, Curried, **'86** 76
Rice and Shrimp, Curried, **'83** 231
Rice, Curry-Spiced, **'86** M226
Rice Mix, Fruited Curry-, **'86** 326
Rice Mold, Curried, **'85** 36
Rice, Quick Curried, **'86** 81
Rice with Almonds, Curried, **'83** M285
Rice with Curry, Raisin, **'85** 83
Rice with Pineapple, Curried, **'79** 142
Salad, Curried Apple-Raisin, **'80** 24
Salad, Curried Broccoli, **'86** 225
Salad, Curried Chicken, **'79** 219; **'84** 66;
　'85 96; **'86** 131
Salad, Curried Chicken-and-Orange, **'87** 144
Salad, Curried Rice, **'80** 84; **'85** 147, 220
Salad, Curried Tuna, **'86** 208
Salad, Curried Turkey, **'88** 140
Salad, Curry Spinach, **'80** 242
Salad, Hot Indian Curry, **'83** 23
Salad with Asparagus, Curried
　Chicken, **'81** 36
Salad with Grapes, Curried Tuna, **'87** 201
Sauce, Curry, **'79** 156; **'83** 138; **'84** M71
Sauce, Halibut with Orange-Curry, **'87** 91
Sauce, Pineapple-Curry, **'79** 252
Shrimp, Curried, **'84** 110
Shrimp Curry, Sour Cream, **'80** 83
Shrimp Curry, Sour Cream and, **'81** 10

Shrimp Malai Curry, **'84** 110
Shrimp, Quick Curried, **'84** M198
Snapper, Honey-Curried, **'85** 181
Soup, Curried, **'81** 130
Soup, Curried Carrot, **'82** 157
Soup, Curried Chicken, **'86** 34
Soup, Curried Turkey, **'86** 332
Spread, Broccamoli Curry, **'88** 55
Spread, Curried Shrimp, **'87** 158
Steak, Curried Beef, **'88** 60
Vegetables with Curry, Stir-Fried, **'87** 51

Custards

Almond Creme Custard with
　Raspberries, **'88** 174
Amaretto Custard,
　Chocolate-Topped, **'87** M37
Amaretto Custard, Range-Top, **'87** 77
Amaretto Custard with
　Raspberries, **'86** 152
Ambrosia, Custard Sauce, **'84** 256
Baked Custard, **'80** 219
Baked Custard, Creamy, **'86** 7
Baked Custard, Easy, **'85** 52
Baked Vanilla Custard, **'82** 129
Boiled Custard, Favorite, **'81** 181
Boiled Custard, Perfect, **'81** 34
Cake, Chocolate Custard, **'88** 175
Chocolate Custard, **'88** 258
Coconut Custard, **'86** 109
Crema, **'80** 175
Crème Pâtissière, **'84** 207
Filling, Creamy Custard, **'81** 180
Filling, Custard, **'82** 52, 298; **'85** 281
Filling, Egg Custard, **'87** 14
Flan Almendra, **'80** 199
Flan, Flaming, **'85** 313
Flan, Orange, **'84** 95
Flan, Pumpkin, **'82** 217
Flans, Individual, **'85** 52
Flan, Spanish, **'85** 51, 311
Lemon Custard in Meringue Cups, **'80** 295;
　'81 172
Mexican Custard, Light, **'88** 149
Napoleon Cream, **'84** 138
Orange Custard Pudding, **'88** 174
Peach Custard Dessert, Fresh, **'86** 162
Pears in Custard, Poached, **'88** 20
Pie, Apple Custard, **'88** 236
Pie, Carrot Custard, **'79** 45
Pie, Coconut Custard, **'82** 33
Pie, Custard Pecan, **'87** 184

Pie, Old-Fashioned Egg Custard, '82 261
Pie, Perfect Custard, '82 92
Pumpkin Custard, '88 279
Sauce, Custard, '85 41; '88 154, 251, 259
Sauce, Fresh Berries with Raspberry
    Custard, '88 163
Squash, Custard-Filled Acorn, '86 334
Stirred Custard, Old-Fashioned, '85 52
Stirred Custard over Fruit, '84 83

D

Dates
Balls, Date-Nut, '85 10
Balls, Peanut-Date, '81 92
Bars, Date, '84 313
Bars, Date-Nut, '80 166
Bars, Date-Oat, '80 M172
Bars, Layered Oatmeal-Date, '85 10
Bars, No-Bake Date, '79 256
Bars, Nutty Date, '84 153
Bread, Chocolate Date-Nut, '81 284
Bread, Date-Nut, '85 306
Bread, Persimmon Date-Nut, '82 218
Bread, Wine-Date Nut, '82 253
Brownies, Date-and-Almond, '88 217
Cake, Date Nut, '79 176; '80 5
Cake, Fresh Apple-Date, '83 300
Cake, Pumpkin Date, '79 251
Cake, Queen Bee, '81 237
Cake Squares, Apple-Date Dream, '85 10
Candy, Date Loaf, '80 302
Cheese, Nutty Date Dessert, '87 299
Chocolate Date-Nut Delight, '88 168
Conserve, Brandied Date, '85 315
Cookies, Christmas Date, '88 287
Cookies, Oatmeal-Date, '82 109
Cookies, Oatmeal-Date Sandwich, '83 257
Cookies, Rolled Fruit, '80 15
Cupcakes, Date, '84 7
Dressing, Date, '87 57
Filling, Apple-Date, '83 301
Filling, Date, '80 15; '83 257; '86 314
Filling, Date Cream, '81 303
June Bugs, '85 11
Loaf, Blue Ribbon Date-Walnut, '80 15
Loaf, Date-Nut, '85 10
Logs, Date, '79 274
Muffins, Carrot-Date-Nut, '86 262
Muffins, Date, '79 142
Muffins, Date-Nut, '84 75
Muffins, Surprise Date, '79 216
Pastries, Date-Filled Cheese, '83 259
Pie, Date-Pecan, '80 15
Pie, Dried Fruit, '83 249
Pudding, Steamed Date, '79 86
Roll, Date Nut, '79 249
Rollups, Date-Cream Cheese, '83 298
Salad, Festive Fruit, '80 16
Sauce, Date-Nut Sundae, '82 167
Spread, Breakfast Date, '84 7
Spread, Date-Walnut, '87 292
Stuffed Dates, Apricot-, '80 250
Desserts. *See also* specific types.
After Dinner-Drink Dessert, '82 100
Alaska, Peachy Melba, '88 266
Alaskas, Brownie, '83 299
Amaretto Cream Tortoni, '85 161

Ambrosia, Baked, '83 303
Ambrosia, Brunch, '83 57
Ambrosia, Honey Bee, '83 267
Ambrosia, Layered, '88 304
Apple Brown Betty, '83 213
Apple-Cranberry Crunch, '86 300; '87 178
Apple Crisp, Delicious, '82 303
Apple Crisp, Granola, '85 78
Apple Delight, '80 109
Apple Dumplings, '82 273
Apple Dumplings with Orange Hard
    Sauce, '88 224
Apple Flan, '81 309
Apple Fritters, '82 273
Apple Kuchen, '79 24
Apple-Nut Crunch, '82 M238
Apple Rings, '85 232
Apple Rings, Cinnamon, '82 M237
Apples and Cream, Brandied, '82 M237
Apples, Baked Mincemeat-Filled, '80 276
Apples, Brandied, '81 248
Apples, Chilled Poached Lemon, '86 182
Apples, Golden, '82 254
Apples, Imperial Baked, '82 273
Apples, Melting, '88 19
Apples, Old English Caramel, '85 231
Apples, Orange-Pecan Baked, '85 45
Apple Squares, Sour Cream, '82 262
Apples with Brandied Date Conserve,
    Cinnamon, '85 315
Apples with Orange Sauce, Baked, '84 314
Apricot Cream, Peachy-, '86 163
Avocado Whip, '79 107
Banana-Berry Supreme, '81 205
Banana Cream Dessert, '81 180
Banana Flip, '83 303
Banana-Peach Flambé, '85 316
Bananas, Candied, '83 179
Bananas Foster, '79 18; '83 M114;
    '86 139; '88 20
Bananas Foster, Elegant, '81 59
Bananas Foster for Two, '80 115
Bananas Foster, Tropical, '79 231
Bananas, Praline, '84 313
Bananas, Regal, '85 46
Bananas Supreme, '84 256
Bananas with Orange Sauce, Baked, '79 115
Bavarian Cream with Fresh Fruit, '88 137
Bavarian Dessert, Light, '86 6
Berries on Snow, '82 227
Berries with Raspberry Custard Sauce,
    Fresh, '88 163
Berry Basket, Summer, '84 158
Berry Compote, '81 275
Berry Grapefruit Cup, '79 242
Berry-Peach Compote, '82 133
Biscuits, Sweet Little, '85 305
Blackberries and Dumplings, '86 196
Blackberry Flan, '79 182
Blueberries and Cointreau, '82 100
Blueberry-Amaretto Squares, '83 220
Blueberry Crumble, '81 84
Blueberry Crunch, Fresh, '82 143
Blueberry Dream, '88 94
Boysenberries and Cream
    Supreme, '82 133
Brandy Float, Blazing, '85 314
Bread, Fry, '85 155
Brownie Ice Cream Sandwich
    Shells, '88 195
Buñuelos, '80 199

Buñuelos, King-Size, '86 5
Butter-Nut Strips, '82 167
Butterscotch Fantastic, '83 76
Cakes, Funnel, '83 250
Cakes, Spanish Wind, '84 157
Cannoli, '80 58
Cantaloupe Compote, '81 147
Cantaloupe Cream Delight, '82 179
Caramel Surprise, '88 202
Champagne Delight, '83 304
Charlotte, Macaroon, '81 296
Charlotte, Peach, '79 68
Charlotte Russe, '80 71; '82 M142
Charlotte Russe, Fresh Lemon, '80 13
Charlotte Russe, Lemon, '84 192
Charlotte Russe, Wine Jelly and, '82 305
Cheese Blintzes, '82 146; '83 71
Cheese, Chunky Cream, '85 306
Cheese Dessert, Creamy Cottage, '87 191
Cheese, Fruited Cream, '85 306
Cheese Kuchen, '86 84
Cheese Molds, Heavenly Dessert, '85 209
Cheese, Nutty Date Dessert, '87 299
Cheese Squares, Lemony Cream, '82 159

Cherries à la Mode, '88 202
Cherries Jubilee, '79 18; '83 139
Cherries Jubilee, Quick, '82 M100
Cherries Jubilite, '86 317
Cherries Sabayon, '88 178
Cherry-Berry on a Cloud, '79 94
Cherry Compote, '83 139
Cherry Dessert, Holiday, '80 255
Chocolate
    Almond Dessert, Chocolate-, '82 306
    Almond Meringue Fingers,
        Chocolate-, '84 158
    Almond Velvet, Chocolate, '81 148
    Brownie-Mint Dessert, '82 227
    Buttercream, Chocolate, '84 156
    Charlotte Russe, Chocolate, '87 74
    Chilled Chocolate Dessert, '83 177
    Coffee Mallow, '80 109
    Cream, Heavenly Chocolate, '88 128
    Crêpes, Chocolate Dream, '86 164
    Cups, Chocolate, '80 207
    Cups, Chocolate Lace, '87 133
    Cups, Chocolate-Mint, '80 71
    Cups, Chocolate-Walnut, '85 213
    Cups, Miniature Chocolate, '87 132
    Date-Nut Delight, Chocolate, '88 168
    Dream Dessert, Chocolate, '83 198
    Easy Chocolate Dessert, '79 75
    Ladyfinger Dessert, Chocolate, '86 162
    Mint Dessert, Chocolate-, '82 100
    Mint Dessert, Cool Chocolate-, '80 109

Desserts, Chocolate *(continued)*

Peanut-Chocolate Dessert, '80 86
Pots de Chocolat, Petits, '82 272
Pots de Crème, '81 15; '84 M145
Pots de Crème, Mocha, '88 M45
Pots de Crème,
  Rum-Flavored, '85 102
Roll, Chocolate Cream, '85 317
Roll, Chocolate Mousse, '83 290
Roulage, Chocolate-Mocha, '80 216
Rum Dessert, Chocolate-, '81 247
Shells with Kahlúa Cream,
  Chocolate, '88 195
Squares, Chocolate-Blueberry
  Dessert, '87 299
Strawberry-Chocolate Combo, '85 96
Sundae Dessert, Hot Fudge, '84 313
Supreme, Chocolate, '84 94
Trifle, Chocolate, '88 258
Truffle Dessert, Chocolate, '88 281
Waffles with Strawberry Cream,
  Chocolate, '88 153
Coconut Cloud, '80 70
Coconut Dessert, Chilled, '83 116
Cœur à la Crème, Christmas, '86 278
Coffee-Almond Tortoni, '81 30
Crackers, Dessert, '87 3
Cranberries, Brandied, '86 269
Cranberries Jubilee, '85 312
Cranberry Apple Dessert, '80 253
Cranberry Jubilee, Tasty, '84 305
Cranberry Supreme, '85 280
Cranberry Surprise Dessert, '79 242
Cream, Bavarian, '86 M165
Cream, Molded French, '85 311
Cream Puffs, Captivating, '81 180
Cream Puffs, Java, '81 187
Cream Puffs, Strawberry, '81 95
Cream Puffs, Tutti-Frutti, '79 231
Crème Celeste, '88 94
Crème d'Ange, '83 91
Crème Pâtissière, '84 207
Crêpes, Basic Dessert, '82 157; '86 275
Crêpes, Dessert, '86 260; '87 290;
  '88 134
Crêpes, Dixie Dessert, '79 222
Crêpes Flambé, Cherry, '79 18
Crêpes, Strawberry Dessert, '83 122
Crêpes Suzettes, Light, '83 71
Custard Dessert, Fresh Peach, '86 162
Date-Nut Balls, '85 10
Doughnuts, Orange Spiced, '79 136
Drink, Creamy Dessert, '86 131
Drink, Simply Super Dessert, '83 303
Éclairs, Minted Miniature, '88 66
Éclairs with Pecan Sauce, '83 219
Flan, '88 247
Frappé, Hawaiian, '81 178
Frozen
  Amaretto Freeze, '82 182
  Amber Bombe, '80 255
  Apricot Fluff, Frozen, '86 242
  Apricot Freeze, '82 10
  Baked Alaska, '84 105; '85 295
  Baked Alaska, Apple, '80 226
  Baked Alaska, Brownie, '80 66
  Baked Alaska, Chocolate
    Mousse, '85 195
  Banana Pops, '83 60; '84 44
  Banana Split Alaskas, '87 10

Banana Split Pie, Layered, '83 189
Cantaloupe Cream, Frozen, '82 159
Cherry Cordial Dessert, '84 312
Chocolate-Coffee Frozen
  Dessert, '85 172
Chocolate Dessert, Frozen, '83 76
Chocolate Mint Freeze, '88 167
Choco-Maple Frozen Dessert, '86 300;
  '87 178
Citrus Cup, Snowball, '79 2
Coffee Dessert, Light, '88 260
Coffee Ice Cream Crunch, '82 182
Coffee Tortoni, Creamy, '88 268
Cranberry Sorbet, '82 251
Elegant Ending, '86 145
Fruit Cream Freeze, '82 144
Fruit Freeze, Holiday, '88 283
Fruit Ice, Mixed, '88 85
Fruit Pops, '87 168
Fudge-Peanut Ice Cream
  Dessert, '88 167
Grand Marnier Cream, '84 312
Grasshopper Freeze, Creamy, '81 180
Honeydew Granita, '87 162
Ice Cream Bombe, '82 305

Ice Cream Delight, '80 69
Ice Cream Dessert, Layered, '83 189;
  '84 94, 105; '86 163
Ice Cream Dessert, Mint, '88 66
Ice Cream Pie, Kona, '83 189
Ice Cream Sandwiches, Chocolate
  Cookie, '87 147
Ice Cream Treats, Crunchy, '86 300;
  '87 178
Lemon-Chiffon Frozen Yogurt, '85 54
Lemon Cream, Frozen, '83 118
Lime-Mint Refresher, '82 144
Little Bits, '79 196
Macaroon-Sherbet Frozen
  Dessert, '79 212
Mint Patty Alaska, '80 219
Mocha Alaska Dessert, '84 191
Mocha Dessert, Frozen, '84 311
Mocha Freeze, Royal, '84 53
Mocha Squares, Frozen, '81 187
Orange Alaska, '83 177
Orange-Banana Pops, '82 129
Ozark Pudding, '88 127
Peach Freeze, Creamy, '82 144
Peanut Butter Delight, Frozen, '88 137
Pineapple Delight, Fresh, '79 111
Pineapple-Orange Bars, '82 129

Pumpkin Dessert, Frozen, '88 167
Rainbow Delight, Frozen, '84 105
Raspberry Dessert, Frozen, '84 192
Sherbet Ambrosia Cups, '82 159
Sherbet Dessert, Layered, '87 109
Strawberry Delight, Frozen,
  '82 112, 174
Strawberry Frost, '82 24; '83 154
Strawberry Popsicles,
  Smoothie, '82 112
Strawberry Puff, '82 5
Toffee Ice Cream Dessert, '87 110
Vanilla Frozen Yogurt, '87 125
Vanilla Soufflé, Frozen, '79 230;
  '82 173
Watermelon Frost, '86 196
Fruit
  Bake, Nutty Fruit, '83 127
  Caribbean Fruit Dessert, '84 314
  Cheese, Luscious Fresh Fruit
    with, '79 153
  Chilled Fruit with Dressing, '85 222
  Combo, Fresh Fruit, '86 178
  Compote, Baked Fruit, '80 276;
    '84 314
  Compote, Baked Mustard Fruit, '85 47
  Compote, Champagne Fruit, '81 309;
    '82 124
  Compote, Chilled Fruit, '83 123
  Compote, Fresh Fruit, '79 162;
    '82 197, 272; '84 82
  Compote, Fruit, '86 330
  Compote, Gingered Fruit, '88 184
  Compote, Hot Fruit, '81 203; '83 53
  Compote, Warm Praline Fruit, '85 260
  Compote, Wine Fruit, '81 272
  Cup, Fruit, '81 141
  Cup with Rum, Fruit, '83 55
  Flame, Sherried Fruit, '85 313
  Flaming Fruit Dessert, '83 302
  Fondue, Fruitcake, '84 258
  Fresh Fruit with Cheese,
    Luscious, '79 153
  Gingered Fruit, '83 151
  Glazed Fruit, '85 83
  Hot Fruit Delight, '83 281
  Kabobs with Mint Marinade, '82 157
  Lemon Curd, Fresh Fruit with, '88 21
  Medley, Chinese Fruit, '83 22
  Medley, Fancy Fruit, '84 82
  Medley, Fresh Fruit, '81 141
  Medley, Frosty Fruit, '82 226
  Medley of Fruit, Tropical, '86 53
  Meringue Shells, Fruited, '87 32
  Orange, Fruit Dessert, '84 314
  Rainbow Fruit Dessert, '85 108
  Soup Dessert, Fruit, '79 172
  Spiced Fruit Delight, '82 229
  Spiced Fruit Dessert, '82 50
  Tequila, Fruit in, '82 223
  Turnovers, Fruit, '79 150
Gâteau Panache, '83 269
Golden Dream, '82 100
Grape Juice-Fruit Refresher, '86 182
Honeydew-Berry Dessert, '83 120
Ice Cream Ginger Fizz, '83 303
Kahlúa Cream, '87 134
Kahlúa Delight, '83 67
Kahlúa Delight, Make-Ahead, '84 M89
Kahlúa Velvet Dessert, '85 M294
Kiwi and Cream in Meringue Cups, '81 279

Kiwi-Berry Pizza, '86 198
Kiwi Jubilee, '83 120
Lemon-Cream Cheese
  Dessert, '84 95
Lemon Cups, Baked, '87 128
Lemon Delight, '82 227
Lemon Dessert, Layered, '88 134
Little Nothings, '79 135
Madeleines, '88 79
Mango Pan Dowdy, '83 150
Maple Nut Dessert, '81 84
Maraschino Russian Cream, '79 231

Melon Ball Compote, '85 157
Melon Balls in Watermelon Sauce, '79 177
Melon-Mint Julep, '86 196
Melons in Mint Sauce, '85 164
Melon Wedges with Berry Sauce, '86 178
Meringue Cream Cups, Lemon, '84 23
Meringue Flowers, '84 156
Meringue, Piping, '84 156
Meringues, Baked Pear, '85 232
Meringues, Strawberry, '84 188
Mocha-Almond Dessert, '80 289; '81 62
Mocha Chiffon, '86 75
Nectarines Royale, '85 132
Orange-Apple Crisp, '80 295
Orange Baskets, '81 308
Orange Chantilly Cream, '84 156
Orange-Coconut Cream, '84 24
Orange Cream, '81 12
Orange Cream Dessert, '80 254; '84 165
Orange Dip, Creamy, '84 117
Orange Elegance, Baked, '80 13
Orange Flambé, Dessert, '85 313
Orange Flan, '84 95
Orange Molded Dessert, '83 302
Oranges, Frosted, '83 270
Oranges, Wine-Poached, '84 M323
Orange-Tapioca Crème, '82 M283
Orange Tapioca Fluff, '87 31
Pancakes, Dessert Ginger, '88 153
Pancakes, Luau Dessert, '88 154
Parfaits
    Blackberries-and-Cream Parfait, '87 129
    Chocolate-Crème de Menthe
      Parfaits, '85 161
    Chocolate-Peppermint Parfaits, '88 65
    Coffee Crunch Parfaits, '82 159
    Eggnog Bavarian Parfait, '79 255
    Kiwi Parfait, '86 199; '87 55
    Lime Parfaits, '80 153
    Mocha-Mallow Parfaits, '80 219
    Orange Parfaits, Chilled, '80 219
    Peach Parfait, '82 166
    Peanut Butter Parfaits,
      Crunchy, '79 176; '80 6

Pineapple Parfait, '84 83
Speedy Parfaits, '83 76
Strawberry-Lemon Parfaits, '84 198
Strawberry Parfait, '79 99
Strawberry Parfaits, Frosty, '85 213
Strawberry Parfait, Surprise, '86 151
Strawberry-Yogurt Parfait,
  Crunchy, '79 124
Peach Almond Cream, '82 108
Peach Cream, Bavarian, '82 171
Peach Dessert, Quick, '85 178
Peach Dessert, Spiced, '83 9
Peach Dumplings, '85 177
Peaches, Brandy, '85 275
Peaches Champagne, '79 146
Peaches Foster, '86 240
Peaches, Gingersnap, '85 M329
Peaches in Wine Sauce, '79 184
Peaches, Macaroon-Stuffed, '79 178
Peaches with Ginger, Oven-Baked, '82 170
Peaches with Nutty Dumplings,
  Spiced, '87 164
Peaches with Rum, Ginger, '84 M323
Peach Halves, Stuffed, '86 196
Peach Melba, '81 83; '83 M114
Peach Split, '85 277
Peachy Melt-Away Dessert, '87 298
Pear Fans with Raspberry-Orange Sauce,
  Poached, '88 22
Pears, Almond-Stuffed, '83 207
Pears Belle Helene, '86 164
Pears Flambé, Orange-Poached, '85 313
Pears, Flaming, '84 313
Pears in Custard, Poached, '88 20
Pears in Red Wine, '82 254
Pears in Wine, Poached, '82 194
Pears, Lemon Poached, '82 74
Pears, Maple-Sugared, '81 232
Pears Poached in Red Wine, '83 302
Pears, Spicy Coconut, '83 207
Pears with Berry Sauce,
  Wine-Poached, '86 144
Pears with Raspberry Sauce,
  Poached, '84 213; '87 69; '88 223
Pecans, Sugared, '82 167
Peppermint Bavarian, '80 153
Peppermint Wafer Dessert, '79 176; '80 7
Pineapple-Almond Delight, '85 96
Pineapple Dessert Chimichangas, '86 4
Pineapple, Meringue-Topped, '84 178
Pineapple 'n' Cream, '88 202
Pineapple, Scalloped, '79 106; '82 254
Pineapple with Natillas Sauce,
  Baked, '83 179
Pizzelles, '83 298
Plum Crunch, Layered, '86 174
Port Wine Jelly with Whipped
  Cream, '84 254
Profiteroles, '84 208
Prune Bavarian, '86 223
Pumpkin Chiffon, '82 216; '86 283;
  '88 260
Pumpkin Chiffon Dessert, '88 128
Pumpkin Flan, '82 217
Pumpkin Mold, '82 311
Pumpkin-Orange Delight, '86 321
Raspberry Dream, '83 108
Raspberry-Jellyroll Dessert, '85 95
Raspberry Prunes, '82 124
Rhubarb-Strawberry Bavarian, '86 140
Rhubarb Whip, '79 112

Rice Cream with Mandarin
  Oranges, '85 317
Sauces
    Almond-Vanilla Custard
      Sauce, '88 M177
    Amaretto-Strawberry Sauce, '87 M165
    Apple Dessert Sauce, '87 M165
    Apple Dessert Sauce, Spicy, '82 177
    Apple Topping, Spicy, '87 125
    Apricot Sauce, '82 212
    Apricot-Walnut Hard Sauce, '88 153
    Banana-Pineapple Sauce, '83 48
    Banana Sundae Sauce, '84 275
    Berry Sauce, '87 290; '88 135

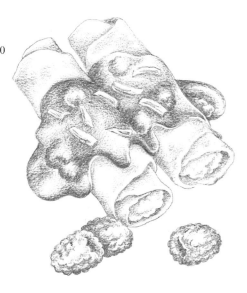

Blackberry Sauce, '86 152
Blueberry Sauce, '88 155
Blueberry Topping, '87 125
Bourbon Praline Sauce, '81 170
Brandied Hard Sauce, '80 264;
  '83 250; '85 313
Brandy-Butter Sauce, '79 230
Brandy-Macadamia Sauce, '82 311
Brandy Sauce, '88 279
Buttered Rum Sauce, '83 249
Buttered Rum Sauce, Hot, '88 204
Butterscotch-Pecan Sauce, '82 212
Caramel-Raisin Sauce, '88 127
Caramel Sauce, '79 79
Caramel Sauce, Easy, '87 38
Cherry-Pineapple Topping, '87 126
Cherry Sauce, '79 91
Cherry Sauce, Elegant, '79 M156
Chocolate-Cherry Sauce, '85 189
Chocolate Cherry Sauce, '87 M165
Chocolate Mint Sauce, Quick, '86 M58
Chocolate-Orange Sauce, '86 165
Chocolate-Peanut Butter Sauce,
  '79 91, M156
Chocolate-Praline Sauce, '85 M295
Chocolate Sauce, '83 189; '84 208,
  313; '86 322
Chocolate Sauce, Classic, '85 207
Chocolate Sauce, Creamy, '88 M177
Chocolate Sauce, Double, '83 79

Desserts, Sauces *(continued)*

Chocolate Sauce, Heavenly, '79 79; '82 167
Chocolate Sauce Supreme, '85 189
Cinnamon-Blueberry Sauce, '86 11
Cinnamon-Fudge Sauce, '85 141
Coconut-Orange Sauce, '85 189
Coconut Sauce, Creamy Light, '82 177
Cranberry Jubilee, Tasty, '85 189
Cranberry Sauce, '86 278; '88 280
Crème Fraîche Sauce, '79 281
Custard Sauce, '85 41; '88 154, 251, 259
Date-Nut Sundae Sauce, '82 167
Fig Sauce, '79 140
Fruit Dessert Sauce, Hot, '87 299
Fruit Sauce, Quick, '82 212
Fudge Sauce, Easy Hot, '84 69

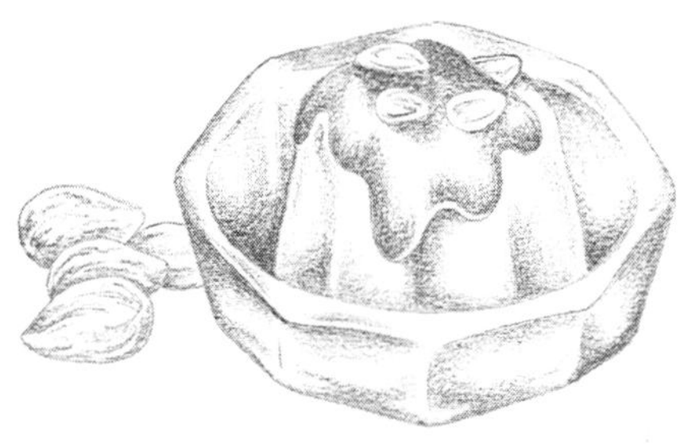

Fudge Sauce, Hot, '82 181, 295; '84 143
Fudge Sauce, Quick Hot, '82 212
Golden Sauce, '88 267
Hard Sauce, '80 265; '82 14
Hard Sauce, Special, '86 318
Honey-Orange Sauce, '85 108
Honeyscotch Sundae Sauce, '82 167
Hot Cinnamon Sauce, Apple Pie with, '88 210
Kahlúa Chocolate Sauce, '85 155
Lemon Dessert Sauce, '87 M165
Lemon Sauce, '84 258, 306; '85 77, 190
Lemon Sauce, Tart, '85 191
Mango Sauce, '83 120
Melba Sauce, '87 77
Mint Sauce, Party, '82 212
Orange Dessert Sauce, '87 58
Orange Hard Sauce, '88 225
Orange Sauce, Fresh, '85 209
Peach-Berry Sauce, '87 M165
Peach-Blueberry Pancake Sauce, '82 177
Peach Blueberry Sauce, '81 170
Peach-Praline Sauce, '85 161
Peach Sauce, '84 144
Peach Sauce, Creamy, '85 189
Peach Sauce, Fresh, '87 167
Peanut Butter Ice Cream Sauce, '84 30
Peanut Dessert Sauce, '86 M251
Pecan Sauce, '83 219
Piña Colada Topping, Chunky, '87 125
Pineapple Ice Cream Sauce, '81 M289

Pineapple-Rhubarb Sauce, '88 94
Pineapple-Rum Sauce, '84 275
Praline Ice Cream Sauce, '85 189
Praline Ice Cream Sauce, Southern, '86 M227
Praline Sauce, '83 25; '84 143
Raspberry-Amaretto Sauce, '88 130
Raspberry-Orange Sauce, '88 22
Raspberry-Peach Topping, '87 126
Raspberry Sauce, '82 289; '83 108; '84 73, 213; '87 69, 117, 183; '88 267
Raspberry Sauce, Crimson, '79 91; '85 30
Raspberry Sauce Dessert, '80 147
Raspberry Sauce Flambé, '84 142
Rhubarb Sauce, Chilled, '88 94
Rum-Butter Sauce, '86 301
Rum-Fruit Sauce, '84 312
Rum-Raisin Sauce, '84 7
Rum Sauce, '88 32
Rum Sauce, Brown Sugar-, '85 231
Rum Sauce, Hot, '79 86
Sherry Sauce, '84 109
Strawberry-Banana Topping, '87 125
Strawberry Sauce, '84 144; '87 93, 198
Strawberry Sauce, Brandied, '88 196
Strawberry Sauce, Fresh, '82 177
Strawberry Sauce, Peaches with, '85 8
Strawberry Sauce with Crunchy Topping, '81 170
Strawberry Sauce with Dumplings, '84 314
Taffy Dessert Sauce, '86 20
Watermelon Sauce, Melon Balls in, '79 177
Savarin, '79 171
Sopaipillas, '80 197; '88 112
Sopaipillas, Pineapple, '83 179
Soufflé, Banana Daiquiri, '84 317
Soufflé, Brandy Alexander, '82 173; '83 M114
Soufflé, Chilled Devonshire, '88 279
Soufflé, Chilled Orange, '84 317; '86 189
Soufflé, Chocolate-Mint, '81 16
Soufflé, Coconut, '85 212
Soufflé, Cold Lemon-Lime, '84 24
Soufflé, Elegant Daiquiri, '80 69
Soufflé, Frozen Orange, '79 211
Soufflé, Frozen Vanilla, '79 230; '82 173
Soufflé, Grand Marnier, '79 281
Soufflé, Grasshopper, '81 248; '86 188
Soufflé, Kahlúa, '82 173
Soufflé, Lemon, '82 170
Soufflé, Light Chocolate, '83 278
Soufflé, Orange Dessert, '83 206
Soufflé, Pineapple Dessert, '80 153
Soufflé, Raspberry, '86 188
Soufflé, Raspberry-Topped, '85 317
Soufflé, Tart Lemon, '85 82
Strawberries, Almond Cream with Fresh, '87 93
Strawberries and Cream, '82 100
Strawberries, Deep-Fried, '84 109
Strawberries Jamaica, '85 161
Strawberries Juliet, '84 82
Strawberries Marsala, '88 171
Strawberries Romanoff, '84 108; '88 95
Strawberries, Ruby, '82 100
Strawberries Sabayon, '79 94

Strawberries with Brandied Orange Juice, '82 160
Strawberries with French Cream, '83 191
Strawberries with Strawberry Cream, '84 108
Strawberries with Walnuts, Stuffed, '85 122; '86 124
Strawberries Zabaglione, '81 95
Strawberry Cheese Delight, '79 50
Strawberry Coconut Nests, '88 136
Strawberry-Cream Cheese Dessert, '83 123
Strawberry Delight, '81 85
Strawberry Dessert, '83 123
Strawberry Dessert, Chilled, '84 164
Strawberry Dessert, Glazed, '84 33
Strawberry Frost, '81 279; '82 24
Strawberry-Lemon Dessert, '86 162
Strawberry Napoleons, '81 126
Strawberry Pizza, '79 94
Strawberry Shortcake Squares, '85 122
Strawberry Swirl, '84 108
Strawberry Yogurt Delight, '85 77
Sundae Dessert, Hot Fudge, '86 322
Sundaes, Cocoa-Kahlúa, '83 M58
Sundaes Flambé, Peach, '81 88
Sundaes, Hot Strawberry, '81 M5
Sundaes, Mauna Loa, '80 126
Sundaes, Quick Pear, '86 71
Toffee Dessert, English, '88 136

Trifle, Easy Strawberry, '88 201
Trifle, Lemon-Blueberry, '88 210
Trifle, Raspberry, '88 259
Trifle, Rum, '86 322
Trifle, Savannah, '80 121
Tropical Snow, '86 34
Vacherin Moka, '80 55
Vanilla Cream, '83 M115
Vanilla Sherry Dessert, Glorified, '81 85
Waffle, Whole Wheat Dessert, '79 92
White Christmas Dessert, '82 261
Wine Jelly, Rosy, '85 306
Yule Log, '79 281; '82 289
Doughnuts
Applesauce Doughnuts, '81 203
Banana Doughnuts, '86 137
Beignets, '84 56
Cake Doughnuts, Quick, '82 226
Chocolate-Covered Doughnuts, '84 55
Chocolate Doughnuts, '83 95
Cinnamon Puffs, '81 209
Dutch Doughnuts, '81 50
Fry Bread, '84 140
Glazed Doughnuts, '83 94

Jelly-Filled Doughnuts, '84 55
Orange Spiced Doughnuts, '79 136
Pineapple Drop Doughnuts, '83 95
Potato Doughnuts, Chocolate-Glazed, '85 6
Potato Doughnuts, Old-Fashioned, '84 56
Puffs, Doughnut, '86 85
Puffs, Wheat Quick Doughnut, '85 278
Spice Doughnuts, '84 56
Whole Wheat Doughnuts, '84 56

Dove
Enchiladas, Dove, '85 270
Gumbo, Dove and Sausage, '81 199
Roasted Doves, Pan-, '87 240

Dressings. *See* Stuffings and Dressings.

Duck and Duckling
Baked Duck, Sherried, '79 224
Blackberry Sauce, Ducklings with, '82 251
Breasts with Raspberry Sauce,
    Duck, '87 240
Casserole, Duck and Wild Rice, '79 224
Enchiladas with Red Pepper-Sour Cream,
    Smoked Duck, '87 121
Gumbo, Duck, Oyster, and
    Sausage, '79 226
Gumbo Ya Ya, '87 210
Holiday Duckling, '80 251
Marinated Duck Breasts,
    Charcoaled, '79 226
Orange Duck, Chafing Dish, '79 226
Orange Gravy, Duck with, '81 259
Pâté, Duck, '79 226
Pâté, Duck Liver, '79 227
Pecan Stuffing, Wild Duck with, '85 269
Prairie Wings Mallard, '83 252
Roast Ducklings with Cherry
    Sauce, '86 312
Roast Duckling with Orange Sauce, '81 125
Roast Duckling with Wine Jelly, '88 243
Roast Duck with Sweet Potato-Eggplant
    Gravy, '83 90
Roast Long Island Duckling, '84 87
Smoked Duck Breasts, '87 121
Wild Duck, Buffet, '86 268

Dumplings
Apple Dumplings, '82 273
Apple Dumplings, Old-Fashioned, '84 226
Apple Dumplings with Orange Hard
    Sauce, '88 224
Beef Stew with Dumplings, '84 3
Blackberries and Dumplings, '86 196
Chicken and Dumplings, Country, '85 254
Chicken and Dumplings, Easy, '86 21
Chicken and Dumplings,
    Old-Fashioned, '79 55; '83 228
Chicken and Dumplings with
    Vegetables, '85 M56
Chicken Stew and Dumplings, '84 4
Cornmeal Dumplings, Turnip Greens
    with, '82 211
Drop Dumplings, Burgundy Stew
    with, '83 125
Old-Fashioned Dumplings, '81 191
Parsley Dumplings, Beef Stew with, '81 76;
    '82 13; '85 M246
Peach Dumplings, '80 143; '85 177
Peas and Dumplings, Green, '80 102
Potato Dumplings, Venison Stew
    with, '87 304
Shrimp with Dumplings, Stewed, '79 31
Strawberry Sauce with Dumplings, '84 314
Tomato Dumplings, '88 144

E

Eggnog
Bread, Eggnog, '83 294
Breakfast Nog, Speedy, '82 47
Christmas Eggnog, '87 242
Coconut Nog, '83 275
Coffee Nog, Brandied, '86 329
Coffee Nog, Irish, '84 258
Cookies, Eggnog Christmas, '79 255
Creamy Eggnog, '80 259; '83 303;
    '85 300
Edenton Eggnog, '84 251
Eggnog, '83 318
Holiday Brew, '81 265
Holiday Eggnog Deluxe, '79 232
Irish Cream Nog, '82 312
Orange Spiced Nog, '82 48
Parfait, Eggnog Bavarian, '79 255
Pie, Eggnog, '80 254; '83 205; '86 317;
    '87 295
Pie, Eggnog Chiffon, '86 281
Pie, Fluffy Eggnog, '81 M269
Punch, Coffee-Eggnog, '86 281
Punch, Holiday Eggnog, '86 281
Salad, Eggnog Christmas, '86 281
Sparkling Eggnog, '79 232

Tarts, Creamy Eggnog, '79 255
Thick and Creamy Eggnog, '80 261

Eggplant
Almonds, Eggplant with, '79 179
Appetizer, Eggplant, '83 187
Bake, Eggplant, '80 82
Bake, Eggplant-Sausage, '85 221
Caponata, '87 166
Casserole, Easy Eggplant, '80 202
Casserole, Eggplant, '81 205; '84 217
Casserole, Eggplant and Noodle, '82 230
Casserole, Eggplant-and-Tomato, '83 187
Casserole, Eggplant-Sausage, '84 215
Casserole, Elegant Eggplant, '82 168
Casserole, Flavorful Eggplant, '79 92
Casserole, Moussaka, '79 179
Casserole, Potato-Eggplant, '87 166
Casserole, Super Eggplant, '80 202
Caviar, Eggplant, '88 262
Crawfish on Eggplant, Soft-Shell, '88 222
Creole Eggplant, '82 107; '83 86
Creole, Eggplant, '86 110
Easy Eggplant, '87 M151
Fried Eggplant, '79 178; '83 187; '88 111
Fried Eggplant, French-, '81 204

Fried Eggplant, Parmesan, '79 189
Fried Parmesan Eggplant, '87 166
Gravy, Roast Duck with Sweet
    Potato-Eggplant, '83 90
Grilled Eggplant, '80 202
Italian Eggplant, '84 216
Italian-Style Eggplant and Zucchini, '79 289;
    '80 26
Jackstraw Eggplant, '82 230
Julienne, Eggplant, '85 221
Lebanese Eggplant, '81 24
Main Dish, Sausage-Eggplant, '80 211
Medley, Eggplant-Shrimp, '79 188
Mexican Eggplant, '83 187
Mexicano, Eggplant à la, '82 229
Moussaka, '87 166
Parmesan, Eggplant, '82 230; '83 186;
    '84 215; '86 53
Parmigiana, Chicken-Eggplant, '82 212
Parmigiana, Eggplant, '81 19; '82 186
Patties, Eggplant, '83 186
Pizza, Eggplant, '85 221
Ratatouille, '84 105, 243
Ratatouille, Eggplant-Zucchini, '81 205
Ratatouille Niçoise, '81 22
Ratatouille, Quick-and-Easy, '80 212
Sandwiches, Baked Eggplant, '82 230
Sautéed Eggplant and Zucchini, '82 96
Soup, Eggplant Supper, '85 221
Spanish Eggplant, '79 21
Spread, Eggplant, '86 278
Squash, Eggplant and, '83 187
Stuffed Eggplant, '80 158
Stuffed Eggplant, Baked, '81 133
Stuffed Eggplant, Beefy, '81 204
Stuffed Eggplant, Cheesy, '79 188; '82 208
Stuffed Eggplant Creole, '82 230
Stuffed Eggplant, Ham-, '80 162
Stuffed Eggplant, Mushroom-, '83 136
Stuffed Eggplant, Ratatouille-, '83 187
Stuffed Eggplant, Ratatouille-Bran, '86 44
Stuffed Eggplant, Rolled, '80 63
Stuffed Eggplant, Sausage, '81 204
Stuffed Eggplant, Seafood, '79 187
Supper, Beef-and-Eggplant, '84 291
Supreme, Eggplant, '79 188; '86 170
Tophats, Eggplant, '79 188

Eggs
au Gratin, Broccoli-and-Eggs, '85 289
au Gratin, Potatoes and Eggs, '79 107
Bake, Breakfast, '85 45
Baked Egg Crisps, '83 57
Baked Eggs Florentine, '86 M12
Baked Eggs in Spinach Nests, '82 70
Bake, Egg and Rice, '83 119
Bake, Sausage Egg, '81 225
Bake, Smoked Sausage-Egg, '85 248
Bedeviled Eggs, '86 67
Benedict, Bacon-and-Tomato Eggs, '87 195
Benedict, Easy Eggs, '80 M268
Benedict, Eggs, '79 40, 254; '85 49
Benedict with Cheese Sauce, Eggs, '81 225
Brandied Cream Sauce, Eggs in, '82 70
Bread, Butter-Egg, '85 269
Bread, County Fair Egg, '87 68
Bread, Easter Egg, '84 94
Breakfast Eye-Openers, '82 231
Breakfast, Farmer's, '81 44
Brunch Eggs, '85 44
Bruncheon Eggs, '83 83
Brunch, Texas, '82 70

Eggs *(continued)*

Bunwiches, **'80** 92
Casserole, Apple-Egg, **'85** 44
Casserole, Bacon and Egg, **'81** 225
Casserole, Breakfast Ham and Egg, **'79** 253
Casserole, Broccoli-and-Egg, **'86** 324
Casserole, Brunch Egg, **'86** 329
Casserole, Cheese-Egg-Zucchini, **'84** 114
Casserole, Cheesy Egg, **'81** 244; **'86** 15
Casserole, Cheesy Potato-Egg, **'84** 5
Casserole, Crab-Egg, **'80** 260
Casserole, Egg, **'83** 311
Casserole, Egg-and-Bacon, **'85** 248
Casserole, Egg-and-Cheese, **'84** 293
Casserole, Egg-Mushroom, **'83** 49
Casserole, Egg Soufflé, **'83** 55
Casserole, Sausage Breakfast, **'81** 270
Casserole, Sausage-Egg, **'86** M12
Casserole, Spinach and Egg, **'82** 270
Casserole, Squash and Egg, **'80** 146
Casserole, Zucchini-Egg, **'84** M113
Chile Eggs, **'88** 80
Cottage Eggs, **'85** 44
Crabmeat and Eggs New Orleans, **'82** 45
Creamed Eggs à la Asparagus, **'81** 201
Creamed Eggs, Broccoli and, **'83** 84
Creamed Eggs in Patty Shells, **'80** M267
Creamed Eggs in Toast Cups, **'83** 83
Creole Eggs, **'82** 42
Creole, Skillet Eggs, **'85** 143
Crêpes, Ham-and-Egg, **'83** 204
Crêpes with Mushroom Sauce, Ham-and-Egg, **'82** 46
Croquettes, Tuna-Egg, **'80** 275
Delight, Bacon-and-Egg, **'85** 143
Delight, Crab-and-Egg, **'84** 261
Delight, Mushroom-Egg, **'83** 14
Dip, Festive Egg, **'79** 285
Dressing, Egg, **'86** 79
Florentine, Eggs, **'79** 39; **'83** 56
Florentine-Style Eggs, **'82** 38
Foo Yong, Egg, **'80** 19; **'86** 232
Foo Yong Patties, **'80** 223
Foo Yong, Shrimp Egg, **'83** 22
Frittata, Broccoli-Cheese, **'81** 243
Frittata, Spinach, **'81** 53
Ham and Eggs à la Swiss, **'88** 158
Ham and Eggs, Creamed, **'82** 40
Ham and Eggs, Creamy, **'87** 286
Ham and Eggs on Toast with Cheese Sauce, **'81** 43
Ham and Eggs, Savory, **'82** 231
Hard-Cooked Eggs, **'82** 280
Hash Brown Skillet Breakfast, **'82** 5
Herb Sauce, Eggs in, **'88** 80
Hominy, Bacon, Eggs, and, **'85** 143
Huevos Rancheros, **'82** 197
Medley, Cheddary Egg, **'81** M176
Mexicana, Eggs, **'82** 146
Migas, **'87** 180
Mound, Frosted Egg, **'79** 33
Mushroom Eggs, Sherried, **'83** 49
Mushrooms and Eggs in Patty Shells, **'85** 143
Mushrooms and Eggs, Saucy, **'79** 138
Nests, Fluffy Egg, **'79** 128
Omelets
- Broccoli-Mushroom Omelet, **'85** 45
- Cheese Omelet, Zippy, **'87** 287
- Cheesy Picante Omelet, **'86** 95
- Chicken Liver Omelet, **'82** 44
- Fluffy Omelet, **'84** 56
- George's Omelets, **'80** 68
- Ham and Cheese Omelet, **'79** 262; **'80** 123
- Mexican Omelet, **'79** 128; **'81** 225
- Mexican Omelet, Easy, **'88** 114
- Mushroom Omelet, Rolled, **'82** 70
- Mushroom Sauce, Puffy Omelets with, **'85** 40
- Olé Omelet, **'87** M124
- Oyster Omelets, Smoked, **'84** 96
- Potato-Sprout Omelet, **'79** 128
- Primavera, Omelet, **'87** 71
- Rising Sun Omelet, **'82** 281; **'83** 42
- Sandwich, Omelet, **'86** 95
- Sausage Filling, Omelet with, **'81** 43
- Sausage Omelet, Puffy, **'80** M268
- Shrimp-and-Cheddar Omelet, **'84** 57
- Sour Cream-Ham Omelet, **'79** 261
- Spanish Omelet, **'81** 201; **'83** 243; **'84** 101
- Spanish-Style Omelets, **'83** 188
- Spinach-Cheese Omelet, **'83** 119
- Sunrise Omelet, **'83** 289
- Swiss Oven Omelet, **'80** 189
- Tex-Mex Omelet con Carne, **'81** 209
- Vegetable Omelet, Beefy, **'83** 188
- Vegetable Omelet, Cheddar-, **'83** 205
- Vegetable Omelet, Cheesy, **'85** 49
- Vegetable Omelet, Fresh, **'84** 211
- Vegetable Omelet, Golden, **'82** M123
- Vegetable Omelet, Puffy, **'83** 188
- Vegetarian Omelet, **'84** 114
- White Wine Omelet, **'79** 103
- Yogurt-Avocado Omelet, **'81** 33
- Zucchini Omelet, **'81** 99

Paint, Egg Yolk, **'86** 322
Patty Shells, Mushrooms and Eggs in, **'88** 197
Peanut Butter Easter Eggs, **'87** 86
Pickled Eggs, Beet, **'84** 287
Pickled Eggs, Rosy, **'86** 68
Pickled Eggs, Spiced, **'84** 288
Pie, Egg-Stra Special Chicken, **'86** 264
Pie, Old-Fashioned Egg Custard, **'82** 261
Pizza, Breakfast, **'85** 44
Poached Eggs, Basic, **'82** 58
Poached Eggs, French-Style, **'82** 58
Puff, Egg-and-Cheese, **'85** 45
Rancheros, Easy Eggs, **'88** 81
Rice, Egg Fried, **'79** 252; **'80** 19
Roulade with Mushroom Filling, Egg, **'88** 84
Salad, Asparagus-and-Egg, **'86** 305
Salad, Deviled Egg, **'83** 124
Salad, Egg-Rice, **'84** 18; **'86** 169
Salad, Green Vegetable and Egg, **'79** 191
Salad, Ham-and-Egg Potato, **'86** 84
Salad, Ham 'n Egg, **'81** 36
Salad, Tossed Shrimp-Egg, **'80** 4
Salad, Tuna-Egg, **'81** 135
Sandwiches, Breakfast, **'82** M123
Sandwiches, Confetti, **'79** 236
Sandwiches, Eggsclusive, **'79** 164; **'80** 130
Sandwiches, Eggs-Tra Special, **'81** 240; **'83** 69
Sandwiches, Open-Faced Cheesy Egg, **'86** 67
Sandwiches, Open-Face Egg, **'83** 292; **'84** 78; **'86** 160
Saucy Eggs, **'83** 84
Saucy Eggs on Toast, **'81** 209
Scotch Eggs, **'79** 261; **'83** 289
Scrambled
- Bacon-and-Eggs Scramble, **'80** M267
- Buttermilk Scrambled Eggs, **'79** 72
- Casserole, Scrambled Egg, **'80** 51; **'86** 241
- Cottage Cheese Scrambled Eggs, **'81** 142
- Cottage-Scrambled Eggs, **'80** 49
- Country Eggs, **'86** 330
- Country-Style Scrambled Eggs, **'79** 22
- Cream Cheese Scrambled Eggs, **'81** 287
- Home-Style Scrambled Eggs, **'84** 66
- Mexican-Style Scrambled Eggs, **'85** 50
- Onion Scrambled Eggs, Creamy, **'83** M203
- Shrimp and Crab Scrambled Eggs, **'79** 261
- Sonora, Eggs, **'80** 196
- Spanish Scrambled Eggs, **'83** 49; **'84** 60
- Special Scrambled Eggs, **'81** 103
- Supreme, Scrambled Eggs, **'79** 39
- Tostadas, Scrambled Egg, **'86** 95
- Wild Rice, Scrambled Eggs with, **'80** 42

Soufflés, Little Egg, **'83** 57
Soufflé, Three-Egg Cheese, **'87** 234
Soup, Egg Drop, **'83** 21; **'86** 16
Soup, Egg-Drop, **'85** M12
Soup, Egg Flower, **'81** 307; **'82** 313; **'83** 65
Spread, Cottage-Egg Salad, **'82** 146
Spread, Egg Salad, **'86** 127
Spread, Egg, Sour Cream, and Caviar, **'85** 279
Spread, Ham-and-Egg, **'79** 59
Spread, Vegetable-Egg, **'87** 106
Strata, Cheese-Rice, **'81** 176
Strata, Sausage, **'84** 101
Strata, Tomato-Cheese, **'81** 209
Stuffed
- Creamed Eggs, **'86** 67
- Creamy Stuffed Eggs, **'84** 143
- Crunchy Stuffed Eggs, **'86** 67
- Deluxe, Eggs, **'82** 79
- Deviled Eggs, **'86** 176
- Deviled Eggs, Bacon, **'86** 136
- Deviled Eggs, Best, **'80** 159
- Deviled Eggs, Creamed, **'82** 79
- Deviled Eggs, Easy, **'82** 127
- Deviled Eggs, Nippy, **'80** 217
- Deviled Eggs, Pimiento-, **'84** 143
- Deviled Eggs, Saucy, **'82** 80
- Deviled Eggs Surprise, **'79** 83
- Deviled Eggs with Smoked Oysters, **'84** 161
- Deviled Eggs, Zesty, **'84** 205
- Devil's Island Eggs, **'82** 79
- Eggs, Stuffed, **'80** 155; **'88** 95
- Mustard Eggs, Spicy, **'84** 143
- Pecan-Stuffed Eggs, **'80** 78
- Shrimp-Curried Eggs, Saucy, **'84** 143
- Tomato Slices, Stuffed Eggs-and-, **'84** 152
- Tuna-Stuffed Eggs, **'83** 83

Sunny-Side-Up Eggs, **'79** 38
Tacos, Breakfast, **'80** 43

Tomatoes, Bacon-and-Egg-Stuffed, **'80** 162
Tortillas, Chorizo and Egg, **'81** 193
Tortillas, Egg-and-Sausage, **'83** 246; **'84** 42
Tulsa Eggs, **'87** 95

Enchiladas
American Enchiladas, **'81** 170
Bean Enchiladas, Spicy, **'88** 18
Casserole, Enchilada, **'87** 287
Casserole, Firecracker Enchilada, **'80** 260
Casserole, Green Enchilada, **'79** 76
Casserole, Sour Cream Enchilada, **'82** 113
Cheese Enchiladas, **'81** 194; **'85** 154
Cheese Enchiladas, Saucy, **'84** 220
Chicken Enchiladas, **'80** 301; **'86** 296
Chicken Enchiladas, Easy, **'82** 89; **'86** 231
Chicken Enchiladas with Spicy Sauce, **'84** 76
Dove Enchiladas, **'85** 270
Duck Enchiladas with Red Pepper-Sour
  Cream, Smoked, **'87** 121
Green Chile-Sour Cream
  Enchiladas, **'84** 234
Hot and Saucy Enchiladas, **'81** 141; **'82** 6
New Mexican Flat Enchiladas, **'85** 244
Pie, Enchilada, **'83** 155
Sauce, Enchilada, **'81** 194
Sauce, Red Chile Enchilada, **'85** 245
Skillet Enchiladas, **'82** 89
Soup, Chicken Enchilada, **'86** 22
Sour Cream Enchiladas, **'83** 200; **'87** 37
Sour Cream Enchiladas, Cheesy, **'79** 25
Spinach Enchiladas, **'83** 60; **'84** 14
Terrificas, Enchiladas, **'84** 32

Escargots
Provençal, Escargots, **'82** 238; **'83** 156

Escarole
Cooked Escarole, Easy, **'84** 85
Salad, Escarole-and-Bacon, **'84** 85

F

Fajitas
Beef Fajitas, **'88** 233
Chicken Fajitas, **'88** 231
Fajitas, **'84** 233
Favorite Fajitas, **'86** 114

Fettuccine
Alfredo, Fettuccine, **'80** 236; **'86** 158
Chicken-Pecan Fettuccine, **'86** 52
Parsley, Fettuccine with, **'83** 115
Shrimp Élégante, **'83** 48
Spinach, Fettuccine and, **'88** 90
Spinach Fettuccine, Easy Chicken with, **'88** 89
Spinach Fettuccine, Fresh, **'83** 60
Spinach Fettuccini, **'82** 179
Spinach Sauce, Fettuccine with, **'84** 329
Supreme, Fettuccine, **'83** 288; **'86** 333
Vegetable Fettuccine, **'83** 312

Figs
Cake, Easy Fig Coffee, **'80** 116
Cake, Fig, **'79** 32
Cake, Fig Preserve, **'79** 140; **'84** 316
Cobbler, Fig, **'79** 140
Cobbler, Super Fig, **'86** 206
Ice Cream, Fig, **'87** 139
Jam, Fig, **'86** 206
Muffins, Fig, **'86** 206
Pickled Figs, **'79** 140
Preserves, Fig, **'79** 140; **'82** 150

Sauce, Fig, **'79** 140
Snacks, Sliced Fig, **'86** 206
Fillings. *See* Frostings.
Fish. *See also* specific types and Seafood.
Almond Baked Fish, **'88** 270
Amandine, Fillet of Fish, **'80** M54
Amandine, Fish, **'85** 179
Amandine, Orange Lake, **'80** 99
Asparagus Divan, Fish-, **'87** 128
Aspic, Fish 'n, **'84** 190
Baked Fillets, Creamy, **'84** 91
Baked Fillets in Lemon-Celery
  Sauce, **'84** 91
Baked Fish, Curried, **'87** 5
Baked Fish Fillets, Creamy, **'85** 217
Baked Fish Fillets, Crunchy, **'85** 217
Baked Fish, Southern, **'82** 73
Baked Fish with Barbecue Sauce, **'84** 92
Bake, Fast Fish, **'85** 218
Bake, Saucy Fish, **'79** 75
Beer-Batter Fish, **'85** 68
Bluefish Chowder, **'84** 282
Broiled Fish Fillets Piquante, **'84** 91
Broiled Herb Fish Fillets, **'79** 99
Cakes, Fish, **'85** 54
Captain's Spicy One, **'81** 125
Casserole, Green Chile-and-Fish, **'84** 32
Catfish Amandine, Mandarin, **'84** 183
Catfish, Barbecued, **'80** 157
Catfish, Crisp Fried, **'82** 242
Catfish, Crisp-Fried, **'88** 110
Catfish, Crown Room's
  Shrimp-Stuffed, **'84** 182
Catfish Eldorado de Colorado, **'84** 183
Catfish, Fried, **'82** 135; **'83** 169
Catfish Fry, **'84** 184
Catfish, Golden Fried, **'80** 99
Catfish Kiev-Style, **'84** 184
Catfish, Lemon Barbecued, **'88** 271
Catfish Meunière, **'80** 57
Catfish, Middendorf's Broiled
  Manchac, **'84** 183
Catfish Parmesan, **'79** 184; **'86** 210
Catfish Pecan, **'85** 53
Catfish Sesame, **'81** 106
Catfish, Smoked, **'84** 47
Catfish, Soufflé-Stuffed, **'84** 183
Catfish, Southern Oven-Fried, **'87** 163
Catfish Stew, Cajun-Style, **'88** 12
Catfish Stir, **'84** 184
Ceviche in Avocado Shells, **'81** 33
Ceviche (Marinated Raw Fish), **'80** 194;
  '82 220
Ceviche, Mexican-Style, **'88** 115
Chart, Fat and Lean Fish, **'85** 180
Chowder, Basque Fish, **'86** 36
Chowder, Creamy Fish, **'79** 16
Chowder, Fish, **'79** 152; **'84** M38
Chowder, Tasty Fish, **'80** 188
Corned Fish, **'79** 32
Crawfish Étouffée, **'83** 91
Crawfish on Eggplant, Soft-Shell, **'88** 222
Crawfish Salad, Dilled, **'83** 126
Crawfish Spaghetti, **'85** 104
Creole Fish, **'87** M79
Crust, Fish in a, **'84** 294
Delight, Fish, **'86** M212
en Papillote, Fish with Snow Peas, **'86** 144
Fillets, Apple-Carrot Stuffed, **'88** M192
Fillets, Lemon-Coated, **'80** M53

Fillets, Parmesan, **'86** M112
Fillets, Spanish-Style, **'86** M112
Florentine, Fish, **'86** 35
Florentine in Parchment, Fish, **'87** 22
Flounder Ambassador, **'86** 234
Flounder au Fromage, Baked, **'86** 234
Flounder, Baked, **'79** 31
Flounder, Broiled, **'88** 28
Flounder, Cheesy Broiled, **'84** 69
Flounder, Crab-Stuffed, **'80** 120; **'81** 176

Flounder, Creole-Style, **'85** 180
Flounder, Crispy Fried, **'84** 93
Flounder Dijon, **'85** 95
Flounder Fillets, Grilled, **'83** 213
Flounder Fillets in Shrimp Sauce, **'83** 227
Flounder Fillets, Stuffed, **'86** 234
Flounder-Grapefruit Broil, **'85** 53
Flounder in Wine Sauce, Fillet of, **'80** 179;
  '81 30
Flounder Nicole, **'85** 217
Flounder, Pesto Broiled, **'86** 150
Flounder Rolls, Vegetable-Stuffed, **'87** 6
Flounder Rolls with Citrus Sauce,
  Stuffed, **'85** 180
Flounder, Seasoned Fried, **'79** 214
Flounder Stuffed with Shrimp, **'88** 51
Flounder Supreme, Baked, **'79** 75
Flounder Thermidor, **'85** 190
Flounder-Vegetable Medley, **'85** 217
Flounder with Hollandaise-Shrimp
  Sauce, **'86** 234
Fresh Fish, Preparing, **'82** 127
Fried Fish, **'79** 151
Fried Fish, Crispy, **'84** 92
Fried Fish Fillets, Oven-, **'79** 75
Fried Fish, Golden, **'82** 134
Gourmet Fish, **'86** 71
Greek Fish with Vegetable Sauce, **'82** 72
Grilled Fish with Heather Sauce, Catfish
  Inn's, **'84** 182
Grill Fish, How to Charcoal-, **'84** 48
Grouper, Creamy Baked, **'85** 292
Grouper, Grilled, **'86** 185
Grouper Macadamia, **'85** 127
Grouper Sauté, Shrimp-and-, **'87** 91
Grouper Spectacular, **'84** 163
Grouper with Confetti
  Vegetables, **'88** M189
Gumbo, Easy Fish, **'81** 6
Haddock, Baked, **'80** 179; **'81** 30
Haddock Fillets with Zucchini
  Stuffing, **'88** M191
Haddock Italiano, **'81** M4
Halibut, Chinese-Style Fried, **'80** 179;
  '81 30

Fish *(continued)*

Halibut Steaks Italiano, '88 M191
Halibut with Cider, '79 182
Halibut with Orange-Curry Sauce, '87 91
Halibut with Swiss Sauce, '83 M195
Herb-Coated Fish, '86 M112
Herbed Fish and Potato Bake, '79 287;
    '80 34
Heroes, Neptune, '84 281
Herring Dip, Yogurt, '80 232
Huachinango à la Veracruzana
    (Veracruz-Style Red Snapper), '80 193
Italian Fish, '88 270
Italian Fish, Easy, '86 M112
Mackerel Creole, '80 126
Mackerel, Lemon-Baked, '79 182
Mackerel, Smoked Salmon or, '84 46
Mahi Mahi, Macadamia, '88 164
Marinated Beer-Battered Fish, '86 180
Monkfish, Greek-Style, '87 M79
Monterey, Fish, '84 293
Mullet, Festive, '79 75
Mullet, Smoked, '84 47
Orange Roughy, Kiwi, '87 193
Orange Roughy with Spinach
    Pesto, '88 M192
Papillote, Ocean, '84 M287
Perch Fillets, Buttery Baked, '81 134
Poached Fish in Creamy Swiss
    Sauce, '80 M53
Redfish Court Bouillon, '83 290; '84 93
Rolls, Vegetable-Filled Fish, '86 M251
Rollups, Shrimp-Stuffed, '82 234
Salad, Smoked Fish-Potato, '84 233
Salad, Smoky Seafood, '84 46
Salmon Mousse, Irresistible, '79 284
Salmon or Mackerel, Smoked, '84 46
Salmon Steaks, Baked, '85 54
Sautéed Seafood Platter, '83 89
Scamp, Tangy Broiled, '87 5
Seasoning Blend, Fish-and-Seafood, '88 28
Seviche Cocktail, '83 258
Shad Roe with Lemon-Butter Sauce,
    Baked, '84 252
Shark, Marinated, '79 151
Skillet Fish Dinner, '88 199
Smoked Fish Log, '85 144
Snapper à l'Orange, Baked, '85 181
Snapper and Stuffing, Baked, '82 72
Snapper, Caribbean, '87 5
Snapper Chowder, Red, '85 217
Snapper, Company Red, '82 72
Snapper Destin, '88 222
Snapper, Honey-Curried, '85 181
Snapper in Wine Sauce, Red, '85 138
Snapper Louisiane, Red, '85 217
Snapper, Orangy, '88 23
Snapper, Poached, '83 101
Snapper, Poached Red, '85 127
Snapper Rolls, Cucumber-Stuffed
    Red, '83 176
Snapper Rome, Fillet of, '80 57
Snapper, Stuffed, '87 138
Snapper Veracruz, Red, '88 149
Snapper with Dill, '84 190
Snapper with Lime, Stuffed Red, '83 246
Snapper with Tarragon Stuffing,
    Baked, '82 136
Sole Divan, '87 21
Sole Fillets, Herbed, '82 21

Sole Fillets in Wine Sauce, '81 109
Sole in Papillote, '82 22
Sole Provençal, Fillet of, '85 78
Sole, Saucy, '82 M68
Sole Véronique, '85 181
Sole with Cucumber Sauce, '84 M286
Steaks, Soy Fish, '86 M112
Stew, Fish-and-Vegetable, '87 220
Surprise, Fish, '84 231
Sweet-and-Sour Fish, '80 M54
Swordfish, Foil-Baked, '87 5
Swordfish, Skewered, '86 256
Tomato Sauce, Fish in, '85 75
Trout Delmonico, '80 57
Trout Florentine, Cheesy, '85 53
Trout in Wine Sauce, '80 180; '81 31
Trout Laurie, '88 270
Trout, Smoked, '84 47
Trout Spread, Smoked, '84 47
Trout, Sunshine, '84 M286
Trout with Ginger and Soy Sauce,
    Grilled, '85 228
Veracruz Fish with Shrimp, '86 130

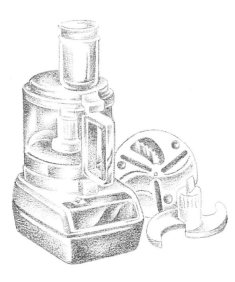

Food Processor
Appetizers
    Artichoke-Caviar Mold, '87 239
    Cheese Ring, Strawberry-, '86 14
    Dip, Blue Cheese, '80 285
    Dip, Cheese-Garlic, '80 192
    Dip, Herbal, '86 14
    Dip, Hot Cheesy Beef, '80 85
    Dip, Spinach, '86 159
    Dip, Sugar Snap, '88 91
    Dip, Yogurt Herring, '80 232
    Guacamole in Shells, '86 74
    Mousse, Salmon Dill, '81 21
    Mousse, Shrimp, '87 251
    Olive Quiche Appetizers, '86 159
    Pasta Bites, Pesto-Cheese, '87 251
    Pastry, Processor, '87 67
    Pâté, Chicken Liver, '81 235;
        '88 M132
    Pâté, Mock, '87 251
    Pâté with Cognac, '86 159
    Pâté with Dill Sauce, Shrimp, '85 39
    Pinwheels, Black-Eyed Pea, '85 300

Salsa Cruda, '87 180
Sandwiches, Dainty Cucumber, '81 119
Shrimp Toast, '86 91
Spread, Country Ham, '87 8
Spread, Fiery Tomato-Cheese, '87 196
Spread, Sherried Liver, '80 86
Spread, Shrimp, '87 111
Spread, Sombrero, '87 111
Spread, Superb Crab, '81 235
Spread, Tipsy Cheese, '80 150
Beverages
    Coffee, Praline-Flavored, '87 69
    Lemonade, Strawberry, '80 160
    Milkshake, Banana, '85 47
Breads
    Apple-Nut Bread, '85 281
    Baguettes, '85 70
    Biscuits, Beaten, '86 54
    Biscuits, Easy Processor, '84 218
    Biscuits, Refrigerator Yeast, '85 48
    Cheese Bread, Crusty, '86 233
    Cream Cheese Loaves,
        Processor, '85 48
    Muffins, Blueberry-Cream
        Cheese, '86 14
    Muffins, Cinnamon-Pecan, '84 219
Butter, Green Peppercorn, '88 60
Crêpes, Basic Processor, '87 289; '88 135
Crêpes, Mushroom-Cheese, '87 289;
    '88 135
Desserts
    Apple Crisp, '84 122
    Cake, Fresh Coconut, '85 281
    Cake, Fresh Coconut-Carrot, '80 299
    Cheesecake with Orange-Pineapple
        Glaze, Lemon, '81 60
    Cheesecake, Yam, '81 224
    Cheese, Nutty Date Dessert, '87 299
    Coconut Puffs, '87 277
    Crêpes, Dessert, '87 290; '88 134
    Crêpes, Strawberry Ice
        Cream, '87 290; '88 135
    Crust, Pecan, '86 317
    Cupcakes, Mocha, '85 250
    Flan, Apple, '81 309
    Frosting, Cream Cheese, '80 299;
        '86 337; '87 58
    Frosting, Fluffy Chocolate, '86 336;
        '87 58
    Frosting, Snow Peak, '85 281
    Ice, Apricot Yogurt, '81 177
    Ice Cream, Mango, '86 216
    Ice Cream, Peach, '86 15
    Ice, Peach, '81 178
    Mousse, Elegant
        Amaretto-Chocolate, '86 337
    Pastry Shells, Cream Cheese, '86 13
    Phyllo Nests, Nutty, '87 277
    Pie Dough, Quick Food
        Processor, '84 219
    Pie, Pumpkin-Pecan, '85 233, 282
    Pies, Miniature Pecan, '86 13
    Sherbet, Instant Fruit, '85 158
    Sorbet, Avocado, '88 117
    Sorbet, Banana-Orange, '88 117
    Sorbet, Cranberry Juice, '85 259
    Sorbet, Pear-Lemon, '88 116
    Sorbet, Strawberry, '88 117
    Tart Shells, '88 4
Dressing, Cornbread-Sausage, '85 280
Dressing, Pecan-Sage, '80 262

Eggs and Omelets
    Scotch Eggs, '83 289
Fruit Nuggets, Dried, '86 326
Main Dishes
    Chicken Pie, Double-Crust, '87 111
    Chili, Zippy, '87 110
    Meatballs, Quick Processor, '87 111
    Oysters St. Jacques, '80 103
    Pizza, Pesto, '87 182
    Spareribs, Peach-Glazed, '86 14
    Steak, Herb-Marinated
        Flank, '85 275
    Turkey, Galantine of, '85 150
Marmalade, Delicious Fruit, '81 285
Pancakes, Pumpkin, '80 228
Pancakes, Strawberry, '84 219
Pizza, Deep-Dish Mediterranean, '80 163
Pizza Supreme, '81 214
Relish, Cranberry, '85 258, 264; '86 283
Relish, Cranberry-Nut, '86 275
Relish, Cranberry-Pear, '85 232
Relish, Easy Tomato, '80 126
Salad Dressings
    French Dressing, Creamy, '81 60
    Lemon Dressing, Creamy, '88 M193
    Pesto Salad Dressing, '86 150
    Poppy Seed Dressing, '86 305
    Russian-Style Salad Dressing,
        '86 305
Salads
    Cranberry Salad, Jellied, '85 281
    Guacamole Salad, '87 181
    Relish Salad, '84 121
    Spinach-Mustard Twist, '86 209
    Tomato-Artichoke Aspic, '86 92
Salsa, Hot Mexican, '85 136
Salsa Picante, Homemade, '81 67
Sauces and Gravies
    Berry Sauce, '87 290; '88 135
    Dessert Sauce, Orange, '87 58
    Devonshire Sauce, Processor, '86 337;
        '87 58
    Green Sauce, Herbed, '86 244
    Orange Dessert Sauce, '86 337
    Peanut Hot Sauce, '86 305
    Pesto, Fresh, '86 150
    Pizza Sauce, '80 163
    Pumpkin Seed Sauce, '88 246
    Seafood Sauce, '86 304
    Tomato Sauce, Italian-Style, '87 182
    Tomato Sauce, Refrigerator, '85 188
Soups and Stews
    Avocado Soup, Chilled, '81 34
    Bean Soup, '80 25
    Brunswick Stew, '80 264
    Brunswick Stew, Blakely, '87 4
    Cauliflower Soup, Creamy, '82 76
    Gazpacho, '80 266
    Melon Soup, Swirled, '87 162
    Mushroom Soup, Cream
        of, '85 93, 261
    Strawberry Soup Supreme, '81 M144
    Tomato Soup with Parmesan Cheese,
        Cream of, '86 161
Spread, Benedictine Sandwich, '80 299
Spread, Corned Beef, '87 196
Terrine with Goat Cheese, Black
    Bean, '87 120
Vegetables
    Asparagus with Basil Butter, '85 40
    Carrots, Honey-Glazed, '84 121

Loaf, Pureed
    Vegetable-Cheese, '85 297
Okra and Tomatoes, Fresh, '81 M165
Peppers, Ham-and-Corn Stuffed, '81 87
Potato-Apple Bake, Sweet, '86 282
Potato Casserole, Processor, '86 159
Potato Pancake, '85 20
Ratatouille Niçoise, '81 22
Squash Casserole, Jiffy, '81 M144
Tomatoes, Crab-Stuffed Cherry, '88 78
Tomatoes, Spinach-Stuffed
    Baked, '86 14
Waffles, Crunchy Walnut, '85 48
Frankfurters
    Appetizer Franks, Saucy, '84 M12
    Appetizers, Bourbon Frankfurter, '85 207
    Bacon-Wrapped Franks, '81 202
    Barbecued Frankfurters, '83 144;
        '84 M12
    Barbecued Frankfurters, Oven-, '83 11
    Barbecued Franks, '85 192
    Barbecue, Tangy Frank, '79 63

Beans and Franks, '85 142
Beans and Franks, Hawaiian
    Baked, '80 136
Beans-and-Franks, Polynesian, '84 M11
Beans, Stove-Top Franks 'n', '88 201
Beany Hot Dogs, '82 190
Cabbage with Apples and Franks, '87 42
Casserole, Hot Doggie, '88 200
Casserole, Layered Frankfurter, '79 64
Chafing Dish Franks, '83 143
Chili-Cheese Dogs, '81 M176
Corn Dog Bites, '85 245
Corn Dogs, Favorite, '83 144
Corn Relish Dogs, '85 192
Crusty Franks, '80 166
Delicious, Hot Dogs, '81 202
Family-Style Franks, '79 54
Grilled Stuffed Franks, '82 163
Hash Browns, Franks and, '80 166
Hawaiian Franks, '81 202
Jubilee, Hot Dog, '81 113
Kraut and Franks, Beany, '79 64
Mexicali Hot Dogs, '82 131
Pickled Party Franks, '83 174
Potatoes, Cheesy Frank-Topped, '83 3
Potatoes, Frank-Filled, '84 M11
Potluck Dish, Frankaroni, '88 201
Sandwiches, Frankfurter, '84 M11
Saucy Franks, '88 201
Skillet Dinner, Frankfurter, '80 166
Skillet, Frankfurter-Cabbage, '80 166

Skillet, Hot Dog and Spaghetti, '83 144
Sloppy Joe Dogs, '85 192
Soup, Split Pea and Frankfurter, '79 64
Spanish Frankfurters, '80 166
Spicy Frankfurters, '81 202
Stuffed Franks and Potatoes, '81 202
Tipsy Franks, '85 52
French Toast
    Almond French Toast, '88 62
    Amandine, Baked Toast, '82 47
    au Fromage, French Toast, '88 288
    Baked French Toast, Oven-, '82 47
    Cinnamon French Toast, '84 211
    Cottage-Topped French Toast, '85 49
    Easy French Toast, '82 M172
    Macadamia French Toast, '86 96
    Orange Butter, French Toast with, '81 42
    Orange French Toast, '83 292; '84 78;
        '86 329
    Orange Sauce, French Toast with, '82 47
    Overnight French Toast Deluxe, '79 216
    Slender French Toast, '86 103
    Waffled French Toast, '82 47
Fritters
    Apple Fritter Rings, '88 44
    Apple Fritters, '81 105; '82 273; '85 14
    Apple Holiday Fritters, '86 314
    Banana Fritters, '79 213
    Blueberry Fritters, '85 152
    Broccoli Fritters, Cheesy, '79 53
    Clam Fritters, '79 151; '86 71
    Corn Fritters, '86 192
    Corn Fritters, Golden, '80 165; '81 128
    Corn Fritters, Skillet-Fried, '85 14
    Ham Fritters, '82 39
    Ham Fritters with Creamy Sauce, '81 105
    Okra, Fritter-Fried, '86 218
    Okra Fritters, '79 160
    Orange Fritters, Puffy, '81 169
    Oyster Fritters, '79 31
    Pear Fritters, Ol' Timey, '86 51
    Pecan Fritters, Chocolate-Covered, '79 205
    Pineapple Fritters, '88 112
    Potato Fritters, Golden Sweet, '79 9
    Sweet Potato Fritters, '88 44
    Zucchini Fritters, '81 163
    Zucchini Fritters, Cheesy, '88 44
Frog Legs
    Crispy Frog Legs, '80 99
    Fried Frog Legs, '88 110
Frostings, Fillings, and Toppings
    Almond-Butter Frosting, '86 107
    Almond Cream Filling, '85 320
    Almond Filling, '87 301
    Almond Filling, Ground, '87 14
    Almond Topping, '85 152; '86 200
    Amaretto Filling, '87 241
    Amaretto Frosting, '86 246
    Apple-Date Filling, '83 301
    Apple Filling, '85 5
    Apple Filling, Dried, '85 242; '87 229
    Apricot Filling, '83 84; '86 107
    Apricot Frosting, '81 192
    Apricot Glaze, '80 280; '82 8; '86 197
    Apricot Glaze for Ham, '85 256
    Apricot Glaze, Sweet, '82 304
    Apricot-Kirsch Glaze, '87 14
    Banana-Nut Frosting, '79 115
    Beef Filling, '80 81
    Berry Glaze, '83 225
    Biscuit Topping, '86 157, 265

Frostings, Fillings, and Toppings *(continued)*

Blueberry Glaze, '83 143
Bourbon Frosting, '88 236
Brandy Cream Frosting, '86 239
Brandy Glaze, Powdered Sugar-, '86 291
Broccoli Filling, '81 44
Brown Sugar Frosting, '79 13; '87 296
Brown Sugar Glaze, '83 312
Brown Sugar Meringue Frosting, '81 70
Brown Sugar Topping, '81 162
Buttercream Frosting, '85 322
Butter Cream Frosting, '88 279
Buttercream Icing, '83 73
Buttercream, Spiced, '84 226
Butter Frosting, '80 129
Butter Frosting, Browned, '86 248
Butter Frosting, Williamsburg, '81 120;
'82 23
Buttermilk Frosting, '85 249
Buttermilk Glaze, '79 140; '81 70; '84 316
Butter Pecan Frosting, '80 229
Caramel Drizzle, '86 247
Caramel Filling, '88 278
Caramel Frosting, '81 278, M289; '82 314;
'83 43; '84 39, 263; '86 239; '87 265
Caramel Frosting, Creamy, '81 71
Caramel Frosting, Easy, '87 39
Caramel Frosting, Favorite, '83 106
Caramel Glaze, '85 320
Carob Frosting, '85 218
Carolina Dream Frosting, '88 278
Catsup Topping, '81 170

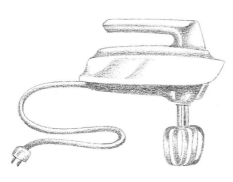

Chantilly Cream, '83 91
Chantilly Crème, '80 280
Cheese Topping, '86 233
Cherry Filling, '83 302; '84 225; '88 178
Cherry Frosting, '86 217
Cherry Glaze, '83 143
Chicken Divan Filling, '81 91
Chicken Filling, '81 200
Chicken Filling, Curried, '88 125
Chicken Filling Luau, '79 81
Chicken-Olive Filling, '81 227
Chicken Salad Filling, '87 106
Chocolate-Almond Frosting, '83 241
Chocolate Buttercream, '84 156
Chocolate Candy Frosting, '81 238
Chocolate-Coffee Frosting, '84 36; '88 269
Chocolate Filling, Rich, '79 68
Chocolate Frosting, '80 M171; '81 265;
'82 262; '83 79, 99, M233, 253;
'84 200; '85 323; '86 8, 93, 138, 239,
314; '87 M97, 198, 199, 293

Chocolate Frosting, Creamy, '85 314;
'86 316; '87 241
Chocolate Frosting, Fluffy, '86 336;
'87 58
Chocolate Frosting, Rich, '84 304
Chocolate Frosting, Satiny, '85 126
Chocolate Fudge Frosting, '83 105
Chocolate Glaze, '81 119; '83 220; '84 10,
55, 253; '85 6; '86 315, 316
Chocolate Glaze, Creamy, '82 88
Chocolate-Honey Glaze, '82 306
Chocolate-Marshmallow Frosting, '83 245
Chocolate Nut Frosting, '80 140
Chocolate-Peanut Butter Frosting, '84 240;
'87 222
Chocolate-Peanut Topping, '79 222
Chocolate Rum Frosting, '79 67
Chocolate Truffle Filling, '87 69
Cinnamon-Cream Frosting, '84 311
Cinnamon Frosting, Buttery, '81 M139
Cinnamon Glaze, '88 83
Cinnamon-Pecan Topping, '85 277
Citrus Glaze, '82 128
Cocoa Frosting, '86 60
Coconut Chocolate Frosting, '79 13
Coconut Cream Cheese Frosting, '86 60
Coconut Cream Filling, '84 200
Coconut Filling, '81 265
Coconut Frosting, '82 262
Coconut Frosting, Creamy, '80 287
Coconut Frosting, Nutty, '86 8
Coconut-Pecan Frosting, '81 296;
'83 M233; '84 43, 322
Cola Frosting, '81 238
Cranberry Glaze, '84 306; '86 171;
'88 244
Cream Cheese Frosting, '79 45; '80 140,
253, 299; '82 135, 244; '83 105, 215,
M233; '84 201, 255, 315, 316; '85 118,
121; '86 217; '87 58
Cream Cheese Frosting, Deluxe, '80 120
Cream Cheese Frosting, Fluffy, '80 245
Cream Cheese Frosting, Nutty, '85 117
Cream Cheese Glaze, '84 150
Cream Filling, '83 220; '84 37; '87 198
Cream, Luscious Pastry, '82 304
Cream, Mock Devonshire, '81 288
Cream Topping, Spicy, '85 177
Crème Chantilly, '87 9
Crème de Menthe Frosting, '86 245
Crème Pâtissière, '83 225
Crumb Topping, '83 183; '88 216
Custard Filling, '82 52, 298; '85 281
Custard Filling, Creamy, '81 180
Custard Filling, Egg, '87 14
Date Cream Filling, '81 303
Date Filling, '80 15; '83 257; '86 314
Decorating Techniques, Cake, '83 72, 240
Decorator Frosting, '82 20, 307; '83 106;
'87 86
Decorator Frosting, Creamy, '79 117
Divinity Frosting, '79 229
Drizzle Glaze, '87 94
Fluffy Filling, '81 192; '86 246
Fluffy Frosting, '79 246; '86 235;
'88 268
Fruit Dressing, Nutty, '88 68
Fruit Filling, Crêpes with, '81 96
Fruit Fluff, Tropical, '88 68
Fruit-Nut Filling, '80 289
Fruit Topping, '81 42; '87 225

Fruity Dessert Topping, '82 167
Fudge Frosting, '81 303; '87 296
Fudge Frosting, Quick, '81 278
Ginger Cream Topping, '84 312
Glaze, Dijon, '87 54
Glaze, Topping, '87 69
Heavenly Frosting, '80 140
Honey Chocolate Frosting, '79 83
Honey Filling, '88 287
Honey Glaze, '88 287
Honey-Nut Glaze, '87 15
Honey Topping, '83 154
Honey-Walnut Filling, '80 21
Horseradish Glaze, Carrots with, '85 66
Kahlúa Glaze, '86 292
Lemon Buttercream Frosting, '83 301;
'86 61
Lemon-Butter Cream Frosting, '85 117
Lemon-Cheese Filling, '79 68; '88 7
Lemon Cream, '82 237
Lemon-Cream Cheese Frosting, '81 157
Lemon Cream Filling, '84 23; '87 14
Lemon Curd, '87 139
Lemon Filling, '81 172; '84 137; '85 191;
'86 235; '87 293

Lemon Filling, Creamy, '80 70
Lemon Frosting, '85 191; '86 217
Lemon Frosting, Creamy, '79 93
Lemon Glaze, '79 285; '86 194; '87 41
Lemon-Orange Filling, '81 71
Lemon-Pineapple Topping, '86 60
Maple Frosting, '82 217; '85 322
Meringue, Cooked, '86 130
Meringue, Easy Cooked, '82 207; '83 158
Meringue Frosting, '86 336; '87 84
Mint Frosting, '88 80
Mocha Butter Cream Frosting, '79 281
Mocha-Buttercream Frosting, '86 26
Mocha Cream Filling, '81 187; '84 305
Mocha Filling, '80 55; '82 262
Mocha Frosting, '83 301; '84 316; '87 224
Mocha Frosting, Creamy, '82 289; '84 311
Mushroom Filling, '81 89; '88 84
Napoleon Cream, '84 138
Never Fail Frosting, '86 314
Nut-and-Fruit Filling, '84 263
Nutty Topping, '85 256; '86 16
Omelet Filling, Greek, '80 68
Omelet Filling, Spanish, '80 68
Orange Buttercream Frosting, '80 70
Orange Butter Frosting, '83 300
Orange-Cream Cheese Frosting, '81 70;
'82 16
Orange Cream Frosting, '81 207; '82 14
Orange Filling, '79 229; '86 336; '87 84;
'88 224
Orange Frosting, '81 7; '86 61; '88 119

Orange Frosting, Creamy, **'83** 24, 241
Orange Glaze, **'79** 2; **'80** 257; **'81** 34, 107; **'82** 75, 206; **'83** 33, 114, 140, 267; **'84** 161; **'86** 298
Orange Glaze, Nutty, **'80** 45
Orange-Lemon Frosting, **'88** 92
Orange-Pineapple Glaze, **'81** 60
Orange Topping, Whipped, **'80** 254
Paint, Egg Yolk, **'86** 322
Papaya Topping, **'86** 181
Peanut Butter Frosting, **'83** 223; **'84** 153; **'85** 34
Peanut Butter-Fudge Frosting, **'87** 184
Peanut Butter Swirl Frosting, **'86** 109
Peanut Frosting, Creamy, **'80** 87
Pecan Frosting, **'86** 86
Peppermint Filling, **'81** 119
Pimiento Topping, **'83** 93
Pineapple Filling, **'80** 140; **'83** 179; **'84** 153
Pineapple Glaze, **'83** 143; **'85** 38
Pineapple Topping, **'86** 239
Powdered Sugar Glaze, **'79** 24; **'82** 92, 283; **'83** 83, 295; **'85** 55
Praline Glaze, **'82** 196
Quick Pour Frosting, **'85** 119
Raspberry Topping, **'85** 317
Ricotta Filling, **'80** 58
Royal Icing, **'80** 278; **'81** 21; **'83** 73; **'84** 303; **'85** 323; **'87** 295; **'88** 309
Rum Cream, **'88** 154, 224
Rum Cream Topping, **'80** 255
Rum Glaze, Buttered, **'83** 220
Sea Foam Frosting, **'81** 211
Seven-Minute Double Boiler Frosting, **'81** 278
Seven-Minute Frosting, **'80** 289; **'83** 299, 301; **'87** 296
Shrimp Salad Filling, **'87** 106
Snow Peak Frosting, **'82** 53; **'85** 281
Snowy Glaze, **'82** 295
Sour Cream Topping, **'85** 298; **'86** 120
Spinach-Mushroom Filling, **'80** 215
Spinach-Ricotta Filling, **'81** 53
Strawberry Cream, **'88** 153
Strawberry Glaze, **'80** 35; **'83** 142
Strawberry Topping, **'86** 32
Streusel, **'85** 326
Streusel Topping, **'88** 154, M275
Sugar Glaze, **'86** 161
Tips for Piping Icing, **'84** 302
Toffee Frosting, English, **'85** 125
Vanilla Cream, **'81** 248
Vanilla Frosting, **'84** 36; **'85** 236
Vanilla Glaze, **'85** M89
Vanilla-Rum Frosting, **'85** 324
Vegetable Topping, **'79** 79
Whipped Cream Frosting, **'83** 229; **'85** 125; **'87** 263
Whipped Cream Topping, **'87** 264
Whipped Topping, Reduced-Calorie, **'85** 55
White Chocolate Frosting, **'88** 280
White Frosting, **'83** 268
White Frosting, Fluffy, **'81** 278
White Frosting, Lemony, **'88** 7
White Frosting, Luscious, **'81** 71
Yogurt-Cheese Topping, **'88** 55
Fruit. *See also* specific types.
Baked Fruit, Gingered, **'81** 232
Baked Fruit Medley, **'81** 297
Bake, Hot Fruit, **'81** 270

Bake, Nutty Fruit, **'83** 127
Balls, Fruit, **'82** 296; **'84** 299
Bars, Fruit and Nut Granola, **'81** 49
Bavarian Cream with Fresh Fruit, **'88** 137
Beverage, Blender Fruit, **'83** 318
Boats, Honeydew Fruit, **'81** 147
Bowl, Sparkling Fresh Fruit, **'80** 146
Braid, Fruit-and-Cheese, **'86** 214
Brandied Fruit, Hot, **'80** 48
Brandied Fruit Starter, **'82** 249
Bread, Cranberry Fruit-Nut, **'79** 275
Bread, Kahlúa Fruit-Nut, **'79** 235
Cake, Fruit-and-Cereal Brunch, **'88** 263
Cake, Fruit and Spice, **'87** M97
Cake, Fruited Pound, **'81** 265
Cake, Fruity Ice Cream, **'87** 110
Cake, Spicy Fruited Carrot, **'85** 117
Cake, Stately Fruit-and-Nut, **'84** 226
Canapés, Fruit-Topped, **'85** 80
Canning and Preserving
    Apple Rings, Cinnamon, **'85** 107
    Berries (except Strawberries), **'80** 128
    Dehydration Chart, Fruit and Vegetable, **'84** 147
    Freezing Chart, Fruit, **'85** 187
    Juices, Fruit, **'85** 107
    Peaches, **'80** 128
    Peaches and Pears, **'85** 106
    Peaches, Honey-Sweet, **'85** 107
Cascade, Fruit, **'86** 104
Cheesecake, Fruit-Glazed, **'80** 24
Cheese, Fruited Cream, **'85** 306
Chicken en Crème, Fruited, **'83** 264
Chicken, Fruit-Glazed, **'80** 211
Chicken with Almond Rice, Spiced Fruited, **'81** 195
Chicken with Almond Sauce, Spiced Fruited, **'81** 195
Chilled Fruit with Dressing, **'85** 222
Chutney, Autumn Fruit, **'88** M230
Combo, Fresh Fruit, **'86** 178
Compote, Baked Fruit, **'80** 276; **'84** 314; **'87** 228
Compote, Baked Mustard Fruit, **'85** 47
Compote, Champagne Fruit, **'81** 309; **'82** 124
Compote, Chilled Fruit, **'83** 123
Compote, Fresh Fruit, **'79** 162; **'82** 197, 272; **'84** 82
Compote, Fruit, **'86** 330
Compote, Gingered Fruit, **'88** 184
Compote, Hot Fruit, **'81** 203; **'83** 53; **'86** 324
Compote, Warm Praline Fruit, **'85** 260
Compote, Wine Fruit, **'81** 272
Compote with Raspberry Puree, Fruit, **'88** 81
Conserve, Dried Fruit, **'82** 308
Cookies, Bourbon Fruit, **'86** 334
Cookies, Fruitcake, **'79** 291; **'86** 320 **'88** 286
Cookies, Holiday Fruitcake, **'81** 301
Cookies, Rolled Fruit, **'80** 15
Cookies, Spicy Holiday Fruit, **'83** 298
Cooler, Four-Fruit, **'86** 101
Cooler, Fruited Wine, **'86** 176
Cream Freeze, Fruit, **'82** 144
Cream Puffs, Tutti-Frutti, **'79** 231
Crêpes, Tropical, **'86** 275
Crêpes, Tropical Fruit, **'87** 77
Cup, Appetizer Fruit, **'86** 131

Cup, Fruit, **'81** 141
Cups, Honeydew Fruit, **'82** 179
Cup, Snowball Citrus, **'79** 2
Cups, Royal Fruit, **'81** 146
Cup, Tipsy Fruit, **'81** 268
Cup, Vanilla Fruit, **'80** 183
Curried Fruit, Almond-, **'83** 261
Curried Fruit Bake, **'87** 241
Curried Fruit, Hot, **'79** 225; **'81** 264; **'84** 287
Custard over Fruit, Stirred, **'84** 83
Delight, Fruit, **'86** 131
Delight, Winter Fruit, **'80** 243
Dessert, Caribbean Fruit, **'84** 314
Dessert, Flaming Fruit, **'83** 302
Dessert, Rainbow Fruit, **'85** 108
Dip, Coconut-Honey Fruit, **'84** 171
Dip, Fresh Fruit, **'80** 265
Dip, Fruited Cream Cheese, **'88** 261
Dip, Fruited Yogurt, **'84** 171
Dip, Heavenly Fruit, **'81** 160
Dip, Marshmallow Fruit, **'84** 171
Dressing, Avocado Fruit Salad, **'82** 93
Dressing, Baked Fruit, **'87** 253
Dressing, Fluffy Fruit, **'79** 69
Dressing for Fruit, Salad, **'86** 40

Dressing for Fruit Salad, **'87** 81
Dressing, Fresh Fruit, **'87** 134
Dressing, Fruit-and-Pecan, **'84** 252
Dressing, Fruited Cornbread, **'80** 262
Dressing, Fruit Salad, **'79** 69
Dressing, Lime-Honey Fruit Salad, **'87** 81
Dressing, Marmalade-Fruit, **'84** 171
Dressing, Nutty Fruit, **'88** 68
Dressing, Tangy Coconut-Fruit, **'84** 171
Dressing, Whipped Cream Fruit, **'79** 270
Drink, Three-Fruit, **'79** 38; **'80** 50; **'87** 199
Drink, Tropical Fruit, **'85** 43
Filling, Crêpes with Fruit, **'81** 96
Filling, Fruit-Nut, **'80** 289
Filling, Lemon Crêpes with Fruit, **'82** 46
Filling, Tutti-Frutti, **'79** 231
Float, Frosty Fruit, **'87** 159
Freeze, Holiday Fruit, **'88** 283
Fresh Fruit, Mint Dip with, **'87** 146
Fresh Fruit with Cheese, Luscious, **'79** 153
Fresh Fruit with Lemon Sauce, **'82** 290
Fruitcakes
    Applesauce Fruitcake, **'83** 258
    Aronowitz Fruitcake, **'86** 285
    Bourbon Fruitcake, **'85** 315
    Brandy Fruitcake, **'82** 261

Fruit, Fruitcakes *(continued)*

Burgundy Fruitcake, **'85** 292
Favorite Fruitcake, Family, **'88** 284
Fondue, Fruitcake, **'84** 258
Japanese Fruitcake, **'83** 268
Jeweled Fruitcake, **'88** 260
Kentucky Fruitcake, **'86** 266
Layered Fruitcake, **'87** 265
Lemon Fruitcake, **'83** 258
Mom's Fruitcake, **'85** 321
Old-South Fruitcake, **'79** 289
Regal Fruitcake, **'83** 257
Sherry-Nut Fruitcake, **'84** 266
Spice Cake, Fruit and, **'87** M97
White Fruitcake, **'80** 280; **'85** 316
Zucchini Fruitcake, **'88** 284
Garnishes, **'82** 280
Gingered Fruit, **'83** 151
Glazed Fruit, **'85** 83
Goose, Fruit- and Pecan-Stuffed, **'83** 268
Goose, Fruited Stuffed Wild, **'88** 248
Goose, Fruit Stuffed, **'83** 320
Granola, Fruity, **'84** 148
Ham Slice, Fruited, **'83** M317
Hawaiian Fruit Dish, **'82** 112
Hot Fruit Delight, **'83** 281
Ice Cream, Tutti-Frutti, **'86** 129
Ice, Fruit, **'86** 176
Ice, Mixed Fruit, **'81** 178; **'88** 85
Ice Tropical, **'79** 174
Juicy, Breakfast Fruit, **'86** 176
Kabobs, Fruit, **'86** 181
Kabobs, Turkey-and-Fruit, **'88** 140
Kabobs with Coconut Dressing,
  Fruit, **'87** 251
Kabobs with Mint Marinade, Fruit, **'82** 157
Lemon Curd, Fresh Fruit with, **'88** 21
Lemon Freeze, Fruity, **'82** 145
Marinated Fruit Bowl, **'80** 297
Marmalade, Delicious Fruit, **'81** 285
Medley, Chilled Fruit, **'84** 60
Medley, Chinese Fruit, **'83** 22
Medley, Fancy Fruit, **'84** 82
Medley, Fresh Fruit, **'81** 141
Medley, Frosty Fruit, **'82** 226
Medley, Fruit Cup, **'85** 47
Medley, Midsummer Fruit, **'88** 182
Medley, Minted Fruit, **'80** 182
Medley of Fruit, Tropical, **'86** 53
Mélange Delight, Fruit, **'81** 302
Mélange, Fruit, **'88** M295
Mélange, Melon, **'84** 139
Meringue Shells, Fruit-Filled, **'86** 151
Mixed Fruit, Unsweetened, **'83** 182
Muffins, Fruited Wheat, **'79** 93
Nuggets, Dried Fruit, **'86** 326
Oatmeal, Fruited, **'88** 19
Picks, Fruit on, **'80** 159
Pie, Crispy-Crust Fruit, **'88** 68
Pie, Fruitcake, **'80** 237
Pie, Fruit-Topped Vanilla Cream, **'84** 49
Pie, Japanese Fruit, **'80** 238
Pies, Baked Fruit, **'84** 7
Pops, Fruit, **'87** 168
Pork Chops, Fruited, **'87** 194
Pork Chops, Fruited Stuffed, **'86** 197
Pork Chops, Fruit-Stuffed, **'82** 136
Pork Chops with Rice, Fruit-Glazed, **'82** 73
Pork Pilaf, Fruited, **'82** 246
Pork Tenderloins, Fruit-Stuffed, **'87** 270

Pudding Compote, Fresh Fruit, **'86** 151
Pudding, Fruited Rice, **'86** 95
Puff, Giant Fruit, **'85** 72
Punch, Fruit, **'83** 52
Punch, Golden Fruit, **'80** 299; **'83** 56
Punch, Holiday Fruit, **'79** 232
Punch, Hot Fruit, **'83** 33
Punch, Party Fruit, **'82** 137
Punch, Spiced Fruit, **'88** 2
Punch, Spirited Fruit, **'81** 100
Punch, Summertime Fruit, **'80** 160
Punch, Tropical Fruit, **'81** 51; **'83** 176
Refresher, Four-Fruit, **'79** 174
Refresher, Grape Juice-Fruit, **'86** 182
Rhapsody, Fruit, **'80** 158
Rice, Far East Fruited, **'81** 175
Rice Mix, Fruited Curry-, **'86** 326
Rice Pilaf, Fruit-and-Vegetable, **'84** 196

Salads
Ambrosia, Fresh Fruit, **'88** 184
Apricot Fruit Salad, **'82** 132
Avocado Fruit Salad, **'87** 41
Banana-Mixed Fruit Salad, **'79** 270
Cabbage and Fruit Salad, **'79** 286
Cantaloupe, Fruit-Filled, **'83** 120
Carrot-and-Seed Salad, Fruity, **'86** 223
Carrot-Fruit Toss, **'82** 235
Chef Salad, Fruited, **'85** 222
Chef's Fruit Salad, **'86** 35
Cherry Fruit Salad, **'87** 236
Chicken-Avocado Salad,
  Fruited, **'82** 101
Chicken-Fruit Salad, **'82** 79
Chicken Salad, Fruited, **'84** 25, 290;
  '88 88
Chicken Salad, Fruity, **'83** 157
Chicken Salad in Avocados,
  Fruited, **'87** 41
Chicken Salad with Fruit, **'82** 171
Citrus Dressing, Fruit Salad
  with, **'88** 6
Coconut Fruit Bowl, **'83** 111
Coconut Salad, Chunky
  Fruit-and-, **'84** 24
Coleslaw, Fruited, **'83** 209; **'85** 139
Coleslaw, Three-Fruit, **'86** 250
Colorful Fruit Salad, **'82** 113
Cottage Cheese-and-Fruit Salad, **'86** 16
Cottage-Fruit Split, **'86** 169
Creamy Fruit Salad, **'84** 265
Curried Fruit Salad, **'85** 107
Date Dressing, Fruit Salad
  with, **'87** 57
Dressed-Up Fruit, **'82** 5
Easy Fruit Salad, **'80** 221
Easy Patio Fruit Salad, **'88** 184
Fall Salad with Ginger
  Dressing, **'82** 194
Festive Fruit Salad, **'80** 16

Fresh Fruit Cup with Mint
  Dressing, **'80** 183
Fresh Fruit Salad, **'82** 165
Fresh Fruit Salad with Celery-Honey
  Dressing, **'80** 42
Frisky Fruit Salad, **'85** 46
Frozen Fruit Salad, **'83** 110
Frozen Fruit Salad, Dreamy, **'79** 126
Frozen Fruit Salad, Luscious, **'81** 204
Frozen Salad Christmas
  Wreath, **'79** 241
Fruit Salad, **'83** 209
Glazed Fruit Salad, **'83** 48; **'84** 290
Ham Salad, Fruited, **'81** 36, 146
Heavenly Salad, **'81** 252
Holiday Fruit Salad, **'87** 236
Honeydew Fruit Bowl, **'84** 186
Honey Dressing, Fruit Salad
  with, **'87** 129
Honey Fruit Salad, **'80** 276
Hurry-Up Fruit Salad, **'87** 236
Jicama-Fruit Salad, **'86** 83
Layered Fruit Salad, **'84** 290
Lemonade Fruit Salad, **'84** 24
Lettuce and Fruit Salad with Poppy
  Seed Dressing, **'80** 152
Main Dish Fruit Salad, **'83** 119
Marinated Fruit Deluxe, **'81** 146
Melon-Citrus Mingle, **'79** 177
Mint Sauce, Fruit Salad with, **'88** M96
Mixed Fruit Cup, **'87** 233
Nut Salad, Cheesy Fruit-'n'-, **'87** 56
Old-Fashioned Fruit Salad, **'82** 80
Persimmon Fruit Salad, **'79** 206
Pineapple Cream Dressing, Fruit Cups
  with, **'83** 81
Pineapple Dressing, Fruit Salad
  with, **'85** 207
Pineapple-Fruit Salad, Icy, **'87** 9
Platter, Fruit Salad, **'83** 261
Poppy Seed Dressing, Fruit Salad
  with, **'88** 78
Potato Salad, Fruity, **'85** 214
Quick-and-Easy Fruit Salad, **'81** 99
Raspberry Fruit Mounds, **'79** 35
Refreshing Fruit Salad, **'85** 92
Rum, Fruit Cup with, **'83** 55
Shrimp Salad, Fruited, **'86** 156
Sour Cream Fruit Salad, **'80** 138
Sparkling Fruit Salad, **'82** 266
Spiced Autumn Fruit Salad, **'87** 228
Springtime Fruit Salad, **'81** 96
Summer Fruit Salad, **'82** 164
Summer Salad, Favorite, **'80** 158
Sweet-and-Sour Fruit Salad, **'80** 13;
  '84 125
Tropical Fruit Salad with Fresh Mint
  Dressing, **'84** 126
Turkey-Fruit Salad, **'79** 56
Turkey Fruit Salad, **'83** 233; **'84** 244
Turkey Salad, Fruitful, **'84** 197
Watermelon Fruit Basket, **'84** 161
Winter Fruit Salad, **'80** 248; **'82** 23
Wreath, Della Robbia Fruit, **'87** 294
Yogurt Fruit Salad, **'81** 114
Sauce, Fruit, **'81** 177
Sauce, Hot Fruit Dessert, **'87** 299
Sauce, Quick Fruit, **'82** 212
Sauce, Rum-Fruit, **'84** 312
Shake, Frosty Fruit, **'87** 23
Shells, Fruited Meringue, **'87** 32

Sherbet, Freezer Fruit, **'86** 334
Sherbet, Frozen Fruit, **'79** 155
Sherbet, Fruit Punch, **'86** 129
Sherbet, Instant Fruit, **'85** 158
Sherried Fruit Casserole, **'80** 284
Sherried Fruit Flame, **'85** 313
Sherried Fruit Mélange, **'80** 158
Slush, Refreshing Fruit, **'82** 35
Slushy, Fruit, **'80** 146
Smoothie, Fruited Honey-Yogurt, **'88** 231
Soup, Chilled Fresh Fruit, **'88** 160
Soup, Cold Fresh Fruit, **'87** 157
Soup Dessert, Fruit, **'79** 172
Soup, Dried Fruit, **'79** 23
Soup, Fruit, **'87** 98
Soup, Swedish Fruit, **'82** 313; **'83** 65
Soup, Yogurt Fruit, **'86** 176
Spareribs, Fruit-Stuffed, **'79** 14
Spiced Fruit, **'79** 23
Spiced Fruit Delight, **'82** 229
Spiced Fruit Dessert, **'82** 50
Spiced Fruit, Warm, **'86** 39
Spiced Winter Fruit, **'83** 262
Spread, Fruit, **'85** 135
Spread, Fruit and Cheese, **'81** 245
Spread, Nutty Fruit-and-Cheese, **'87** 246
Spread, Sugarless Fruit, **'84** 60
Squares, Christmas Fruit, **'88** 282
Squash, Fruited Acorn, **'85** 235
Squash, Fruit-Stuffed Acorn, **'81** 295
Strudel, Fruit Basket, **'87** 276
Syrup, Apricot Fruit, **'82** 10
Syrup, Fruit, **'86** 176

Tart, Fancy Fruit, **'82** 128
Tart, Fresh Fruit, **'84** 178
Tart, Open-Face Fruit, **'84** 207
Tart, Rainbow Fruit, **'82** 304
Tea, Christmas Fruit, **'83** 275
Tea, Fruited Mint, **'88** 79
Tea, Hot Spiced Fruit, **'87** 242
Tequila, Fruit in, **'82** 223
Topping, Fruit, **'81** 42; **'87** 225
Topping, Fruity Dessert, **'82** 167
Tropical Fruit Fluff, **'88** 68
Turnovers, Fruit, **'79** 150
Twists, Fruit-Nut, **'82** 253
Wine, Fruit in White, **'81** 48
Winter Fruit with Custard Sauce, **'88** 251
Wontons, Fruit-Filled, **'85** 287

G

Game. *See also* specific types.
Chili, Double-Meat, **'80** 12
Dove and Sausage Gumbo, **'81** 199
Dove Enchiladas, **'85** 270
Doves, Pan-Roasted, **'87** 240
Duck and Wild Rice Casserole, **'79** 224
Duck, Buffet Wild, **'86** 268
Duckling, Holiday, **'80** 251
Duckling, Roast Long Island, **'84** 87
Ducklings with Blackberry Sauce, **'82** 251
Ducklings with Cherry Sauce, Roast, **'86** 312
Duckling with Orange Sauce, Roast, **'81** 125
Duckling with Wine Jelly, Roast, **'88** 243
Duck, Oyster, and Sausage Gumbo, **'79** 226
Duck, Sherried Baked, **'79** 224
Duck with Orange Gravy, **'81** 259
Duck with Pecan Stuffing, Wild, **'85** 269
Duck with Sweet Potato-Eggplant Gravy, Roast, **'83** 90
Goose, Fruited Stuffed Wild, **'88** 248
Goose with Currant Sauce, Wild, **'87** 240
Mallard, Prairie Wings, **'83** 252
Pheasant Muscatel, **'85** 269
Quail Breasts, Southern, **'85** 270
Quail, Fried, **'82** 45
Quail, Grilled Breakfast, **'88** 220
Quail, Magnificent, **'82** 214
Quail, Marinated, **'80** 221
Quail, Seasoned Fried, **'88** 220
Quail Superb, **'81** 303
Quail with Gravy, Georgia, **'87** 240
Quail with Mushrooms, **'85** 138
Quail with Mushrooms, Baked, **'81** 259
Quail with Onion Gravy, Fried, **'82** 214
Quail with Red Plum Sauce, **'80** 48
Rabbit, Hickory Barbecued, **'82** 216
Squab, Baked Stuffed, **'82** 260
Stew, Hunter's, **'85** 270
Venison and Tomatoes, **'85** 270
Venison Burgers, **'87** 304
Venison Chili, **'82** 216; **'86** 3; **'87** 304
Venison, Country-Fried, **'81** 233
Venison Kabobs, **'82** 215; **'88** 249
Venison Roast, **'82** 226
Venison Roast with Red Wine Gravy, **'85** 270
Venison Sausage Balls, **'80** 42
Venison Sausage Stew, **'87** 238
Venison Soup, **'82** 216
Venison Steak, Country-Fried, **'83** 262
Venison Steaks, Country-Style, **'82** 215
Venison Steaks, Grilled, **'82** 215
Venison Stew, **'86** 294
Venison Stew with Potato Dumplings, **'87** 304
Venison Tenderloin Appetizers, **'88** 249
Venison-Vegetable Bake, **'87** 304
Garnishes
Broccoli Bouquet, **'87** 115
Butter Balls, **'82** 189
Butter Curls, **'82** 51, 189
Carrot Curls, **'85** 338
Carrot Flowers, **'85** 338
Celery Fans, **'85** 339

Chocolate Curls, **'85** 338
Chocolate Hearts and Shavings, **'86** 26
Chocolate Leaves, **'88** 281
Citrus Cups, **'85** 339
Citrus Cups, Notched, **'82** 280
Cranberries, Frosted, **'82** 280; **'85** 339
Eggs, Hard-Cooked, **'82** 280
Grapes, Frosted, **'82** 51; **'85** 339
Green Onion Fans, **'85** 339
Guide, Garnishing, **'82** 138
Lemon or Orange Rose, **'85** 338
Lemon Roses, **'82** 280
Lemon Slices, Fluted, **'82** 51
Marinade, Dill, **'87** 115
Marinade, Garlic-and-Oregano, **'87** 115
Marinade, Sweet-and-Sour, **'87** 115
Mushrooms, Aztec, **'82** 51
Mushrooms, Fluted, **'82** 280; **'85** 338
Onion Mum, **'85** 339
Onion Rose, **'87** 114
Piped Garnishes, **'82** 280

Radish Rose, **'85** 339
Squash Buttercup, **'87** 114
Tomato Flower, Marinated Pasta in, **'87** 115
Tomato or Green Pepper Cups, **'85** 339
Tomato Rose, **'82** 51; **'85** 338
Vegetable and Fruit Garnishes, **'82** 280
Zucchini Fan, **'87** 114
Goose
Stuffed Goose, Fruit-, **'83** 320
Stuffed Goose, Fruit- and Pecan-, **'83** 268
Wild Goose, Fruited Stuffed, **'88** 248
Wild Goose with Currant Sauce, **'87** 240
Granola
Bars, Coconut Granola, **'85** 202
Bars, Fruit and Nut Granola, **'81** 49
Bars, Granola, **'83** 305
Bread, Honey-Granola, **'86** 56
Chocolate Morsels, Granola with, **'86** 69
Crisp, Granola Apple, **'85** 78
Crunchy Granola, **'81** 218; **'84** 144
Easy Granola, **'81** 49
Fruity Granola, **'84** 148
Granola, **'79** 190
Homemade Granola, **'84** 58
Mix, Granola Snack, **'86** 229
Orange Granola, Sunny, **'84** 212
Peanut Butter Granola, **'82** 296
Sunshine Granola, **'79** 37

Granola *(continued)*

Toasty Granola, **'79** 37
Whole Wheat Granola, **'82** 167

Grapefruit
Aspic, Grapefruit, **'80** 297; **'82** 112;
  '83 153
Biscuits, Grapefruit Juice, **'83** 10
Broiled Grapefruit, **'85** 7
Broiled Grapefruit, Holiday, **'88** 251
Broiled Grapefruit, Sherried, **'80** 50
Broil, Flounder-Grapefruit, **'85** 53
Cooler, Grapefruit, **'88** 81
Cup, Berry Grapefruit, **'79** 242
Delight, Winter Fruit, **'80** 243
Dressing, Grapefruit French, **'80** 101
Dressing, Grapefruit Salad, **'84** 262
Drink, Three-Fruit, **'80** 50
Ice, Pink Grapefruit, **'85** 304
Marmalade, Combination Citrus, **'80** 50
Marmalade, Grapefruit, **'82** 308
Minted Grapefruit, **'88** 81
Refresher, Grapefruit, **'88** 85
Refresher, Grapefruit-Orange, **'82** 174
Salad, Avocado-Grapefruit, **'85** 26
Salad, Congealed Grapefruit, **'84** 325;
  '85 279

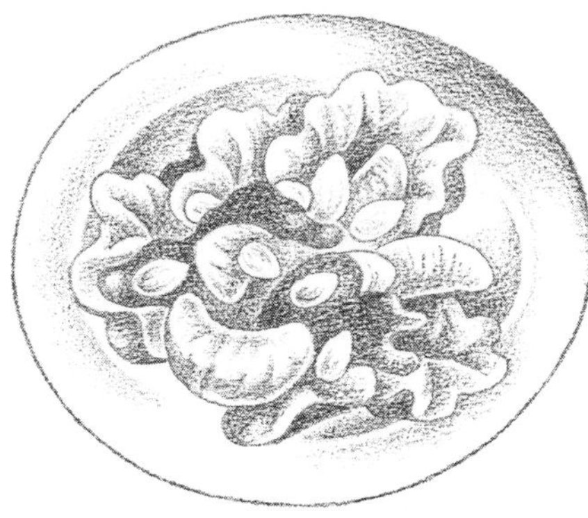

Salad, Grapefruit, **'83** 124; **'84** 325;
  '88 122
Salad, Grapefruit-and-Shrimp, **'88** 5
Salad, Grapefruit-Avocado, **'83** 316; **'84** 16
Salad, Grapefruit Combo, **'80** 50
Salad, Grapefruit Congealed, **'83** 190
Salad, Grapefruit-Cucumber, **'80** 100
Salad, Grapefruit Winter, **'84** 24
Supreme, Grapefruit, **'80** 50

Grapes
Carrots with Grapes, Glazed, **'82** 287
Chicken Véronique, **'84** 260; **'85** 302
Frosted Grapes, **'82** 51
Granita, Grape, **'88** 118
Green Grapes Supreme, **'88** 81
Ham Véronique, **'85** 90
Ice Cream, Scuppernong, **'88** 216
Ice, Grape, **'83** 162
Ice, Muscadine, **'82** 202
Jelly, Grape-Burgundy Freezer, **'85** 130
Jelly, Wild Muscadine, **'79** 32
Mold, Double Grape-Cantaloupe, **'79** 173
Pie, Grape, **'85** 212
Pie, Grape Juice, **'79** 123
Pie, Muscadine, **'82** 202

Pie, Scuppernong, **'88** 216
Punch, Sparkling Grape, **'82** 48
Refresher, Grape Juice-Fruit, **'86** 182
Salad, Marinated Chicken-Grape, **'85** 74
Salad Mold, Grape, **'83** 120
Salad Véronique, Macaroni, **'85** 164
Salad with Grapes, Chicken, **'86** 117
Sauce, Pears in Muscadine, **'88** 216
Sauce, White Grape, **'80** 38
Scallops Véronique, **'83** 144
Slaw, Grape-Poppy Seed, **'86** 225
Sole Véronique, **'85** 181
Tart, Green Grape, **'87** 77
Tea, White Grape Juice, **'87** 57
Tuna Salad with Grapes, Curried, **'87** 201

Gravies. *See also* Sauces.
Chive Gravy, Beef and Broccoli
  with, **'88** 214
Cream Gravy, **'88** 15
Cream Gravy, Country-Fried Steak
  with, **'84** 8
Cream Gravy, Fried Chicken with, **'85** 241
Currant Gravy, **'83** 276
Dill-Cream Gravy, Pork Chops with, **'84** 81
Fried Ripe Tomatoes with Gravy, **'82** 180
Giblet Gravy, **'79** 283; **'88** 253
Gravy, **'88** 303
Ham with Gravy, Virginia, **'86** 15
Onion Gravy, Fried Quail with, **'82** 214
Orange Gravy, **'81** 259
Pea Gravy, Black-Eyed, **'87** 12
Red-Eye Gravy, Country Ham with, **'79** 37
Redeye Gravy, Country Ham with, **'86** 254
Red-Eye Gravy, Ham and, **'88** 221
Sour Cream Gravy, Pot Roast with, **'79** 17
Sweet Potato-Eggplant Gravy, Roast Duck
  with, **'83** 90
Wine Gravy, Pot Roast in White, **'81** 299
Wine Gravy, Venison Roast with
  Red, **'85** 270

Greens. *See also* specific types.
Bake, Grits 'n Greens Dinner, **'84** 281
Chard, Buttered, **'83** 36
Chard with Tomatoes, Swiss, **'83** 36
Collard Greens, Seasoned, **'82** 211
Collards, **'79** 32
Collards, Southern-Style, **'82** 107
Escarole-and-Bacon Salad, **'84** 85
Escarole, Easy Cooked, **'84** 85
Kale, Scalloped, **'86** 224
Kale, Sweet-and-Sour, **'80** 298
Mustard Greens and Potatoes, **'86** 224
Turnip Greens and Ham Hock,
  Southern, **'80** 119
Turnip Greens, Old-Fashioned, **'85** 255
Turnip Greens, Saucy, **'83** 12
Turnip Greens with Cornmeal
  Dumplings, **'82** 211
Turnip Greens with Turnips, **'84** 230
Turnip Salad, **'85** 235
Watercress-and-Mushroom Salad, **'88** 104
Watercress Mousse, **'88** 104
Watercress Soup, **'88** 104
Watercress Spread, **'88** 103

Grits
Bake, Grits 'n Greens Dinner, **'84** 281
Casserole, Cheesy Grits, **'81** 270
Casserole, Garlic Grits, **'81** 47
Casserole, Grits-Sausage, **'84** 75; **'86** 241
Cheese-and-Garlic Grits, Baked, **'83** 292;
  '84 78

Cheese Grits, **'86** 242
Cheese Grits, Baked, **'80** 49, 99; **'83** 311;
  '85 41
Cheese Grits, Garlic, **'80** 47; **'81** 197
Cheese Grits, Gruyère, **'81** 47
Cheese Grits, Jalapeño, **'85** 43
Cheese Grits, Quick, **'83** M203
Cheese Grits, Sliced, **'84** 75
Country Grits and Sausage, **'83** 54
Fried Grits, **'83** 292; **'84** 78
Garlic-Cheese Grits, **'86** 180; **'88** 126
Good Morning Grits, **'87** 156
Grillades and Grits, **'88** 126
Nassau Grits, **'81** 47
Orange Grits, **'81** 47
Patties, Grits, **'83** 52
Pie, Crustless Grits-and-Ham, **'86** 103
Sausage Grits, **'86** 92
Scrambled Grits, **'80** 48
Shrimp Stew and Grits, **'80** 118
Soufflé, Grits, **'80** 30
Soufflé, Mexican Grits, **'79** 55
Spoonbread, Grits, **'79** 38
Stew over Grits, Shrimp, **'88** 126
Timbales, Grits, **'88** 223

Gumbos
Beef Gumbo, Ground, **'87** 283
Chicken and Oyster Gumbo, **'81** 198
Chicken Gumbo, **'79** 199
Chicken Gumbo, Easy, **'83** 156
Chicken Gumbo with Smoked
  Sausage, **'81** 199
Chicken-Ham-Seafood Gumbo, **'81** 6
Combo Gumbo, **'81** 198
Crab and Shrimp Gumbo, **'81** 200
Creole Gumbo, **'86** 228
Creole Gumbo, Quick, **'82** 87
Dove and Sausage Gumbo, **'81** 199
Duck, Oyster, and Sausage
  Gumbo, **'79** 226
Fish Gumbo, Easy, **'81** 6
Ham and Seafood Gumbo, **'81** 199
Okra Gumbo, **'86** 210
Okra Gumbo, Deep South, **'79** 48
Okra Gumbo Freezer Mix, **'86** 210
Seafood Gumbo, **'79** 198, 286; **'80** 34;
  '81 5; **'83** 90; **'84** 87, 92; **'87** 210
Seafood Gumbo, Champion, **'86** 293
Seafood Gumbo, Creole, **'82** 278
Seafood Gumbo with Whole Crabs, **'85** 2
Seafood-Okra Gumbo, Light, **'86** 155
Shrimp Gumbo, **'81** 199
Shrimp Gumbo, Quick, **'86** 71
Southern Gumbo, **'82** 242
Texas Ranch-Style Gumbo, **'82** 226
Turkey Gumbo, **'82** 268; **'85** 258
Ya Ya, Gumbo, **'87** 210

H

Ham. *See also* Pork.
Appetizers, Meat-and-Cheese, **'87** 7
Bake, Chicken, Ham, and Cheese, **'87** 217
Baked
    Apples, Baked Ham and, **'82** M237
    Apricot Baked Ham, **'84** 160
    Cranberry-Raisin Sauce, Baked Ham
      with, **'88** 244
    Festive Baked Ham, **'83** 263
    Glazed Ham, Molasses-, **'84** 24
    Glazed Ham, Sunshine-, **'84** 252
    Glazed Stuffed Ham, **'84** 321
    Maple-Raisin Sauce, Baked Ham
      with, **'83** 215
    Marinated Baked Ham, **'86** 94;
      '88 133
    Orange Sauce, Baked Ham
      with, **'86** 294
    Pineapple-Baked Ham, **'86** 48
    Plum Ham, **'80** 110
    Royale, Ham, **'84** 260
    Slice, Baked Ham, **'83** 12
    Strata, Baked Ham, **'83** 283
Bake, Ham-Rice-Tomato, **'87** 78
Bake, Harvest Ham, **'79** 210
Bake, Layered Ham and Turkey, **'79** 252
Balls, Appetizer Ham, **'82** 39
Balls, Fried Ham-and-Cheese, **'84** 221
Balls, Ham, **'84** 91; **'86** 256
Balls with Spiced Cherry Sauce,
  Ham, **'81** 112; **'82** 12
Barbecued Ham Slices, **'81** 110
Beans with Ham, Baked, **'80** 136
Biscuits, Ham-Filled Angel, **'80** 159
Biscuits, Petite Ham and Cheese, **'79** 193
Bread, Ham-and-Cheese, **'86** 213
Broiled Ham, Cranberry, **'88** 301
Cakes, Hawaiian Ham, **'79** 252
Casserole, Apple Ham, **'79** 213
Casserole, Breakfast Ham and
  Egg, **'79** 253
Casserole, Cheesy Ham-and-Potato, **'84** 326
Casserole, Golden Ham, **'82** 119
Casserole, Ham and Broccoli, **'81** 133
Casserole, Ham-and-Cheese, **'87** 78
Casserole, Ham and Lima, **'79** 192
Casserole, Ham and Noodle, **'80** 300
Casserole, Ham-and-Potato, **'83** M87
Casserole, Ham-and-Rice, **'84** 75
Casserole, Macaroni-Ham, **'81** M177;
  '83 283
Casserole, Quick Ham-Broccoli, **'82** 40
Casserole, Vegetable-and-Ham, **'84** 91
Cheese Chips, Ham-, **'82** 34
Cheese Toss, Ham and, **'79** 55
Cheesy Chicken-and-Ham Bundles, **'84** 261
Cheesy Ham-and-Turkey Specials, **'84** 14
Cheesy Ham Dinner, **'84** 90
Cheesy Ham Nuggets, **'81** 290
Cheesy Ham Towers, **'82** M77
Chowder, Creamy Ham, **'88** M53
Chowder, Ham and Corn, **'79** 16
Chowder, Ham-and-Corn, **'82** 40
Chowder, Ham 'n Cheese, **'79** 199
Citrus-and-Spice Ham, **'88** 40
Coleslaw, Ham, **'84** 195
Cordon Bleu, Chicken, **'81** 304; **'82** 83

Cordon Bleu, Company Chicken, **'82** 274
Cordon Bleu, Veal, **'87** 219
Country Ham
  Biscuits, Country Ham in
    Heart, **'86** 105
  Bread with Herb Butter, Country
    Ham, **'86** 255
  Brown Sugar Glaze, Smithfield Ham
    with, **'86** 253
  Cider-Baked Country Ham, **'82** 198
  Cider, Country Ham in Apple, **'80** 251
  Cornbread, Crab with Chile, **'86** 254
  Kentucky Hot Brown, **'86** 254
  Kentucky Jack, **'86** 254
  Loaves, Country Ham, **'86** 255
  Oysters and Ham, Edwards', **'86** 253
  Quiche, Country Ham, **'87** 287
  Red-Eye Gravy, Country Ham
    with, **'79** 37
  Redeye Gravy, Country Ham
    with, **'86** 254
  Roasted Country Ham,
    Edwards', **'86** 253
  Spread, Country Ham, **'87** 8
  Stuffed Country Ham,
    Maryland, **'88** 49
  Swirls, Veal-and-Smithfield
    Ham, **'86** 253
  Virginia Ham with Gravy, **'86** 15
  Wine, Country Ham in, **'81** 260
Creamed Ham and Chicken, **'81** M74
Creamed Ham and Eggs, **'82** 40
Creamy Ham Medley, **'84** 90
Creamy Ham Towers, **'79** 138
Crêpes, Ham-and-Egg, **'83** 204
Crêpes with Mushroom Sauce,
  Ham-and-Egg, **'82** 46
Croquettes, Ham, **'82** 119
Cured Ham and Biscuits, **'85** 320
Curried Ham and Peaches, **'82** 60
Curried Ham Steak, **'82** 120
Curried Ham with Rice, **'80** 111
Delight, Ham-Asparagus, **'86** 48
Deviled Delight, **'83** 130
Deviled Ham Twists, **'82** 86
Dinner, Corn-and-Ham Skillet, **'83** 190
Dinner, Ham-Asparagus, **'80** 10
Dinner, Ham Skillet, **'85** 179
Eggplant, Ham-Stuffed, **'80** 162
Eggs à la Swiss, Ham and, **'88** 158
Eggs, Creamy Ham and, **'87** 286
Eggs on Toast with Cheese Sauce, Ham
  and, **'81** 43
Eggs, Savory Ham and, **'82** 231
Fritters, Ham, **'82** 39
Fritters with Creamy Sauce, Ham, **'81** 105
Fruited Ham Slice, **'83** M317
Glazed Ham, Cranberry, **'81** 274
Glazed Ham, Cranberry-Orange, **'81** 295
Glazed Ham, Honey-Orange, **'83** 320
Glazed Ham Slice, Honey-, **'81** 104
Glazed Ham, Sweet-and-Sour, **'88** M15
Glazed Ham, Sweet-Sour, **'83** 311
Grilled Ham, Golden, **'79** 90
Gumbo, Chicken-Ham-Seafood, **'81** 6
Gumbo, Combo, **'81** 198
Gumbo, Ham and Seafood, **'81** 199
Hideaways, Ham, **'81** 29
Hopping John with Ham, **'81** 7
Hot Rods, Ham, **'86** 136
Jambalaya, Creole, **'87** 210

Jambalaya de Covington, **'87** 211
Kabobs, Honey Ham, **'80** 156
Kabobs, Swiss-Ham, **'81** 124
Loaf, Cranberry-Ham, **'82** M77
Loaf, Glazed Ham, **'79** 187
Loaf, Ham, **'79** 180; **'80** 272
Loaf, Hawaiian Ham, **'79** 71
Loaf, Pineapple Upside-Down Ham, **'79** 253
Loaf, Saucy Ham, **'86** M328
Loaf, Spicy Ham, **'80** 110
Loaf, Supreme Ham, **'79** 242
Loaf, Upside-Down Ham, **'82** 40
Noodles, Ham and Swiss on, **'87** 108

Omelet, Ham and Cheese, **'79** 262;
  '80 123
Omelet, Sour Cream-Ham, **'79** 261
Pâté, Ham, **'85** 279
Patties, Ham, **'81** 99
Patties, Ham-Sprout, **'85** 51
Patties, Pineapple-Ham, **'80** 110
Peas and Ham, Southern, **'85** 138
Peas with Ham Hocks, Black-Eyed, **'79** 122
Peppers, Ham-and-Corn Stuffed, **'81** 87
Peppers, Ham-Stuffed Green, **'80** 65
Peppers with Rice and Ham,
  Stuffed, **'82** 131
Pie, Crustless Grits-and-Ham, **'86** 103
Pie, Golden Ham, **'87** 78
Pie with Cheese Crust, Ham, **'80** 286
Pie, Zucchini-Ham-Cheese, **'80** 272
Pilaf Mold, Ham, **'86** 222
Pineapple-Flavored Ham, **'87** 160
Pocket, Ham and Swiss in the, **'83** 31
Potatoes, Ham Stuffed, **'79** 210
Potatoes, Ham-Stuffed New, **'88** 211
Potatoes, Jalapeño-Ham Stuffed, **'81** M161
Potatoes with Ham Bits, Creamy, **'87** 191
Praline Ham, **'85** 302
Prosciutto, Pizza with Artichoke
  and, **'87** 182
Puffs, Ham-and-Cheese, **'86** 277
Puffs, Ham-Filled Party, **'84** 116
Quiche, Cheesy Ham, **'79** 127
Quiche, Cheesy Jalapeño, **'84** 31
Quiche, Crustless Ham, **'84** 235
Quiche, Ham, **'80** 110
Quiche, Ham-and-Mushroom, **'81** 11
Quiche, Ham-and-Vegetable, **'84** 326
Quiche, Ham-Cheese, **'79** 26
Raisin Ham, **'80** 124
Raisin Sauce, Ham with, **'82** M76
Red-Eye Gravy, Ham and, **'88** 221
Rice, Savannah Red, **'80** 119
Rice Toss, Ham-, **'82** 40

Ham (continued)

Ring, Chili-Sauced Ham, '81 M122
Ring, Ham, '84 91
Roast, Peachy Ham, '86 118
Roll, Ham-and-Cheese, '79 234
Rolls, Ham, '79 153
Rolls, Ham-and-Broccoli, '86 212; '87 82
Rolls, Ham-and-Cheese, '82 3
Rolls, Ham-Asparagus, '79 41
Rolls, Hearty Salad, '81 206
Rolls, Rice-Stuffed Ham, '83 190
Rolls, Spinach-Ham, '88 78
Roll-Ups, Ham and Spinach, '81 143
Rollups, Ham-and-Swiss, '85 113
Rollups, Spinach-and-Ham, '86 84
Salad Boats, '80 93
Salad, Congealed Ham, '81 36
Salad, Crunchy Baked Ham, '83 23
Salad, Fruited Ham, '81 36, 146
Salad, Ham-and-Apple, '88 139
Salad, Ham-and-Cheese, '88 138
Salad, Ham-and-Egg Potato, '86 84
Salad, Ham and Macaroni, '79 220
Salad, Ham and Potato, '80 272
Salad, Ham 'n Egg, '81 36
Salad, Ham-Noodle, '85 249
Salad, Hawaiian Ham-Sweet
   Potato, '82 232
Salad, Hearty Ham, '82 40
Salad, Macaroni-Ham, '85 218
Salad, Mandarin Ham-and-Rice, '87 145
Salad, Spicy Italian Ham, '85 74
Sandwiches, Asparagus-and-Ham
   Melt, '88 M96
Sandwiches, Baked Ham, '81 29
Sandwiches, Creamy Blue
   Cheese-Ham, '87 279
Sandwiches, Denver Pita, '86 M12
Sandwiches, Ham-and-Cheese Pita, '87 202;
   '88 44
Sandwiches, Hot Ham, '79 214
Sandwiches, Hot Ham-and-Cheese, '85 299
Sandwiches, Meal-in-One, '80 218
Sandwiches, Monte Cristo, '83 134
Sandwiches, Open-Faced, '79 214
Sandwiches, Open-Face Ham, '82 40;
   '85 8
Sandwiches, Tangy Ham-and-Swiss, '85 164
Sandwiches, Virginia Ham, '80 155
Sandwiches, Yummy, '81 229
Sandwich, Tangy Ham Salad, '80 272
Sandwich, Tex-Mex Ham-and-Cheese,
   '86 4
Sauce, Steak with
   Ham-and-Mushroom, '83 109
Skillet Ham-and-Vegetables, '84 90
Skillet, Ham-Noodle, '87 78
Skillet, Ham Spaghetti, '83 283
Smoked Ham, '86 92
Soup, Chicken, Ham, and Oyster, '79 198
Soup, Ham-and-Bean, '84 4
Soup, Hearty Ham, '82 4
Spread, Cold Ham, '82 248
Spread, Deviled Ham, '79 81
Spread, Ham, '86 126
Spread, Ham-and-Egg, '79 59
Spread, Ham and Pimiento, '80 285;
   '81 56
Spread, Ham Salad, '87 92
Spread, Hawaiian Ham, '87 106

Squash, Ham-Stuffed Acorn, '81 239;
   '83 66
Stew, Blakely Brunswick, '87 4
Stir-Fry, Easy Ham, '86 332
Stir-Fry, Ham and Zucchini, '79 47
Strata, Ham and Broccoli, '80 261
Stroganoff, Ham, '82 40
Stromboli, '88 272
Stuffed Ham, '86 323
Superburgers, '79 89
Supper, Top-of-Stove, '86 332
Tart Milan, '87 70
Tart, Supreme Ham, '84 22
Tetrazzini, Ham, '82 M77; '84 241
Turnip Greens and Ham Hock,
   Southern, '80 119
Turnovers, Chile-Ham, '88 64
Turnovers, Party Ham, '82 39
Véronique, Ham, '85 90
Waffles, Ham, '80 44
Zucchini, Ham and Cheese Stuffed, '79 157

Hearts of Palm
Salad, Different Vegetable, '82 143
Salad, Hearts of Palm, '81 252
Salad, Hearts-of-Palm, '87 138

Hominy
Bacon, Eggs, and Hominy, '85 143
Bake, Chili Hominy, '81 282; '82 58
Bake, Hominy-Sausage, '88 51
Casserole, Cheesy Hominy, '83 170
Casserole, Chile-Hominy, '81 29
Casserole, Hominy-Chili, '86 255
Caviar, Texas, '86 218
Cheese Hominy, Hot, '84 77
Chiles and Cheese, Hominy with, '86 78
Gold Coast Hominy, '83 52
Jalapeño Hominy, '82 51
Mexican Hominy, '86 255
Salad, Hominy-Bean, '88 266
Skillet, Hominy-Sausage, '81 29
Soup, Southwest, '86 255

Honey
Ambrosia, Honey Bee, '83 267
Apple Quarters, Honey-Baked, '86 93
Apples, Honey-Baked, '83 234; '84 244
Bananas, Honey-Baked, '81 268
Bread, Applesauce-Honey Nut, '87 300
Bread, Honey-Cinnamon Swirl, '88 287
Bread, Honey-Granola, '86 56
Bread, Honey Oatmeal, '80 60
Bread, Honey Wheat, '85 18, 268
Bread, Whole Wheat Honey, '82 65;
   '83 106
Brownies, Heavenly Honey, '79 83
Buns, Honey Oatmeal, '83 154
Butter, Honey-Orange, '79 36; '85 19
Cake, Honey-Oatmeal, '87 222
Carrots, Honey-Glazed, '80 115; '84 121;
   '85 18
Carrots, Honey-Kissed, '84 122
Chicken, Honey, '82 55; '88 67
Chicken, Honey-Curry, '87 36
Cornbread, Honey, '83 286; '84 17
Dip, Coconut-Honey Fruit, '84 171
Dip, Peanut Butter-Honey, '85 19
Dressing, Celery-Honey, '80 42
Dressing, Honey, '79 242; '83 146;
   '87 129
Dressing, Honey French, '87 81
Dressing, Honey-Lime, '83 139
Dressing, Lime-Honey Fruit Salad, '87 81

Dressing, Tomato-Honey French, '81 105
Filling, Honey, '88 287
Filling, Honey-Walnut, '80 21
Frosting, Honey Chocolate, '79 83
Glaze, Chocolate-Honey, '82 306
Glaze, Honey, '88 287
Glaze, Honey-Nut, '87 15
Ham, Honey-Orange Glazed, '83 320
Ham Slice, Honey-Glazed, '81 104
Kabobs, Honey Ham, '80 156
Leeks, Honey-Glazed, '86 62
Loaves, Hint o' Honey, '81 104
Mousse, Honeyed Chocolate, '87 223
Muffins, Banana-Honey-Nut, '88 62
Muffins, Honey Bran, '88 171
Muffins, Honey-Oatmeal, '84 229
Muffins, Honey-Wheat, '83 96; '88 263
Muffins, Oatmeal-Honey, '83 95
Muffins, Orange-Honey, '88 284
Muffins, Peanut Butter-Honey, '82 56
Onions, Honey, '81 86
Peaches, Honey-Sweet, '85 107
Pears, Pineapple-Honey, '86 94
Pecans, Honeycomb, '84 300
Pecans, Sugar-and-Honey, '86 319
Preserves, Honeyed Peach, '85 130
Rice, Honey, '85 83
Rings, Honey Apple, '80 243
Rolls, Dilled Honey-Wheat, '83 254
Rolls, Honey Wheat, '83 278
Rolls, Super Honey, '80 115
Salad, Honey Fruit, '80 276
Sauce, Cinnamon-Pecan-Honey
   Pancake, '88 46
Sauce, Honey-Butter, '85 18
Sauce, Honey-Lemon Mustard, '84 275
Sauce, Honey-Lime, '82 85
Sauce, Honey-Mustard, '85 13
Sauce, Honey-Orange, '85 108
Sauce, Honeyscotch Sundae, '82 167
Smoothie, Fruited Honey-Yogurt, '88 231
Snapper, Honey-Curried, '85 181
Spareribs, Honey-Glazed, '82 163
Spread, Honey, '81 229
Spread, Honey-Nut, '87 157
Swirl, Honey-Walnut, '80 21
Syrup, Maple-Honey-Cinnamon, '85 19
Tea, Honey, '81 105
Topping, Honey, '83 154
Twist, Honey, '79 80
Whip, Peaches with Honey-Lime, '85 108

Honeydew. *See* Melons.
Hors d'Oeuvres. *See* Appetizers.
Hot Dogs. *See* Frankfurters.

I

Ice Creams and Sherbets
Alaska, Apple Baked, '80 226
Alaska, Baked, '84 105; '85 295
Alaska, Brownie Baked, '80 66
Alaska, Mint Patty, '80 219
Alaskas, Banana Split, '87 10
Amaretto Freeze, '82 182
Ambrosia Cups, Sherbet, '82 159
Apricot Sherbet, '81 177
Apricot Yogurt Ice, '81 177

Avocado Ice, '83 179
Avocado Sherbet, '83 162
Avocado Sorbet, '88 117
Balls, Almond Ice Cream, '86 315
Balls, Easy Ice Cream, '84 106
Banana-Orange Sherbet, '83 162
Banana-Orange Sorbet, '88 117
Bananas Foster, Elegant, '81 59
Banana Split Ice Cream, '80 176
Banana Split Pie, Layered, '83 189
Beverages
    Almond Float, Nutmeg-, '84 106
    Amaretto Breeze, '83 172
    Apple Juice Shrub,
      Shenandoah, '79 282
    Banana Flip, '83 303
    Banana-Pineapple Milk Shake, '84 59
    Banana Smoothie, '87 160
    Brandy Cream, '84 312
    Champagne Delight, '83 304
    Chocolate-Mint Smoothie, '84 166
    Coffee Floats, Maple-, '86 195
    Coffee Punch, Creamy, '81 50
    Coffee Refresher, Velvet, '79 149
    Cranberry Float, Sparkling, '86 195
    Cranberry-Orange Soda, '79 148
    Cranberry Shake, '83 171
    Fruit Float, Frosty, '87 159
    Ginger Fizz, Ice Cream, '83 303
    Golden Dream, '82 100
    Kahlúa Velvet Frosty, '82 244
    Lime Cooler, '87 160
    Lime Fizz, '81 172
    Lime-Pineapple Punch, '83 142
    Mocha Punch, '84 166
    Orange Milk Shake, '84 166
    Orange Shake, Peachy, '81 156
    Orange Sherbet Party Punch, '83 142
    Peach Frosty, '81 156
    Peanut Butter Milkshakes, '85 198
    Peanut Butter Shake, '82 48
    Pineapple Sherbet Float, '79 148
    Punch, Double Sherbet, '79 232
    Punch, Parsonage, '79 148
    Raisin Shake, Amazin', '86 195
    Rum Coffee Cream, Icy, '83 172
    Shake, Pep, '79 38
    Strawberry-Banana Float, '87 160
    Strawberry Milkshake, Fresh, '82 113
    Strawberry-Pineapple Shake, '84 166
    Strawberry Punch, Creamy, '86 195
    Strawberry Smoothie, '86 183
    Strawberry Soda,
      Old-Fashioned, '79 149
    Tahitian Flower, '87 159
    Vanilla Frosty, French, '79 148
    Whispers, '86 317
Black Forest Ice Cream, '88 203
Blueberry Ice Cream, '88 203
Blueberry-Kirsch Sorbet, '83 120
Bombe, Amber, '80 255
Bombe, Ice Cream, '82 305
Bourbon Ice Cream, '87 139
Brownie Dessert, Special-Occasion, '87 139
Buttermilk Sherbet, '84 184
Butter Pecan Ice Cream, '80 176; '86 129;
  '88 202
Cake for Grown-Ups, Ice Cream, '88 M192
Cake, Fruity Ice Cream, '87 110
Cake, Ice Cream, '86 321
Cake, Ice Cream Angel, '83 23

Cake, Praline Ice Cream, '80 84
Candy Crunch Ice Cream, '79 166
Cantaloupe Ice Cream, '79 177
Cantaloupe Sherbet, '88 183
Cantaloupe Sherbet, Frosty, '82 144
Caramel-Vanilla Helado (Caramel-Vanilla Ice
  Cream), '81 67
Cherry Ice Cream, '84 184
Cherry-Nut Ice Cream, '86 129
Cherry-Pecan Ice Cream, '88 203
Chocolate Chunk-Peanut Butter Ice
  Cream, '85 297; '86 120
Chocolate-Covered Peanut Ice
  Cream, '88 203
Chocolate Ice Cream, '80 176; '86 129
Cider Ice, '83 162
Coconut Ice Cream, Fresh, '79 166
Coffee Ice Cream, '88 202
Coffee Ice Cream Crunch, '82 182
Coffee-Kahlúa Granita, '88 118
Cookies and Cream Ice Cream, '88 203
Cranberry-Apple Ice, '82 290
Cranberry Ice, Tangy, '87 305
Cranberry Juice Sorbet, '85 259
Cranberry-Orange Ice, Tart, '86 317
Cranberry Sherbet, '88 280
Cranberry Sorbet, '82 251
Crêpes, Coffee Ice Cream, '84 85
Crêpes, Strawberry Ice Cream, '87 290
Delight, Ice Cream, '80 69
Dessert, Layered Ice Cream, '83 189;
  '84 94, 105; '86 163
Dessert, Layered Sherbet, '87 109
Dessert, Mint Ice Cream, '88 66
Double-Chocolate Ice Cream, '88 203
Fig Ice Cream, '87 139
Fried Ice Cream, Coconut, '85 141
Fried Ice Cream, French-, '85 141
Fried Ice Cream Puffs, '85 141
Fruit Ice, '86 176
Fruit Ice, Mixed, '81 178
Fruit Punch Sherbet, '86 129
Fruit Sherbet, Freezer, '86 334
Fruit Sherbet, Frozen, '79 155
Fruit Sherbet, Instant, '85 158
Fudge-Peanut Ice Cream Dessert, '88 167
Grapefruit Ice, Pink, '85 304
Grape Granita, '88 118
Grape Ice, '83 162
Hawaiian Frappé, '81 178
Italian-Style Ice Cream, '79 245
Kiwi Ice, '84 315
Lemonade Ice Cream, '88 202
Lemon Cream Sherbet, '79 114
Lemon Ice Cream, '79 142; '83 170
Lemon Ice Cream Tarts, '80 152
Lime Sherbet, '82 159
Lime Sherbet, Creamy, '84 165
Loaf, Pink Lemonade Ice Cream, '88 202
Log, Ice Cream Yule, '83 253
Macaroon-Sherbet Frozen Dessert, '79 212
Making Ice Cream, About, '82 171
Mango Ice Cream, '86 216
Mango Sorbet, '86 196
Mexican Sherbet, '79 155
Mint-Chocolate Chip Ice Cream, '88 202
Mint Sherbet, Fresh, '88 23
Mocha Ice Cream, '88 202
Muscadine Ice, '82 202
Orange Granita, '88 118
Orange-Pineapple Ice Cream, '86 117

Orange Sherbet, '79 155
Orange Sherbet Salad, '81 154
Parfaits, Chocolate-Crème de
  Menthe, '85 161
Parfaits, Coffee Crunch, '82 159
Parfait, Strawberry, '79 99
Parfait, Surprise Strawberry, '86 151
Peach Ice, '81 178
Peach Ice Cream, '81 184; '82 171;
  '83 159; '86 15

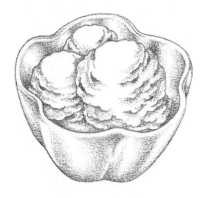

Peach Ice Cream, Creamy, '85 177
Peach Ice Cream, Deluxe, '80 176
Peach-Yogurt Ice, '84 83
Peanut Butter Ice Cream, '81 103;
  '88 64, 203
Pear-Lemon Sorbet, '88 116
Peppermint Ice Cream, '80 176; '86 129
Pie, Absolutely Divine Ice Cream, '82 181
Pie, Caramel Ice Cream, '82 181
Pie, Carrot Ice Cream, '86 200
Pie, Chocolate-Ice Cream, '87 224
Pie, Chocolate-Mint Ice Cream, '81 144
Pie, Coffee Ice Cream, '79 231
Pie, Heavenly Ice Cream, '82 181
Pie, Kona Ice Cream, '83 189
Pie, Lemon Ice Cream, '80 70
Pie, Peanutty Ice Cream, '82 56
Pie, Peppermint Candy-Ice Cream, '87 260
Pie, Pumpkin Ice Cream, '81 272
Pie, Pumpkin-Ice Cream, '87 243
Pie with Meringue-Pecan Crust, Ice
  Cream, '88 127
Pie with Rum-Fruit Sauce, Ice
  Cream, '84 312
Pineapple-Mint Ice Cream, '84 186
Pineapple Sherbet, '81 177; '84 83
Pineapple Sherbet, Creamy, '79 155
Pralines and Cream Ice Cream, '82 184;
  '83 159
Rainbow Candy Ice Cream, '88 202
Raspberry Ice Cream, '80 176
Raspberry Ice Cream, Fresh, '86 152
Raspberry Liqueur Granita, '88 117
Raspberry Sherbet, '83 162
Roll, Chocolate-Frosted Ice Cream, '84 200
Roll, Strawberry Ice Cream, '84 105
Salad, Ice Cream, '79 126
Sandwiches, Chocolate Cookie Ice
  Cream, '87 147
Sandwich Shells, Brownie Ice
  Cream, '88 195
Scuppernong Ice Cream, '88 216
Snow Ice Cream, '88 10

Ice Creams and Sherbets (*continued*)

Straw-Ba-Nut Ice Cream, '80 177
Strawberry-Banana-Nut Ice Cream, '88 203
Strawberry-Champagne Sorbet, '83 162
Strawberry Ice, '84 175; '85 108
Strawberry Ice Cream, '80 177
Strawberry Ice Cream Crêpes, '88 135
Strawberry Ice Cream, Homemade, '84 184
Strawberry Ice Cream,
    Old-Fashioned, '79 94
Strawberry Ice Cream, Very, '81 155
Strawberry-Orange Ice, '86 196
Strawberry Sherbet, '82 112, 160
Strawberry Sorbet, '88 117
Sundae Dessert, Hot Fudge, '84 313
Sundaes, Cocoa-Kahlúa, '83 M58
Sundaes Flambé, Peach, '81 88
Sundaes, Hot Strawberry, '81 M5
Sundaes, Mauna Loa, '80 126
Sundaes, Quick Pear, '86 71
Sundaes, Spicy Apple Ice Cream, '86 M195
Tea Granita, Mint, '88 117
Toffee Ice Cream, '88 202
Toffee Ice Cream Dessert, '87 110
Treats, Crunchy Ice Cream, '86 300;
    '87 178
Tutti-Frutti Ice Cream, '86 129
Vanilla Ice Cream, '80 176; '86 129
Vanilla Ice Cream, Basic, '88 202
Vanilla Ice Cream, Country, '82 143
Vanilla Ice Cream Spectacular, '82 166
Watermelon Sherbet, '79 155
Watermelon Sherbet, Light, '81 147
Wine Ice, '83 163

J

Jams and Jellies
Apple-Cranberry Conserve, '82 308
Apple Jelly, '82 149
Apple Marmalade, '79 120
Apple-Mint Jelly, '87 134
Apricot Jam, Golden, '80 31
Banana Jam, '82 296
Basil Jelly, '82 301
Blackberry Jam, '82 149
Blackberry Jam, Freezer, '84 M181
Blackberry Jelly, '82 149
Blueberry Conserve, '82 149
Blueberry Jam, '79 120; '85 130
Carrot-Citrus Marmalade, '81 148
Christmas Brunch Jam, '81 286
Christmas Jam, '88 288
Citrus Marmalade, '80 101
Citrus Marmalade, Combination, '80 50
Citrus Marmalade, Mixed, '81 43
Crabapple Jelly, '79 120; '81 217
Cranberry Conserve, '79 243; '85 266
Cranberry-Wine Jelly, '81 290
Fig Jam, '86 206
Fig Preserves, '79 140; '82 150
Freezer Jelly, Christmas, '86 M288
Fruit Conserve, Dried, '82 308
Fruit Marmalade, Delicious, '81 285
Grape-Burgundy Freezer Jelly, '85 130
Grapefruit Marmalade, '82 308
Green Tomato Jam, '79 121
Mango-Pineapple Preserves, '79 137
Mint Jelly, '79 121; '82 301
Muscadine Jelly, Wild, '79 32
Orange Marmalade, '81 42
Orange-Pineapple Marmalade, '82 150
Peach-Banana Jam, Rosy, '80 142
Peach Conserve, '79 120
Peach Jam, Freezer, '83 182; '84 M182
Peach-Orange Marmalade, '82 150
Peach-Plum Freezer Jam, '85 130
Peach Preserves, '81 147
Peach Preserves, Honeyed, '85 130
Peach Preserves, Old-Fashioned, '82 150
Pear Jam, Paradise, '84 300
Pear Marmalade, '79 196
Pear Preserves, '82 195
Pepper Jelly, '79 121
Pepper Jelly, Unusual Green, '82 132
Pineapple Jam, '81 147
Plum Jelly, '82 150
Port Wine Jelly with Whipped
    Cream, '84 254
Raspberry Freezer Jam, '84 M181
Rose Geranium Jelly, '82 301
Rosemary Jelly, '82 301
Sage Jelly, '82 301
Strawberry Freezer Jam, '84 M182
Strawberry Jelly, '81 147
Strawberry-Pineapple Marmalade, '85 130
Strawberry Preserves, '79 120; '81 96
Strawberry Preserves Deluxe, '82 150
Strawberry Preserves, Freezer, '82 112
Thyme Jelly, '82 301
Watermelon Preserves, '79 120
Wine Jelly, '88 243
Wine Jelly, Rosy, '85 306

Jicama
Fried Jicama, French-, '81 88
Parsleyed Jicama, '81 88
Salad, Jicama, '87 123
Salad, Jicama-and-Orange, '88 246
Salad, Jicama-Fruit, '86 83
Salad, Jicama-Orange, '86 83

K

Kabobs
Beef Kabobs, '85 110
Beef Kabobs Deluxe, '82 182
Beef Kabobs, Marinated, '82 105; '85 159
Beef Kabobs, Pineapple-, '83 212
Beef Kabobs, Saucy, '83 109
Beef Kabobs, Spirited, '87 142
Beef Kabobs, Teriyaki, '80 207
Beef Kabobs with Rice, Marinated, '84 32
Cantaloupe Wedges, Grilled, '87 162
Chicken-Avocado Kabobs, '82 9; '83 68
Chicken, Garlic-Grilled, '87 180
Chicken Kabobs, '87 141
Chicken Kabobs, Good-and-Easy, '85 87
Chicken Kabobs, Marinated, '84 M144
Chicken Kabobs, Pineapple-, '86 M328
Chicken Kabobs, Sesame, '82 165
Chicken Kabobs, Soy-, '86 156
Chicken Kabobs Supreme, '81 124
Chicken Livers en Brochette, '84 222
Fruit Kabobs, '86 181
Fruit Kabobs with Coconut
    Dressing, '87 251
Fruit Kabobs with Mint Marinade, '82 157
Ham Kabobs, Honey, '80 156
Ham Kabobs, Swiss-, '81 124
Hawaiian Kabobs, '85 157
Hot-and-Spicy Kabobs, '87 193

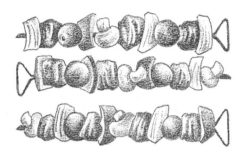

Lamb Kabobs, '85 159; '86 90
Lamb Kabobs, Savory, '80 184
Lamb Shish Kabobs, '79 142
Liver Kabobs, '80 185
Oysters Brochette, '80 56
Pork Kabobs, Spicy, '82 182
Rumaki Kabobs, '82 182
Salmon Kabobs, '81 182
Scallop-Bacon Kabobs, '81 111
Scallop Kabobs, Grilled, '83 101
Scallop Kabobs, Sea, '82 162
Scallops en Brochette with
    Vegetables, '80 163
Seafood Brochette, '87 96
Shish Kabobs, '82 182; '85 M112
Shish Kabobs, Overnight, '81 124
Shish Kabobs Teriyaki, '85 37
Shrimp, Grilled Marinated, '87 173
Shrimp Kabobs, '80 150, 184
Shrimp Kabobs, Marinated, '84 276;
    '85 158
Shrimp, Marinated and Grilled, '87 141
Sirloin Kabobs, Marinated, '82 162
Steak-and-Shrimp Kabobs, '80 184
Steak Kabobs, '82 4
Steak Kabobs, Barbecued, '79 89
Steak Kabobs, Marinated, '80 184
Steak on a Stick, '83 109
Steak with Vegetables, Skewered, '81 124
Turkey-and-Fruit Kabobs, '88 140
Vegetable Kabobs, Fresh, '81 158
Vegetable Kabobs, Marinated, '83 M195
Vegetable Kabobs, Tangy
    Marinated, '88 142
Venison Kabobs, '82 215; '88 249

Kiwifruit
Icc, Kiwi, '84 315
Jubilee, Kiwi, '83 120
Meringue Cups, Kiwi and Cream
in, '81 279
Muffins, Kiwifruit, '87 255
Orange Roughy, Kiwi, '87 193
Parfait, Kiwi, '86 199; '87 55
Pizza, Kiwi-Berry, '86 198; '87 55
Salad, Spinach-Kiwifruit, '87 305
Tart, Kiwifruit-Peach, '88 20

L

Lamb
Barbecued Lamb, '79 58
Burgers, Mesquite-Grilled Lamb, '88 59
Burgoo, Five-Meat, '87 3
Casserole, Moussaka, '79 179
Chops, Barbecued Lamb, '79 89
Chops, Broiled Lamb, '85 22
Chops Dijonaise, Gourmet Lamb, '82 93
Chops, Dijon Lamb, '84 277
Chops, Orange Lamb, '83 35
Chops Teriyaki, Lamb, '85 109
Chops, Teriyaki Lamb, '87 60
Chops with Shrimp, Lamb, '88 58
Curried Lamb with Rice, '82 93
Curried Lamb with Rice Mold, '85 36
Curry with Rice, Lamb, '80 83; '81 10
Fillets of Lamb with Vegetables, '85 36
Hawaii, Lamb, '81 58
Kabobs, Lamb, '85 159; '86 90
Kabobs, Lamb Shish, '79 142
Kabobs, Overnight Shish, '81 124
Kabobs, Savory Lamb, '80 184
Kabobs, Shish, '82 182; '85 M112
Kabobs Teriyaki, Shish, '85 37
Leg of Lamb, '86 90
Leg of Lamb, Glazed, '86 90
Leg of Lamb, Half of, '86 90
Leg of Lamb, Roast, '87 96
Leg of Lamb, Stuffed, '82 93; '87 248
Meatballs with Yogurt Sauce,
Lamb, '85 132
Moussaka, '87 166
Pilaf, Hearty Lamb, '83 101
Pockets with Dilled Cucumber Topping,
Lamb, '87 104
Rack of Lamb with Herb Mustard
Glaze, '81 260
Roasted Lamb Rosemary, '88 244
Roasted Rosemary Lamb, '86 89
Roast of Lamb, Crown, '81 58
Salad, Spinach-Lamb, '85 58
Shanks Milanaise, Lamb, '82 93
Steaks with Béarnaise Sauce, Lamb, '85 37
Stew-in-a-Loaf, Lamb, '85 37
Stew, Lamb, '79 293; '88 58
Lasagna
Beefy Lasagna, '80 81
Cheesy Lasagna, '82 224; '88 299
Chicken Lasagna, '87 M302; '88 90
Florentine, Lasagna, '88 196
Garden Lasagna, '83 119
Lasagna, '82 119; '83 M6
Lean Lasagna, '86 37
Pizza, Lasagna, '85 285

Quick Lasagna, '84 220
Quick 'n Easy Lasagna, '80 M10
Sausage Lasagna, '83 288
Sausage-Lasagna Rollups, '80 236
Sausage Pinwheels, Lasagna, '79 6
Simple Lasagna, '81 188
South-of-the-Border Lasagna, '84 31
Spinach Lasagna, '79 25; '81 243
Spinach Lasagna, Cheesy, '80 32; '83 204
Squash Lasagna, Spaghetti, '84 127
Tofu Lasagna, '83 312
Tuna Lasagna, '83 44; '84 123
Turkey Lasagna, '83 239
Two, Lasagna for, '81 91
Vegetable Lasagna, '84 201
Vegetable Lasagna, Cheesy, '79 84
Vegetable Lasagna, Colorful, '87 19
Vintage Lasagna, '79 194
Zesty Lasagna, '87 M188
Zucchini Lasagna, '85 194

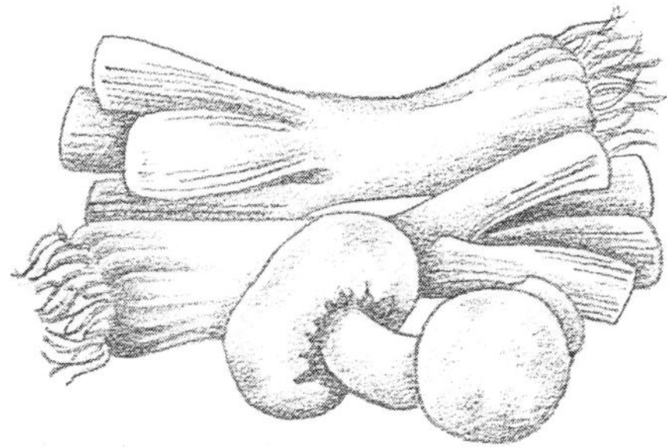

Leeks
Dilly Leek Combo, '82 26
Dip, Creamy Leek, '86 77
Glazed Leeks, '82 26
Glazed Leeks, Honey-, '86 62
Medley, Carrot-and-Leek, '88 102
Orange Sauce, Leeks in, '88 86
Quiche, Cheddar-Leek, '88 198
Soup, Carrot-Leek, '86 34
Soup, Leek-and-Potato, '84 112
Soup, Leek-Vegetable, '86 304
Soup, Watercress-and-Leek, '86 161
Tarragon Leeks, '84 66
Lemon
Apples, Chilled Poached Lemon, '86 182
Beans, Lemon-Mint, '88 22
Beans, Lemony Green, '85 190
Beverages
Buttered Lemonade, Hot, '88 208
Cooler, Lemon, '82 48
Cranberry Lemonade, Spiced, '87 292
Fresh Squeezed Lemonade, '81 172
Mist, Orange-Lemon, '79 288; '80 35
Orange-Mint Lemonade, '88 82
Punch, Lemon Balm, '80 42
Punch, Sparkling Lemonade, '88 276
Punch, Strawberry-Lemonade, '85 116
Sipper, Sunshine, '86 179
Slush, Pink Lemonade, '80 151
Strawberry Lemonade, '80 160
Syrup, Cherry-Lemonade, '86 214
Tea, Almond-Lemonade, '86 229
Tea Cubes, Lemonade with
Frozen, '85 161
Tea, Lemon, '82 156
Tea, Lemon-Mint, '85 162
Bread, Blueberry-Lemon, '85 190
Bread, Lemon, '79 275; '87 256

Bread, Lemon-Nut, '79 24
Bread, Lemon-Pecan, '83 54
Broccoli Goldenrod, Lemon-, '84 M89
Broccoli, Lemon, '88 119
Brussels Sprouts with Celery,
Lemony, '85 25
Butter, Asparagus in Lemon, '80 M123
Butter, Asparagus with Lemon, '87 M151
Butter, Shrimp in Lemon, '84 163
Cabbage, Lemon-Butter, '88 156
Canapés, Lemon-Cheese, '87 93
Carrots, Lemon, '82 300; '83 111
Carrots, Lemon-Glazed, '84 16
Catfish, Lemon Barbecued, '88 271
Cauliflower, Easy Lemon, '83 322
Cheese Patty, Lemon-Pepper, '84 117
Chicken and Vegetables, Lemon, '88 118
Chicken, Baked Lemon, '85 190
Chicken Cutlets with Lemon, '85 8
Chicken, Grilled Yogurt-Lemon, '81 111
Chicken in Lemon and Wine, '83 281
Chicken, Lemon, '81 M138; '86 173
Chicken, Lemonade, '82 163
Chicken, Lemon-Fried, '79 77
Chicken, Lemon Fried, '82 275
Chicken, Lemon-Frosted, '88 170
Chicken, Lemon-Herb, '85 127
Chicken Nuggets, Lemon-, '86 337;
'87 283
Chicken Piccata, Herbed, '88 28
Chicken, Sweet-and-Sour Lemon, '84 93
Chicken, Sweet Lemon, '79 218
Chicken, Sweet Lemon-, '84 69
Cornish Hens, Lemon Roasted, '82 260
Cream, Strawberries 'n Lemon, '85 120
Crêpes with Fruit Filling, Lemon, '82 46
Cutlets, Lemon-Flavored, '79 105
Desserts
Apples, Chilled Poached
Lemon, '86 182
Bars Deluxe, Lemon, '79 35
Bars, Lemon Yogurt Wheat, '79 93
Bars, Tangy Lemon, '86 217
Cake, Easy Lemon, '83 24
Cake, General Robert E. Lee
Orange-Lemon, '88 92
Cake, Glazed Lemon, '86 70
Cake, Lemon Angel, '80 147
Cake, Lemon-Coconut Cream, '81 179
Cake, Lemon-Coconut Sheet, '85 117
Cake, Lemon Gold, '83 301
Cake, Lemon-Pineapple, '86 60, 239
Cake, Lemon Pound, '82 88
Cake, Lemon Pudding, '83 106
Cake, Lemon-Sour Cream
Pound, '87 38
Cake, Lemon Tea, '82 169
Cake, Lightly Lemon Coffee, '81 14
Cake, Luscious Lemon Layer, '86 61
Cake, Old-Fashioned Lemon
Layer, '85 191
Cake Roll, Elegant Lemon, '80 70
Cake, Tart Lemon-Cheese, '88 7
Charlotte Russe, Fresh Lemon, '80 13
Charlotte Russe, Lemon, '84 192
Cheesecake, Lemon, '86 194
Cheesecake with Orange-Pineapple
Glaze, Lemon, '81 60
Cookies, Lemonade, '79 51
Cookies, Lemon Crinkle, '81 287
Cookies, Lemony Cutout, '85 323

Lemon, Desserts *(continued)*

Cookies, Sunshine Lemon, **'86** 69
Cream Cheese Dessert,
  Lemon-, **'84** 95
Cream Cheese Squares,
  Lemony, **'82** 159
Cream, Frozen Lemon, **'83** 118
Cream, Lemon, **'82** 237
Cream Puffs,
  Strawberry-Lemon, **'87** 75
Cupcakes, Lemon Moist, **'82** 112;
  '83 153
Cups, Baked Lemon, **'87** 128
Curd, Fresh Fruit with Lemon, **'88** 21
Curd, Lemon, **'87** 139
Custard in Meringue Cups,
  Lemon, **'80** 295; **'81** 172
Dainties, Lemon Pecan, **'80** 208
Delight, Lemon, **'82** 227
Filling, Creamy Lemon, **'80** 70
Filling, Lemon, **'81** 172; **'84** 137;
  '85 191; **'86** 235; **'87** 293
Filling, Lemon-Cheese, **'79** 68; **'88** 7
Filling, Lemon Cream, **'84** 23; **'87** 14
Filling, Lemon-Orange, **'81** 71
Frosting, Creamy Lemon, **'79** 93
Frosting, Lemon, **'85** 191; **'86** 217
Frosting, Lemon Buttercream, **'83** 301;
  '86 61
Frosting, Lemon-Butter
  Cream, **'85** 117
Frosting, Lemon-Cream
  Cheese, **'81** 157
Frosting, Lemony White, **'88** 7
Frosting, Orange-Lemon, **'88** 92
Fruitcake, Lemon, **'83** 258
Glaze, Lemon, **'79** 285; **'86** 194;
  '87 41
Ice Cream, Lemon, **'79** 142; **'83** 170
Ice Cream, Lemonade, **'88** 202
Layered Lemon Dessert, **'88** 134
Loaf, Lemon-Cream Tea, **'84** 50
Logs, Hazelnut-Lemon, **'84** 117
Melting Moments, **'85** 191
Meringue, Chocolate Pudding with
  Lemon, **'88** 258
Meringue Cream Cups, Lemon, **'84** 23
Mousse, Strawberry-Lemon, **'82** 128
Parfaits, Strawberry-Lemon, **'84** 198
Pastry Shell, Lemon in, **'84** 137
Pears, Lemon Poached, **'82** 74
Pie, Angel, **'79** 123
Pie, Apple-Lemon Chess, **'86** 220
Pie, Buttermilk Lemon, **'81** 120;
  '82 23
Pie, Buttermilk-Lemon, **'88** 297
Pie, Buttermilk-Lemon Cream, **'88** 99
Pie, Deluxe Lemon Meringue, **'81** 172
Pie, Frozen Lemon Cream, **'82** 86
Pie, Lemon Cheese, **'81** 136; **'82** 146
Pie, Lemon Chess, **'79** 32; **'82** 196
Pie, Lemon-Cottage Cheese, **'79** 44
Pie, Lemon Cottage Cheese, **'81** 143
Pie, Lemon Ice Cream, **'80** 70
Pie, Lemon Meringue, **'85** M112;
  '86 130
Pie, Lemon-Orange, **'85** 172
Pie, Lemon-Sour Cream, **'82** 169
Pie, Lemon Sponge, **'83** 192
Pie, Lemon-Strawberry, **'88** 127

Pie, Lemon Twirl, **'84** 94
Pie, Slice of Lemon, **'84** 23
Pie, Tart Lemon-Apple, **'80** 100
Pie, Whipped Lemon, **'79** 124
Pudding, Layered Lemon, **'82** 128
Pudding, Lemon, **'79** 86; **'81** 99
Pudding, Lemon Fluff, **'85** 304
Pudding, Old-Fashioned Lemon
  Bread, **'88** 95
Roll, Snow-Capped Lemon, **'79** 68
Sauce, Lemon, **'84** 258, 306;
  '85 77, 190
Sauce, Tart Lemon, **'85** 191

Sherbet, Lemon Cream, **'79** 114
Sorbet, Pear-Lemon, **'88** 116
Soufflé, Cold Lemon-Lime, **'84** 24
Soufflé, Lemon, **'82** 170, 252
Soufflés, Quick Lemon Sauce, **'88** 43
Soufflé, Tart Lemon, **'85** 82
Soufflé with Raspberry-Amaretto Sauce,
  Frozen Lemon, **'88** 130
Sponge Cups, Lemon, **'83** 10
Squares, Golden Carrot-Lemon, **'80** 40
Squares, Lemon, **'81** 197
Strawberry-Lemon Dessert, **'86** 162
Tarts, Dainty Lemon, **'82** 304
Tarts, Golden Lemon, **'85** 191
Tart Shells, Lemon, **'88** 195
Tarts, Lemon, **'82** 156; **'83** 79
Tarts, Lemon-Cheese, **'79** 2
Tarts, Lemon Ice Cream, **'80** 152
Tarts, Lemon-Sour Cream, **'81** 304
Topping, Lemon-Pineapple, **'86** 60
Trifle, Lemon-Blueberry, **'88** 210
Yogurt, Lemon-Chiffon Frozen, **'85** 54
Yummies, Lemon, **'81** 301
Zephers, Lemon, **'81** 172
Dressing, Chilled Broccoli with
  Lemon, **'88** 270
Dressing, Creamy Lemon, **'88** M193
Dressing, Green Salad with Lemony
  French, **'85** 67
Dressing, Lemon Cream, **'82** 170
Dressing, Lemon-Herb Salad, **'82** 67
Dressing, Lemon-Pepper, **'87** 55
Dressing, Lemon Salad, **'79** 8
Dressing, Tomato Slices with
  Lemon, **'87** 167
Fillets, Lemon-Coated, **'80** 53
Flounder Thermidor, **'85** 190
Freeze, Fruity Lemon, **'82** 145

Knots, Glazed Lemon, **'86** 290
Linguine with Garlic and Lemon, **'88** 91
Mackerel, Lemon-Baked, **'79** 182
Marmalade, Citrus, **'80** 101
Mayonnaise, Lemon-Cream, **'85** 264
Mold, Cheesy Lemon, **'79** 241
Mold, Lemon-Cucumber, **'87** 90
Muffins, Blueberry-Lemon, **'79** 7
Muffins, Fresh Lemon, **'79** 161
Muffins, Lemon, **'88** 119, M275
Pork Chops, Lemon-Herb, **'84** 81
Pork Chops, Lemony, **'88** 118
Potatoes, Lemon and Nutmeg, **'80** 36
Potatoes, Lemon-Buttered New, **'84** 149
Potatoes, Lemon-Herb Stuffed, **'83** 173
Potatoes, Lemon-Steamed, **'86** 177
Potatoes, Lemony New, **'82** 158
Potato Wedges, Lemon, **'88** 21
Relish, Lemony Cranberry, **'79** 243
Ribs, Lemon Baked, **'81** 166
Ribs, Lemon Grilled, **'81** 154
Roses, Lemon, **'82** 280
Salad, Cauliflower-Lemon, **'81** 23
Salad, Lemonade Fruit, **'84** 24
Salad, Lemon-Cheese, **'85** 240
Salad, Lemon-Cranberry Congealed, **'87** 311
Salad, Lemon-Onion, **'85** 252
Salad, Lemon-Vegetable Congealed, **'85** 22
Salad, Lemony Apple-Bran, **'86** 223
Sauce and Pecans, Broccoli with
  Lemon, **'86** 71
Sauce, Asparagus with Lemon, **'86** 62
Sauce, Baked Fillets in
  Lemon-Celery, **'84** 91
Sauce, Brussels Sprouts in Lemon, **'82** 269
Sauce, Honey-Lemon Mustard, **'84** 275
Sauce, Lemon, **'82** 290; **'85** 77, 190
Sauce, Lemon-Butter, **'84** 252
Sauce, Lemon Dessert, **'87** M165
Sauce, Lemon Meunière, **'88** 222
Sauce, Lemon Parsley, **'81** 106
Sauce, Lemony Barbecue, **'88** M177
Sauce, Lemony Cheese, **'84** 183
Sauce, New Potatoes with Lemon, **'86** 130
Sauce, Shrimp in Lemon Garlic, **'83** 67
Scones, Lemon-Raisin, **'87** 69
Shrimp, Lemon-Garlic Broiled, **'82** 29;
  '86 182
Shrimp, Luscious Lemon, **'88** 150
Slaw or Salad Dressing,
  Lemon-Yogurt, **'88** 54
Slices, Fluted Lemon, **'82** 51
Spareribs, Lemony Sweet, **'80** 73
Spinach, Creamy Lemon, **'82** 302
Spinach with Feta, Lemon, **'85** 190
Spirals, French Lemon, **'81** 94
Sprouts, Lemon, **'85** 288
Steak with Brandy Sauce,
  Lemon-Butter, **'85** 78
Veal Piccata, Lemon, **'86** 118
Veal with Artichoke Hearts,
  Lemon, **'87** 219
Vermicelli, Lemon, **'84** 329
Vinegar, Lemon-Mint, **'85** 124
Vinegar, Raspberry-Lemon, **'87** 134
Vinegar, Spicy Oregano-Lemon, **'85** 124

Lime

Butter, Chicken with Lime, **'84** 68
Cooler, Lime, **'87** 160
Daiquiris, Freezer Lime, **'79** 141
Dressing, Honey-Lime, **'83** 139

Dressing, Lime, '79 2; '83 120
Dressing, Lime-Honey Fruit Salad, '87 81
Dressing, Lime-Parsley, '85 131
Dressing, Lime Sherbet, '80 221
Fizz, Lime, '81 172
Fuzz Buzz, '82 160
Loaf, Lime Layer, '85 96
Margaritas, Frosted, '84 115
Margaritas, Frosty, '83 172
Margaritas, Pitcher, '83 175
Marmalade, Citrus, '80 101
Mousse Freeze, Luscious Lime, '81 173
Parfaits, Lime, '80 153
Pie, Lime Chiffon, '86 130
Pie, Lime Fluff, '84 43
Punch, Foamy Lime, '82 264
Punch, Lime, '84 58
Punch, Lime-Pineapple, '83 142
Punch, Orange-Lime, '82 160
Refresher, Lime-Mint, '82 144
Rice, Lime-Flavored, '84 175
Salad, Emerald, '81 143
Salad, Frosted Lime-Cheese, '79 286
Salad, Pear-Lime, '84 152
Salad, Pineapple-Lime, '84 320
Salad, Snowy Emerald, '87 311
Sauce, Honey-Lime, '82 85
Sherbet, Creamy Lime, '84 165
Sherbet, Lime, '82 159
Snapper with Lime, Stuffed Red, '83 246
Sopa de Lima, '79 211
Soufflé, Cold Lemon-Lime, '84 24
Soup, Lime, '88 31
Squares, Lime, '79 2
Tart, Lime-Pineapple, '88 6
Whip, Peaches with Honey-Lime, '85 108

Linguine
Carbonara, Linguine, '87 108
Clam Sauce, Linguine in, '81 83
Clam Sauce, Linguine with, '84 124;
  '88 90
Clam Sauce with Linguine, '84 9
Garlic and Lemon, Linguine with, '88 91
Pasta Verde, '84 201
Salad, Pasta, '84 139
Seafood Linguine, '79 227
Seafood Sauce, Linguine with, '83 232
Tomato-Cream Sauce, Linguine
  with, '86 158
Whole Wheat Linguine, '84 177
Liver
Barbecued Liver, '85 219
Beef Liver Patties, '81 277
Calf's Liver with Vegetables, '85 219
Chicken Liver and Bacon Roll-Ups, '80 200;
  '81 57
Chicken Liver Omelet, '82 44
Chicken Liver Pâté, '79 153; '81 235;
  '83 108; '84 205
Chicken Livers and Potatoes, '82 218
Chicken Livers and Rice Dish, '82 218
Chicken Livers en Brochette, '84 222
Chicken Livers in Italian Sauce, '83 117
Chicken Livers in Orange Sauce, '82 218
Chicken Livers in Wine Sauce, '81 104
Chicken Livers, Party, '83 242
Chicken Livers Risotto, '82 218
Chicken Livers, Sautéed, '80 200; '81 57
Chicken Livers, Scrumptious, '84 230
Chicken Livers Stroganoff, '80 200; '81 57
Chicken Livers Supreme, '81 298
Chicken Livers with Marsala Wine
  Sauce, '81 76
Chicken Livers with Mushrooms, '81 133
Chicken Livers with Rice, '80 200; '81 58;
  '84 292
Chicken Liver Turnovers, '79 141
Creamy Liver and Noodle Dinner, '80 11
Creole Liver, '85 219; '86 108
Creole Sauce, Liver in, '87 33
Duck Liver Pâté, '79 227
French-Style Liver, '80 10
Gravy, Liver and, '80 10
Herbs, Liver with, '81 277
Italiano, Liver, '85 219
Kabobs, Liver, '80 185
Loaf, Skillet Liver, '80 11
Pâté, Country, '86 66
Pâté, Liver-Cheese, '85 276
Pâté with Cognac, '86 159
Rumaki, '80 M136
Rumaki Kabobs, '82 182
Saucy Liver, '81 277
Sauté, Liver, '81 277
Spanish-Style Liver, '80 11
Spread, Sherried Liver, '80 86
Stroganoff, Liver, '79 54
Sweet-and-Sour Liver, '81 277
Lobster
Beef Tenderloin, Lobster-Stuffed, '87 248
Clambake, Backyard, '81 92
Creamy Lobster, '79 181
How to Cook Lobster, '81 169
Orange Sauce, Lobster Tails with
  Spiced, '86 155
Salad, Lobster and Orange, '82 207
Taco with Yellow Tomato Salsa and Jicama
  Salad, Warm Lobster, '87 122
Thermidor, Lobster, '85 103

M

Macaroni
Beef and Macaroni, Ground, '85 218
Beef and Macaroni, Skillet, '82 130
Beef-Macaroni Combo, '79 194
Casserole, Chicken-Macaroni, '85 219
Casserole, Macaroni, '84 220; '87 154
Casserole, Macaroni and Chicken, '80 260
Casserole, Macaroni-Ham, '81 M177;
  '83 283
Casserole, Spinach-Beef-Macaroni, '83 313
Cheese, Baked Macaroni and, '82 199
Cheese Deluxe, Macaroni-and-, '79 84
Cheese Deluxe, Macaroni and, '80 236
Cheese, Macaroni and, '83 M7;
  '88 M147, M190
Cheese Macaroni, Double, '82 224
Cheese Puff, Macaroni and, '79 5
Cheese, Tasty Macaroni and, '83 288
Cheese, Thick-and-Rich Macaroni
  and, '84 329
Cheese with Wine, Macaroni-and-, '86 78
Cheesy Macaroni-Mushroom Bake, '81 243
Dinner, Sausage Skillet, '83 29

Glorious Macaroni, '84 76
Oysters with Macaroni, Scalloped, '80 297
Peppers,
  Macaroni-and-Cheese-Stuffed, '80 65
Salad, Acini di Pepe, '83 163
Salad, Barbecue Macaroni, '82 276
Salad, Confetti Macaroni, '82 132; '85 297
Salad, Crunchy Macaroni, '82 24
Salad, Dilled Macaroni-Cheese, '86 208
Salad, Festive Macaroni-Shrimp, '85 165
Salad for Two, Macaroni, '81 31
Salad, Garden Macaroni, '84 290
Salad, Gourmet Macaroni, '81 253
Salad, Ham and Macaroni, '79 220
Salad, Hearty Macaroni, '84 90
Salad, Macaroni, '87 92
Salad, Macaroni-Chicken, '85 296; '86 302
Salad, Macaroni-Crabmeat, '81 153
Salad, Macaroni-Ham, '85 218
Salad, Macaroni-Salmon, '82 232
Salad, Macaroni Shell, '87 38
Salad, Macaroni-Shrimp, '85 121
Salad, Macaroni-Vegetable, '86 209
Salad, Olive Clubhouse, '81 114
Salad, Overnight Pasta, '82 276
Salad, Pineapple Macaroni, '79 220
Salad, Refreshing Macaroni, '80 177
Salad, Salmon-and-Macaroni, '81 114
Salad, Shrimp Macaroni, '79 220
Salad, Shrimp-Macaroni, '85 219
Salad, Spiral Macaroni, '82 276
Salad, Sweet-and-Sour Macaroni, '85 166
Salad, Taco Macaroni, '85 165
Salad, Tuna Macaroni, '83 44, 145
Salad, Tuna-Macaroni, '84 66
Salad, Turkey Macaroni, '83 282
Salad Véronique, Macaroni, '85 164
Salad, Whole Wheat
  Macaroni-Tuna, '84 193
Supper Supreme, Sunday, '79 76
Tomatoes, Tuna-Mac in, '87 188
Toss, Corkscrew Macaroni, '83 163
Treat, Tuna-Macaroni, '82 131
Mangoes
Beef and Rice, Mango-, '88 138
Cake, Mango, '83 150
Crêpes, Mango-Pineapple, '86 216
Frappé, Mango, '86 216

Mangoes *(continued)*

Ice Cream, Mango, **'86** 216
Orange Smoothie, Mango-, **'86** 216
Pan Dowdy, Mango, **'83** 150
Pie, Green Mango, **'79** 137
Pie, Mango-Ginger, **'88** 138
Preserves, Mango-Pineapple, **'79** 137
Salad, Fresh Mango, **'84** 126
Salad, Mango, **'79** 137
Salad with Mango, Chicken, **'86** 215
Sauce, Mango, **'83** 120
Sauce, Mango-Spiced Rum, **'86** 215
Sorbet, Mango, **'86** 196

Manicotti

Cheesy Manicotti, **'83** 216
Chicken Manicotti, Creamy, **'85** 60
Quick Manicotti, **'79** 6
Special Manicotti, **'88** 50
Spinach Manicotti, **'82** 199
Stuffed Manicotti, **'83** M6
Stuffed Manicotti, Saucy, **'83** 288
Stuffed Manicotti, Spinach-, **'88** 255
Zucchini Manicotti, **'84** 194

Marinades. *See* Sauces.

Marshmallows

Ambrosia, Carrot-Marshmallow, **'80** 5
Brownies, Chewy Marshmallow, **'83** 306
Brownies, Choco-Mallow, **'87** 198
Cake, No-Egg Chocolate
    Marshmallow, **'87** 97
Dip, Marshmallow Fruit, **'84** 171
Frosting, Chocolate-Marshmallow, **'83** 245
Parfaits, Mocha-Mallow, **'80** 219
Pudding, Banana-Mallow, **'86** 139

Mayonnaise

Aioli (garlic mayonnaise), **'88** 221
Anchovy Mayonnaise, **'86** 179
Cake, Chocolate Mayonnaise, **'83** 99
Dip, Artichokes with
    Herb-Mayonnaise, **'84** 67
Dressing, Mayonnaise, **'86** 11
Herbed Mayonnaise, **'82** 85, 192
Homemade Mayonnaise, **'80** 155
Homemade Mayonnaise, Easy, **'84** 12
Lemon-Cream Mayonnaise, **'85** 264
Muffins, Mayonnaise, **'86** 16
Parmesan Mayonnaise, **'86** 79
Russian Mayonnaise, **'80** 137
Sauce, Herb-Mayonnaise, **'85** 73
Tasty Mayonnaise, **'82** 192
Wine Mayonnaise, Hot, **'81** 83

Meatballs

Bacon Meatballs, Burgundy, **'80** 283
Bacon-Wrapped Meatballs, **'79** 81
Beef Balls Heidelberg, **'83** 164; **'84** 39
Brandied Meatballs, **'83** 78
Chafing Dish Meatballs, **'81** 260
Chestnut Meatballs, **'79** 110
Chinese Meatballs, **'83** 116; **'87** 194
Cocktail Meatballs, **'79** 63, 207
Creole, Meatball-Okra, **'83** 156
Creole, Meatballs, **'82** 233
Español, Meatballs, **'82** 110
Flavorful Meatballs, **'84** 206
Golden Nugget Meatballs, **'82** 233
Gravy, Meatballs in, **'79** 136
Ham Balls, **'84** 91; **'86** 256
Ham Balls, Appetizer, **'82** 39
Hawaiian Meatballs, **'85** 86
Hawaiian Meatballs, Tangy, **'79** 129

Lamb Meatballs with Yogurt Sauce, **'85** 132
Mock Meatballs, **'81** 243
Mushroom-Meatball Stroganoff, **'85** 85
Oven-Barbecued Meatballs, **'82** 233
Pizza Meatballs, **'85** 86
Polynesian Meatballs, **'80** 207
Processor Meatballs, Quick, **'87** 111
Red Delicious Meatballs, **'85** 85
Royal Meatballs, **'87** 268; **'88** 102
Saucy Meatballs, **'85** 68
Saucy Party Meatballs, **'80** 149
Sauerbraten Meatballs, **'85** 85
Sauerkraut Meatballs, **'86** 257
Spaghetti-and-Herb Meatballs, **'84** 75
Spaghetti with Meatballs, **'81** 38
Spiced Meatballs, **'79** 284
Spicy Meatballs and Sausage, **'79** 163
Stew, Meatball, **'79** 198
Stroganoff, Meatball, **'81** 297
Swedish Meatballs, **'80** 80; **'86** 256
Sweet-and-Sour Meatballs, **'82** 233, 247;
    '86 240
Sweet-and-Sour Party Meatballs, **'79** 233
Tamale Meatballs, **'80** 194
Veal Meatballs, European, **'85** 30
Venison Sausage Balls, **'80** 42
Zesty Meatballs, **'80** 250

Meat Loaf. *See* Beef, Ground/Meat Loaf.

Melons

Balls, Mellowed-Out Melon, **'88** 182
Balls, Minted Melon, **'87** 162
Bowl with Cucumber-Mint Dressing, Melon
    Ball, **'87** 153
Cantaloupe-Cheese Salad, **'88** 184
Cantaloupe Compote, **'81** 147
Cantaloupe Cooler Salad, **'79** 176
Cantaloupe Cream Delight, **'82** 179
Cantaloupe Cream, Frozen, **'82** 159
Cantaloupe Cream Pie, **'79** 177
Cantaloupe, Fruit-Filled, **'83** 120
Cantaloupe Ice Cream, **'79** 77
Cantaloupe Meringue Pie, **'88** 182
Cantaloupe Mold, Double-Grape, **'79** 173
Cantaloupe-Pecan Salad, **'86** 178
Cantaloupe Pie, **'86** 163
Cantaloupe Punch, **'81** 147
Cantaloupe Salad, **'86** 182
Cantaloupe Sherbet, **'88** 183
Cantaloupe Sherbet, Frosty, **'82** 144
Cantaloupe Soup, **'83** 120; **'88** 160
Cantaloupe Soup, Chilled, **'81** 156
Cantaloupe Soup, Fresh, **'84** 190
Cantaloupe, Southern Plantation, **'82** 179
Cantaloupe Wedges, Grilled, **'87** 162
Citrus Mingle, Melon-, **'79** 177
Compote, Melon Ball, **'85** 157
Cooler, Melon, **'81** 146
Cooler, Melon Ball, **'86** 131
Filled Melon, Berry-, **'86** 93
Fruit Bowl, Sparkling Fresh, **'80** 146
Fruit Cup with Mint Dressing, Fresh, **'80** 183
Fruit Deluxe, Marinated, **'81** 146
Fruited Ham Salad, **'81** 146
Fruit Medley, Minted, **'80** 182
Honeydew-Berry Dessert, **'83** 120
Honeydew Fruit Boats, **'81** 147
Honeydew Fruit Bowl, **'84** 186
Honeydew Fruit Cups, **'82** 179
Honeydew Granita, **'87** 162
Honeydew Salad with Apricot Cream
    Dressing, **'84** 191

Julep, Melon-Mint, **'86** 196
Julep, Rainbow Melon, **'80** 183
Mélange, Melon, **'84** 139
Minted Melon Cocktail, **'81** 146
Mint Sauce, Melons in, **'85** 164
Salad, Avocado-Melon, **'82** 164
Salad, Congealed Melon Ball, **'84** 125

Salad, Summertime Melon, **'82** 101
Salad with Dill Dressing, Melon, **'88** 182
Soup, Melon, **'80** 182
Soup, Swirled Melon, **'87** 162
Watermelon Frost, **'86** 196
Watermelon Fruit Basket, **'84** 161
Watermelon Preserves, **'79** 120
Watermelon Rind Pickles, **'81** 174
Watermelon Salad with Celery-Nut
    Dressing, **'80** 182
Watermelon Sauce, Melon Balls in, **'79** 177
Watermelon Sherbet, **'79** 155
Watermelon Sherbet, Light, **'81** 147
Watermelon Sparkle, **'84** 191
Wedges with Berry Sauce, Melon, **'86** 178

Meringues

Asparagus Meringue, **'88** 131
Baked Pear Meringues, **'85** 232
Bars, Meringue-Chocolate Chip, **'84** 118
Basket, Summer Berry, **'84** 158
Cake, Brown Sugar Meringue, **'81** 70
Cake, Orange Meringue, **'86** 336; **'87** 84
Cakes, Spanish Wind, **'84** 157
Cooked Meringue, **'86** 130
Cooked Meringue, Easy, **'82** 207; **'83** 158
Cookies, Forget 'em, **'83** 256
Cookies, Meringue Kiss, **'86** 121
Cookies, Meringue Surprise, **'86** 320
Cups, Kiwi and Cream in
    Meringue, **'81** 279
Cups, Lemon Custard in
    Meringue, **'80** 295; **'81** 172
Cups, Lemon Meringue Cream, **'84** 23
Fingers, Chocolate-Almond
    Meringue, **'84** 158
Flowers, Meringue, **'84** 156
Frosting, Brown Sugar Meringue, **'81** 70
Frosting, **'86** 336; **'87** 84
Holiday Meringues, **'88** 280
Meringue, **'87** 207
Peach Melba Meringues, **'87** 76
Pineapple, Meringue-Topped, **'84** 178
Piping Meringue, **'84** 156
Shell, Cinnamon Meringue, **'82** 263
Shells, Fruited Meringue, **'87** 32
Shells, Fruit-Filled Meringue, **'86** 151
Strawberry Meringues, **'84** 188
Strawberry Meringue Torte, **'88** 136

Torte, Toffee Meringue, '87 118
Vacherin Moka, '80 55
Microwave
　Appetizers
　　Bacon-Chestnut Wraps, '84 M216
　　Brie Appetizer, Bit-of-, '88 M8
　　Canapés, Green Onion, '84 M216
　　Cheese Log, Toasted Pecan, '86 M288
　　Cheese Sticks, Peppery, '81 M289
　　Crab-Zucchini Bites, '84 M216
　　Dip, Chipped Beef, '88 M8
　　Dip, Creamy Crab, '80 M135
　　Dip, Hot Artichoke Seafood, '85 M212
　　Dip, Shrimp, '88 M261
　　Franks, Saucy Appetizer, '84 M12
　　Mix, Spicy Party, '81 M138
　　Mushrooms, Shrimp-Stuffed, '80 M135
　　Mushrooms, Spinach-Stuffed, '88 M261
　　Mushrooms, Tipsy, '84 M216
　　Nachos, Make-Ahead, '80 M135
　　Nuts, Sherry-Orange, '86 M289
　　Pâté, Chicken Liver, '88 M132
　　Pecans, Spicy, '81 M289
　　Popcorn, Caramel, '86 M212
　　Popcorn, Garlic, '83 M315
　　Potato Skins, Cheese, '84 M239
　　Rumaki, '80 M136
　　Spread, Chicken Salad Party, '88 M8
　　Spread, Hot Beef, '84 M216
　　Spread, Seafood, '86 M58
　Apples, Rosy Cinnamon, '87 M37
　Beverages
　　Café Colombian Royal, '80 M290
　　Chocolate, Creole Hot, '80 M290
　　Chocolate, Flaming Brandied, '80 M290
　　Chocolate Mix, Deluxe Hot, '80 M290
　　Coffee, Mocha, '85 M329
　　Tomato Cocktail, '83 M203
　Blanching Chart, Microwave, '80 M181
　Breads
　　Caramel Ring, Easy, '85 M89
　　Cheese-Herb Bread, '84 M144
　　Chocolate Loaf Bread, '88 M188
　　Coffee Cake, Cinnamon, '83 M203
　　Coffee Cake, Orange, '85 M88
　　Coffee Cake Ring, '85 M89
　　Coffee Ring, Sugarplum, '83 M37
　　Muffins, Apple-Bran, '85 M89
　　Muffins, Cheesy Cornbread, '88 M275
　　Muffins, Cinnamon-Nut, '85 M88
　　Muffins, Corn, '82 M282
　　Muffins, Cranberry Streusel
　　　Cake, '88 M274
　　Muffins, Lemon, '88 M275
　　Muffins, Whole Wheat Bran, '88 M274
　　Rolls, Cherry-Almond, '84 M198
　　Toast, Easy French, '82 M172
　　Whole Wheat-Rye Bread, '83 M37
　Chutney, Autumn Fruit, '88 M230
　Croutons, '86 M288
　Croutons, Microwave, '86 M227
　Desserts
　　Apple-Nut Crunch, '82 M238
　　Apple Rings, Cinnamon, '82 M237
　　Apples and Cream,
　　　Brandied, '82 M237
　　Apples, Easy Baked, '82 M238
　　Bananas Foster, '83 M114
　　Bars, Blackberry Jam, '82 M185
　　Bars, Chewy Peanut, '80 M172
　　Bars, Date-Oat, '80 M172

　　Bars, Peanut
　　　Butter-and-Fudge, '80 M172
　　Bavarian Cream, '86 M165
　　Brownies, Chocolate-Mint, '85 M294
　　Brownies, Nutty Fudge, '80 M171
　　Brownies, Quick, '87 M302
　　Cake, Fruit and Spice, '87 M97
　　Cake, German Chocolate, '83 M233
　　Cake, No-Egg Chocolate
　　　Marshmallow, '87 M97
　　Cake, Old-Fashioned Carrot, '83 M232
　　Cake, Peanut Butter, '83 M233
　　Charlotte Russe, '82 M142
　　Cheesecake,
　　　Chocolate-Amaretto, '85 M294
　　Cheesecake, Pear-Berry, '82 M141
　　Cherries Jubilee, Quick, '82 M100
　　Cobbler, Apple-Pecan, '84 M198
　　Cookies, Chocolate-Almond
　　　Surprise, '88 M45
　　Cookies, Doubly-Good
　　　Chocolate, '82 M185
　　Cookies, Nutty Oatmeal-Chocolate
　　　Chip, '82 M185

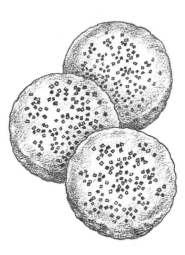

　　Cookies, Spice, '87 M278
　　Cookies, Wedding, '82 M185
　　Cream, Vanilla, '83 M115
　　Crème, Orange-Tapioca, '82 M283
　　Crust, Graham Cracker, '88 M45
　　Crust, Microwaved Graham
　　　Cracker, '82 M141
　　Cupcakes,
　　　Cinnamon-Chocolate, '81 M139
　　Custard, Chocolate-Topped
　　　Amaretto, '87 M37
　　Divinity, Peanut, '87 M278
　　Frosting, Buttery Cinnamon, '81 M139
　　Frosting, Caramel, '81 M289
　　Frosting, Chocolate, '80 M171;
　　　'83 M233; '87 M97
　　Frosting, Coconut-Pecan, '83 M233
　　Frosting, Cream Cheese, '83 M233
　　Fudge, Double-Good, '79 M263
　　Fudge, Double Good, '87 M278
　　Fudge, Quick-and-Easy, '88 M190
　　Ice Cream Cake for
　　　Grown-Ups, '88 M192
　　Jam Squares, '81 M289
　　Kahlúa Delight, Make-Ahead, '84 M89

　　Kahlúa Velvet Dessert, '85 M294
　　Millionaires, '79 M262
　　Oranges, Wine-Poached, '84 M323
　　Pastry, Basic, '81 M268
　　Pastry, Basic Microwave, '82 M142;
　　　'85 M113
　　Pastry, Double-Crust, '82 M298
　　Peaches, Gingersnap, '85 M329
　　Peach Melba, '83 M114
　　Peanut Brittle, '79 M263
　　Peanut Butter
　　　Slice-and-Bakes, '82 M185
　　Pecan-Coconut Clusters, '86 M251
　　Pie, Best-Ever Chocolate, '88 M45
　　Pie, Caramel-Banana, '86 M165
　　Pie, Cranberry-Apple
　　　Holiday, '81 M269
　　Pie, Double Chocolate, '82 M282
　　Pie, Easy Cherry, '82 M299
　　Pie, Festive Pumpkin, '81 M269
　　Pie, Fluffy Eggnog, '81 M269
　　Pie, Glazed Strawberry, '82 M142
　　Pie, Lemon Meringue, '85 M112
　　Pie, Nutty Cranberry, '82 M298
　　Pie, Old-Fashioned Apple, '82 M299
　　Pie, Old-Fashioned Pecan, '81 M269
　　Pie, Quick Pumpkin, '88 M230
　　Pots de Crème, '84 M145
　　Pots de Crème, Mocha, '88 M45
　　Pralines, '86 M288
　　Pralines, Southern, '79 M263
　　Pudding, Brown
　　　Sugar-Pecan, '86 M165
　　Pudding, Chocolate-Almond, '82 M142
　　Pudding, Mandarin-Almond, '85 M12
　　Soufflé, Brandy Alexander, '83 M114
　　Sundaes, Cocoa-Kahlúa, '83 M58
　　Sundaes, Hot Strawberry, '81 M5
　　Sundaes, Spicy Apple Ice
　　　Cream, '86 M195
　　Toffee, Nutty, '79 M263
　Eggs and Omelets
　　Baked Eggs Florentine, '86 M12
　　Benedict, Easy Eggs, '80 M268
　　Creamed Eggs in Patty
　　　Shells, '80 M267
　　Medley, Cheddary Egg, '81 M176
　　Olé Omelet, '87 M124
　　Sausage Omelet, Puffy, '80 M268
　　Scramble, Bacon-and-Eggs, '80 M267
　　Scrambled Eggs, Creamy
　　　Onion, '83 M203
　　Vegetable Omelet, Golden, '82 M123
　Fruit Mélange, '88 M295
　Grits, Quick Cheese, '83 M203
　Jam, Freezer Blackberry, '84 M181
　Jam, Freezer Peach, '84 M182
　Jam, Raspberry Freezer, '84 M181
　Jam, Strawberry Freezer, '84 M182
　Jelly, Christmas Freezer, '86 M288
　Macaroni and Cheese, '83 M7;
　　'88 M147, M190
　Main Dishes
　　Beans-and-Franks, Polynesian,
　　　'84 M11
　　Beef Casserole, Easy, '86 M58
　　Beef Casserole, Layered, '82 M203
　　Beef with Pea Pods,
　　　Oriental, '86 M328
　　Casserole, Mexi, '83 M87
　　Chicken alla Romano, '83 M58

Microwave, Main Dishes *(continued)*

Chicken and Cashews,
Ginger, '85 M11
Chicken and Dumplings with
Vegetables, '85 M56
Chicken and Spinach Rollups, '82 M68
Chicken-and-Vegetable Platter, '88 M52
Chicken and Vegetables
Vermouth, '87 M37
Chicken-Asparagus Rolls, '86 M211
Chicken, Crispy Parmesan, '80 M76
Chicken, Crunchy Spiced, '85 M57
Chicken Divan, '80 M10; '87 M218
Chicken Divan Casserole, '82 M203
Chicken Divan Quiche, '88 M125
Chicken in a Bag, '86 M57
Chicken Kabobs, Marinated, '84 M144
Chicken Kabobs, Pineapple-, '86 M328
Chicken Lasagna, '87 M302
Chicken, Lemon, '81 M138
Chicken, Orange, '86 M140
Chicken, Pineapple, '83 M194
Chicken, Tangy Herbed, '87 M302
Chicken Teriyaki, '80 M76
Chicken Tetrazzini, '80 M75
Chicken Tetrazzini, Cheesy, '83 M87
Chicken Toss, Quick, '87 M124
Chicken with Noodles,
Sesame, '88 M125
Chicken with Pecan-Rice
Dressing, '85 M57
Chicken with Wild Rice,
Elegant, '80 M76
Chicken, Zesty Barbecued, '80 M76
Chili-Cheese Dogs, '81 M176
Chili, Turkey-Bean, '88 M213
Cornish Hens, Orange-Glazed
Stuffed, '84 M89
Crab Imperial, Pineapple-, '84 M286
Crabmeat and Mushrooms on Toast
Points, '82 M91

Crêpes, Sherried Beef, '85 M29
Dinner, Easy Steamed, '83 M314
Filet Mignon Patties, Mock, '82 M68
Fillets, Apple-Carrot Stuffed, '88 M192
Fillets, Lemon-Coated, '80 M53
Fillets, Parmesan, '86 M112
Fillets, Spanish-Style, '86 M112
Fish Amandine, Fillet of, '80 M54
Fish, Creole, '87 M79
Fish Delight, '86 M212
Fish, Easy Italian, '86 M112
Fish, Herb-Coated, '86 M112
Fish in Creamy Swiss Sauce,
Poached, '80 M53
Fish Rolls, Vegetable-Filled, '86 M251

Fish Steaks, Soy, '86 M112
Fish, Sweet-and-Sour, '80 M54
Frankfurters, Barbecued, '84 M12
Grouper with Confetti
Vegetables, '88 M189
Haddock Fillets with Zucchini
Stuffing, '88 M191
Haddock Italiano, '81 M4
Halibut Steaks Italiano, '88 M191
Halibut with Swiss Sauce, '83 M195
Ham and Apples, Baked, '82 M237
Ham and Chicken, Creamed, '81 M74
Ham-Asparagus Dinner, '80 M10
Hamburger Patties, '82 M172
Ham Casserole, Macaroni-, '81 M177
Ham Loaf, Cranberry-, '82 M77
Ham Loaf, Saucy, '86 M328
Ham Ring, Chili-Sauced, '81 M122
Ham Slice, Fruited, '83 M317
Ham, Sweet-and-Sour Glazed, '88 M15
Ham Tetrazzini, '82 M77
Ham Towers, Cheesy, '82 M77
Ham with Raisin Sauce, '82 M76
Kabobs, Shish, '85 M112
Lasagna, '83 M6
Lasagna, Quick 'n Easy, '80 M10
Lasagna, Zesty, '87 M188
Manicotti, Stuffed, '83 M6
Meat Loaf, Basic, '88 M14
Meat Loaf, Cheesy Pizza, '81 M121
Meat Loaf, Easy, '88 M214
Meat Loaf, Oriental, '81 M122;
'83 M194
Meat Loaf, Swedish, '81 M121
Meat Loaf, Vegetable, '85 M29
Monkfish, Greek-Style, '87 M79
Orange Roughy with Spinach
Pesto, '88 M192
Oysters on the Half Shell,
Dressed, '87 M79
Paella, Party, '88 M189
Papillote, Ocean, '84 M287
Peppers, Hearty Stuffed, '88 M214
Pineapple Loaves, Individual, '81 M121
Pizza, Jiffy Jazzed-Up, '83 M314
Pork Casserole, Cheesy, '81 M74
Pork Chop, Saucy, '86 M140
Pork Chops, Pineapple, '87 M124
Potatoes, Frank-Filled, '84 M11
Pot Roast, Basic, '81 M208
Pot Roast, Company, '88 M14
Pot Roast with Vegetables, '81 M208
Pot Roast with Vegetables,
Marinated, '88 M52
Quiche, Benedict, '80 M107
Quiche, Crab, '82 M122
Quiche Lorraine, '80 M108
Quiche, Spicy Sausage, '80 M108
Quiche, Spinach-Mushroom, '81 M74
Quiche, Vegetable, '87 M219
Salmon Patties, Open-Faced, '87 M218
Sausage and Rice Casserole,
Oriental, '82 M123
Sausage Casserole, Easy, '87 M189
Sausage Dinner, Beefy, '80 M9
Sausage-Egg Casserole, '86 M12
Sausage Jambalaya
Casserole, '82 M203
Shrimp, Garlic-Buttered, '86 M226
Shrimp in Cream Sauce, '84 M286
Shrimp, Quick Curried, '84 M198

Sloppy Joes, Pocket, '85 M328
Sole, Saucy, '82 M68
Sole with Cucumber Sauce, '84 M286
Spaghetti, Easy, '83 M317
Spaghetti Pie, '81 M32
Steak, Onion-Smothered, '87 M189
Taco Pies, Individual, '82 M282
Tacos, Jiffy, '83 M318
Tacos, Microwave, '88 M213
Tortilla Pie, '85 M211
Trout, Sunshine, '84 M286
Tuna Casserole, Easy, '82 M203
Veal and Carrots in Wine
Sauce, '86 M139
Veal, Italian Style, '82 M68
Zucchini, Beef-Stuffed, '86 M139
Mustard, Coarse-and-Sweet, '86 M288
Noodles, Cheesy Parmesan, '83 M7
Pastry, Microwaved Quiche, '81 M74;
'82 M122
Pastry, Quiche, '80 M107
Peaches with Rum, Ginger, '84 M323
Pears, Marmalade Breakfast, '83 M203
Pineapple, Scalloped, '84 M323
Pumpkin, Cooked Fresh, '88 M230
Pumpkin Seeds, Toasted, '88 M230
Relish, Cranberry-Orange, '81 M289
Relish, Spicy Apple, '84 M323
Rice, Almond, '85 M112
Rice, Basic Long-Grain, '83 M285
Rice, Basic Quick-Cooking, '83 M285
Rice, Chicken-Flavored, '84 M144
Rice, Curry-Spiced, '86 M226
Rice, Herbed, '83 M285
Rice, Oriental, '85 M12, 146

Rice, Parsleyed, '83 M58
Rice with Almonds, Curried, '83 M285
Salad Dressings
Vinaigrette Dressing and
Croutons, '86 M288
Salads
Artichokes with Orzo Salad, '88 M193
Beef Salad, Tangy, '87 M218
Chicken Salad, Special, '88 M193
Fast-and-Easy Salad, '85 M328
Fruit Salad with Mint Sauce, '88 M96
Pork-and-Spinach Salad,
Mandarin, '88 M126
Potato Salad, Chunky, '81 M138
Potato Salad, German-Style, '88 M194
Spinach Salad, Sweet-Sour, '85 M112
Spinach Salad, Wilted, '81 M4
Taco Salad Cups, '85 M29
Tuna Salad, Cheese-Sauced, '87 M124
Sandwiches
Asparagus-and-Ham Melt
Sandwiches, '88 M96

Breakfast Sandwiches, '82 M123
Brown Bread-Cream Cheese
  Sandwiches, '87 M6
Burgers, Pizza, '80 M201
Crabmeat Sandwiches,
  Deluxe, '81 M74
Frankfurter Sandwiches, '84 M11
Grilled Cheese Sandwiches, '82 M172
Hot Brown Sandwiches, '80 M202
Pita Sandwiches, Denver, '86 M12
Pita Sandwiches, Hot, '87 M6
Pizza Sandwiches,
  Open-Face, '84 M198
Pork Sandwiches, Party, '88 M273
Reuben Sandwiches, '80 M201
Tuna Sandwiches, Hot, '86 M194
Sauces and Gravies
  Almond-Vanilla Custard
    Sauce, '88 M177
  Amaretto-Strawberry Sauce, '87 M165
  Apple Dessert Sauce, '87 M165
  Barbecue Sauce, Lemony, '88 M177
  Béchamel Sauce, '84 M239
  Cheese Sauce, '79 M156; '82 M123
  Cherry Sauce, Elegant, '79 M156
  Chocolate Cherry Sauce, '87 M165
  Chocolate Mint Sauce, Quick, '86 M58
  Chocolate-Peanut Butter
    Sauce, '79 M156
  Chocolate-Praline Sauce, '85 M295
  Chocolate Sauce, Creamy, '88 M177
  Crab Marinara Sauce,
    Quick, '85 M151
  Cream Sauce, Sherried, '85 M152
  Curry Sauce, '79 M156; '84 M71
  Dill Sauce, '84 M70
  Dill Sauce, Creamy, '79 M156
  Garlic-Cheese Sauce, '84 M70
  Hollandaise Sauce, '80 M107, M268;
    '88 M177
  Horseradish-Mustard Sauce,
    Creamy, '88 M177
  Horseradish Sauce, '88 M273
  Lemon Dessert Sauce, '87 M165
  Mint Sauce, '88 M96
  Mushroom Sauce, '84 M70
  Mustard Sauce, '84 M70
  Orange Sauce, '84 M286
  Parsley-Garlic Sauce, '84 M70
  Peach-Berry Sauce, '87 M165
  Peanut Dessert Sauce, '86 M251
  Pineapple Ice Cream Sauce, '81 M289
  Praline Ice Cream Sauce,
    Southern, '86 M227
  Sour Cream Sauce, '82 M68
  Swiss Sauce, '83 M195
  Taco Sauce, '82 M283
  Tomato Sauce, Herbed
    Fresh, '85 M151
  Tomato Sauce, Italian, '82 M68
  Vegetable-Cheese Sauce, '85 M152
  White Sauce, Basic, '79 M156
Soups and Stews
  Bacon-Beer Cheese Soup, '87 M7
  Beef Stew with Parsley
    Dumplings, '85 M246
  Broccoli Soup, '86 M194
  Broccoli Soup, Cream of, '80 M225
  Cauliflower Soup, Cream of, '87 M7
  Cheese Soup,
    Bacon-Topped, '80 M224

Cheese Soup, Monterey
  Jack, '85 M211
Chicken Soup, Quick, '86 M72
Chili, Basic, '82 M11
Chili, Beefy Sausage, '82 M11
Chili, Cheese-Topped, '82 M11
Chili, Chunky, '82 M11
Chili with Rice, '82 M11
Chowder, Corn, '84 M38
Chowder, Creamy Ham, '88 M53
Chowder, Fish, '84 M38
Chowder, New England Clam, '86 M72
Crab Soup, Creamy, '80 M224
Egg-Drop Soup, '85 M12
Mushroom Soup, '86 M73
Mushroom Soup, Curried, '84 M89
Onion Soup, French, '86 M212
Onion Soup, Shortcut
  French, '85 M328
Pea Soup, Spring, '88 M96
Potato-Bacon Soup, '84 M38
Potato Soup, Cream of, '80 M224
Strawberry Soup Supreme, '81 M144
Tomato-Celery Soup, '83 M58
Tomato-Vegetable Soup, '81 M177
Vegetable Soup, Beefy, '84 M38
Topping, Streusel, '88 M275
Vegetables
  Acorn Rings, Easy Glazed, '81 M231
  Asparagus in Lemon Butter, '80 M123
  Asparagus-Pea Casserole, '88 M294
  Asparagus with Lemon
    Butter, '87 M151
  Beans Amandine, Green, '82 M20
  Beans, Bacon-Topped
    Green, '80 M123
  Beans, Green, '87 M151
  Beans, Herbed Green, '83 M147;
    '88 M190
  Beans, Marinated Italian, '86 M226
  Beans, Nutty Green, '88 M187
  Beans, Tangy Green, '85 M142

Beets, Harvard, '83 M195
Beets with Sour Cream
  Dressing, '88 M295
Broccoli au Gratin, '82 M20
Broccoli, Chinese, '85 M12
Broccoli Goldenrod, Lemon-, '84 M89
Broccoli, Marinated Fresh, '81 M139
Broccoli-Swiss Cheese
  Casserole, '85 M211
Carrots-and-Celery,
  Scalloped, '84 M112
Carrots, Orange-Glazed, '81 M165
Carrots, Spice-Glazed, '83 M58
Corn Fix-Up, Quick, '81 M4

Corn, Mexi-, '82 M21
Corn on the Cob,
  Microwaved, '80 M122
Corn on the Cob, Parmesan, '88 M187
Corn on the Cob, Spicy, '87 M151
Corn, Seasoned Fresh, '83 M147
Corn, Southern-Style
  Creamed, '81 M165
Eggplant, Easy, '87 M151
Fresh Vegetables,
  Microwaving, '82 M138
Garden Harvest, '85 M142
Julienne Vegetables with
  Walnuts, '86 M251
Kabobs, Marinated
  Vegetable, '83 M195
Mixed Vegetables, '83 M195
Okra and Tomatoes, Fresh, '81 M165
Okra, Corn, and Peppers, '87 M151
Okra Medley, '88 M185
Onion-Potato Bake, '83 M195
Onions and Peppers,
  Sautéed, '83 M148
Onions, Micro-Baked, '82 M32
Peas and Tomatoes, Basil
  Snow, '88 M185
Peas, Fresh Black-Eyed, '81 M165
Peas in a Potato Nest, '84 M239
Peas with Almonds, Curried, '88 M294
Pepper Cups, Hot
  Vegetable, '88 M188
Platter, Vegetable, '88 M187
Potato Casserole, Creamy, '84 M113
Potatoes, Cheesy
  Bacon-Stuffed, '81 M61
Potatoes, Creamy Cheese, '88 M146
Potatoes, Herbed New, '83 M148
Potatoes, Jalapeño-Ham
  Stuffed, '81 M61
Potatoes, Micro-Baked, '81 M61
Potatoes, Orange-Baked
  Sweet, '88 M294
Potatoes, Quick Browned, '82 M172
Potatoes, Seasoned New, '87 M151
Potatoes, Shrimp-Sauced, '81 M61
Potatoes, Summertime, '86 M195
Potatoes with Béchamel Sauce,
  Stuffed, '84 M239
Potatoes with Chives, '81 M61
Potatoes with Hot Bacon
  Dressing, '88 M294
Potato Fans, Parmesan, '84 M240
Potato Fans, Parmesan-, '88 M190
Spinach Delight, '84 M144
Squash-and-Pepper Toss,
  Crisp, '87 M152
Squash, Apple-Stuffed
  Butternut, '81 M232
Squash Bake, Cheddar-, '84 M113
Squash Casserole, Jiffy, '81 M144
Squash, Country Club, '88 M16
Squash, Cranberry-Filled
  Acorn, '81 M231
Squash Medley, Fresh, '81 M165
Squash Ring, Butternut, '81 M232
Squash, Sausage-Stuffed
  Acorn, '81 M231
Squash Toss, Simple, '85 M142
Squash with Meat Sauce,
  Spaghetti, '88 M180
Stir-Fry, Vegetable, '82 M172

Microwave, Vegetables *(continued)*

    Tomatoes, Zippy Mustard, **'86** M226
    Zucchini Boats, **'85** M143
    Zucchini-Egg Casserole, **'84** M113
    Zucchini, Italian, **'83** M147

Mincemeat
Apples, Baked Mincemeat-Filled, **'80** 276
Bars, Mincemeat-Spice, **'88** 231
Cake, Mincemeat Spice, **'79** 246
Cakes, Mini-Mincemeat Nut, **'88** 257
Cookies, Mincemeat, **'79** 51
Cookies, Mincemeat Drop, **'79** 246
Cookies, Mincemeat Sweetheart, **'87** 293
Cookies, Pear Mincemeat, **'84** 264
Homemade Mincemeat, **'79** 245
Peaches, Mincemeat, **'85** 178
Peaches with Mincemeat, Brandied, **'81** 47
Pear Mincemeat, **'79** 196; **'84** 264;
   '88 226
Pie, Apple-Mincemeat, **'85** 316
Pie, Holiday Mincemeat, **'80** 282; **'87** 213
Pie, Mincemeat-Cheese, **'80** 253
Pie, Mincemeat Chiffon, **'79** 245
Pie, Mincemeat-Peach, **'80** 295; **'81** 188
Pie, Pear-Mince, **'81** 271
Pie, Pear Mincemeat, **'84** 264; **'88** 226
Pudding, Steamed Mincemeat, **'80** 264
Salad, Holiday Mincemeat, **'85** 263

Mousses
Amaretto-Chocolate Mousse, **'86** 50
Amaretto-Chocolate Mousse,
   Elegant, **'86** 337
Amaretto Mousse, **'86** 188
Apricot Mousse, **'82** 72
Asparagus Mousse Salad, **'86** 252
Cake, Chocolate Mousse, **'87** 264
Caviar Mousse, **'82** 71; **'85** 86
Chocolate Mousse, **'88** 280
Chocolate Mousse Baked Alaska, **'85** 195
Chocolate Mousse, Blender, **'82** 71
Chocolate Mousse, Blender-Quick, **'80** 269
Chocolate Mousse, Brandy-, **'85** 102
Chocolate Mousse, Creamy, **'87** 133
Chocolate Mousse, Honeyed, **'87** 223
Chocolate Mousse, Quick, **'85** 87
Chocolate Mousse Roll, **'88** 280
Chocolate-Orange Mousse, **'81** 16, 205
Chocolate Rum Mousse, **'86** 189
Coffee Mousse, **'84** 126
Coffee-Nut Mousse, **'86** 319
Crab Mousse, **'79** 117
Crème de Menthe Mousse, **'80** 109
Cucumber Mousse, **'79** 11; **'88** 121
Horseradish Mousse, **'84** 126
Lime Mousse Freeze, Luscious, **'81** 173
Mustard Mousse, **'84** 127; **'86** 184
Orange Mousse, **'86** 69
Oyster Mousse, **'81** 245
Oyster Mousse, Smoked, **'84** 320
Peach Macaroon Mousse, **'80** 153
Peach Mousse, **'85** 54
Peppermint Candy Mousse, **'82** 71
Pie, Chocolate-Amaretto Mousse, **'80** 180;
   '81 30
Pie, Chocolate Mousse, **'81** 136
Pineapple Mousse, Elegant, **'79** 230
Quick-as-a-Wink Mousse, **'84** 311
Raspberry Mousse, **'81** 34
Rhubarb Mousse, **'88** 93
Roquefort Mousse, **'82** 71

Salmon Dill Mousse, **'81** 21
Salmon Mousse, Irresistible, **'79** 284
Sherried Mousse, **'81** 247
Shrimp Mousse, **'79** 57; **'87** 196, 251
Strawberry-Lemon Mousse, **'82** 128
Strawberry Mousse, **'81** 95
Strawberry Mousse, Fresh, **'82** 72
Tuna Mousse, **'80** 275
Watercress Mousse, **'88** 104

Muffins
Almond Muffins, Peachy-, **'86** 301
Apple-Bran Muffins, **'85** M89
Apple Muffins, **'83** 96; **'84** 193; **'87** 23
Apple Muffins, Fresh, **'84** 264
Apple Muffins, Spiced, **'79** 60
Apple-Oat Muffins, Spicy, **'86** 45
Applesauce Muffins, **'84** 284
Applesauce Muffins, Bite-Size, **'82** 104
Applesauce Spice Muffins, **'88** 236
Banana Bran Muffins, **'83** 48
Banana-Honey-Nut Muffins, **'88** 62
Banana Muffins, **'80** 88; **'84** 75
Banana-Oatmeal Muffins, **'84** 20
Banana-Oat Muffins, **'87** 188
Banana-Orange Muffins, **'84** 148
Banana Surprise Muffins, **'82** 105
Blueberry Buttermilk Muffins, **'80** 16
Blueberry-Cream Cheese Muffins, **'86** 14
Blueberry Ice Cream Muffins, **'82** 143
Blueberry-Lemon Muffins, **'79** 7

Blueberry Muffins, **'80** 143
Blueberry Muffins, Easy, **'81** 197
Blueberry Muffins, Golden, **'79** 235
Blueberry Muffins, Old-Fashioned, **'86** 161
Blueberry Muffins with Streusel
   Topping, **'88** 129
Blueberry-Oatmeal Muffins, **'87** 24
Blueberry Streusel Muffins, **'80** 46
Bran-Buttermilk Muffins, **'85** 7
Bran Muffins, **'84** 53
Bran Muffins, Easy, **'83** 55
Bran Muffins, Ever-Ready, **'81** 106
Bran Muffins for Two, **'84** 211
Bran, Muffins Made of, **'86** 103
Bran Muffins, Quick, **'86** 85
Bran Muffins, Refrigerator, **'79** 6
Bran Muffins, Sour Cream-, **'87** 98
Bran Muffins, Spiced, **'84** 229
Breakfast Bites, **'86** 15
Carrot-and-Raisin Muffins, **'87** 24
Carrot-Date-Nut Muffins, **'86** 262
Carrot-Pineapple Muffins, **'81** 6
Carrot-Wheat Muffins, **'88** 9
Cheese-and-Pepper Muffins, **'84** 139
Cheese Muffins, Marvelous, **'83** 96
Cherry Muffins, **'82** 105

Cinnamon-Nut Muffins, **'85** M88
Cinnamon-Pecan Muffins, **'84** 219
Coconut-Molasses Muffins, **'82** 210
Coffee Cake Muffins, **'79** 7
Cornbread Muffins, Cheesy, **'88** M275
Cornbread Muffins, Southern, **'85** 201
Cornmeal Muffins, **'80** 90; **'88** 92
Corn Muffins, **'82** M282; **'84** 16
Corn Muffins, Quick, **'88** 15
Corn Muffins, Sage-, **'83** 207
Corn Muffins, Tomato, **'81** 137
Cranberry Muffins, **'81** 249
Cranberry-Pecan Muffins, **'84** 269
Cranberry Streusel Cake Muffins, **'88** M274
Date Muffins, **'79** 142
Date Muffins, Surprise, **'79** 216
Date-Nut Muffins, **'84** 75
Egg Muffins, One-, **'83** 9
English Muffins, **'87** 49; **'88** 76
English Muffins, Raisin, **'80** 75
Fiber Muffins, High-, **'85** 250
Fig Muffins, **'86** 206
Gingerbread Muffins, **'81** 285
Gingerbread Muffins, Last-Minute, **'82** 105
Grain Muffins, Four-, **'80** 46
Honey Bran Muffins, **'88** 171
Honey-Oatmeal Muffins, **'84** 229
Honey-Wheat Muffins, **'83** 96; **'88** 263
Jam Muffins, **'79** 7
Jelly-Filled Muffins, **'80** 16
Kiwifruit Muffins, **'87** 255
Lemon Muffins, **'88** 119, M275
Lemon Muffins, Fresh, **'79** 161
Magic Muffins, **'79** 244
Mayonnaise Muffins, **'83** 57; **'86** 16
Merry Muffins, **'82** 253
Mix, Quick Bread, **'81** 90
Muffins, **'81** 90
Nut Crunch Muffins, Best Ever, **'82** 65;
   '83 106
Nut Muffins, Tasty, **'79** 208
Nutty Muffins, **'86** 141
Oatmeal Bran Muffins, **'81** 236
Oatmeal-Honey Muffins, **'83** 95
Oatmeal Muffins, **'82** 129, 210;
   '84 72, 140
Oatmeal Muffins, Best-Ever, **'84** 242
Orange-Honey Muffins, **'88** 284
Orange Juice Muffins with Honey
   Spread, **'81** 229
Orange Muffins, **'79** 236; **'81** 107; **'83** 54
Orange Muffins, Streusel-Topped, **'84** 74
Orange-Oatmeal Muffins, **'85** 202
Orange-Pecan Muffins, **'83** 96
Peach Muffins, Special, **'84** 74
Peanut Butter-Honey Muffins, **'82** 56
Peanut Butter Muffins, **'80** 86; **'87** 158
Pecan Muffins, **'80** 16
Pecan Muffins, Chunky, **'88** 9
Pecan Muffins, Country, **'83** 222
Pineapple Muffins, **'81** 14, 250
Plum Good Muffins, **'83** 96
Poppy Seed Muffins, **'81** 63
Potato Muffins, Sweet, **'81** 224; **'85** 6;
   '87 280
Prune Muffins, Miniature, **'85** 223
Pumpkin Muffins, **'79** 206, 275; **'81** 272
Pumpkin Muffins, Nutty, **'86** 291
Raisin Muffins, Breakfast, **'84** 59
Raisin-Pecan Ginger Muffins, **'88** 9
Sausage-Cheese Muffins, **'86** 213

Sausage Muffins, **'88** 52
Sesame Cheese Muffins, **'86** 16
Sour Cream Muffins, Mini, **'88** 283
Squash Muffins, Yellow, **'81** 163
Sunshine Muffins, **'86** 9
Tea Muffins, **'82** 105
Tropical Muffins, **'84** 299
Wheat Germ-Prune Muffins, **'81** 106
Wheat Muffins, Fruited, **'79** 93
Whole Wheat Bran Muffins, **'88** M274
Whole Wheat Raisin Muffins, **'85** 207
Yam Muffins, **'79** 7
Yeast Muffins, Quick, **'84** 69
Yogurt Muffins, **'88** 55
Zucchini Muffins, **'83** 121; **'86** 146

Mushrooms

Appetizers, Chicken-Mushroom, **'88** 210
Asparagus and Mushrooms, **'85** 108
au Gratin, Mushrooms, **'81** 108
Aztec Mushrooms, **'82** 51
Bake, Cheesy Macaroni-Mushroom, **'81** 243
Baked Mushrooms, Creamy, **'87** 127
Bake, Windsor Mushroom, **'88** 132
Balls, Cheese and Mushroom, **'79** 63
Beans with Mushrooms, Green, **'82** 21
Beef Tenderloin with Mushrooms, **'87** 115
Bisque, Brisk Mushroom, **'81** 190
Bundles, Chicken-Mushroom, **'80** 157
Canapés, Mushroom, **'80** 285
Casserole, Egg-Mushroom, **'83** 49
Casserole, Mushroom-Artichoke, **'87** 241
Casserole, Mushroom-Cheese, **'83** 216
Casserole, Mushroom-Potato, **'84** 5
Casserole, Sausage-Mushroom
   Breakfast, **'86** 95
Champignons au Vin, **'79** 47
Chicken and Mushrooms in Wine
   Sauce, **'81** 109
Chicken Livers with Mushrooms, **'81** 133
Chicken-Mushroom Dinner, **'81** 3
Chowder, Mushroom, **'79** 16
Consommé aux Champignons, **'79** 48
Crabmeat and Mushrooms on Toast
   Points, **'82** M91
Creamed Mushrooms in Wild Rice
   Ring, **'80** 270
Creamed Mushrooms on Toast, **'81** 190
Crêpes, Cheese and Mushroom, **'81** 88
Crêpes, Coquilles St. Jacques, **'83** 13
Crêpes, Mushroom-Cheese, **'87** 289;
   '88 135
Curried Mushrooms, **'84** 214
Dressing, Whole Wheat-Mushroom, **'84** 283
Drunk Mushrooms, **'83** 174
Egg Delight, Mushroom-, **'83** 14
Eggplant, Mushroom-Stuffed, **'83** 136
Filling in a Peel, Mushroom, **'84** 214
Filling, Mushroom, **'81** 89; **'82** 259;
   '83 51; **'88** 84
Filling, Spinach-Mushroom, **'80** 215

Fluted Mushrooms, **'82** 280
Fresh Mushrooms, Savory, **'85** 268
Fried Mushrooms, French-, **'82** 78
Fried Mushrooms with Tartar Sauce,
   French-, **'86** 233
Heavenly Mushrooms, **'87** 281
Herbed Mushrooms, **'84** 214; **'88** 176
Logs, Mushroom, **'84** 206
Marinated Herb Mushrooms, **'86** 327
Marinated Mushroom Caps, **'83** 128
Marinated Mushrooms, **'80** 82, 270;
   '81 69; **'86** 135
Marinated Mushrooms, Easy, **'86** 217
Marinated Mushrooms, Mexican, **'81** 66
Marinated Mushrooms, Special, **'83** 13
Muffin Stacks, Mushroom-Topped, **'80** 271
Newburg, Mushroom, **'88** 252
Noodles and Mushrooms, Cheesy, **'79** 84
Omelet, Broccoli-Mushroom, **'85** 45
Omelet, Rolled Mushroom, **'82** 70
Panuchos, Mushroom, **'83** 51
Pastry Cups, Mushroom-Almond, **'88** 210
Patty Shells, Mushrooms and Eggs
   in, **'85** 143; **'88** 197
Patty Shells, Mushrooms in, **'80** 283
Peas and Mushrooms, **'83** 141
Peas and Mushrooms, Buttered, **'82** 204
Peas with Mushrooms, Creamy, **'84** 196
Peas with Mushrooms, Green, **'80** 101
Pizza, Cheese-and-Mushroom, **'83** 226
Potatoes, Mushroom-Dill-Topped, **'86** 41
Potatoes, Mushroom Scalloped, **'87** 191
Pot Roast, Mushroom, **'79** 17
Quail with Mushrooms, **'85** 138
Quail with Mushrooms, Baked, **'81** 259
Quiche, Ham-and-Mushroom, **'81** 11
Quiche Lorraine, Mushroom-, **'86** 242
Quiche, Mushroom, **'80** 222; **'81** 244
Quiche, Spinach-Mushroom, **'81** M74
Quiche, Zucchini-Mushroom, **'79** 127
Rollups, Mushroom, **'85** 318
Salad, Fabulous Mushroom, **'81** 190
Salad, Marinated Mushroom, **'88** 215
Salad, Mushroom-and-Pepper, **'86** 68
Salad, Mushroom-Zucchini, **'85** 8
Salad, Spinach and Mushroom, **'80** 112
Salad, Watercress-and-Mushroom, **'88** 104
Salad with Fresh Mushrooms, Rice, **'80** 231
Sandwiches, Toasted Mushroom, **'87** 281
Sauce, Beef Tenderloin with
   Mushroom, **'88** 3
Sauce, Beef Tenderloin with
   Mushroom-Sherry, **'87** 306
Sauce, Broiled Tomatoes with
   Mushroom, **'81** 103
Sauce, Chicken Florentine with
   Mushroom, **'87** 250
Sauce, Mushroom, **'81** 90, 200; **'82** 46;
   '83 71, 205, 212; **'84** M70; **'85** 40;
   '86 198; **'87** 36, 186, 284
Sauce, Mushroom-Cheese, **'83** 190; **'86** 48
Sauce, Mushroom-Dill, **'80** 271
Sauce, Mushroom-Wine, **'84** 84; **'86** 24
Sauce, Onion-Mushroom, **'85** 224; **'86** 84
Sauce, Steak with
   Ham-and-Mushroom, **'83** 109
Sauce, Steak with Mushroom, **'83** 212
Sauce Supreme on Vermicelli,
   Mushroom, **'86** 158
Saucy Mushrooms and Eggs, **'79** 138
Sautéed Mushrooms, **'84** 35

Sautéed Mushrooms, Easy, **'81** 131
Sautéed Mushroom Spectacular, **'83** 206
Scallops and Mushrooms, Creamy, **'83** 144
Seasoned Mushrooms, **'83** 291
Sherried Mushroom Eggs, **'83** 49
Sherried Mushrooms, **'83** 13
Shrimp-Mushroom Italienne, Green Pasta
   with, **'79** 170
Soufflés, Mushroom, **'87** 282
Soup, Chunky Mushroom, **'88** 12
Soup, Cream of Mushroom, **'84** 5;
   '85 93, 261
Soup, Creamy Avocado-Mushroom, **'85** 25
Soup, Creamy Mushroom, **'79** 243;
   '81 307
Soup, Curried Mushroom, **'84** M89
Soup, Elegant Mushroom, **'83** 99
Soup, Fresh Mushroom, **'81** 109
Soup, Mushroom, **'82** 286; **'86** M73
Soup, Mushroom-Onion, **'80** 25
Soup, Oyster-and-Mushroom, **'87** 39
Sour Cream-Dill Sauce, Mushrooms
   in, **'84** 215
Spaghetti with Mushrooms, Spicy, **'85** 2
Spinach with Mushrooms, **'80** 19
Spread, Hot Mushroom, **'81** 190
Squash, Mushroom-Stuffed Yellow, **'84** 154
Steak and Mushrooms, Flank, **'87** 61
Stems, Mushrooms with, **'86** 258
Stir-Fried Mushrooms with Bacon, **'80** 123
Stroganoff, Mushroom, **'81** 298
Stroganoff, Mushroom-Meatball, **'85** 85
Stuffed Mushroom Appetizers, **'88** 210
Stuffed Mushroom Caps, Crab-, **'84** 160
Stuffed Mushroom Delight, **'87** 281
Stuffed Mushrooms, **'79** 212; **'81** 239;
   '83 13, 66, 126, 136
Stuffed Mushrooms, Black Olive-, **'86** 258
Stuffed Mushrooms, Cheese 'n'
   Bacon-, **'86** 258
Stuffed Mushrooms, Chicken-, **'80** 162
Stuffed Mushrooms, Crab-, **'81** 190
Stuffed Mushrooms, Crawfish-, **'86** 258
Stuffed Mushrooms, Elegant
   Cheese-, **'81** 57
Stuffed Mushrooms, Flavor-, **'85** 288
Stuffed Mushrooms Florentine, **'82** 270
Stuffed Mushrooms, Italian
   Sausage-, **'83** 127
Stuffed Mushrooms, Parmesan, **'83** 115
Stuffed Mushrooms, Pâté-, **'85** 118
Stuffed Mushrooms, Pecan-, **'84** 261
Stuffed Mushrooms, Pesto-, **'86** 150
Stuffed Mushrooms, Pistachio-, **'86** 141
Stuffed Mushrooms, Ricotta-, **'85** 20
Stuffed Mushrooms, Sausage-, **'80** 248
Stuffed Mushrooms, Seasoned, **'84** 206
Stuffed Mushrooms, Shrimp-, **'80** M135
Stuffed Mushrooms, Spinach-, **'86** 81;
   '88 131, M261
Stuffed with Crab, Mushrooms, **'82** 249
Supreme, Mushrooms, **'84** 214
Tarts, Hot Sherried Mushroom, **'83** 78
Tarts, Mushroom, **'88** 161
Tipsy Mushrooms, **'84** M216
Tomatoes, Mushroom-Stuffed, **'86** 218
Turnovers, Tiny Mushroom, **'86** 24
Vegetable Mushroom Caps, **'81** 246
Vermicelli with Mushrooms, **'79** 195
Wild Rice and Mushrooms, **'83** 278
Wine Sauce, Mushrooms with, **'85** 292

Mustard

Brussels Sprouts with Shallots and Mustard, '85 258
Coarse-and-Sweet Mustard, '86 M288
Compote, Baked Mustard Fruit, '85 47
Dressing, Mustard, '80 112
Flounder Dijon, '85 95
Herbed Mustard, '87 134
Homemade Mustard, '81 77
Homemade Mustard, Zesty, '82 55
Horseradish Mustard, Lower Sodium, '86 325
Hot German Mustard, '82 298
Hot Mustard, Chinese, '85 12
Hot Sweet Mustard, '85 12
Mousse, Mustard, '84 127; '86 184
Sauce, Chilled Asparagus in Mustard, '88 130
Sauce, Creamy Horseradish-Mustard, '88 M177
Sauce, Creamy Mustard, '80 272; '86 257; '87 232
Sauce, Extra-Special Mustard, '79 82
Sauce, Honey-Lemon Mustard, '84 275
Sauce, Honey-Mustard, '85 13
Sauce, Light Mustard, '82 178
Sauce, Mild Mustard, '85 224; '86 84
Sauce, Mock Mustard-Hollandaise, '87 269
Sauce, Mustard, '80 222, 283; '83 21, 321; '84 M70, 289; '85 148; '86 185; '87 22
Sauce, Mustard Cream, '88 61
Sauce, Mustard-Sour Cream, '81 68
Sauce, Sausage Sandwiches with Mustard, '84 250
Sauce, Stone Crab Mustard, '80 3
Sauce, Sweet Mustard, '85 12
Spread, Mustard, '86 105

N

Nectarines

Apple Juice, Nectarines in, '83 183
Butter, Nectarine, '79 175
Cocktail, Nectarine, '85 107
Royale, Nectarines, '85 132
Salad, Nectarine Chicken, '79 175

Noodles

Bake, Hamburger-Noodle, '81 140
Bake, Pork-and-Noodle, '88 98
Bake, Sausage-Noodle, '81 92
Bake, Sour Cream-Noodle, '79 55
Bake, Taco Beef-Noodle, '81 141
Beef and Noodles, Easy, '83 288
Caraway Buttered Noodles, '87 230
Casserole, Beef-and-Noodles, '84 72
Casserole, Chicken and Green Noodle, '80 32
Casserole, Eggplant and Noodle, '82 230
Casserole, Ham and Noodle, '80 300
Casserole, Sausage and Noodle, '82 123
Cheesy Noodles and Mushrooms, '79 84
Chicken with Noodles, Sesame, '88 M125
Chili with Noodles, '81 282; '82 57
Crispy Noodles, Chow Mein over, '85 286
Dinner, Beefy Noodle, '81 179
Dinner, Creamy Liver and Noodle, '80 11
Dinner, Pork-and-Noodles Skillet, '88 199

Green Noodles, '80 211
Ham and Swiss on Noodles, '87 108
Italian Sauce with Noodles, '84 250
Orange Noodles, '84 177
Parmesan Noodles, '83 118
Parmesan Noodles, Cheesy, '83 M7
Parslied Noodles, '85 31
Rice Noodles, Shredded Beef over, '85 74
Ring, Noodle, '85 285
Salad, Ham-Noodle, '85 249
Salad, Ramen Noodle, '88 41
Scallops and Pasta, Fresh, '83 164
Skillet, Ham-Noodle, '87 78
Soup, Chicken Noodle, '80 264
Spinach Noodles, Chicken and, '82 19
Spinach with Noodles, Creamed, '84 29
Stew with Noodles, Hungarian, '80 263
Veal Sauce, Noodles with, '80 236
White Noodles, '80 211

O

Oatmeal

Bars, Apricot-Oatmeal, '86 216
Bars, Chocolate-Topped Oatmeal, '86 110
Bars, Date-Oat, '80 M172
Bars, Layered Oatmeal-Date, '85 10
Bars, Oatmeal-Caramel, '85 247
Bars, Yummy Fudge, '87 158
Bread, Blueberry-Oatmeal, '83 139
Bread, Caraway-Raisin Oat, '86 44
Bread, Honey Oatmeal, '80 60
Bread, Oatmeal, '81 236, 300
Bread, Oatmeal Raisin, '81 14
Bread, Oatmeal-Raisin, '83 59
Bread, Oat-Molasses, '82 139
Bread, Round Oatmeal, '84 20
Bread, Whole Wheat-Oatmeal, '87 85
Breakfast Oatmeal, Swiss Style, '81 49
Brownies, Oatmeal, '87 199
Buns, Honey Oatmeal, '83 154
Cake, Dutch Oatmeal, '83 95
Cake, Golden Apple-Oatmeal, '86 301
Cake, Honey-Oatmeal, '87 222
Cake, Oatmeal-Coconut Coffee, '83 312
Cookies, Apple-Nut, '80 228
Cookies, Apple-Oatmeal, '85 215
Cookies, Banana Oatmeal, '79 217
Cookies, Chocolate Chip-Oatmeal, '84 119
Cookies, Chocolate-Oatmeal, '80 105
Cookies, Cinnamon Oatmeal, '84 72
Cookies, Crispy Oat, '88 203
Cookies, Crunchy Oatmeal, '85 202
Cookies, Date-Filled Oatmeal, '86 314
Cookies, Easy Oatmeal, '80 105
Cookies, Frosted Oatmeal-Raisin, '79 290
Cookies, Giant Oatmeal-Spice, '80 105
Cookies, Lace, '86 8
Cookies, Nutty Oatmeal, '81 130
Cookies, Nutty Oatmeal-Chocolate Chip, '82 M185
Cookies, Oatmeal-Coconut, '80 218
Cookies, Oatmeal-Date, '82 109
Cookies, Oatmeal-Date Sandwich, '83 257
Cookies, Oatmeal-Peanut Butter, '85 171
Cookies, Oatmeal-Raisin, '87 221
Cookies, Old-Fashioned Oatmeal, '80 106; '85 250

Cookies, Orange-Glazed Oatmeal, '80 60
Cookies, Peanut Butter-Oatmeal, '81 218; '84 72
Cookies, Peanutty Oatmeal, '80 106; '83 95
Cookies, Slice-and-Bake Oatmeal, '80 105
Cookies, Special Oatmeal, '81 236
Cookies, Spicy Oatmeal, '81 197
Cookies, Take-Along Breakfast, '84 59
Crackers, Oatmeal-Wheat Germ, '84 236
Crispies, Oat, '83 96
Crispies, Oatmeal Nut, '80 208
Fruited Oatmeal, '88 19
Granola Bars, '83 305
Granola, Crunchy, '81 218; '84 144
Granola, Easy, '81 49
Granola, Fruity, '84 148
Granola, Homemade, '84 58
Granola, Sunny Orange, '84 212
Krispies, Oatmeal, '85 115
Loaf, Banana-Oat Tea, '87 256
Loaf, Pumpkin-Oatmeal, '81 49
Mix, Rolled Oats, '84 72
Muffins, Banana-Oat, '87 188
Muffins, Banana-Oatmeal, '84 20
Muffins, Best-Ever Oatmeal, '84 242
Muffins, Blueberry-Oatmeal, '87 24
Muffins, Honey-Oatmeal, '84 229
Muffins, Oatmeal, '82 129, 210; '84 72, 140
Muffins, Oatmeal Bran, '81 236
Muffins, Oatmeal-Honey, '83 95
Muffins, Orange-Oatmeal, '85 202
Muffins, Spicy Apple-Oat, '86 45
Pancakes, Oatmeal, '80 44
Pancakes, Oatmeal-Brown Sugar, '88 203
Piecrust, Crisp Cereal, '83 100
Piecrust, Oatmeal, '79 79
Waffles, Oatmeal-Nut, '83 96

Okra

Bake, Okra-Tomato, '80 298; '81 26
Casserole, Okra, '79 160
Cheese, Okra with, '80 185
Chowder, Quick Okra, '80 185
Corn, and Peppers, Okra, '87 M151
Cream, Okra and Corn in, '79 160
Creole, Meatball-Okra, '83 156
Creole Okra, '81 182
Creole, Okra-Corn, '83 157
Fingers, Okra, '85 196
Fresh Okra and Tomatoes, '87 89
Fried Okra, '79 122; '86 211; '87 89; '88 111
Fried Okra, Crispy, '86 169
Fried Okra, French-, '82 126
Fried Okra, Fritter-, '86 218
Fried Okra, Old-Time, '80 185
Fritters, Okra, '79 160
Fry, Okra-Potato, '81 159
Gumbo, Deep South Okra, '79 48
Gumbo Freezer Mix, Okra, '86 210
Gumbo, Light Seafood-Okra, '86 155
Gumbo, Okra, '86 210
How to Can Okra, '80 127
Medley, Okra, '88 M185
Medley, Okra-Corn-Tomato, '81 159
Pickles, Okra, '81 173
Pilaf, Okra, '80 185; '82 126
Plantation Okra, '82 126
Puffs, Okra, '83 157
Sautéed Corn and Okra, '84 158

Soup, Charleston Okra, **'87** 156
Soup, Sausage and Okra, **'80** 209
Stewed Okra, Southern, **'82** 134
Stew, Old-Fashioned Okra, **'84** 158
Surprise, Okra, **'79** 160; **'84** 158
Tomato Combo, Okra-, **'83** 157
Tomatoes and Okra, **'86** 170; **'87** 164
Tomatoes, Fresh Okra and, **'81** M165
Tomatoes, Okra and, **'80** 185; **'81** 139
Tomatoes, Okra and Green, **'79** 160
Tomatoes with Okra, **'85** 106
Olives
Antipasto, Easy, **'85** 114
Appetizers, Cheesy Olive, **'85** 113
Appetizers, Cheesy-Olive, **'87** 246
Ball, Blue Cheese-Olive, **'82** 248
Ball, Olive Cheese, **'80** 258
Black Olives, Shrimp Spaghetti with, **'85** 13
Black Olive-Stuffed Mushrooms, **'86** 258
Casserole, Turkey-Olive, **'87** 268
Chalupas, Chicken-Olive, **'81** 227
Chicken-and-Rice Valencia, **'85** 113
Filling, Chicken-Olive, **'81** 227
Ham-and-Swiss Rollups, **'85** 113
Potatoes, Olive, **'80** 114
Salad, Mexican Olive, **'85** 84
Salad, Olive Clubhouse, **'81** 114
Salad, Olive-Potato, **'85** 114
Spread, Antipasto, **'81** 25
Spread, Cheese-Olive, **'79** 82
Spread, Cream Cheese-Olive, **'82** 35
Spread, Creamy Olive, **'81** 290
Spread, Tomatoes with Olive, **'85** 114
Stuffed Olives, Almond-, **'88** 95
Toss, Cauliflower-Olive, **'85** 198; **'86** 147
Toss, Tomato-Olive Pasta, **'86** 209
Omelets. *See also* Eggs/Omelets.
Broccoli-Mushroom Omelet, **'85** 45
Cheese Omelet, Zippy, **'87** 287
Cheesy Picante Omelet, **'86** 95
Chicken Liver Omelet, **'82** 44
Filling, Greek Omelet, **'80** 68
Filling, Spanish Omelet, **'80** 68
Fluffy Omelet, **'84** 56
George's Omelets, **'80** 68
Ham and Cheese Omelet, **'79** 262; **'80** 123
Mexican Omelet, **'79** 128; **'81** 225
Mushroom Omelet, Rolled, **'82** 70
Mushroom Sauce, Puffy Omelets with, **'85** 40
Omelet, Olé, **'87** M124
Oyster Omelets, Smoked, **'84** 96
Potato-Sprout Omelet, **'79** 128
Primavera, Omelet, **'87** 71
Rising Sun Omelet, **'82** 281; **'83** 42
Sandwich, Omelet, **'86** 95
Sausage Filling, Omelet with, **'81** 43
Sausage Omelet, Puffy, **'80** M268
Shrimp-and-Cheddar Omelet, **'84** 57
Sour Cream-Ham Omelet, **'79** 261
Spanish Omelet, **'81** 201; **'83** 243; **'84** 101
Spanish-Style Omelets, **'83** 188
Spinach-Cheese Omelet, **'83** 119
Sunrise Omelet, **'83** 289
Swiss Oven Omelet, **'80** 189
Tex-Mex Omelet con Carne, **'81** 209
Vegetable Omelet, Beefy, **'83** 188
Vegetable Omelet, Cheddar-, **'83** 205
Vegetable Omelet, Cheesy, **'85** 49
Vegetable Omelet, Fresh, **'84** 211
Vegetable Omelet, Golden, **'82** M123
Vegetable Omelet, Puffy, **'83** 188
Vegetarian Omelet, **'84** 114
Wine Omelet, White, **'79** 103
Yogurt-Avocado Omelet, **'81** 33
Zucchini Omelet, **'81** 99
Onions
Bake, Cheese Onion, **'82** 32
Baked Onions, Micro-, **'82** M32
Baked Onions, Spicy, **'84** 65
Bake, Onion-Potato, **'83** M195
Barbecued Onions, **'88** 86
Beans and Scallions, Fresh Lima, **'82** 133
Bean Sauce, Pork-and-Onions with, **'85** 76
Beef and Onions, Smothered, **'85** 293
Beef Burgundy with Pearl Onions, **'81** 108
Bread, Easy Onion, **'81** 162
Bread, Easy Onion-Dill, **'85** 5
Bread, Onion-Cheese, **'79** 180; **'81** 8
Bread, Onion-Cheese Supper, **'83** 112
Bread, Onion-Parmesan, **'84** 284
Bread, Toasted Onion-Herb, **'83** 266
Buns, Cheesy Onion, **'85** 5
Buns, Onion-Cheese, **'88** 218
Butter, Onion, **'86** 253
Carrots with Bacon and Onion, Glazed, **'87** 200
Casserole, Cheesy Onion, **'79** 101
Cheese Onions, Sherried, **'82** 32
Chicken, Onion-Crusted, **'88** 40
Cornbread, Onion, **'88** 283
Cornbread, Onion-Topped, **'84** 153
Creole Onions, **'82** 32
Deluxe, Broccoli-Onion, **'81** 75
Dip, Cheesy Onion, **'83** 145
Dip, Chunky Onion, **'84** 257
Dip, Cream Cheese-Onion, **'79** 236
Dressing, Green Pepper-Onion Salad, **'84** 12
Dressing, Onion-French, **'84** 283
Eggs, Creamy Onion Scrambled, **'83** M203
Fried
Crisp Fried Onion Rings, **'84** 65
Crispy Fried Onion Rings, **'80** 108
Crispy Onion Rings, **'86** 110
Deluxe Fried Onion Rings, **'80** 108
Easy Onion Rings, **'80** 108
Favorite Fried Onion Rings, **'81** 86
French-Fried Onion Rings, **'88** 111
French-Fried Onion Rings Supreme, **'80** 109
Green Onions, Fried, **'81** 106
Rings, Fried Onion, **'83** 85; **'85** 69
Glazed Carrots and Onions, **'83** 25; **'87** 128
Glazed Onions, **'84** 104
Glazed Pearl Onions, **'85** 258
Gourmet Onions, **'81** 86
Gravy, Fried Quail with Onion, **'82** 214
Green Onion Canapés, **'84** M216
Green Onion Hoecakes, **'88** 112
Green Onion Quiche, Cheesy, **'83** 194; **'84** 42
Green Onion Relish, **'84** 65
Green Onion Teasers, **'82** 42
Grilled Squash and Onion, **'79** 150
Herbed Carrots and Onions, **'87** 31
Herbed Onions, **'84** 149
Honey Onions, **'81** 86
Hush Puppies, Onion, **'85** 14
Italian Dressing, Tomato, Onion, and Cucumber in, **'81** 83
Loaves, Onion Twist, **'84** 300
Peas with Onions, Buttered, **'80** 242
Pickled Refrigerator Onion Rings, **'84** 265
Pie, Onion, **'82** 191
Pie, Onion-Cheese, **'88** 86
Quiche, Onion, **'83** 121
Relish, Pepper-Onion, **'84** 180
Rice, Seasoned Onion, **'82** 166
Rolls, Poppy Seed Onion, **'81** 63
Salad Bowl, Spinach-and-Onion, **'81** 157
Salad, Lemon-Onion, **'85** 252
Salad, Tomato-Cucumber-Onion, **'81** 239
Salad, Vidalia-Tomato, **'84** 65

Sandwiches on Salt-Rising Bread, Vidalia, **'79** 145
Sauce, Brussells Sprouts in Onion, **'81** 308
Sauce, Onion, **'82** 72; **'87** 248
Sauce, Onion Cream, **'87** 232
Sauce, Onion-Mushroom, **'85** 224; **'86** 84
Sauce, Onion-Parsley, **'85** 148
Sauce, Pepper-Onion, **'84** 125
Sautéed Onions and Peppers, **'83** M148
Selecting and Storing Onions, **'84** 65
Shells, Cheese and Limas in Onion, **'81** 86
Soufflé, Onion, **'79** 247
Soup
Cheese Onion Soup, Double-, **'85** 227
Cheese Soup, Onion-, **'87** 81
Classic Onion Soup, **'84** 65
Double Cheese-Topped Onion Soup, **'79** 49
Easy Onion Soup, **'85** 226
French Onion-Beef Soup, **'87** 54
French Onion Soup, **'79** 49; **'80** 188; **'83** 126; **'85** 226; **'86** M212
French Onion Soup, Shortcut, **'85** M328
French Onion Soup, Toasty, **'81** 306
Green Onion Soup, **'84** 112
Green Onion Soup, Creamed, **'83** 82
Mushroom-Onion Soup, **'80** 25
Oven-Browned Onion Soup, **'79** 49
Rich Onion Soup, **'85** 226
Superb Onion Soup, **'81** 86
Vichyssoise, **'86** 181
Sour Cream, Cucumber and Onion in, **'81** 69
Spread, Braunschweiger-Onion, **'79** 82
Squares, Creamy Onion, **'79** 48
Squares, Sausage-Onion, **'83** 112
Steak, Onion-Smothered, **'87** M189
Stew, Beef-and-Onion, **'87** 18
Stuffed Baked Onions, **'82** 32
Stuffed Onions and Wine, **'85** 268
Stuffed Onions, Baked, **'83** 135
Stuffed Onions, Broccoli-, **'84** 154

Onions *(continued)*

    Stuffed with Peas, Onions, **'84** 68
    Stuffing, Rice-and-Onion, **'88** 246
    Sweet-Hot Onions, **'85** 139
    Turnips and Onions, **'83** 242
    Veal and Onions, Herbed, **'79** 108
On The Light Side. *See* Cooking Light.
Oranges
    Appetizer, Orange-Berry, **'85** 81
    Apples, Orange-Glazed, **'82** 51
    Asparagus with Orange Butter Sauce, **'85** 43
    Asparagus with Orange Sauce, **'83** 46
    Bake, Butternut-Orange, **'86** 295
    Baked Oranges, **'79** 247
    Bake, Sweet Potato-Orange, **'83** 226
    Beets, Orange-Ginger, **'80** 137
    Beets, Orange-Glazed, **'81** 167; **'85** 289;
      '86 187
    Beverages
        Blush, Orange, **'80** 51
        Breakfast Eye-Opener, **'87** 199
        Citrus Cooler, **'82** 160
        Cocktail, Orange-Champagne, **'79** 39
        Cocktail, Tomato-Orange Juice, **'83** 169
        Coffee, Viennese Orange, **'84** 54
        Flip, Orange-Banana, **'82** 48
        Flips, Orange Blossom, **'80** 51
        Frosty, Orange, **'86** 101
        Frosty Sours, **'81** 156
        Liqueur, Orange, **'81** 287
        Magnolia Blossoms, **'87** 72
        Magnolias, **'82** 196
        Mist, Orange-Lemon, **'79** 288; **'80** 35
        Nog, Orange Spiced, **'82** 48
        Pick-Me-Up, Orange, **'80** 232
        Punch, Citrus Party, **'83** 141
        Punch, Orange Blossom, **'83** 142
        Punch, Orange-Lime, **'82** 160
        Punch, Orange-Mint, **'82** 121
        Punch, Orange Sherbet Party, **'83** 142
        Punch, Orange Soda, **'87** 214
        Punch, Pineapple-Orange, **'85** 236
        Punch, Refreshing Orange, **'81** 39
        Refresher, Grapefruit-Orange, **'82** 174
        Sangría, **'81** 67
        Sangría, Easy Citrus, **'80** 218
        Sangría, Orange, **'81** 237
        Shake, Orange Milk, **'84** 166
        Shake, Peachy Orange, **'81** 156
        Shake, Strawberry-Orange
          Breakfast, **'87** 186
        Shake, Tropical, **'87** 200
        Slush, Banana-Orange, **'80** 48; **'81** 155
        Slush, Orange, **'82** 49
        Slush, Strawberry-Orange, **'83** 172
        Smoothie, Mango-Orange, **'86** 216
        Smoothie, Tropical, **'81** 50
        Soda, Cranberry-Orange, **'79** 148
    Breads
        Anise-Orange Bread, **'83** 295
        Baba au Orange, **'86** 138
        Biscuits, Orange, **'88** 85
        Blueberry-Orange Bread, **'87** 140
        Breakfast Ring, Orange, **'81** 229
        Coffee Cake, Cranberry-Orange, **'82** 283
        Coffee Cake, Orange, **'85** M88
        Coffee Cake, Orange Marmalade
          Swirl, **'81** 107
        Coffee Cake, Orange-Pecan, **'86** 86
        Coffee Ring, Caramel-Orange, **'80** 45

        Cranberry Bread, Orange-, **'85** 266
        Cranberry-Orange Bread, **'87** 244
        Cream Cheese Bread,
          Orange-, **'82** 210
        Muffins, Banana-Orange, **'84** 148
        Muffins, Orange, **'79** 236; **'81** 107;
          '83 54
        Muffins, Orange-Honey, **'88** 284
        Muffins, Orange-Oatmeal, **'85** 202
        Muffins, Orange-Pecan, **'83** 96
        Muffins, Streusel-Topped
          Orange, **'84** 74
        Muffins with Honey Spread, Orange
          Juice, **'81** 229

        Nut Bread, Blueberry-Orange, **'84** 141
        Nut Bread, Cranberry-Orange, **'80** 288
        Nut Bread, Orange-, **'82** 75
        Nut Loaf, Orange, **'80** 226
        Pecan Bread, Glazed Orange-, **'81** 250
        Pecan Bread, Orange-, **'79** 148
        Pecan Loaves, Orange-, **'79** 215
        Puffs, Upside-Down Orange, **'83** 57
        Pumpkin Bread, Orange-, **'87** 300
        Rolls, Frosted Hot Orange, **'80** 257
        Rolls, Luscious Orange, **'86** 298
        Rolls, Orange, **'80** 22; **'82** 17; **'88** 79
        Rolls, Orange Butter, **'82** 206; **'83** 33
        Rye Bread, Swedish Orange-, **'85** 111
        Tea Bread, Orange, **'79** 234
        Toast, Orange French, **'83** 292;
          '84 78; **'86** 329
        Toast, Orange Praline, **'79** 36
        Toast Topper, Orange, **'79** 36
        Toast with Orange Sauce,
          French, **'82** 47
        Whole Wheat Orange Bread, **'85** 5
    Broccoli, Easy Orange, **'85** 267
    Broccoli with Orange Sauce, **'80** 243
    Broiled Orange Halves, **'85** 288
    Brussels Sprouts, Orange, **'84** 34
    Butter, Honey-Orange, **'79** 36; **'85** 19
    Butter, Orange, **'81** 8, 42
    Butter, Orange-Pecan, **'84** 75
    Candied Orange Peel, **'81** 286
    Carrots in Orange Sauce, **'82** 107
    Carrots, Orange-Glazed, **'79** 12; **'81** M165
    Carrots, Orange-Raisin, **'80** 24
    Carrots, Orange-Spiced, **'88** 18
    Catfish Amandine, Mandarin, **'84** 183
    Celery in Orange Sauce, **'79** 70
    Chicken à l'Orange, **'84** 277
    Chicken à l'Orange, Stir-Fry, **'83** 82
    Chicken Breasts with Orange Sauce, **'79** 77
    Chicken Breasts with Parslied Rice,
      Orange, **'87** 242

    Chicken, Crispy Mandarin, **'86** 119
    Chicken in Orange-Almond Sauce, **'79** 219;
      '80 13
    Chicken in Orange Sauce, **'83** 8
    Chicken Livers in Orange Sauce, **'82** 218
    Chicken, Orange, **'83** 278; **'86** M140
    Chicken, Orange-Avocado, **'80** 38
    Chicken, Orange Barbecued, **'88** 123
    Chicken Stir-Fry, Kyoto Orange-, **'87** 96
    Chicken Stir-Fry, Orange-, **'84** 68
    Chutney, Cranberry-Orange, **'79** 292
    Chutney, Orange-Cranberry, **'86** 266
    Cornish Hens, Orange-Glazed, **'83** 267
    Cornish Hens, Orange-Glazed
      Grilled, **'86** 250
    Cornish Hens, Orange-Glazed
      Stuffed, **'84** M89
    Cornish Hens with Cranberry-Orange
      Sauce, **'86** 119
    Cornish Hens with Orange Glaze, **'79** 244
    Crêpes, Chocolate-Orange, **'85** 263
    Desserts
        Alaska, Orange, **'83** 177
        Ambrosia, Pineapple-Orange, **'88** 252
        Baked Apples, Orange-Pecan, **'85** 45
        Baked Apples with Orange
          Sauce, **'84** 314
        Baked Bananas with Orange
          Sauce, **'79** 115
        Baked Orange Elegance, **'80** 13
        Bars, Pineapple-Orange, **'82** 129
        Baskets, Orange, **'81** 308
        Cake, Fresh Orange, **'83** 300
        Cake, Fresh Orange Chiffon, **'88** 179
        Cake, General Robert E. Lee
          Orange-Lemon, **'88** 92
        Cake, Mandarin Orange, **'83** 24
        Cake, Mandarin-Rum, **'84** 150
        Cake, Orange, **'86** 61
        Cake, Orange-Cranberry, **'85** 314
        Cake, Orange Liqueur, **'87** 84
        Cake, Orange Marmalade, **'85** 53
        Cake, Orange Meringue, **'86** 336;
          '87 84
        Cake, Orange Nut, **'80** 70
        Cake, Orange-Nut Butter, **'80** 254
        Cake, Orange-Pecan Crunch, **'83** 10
        Cake, Orange Pound, **'87** 84, 221
        Cake, Orange Rum, **'79** 2
        Cake, Orange-Slice, **'81** 264
        Cake, Orange Streusel, **'88** 10
        Cake, Rum-Orange Coconut, **'88** 224
        Cake Squares, Apple-Orange, **'84** 150
        Cake Squares, Orange, **'81** 34
        Cake Squares,
          Orange-Pumpkin, **'83** 242
        Cake, Williamsburg Orange, **'81** 120;
          '82 23
        Cheesecake, Orange, **'81** 84; **'85** 38
        Chocolate-Orange Roll, **'87** 21
        Cookies, Carrot-Orange, **'83** 149
        Cookies, Frosted Orange, **'83** 114
        Cookies, Orange-Chocolate, **'83** 113
        Cookies, Orange-Glazed
          Oatmeal, **'80** 60
        Cookies, Orange-Pecan, **'88** 119
        Cookies, Orange Refrigerator, **'86** 230
        Cream Dessert, Orange, **'80** 254;
          '84 165
        Cream, Orange, **'81** 12
        Cream, Orange Chantilly, **'84** 156

Cream, Orange-Coconut, '84 24
Cream, Orange Whipped, '88 83
Crème, Orange-Tapioca, '82 M283
Crêpes, Amaretto-and-Orange, '86 260
Crêpes, Orange Dream, '82 183
Crispies, Orange, '84 205
Crisp, Orange-Apple, '80 295
Delight, Pumpkin-Orange, '86 321
Dip, Creamy Orange, '84 117
Filling, Lemon-Orange, '81 71
Filling, Orange, '79 229; '86 336;
  '87 84; '88 224
Fingers, Orange, '87 57
Flambé, Dessert Orange, '85 313
Flan, Orange, '84 95
Frosted Oranges, '83 270
Frosting, Creamy Orange, '83 24, 241
Frosting, Orange, '81 7; '86 61;
  '88 119
Frosting, Orange Butter, '83 300
Frosting, Orange Buttercream, '80 70
Frosting, Orange Cream, '81 207;
  '82 14
Frosting, Orange-Cream
  Cheese, '81 70; '82 16
Frosting, Orange-Lemon, '88 92
Fruit Dessert Orange, '84 314

Glazed Oranges and Pineapple, '86 318
Granita, Orange, '88 118
Ice Cream, Orange-Pineapple, '86 117
Ice, Strawberry-Orange, '86 196
Ice, Tart Cranberry-Orange, '86 317
Juice, Strawberries with Brandied
  Orange, '82 160
Molded Dessert, Orange, '83 302
Mousse, Chocolate-Orange,
  '81 16, 205
Mousse, Orange, '86 69
Parfaits, Chilled Orange, '80 219
Peanut Brittle, Orange, '80 302
Pears Flambé,
  Orange-Poached, '85 313
Pears in Orange Sauce,
  Poached, '82 19
Pears, Orange Poached, '80 218
Pie, Lemon-Orange, '85 172
Pie, Orange Ambrosia, '80 237
Pie, Orange Chess, '88 204
Pie, Orange Chiffon, '87 260
Pie, Orange Meringue, '81 12, 309
Pie, Orange-Pecan, '79 282; '83 222
Pie, Sweet Potato-Orange, '88 207
Poached Oranges, Wine-, '84 M323

Pops, Orange-Banana, '82 129
Pudding, Mandarin-Almond, '85 M12
Pudding, Orange, '81 85; '82 111;
  '83 153
Pudding, Orange Custard, '88 174
Rice Cream with Mandarin
  Oranges, '85 317
Sherbet Ambrosia Cups, '82 159
Sherbet, Banana-Orange, '83 162
Sherbet, Orange, '79 155
Shortbread Madeleines,
  Orange, '88 242
Shortcake, Fresh Orange, '80 100
Sorbet, Banana-Orange, '88 117
Soufflé, Chilled Orange, '84 317;
  '86 189
Soufflé, Frozen Orange, '79 211
Soufflé, Grand Marnier, '79 281
Soufflé, Orange Dessert, '83 206
Special, Orange Blossom, '79 48
Squares, Orange-Crunch, '86 136
Tapioca Fluff, Orange, '87 31
Tarts, Frozen Orange, '80 154
Topping, Whipped Orange, '80 254
Dip, Creamy Orange, '87 247
Dip, Orange Sour Cream, '79 208
Dip, Spicy Orange, '85 230
Doughnuts, Orange Spiced, '79 136
Dressing, Marmalade-Fruit, '84 171
Dressing, Orange, '81 141
Dressing, Orange Blossom, '82 266
Dressing, Orange-Coconut, '80 158
Dressing, Orange-Poppy Seed, '87 187
Dressing, Orange-Yogurt, '85 304
Duck, Chafing Dish Orange, '79 226
Fritters, Puffy Orange, '81 169
Granola, Sunny Orange, '84 212
Gravy, Orange, '81 259
Grits, Orange, '81 47
Halibut with Orange-Curry Sauce, '87 91
Ham, Cranberry-Orange Glazed, '81 295
Lamb Chops, Orange, '83 35
Lemonade, Orange-Mint, '88 82
Lobster Tails with Spiced Orange
  Sauce, '86 155
Marmalade, Orange, '81 42
Marmalade, Orange-Pineapple, '82 150
Marmalade, Peach-Orange, '82 150
Noodles, Orange, '84 177
Nuts, Sherry-Orange, '86 M289
Pancakes, Orange-Yogurt, '87 225
Pears, Marmalade Breakfast, '83 M203
Pears, Orange-Glazed, '79 247
Pecans, Orange, '84 299; '87 292
Popcorn, Orange, '86 230
Porc à l'Orange, '80 242
Pork Chops, Orange, '84 81
Pork Chops, Orange-Cranberry, '86 335;
  '87 84
Pork Chops, Orange-Glazed, '81 234;
  '82 25; '83 39
Potatoes, Coconut-Orange Sweet, '84 252
Potatoes in Orange Cups, Sweet, '82 272
Potatoes, Orange-Baked
  Sweet, '88 M294
Potatoes, Orange-Glazed Sweet, '81 223;
  '83 280
Potatoes, Orange Sweet, '86 279
Potato-Stuffed Orange Cups,
  Sweet, '81 223
Prunes, Orange-Spiced, '85 224

Relish, Cranberry-Orange, '81 M289;
  '88 254
Rice, Orange, '79 43; '81 175; '82 200
Roast, Orange Marinated Chuck, '85 179
Salads
  Ambrosia Supreme, Orange, '79 37
  Aspic, Orange-and-Carrot, '86 199
  Beet Salad, Orange-and-, '88 43
  Carrot Salad, Orange-, '80 89;
    '84 325
  Carrot-Tangerine Salad, '83 316;
    '84 16
  Cauliflower Salad, Orange-, '82 266
  Cherry-Orange Salad, '79 74; '82 56
  Chicken-and-Orange Salad,
    Curried, '87 144
  Chicken Salad, Persian, '81 12
  Congealed Salad,
    Pineapple-Orange, '83 218
  Cottage Cheese Salad, Orange-,
    '79 44
  Creamy Orange Salad, '84 124
  Cups, Citrus Salad in Orange, '85 47
  Cups, Orange, '86 92
  Cups, Orange Salad, '85 40
  Frosted Orange Salad, '81 154;
    '83 123

  Jeweled Orange Salad, '83 210
  Jicama-and-Orange Salad, '88 246
  Jicama-Orange Salad, '86 83
  Lobster and Orange Salad, '82 207
  Mandarin Chicken, Carousel, '79 88
  Mandarin Ham-and-Rice Salad, '87 145
  Mandarin Orange and Pineapple
    Salad, '82 266
  Mandarin Orange Salad, '81 252;
    '84 161
  Mandarin Pork-and-Spinach
    Salad, '88 M126
  Mandarin Rice Salad, '88 271
  Mandarin Salad Molds, '85 54
  Mandarin Spinach Salad, '85 163
  Pear Salad, Orange-, '84 164
  Quick Orange Salad, '87 80
  Romaine Salad, Orange-, '84 325;
    '87 239
  Sesame-Citrus Green Salad, '86 33
  Sherbet Salad, Orange, '81 154
  Shrimp-and-Orange Rice Salad,
    Zesty, '87 155
  Shrimp Salad, Orange-, '84 197
  Slaw, Cabbage-Orange, '79 135
  Spinach-and-Orange Salad, '86 15
  Spinach Salad, Orange-, '83 316;
    '84 16

Oranges, Salads (continued)

Sunshine Delight, **'86** 117
Surprise Salad, Orange, **'79** 12
Walnut Salad, Orange, **'80** 246
Sauces and Glazes
Chocolate-Orange Sauce, **'86** 165
Coconut-Orange Sauce, **'85** 189
Dessert Sauce, Orange, **'86** 337;
'87 58
Fresh Orange Glaze, **'88** 179
Fresh Orange Sauce, **'85** 209
Hard Sauce, Orange, **'88** 225
Honey-Orange Sauce, **'85** 108
Leeks in Orange Sauce, **'88** 86
Liqueur Sauce, Orange, **'86** 142
Mandarin Sauce, **'84** 60
Nutty Orange Glaze, **'80** 45
Orange Glaze, **'79** 2; **'80** 257; **'81** 34,
107; **'82** 75, 206; **'83** 33, 114, 140,
267; **'84** 161; **'86** 298
Orange Sauce, **'82** 47; **'83** 10, 277;
'84 M286; **'86** 294
Peas in Orange Sauce, Green,
'88 97
Pineapple Glaze, Orange-,
'81 60
Pineapple-Orange Sauce, **'84** 14
Raspberry-Orange Sauce, **'88** 22
Syrup, Orange, **'80** 228
Scampi, Orange, **'85** 303
Slices, Spicy Orange, **'81** 12
Snapper à l'Orange, Baked, **'85** 181
Snapper, Orangy, **'88** 23
Soup, Carrot-Orange, **'79** 172
Spareribs, Orange-Glazed, **'84** 296

Spareribs with Orange Barbecue
Sauce, **'83** 11
Special, Orange Blossom, **'88** 158
Spread, Orange Cheese, **'87** 292
Squash à l'Orange, **'85** 230
Turkey-Orange Skillet, Oriental, **'86** 284
Oysters
Bacon, Oysters in, **'83** 211
Baked Oysters, Bacon-, **'86** 132
Baked Oysters over Toast Points, **'84** 214
Bake, Oyster-and-Corn, **'83** 34; **'84** 44
Barbecued Oysters, **'82** 247
Bienville, Oysters, **'79** 182

Bisque, Oyster, **'83** 252
Brochette, Oysters, **'80** 56
Buccaneer, Oysters, **'87** 40
Casino on Cornbread, Oysters, **'79** 34
Casino, Oysters à la, **'80** 296
Casserole, Oyster, **'79** 228
Casserole, Oyster-and-Spinach, **'83** 34;
'84 44
Casserole, Oyster-and-Wild Rice, **'83** 34;
'84 44
Casserole, Wild Rice-Oyster, **'86** 256
Chowder, Oyster, **'83** 229
Chowder, Oyster-Corn, **'83** 211
Creamy Oysters and Crabmeat, **'83** 211
Crêpes, Virginia, **'79** 264
Dip, Smoked Oyster, **'79** 233
Dressed Oysters on the Half
Shell, **'87** M79
Dressing, Oyster, **'79** 250
Dressing, Oyster Bread, **'82** 251
Fresh Oysters, Preparing, **'82** 127
Fried Oyster Bubbles, **'80** 296
Fried Oysters, **'85** 104
Fried Oysters, Delicious, **'83** 212
Fried Oysters, Southern, **'88** 111
Fried Raw Oysters, **'81** 135; **'82** 14
Fritters, Oyster, **'79** 31
Fry, Hangtown, **'80** 297
Gino, Oysters à la, **'81** 126
Gumbo, Chicken and Oyster, **'81** 198
Gumbo, Duck, Oyster, and
Sausage, **'79** 226
Gumbo, Seafood, **'83** 90; **'87** 210
Ham, Edwards' Oysters and, **'86** 253
Johnny Reb, Oysters, **'82** 42
Landmark, Oyster, **'84** 88
Loaves, Spinach-Oyster, **'84** 213
Mornay, Seafood, **'83** 67
Mousse, Oyster, **'81** 245
Mousse, Smoked Oyster, **'84** 320
Nachos, Texas Oyster, **'87** 39
Omelets, Smoked Oyster, **'84** 96
Patty Shells, Oysters in, **'83** 212;
'85 257
Pie, Creole Oyster, **'84** 214
Pie, Turkey-and-Oyster, **'82** 267
Poor Boys, Oyster-and-Bacon, **'87** 40
Rockefeller, Southern Oysters, **'80** 212
Sandwich, Oyster Submarine, **'80** 92
Sautéed Oysters, **'86** 132
Sautéed Seafood Platter, **'83** 89
Scalloped Oysters, **'79** 225; **'84** 213;
'86 132
Scalloped Oysters with Macaroni,
'80 297
Shrimp Sauce, Oysters in, **'87** 40
Smoked Oysters, Deviled Eggs
with, **'84** 161
Smoky Oysters Supreme, **'87** 60
Soup, Chicken, Ham, and Oyster,
'79 198
Soup, Oyster, **'79** 228; **'83** 211
Soup, Oyster-and-Mushroom, **'87** 39
Soup, Oyster-Cheese, **'84** 213
Stew, Company Oyster, **'80** 297
Stew, Golden Oyster, **'86** 132
Stew, Holiday Oyster, **'85** 264
Stew, Oyster, **'80** 221
St. Jacques, Oysters, **'80** 103
Stuffing, Roast Turkey with
Oyster, **'80** 251

P

Pancakes
Apple Pancakes with Cider Sauce,
Spicy, **'87** 224
Applesauce Pancakes, **'79** 114
Apricot Delight, **'81** 42
Blueberry Buttermilk Pancakes, **'79** 114
Blueberry Pancakes, **'85** 152
Blueberry Pancakes, Sour Cream, **'81** 164
Buttermilk Griddle Cakes, **'81** 120; **'82** 22
Buttermilk Pancakes, **'83** 243; **'84** 101
Cornmeal Batter Cakes, **'87** 16
Cornmeal Pancakes, Hearty, **'88** 129
Cottage Cheese Pancakes, **'79** 115
Dessert Ginger Pancakes, **'88** 153
Dessert Pancakes, Luau, **'88** 154
Filled Pancake, Apple-, **'86** 96
Fluffy Pancakes, **'86** 137
Fruit Topping, Pancakes with, **'81** 42
Gingerbread Pancakes, **'84** 242
Island Pancakes, **'87** 225
Oatmeal-Brown Sugar Pancakes, **'88** 203
Oatmeal Pancakes, **'80** 44
Orange-Yogurt Pancakes, **'87** 225
Pancakes, **'81** 90
Potato Pancake, **'85** 20
Potato Pancakes, **'79** 115
Potato Pancakes, Moist, **'80** 36
Potato Pancakes, Sweet, **'87** 280
Pumpkin Pancakes, **'80** 228
Quick Bread Mix, **'81** 90
Rice Pancakes, **'85** 147
Sauce, Cinnamon-Pecan-Honey
Pancake, **'88** 46
Sauce, Peach-Blueberry Pancake, **'82** 177
Sausage Rollups, Pancake-, **'83** 246; **'84** 42
Sour Cream Pancakes, **'79** 213
Sour Cream Pancakes, Fluffy, **'79** 209
Strawberry Pancakes, **'84** 219
Supper Pancake, **'86** 242
Vegetable Pancakes, **'88** 297
Wheat Germ-Banana Pancakes, **'79** 114
Wheat Germ Pancakes, **'86** 242
Wheat Pancakes, Shredded, **'84** 59
Wheat Quick Pancakes, **'85** 278
Whole Wheat Pancakes, **'83** 18
Parsnips
Candied Parsnips, **'86** 224
Soufflé, Golden Parsnip, **'83** 266
Sugar-Crusted Parsnips, **'88** 229
Pastas. See also specific types.
Antipasto, Pasta, **'85** 286
Artichoke Hearts, Pasta with, **'86** 209
Bean-Salami Pasta Toss, Kidney, **'85** 165
Bites, Pesto-Cheese Pasta, **'87** 251
Broccoli and Sausage, Pasta with, **'87** 109
Broccoli Pasta, **'84** 176
Cannelloni, **'85** 60
Cheeses, Pasta Stuffed with Five, **'88** 197
Chicken-and-Broccoli Pasta, **'87** 286
Chicken, Bird's-Nest, **'88** 152
Clam Sauce, Pasta with, **'84** 291
Crab Bake, Quick, **'87** 192
Dressing, Pasta Salad, **'86** 121
Frittata, Pasta, **'85** 286
Garden Pasta, **'82** 199
Green Pasta with Shrimp-Mushroom
Italienne, **'79** 170

Mexican Luncheon, '87 192
Minestrone, '82 4
Oregano Pasta, '84 176
Pepperoni Pasta, '83 105
Pie, Broccoli-and-Turkey Pasta, '88 269
Pie, Spinach-Pasta, '85 286
Pimiento Pasta, '84 176
Platter, Cold Pasta, '88 42
Primavera, Almost Pasta, '86 38
Primavera, Pasta, '85 86
Primavera, Tomato-Pasta, '86 209
Provençale, Pasta, '88 90
Ravioli, Homemade, '87 230
Ravioli Pasta, Homemade, '87 231
Rotelle, Chicken and Tomato with, '87 108
Rotelle, Shrimp, '85 165
Rotini Romano, '87 193
Salad, Acini di Pepe, '83 163
Salad, Broccoli-Cauliflower Pasta, '88 269
Salad, Chicken Pasta, '88 89
Salad, Crabmeat-Shrimp Pasta, '86 208
Salad, Crunchy Pasta, '85 166
Salad, Crunchy Rotelle, '86 209
Salad, Garden Pasta, '86 188
Salad, Italian, '87 145
Salad, Main-Dish Pasta, '82 199
Salad, Overnight Pasta, '82 276
Salad, Pasta, '84 139; '86 120; '87 36
Salad, Pasta-and-Shrimp, '83 163
Salad, Pasta-Bean, '86 169
Salad, Pistachio-Pasta, '86 141
Salad, Rotini, '88 42
Salad, Salmon-Pasta, '87 9
Salad, Seashell, '86 209
Salad, Shrimp Vermicelli, '88 139
Salad, Tarragon Pasta-Chicken, '87 155
Salad, Vermicelli Vinaigrette, '82 189
Salad, Ziti-Cheddar, '85 165
Salmon Carbonara, '83 43
Sauerkraut Salad, Crunchy, '87 9
Sausage and Mixed Vegetables, Pasta
   with, '84 249
Scallops and Pasta, Fresh, '83 164
Seafood Delight, '86 208
Seashell-Provolone Casserole, '80 189
Seashells Florentine, Jumbo, '79 6
Shells, Cheesy Beef-Stuffed, '83 217
Shells, Salmon Salad, '85 286
Shells, Spinach-Stuffed, '85 60; '87 20
Shrimp Élégante, '83 48
Shrimp Marinara, '84 233
Shrimp-Pasta Medley, '88 302
Snappy Pasta, '83 164
Spinach-Mustard Twist, '86 209
Straw and Hay Pasta, '80 211
Tetrazzini, Chicken, '79 268
Tetrazzini, Ham, '82 M77
Tomato-Olive Pasta Toss, '86 209
Tortellini, Italian Sausage Soup with, '88 46
Tortellini Salad, Chicken, '87 288
Tortellini with Tomato Sauce,
   Spinach, '88 302
Toss, Pasta-Basil, '87 33
Tuna Pasta, Stuffed Tomato with, '88 54
Vegetable Sauce, Pasta with, '83 163
Vegetables, Pasta and Garden, '87 192
Verde, Pasta, '84 201
Vermicelli, Anchovy-Garlic Sauce
   over, '86 158
Vermicelli and Sprouts with Red Clam
   Sauce, '86 143

Vermicelli, Lemon, '84 329
Vermicelli, Mushroom Sauce Supreme
   on, '86 158
Vermicelli, Scallop-Vegetable, '87 143
Vermicelli, Shrimp and Feta Cheese
   on, '87 108
Vermicelli with Clam Sauce, '85 295
Vermicelli with Mushrooms, '79 195
Vermicelli with Tomato Sauce, '83 164
Pâtés. See Appetizers/Pâtés.
Peaches
Alaska, Peachy Melba, '88 266
Ambrosia, Peach, '83 53
Baked Peaches and Sausage, '82 50
Baked Peaches, Spicy, '86 39
Baked Peaches with Ginger,
   Oven-, '82 170
Bellinis, '88 77
Brandied Peaches with Mincemeat, '81 47
Brandy Peaches, '85 275
Bread, Georgia Peach, '79 161
Bread, Peach, '82 170
Butter, Peach, '82 308
Cake, Fresh Peach, '85 178
Cake, Peaches and Cream, '80 142
Cake, Peach Upside-Down, '87 8
Cake, Peachy Picnic, '79 178
Champagne, Peaches, '79 146
Charlotte, Peach, '79 68
Cheesecake, Peaches 'n' Cream, '88 137
Chicken Breasts, Peach-Stuffed, '79 177
Chicken Peach Dinner, '79 77
Chutney, Peach, '84 179
Cobbler, Fresh Peach, '82 139
Cobbler, Grenadine-Peach, '85 178
Cobbler, Lattice-Topped Peach, '79 154

Cobbler, No-Dough
   Blueberry-Peach, '86 177
Cobbler, Old-Fashioned Peach, '82 170
Cobbler, Peach, '83 175; '84 178
Cobbler, Peach-Caramel, '86 300; '87 178
Cobbler, Peachy Blueberry, '80 143
Cobbler, Quick Peach, '79 215; '81 142
Cobbler, Spicy Peach, '85 178
Cobbler Supreme, Peach, '81 184
Compote, Berry-Peach, '82 133
Conserve, Peach, '79 120
Cooler, Peach, '85 198; '86 6
Crabapple Peaches, Broiled Pork Chops
   with, '81 83
Cream, Bavarian Peach, '82 171
Cream, Peach Almond, '82 108
Cream, Peaches 'n' Almond, '86 229
Cream, Peachy-Apricot, '86 163
Crêpes, Fresh Peach, '84 186
Crêpes, Peach, '82 184

Crisp, Peach, '83 113
Crumble, Easy Peach, '83 116
Curried Ham and Peaches, '82 60
Custard Dessert, Fresh Peach, '86 162
Dessert, Peachy Melt-Away, '87 298
Dessert, Quick Peach, '85 178
Dip, Creole Peach, '80 142
Dumplings, Peach, '80 143; '85 177
Flambé, Banana-Peach, '85 316
Flambé, Peach Sundaes, '81 88
Flip, Peach, '79 217
Foster, Peaches, '86 240
Freeze, Creamy Peach, '82 144
Frost, Peach, '84 164
Frosty, Peach, '81 156; '83 318
Fuzz Buzz, '82 160
Ginger Peaches with Rum, '84 M323
Gingersnap Peaches, '85 M329
Ham Roast, Peachy, '86 118
Honey-Lime Whip, Peaches with, '85 108
Honey-Sweet Peaches, '85 107
Ice Cream, Creamy Peach, '85 177
Ice Cream, Deluxe Peach, '80 176
Ice Cream, Peach, '81 184; '82 171;
   '83 159; '86 15
Ice, Peach, '81 178
Ice, Peach-Yogurt, '84 83
Jam, Freezer Peach, '83 182; '84 M182
Jam, Peach-Plum Freezer, '85 130
Jam, Rosy Peach-Banana, '80 142
Marmalade, Peach-Orange, '82 150
Melba, Peach, '81 83; '83 M114
Meringues, Peach Melba, '87 76
Mincemeat Peaches, '85 178
Mold, Peachy Berry Cream, '83 130
Mousse, Peach, '85 54
Mousse, Peach Macaroon, '80 153
Muffins, Peachy-Almond, '86 301
Muffins, Special Peach, '84 74
Nest, Peaches in a Garden, '87 154
Parfait, Peach, '82 166
Pears, Peaches and, '85 106
Pickled Peaches, Perfect, '85 178
Pickles, Peach, '85 177
Pie, Fresh Peach, '82 170
Pie, Luscious Peach, '81 136
Pie, Mincemeat-Peach, '80 295; '81 188
Pie, Peach-Cranberry, '83 249
Pie, Peaches-and-Cream, '81 184
Pie, Rhubarb-Peach, '86 140
Pies, Delicious Fried, '83 84
Pies, Easy Peach Fried, '85 178
Pies, Fried Peach, '81 272
Pies, Little Peach, '86 303
Pork Steaks, Peachy, '79 166
Potatoes and Peaches, Sweet, '86 11
Preserves, Cream Cheese and
   Peach, '84 264
Preserves, Honeyed Peach, '85 130
Preserves, Old-Fashioned Peach, '82 150
Preserves, Peach, '81 147
Pudding, Peachy Bread, '88 175
Puffs, Peach Sweet Potato, '87 280
Refresher, Peach, '86 103
Relish, Peach, '85 136
Ring, Spicy Peach-Cranberry, '85 264
Salad, Frosted Peach, '82 145
Salad, Frozen Peach, '82 54
Salad, Georgia Peach, '80 142
Salad, Peaches-and-Cream, '83 108
Salad, Peach Party, '84 290

Peaches *(continued)*

Salad, Peach Pinwheel, **'79** 11
Salad, Pickled Peach, **'80** 104; **'85** 264
Salad Supreme, Easy Peach, **'79** 177
Sauce, Creamy Fresh Peach, **'79** 177
Sauce, Creamy Peach, **'85** 189
Sauce, Fresh Peach, **'87** 167
Sauce, Peach, **'84** 144
Sauce, Peach-Berry, **'87** M165
Sauce, Peach-Blueberry, **'81** 170
Sauce, Peach-Blueberry Pancake, **'82** 177
Sauce, Peach-Praline, **'85** 161
Shake, Peachy Orange, **'81** 156
Shake, Pep, **'79** 38
Slaw, Party Peach, **'86** 250
Smash, Peach, **'88** 161
Soup, Peach, **'83** 120, 180
Soup, Peach-Plum, **'87** 157
Spareribs, Peach-Glazed, **'86** 14
Spiced Peach Dessert, **'83** 9
Spiced Peaches, Brandy, **'80** 142
Spiced Peaches, Ginger, **'86** 15
Spiced Peaches with Nutty
 Dumplings, **'87** 164
Split, Peach, **'85** 277
Spread, Peachy-Raisin, **'86** 326
Strawberry Sauce, Peaches with, **'85** 8
Stuffed Peaches, Macaroon-, **'79** 178
Stuffed Peach Halves, **'86** 196
Tart, Kiwifruit-Peach, **'88** 20
Topping, Raspberry-Peach, **'87** 126
Wine Sauce, Peaches in, **'79** 184

Peanut Butter

Balls, Chocolate-Peanut Butter, **'80** 87
Balls, No-Cook Candy, **'85** 14
Balls, Peanut Butter-Chocolate, **'80** 269
Bars, Peanut Butter, **'84** 243
Bars, Peanut Butter-and-Fudge,
 '80 M172
Bars, Peanut Butter 'n' Jelly, **'83** 305
Bread, Peanut Butter, **'86** 171; **'88** 64
Brownies, Chocolate Chip-Peanut
 Butter, **'84** 73
Brownies, Peanut Butter, **'87** 199
Cake, Chocolate-Peanut Butter, **'84** 240
Cake, Fudgy Peanut Butter, **'85** 91
Cake, Peanut Butter, **'79** 51; **'83** M233
Cake, Peanut Butter-and-Jelly, **'85** 34
Cake, Peanut Butter-Banana, **'80** 87
Cake, Peanut Butter Swirl, **'86** 109
Cheese Ball, Peanut Butter-, **'86** 136
Chicken, Peanut
 Butter-Marmalade, **'81** 282; **'82** 30
Cones, Chocolate-Peanut Butter, **'85** 14
Cookies, Chocolate-Peanut Butter, **'85** 90
Cookies, Choco Surprise, **'80** 60
Cookies, Crisp Peanuttiest, **'88** 65
Cookies, Double Chip, **'81** 301
Cookies, Double Peanut Butter, **'80** 209
Cookies, Freezer Peanut Butter-Chocolate
 Chip, **'86** 230
Cookies, Miracle, **'83** 149
Cookies, Monster, **'84** 36
Cookies, Oatmeal-Peanut Butter,
 '85 171
Cookies, Peanut Butter, **'82** 56; **'87** 58
Cookies, Peanut Butter-Chocolate
 Kiss, **'86** 49
Cookies, Peanut Butter-Cinnamon, **'84** 30
Cookies, Peanut Butter-Coconut, **'83** 113

Cookies, Peanut Butter-Oatmeal, **'81** 218;
 '84 72
Cookies, Quick Peanut Butter, **'86** 109
Cooler, Peanut Butter, **'84** 115
Creams, Peanut Butter, **'79** 273
Crisps, Peanut Butter, **'79** 50
Cupcakes, Chocolate Surprise, **'85** 91
Cups, Chocolate-Peanut Butter, **'85** 14
Dip, Peanut Butter, **'86** 135
Dip, Peanut Butter-Honey, **'85** 19
Eggs, Peanut Butter Easter, **'87** 86
Fingers, Peanut Butter, **'79** 256
Frosting, Chocolate-Peanut Butter, **'84** 240;
 '87 222
Frosting, Creamy Peanut, **'80** 87
Frosting, Peanut Butter, **'83** 223; **'84** 153;
 '85 34
Frosting, Peanut Butter-Fudge, **'87** 184
Frosting, Peanut Butter Swirl, **'86** 109
Frosts, Peanut Butter, **'84** 153
Frozen Peanut Butter Delight, **'88** 137
Fudge, Chocolate-Peanut Butter, **'87** 257
Fudge, Double-Good, **'79** M263
Fudge, Double Peanut, **'85** 91
Fudge, Marbled Peanut Butter, **'88** 65
Fudge, Peanut Butter, **'80** 302
Granola, Peanut Butter, **'82** 296
Ice Cream, Chocolate Chunk-Peanut
 Butter, **'85** 297; **'86** 120
Ice Cream, Peanut Butter, **'81** 103;
 '88 64, 203
Logs, No-Bake Peanut Butter, **'84** 211
Milkshakes, Peanut Butter, **'85** 198
Muffins, Peanut Butter, **'80** 86; **'87** 158
Muffins, Peanut Butter-Honey, **'82** 56
Parfaits, Crunchy Peanut Butter, **'79** 176;
 '80 6
Pie, Chocolate-Peanut Butter, **'85** 91
Pie, Chocolate-Peanut Butter Swirl, **'87** 262
Pie, Peanut Butter, **'85** 275; **'86** 109
Pie, Peanut Butter Cream, **'79** 50; **'88** 65
Pie, Peanut Butter Meringue, **'84** 30
Pie, Tin Roof, **'85** 91
Pudding, Peanut Butter, **'85** 95; **'88** 32
Sandwiches, Peanut-Cheese-Raisin, **'88** 140
Sandwich, Peanut Butter Breakfast, **'82** 55
Sauce, Chocolate-Peanut Butter,
 '79 91, M156
Sauce, Peanut Butter Barbecue, **'81** 233
Sauce, Peanut Butter Ice Cream, **'84** 30
Shake, Peanut Butter, **'82** 48
Slice-and-Bakes, Peanut Butter, **'82** M185
Snaps, Peanut Butter, **'81** 237
Soup, Cream of Peanut Butter, **'84** 29
Soup, Creamy Peanut, **'79** 50
Squares, Chocolate Chip-Peanut
 Butter, **'84** 118
Squares, Peanut Butter, **'83** 116
Squares, Peanut Butter-Chocolate
 Candy, **'82** 56
Temptations, Peanut Butter, **'84** 29
Tiger Butter, **'86** 48
Yummies, Peanut Butter, **'83** 223

Peanuts

Apples, Peanutty Stuffed, **'85** 25
Balls, Peanut-Date, **'81** 92
Bananas, Nutty, **'79** 251
Bars, Chewy Peanut, **'80** M172
Bars, Fruit and Nut Granola, **'81** 49
Bread, Peanut, **'87** 184
Brittle, Golden Peanut, **'83** 223

Brittle, Never-Fail Peanut, **'79** 273
Brittle, Orange Peanut, **'80** 302
Brittle, Peanut, **'79** M263; **'80** 87; **'84** 298
Brittle with Crushed Peanuts, **'87** 184
Cake, Chocolate-Caramel-Nut, **'83** 23
Cake, Chocolate-Peanut Cluster, **'87** 184
Cake, Super Peanutty Layer, **'83** 222
Candied Popcorn and Peanuts, **'82** 295
Chicken with Peanuts, Oriental, **'82** 236
Chili Nuts, Hot, **'81** 254
Clusters, Chocolate-Peanut, **'81** 16
Clusters, Nut, **'81** 254
Clusters, Peanut, **'87** 184
Clusters, Peanutty, **'83** 143
Cookies, Chocolate-Peanut, **'83** 223
Cookies, Crisp Peanuttiest, **'88** 65
Cookies, Peanutty Oatmeal, **'80** 106;
 '83 95
Cookies, Salted Peanut, **'87** 92
Crust, Peanut-Graham Cracker, **'79** 50
Dessert, Fudge-Peanut Ice Cream, **'88** 167
Dessert, Peanut-Chocolate, **'80** 86
Divinity, Peanut, **'85** 233; **'87** M278
Dressing, Roast Turkey with
 Peanut, **'79** 283
Frosting, Creamy Peanut, **'80** 87
Fruit Dressing, Nutty, **'88** 68
Fudge, Double Peanut, **'85** 91
Ice Cream, Chocolate-Covered
 Peanut, **'88** 203
Pie, Caramel-Peanut, **'86** 259
Pie, Peanut Raisin, **'79** 85
Pie, Peanutty Ice Cream, **'82** 56
Puff Nibbles, **'84** 191
Salad, Green Bean-Peanut, **'86** 117
Salad, Nutty Cabbage, **'87** 42
Salad, Nutty Green, **'87** 168
Salad, Peanut-Apple, **'80** 5
Sauce, Peanut Dessert, **'86** M251
Sauce, Peanut Hot, **'86** 305
Sauce, Pork Chops with Peanut, **'83** 29
Slaw, Banana-Nut, **'86** 250
Slaw, Nutty Cabbage, **'88** 218
Slaw, Peanut, **'85** 139
Slaw, Peanutty-Pear, **'86** 250
Snack, Toasted Cereal, **'85** 215
Soup, Chilled Peanut, **'79** 130
Soup, Creamy Peanut, **'79** 50
Soup, Peanut, **'87** 184
Spicy Nuts, **'82** 161
Squares, Caramel-Peanut, **'85** 247
Sugared Peanuts, **'82** 249

Pears

Belle Helene, Pears, **'86** 164
Bread, Pear, **'80** 218
Breakfast Pears, Marmalade, **'83** M203
Breakfast Treat, Pear, **'87** 72
Butter, Pear, **'85** 130
Butter, Spiced Pear, **'80** 218
Cake, Pear Preserve, **'85** 52
Cake, Upside-Down Sunburst, **'87** 9
Cake with Caramel Drizzle, Pear, **'86** 247
Casserole, Pear-Sweet Potato, **'86** 280
Cheesecake, Pear-Berry, **'82** 141
Cheesecake, Pear-Glazed, **'79** 67
Cobbler, Best Ever Pear, **'82** 194
Coconut Pears, Spicy, **'83** 207
Cookies, Pear Mincemeat, **'84** 264
Cream, Pears in Orange, **'84** 245
Crisp, Cranberry-Pear, **'83** 207
Crumble, Pear, **'85** 221

Delight, Pineapple-Pear, '82 54
Dressing, Pear, '83 146
Filled Pears, Cheese-, '81 268
Flaming Pears, '84 313
Fritters, Ol' Timey Pear, '86 51
Glazed Pears, Orange-, '79 247
Jam, Paradise Pear, '84 300
Marmalade, Pear, '79 196
Meringues, Baked Pear, '85 232
Mincemeat, Pear, '79 196; '84 264;
  '88 226
Muscadine Sauce, Pears in, '88 216
Peaches and Pears, '85 106
Pickles, Mustard Pear, '79 196
Pie, Apple-Pear, '83 249
Pie, Deep-Dish Pear, '80 219
Pie, Delicious Pear, '88 226
Pie, Double-Crust Pear, '82 194
Pie, French Pear, '87 213
Pie, Natural Pear-Apple, '88 226
Pie, Pear Crumble, '83 207
Pie, Pear-Mince, '81 271
Pie, Pear Mincemeat, '84 264; '88 226
Pie, Pear Streusel, '83 234; '84 244
Pie, Tennessee Pear, '85 230
Pineapple-Honey Pears, '86 94
Poached in Red Wine, Pears, '83 302
Poached Pear Fans with Raspberry-Orange
  Sauce, '88 22
Poached Pears Flambé, Orange-, '85 313

Poached Pears in Custard, '88 20
Poached Pears in Orange Sauce, '82 19
Poached Pears in Wine, '82 194
Poached Pears, Lemon, '82 74
Poached Pears, Orange, '80 218
Poached Pears with Berry Sauce,
  Wine-, '86 144
Poached Pears with Raspberry
  Sauce, '84 213; '87 69; '88 223
Preserves, Pear, '82 195
Relish, Cranberry-Pear, '85 232
Relish, Pear, '79 196
Ruby Pears, '81 288
Salad, Blue Cheese-Pear-Apple, '81 224
Salad, Crunchy Pear, '83 234; '84 244
Salad, Festive Fruit, '80 16
Salad, Festive Pear-and-Spinach, '85 131
Salad, Orange-Pear, '84 164
Salad, Pear-and-Celery, '87 56
Salad, Pear-Lime, '84 152
Salad, Royal Pear, '84 265
Slaw, Peanutty-Pear, '86 250
Sorbet, Pear-Lemon, '88 116
Stuffed Pears, Almond-, '83 207

Stuffed with Cheese, Pears, '82 290
Sugared Pears, Maple-, '81 232
Sundaes, Quick Pear, '86 71
Tart, Pear, '82 304
Wild Rice, Cranberry-Pear, '83 279
Wine, Pears in Red, '82 254

Peas
Baked Peas, Chinese-Style, '86 305
Black-Eyed
  Best Ever Plain Ole Peas, '88 2
  Cajun Peas, '88 3
  Casserole, Reunion Pea, '87 11
  Caviar, Texas, '86 218
  Chinese Peas, '88 3
  Creole Black-Eyed Peas, '86 252
  Creole Black-Eyes and Rice, '85 6
  Delight, Tomato-Pea, '84 196
  Dinner, Black-Eyed Pea Skillet, '86 6
  Dip, Black-Eyed Pea, '81 8
  Flips, Pea, '80 7
  Fresh Black-Eyed Peas, '81 M165
  Gravy, Black-Eyed Pea, '87 12
  Ham Hocks, Black-Eyed Peas
    with, '79 122
  Hearty Black-Eyed Peas, '85 7
  Hopping Good Peas, '80 7
  Hopping John, '80 7
  Hopping John, Skillet, '79 10
  Hopping John with Ham, '81 7
  Jalapeño Black-Eyed Peas, '88 166
  Jambalaya, Good Luck, '87 11
  Marinated Black-Eyed Peas, '82 156;
    '88 101
  Mexican Black-Eyed Peas, '84 327
  Mexicano, Black-Eyed Peas, '79 10
  Mexi-Peas, '88 3
  Pickled Black-Eyed Peas, '79 10
  Pinwheels, Black-Eyed Pea, '85 300;
    '86 18
  Rice, Black-Eyed Peas with, '83 12
  Salad, Black-Eyed Pea, '80 112;
    '86 225; '88 92, 221
  Salad, Hot Bacon and
    Black-Eyed, '85 7
  Salad, Mexi-Pea, '81 7
  Salad, Overnight Black-Eyed
    Pea, '81 280
  Salad, Plentiful P's, '87 12
  Sausage, Black-Eyed Peas with, '86 7
  Seasoned Black-Eyed Peas, '85 138
  Soup, Beefy Black-Eyed, '85 6
  Southern-Style Black-Eyed
    Peas, '82 107
  South-of-the-Border Black-Eyed
    Peas, '86 7
  Spaghetti, Black-Eyed Pea, '81 7
  Special, Black-Eyed Pea, '86 7
  Spicy Black-Eyed Peas,
    Hot-and-, '84 9
  Spicy Hot Black-Eyed Peas, '81 8
  Spread, Black-Eyed Pea, '86 77
  Sweet-and-Sour Black-Eyed
    Peas, '85 290
  Sweet-and-Sour Peas, '88 3
  Vinaigrette, Black-Eyed Pea, '86 7
Casserole, Curry Pea, '87 154
English
  Baked Tuna and Peas in Wine
    Sauce, '83 196
  Braised Rice and Peas, '79 101
  Broil, Tomato-English Pea, '83 192

Buttered Peas and
  Mushrooms, '82 204
Buttered Peas with Onions, '80 242
Casserole, Asparagus-and-English
  Pea, '86 324
Casserole, Asparagus and
  Peas, '80 152
Casserole, Asparagus-Pea, '88 M294
Casserole, Cauliflower-Pea, '85 260
Casserole, Cheesy English
  Pea, '83 216
Casserole, English
  Pea-Pimiento, '83 207
Casserole, Quick Fresh English
  Pea, '84 145
Casserole Supreme, Pea, '82 281;
  '83 32
Cauliflower and Peas with Curried
  Almonds, '79 221; '80 82
Cauliflower, Peas and, '82 288
Celery, Deluxe Peas and, '81 267
Continental, Peas, '84 254
Country-Style Peas, '80 101
Country Style, Peas, '81 101
Creamed Peas and New
  Potatoes, '79 102
Creole Peas, Quick, '84 123
Curried Peas with Almonds, '88 M294
Deluxe English Peas, '84 68
Deviled Peas in Toast Cups, '86 280
Dumplings, Green Peas and, '80 102
Glazed English Peas, '83 111
Italian Peas, '81 83
Lettuce Peas, French, '86 62
Medley, English Pea, '85 236
Medley, Spring Pea, '83 141
Minted Peas, '83 141; '87 56
Mushrooms, Creamy Peas
  with, '84 196
Mushrooms, Green Peas with, '80 101
Mushrooms, Peas and, '83 141
Onions Stuffed with Peas, '84 68
Orange Sauce, Green Peas in, '88 97
Party Peas, '79 102
Pignoli, Peas, '83 190
Potato Nest, Peas in a, '84 M239
Rice, Holiday Peas and, '86 328
Rice, Peas and, '88 97
Rice with Green Peas, '87 45
Salad, Cauliflower-Pea, '87 231
Salad, Cheddar-Pea, '84 82
Salad, Chicken-Pea, '83 218
Salad, Creamy Pea, '80 111
Salad, English Pea, '81 280
Salad, English Pea-and-Apple, '87 24
Salad, Marinated English Pea, '82 54
Salad, Marinated Pea, '81 204
Salad, Peas-and-Asparagus, '83 141
Salad, Rice-Pea, '85 163
Salad, Savory Cauliflower and
  Pea, '81 280
Salad, Special Pea, '83 239
Sauce, Green Pea, '83 22
Scallions, Peas and, '80 101
Sherry, Peas with, '80 102
Soup, Chilled Pea, '84 181
Soup Élégante, Pea, '79 53
Soup, Fresh Pea, '86 181
Soup, Peppery Pea, '82 271
Soup, Spring Pea, '88 M96
Special Peas, '88 97

Peas *(continued)*

Ham, Southern Peas and, **'85** 138
Medley, Peas-and-Corn, **'85** 138
Salad, Three Pea, **'84** 290
Snow
  Appetizers, Sugar Snap Pea, **'86** 115
  Basil Snow Peas and
    Tomatoes, **'88** M185
  Beef and Snow Peas, Oriental, **'79** 105
  Beef with Pea Pods,
    Oriental, **'86** M328
  Chicken with Snow Peas, **'83** 137
  Chinese Peas, Easy, **'83** 206
  Crunchy Snow Peas and Dip, **'86** 62
  Dip, Sugar Peas with, **'86** 170
  Dip, Sugar Snap, **'88** 91
  en Papillote, Fish with Snow
    Peas, **'86** 144
  Medley, Cauliflower-Snow
    Pea, **'87** 305
  Peas and Snow Peas, **'88** 67
  Piquant, Snow Peas, **'79** 21
  Salad, Sugar Snap Pea, **'86** 115

  Sesame Snow Peas and Red
    Pepper, **'84** 175
  Shrimp Combo, Snow Pea-, **'79** 57
  Shrimp with Snow Peas, **'85** 75
  Skillet Snow Peas with Celery,
    '84 123
  Stir-Fried Peas and Peppers, **'87** 51
  Stir-Fry, Beef and Pea, **'82** 98
  Stir-Fry Beef and Pea Pods, **'80** 19
  Stir-Fry, Beef and Snow Pea, **'82** 98
  Stir-Fry Beef and Snow Peas, **'83** 22
  Stir-Fry, Potato-Snow Pea, **'86** 173
  Stuffed Snow Peas, **'84** 80
  Stuffed Snow Peas, Crab-, **'85** 288
  Tomatoes, Snow Peas and, **'83** 111
  Vegetable Medley, Spring, **'86** 115
Soup, Country-Style Pea, **'86** 267
Soup, Split Pea, **'88** 235
Soup, Split Pea and Frankfurter, **'79** 64

Pecans
Apples, Orange-Pecan Baked, **'85** 45
Ball, Deviled Pecan, **'80** 258
Ball, Party Pecan Cheese, **'81** 235
Ball, Pecan Cheese, **'83** 127
Balls, Date-Nut, **'85** 10
Ball, Tuna-Pecan, **'87** 94
Barbecued Pecans, **'83** 222
Bars, Pecan, **'82** 209
Beans, Nutty Green, **'88** M187
Bites, Cheesy Pecan, **'82** 248
Bread, Apple-Nut, **'85** 281
Bread, Applesauce Nut, **'81** 305
Bread, Banana-Nut, **'86** 8, 70
Bread, Banana-Nut-Raisin, **'81** 59
Bread, Cheddar-Nut, **'85** 41

Bread, Cherry Nut, **'81** 306; **'82** 36
Bread, Chocolate Date-Nut, **'81** 284
Bread, Glazed Orange-Pecan, **'81** 250
Bread, Kahlúa Fruit-Nut, **'79** 235
Bread, Lemon-Pecan, **'83** 54
Bread, Maraschino Cherry Nut, **'79** 234
Bread, Orange-Nut, **'82** 75
Bread, Orange-Pecan, **'79** 148
Bread, Persimmon Date-Nut, **'82** 218
Bread, Pineapple-Nut, **'79** 215
Bread, Pineapple-Pecan Loaf, **'87** 256
Bread, Prune-Nut, **'87** 255
Bread, Pumpkin-Nut, **'83** 294
Bread, Pumpkin-Pecan, **'87** 221
Bread, Quick Cherry-Nut, **'85** 55
Bread, Strawberry-Nut, **'79** 24
Bread, Wine-Date Nut, **'82** 253
Brittle, Chocolate, **'83** 315
Broccoli with Lemon Sauce and
  Pecans, **'86** 71
Brownies, Chocolate-Pecan, **'81** 64
Brownies, Nutty Blonde, **'81** 64
Brownies, Nutty Cocoa, **'81** 64
Brownies, Nutty Fudge, **'80** M171
Buns, Nutty, **'86** 290
Butter, Orange-Pecan, **'84** 75
Cake, Apple-Pecan Coffee, **'84** 242
Cake, Bourbon-Pecan, **'84** 25
Cake, Butter Pecan, **'80** 229
Cake, Caramel-Filled Butter Pecan, **'88** 278
Cake, Cinnamon-Pecan Coffee, **'87** 69
Cake, Date Nut, **'79** 176; **'80** 5
Cake, Kentucky Pecan, **'84** 263
Cake, Orange Nut, **'80** 70
Cake, Orange-Nut Butter, **'80** 254
Cake, Orange-Pecan Coffee, **'86** 86
Cake, Orange-Pecan Crunch, **'83** 10
Cake, Pecan-Topped Coffee, **'81** 41
Cake, Pineapple-Pecan
  Upside-Down, **'84** 25
Cake, Praline Pound, **'82** 88
Cake, Rich Chocolate-Nut, **'86** 8
Cake with Praline Glaze, Pecan, **'82** 196
Candied Nuts, **'81** 261
Candy, Chocolate-Nut Log, **'86** 335
Carrots and Celery with Pecans, **'84** 254
Catfish Pecan, **'85** 53
Cheesecake, Butter Pecan, **'86** 61
Cheesecake, Pecan, **'85** 38
Chews, Chocolate-Nut, **'81** 92
Chicken, Nutty Oven-Fried, **'85** 160
Chicken, Oven-Fried Pecan, **'84** 288
Chicken, Sweet-and-Sour, **'79** 106
Chocolate Date-Nut Delight, **'88** 168
Clusters, Pecan, **'81** 266
Clusters, Pecan-Coconut, **'86** M251
Clusters, Roasted Pecan, **'85** 233
Cobbler, Apple-Pecan, **'84** M198
Coffee 'n' Spice Pecans, **'88** 256
Cookies, Butter Pecan, **'82** 139
Cookies, Butter Pecan Shortbread, **'80** 282
Cookies, Butterscotch-Pecan, **'84** 36
Cookies, Cherry Pecan, **'82** 136
Cookies, Chocolate-Nut Freezer, **'88** 217
Cookies, Easy Pecan, **'80** 208
Cookies, Nutty Oatmeal, **'81** 130
Cookies, Nutty Oatmeal-Chocolate
  Chip, **'82** 185
Cookies, Orange-Pecan, **'88** 119
Cookies, Pecan-Butter, **'83** 113
Cookies, Pecan Crescent, **'85** 324

Crispies, Oatmeal Nut, **'80** 208
Crispies, Pecan-Cheese, **'87** 168
Crisps, Sugar Pecan, **'86** 230
Crunch, Apple-Nut, **'82** M238
Crust, Pecan, **'86** 317
Crust, Spiced Nut, **'87** 295
Cupcakes, Apple-Nut, **'82** 279
Dainties, Lemon Pecan, **'80** 208
Dessert, Maple Nut, **'81** 84
Dressing, Chicken with
  Pecan-Rice, **'85** M57
Dressing, Fruit-and-Pecan, **'84** 252
Dressing, Pecan-Sage, **'80** 262
Dressing, Watermelon Salad with
  Celery-Nut, **'80** 182
Dumplings, Spiced Peaches with
  Nutty, **'87** 164
Eggs, Pecan-Stuffed, **'80** 78
Fettuccine, Chicken-Pecan, **'86** 52
Filling, Fruit-Nut, **'80** 289
Fritters, Chocolate-Covered Pecan, **'79** 205
Frosting, Banana-Nut, **'79** 115
Frosting, Butter Pecan, **'80** 229
Frosting, Chocolate Nut, **'80** 140
Frosting, Coconut-Pecan, **'81** 296;
  '83 M233; **'84** 43, 322
Frosting, Nutty Coconut, **'86** 8
Frosting, Nutty Cream Cheese, **'85** 117
Frosting, Pecan, **'86** 86
Fudge, Cherry Nut, **'83** 315
Fudge, Creamy Pecan, **'84** 321
Fudge, Nutty White, **'81** 253
Fudge, Quick Nut, **'83** 316
Glazed Nuts, **'88** 222
Glazed Pecans, **'81** 254; **'82** 136
Glaze, Honey-Nut, **'87** 15
Goose, Fruit- and Pecan-Stuffed, **'83** 268
Honeycomb Pecans, **'84** 300
Hot Pepper Pecans, **'85** 4
Ice Cream, Butter Pecan, **'80** 176;
  '86 129; **'88** 202
Ice Cream, Cherry-Nut, **'86** 129
Ice Cream, Cherry-Pecan, **'88** 203
Ice Cream, Straw-Ba-Nut, **'80** 177
Ice Cream, Strawberry-Banana-Nut, **'88** 203
Loaf, Date-Nut, **'85** 10
Loaf, Orange Nut, **'80** 226
Loaf, Tasty Apricot-Nut, **'82** 10
Loaves, Orange-Pecan, **'79** 215
Log, Chicken-Pecan, **'81** 290
Log, Toasted Pecan Cheese, **'86** M288
Maple-Nut Coffee Twist, **'86** 290
Muffins, Chunky Pecan, **'88** 9

Muffins, Cinnamon-Nut, **'85** M88
Muffins, Cinnamon-Pecan, **'84** 219
Muffins, Country Pecan, **'83** 222
Muffins, Cranberry-Pecan, **'84** 269

Muffins, Nutty Pumpkin, '86 291
Muffins, Orange-Pecan, '83 96
Muffins, Pecan, '80 16
Muffins, Raisin-Pecan Ginger, '88 9
Mushrooms, Pecan-Stuffed, '84 261
Nuggets, Cherry Nut, '81 286
Orange Nuts, Sherry-, '85 M289
Orange Pecans, '84 299; '87 292
Pepper Pecans, '87 137
Pie, Bourbon-Pecan, '85 90
Pie, Bourbon-Pecan Pumpkin, '87 264
Pie, Caramel-Pecan, '88 282
Pie, Caramel-Pecan Apple, '85 247
Pie, Chocolate Pecan, '80 237; '83 12
Pie, Choco-Pecan, '82 86
Pie, Coconut Pecan, '81 161
Pie, Coconut-Pecan Chess, '81 248
Pie, Coffee Pecan, '82 74
Pie, Custard Pecan, '87 184
Pie, Date-Pecan, '80 15
Pie, Golden Pecan, '81 266
Pie, Grandmother's Pecan, '86 269
Pie, Holiday Pecan, '81 296
Pie, Layered Pecan, '83 305
Pie, Maple-Pecan, '81 266
Pie, Molasses-Pecan, '86 259
Pie, Nutty Cranberry, '82 298
Pie, Nutty Pumpkin, '82 67
Pie, Old-Fashioned Pecan, '81 M269
Pie, Orange-Pecan, '79 282; '83 222
Pie, Pecan, '79 251; '80 57; '85 255
Pie, Pumpkin-Pecan, '85 233, 282
Pie, Raisin-Pecan, '87 213
Pies, Individual Pecan, '85 295
Pies, Miniature Pecan, '79 205; '86 13
Pie, Spicy Pecan, '84 240
Pies, Tiny Pecan, '79 225
Pie, Sweet Potato-Pecan, '83 90
Pie, Texas Pecan, '83 159
Popcorn Balls, Nutty, '88 227
Popovers, Giant Pecan, '83 208
Praline Cheesecake, '83 270
Praline Clusters, Dark, '86 313
Praline Delights, Spicy, '84 299
Praline Fruit Compote, Warm, '85 260
Praline Glaze, '82 196
Praline Ham, '85 302
Praline Ice Cream Cake, '80 84
Praline Ice Cream Sauce, '85 189
Praline Ice Cream Sauce,
   Southern, '86 M227
Praline Pie, Chocolate-, '86 259
Praline Pound Cake, '82 88
Pralines, '79 272; '86 M288
Pralines and Cream Ice Cream, '82 184;
   '83 159
Praline Sauce, '83 25; '84 143
Praline Sauce, Bourbon, '81 170
Praline Sauce, Chocolate-, '85 M295
Praline Sauce, Peach-, '85 161
Pralines, Butterscotch, '81 253
Pralines, Creamy, '80 198
Pralines, Dark, '83 52
Pralines, Maple-Pecan, '83 222
Pralines, New Orleans-Style, '86 335
Pralines, Original Pecan, '81 11
Pralines, Plantation Coffee, '86 241
Pralines, Southern, '79 M263
Pralines, Texas-Size, '79 186
Praline Toast, Orange, '79 36
Pudding, Brown Sugar-Pecan, '86 M165

Pudding, with Hot Rum Sauce,
   Apple-Nut, '79 86
Rice, Nutted, '85 269
Rice, Pecan, '85 53
Roll, Banana-Nut, '85 112
Roll, Date Nut, '79 249
Rolls, Buttered Rum-Nut, '86 291
Rolls, Caramel-Nut, '86 312
Rolls, Pecan, '79 285; '81 62
Roulade, Pecan, '87 183
Salad, Apple-Nut, '80 226
Salad, Beet-Nut, '79 74
Salad, Cantaloupe-Pecan, '86 178
Salad, Creamy Carrot-Nut, '86 331
Salted Pecans, Southern, '80 285
Sauce, Butterscotch-Pecan, '82 212
Sauce, Cinnamon-Pecan-Honey
   Pancake, '88 46
Sauce, Date-Nut Sundae, '82 167
Sauce, Éclairs with Pecan, '83 219
Sauce, Pecan, '83 219
Spiced Pecans, '79 296; '80 31; '81 286
Spicy Curried Nuts, '82 250
Spicy Pecans, '81 M289
Spread, Honey-Nut, '87 157
Squares, Butter Pecan Pie, '81 262
Squares, Easy Pecan, '79 292; '81 230
Squares, Pecan, '79 205
Squares, Twice-Baked Pecan, '79 291
Squash, Apple-and-Pecan-Filled, '88 228
Squash with Molasses and Pecans,
   Acorn, '85 205
Stuffing, Pecan, '79 292; '80 32
Stuffing, Wild Duck with Pecan, '85 269
Sugar-and-Honey Pecans, '86 319
Sugar and Spice Pecans, '82 297
Sugar-and-Spice Pecans, '86 121
Sugared Pecans, '82 167
Sugar Pecans, Brown, '81 266
Sugarplums, Pecan Shortbread, '83 298
Syrup, Chunky Pecan, '85 278
Syrup, Maple-Nut, '80 228
Tarts, Apple-Pecan, '80 282
Tarts, Easy Pecan, '84 313
Tarts, Pecan, '81 266
Tarts, Special Pecan, '87 224
Tassies, Teatime, '84 321
Toasted Chili Pecans, '85 154
Toasted Pecans, '84 321; '86 229
Toasted Pecans, Buttery, '88 77
Toffee, Nutty, '79 M263
Topping, Cinnamon-Pecan, '85 277
Topping, Nutty, '85 256
Torte, Carob-Pecan, '85 218
Torte, Heavenly Pecan, '81 266
Torte, Mocha-Pecan, '86 26
Wafers, Pecan-Cheese, '81 119
Waffles, Pecan, '87 225
Waffles, Pumpkin-Nut, '86 96
Waffles, Southern Chicken-Pecan, '82 231
Zucchini with Pecans, '87 31
Peppermint
Bavarian, Peppermint, '80 153
Brownies, Chocolate-Peppermint, '88 262
Chocolate Mint Freeze, '88 167
Cookies, Peppermint Candy, '88 286
Dessert, Peppermint Wafer, '79 176; '80 7
Filling, Peppermint, '81 119
Flip, Hot Peppermint, '86 329
Ice Cream, Peppermint, '80 176; '86 129
Mints, Party, '79 273; '81 119

Mousse, Peppermint Candy, '82 71
Parfaits, Chocolate-Peppermint, '88 65
Patties, Peppermint, '86 278
Pie, Peppermint Candy-Ice Cream, '87 260
Soufflé, Chocolate Mint, '81 16
Squares, Chocolate-Peppermint, '81 119
Twists, Mint, '86 106
Wreaths, Melt-Away Peppermint, '85 324
Peppers
Chicken Scaloppine with Peppers, '85 78
Chile
   Casserole, Chile-Cheese, '82 90
   Casserole, Chile 'n' Cheese
      Breakfast, '88 57
   Casserole, Chiles Rellenos, '79 84;
      '84 31, 234
   Casserole, Chili-Corn, '88 266
   Casserole, Chili-Rice, '79 54
   Casserole, Green
      Chile-and-Fish, '84 32
   Casserole, Mexican Rice, '83 31
   Casserole, Sausage-Chile
      Rellenos, '88 52

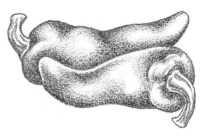

   Chicken with Salsa, Baked
      Chile, '88 147
   Chimichangas (Fried Burritos), '81 196;
      '85 244
   con Queso, Chile, '80 194
   con Queso Supreme, Chile, '80 265
   Cream, Ancho Chile, '87 121
   Dip, Cheese-and-Chile, '83 31
   Dip, Hot Chile, '82 248
   Dip, Hot Chile-Beef, '83 218
   Egg Rolls, Chiles Rellenos, '86 296
   Eggs, Chile, '88 80
   Enchiladas, Green Chile-Sour
      Cream, '84 234
   Enchiladas, New Mexican Flat, '85 245
   Light Chile Verde, '88 148
   Pie, Green Chile-Cheese, '84 234
   Powder, Red Chile, '85 245
   Puerco en Adobo, '88 116
   Quiche, Chile Pepper, '82 224
   Quiche, Green Chile, '83 31
   Quiche, Shrimp, '83 50
   Quiche, Squash-and-Green
      Chile, '88 143
   Rellenos, Chiles (Stuffed
      Chiles), '82 220; '83 150; '88 116
   Rice and Green Chiles, '83 152
   Rice, Chili-Cheesy, '79 43
   Salad, Spicy Chile-Tomato, '88 121
   Salsa with Homemade Tostados, Hot
      Chile, '88 115
   Sauce, Ancho Chile, '87 122
   Sauce, Green Chile, '82 220
   Sauce, Red Chile, '85 245
   Sauce, Red Chile Enchilada, '85 245

Peppers, Chile *(continued)*

Squash, Chile, **'84** 77
Squash, Mexican, **'83** 31
Squash with Green Chiles,
    Stuffed, **'83** 148
Tamales, Hot, **'83** 51
Tamales, Sweet, **'83** 52
Turnovers, Chile-Ham, **'88** 64
Combo, Cucumber-and-Pepper, **'88** 176
Cups, Hot Vegetable Pepper, **'88** M188
Green
    Beef and Green Peppers, **'79** 104
    Beefed-Up Peppers, **'82** 186
    Bread, Pepper, **'85** 156
    Casserole, Peppered Pork
        Chop, **'82** 25
    Chicken Peppers, Devilish, **'80** 65
    Cups, Potato Salad in Pepper, **'79** 78
    Deluxe, Peppers, **'81** 159
    Dressing, Green Pepper-Onion
        Salad, **'84** 12
    Fried Pepper Strips, **'82** 208
    Jelly, Pepper, **'79** 121
    Jelly, Unusual Green Pepper, **'82** 132
    Mexican Green Peppers, **'80** 65
    Muffins, Cheese-and-Pepper, **'84** 139
    Pizza Peppers, **'83** 135
    Potato Salad 'n' Peppers, **'83** 135
    Ratatouille, **'85** 92
    Relish, Pepper, **'83** 183
    Relish, Pepper-Onion, **'84** 180
    Salad, Ruby-and-Emerald, **'85** 79
    Sauce, Pepper-Onion, **'84** 125
    Sausage and Peppers, Italian, **'84** 9
    Sautéed Onions and
        Peppers, **'83** M148
    Sauté, Tomato-Pepper, **'84** 142
    Soup, Green Pepper, **'88** 250
    Stacks, Pepper-Cheese, **'87** 80
    Steak and Rice, Pepper, **'81** 17
    Steak, Pepper, **'81** 273; **'85** 57;
        '88 113
    Steak, Pepper-Beef, **'85** 21
    Stir-Fry Steak, Pepper, **'81** 240

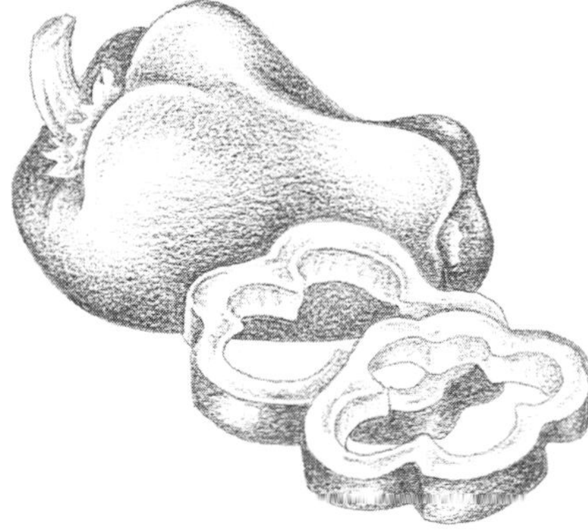

Stuffed Green Peppers, Beefy, **'81** 86
Stuffed Green Peppers, Ham-, **'80** 65
Stuffed Pepper Medley, **'82** 131
Stuffed Peppers, **'81** 239; **'83** 66;
    '84 202
Stuffed Peppers, Beef-, **'84** 154;
    '85 146

Stuffed Peppers, Corn-, **'84** 104
Stuffed Peppers, Curried
    Chicken-, **'87** 19
Stuffed Peppers for Two, **'80** 84
Stuffed Peppers, Ham-and-Corn, **'81** 87
Stuffed Peppers, Hearty, **'88** M214
Stuffed Peppers,
    Macaroni-and-Cheese-, **'80** 65
Stuffed Peppers, Rice-, **'80** 65
Stuffed Peppers, Shrimp-, **'80** 162;
    '86 131, 197
Stuffed Peppers, Spinach-, **'82** 180
Stuffed Peppers with Rice and
    Ham, **'82** 131
Stuffed with Beef, Peppers, **'84** 72
Taco Peppers, **'81** 86
Veal and Peppers, Spaghetti
    with, **'81** 201; **'82** 14
Jalapeño
    Bread, Jalapeño Pepper, **'83** 121
    Casserole, Jalapeño Corn, **'83** 256
    Casserole, Jalapeño Rice, **'81** 66
    Celery, Jalapeño Stuffed, **'79** 70
    Cheese, Shrimp with Herbed
        Jalapeño, **'87** 112
    Cheesy, Jalapeño Peppers, **'80** 195
    Cornbread, Beefy Jalapeño, **'82** 142
    Cornbread, Cheddar-Jalapeño, **'85** 3
    Cornbread, Jalapeño, **'85** 200
    Grits, Jalapeño Cheese, **'85** 43
    Hominy, Jalapeño, **'82** 51
    Loaf, Jalapeño-Cheese, **'84** 76
    Peas, Jalapeño Black-Eyed, **'88** 166
    Potatoes, Jalapeño, **'84** 39
    Potatoes, Jalapeño-Ham
        Stuffed, **'81** M61
    Quiche, Cheesy Jalapeño, **'84** 31
    Quiche, Jalapeño-Corn, **'85** 122
    Quiche Squares, Cheesy Hot, **'79** 124
    Rice, Jalapeño, **'79** 43
    Rice, Jalapeño Hot, **'80** 126
    Salsa Picante, **'84** 108
    Salsa Picante, Homemade, **'81** 67
    Sauce, Jalapeño, **'80** 193
    Sauce, San Antonio Hot, **'84** 291
    Spread, Jalapeño-Cheese, **'82** 248
    Squares, Jalapeño Cheese, **'80** 195
    Stuffed Jalapeños, Shrimp-, **'88** 115
Okra, Corn, and Peppers, **'87** M151
Red Pepper Salad, Broccoli and, **'83** 224
Red Pepper, Sesame Snow Peas
    and, **'84** 175
Red Peppers, Potatoes with
    Sweet, **'87** 192
Roasted Peppers, Marinated, **'87** 90
Salad, Chilled Turkey-and-Pepper
    Stir-Fry, **'88** 140
Salad, Mushroom-and-Pepper, **'86** 68
Salsa, Pepper, **'88** 26
Steak, Red Pepper Round, **'88** 214
Stir-Fried Peas and Peppers, **'87** 51
Strips, Green Beans and Pepper, **'86** 170
Toss, Crisp Squash-and-Pepper, **'87** M152
Persimmons
Bread, Persimmon, **'80** 228
Bread, Persimmon Date-Nut, **'82** 218
Cake, Persimmon, **'79** 205
Cookies, Persimmon-Raisin, **'85** 232
Pie, Persimmon, **'79** 206
Pudding, Persimmon, **'79** 206
Salad, Persimmon Fruit, **'79** 206

Pheasants
Muscatel, Pheasant, **'85** 269
Port Wine Sauce, Pheasants with, **'84** 252
Pickles and Relishes
Antipasto Relish, **'86** 327
Apple Relish, Spicy, **'84** M323
Asparagus, Pickled, **'83** 46
Avocado Relish, **'87** 120
Beet Pickles, **'81** 210
Beet Relish, **'84** 179
Beet Relish, Colorful, **'85** 136
Beets, Easy Pickled, **'80** 137
Beets, Pickled, **'81** 216
Black Bean-Tomatillo Relish, **'87** 121
Broccoli, Pickled, **'81** 308
Cabbage Relish, **'83** 260
Chow Chow, **'82** 196
Chowchow, **'87** 150
Chutney
    Commander's Chutney, **'87** 245
    Cranberry-Amaretto Chutney with
        Cream Cheese, **'87** 244
    Cranberry Chutney, **'80** 243; **'83** 260;
        '84 265
    Cranberry-Orange Chutney, **'79** 292
    Fruit Chutney, Autumn, **'88** M230
    Orange-Cranberry Chutney, **'86** 266
    Pâté, Chutney-Cheese, **'84** 152
    Peach Chutney, **'84** 179
    Plum Chutney, **'84** 179
    Rhubarb Chutney, **'87** 245
    Roll, Chutney, **'83** 259
    Rosy Chutney, **'80** 120
    Tomato-Apple Chutney, **'84** 180
Corn Relish, **'81** 129, 175; **'83** 189;
    '84 107; **'85** 136; **'87** 120, 245
Corn Relish, Easy, **'83** 260
Corn Relish, Virginia, **'79** 283
Cran-Apple Relish, **'84** 300
Cranberry Conserve, **'79** 243
Cranberry-Nut Relish, **'86** 275
Cranberry-Orange Relish, **'81** M289;
    '88 254
Cranberry-Pear Relish, **'85** 232
Cranberry Relish, **'81** 275; **'83** 144;
    '85 258, 264; **'86** 283; **'87** 245
Cranberry Relish, Holiday, **'88** 304
Cranberry Relish, Lemony, **'79** 243
Cranberry Relish, Old-Fashioned, **'82** 297
Cucumber Chips, **'85** 176
Cucumber Pickles, Sour, **'85** 176
Cucumber Relish, **'85** 176
Cucumber Sandwich Pickles, **'81** 174
Dill Pickles, **'81** 174
Dill Pickles, Fried, **'84** 206
Dills, Lazy Wife, **'87** 149
Eggs, Beet Pickled, **'84** 287
Eggs, Spiced Pickled, **'84** 288
Figs, Pickled, **'79** 140
Garden Relish, **'83** 259
Garden Relish, End-of-the-, **'80** 179
Icicle Pickles, Sweet, **'85** 176
India Relish, **'84** 179
Mixed Pickles, **'81** 174
Okra Pickles, **'81** 173
Onion Relish, Green, **'84** 65
Onion Rings, Pickled Refrigerator, **'84** 265
Orange Slices, Spicy, **'81** 12
Peaches, Perfect Pickled, **'85** 178
Peach Pickles, **'85** 177
Peach Relish, **'85** 136

Pear Pickles, Mustard, **'79** 196
Pear Relish, **'79** 196
Pepper-Onion Relish, **'84** 180
Pepper Relish, **'83** 183
Pineapple, Pickled, **'79** 24
Problem Chart, Pickle, **'85** 176
Salad, Relish, **'84** 121
Salsa, **'80** 196
Salsa Cruda, **'87** 180
Salsa, Fresh Summer, **'87** 89
Salsa, Hot Mexican, **'85** 136
Salsa Picante, **'84** 108
Salsa Picante, Homemade, **'81** 67
Salsa, Tomato, **'87** 120
Salsa, Yellow Tomato, **'87** 122
Sauerkraut Relish, **'85** 136
Squash Pickles, **'81** 174; **'87** 150

Sweet Pickles, Quick, **'87** 149
Tomato Pickles, Green, **'87** 134
Tomato Relish, **'85** 188
Tomato Relish, Easy, **'80** 126
Vegetable Relish, Eight-, **'84** 179
Watermelon Rind Pickles, **'81** 174; **'84** 106
Zucchini, Dilled Fresh, **'81** 174
Zucchini Relish, **'87** 200
Pies and Pastries
Almond Combs, **'84** 136
Almond Pie, Toasted, **'86** 163
Ambrosia Pie, **'79** 284
Angel Pie, **'79** 123; **'80** 238
Apple
Autumn Apple Pie, **'79** 205
Berry-Apple Pie, **'88** 251
Brandy-Apple Pie, **'86** 301
Brandy Raisin-Apple Pie, **'83** 192
Cake, Apple Pie, **'82** 226
Chess Pie, Apple-Lemon, **'86** 220
Cider Pie, Apple, **'84** 227
Cinnamon Sauce, Apple Pie with Hot, **'88** 210
Cranberry-Apple Holiday Pie, **'81** M269
Cranberry-Apple Pie, **'79** 264
Cream Cheese Pie, Apple-, **'81** 247
Custard Pie, Apple, **'88** 236
Danish, Deep-Dish Apple, **'86** 161
Dumplings, Old-Fashioned Apple, **'84** 226
Dutch Apple Pie, **'81** 105; **'82** 273
Easy-Crust Apple Pie, **'87** 11
Flan, Apple, **'81** 309
Foldovers, Apple, **'84** 136
Fresh Apple Pie, **'84** 178
Fried Apple Pies, **'81** 217; **'86** 302; **'88** 112, 225
Fried Apple Turnovers, **'81** 161
Grandmother's Apple Pie, **'87** 212
Grated Apple Pie, **'83** 304
Holiday Apple Pie, **'87** 260
Lemon-Apple Pie, Tart, **'80** 100
Mincemeat Pie, Apple-, **'85** 316
No-Crust Apple Pie, **'88** 204
Old-Fashioned Apple Pie, **'82** M299; **'88** 94
Pear-Apple Pie, Natural, **'88** 226
Pear Pie, Apple-, **'83** 249
Red Apple Pie, **'79** 282
Roll, Apple, **'82** 178
Rolls, Luscious Apple, **'88** 225
Strudel, Apple, **'85** 259
Turnovers, Delicious Apple, **'86** 25
Turnovers, Puffy Apple, **'87** 276
Upside-Down Southern Apple Pie, **'88** 226
Apricot Fried Pies, **'86** 269
Apricot Pastries, **'83** 297
Apricot Pie, Yogurt-, **'85** 132
Apricot Pinwheels, **'87** 276
Apricot Surprise Pie, **'88** 99
Banana Cream Pie, **'84** 48; **'87** 207
Banana Pie with Hot Buttered Rum Sauce, **'88** 204
Bavarian Cream Pie, **'79** 281
Blackberry-Apple Pie, **'87** 130
Blackberry Cream Pie, **'81** 132
Blackberry Pie, **'84** 141; **'86** 152
Blackberry Pie, Creamy, **'88** 179
Blackberry Roll, **'82** 178
Blueberry-Cream Cheese Pie, **'88** 154
Blueberry Cream Pie, **'84** 142
Blueberry Cream Pie, Fresh, **'80** 144
Blueberry Kuchen, **'80** 143
Blueberry Pie, Fresh, **'83** 183; **'85** 152
Blueberry-Sour Cream Pie, **'83** 183
Boston Cream Pie, **'83** 220
Bourbon Pie, Kentucky, **'84** 87
Boysenberry Pie, **'82** 133
Brownie Pie, Crustless, **'82** 33
Buttermilk-Lemon Cream Pie, **'88** 99
Buttermilk Lemon Pie, **'81** 120; **'82** 23
Buttermilk-Lemon Pie, **'88** 297
Buttermilk Pie, **'82** 53; **'83** 158; **'88** 93
Buttermilk Pie, Old-Fashioned, **'79** 72
Butterscotch Cream Pie, **'84** 48; **'87** 207
Butterscotch Meringue Pie, **'83** 158
Cannoli, **'80** 58
Cantaloupe Cream Pie, **'79** 177
Cantaloupe Meringue Pie, **'88** 182
Cantaloupe Pie, **'86** 163
Caramel-Banana Pie, **'86** M165
Caramel Banana Pie, Luscious, **'79** 115
Caramel-Peanut Pie, **'86** 259
Caramel Pie, Burnt, **'82** 53
Carrot Custard Pie, **'79** 45
Caviar Pie, **'79** 154
Cheese
Camembert Bars, **'86** 58
Cottage Cheese Pie, **'82** 85
Cream Puffs with Chicken Salad, Cheesy, **'86** 260
Date-Filled Cheese Pastries, **'83** 259
Hors d'Oeuvre Pie, Cheesy, **'88** 91
Lemon Cheese Pie, **'81** 136; **'82** 146
Lemon-Cottage Cheese Pie, **'79** 44
Lemon Cottage Cheese Pie, **'81** 143
Make-Ahead Cheesecake Pie, **'81** 233
Mincement-Cheese Pie, **'80** 253
Phyllo-Cheese Triangles, **'87** 246
Puffs, Mexican Cheese, **'87** 8
Tartlets, Cheese, **'88** 211
Yogurt-Cheese Pie, **'82** 121
Cherry Pie, Easy, **'82** 299
Cherry Pie, Fresh, **'88** 178
Cherry Pie, Prize-Winning, **'82** 57
Cherry Pie, Red, **'83** 192
Cherry Pie, Scrumptious, **'83** 250
Chess Pie, Brown Sugar, **'86** 220
Chess Pie, Old-Fashioned, **'86** 220
Chicken Puffs, Appetizer, **'85** 72

Chocolate
Almond Pie, Creamy Chocolate-, **'85** 102
Amandine, Chocolate Pie, **'83** 300
Amaretto Mousse Pie, Chocolate-, **'80** 180; **'81** 30
Berry Pie, Heavenly Chocolate-, **'85** 102
Best-Ever Chocolate Pie, **'88** M45
Black Bottom Pie, **'82** 53
Bourbon Pie, Chocolate, **'88** 99
Chess Pie, Chocolate, **'81** 161; **'86** 220
Chilled Chocolate Pie, **'88** 99
Chip Pie, Chocolate, **'85** 114
Cream Cheese Pie, Chocolate-, **'80** 69
Cream Pie, Chocolate, **'83** 192; **'84** 49; **'87** 208
Creamy Chocolate Pie, **'85** 298; **'86** 119
Double Chocolate Pie, **'82** M282
Easy Chocolate Pie, **'83** 158
French Silk Pie, **'80** 247
Frozen Chocolate Pie, **'80** 154
Fudge Pie, **'87** 168
Fudge Pie, Sweetheart, **'86** 316
Heavenly Chocolate Pie, **'87** 260
Ice Cream Pie, Chocolate-, **'87** 224
Meringue Pie, Chocolate, **'80** 238; **'82** 206; **'83** 158
Meringue Pie, Chocolate-Filled, **'86** 121
Mocha Crunch Pie, Chocolate-, **'81** 136
Mousse Pie, Chocolate, **'81** 136
Mud Pie, Tipsy, **'80** 255
Peanut Butter Pie, Chocolate-, **'85** 91

Pies and Pastries, Chocolate *(continued)*

Peanut Butter Swirl Pie,
Chocolate-, **'87** 262
Praline Pie, Chocolate-, **'86** 259
Silk Pie, Chocolate, **'88** 67
Whipped Cream Pie,
Chocolate, **'79** 124
Christmas Pie, White, **'88** 281
Cobblers
Apple Cobbler, Easy, **'83** 174
Apple Cobbler for Two, **'85** 261
Apple Crisp, **'84** 122
Apple-Pecan Cobbler, **'84** M198
Apple Walnut Cobbler, **'79** 154
Apple-Walnut Cobbler, **'81** 248
Apricot Cobble Up, **'82** 138
Berry-Cherry Cobbler, **'83** 270
Berry Crisp, **'83** 130
Blackberry-Almond Cobbler, **'81** 132
Blackberry Cobbler, **'82** 139; **'83** 175
Blackberry Cobbler,
Deep-Dish, **'80** 186
Blackberry Cobbler, Deluxe, **'81** 132
Blackberry Cobbler,
New-Fashioned, **'87** 164
Blackberry Cobbler, Southern, **'81** 132
Blueberry Buckle, **'85** 30
Blueberry Cobbler, **'83** 175
Blueberry Cobbler, Easy, **'83** 183
Blueberry Cobbler, Fresh, **'80** 144
Blueberry Cobbler, Peachy, **'80** 143
Blueberry Crisp, **'84** 177
Blueberry Crunch, Fresh, **'82** 143
Blueberry, Huckle-Buckle, **'86** 151
Blueberry-Peach Cobbler,
No-Dough, **'86** 177
Blueberry Pinwheel Cobbler, **'87** 140
Boysenberry Cobbler, **'82** 133
Cherry Cobbler, **'82** 91, 139
Cherry Cobbler, Fresh, **'84** 178
Cherry Slump, **'83** 139
Cranberry-and-Apple Cobbler, **'84** 306
Cranberry Cobbler, **'81** 275
Cranberry Cobbler, Easy, **'86** 260
Cranberry Cobbler Roll, **'80** 288;
'81 248
Cranberry-Pear Crisp, **'83** 207
Fig Cobbler, **'79** 140
Fig Cobbler, Super, **'86** 206
Grenadine-Peach Cobbler, **'85** 178
Peach-Caramel Cobbler, **'86** 300;
'87 178
Peach Cobbler, **'83** 175; **'84** 178
Peach Cobbler, Fresh, **'82** 139
Peach Cobbler,
Lattice-Topped, **'79** 154
Peach Cobbler, Old-Fashioned, **'82** 170
Peach Cobbler, Quick, **'79** 215;
'81 142
Peach Cobbler, Spicy, **'85** 178
Peach Cobbler Supreme, **'81** 184
Peach Crisp, **'83** 113
Peach Crumble, Easy, **'83** 116
Pear Cobbler, Best Ever, **'82** 194
Pear Crumble, **'85** 221
Pineapple-Apple Betty, **'85** 46
Plum Cobbler, Crunchy, **'88** 152
Strawberry-Rhubarb Cobbler, **'88** 93
Strawberry-Rhubarb Cobbler,
Rosy, **'79** 154

Coconut-Caramel Pies, **'87** 260
Coconut Chess Pie, **'86** 220
Coconut Cloud, **'80** 70
Coconut Cream Pie, **'80** 238; **'81** 136;
'82 85; **'84** 49; **'87** 207
Coconut Cream Pie, Fresh, **'80** 289
Coconut Custard Pie, **'82** 33
Coconut Macaroon Pie, **'88** 204
Coconut Pie, Blender, **'84** 236
Coconut Pie, Magic, **'79** 53
Coconut Pie, Mock, **'86** 200
Coconut Pie, Quick, **'83** 115
Coconut-Pineapple Pie, **'84** 256
Coconut Puffs, **'87** 277
Cracker Pie, **'79** 113
Cranberry-Cherry Pie, Tart, **'87** 299
Cranberry Freezer Pie, Festive, **'84** 306
Cranberry Pie, Frosty, **'79** 249
Cranberry Pie, Nutty, **'82** M298
Cranberry Pie, Walnut-, **'87** 259
Cranberry-Raisin Pie, **'80** 283; **'85** 316
Cran-Raspberry Pie, **'87** 244
Cream Horns, **'84** 137
Cream Pie, Texas, **'81** 181
Cream Puffs, Captivating, **'81** 180
Cream Puffs, Java, **'81** 187
Cream Puffs, Strawberry, **'81** 95
Cream Puffs, Strawberry-Lemon, **'87** 75
Cream Puffs, Tutti-Frutti, **'79** 231
Crème de Menthe Pie, Quick, **'88** 127
Custard Pie, Old-Fashioned Egg, **'82** 261
Custard Pie, Perfect, **'82** 92
Daiquiri Pie, **'79** 68
Danish Pastry Puffs, **'85** 311
Dream Pie, **'80** 90

Éclairs with Pecan Sauce, **'83** 219
Eggnog Chiffon Pie, **'86** 281
Eggnog Pie, **'80** 254; **'83** 205; **'86** 317;
'87 295
Eggnog Pie, Fluffy, **'81** M269
Fig Snacks, Sliced, **'86** 206
Fried Pies, Delicious, **'83** 84
Fruitcake Pie, **'80** 237
Fruit Pie, Crispy-Crust, **'88** 68
Fruit Pie, Dried, **'83** 249
Fruit Pie, Japanese, **'80** 238
Fruit Pies, Baked, **'84** 7
Fruit Puff, Giant, **'85** 72
Grape Juice Pie, **'79** 123
Grape Pie, **'85** 212
Grasshopper Freeze, Creamy, **'81** 180
Grasshopper Pie, **'83** 145

Heavenly Pie, **'83** 158
Ice Cream Delight, **'80** 69
Ice Cream Pie, Absolutely Divine, **'82** 181
Ice Cream Pie, Caramel, **'82** 181
Ice Cream Pie, Carrot, **'86** 200
Ice Cream Pie, Chocolate-Mint, **'81** 144
Ice Cream Pie, Coffee, **'79** 231
Ice Cream Pie, Heavenly, **'82** 181
Ice Cream Pie, Kona, **'83** 189
Ice Cream Pie, Lemon, **'80** 70
Ice Cream Pie, Peanutty, **'82** 56
Ice Cream Pie, Peppermint Candy-, **'87** 260
Ice Cream Pie, Pumpkin, **'81** 272
Ice Cream Pie with Meringue-Pecan
Crust, **'88** 127
Ice Cream Pie with Rum-Fruit
Sauce, **'84** 312
Kahlúa Pie, **'83** 191
Lemon Chess Pie, **'79** 32; **'82** 196
Lemon Cream Pie, Frozen, **'82** 86
Lemon in Pastry Shell, **'84** 137
Lemon Meringue Pie, **'85** M112; **'86** 130
Lemon Meringue Pie, Deluxe, **'81** 172
Lemon-Orange Pie, **'85** 172
Lemon Pie, Buttermilk, **'81** 120; **'82** 23
Lemon Pie, Slice of, **'84** 23
Lemon Pie, Whipped, **'79** 124
Lemon-Sour Cream Pie, **'82** 169
Lemon Sponge Pie, **'83** 192
Lemon-Strawberry Pie, **'88** 127
Lemon Twirl Pie, **'84** 94
Lime Chiffon Pie, **'86** 130
Lime Fluff Pie, **'84** 43
Macadamia Pie, **'80** 238
Main Dish
Artichoke Pie, **'79** 25
Beef Pies, Carry-Along, **'80** 224;
'81 56
Beef Roast Pot Pie, **'88** 296
Breakfast Pie, **'86** 242
Broccoli-and-Turkey Pasta Pie, **'88** 269
Broccoli-Beef Pie, **'83** 196
Burrito Pie, Mexican, **'87** 287
Cheese-Beef Pie, **'85** 33
Cheese Pie, Mexican, **'82** 9; **'83** 69
Chicken Breasts Wellington, **'84** 22
Chicken, Company Creamed, **'82** 84
Chicken in Pastry, **'86** 122
Chicken in Phyllo, **'87** 286
Chicken Liver Turnovers, **'79** 141
Chicken Pie, **'81** 281; **'82** 31
Chicken Pie, Biscuit-Topped,
'86 157, 264
Chicken Pie, Cheesy Mexican, **'82** 142
Chicken Pie, Deluxe, **'88** 298
Chicken Pie, Double-Crust, **'87** 111
Chicken Pie, Egg-Stra Special, **'86** 264
Chicken Pot Pie, **'81** 210; **'82** 114;
'84 21
Chicken Pot Pie, Easy, **'83** 156
Chicken Pot Pie, Thick 'n'
Crusty, **'87** 267; **'88** 102
Chicken Pot Pie with Cheese
Crust, **'86** 264
Chicken Salad in Cream Puff
Bowl, **'86** 232
Chicken-Vegetable Pot Pie, **'81** 281;
'82 30
Chile-Cheese Pie, Green, **'84** 234
Chili-Tamale Pie, **'82** 9; **'83** 68
Cornbread-Sausage-Apple Pie, **'87** 171

Corn Burger Pie, '83 156
Country Pie, '83 155
Enchilada Pie, '83 155
Fish in a Crust, '84 294
Grits-and-Ham Pie, Crustless, '86 103
Hamburger Pie, '81 92; '84 13
Ham Pie, Golden, '87 78
Ham Pie with Cheese Crust, '80 286
Ham Tart, Supreme, '84 22
Ham Towers, Cheesy, '82 77
Meat-and-Potato Pie, '84 23
Meat Pie, Mexicali, '81 194
Meat Pie, Old-Fashioned, '82 110
Meat Pie, Reuben, '80 189
Meat Pies, Cornish, '84 23
Meat Pies, Natchitoches, '84 21
Meat Turnovers, '86 326
Oyster Pie, Creole, '84 214
Pancake, Supper, '86 242
Pea Flips, '80 7
Pineapple-Chicken Salad Pie, '80 138
Salmon-Spinach Turnovers, '83 44
Sausage Log, Phyllo, '84 294
Sausage Pizza Pie, Link-, '85 33
Seafood Pie, Hot, '80 32
Shepherd Pie, '83 116
Shrimp Puffs, Luncheon, '85 72
Sombrero Pie, '81 140
Spaghetti Pie, '81 32
Spanakópita, '86 58
Spinach-Pasta Pie, '85 286
Taco Pie, '88 256
Taco Pie, Crescent, '80 80
Taco Pie, Double-Crust, '88 272
Taco Pies, Individual, '82 M282
Tortilla Pie, '85 M211
Tortilla Pie, Montezuma, '83 199
Tuna Pie with Cheese Roll
  Crust, '80 286
Tuna-Rice Pie, '84 123
Turkey-and-Dressing Pie, '84 326
Turkey-and-Oyster Pie, '82 267
Turkey-Cheese Pie, '88 264
Turkey Pie, '80 285
Turkey Pie, Crumb-Crust
  Curried, '86 265
Turkey Pie, Golden, '79 253
Turkey Pie, Lattice-Topped, '81 277;
  '82 7
Turkey Pie, Potato-Topped, '86 265
Turkey Pot Pie, '86 265
Vegetable-Beef Pies, '80 286
Zucchini-Ham-Cheese Pie, '80 272
Mango-Ginger Pie, '88 138
Mango Pie, Green, '79 137
Mexican Fiesta Confection, '82 223
Mincemeat Chiffon Pie, '79 245
Mincemeat-Peach Pie, '80 295; '81 188
Mincemeat Pie, Holiday, '80 282; '83 250;
  '87 213
Mincemeat Pie, Pear, '84 264
Mocha Meringue Pie, '80 242; '88 163
Molasses Pie, '86 20
Muscadine Pie, '82 202
Mushroom-Almond Pastry Cups, '88 210
Napoleons, '84 138
Napoleons, Strawberry, '81 126
Nesselrode Pie, Fluffy, '87 261
Orange Ambrosia Pie, '80 237
Orange Blossom Special, '79 48
Orange Chess Pie, '88 204

Orange Chiffon Pie, '87 260
Orange Meringue Pie, '81 12, 309
Orange Shortcake, Fresh, '80 100
Palmiers, '87 277
Papaya Pie, '86 53
Pastries and Crusts
  Almond Pastry, '85 177
  Basic Microwave Pastry, '82 M142;
    '85 M113
  Basic Pastry, '79 282; '81 M268;
    '82 114; '84 48
  Butter Pastry, Golden, '84 22
  Cereal Piecrust, Crisp, '82 209;
    '83 100
  Cheddar Cheese Pastry, '80 219;
    '82 194
  Cheddar Pastry, '86 206
  Cheese Crust, '80 286; '86 264
  Cheese Pastry, '88 56
  Cheese Rolls, '80 286
  Chocolate-Coconut Crust, '87 261
  Chocolate-Coconut Pie Shell, '82 210;
    '83 100
  Chocolate Crumb Crust, '87 261

  Chocolate Crust, '87 264
  Chocolate Cups, '80 207
  Chocolate Pastry Shell, '87 262
  Cinnamon Meringue Shell, '82 263
  Cookie Crust, Spicy, '88 7
  Cornmeal Pastry, '81 140
  Cracker Crust, '88 97
  Cream Cheese Pastries, '80 250
  Cream Cheese Pastry, '82 39;
    '86 24, 78
  Cream Cheese Pastry Shells, '86 13
  Cream Cheese Pastry Shells,
    Miniature, '87 190
  Cream Cheese Patty Shells, '81 266;
    '82 249
  Cream Cheese Shells, '79 2
  Crumb Crust, Cheesy, '88 86
  Decorating Pie Crusts, '83 248
  Deluxe Piecrust, '79 79
  Double-Crust Pastry, '81 105; '82 85,
    M298; '83 248; '85 191; '87 299;
    '88 94, 178
  Double-Crust Pastry, Flaky, '82 57
  Flaky Pastry, '80 224; '81 56, 210;
    '83 156
  German Pastries, '86 78
  Ginger Snap Crust, '88 138
  Graham Cracker Crust, '79 45; '86 32;
    '87 139, 243; '88 M45, 55, 67

Graham Cracker Crust,
  Microwaved, '82 M141
Graham Cracker Crust,
  Peanut-, '79 50
Heart Tart Pastry, '87 14
Italian Sweet Crust, Plum Pie
  with, '79 162
Make-Ahead Pastry, '82 209; '83 100
Mocha Pastry Shell, '81 136
Never Fail Pastry, '79 79
Nut Crust, Spiced, '87 295
Oatmeal Piecrust, '79 79
Pastry, '82 85, 139, 259; '83 84, 91,
  175; '84 21, 23; '86 24, 25, 242,
  259, 303, 326; '87 212, 267;
  '88 103, 198, 225
Pâté Pastry, '86 65
Pecan Crust, '86 317
Perfect Pastry Mix, '81 142
Perfect Pastry Shell, '81 142
Perfect Piecrust, Making, '82 234
Pizza Crust, '80 233; '83 226; '86 77
Pizza Crust, Crispy, '87 181
Processor Pastry, '87 67
Processor Pie Dough, Quick
  Food, '84 219
Puff Pastry, Basic, '84 135
Puff Pastry, Cream, '85 72
Puff Pastry, Quick, '84 207
Quiche Pastry, '80 M107
Quiche Pastry, Microwaved, '81 M74;
  '82 M122
Rice-Cheese Shell, '82 49
Rice Crust, Crispy, '84 43
Seasoned Pastry, '79 253
Sesame Pastry Shell, '82 67
Shell, Pastry, '84 31, 127; '87 262
Shells, Pastry, '83 93
Shortcake Pastry, '80 100
Spice Crust, '82 298
Tart Crust, '84 178
Tart Shell, '87 77; '88 20
Tart Shells, '82 304; '83 279;
  '85 300; '86 18, 105; '88 4
Tart Shells, Cheese, '88 88
Tart Shells, Cheese Pastry, '85 216
Tart Shells, Tea, '85 120
Timbale Shells, '82 108
Triple-Crust Pastry, '80 186
Whole Wheat Crust, '82 298
Whole Wheat Pastry, '81 229
Peach-Cranberry Pie, '83 249
Peach Cream Pie, Dried, '84 146
Peaches-and-Cream Pie, '81 184
Peach Fried Pies, Easy, '85 178
Peach Pie, Fresh, '82 170
Peach Pie, Luscious, '81 136
Peach Pies, Fried, '81 272
Peach Pies, Little, '86 303
Peanut Butter Cream Pie, '79 50;
  '88 65
Peanut Butter Meringue Pie, '84 30
Peanut Butter Pie, '85 275; '86 109
Peanut-Raisin Pie, '79 85
Pear Crumble Pie, '83 207
Pear Mincemeat Pie, '88 226
Pear-Mince Pie, '81 271
Pear Pie, Deep-Dish, '80 219
Pear Pie, Delicious, '88 226
Pear Pie, Double-Crust, '82 194
Pear Pie, French, '87 213

Pies and Pastries (continued)

Pear Pie, Tennessee, **'85** 230
Pear Streusel Pie, **'83** 234; **'84** 244
Pecan
    Bourbon Pecan Pie, **'85** 90
    Butter Pecan Pie Squares, **'81** 262
    Caramel-Pecan Apple Pie, **'85** 247
    Caramel-Pecan Pie, **'88** 282
    Chocolate Pecan Pie, **'80** 237; **'83** 12
    Choco-Pecan Pie, **'82** 86
    Coconut-Pecan Chess Pie, **'81** 248
    Coconut Pecan Pie, **'81** 161
    Coffee Pecan Pie, **'82** 74
    Custard Pecan Pie, **'87** 184
    Date-Pecan Pie, **'80** 15
    Golden Pecan Pie, **'81** 266
    Grandmother's Pecan Pie, **'86** 269
    Holiday Pecan Pie, **'81** 296
    Individual Pecan Pies, **'85** 295
    Layered Pecan Pie, **'83** 305
    Maple-Pecan Pie, **'81** 266
    Miniature Pecan Pies, **'79** 205; **'86** 13
    Molasses-Pecan Pie, **'86** 259
    Old-Fashioned Pecan Pie, **'81** M269
    Orange-Pecan Pie, **'79** 282; **'83** 222
    Pecan Pie, **'79** 251; **'80** 57; **'85** 255
    Pumpkin-Pecan Pie, **'85** 233, 282
    Raisin-Pecan Pie, **'87** 213
    Spicy Pecan Pie, **'84** 240
    Sweet Potato-Pecan Pie, **'83** 90
    Texas Pecan Pie, **'83** 159
    Tiny Pecan Pies, **'79** 225
Persimmon Pie, **'79** 206
Phyllo Cheesecakes, Little, **'87** 275
Phyllo Nests, Nutty, **'87** 277

Pineapple Phyllo Bundles, **'87** 277
Pineapple Pie, **'80** 237
Pineapple Pie, Double-Crust, **'82** 85
Pistachio Pie, **'80** 56
Plum Cream Pie, Easy, **'86** 174
Plum Kuchen, **'79** 161
Plum Pie, Streusel-Topped, **'88** 153
Plum Pie with Italian Sweet Crust, **'79** 162
Preserve-Filled Foldovers, **'80** 7
Profiteroles, **'84** 208
Pumpkin Chiffon Pie, **'84** 312
Pumpkin Empanadas, **'82** 223
Pumpkin-Ice Cream Pie, **'87** 243
Pumpkin Pie, Autumn, **'87** 213
Pumpkin Pie, Bourbon-Pecan, **'87** 264
Pumpkin Pie, Festive, **'81** M269
Pumpkin Pie, Fluffy, **'80** 283
Pumpkin Pie in Spiced Nut Crust, **'87** 295
Pumpkin Pie, Nutty, **'82** 67
Pumpkin Pie, Quick, **'88** M230

Pumpkin Pie, Rich, **'86** 292
Pumpkin Pie, Sour Cream-, **'84** 263
Pumpkin Pies, Spicy, **'84** 322
Pumpkin Pie Supreme, **'82** 217
Pumpkin Pie, Traditional, **'85** 256
Pumpkin Praline Pie, **'80** 244
Raisin Pie, **'83** 220
Raisin Pie, Spiced, **'84** 148
Raspberry-Nut Strudel, **'83** 304
Rhubarb-Peach Pie, **'86** 140
Rhubarb-Raisin Pie, **'79** 112
Rugelach, **'85** 276
Rum Bisque Pie, **'79** 123
Rum Cream Pie, **'85** 212
Scuppernong Pie, **'88** 216
Sour Cream Pie, **'86** 260
Sour Cream Pie, Tropical, **'79** 176; **'80** 6
Strawberry Angel Pie, **'88** 136
Strawberry-Banana Glazed Pie, **'81** 181
Strawberry-Glaze Pie, **'81** 141
Strawberry Pie, Chilled, **'82** 112
Strawberry Pie, Glazed, **'82** M142
Strawberry Yogurt Pie, **'80** 232
Strawberry-Yogurt Pie, **'85** 122; **'86** 124
Strudel, Fruit Basket, **'87** 276
Tarts
    Almond Tea Tarts, **'85** 120
    Apple Cream Tart, **'84** 207
    Apple-Pecan Tarts, **'80** 282
    Apple Tart, Deluxe, **'84** 227
    Apple Tart with Cheese
      Pastry, **'88** 225
    Apricot Tarts, **'79** 282; **'88** 281
    Blue Cheese Appetizer Tarts, **'85** 300;
      '86 18
    Bouilli, Tarte à la, **'83** 92
    Caramel Tarts, **'82** 43
    Cheese Tart, Herb-, **'87** 98
    Cherry and Blackberry Tart, **'83** 225
    Cherry Tarts, Cheery, **'80** 238
    Chicken Salad Tarts, **'84** 257
    Chocolate-Amaretto Heavenly
      Tarts, **'88** 4
    Cranberry-Cream Cheese
      Tarts, **'80** 154
    Cranberry Holiday Tarts, **'83** 279
    Cranberry-Nut Tart, **'84** 305
    Cranberry Tartlets, Fresh, **'87** 244
    Cream Cheese Tarts, **'84** 74
    Eggnog Tarts, Creamy, **'79** 255
    French Silk Tarts, **'79** 236
    Fruit Tart, Fancy, **'82** 128
    Fruit Tart, Fresh, **'84** 178
    Fruit Tart, Open-Face, **'84** 207
    Fruit Tart, Rainbow, **'82** 304
    Grape Tart, Green, **'87** 77
    Grasshopper Tarts, **'80** 220
    Heart Tarts, **'87** 14
    Kentucky Derby Tarts, **'79** 102
    Kiwifruit-Peach Tart, **'88** 20
    Lady Baltimore Tarts, **'88** 282
    Lemon-Cheese Tarts, **'79** 2
    Lemon Ice Cream Tarts, **'80** 152
    Lemon-Sour Cream Tarts, **'81** 304
    Lemon Tarts, **'82** 156; **'83** 79
    Lemon Tarts, Dainty, **'82** 304
    Lemon Tarts, Golden, **'85** 191
    Lemon Tart Shells, **'88** 195
    Lime-Pineapple Tart, **'88** 6
    Little Bits, **'79** 196
    Milan, Tart, **'87** 70

    Mushroom Tarts, **'88** 161
    Orange Tarts, Frozen, **'80** 154
    Pear Tart, **'82** 304
    Pecan Tarts, **'81** 266
    Pecan Tarts, Easy, **'84** 313
    Pecan Tarts, Special, **'87** 224
    Pommes, La Tarte aux, **'80** 125
    Prune Tarts, Brandied, **'85** 223
    Puddin' Pies, President Tyler's, **'80** 43
    Pumpkin Tarts, No-Bake, **'86** 291
    Sausage 'n' Cheese Tarts, **'88** 51
    Seafood Tartlets, **'87** 247
    Shrimp Tart, **'87** 70
    Strawberry Tart, **'84** 138
    Strawberry Tarts, **'80** 70
    Teatime Tassies, **'84** 321
Tin Roof Pie, **'85** 91
Transparent Pie, **'80** 238

Turnovers, Fried Apricot, **'86** 24
Turnovers, Fruit, **'79** 150
Turnovers, Party Ham, **'82** 39
Turnovers, Roast Beef, **'88** 273
Turnovers, Sausage-Cheese, **'88** 231
Vanilla Cream Pie, Fruit-Topped, **'84** 49
Vegetable
    Bean Pie, Pinto, **'80** 40
    Broccoli-Cheese Pie, **'84** 235
    Carrot Pie, **'83** 117
    Cauliflower-Carrot Pie, **'82** 191
    Corn Pie, Quick and Cheesy, **'82** 191
    Florentine Crêpe Pie, **'79** 34
    Mushrooms in Patty Shells, **'80** 283
    Mushroom Tarts, Hot Sherried, **'83** 78
    Mushroom Turnovers, Tiny, **'86** 24
    Onion-Cheese Pie, **'88** 86
    Onion Pie, **'82** 191
    Potato-Orange Pie, Sweet, **'88** 207
    Ratatouille Pie, **'88** 198
    Spinach Pie, **'82** 191; **'88** 56
    Spinach Pie, Greek, **'85** 59
    Spinach Tarts, **'82** 249
    Squash Chiffon Pie, Butternut, **'83** 296;
      '84 285
    Squash Pie, Butternut, **'80** 40;
      '87 198
    Squash Pie, Spaghetti, **'80** 186
    Squash Pie, Spicy, **'85** 9
    Squash Pie, Spicy Butternut, **'80** 296
    Sweet Potato Cream Pie,
      Southern, **'87** 260
    Sweet Potato Meringue Pie, **'81** 126;
      '83 225
    Sweet Potato Pie, **'79** 207; **'85** 255,
      275; **'86** 269
    Sweet Potato Pie, No-Crust, **'84** 236

Sweet Potato Pie,
Old-Fashioned, **'79** 9
Sweet Potato Pone Pie, **'80** 288
Tomato Pie, **'88** 198
Tomato Pie, Green, **'79** 195
Vegetable Turnovers, **'86** 24
Yam Pie, Louisiana, **'81** 223
Zucchini Pie, Cheesy, **'82** 191
Zucchini Pie, Italian-Style, **'83** 43

Pimiento
Ball, Pimiento Cheese, **'80** 258
Bread, Pimiento-Cheese, **'85** 223
Casserole, English Pea-Pimiento, **'83** 207
Cheese, Chunky Pimiento, **'86** 295
Cheese, Creamy Pimiento, **'86** 296
Cheeses, Pimiento and Three, **'86** 296
Cheese, West Texas Pimiento, **'84** 9
Eggs, Pimiento-Deviled, **'84** 143
Pasta, Pimiento, **'84** 176
Popovers, Pimiento, **'79** 138
Sandwiches, Pimiento Cheese, **'82** 278
Sauce, Cauliflower with Pimiento, **'87** 232
Spread, Garlic Pimiento Cheese, **'79** 58
Spread, Ham and Pimiento, **'80** 285;
'81 56
Spread, Low-Calorie Pimiento
Cheese, **'85** 215
Spread, Pimiento Cheese, **'82** 35; **'83** 93;
'86 127
Topping, Pimiento, **'83** 93

Pineapple
Ambrosia, Pineapple-Orange, **'88** 252
Appetizer, Shrimp-Pineapple, **'85** 80
Bacon-Wrapped Pineapple Chunks, **'84** 25
Baked Pineapple, **'83** 261; **'84** 287
Baked Pineapple with Natillas
Sauce, **'83** 179
Bake, Pineapple, **'79** 251
Bake, Pineapple-Cheese, **'79** 106
Ball, Pineapple Cheese, **'81** 160
Ball, Pineapple-Cheese, **'84** 26
Bars, Pineapple-Orange, **'82** 129
Basket, Summer Berry, **'84** 158
Beans and Franks, Hawaiian
Baked, **'80** 136
Beans, Hawaiian-Style Baked, **'86** 210
Beefburgers Hawaiian, **'86** 137
Beets with Pineapple, **'79** 249; **'82** 204
Betty, Pineapple-Apple, **'85** 46
Boat Aloha, Pineapple, **'80** 102
Boats Ahoy, Pineapple, **'80** 148
Bread, Carrot-Pineapple, **'82** 210
Bread, Pineapple, **'83** 139
Bread, Pineapple-Apricot, **'84** 7
Bread, Pineapple-Carrot, **'79** 106
Bread, Pineapple-Nut, **'79** 215
Bread, Pineapple-Pecan Loaf, **'87** 256
Buns, Easy Pineapple, **'85** 14
Burgers, Pineapple, **'82** 169
Cake, Cajun, **'87** 138
Cake, Coconut-Pineapple Layer, **'80** 140
Cake, Heavenly Pineapple, **'83** 303
Cake, Lemon-Pineapple, **'86** 60, 239
Cake, Pineapple-Pecan
Upside-Down, **'84** 25
Cake, Pineapple Pound, **'79** 148
Cake, Pineapple Upside-Down, **'80** 102;
'88 10
Cake Roll, Coconut-Pineapple, **'84** 304
Cake, Skillet Pineapple
Upside-Down, **'85** 242

Cake, Stacked Pineapple
Upside-Down, **'86** 239
Carrots, Pineapple, **'83** 198
Cheesecake, Pineapple, **'81** 32
Cheesecake, Ultimate Pineapple, **'85** 38
Chicken and Pineapple, **'81** 281; **'82** 30
Chicken Bake, Pineapple, **'82** 120
Chicken, Hawaiian Sesame, **'81** 106
Chicken, Oriental Pineapple, **'84** 288
Chicken, Piña Colada, **'86** 21
Chicken, Pineapple, **'83** M194; **'85** 3
Chicken with Pineapple, Oriental, **'86** 42
Chops, Pineapple-Curry Glazed, **'82** 106
Coleslaw, Curried Pineapple, **'88** 172
Cookies, Pineapple, **'79** 216
Crab Imperial, Pineapple-, **'84** M286
Cream, Pineapple 'n', **'88** 202
Crêpes, Mango-Pineapple, **'86** 216

Delight, Pineapple-Almond, **'85** 96
Delight, Pineapple-Pear, **'82** 54
Dessert Chimichangas, Pineapple, **'86** 4
Dip, Cheesy Pineapple, **'80** 249
Dip, Pineapple-Ginger, **'86** 104
Doughnuts, Pineapple Drop, **'83** 95
Dressing, Fruit Salad with
Pineapple, **'85** 207
Dressing, Pineapple Cream, **'83** 81
Dressing, Pineapple-Poppy Seed, **'85** 55
Drink, Coconut-Pineapple, **'83** 172
Filling, Pineapple, **'80** 140; **'83** 179;
'84 153
Float, Pineapple Sherbet, **'79** 148
Franks, Hawaiian, **'81** 202
Frappé, Hawaiian, **'81** 178
Fresh Pineapple Boats, **'83** 153
Fresh Pineapple Delight, **'79** 111
Fried Pineapple, **'81** 232
Fritters, Pineapple, **'88** 112
Glazed Oranges and Pineapple, **'86** 318
Glaze, Orange-Pineapple, **'81** 60
Glaze, Pineapple, **'83** 143; **'84** 26; **'85** 38
Ham, Citrus-and-Spice, **'88** 40
Ham, Pineapple-Baked, **'86** 48
Ham, Pineapple-Flavored, **'87** 160
Hawaiian Dream Boats, **'86** 151
Ice Cream, Orange-Pineapple, **'86** 117
Ice Cream, Pineapple-Mint, **'84** 186
Jam, Pineapple, **'81** 147
Kabobs, Pineapple-Beef, **'83** 212
Kabobs, Pineapple-Chicken, **'86** M328
Loaf, Hawaiian, **'80** 225
Loaf, Pineapple Upside-Down Ham, **'79** 253

Loaves, Individual Pineapple, **'81** M121
Marmalade, Orange-Pineapple, **'82** 150
Marmalade, Strawberry-Pineapple, **'85** 130
Meatballs, Chinese, **'87** 194
Meatballs, Polynesian, **'80** 207
Meringue-Topped Pineapple, **'84** 178
Milkshake, Pineapple, **'87** 199
Mold, Minted Pineapple, **'85** 240
Mousse, Elegant Pineapple, **'79** 230
Muffins, Carrot-Pineapple, **'81** 6
Muffins, Pineapple, **'81** 14, 250
Muffins, Sunshine, **'86** 9
Nog, Speedy Breakfast, **'82** 47
Parfait, Pineapple, **'84** 83
Patties, Pineapple-Ham, **'80** 110
Pears, Pineapple-Honey, **'86** 94
Phyllo Bundles, Pineapple, **'87** 277
Pickled Pineapple, **'79** 24
Pie, Coconut-Pineapple, **'84** 256
Pie, Double-Crust Pineapple, **'82** 85
Pie, Pineapple, **'80** 237
Pie, Pineapple-Chicken Salad, **'80** 138
Pineapple Topping, Cherry-, **'87** 126
Pork and Pineapple, Polynesian, **'83** 102
Pork Chops, Hawaiian, **'86** 212
Pork Chops, Pineapple, **'87** M124
Pork, Pineapple, **'82** 60
Pork, Pineapple Sweet-and-Sour, **'82** 120
Pork Roast, Pineapple, **'79** 41
Pot Roast, Hawaiian, **'81** 298
Pot Roast, Polynesian, **'80** 59
Preserves, Mango-Pineapple, **'79** 137
Pudding, Pineapple, **'80** 102
Punch, False-Kick, **'82** 121
Punch, Hot Pineapple, **'82** 264
Punch, Lime-Pineapple, **'83** 142
Punch, Pineapple, **'79** 174; **'80** 128
Punch, Pineapple-Mint, **'88** 209
Punch, Pineapple-Orange, **'85** 236
Punch, Spiced Pineapple, **'83** 33
Rice with Pineapple, Curried, **'79** 142
Rolls, Cranberry-Pineapple, **'86** 275
Salad, Cucumber-Pineapple, **'84** 124
Salad Dressing, Pineapple, **'81** 36
Salad, Heavenly Frosted, **'79** 286
Salad, Icy Pineapple-Fruit, **'87** 9
Salad, Mandarin Orange and
Pineapple, **'82** 266
Salad, Pineapple-Buttermilk, **'82** 80
Salad, Pineapple-Celery, **'85** 95
Salad, Pineapple-Cucumber
Congealed, **'83** 118
Salad, Pineapple Daiquiri, **'84** 232
Salad, Pineapple-Lime, **'84** 320
Salad, Pineapple Macaroni, **'79** 220
Salad, Pineapple-Nut Chicken, **'83** 80
Salad, Pineapple-Orange Congealed, **'83** 218
Sauce, Banana-Pineapple, **'83** 48
Sauce, Jezebel, **'81** 29; **'82** 55
Sauce, Pineapple, **'84** 236
Sauce, Pineapple-Curry, **'79** 252
Sauce, Pineapple Ice Cream, **'81** M289
Sauce, Pineapple-Orange, **'84** 14
Sauce, Pineapple-Rhubarb, **'88** 94
Sauce, Pineapple-Rum, **'84** 275
Sauce, Raisin-Pineapple, **'82** 177
Sauce, Sweet-and-Sour Pineapple, **'85** 66
Scalloped Pineapple, **'79** 106; **'82** 254;
'84 M323
Shake, Banana-Pineapple Milk, **'84** 59
Shake, Pineapple-Banana, **'85** 215

Pineapple *(continued)*

Shake, Strawberry-Pineapple, '84 166
Sherbet, Creamy Pineapple, '79 155
Sherbet, Pineapple, '81 177; '84 83
Skewered Pineapple and
  Strawberries, '84 251
Slaw, Apple-Pineapple, '79 241
Slaw, Colorful Pineapple, '86 250
Slicing Pineapples, Instructions for, '82 94
Slush, Pineapple, '88 82
Sopaipillas, Pineapple, '83 179
Soufflé, Pineapple Dessert, '80 153
Spiced Pineapple, '80 102
Spread, Hawaiian Cheese, '87 158
Spread, Pineapple-Cheese, '86 126
Spread, Pineapple-Cream Cheese, '82 35
Spread, Pineapple Sandwich, '84 166
Spritz, Pineapple, '86 94
Squash, Pineapple-Stuffed Acorn, '84 255
Sundaes, Mauna Loa, '80 126
Tart, Lime-Pineapple, '88 6
Topping, Lemon-Pineapple, '86 60
Topping, Pineapple, '86 239
Tropical Snow, '86 34
Wassail, Pineapple-Apricot, '83 275

Pizza

Artichoke and Prosciutto, Pizza
  with, '87 182
Beef-and-Sausage Pizza, Double
  Cheesy, '86 77
Bread, Pizza Batter, '85 56
Breakfast Pizza, '85 44; '88 288
Burger, Pizza, '87 185
Burgers, Easy Pizza, '82 190
Burger Snacks, Pizza-, '84 30
Burgers, Pizza, '80 M201; '81 73
Calzone, '85 94
Casserole, Pizza, '88 273
Casserole, Quick Pizza, '83 266
Cheese-and-Mushroom Pizza, '83 226
Clam Pizza, Baby, '87 182
Cocktail Pizzas, '79 110
Crust, Crispy Pizza, '87 181
Crust, Pizza, '80 233; '83 226; '85 243;
  '86 77
Crust, Thick, '81 214
Crust, Thin, '81 214
Cups, Pizza, '81 215
Deep-Dish Mediterranean Pizza, '80 163
Deep-Dish Pizza Luncheon Pie, '80 286
Deep-Dish Vegetarian Pizza, '85 243
Eggplant Pizza, '85 221
French Bread, Pizza on, '82 131
Gruyère-Chicken Pizza, '87 182
Hamburger Pizza, Quick, '85 243
Homemade Pizza, Best Ever, '80 233
Italian-Style Pizza, Original, '87 182
Jazzed-Up Pizza, Jiffy, '83 M314
Kiwi-Berry Pizza, '86 198; '87 55
Lasagna Pizza, '85 285
Meatballs, Pizza, '85 86
Meat Loaf, Cheesy Pizza, '81 121
Pan Pizza, Quick, '86 160
Party Pizzettes, '80 192
Pepperoni Pizza, Thick 'n' Crusty, '85 244
Peppers, Pizza, '83 135
Pesto Pizza, '87 182
Popcorn, Pizza-Flavored, '85 236
Quiche, Pizza, '86 53
Quick Little Pizzas, '88 227

Salad Pizza, '87 182
Sandwiches, Open-Face Pizza, '82 3;
  '83 85; '84 M198; '85 22
Sandwich, Giant Pizza, '80 93
Sauce, Pizza, '84 33; '85 285
Sausage-Pepperoni Pizza, Spicy, '83 226
Sausage Pizza Pie, Link-, '85 33
Slices, Pizza, '84 269
Snacks, Pizza Party, '86 262
Snacks, Tasty Little Pizza, '79 248
Speedy Pizza, '81 214
Squares, Pizza, '87 168
Strawberry Pizza, '79 94
Supreme, Pizza, '81 214
Tostada Pizza, '81 16; '82 13
Turnovers, Little Pizza, '85 327
Two-Way Pizza, '79 93
Whole Wheat Pizza, '84 33
Zucchini Pizzas, '88 212

Plums

Bread, Sugar Plum, '80 256
Butter, Plum, '88 152
Chutney, Plum, '84 179
Cobbler, Crunchy Plum, '88 152
Crunch, Layered Plum, '86 174
Ham, Plum, '80 110
Jam, Peach-Plum Freezer, '85 130
Jelly, Plum, '82 150
Kuchen, Plum, '79 161

Muffins, Plum Good, '83 96
Pie, Easy Plum Cream, '86 174
Pie, Streusel-Topped Plum, '88 153
Pie with Italian Sweet Crust, Plum, '79 162
Pudding, Flamed Plum, '84 276
Pudding-Gelatin Mold, Plum, '86 300;
  '87 178
Pudding, Light Plum, '86 318
Pudding, Old-Fashioned Plum, '80 264
Pudding, '79 281
Sauce, Chinese Plum, '82 237
Sauce, Gingered Plum, '87 175
Sauce, Plum, '80 249; '82 40; '88 152
Sauce, Quail with Red Plum, '80 48
Sauce, Spicy Plum, '86 11
Slush, Plum, '84 139
Soup, Chilled Purple Plum, '79 162
Soup, Peach-Plum, '87 157
Soup, Plum, '85 107

Popcorn

Bacon-Cheese Popcorn, '86 74
Balls, Nutty Popcorn, '88 227
Cake, Popcorn-Gumdrop, '87 262
Candied Popcorn and Peanuts, '82 295
Caramel Corn, '88 64
Caramel Corn, Baked, '81 218

Caramel Corn Candy, '84 243
Caramel Popcorn, '79 219; '86 M212
Caramel Popcorn, Crispy, '85 247
Cinnamon-Popcorn Crunch, '86 136
Garlic Popcorn, '83 M315
Harvest Popcorn, '84 300
Mix, Curried Popcorn, '86 326
Nutty Popcorn, '85 208
Orange Popcorn, '86 230
Oriental Popcorn, '86 74
Pizza-Flavored Popcorn, '85 236
Pretzel Popcorn, '84 30
Scramble, Popcorn, '87 185
Sesame-Cheese Popcorn, '79 220
Spiced Popcorn Snack, '87 8

Pork. *See also* Bacon, Ham, Sausage.

Backbones, Smoked Country-Style, '82 162
Bake, Pork-and-Noodle, '88 98
Bake, Pork Spaghetti, '81 11
Barbecue
  Chops, Barbecued Pork, '81 10
  Chops, Marinated Barbecued
    Pork, '79 90
  Chops, Oven-Barbecued Pork, '81 234;
    '82 26; '83 40
  Home-Style Barbecue, '88 145
  Pork, Barbecued, '80 72
  Ribs, Apple Barbecued, '80 111
  Ribs, Barbecued, '80 111; '85 159
  Ribs, Country-Style Barbecued, '79 42
  Ribs, Herbed Barbecued, '86 185
  Ribs, Oven-Barbecued Pork, '88 132
  Ribs, Smoky Barbecued, '80 111
  Ribs, Tangy Barbecued, '83 160
  Roast, Barbecued Pork, '82 11
  Roast, Barbecue Pork, '82 97;
    '83 104
  Roast, Berry Barbecued Pork, '80 288
  Shoulder, Barbecued Pork, '81 111;
    '82 11
  Spareribs, Barbecued, '81 112; '82 12;
    '86 232
  Spareribs, Barbecued
    Country-Style, '80 73
  Spareribs, Easy Barbecued, '82 97;
    '83 104
  Spareribs, Saucy Barbecued, '79 14
  Spareribs, Southern Barbecued, '79 90
  Spareribs, Spicy Barbecued, '84 93
  Spareribs, Tangy Barbecued, '82 106
  Spareribs with Orange Barbecue
    Sauce, '83 11
  Spicy Barbecued Pork, '84 296
Bean Sauce, Pork-and-Onions with, '85 76
Brunch Eggs, '85 44
Burgers, Hearty Sauced Pork, '84 125
Burgoo, Five-Meat, '87 3
Burgoo, Harry Young's, '87 3
Burritos, '80 196
Burritos, Meat-and-Bean, '81 194
Calabaza Guisada con Puerco (Pumpkin
  Cooked with Pork), '80 193
Casserole, Cheesy Pork, '81 M74
Casserole, Pork, '83 116
Chalupa, Bean, '80 223
Chalupas, Pork, '83 160
Chile Verde, Light, '88 148
Chili, Double-Meat, '79 269; '80 12
Chops. *See also* Pork/Barbecue.
  Apple-Kraut Pork Chops, '84 50
  Apple Pork Chops, Spicy, '87 230

Apricot-Sauced Pork Chops, '85 22
Arlo, Pork, '87 229
Baked Pork Chops and Apples, '81 10
Bake, Fiesta Pork, '79 265
Braised Pork Chops, Bourbon-, '85 89
Broiled Pork Chops with Crabapple
    Peaches, '81 83
Casserole, Peppered Pork
    Chop, '81 235; '82 25; '83 39
Cheesy Pork Chops, '83 102
Chili Chops, '87 10
Cider-Sauced Pork Chops, '86 213;
    '87 81
Company Pork Chops, '85 109
Costillas Rellenos (Stuffed Pork
    Chops), '82 219
Country Pride Pork Chops, '79 159
Cranberry Pork Chops, '80 288
Creamy Gravy, Pork Chops
    and, '81 207
Creole Pork Chops, '83 102

Dill-Cream Gravy, Pork Chops
    with, '84 81
Dinner, Pork Chop, '80 84; '81 180;
    '88 25
Fiesta, Pork Chops, '86 118
Fruited Pork Chops, '87 194
Glazed Apple Pork Chops, '86 300
Glazed Chops,
    Pineapple-Curry, '82 106
Glazed Pork Chops, '86 185
Glazed Pork Chops, Apple-, '84 212;
    '87 35
Glazed Pork Chops, Orange-, '81 234;
    '82 25; '83 39
Glazed Pork Chops with Rice,
    Fruit-, '82 73
Glazed Pork Steaks, '83 178
Gourmet Pork Chops, '79 180
Grilled Pork Chops, '88 113
Grilled Pork Chops, Hawaiian, '85 159
Grilled Pork Chops, Marinated, '81 110
Hawaiian Pork Chops, '86 212; '87 82
Italiano, Pork Chops, '80 72
Italian, Pork Chops, '79 47
Jardinière, Pork Chops, '81 112;
    '82 12
Lemon-Herb Pork Chops, '84 81
Lemony Pork Chops, '88 118
Meal for Two, Pork Chop, '81 273

Orange-Cranberry Pork
    Chops, '86 335; '87 84
Orange-Glazed Pork Chops, '84 234
Orange Pork Chops, '84 81
Oriental Pork Chops, '84 81
Peanut Sauce, Pork Chops
    with, '83 29
Pineapple Pork Chops, '87 M124
Pleasing Pork Chops, '79 125
Polynesian Pork and Pineapple, '83 102
Rice, Pork Chops and
    Spanish, '83 103; '85 293
Risotti, Pork Chops, '81 234; '82 26
Saucy Company Pork Chops, '83 102
Saucy Pork Chop, '86 M140
Sauerkraut, Pork Chops and, '88 98
Savory Pork Chops, '87 194
Scallop, Pork Chops and
    Potato, '82 114
Sherry-Apple Pork Chops, '88 40
Sherry, Chops in, '79 125
Skillet Dinner, Pork Chop, '79 125
Skillet Pork Chops, Easy, '79 255
Sour Cream Sauce, Pork Chops
    with, '83 102
Special, Pork Chop, '79 81
Stuffed Baked Pork Chops, '79 222;
    '80 64
Stuffed Chops, Barbecued, '87 229
Stuffed Pork Chops, '84 195; '86 89
Stuffed Pork Chops, Apple-, '79 125
Stuffed Pork Chops,
    Apple-Crumb, '81 234; '82 26;
    '83 39
Stuffed Pork Chops, Apricot-, '86 76
Stuffed Pork Chops, Braised, '87 249
Stuffed Pork Chops, Cheese-, '84 81
Stuffed Pork Chops, Easy, '81 10
Stuffed Pork Chops, Fruit-, '82 136
Stuffed Pork Chops, Fruited, '86 197
Stuffed Pork Chops, Rice-, '83 102
Stuffed with Prunes, Pork
    Chops, '84 7
Sweet-and-Sour Pork Chops, '83 160
Vegetable Pork Chops, Skillet, '85 179
Vegetables, Pork Chops and
    Garden, '88 297
Chow Mein, Pork, '80 208
Combo, Vegetable-Pork, '85 113
Curry, Hurry, '79 103
Dinner, Pork and Noodles Skillet, '88 199
Egg Rolls, '86 81
Eggrolls, Shrimp and Pork, '82 240; '83 18
Eggs, Tulsa, '87 95
Hominy, Mexican, '86 255
Hot-and-Spicy Pork, '81 228
Kabobs, Spicy Pork, '82 182
Leg of Pork with Cranberry Glaze, '88 244
Loin Stuffed with Wild Rice, Pork, '84 35
Meatballs in Gravy, '79 136
Meatballs, Sauerkraut, '86 257
Meatballs, Tangy Hawaiian, '79 129
Meat Loaf
    Glazed Ham Loaf, '79 187
    Ham Loaf, '79 180
    Italian Meat Loaf, '79 187
    Mozzarella-Layered Meat Loaf, '79 71
    Pineapple Upside-Down Ham
        Loaf, '79 253
    Savory Meat Loaf, '87 216
    Skillet Liver Loaf, '80 11

    Stuffed Meat Loaf, '79 187
    Supreme Ham Loaf, '79 242
    Swedish Meat Loaf, '81 121
    Triple Meat Loaf, '79 186
Medaillions of Pork with
    Vegetables, '88 223
Oriental, Pork, '81 212
Paella, Chicken-Pork-Shrimp, '82 245
Pâté, Country, '86 66
Pâté en Croûte, '86 65
Pâté with Spinach and Cream,
    Pork, '83 224
Pies, Natchitoches Meat, '84 21
Pie, Sombrero, '81 140
Pilaf, Fruited Pork, '82 246
Pineapple Pork, '82 60
Polynesian Pork, '85 78
Ribs. See also Pork/Barbecue.
    Baked Ribs, Easy, '86 20
    Baked Ribs, Lemon, '81 166
    Chinese Spareribs, '81 10
    Glazed Spareribs, '88 98
    Glazed Spareribs, Honey-, '82 163
    Glazed Spareribs, Orange-, '84 296
    Glazed Spareribs, Peach-, '86 14
    Grilled Ribs, Lemon, '81 154
    Lemony Sweet Spareribs, '80 73
    Oven Ribs, Smoky, '81 166
    Plantation Ribs, '84 217
    Puerco en Adobo, '88 116
    Saucy Oven Spareribs, '80 207
    Saucy-Sweet Ribs, '81 166
    Smoked Ribs, '88 169
    Smoky Ribs, '84 172
    Stuffed Spareribs, Fruit-, '79 14
    Sweet-and-Sour Spareribs, '83 21
Risotto, Pork, '82 60
Roasts
    à l'Orange, Porc, '80 242
    Arista of Pork, '81 260
    Braised Pork, Brown Sugar, '84 36
    Crown Roast of Pork, Royal, '80 252
    Crown Roast of Pork, Stuffed, '86 323
    Crown Roast of Pork with
        Cranberry-Sausage Stuffing, '88 49
    Glazed Pork Loin, '87 229
    Indonesian Pork Roast, '81 227
    Loin of Pork, Roast, '84 276
    Loin, Roast Pork, '88 221
    Mandarin Pork Roast, '83 47
    Marinated Pork Roast, '80 71; '84 260
    Pineapple Pork Roast, '79 41
    Pineapple Sweet-and-Sour
        Pork, '82 120
    Rio Grande Pork Roast, '84 35, 296
    Smoked Pork Shoulder, '82 225
    Stuffed Crown Pork Flambé, '83 263
    Stuffed Pork Loin Roast,
        Prune-, '80 29
    Stuffed Pork Roast, '81 111; '82 12;
        '85 229
    Stuffed Pork Shoulder, '81 11
    Tomato Sauce, Pork Roast
        with, '87 249
    Zesty Pork Roast, '85 179
Salad, Mandarin
    Pork-and-Spinach, '88 M126
Salad, Pork-'n'-Bean, '87 83
Sandwiches, Party Pork, '88 M273
Sausage, Pork, '81 55
Sloppy Joes, Pork, '86 294

Pork (*continued*)

Soup, Guadalajara, '88 30
Soup, Homemade, '79 198
Steaks, Herbed Pork, '80 72
Steaks, Peachy Pork, '79 166
Stew, Bama Brunswick, '87 4
Stew, Brunswick, '80 264
Stew, Sonny Frye's Brunswick, '87 4
Stir-Fried Pork, '87 51
Stir-Fried Pork in Garlic Sauce, '84 141
St. Tammany, Pork, '82 260
Swedish Porkburgers, '79 42
Sweet-and-Pungent Pork, '86 118
Sweet-and-Sour Pork, '79 42; '80 72, 227;
  '81 26, 104, 111; '82 12; '84 218;
  '85 34, 194; '86 241
Tamales, '80 195
Tamales, Hot, '83 51
Tempting Twosome, '81 240
Tenderloin
  Apple-Ginger Pork Tenderloin, '86 75
  Blue Cheese, Pork Tenderloin
    with, '86 76
  Curried Pork Tenderloin, '86 76
  Danish Pork Tenderloin, '82 186
  Grilled Pork Tenderloin, '88 98
  Marinated Pork Tenderloin, '84 175
  Medaillions with Chutney Sauce,
    Pork, '87 35
  Picatta, Pork Tenderloin, '86 76
  Platter, Tenderloin, '79 42
  Roast Pork Tenderloin, '84 35
  Sandwiches, Beef and Pork
    Tenderloin, '80 175
  Stuffed Pork Tenderloins,
    Fruit-, '87 270
  Sunrise Pork Tenderloin, '79 103
  Towers, Pork Tenderloin, '86 75
Terrine, Jeweled Pork, '84 130
Wontons, Crispy Fried, '83 21

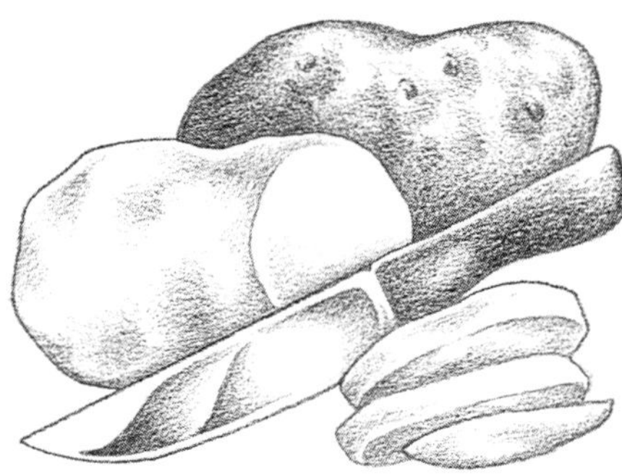

Potatoes
au Gratin, Potatoes and Eggs, '79 107
au Gratin, Potatoes-and-Zucchini, '84 5
Bacon Dressing, Potatoes with
  Hot, '88 M294
Bake, Chive-Potato, '82 229
Bake, Creamy Potato, '82 201; '88 41
Baked. *See also* Potatoes/Stuffed.
  Avocado-Topped Potatoes, '83 3
  Beef and Chicken-Topped Potatoes,
    Creamed, '83 210
  Broccoli-and-Almond-Topped
    Potatoes, '83 3

Broccoli-Topped Baked
  Potatoes, '86 17
Cheese Potato Skins, '84 M239
Cheese Sauce, Baked Potatoes
  with, '83 239
Cheesy Frank-Topped Potatoes, '83 3
Cheesy Potato Skins, '82 78
Chili-Topped Potatoes, '83 3
Crabmeat-Topped Potatoes, '83 3
Frank-Filled Potatoes, '84 M11
Garden Potato Cups, '83 76
Garden-Topped Potatoes, '83 4
Mexican-Topped Potatoes, '83 3
Micro-Baked Potatoes, '81 M61
Million Dollar Potatoes, '83 210
Mushroom-Dill-Topped
  Potatoes, '86 41
Mushroom Filling in a Peel, '84 214
Oven-Baked Potatoes, Easy, '82 202
Salmon-Topped Potatoes, '84 124
Skins, Baked Potato, '86 81
Sweet-and-Sour-Topped Potatoes, '83 4
Taco-Baked Potatoes, '84 119
Bake, Herbed Fish and Potato, '79 287;
  '80 34
Bake, Onion-Potato, '83 M195
Bake, Potato, '83 209
Bake, Potato-Broccoli-Cheese, '80 114
Bake, Potato-Tomato, '86 17
Baskets, Potato, '86 193
Basque-Style Potatoes, '79 46
Beans and Potatoes, Down-Home, '85 254
Beets, Potato-Stuffed, '83 234
Bisque, Spinach-Potato, '86 66
Bread, Old-Fashioned Potato, '86 57
Bread, Potato, '85 56
Breakfast, Farmer's, '81 44
Breakfast Potatoes, Mexican, '81 209
Browned Potatoes, Quick, '82 M172
Brunch for a Bunch, '88 57
Candy, Potato, '79 273
Caraway Potatoes, '85 85
Caraway Potatoes, Cheesy, '86 17
Casserole, Cheesy Ham-and-Potato, '84 326
Casserole, Cheesy Potato, '80 244; '83 53
Casserole, Cheesy Potato-Egg, '84 5
Casserole, Creamy Potato, '84 M113
Casserole, Easy Potato, '80 114
Casserole, Fluffy Potato, '80 268
Casserole, Ham-and-Potato, '83 M87
Casserole, Hash Brown Potato, '81 40
Casserole, Irish Potato, '81 263
Casserole, Italian, '80 81
Casserole, Mashed Potato, '85 296
Casserole, Mushroom-Potato, '84 5
Casserole, Potato, '87 190
Casserole, Potato Breakfast, '80 52
Casserole, Potato-Cheese, '79 101
Casserole, Potato-Eggplant, '87 166
Casserole, Processor Potato, '86 159
Casserole, Saucy Potato, '81 276
Casserole, Saucy Potato-Tomato, '79 46
Casserole, Sausage-Potato, '86 217
Caviar Potatoes, '84 80
Caviar Potatoes, Appetizer, '86 223
Charcoal Potatoes, '88 129
Cheese Potatoes, Creamy, '88 M146
Cheese Potatoes, Double-, '86 6
Cheese Potatoes, Two-, '80 114
Cheesy Potatoes, '82 211
Chicken Livers and Potatoes, '82 218

Chili, Savory Potato, '83 284
Chips, Homemade Potato, '82 25
Chive Potatoes, Cheesy, '79 46
Chives, Potatoes with, '81 M61
Christmas Potatoes, '88 252
Creamed Potatoes, '83 25
Cream-Wine Sauce, Potatoes in, '86 18
Creamy Potatoes with Ham Bits, '87 191
Creole Potatoes, '87 138
Croquettes, Parmesan Potato, '84 210
Croquettes, Potato, '87 116
Deviled Potatoes, Hot, '84 296; '85 196
Doughnuts, Chocolate-Glazed Potato, '85 6
Doughnuts, Old-Fashioned Potato, '84 56
Duchesse, Potatoes, '84 210
Dumplings, Venison Stew with
  Potato, '87 304
Fans, Parmesan Potato, '84 M240
Feta Cheese, Potatoes with, '84 295;
  '85 196
Fluffy Potatoes, '84 296; '85 196
French Fries, Herb, '82 211
Fried Potatoes, Almond-, '82 25
Fried Potatoes, Herb-, '82 25
Fried Potatoes, Oven-, '82 25
Fried Potatoes, Southern-, '82 25
Fried Potato Patties, '82 25
Fry, Okra-Potato, '81 159

Garlic Potatoes, '84 296; '85 196
Gourmet, Potatoes, '80 114
Greens and Potatoes, Mustard, '86 224
Grilled Herb Potatoes, '84 172
Gruyère Potatoes, '83 193
Hash Brown Cheese Bake, '82 50
Hash Brown Potatoes, '81 48
Hash Browns, Company, '79 268; '80 14
Hash Browns, Franks and, '80 166
Hash Brown Skillet Breakfast, '82 5
Herb Butter, Potatoes with, '81 276
Herb Potatoes, '88 134
Jalapeño Potatoes, '84 39
Latkes, '84 318
Lemon and Nutmeg Potatoes, '80 36
Lightbread, Potato, '80 225
Loaves, Potato, '86 162
Lorraine, Potatoes, '87 190
Mashed Potatoes, Jazzy, '87 192
Missy Potatoes, '85 259
Mustard Potatoes, '79 32
Nest, Peas in a Potato, '84 M239
Nests with Savory Shavings,
  Potato, '84 209
New Potatoes, Browned, '86 244
New Potatoes, Cheesy, '85 156
New Potatoes, Creamed Peas and, '79 102
New Potatoes, Green Beans with, '87 164
New Potatoes, Ham-Stuffed, '88 211
New Potatoes, Herbed, '81 102;
  '83 9, M148

New Potatoes, Lemon-Buttered, '84 149
New Potatoes, Lemony, '82 158
New Potatoes, Parsley, '79 122
New Potatoes, Seasoned, '87 M151
New Potatoes with Lemon Sauce, '86 130
New Potatoes with Parsley-Chive
   Sauce, '84 212
Olive Potatoes, '80 114
Omelet, Potato-Sprout, '79 128
Oven Potatoes, Crispy, '82 96
Pancake, Potato, '85 20
Pancakes, Moist Potato, '80 36
Pancakes, Potato, '79 115
Parmesan Potatoes, '82 270
Parmesan-Potato Fans, '88 M190
Parslied Potatoes, '86 18
Peppers, Potatoes with Sweet Red, '87 192
Pie, Meat-and-Potato, '84 23
Pie, Potato-Topped Turkey, '86 265
Potage, Subtle Potato, '80 78
Puffs, Potato, '80 36
Quiche, Crustless Potato, '83 49
Rolls, Feathery Light Potato, '81 305;
   '82 36
Rolls, Homemade Potato, '82 252
Rolls, Potato, '81 300
Rolls, Potato Yeast, '87 53
Rolls, Refrigerated Potato, '83 254
Rolls, Refrigerator Potato, '87 15
Rolls, Southern Potato, '86 299
Rolls, Super Potato, '85 145
Rolls, Supreme Potato, '82 130
Rosemary, Potatoes Anna with, '84 209
Roses, Potato, '81 246
Salads
   Any Day Potato Salad, '81 154
   Bacon-Topped Potato Salad, '85 59
   Bean Salad, Potato-, '82 301
   Broccoli-Potato Salad, Hot, '85 23
   Chunky Potato Salad, '81 M138
   Confetti Potato Salad, '80 5; '88 16
   Corned Beef-Potato Salad, '85 213
   Corned Beef Salad, Potato-, '81 36
   Cottage Cheese-Potato Salad,
      '79 147, 285
   Creamy Potato Salad, '80 178;
      '88 171
   Deluxe Potato Salad, '80 155
   Dill Potato Salad, '85 213
   Dill Potato Salad, Hot, '79 78
   Dutch Potato Salad, Hot, '87 176
   Fish-Potato Salad, Smoked, '84 233
   French-Style Potato Salad, '88 171
   Fruity Potato Salad, '85 214
   Garden Patch Potato Salad, '84 82
   German Potato Salad, '82 134, 239;
      '84 18
   German Potato Salad, Hot, '79 78
   German-Style Potato Salad, '83 23;
      '88 M194
   Grecian Potato Salad, '82 55
   Green Bean-Potato Salad, '83 80
   Ham-and-Egg Potato Salad, '86 84
   Ham and Potato Salad, '80 272
   Herbed Potato Salad, '87 171
   Hot Dutch Potato Salad, '86 297
   Hot Potato Salad, '79 78; '81 276;
      '86 10
   Hot Potato Salad Supreme, '79 78
   Layered Creamy Potato Salad, '81 23
   Mustard Potato Salad, '86 302

New Potato Salad, '84 120, 139
New Potato Salad,
   Asparagus-and-, '86 69
Olive-Potato Salad, '85 114
Parmesan Potato Salad, Hot, '79 78
Parslied Potato Salad, '85 240
Pepper Cups, Potato Salad in, '79 78
Peppers, Potato Salad 'n', '83 135
Pickle-Potato Salad, Sweet, '85 213
Pole Bean-Potato Salad, Hot, '79 74
Salmon-Potato Salad, '87 285
Saucy Potato Salad, '87 123
Savory Potato Salad, '80 30
Sour Cream Potato Salad, '79 104;
   '80 79
Sour Cream-Potato Salad, '84 149
Spring Salad, Mediterranean, '80 148
Sweet and Sour Potato Salad, '80 152
Tuna-Potato Salad, '84 289
Saucy Potatoes for Company, '82 202
Scalloped Potatoes, '82 300; '83 211
Scalloped Potatoes and Turnips, '85 235
Scalloped Potatoes, Cheesy, '83 82
Scalloped Potatoes, Mushroom, '87 191
Scalloped Potatoes, Party, '87 191
Scalloped Potatoes, Skillet, '79 46
Scalloped Potatoes, Special, '88 162
Scalloped Potatoes, Wayside, '79 283
Scalloped Potatoes with Pimiento, '81 75
Scallop, Pork Chops and Potato, '82 114
Seasoned Potatoes, '87 253
Shavings, Savory, '84 209
Shoestring Potato Tuna Bake, '82 211
Shrimp-Sauced Potatoes, '81 M61
Skillet Potatoes, Peppy, '86 110
Skins, Baked Potato, '86 81
Skins, Cheesy Potato, '82 78
Slims, Potato, '81 276
Snow-Capped Potatoes, '84 255
Soufflé Potatoes, '84 295; '85 196
Soup, Asparagus-Potato, '85 23
Soup, Celery-and-Potato, '84 279
Soup, Chilled Cucumber-Potato, '85 93
Soup, Cold Potato-Cucumber, '88 160
Soup, Cream of Potato, '80 M224; '82 21
Soup, Creamy Potato, '81 19, 98; '84 112
Soup, Golden Cream of Potato, '86 302
Soup, Holiday Potato, '79 236
Soup, Leek-and-Potato, '84 112
Soup, Potato, '82 278; '83 292
Soup, Potato-Bacon, '84 M38
Soup, Potato-Beet, '88 156
Soup, Potato-Carrot, '88 297
Soup, Sausage-Potato, '80 25
Soup, Special Potato, '82 3
Soup, Three-Potato, '86 16
Sour Cream Potatoes, '84 39
Special Potatoes, '83 169
Steak 'n Potatoes, Skillet, '81 18
Steamed Potatoes, Lemon-, '86 177
Stir-Fry, Potato-Snow Pea, '86 173
Stuffed
   Bacon-Stuffed Potatoes, '86 193
   Bacon-Stuffed Potatoes,
      Cheesy, '81 M61
   Bacon-Topped Blue Cheese
      Potatoes, '79 46
   Baked Potatoes, Stuffed, '83 322
   Baked Stuffed Potatoes, '84 38
   Béchamel Sauce, Stuffed Potatoes
      with, '84 M239

   Blue Cheese Stuffed Potatoes, '81 276
   Cheese Sauce, Stuffed Potatoes
      with, '87 192
   Chicken-Cheese Stuffed
      Potatoes, '86 55
   Chive-Stuffed Baked Potatoes, '79 52
   Chive-Stuffed Potatoes,
      Creamy, '80 268
   Crab-Stuffed Potatoes, Cheesy, '86 17
   Creamy Stuffed Baked
      Potatoes, '86 55
   Creamy Stuffed Potatoes, '79 211

   Fluffy Stuffed Potatoes, '86 223
   Franks and Potatoes, Stuffed, '81 202
   Ham Stuffed Potatoes, '79 210
   Herb Stuffed Potatoes, '79 211
   Jalapeño-Ham Stuffed
      Potatoes, '81 M61
   Lemon-Herb Stuffed Potatoes, '83 173
   Patchwork Potatoes, '86 54
   Roquefort, Potatoes, '79 211
   Savory Stuffed Potatoes, '81 101
   Shrimp Boats, '79 57
   Shrimp-Stuffed Potatoes,
      Creamy, '80 36
   South-of-the-Border Stuffed
      Potatoes, '86 54
   Tuna Stuffed Potatoes, '79 210
   Twice-Baked Potatoes, '83 227
   Vegetable-Topped Stuffed
      Potatoes, '85 235
   Yogurt-Stuffed Potatoes, '88 24
Summertime Potatoes, '86 M195
Turnips and Potatoes, '79 254
Turnips, Southern, '87 190
Vichyssoise, '86 181
Vinaigrette, Potato-Broccoli, '85 84
Wedges, Beer-Batter Potato, '83 211
Wedges, Lemon Potato, '88 21
Yeast, Potato, '87 53

Potatoes, Sweet
Apple Shells, Sweet Potatoes in, '85 206
Apple-Stuffed Sweet Potatoes, '88 207
Apricot Sweet Potatoes, '82 228
Bake, Southern Sweet Potato, '85 229
Bake, Sweet Potato, '80 287
Bake, Sweet Potato-Apple, '83 25; '86 282
Bake, Sweet Potato-Apricot, '85 206
Bake, Sweet Potato-Orange, '83 226
Balls, Sweet Potato, '86 312
Biscuits, Sweet Potato, '80 287; '84 140
Boats, Sweet Potato, '80 287
Bourbon Sweet Potatoes, '86 324; '87 280

Potatoes, Sweet (*continued*)

Broiled Sweet Potatoes, Coconut-, '84 231
Cake, Sweet Potato, '79 207
Cake, Sweet Potato Loaf, '81 224
Cake, Sweet Potato Pound, '83 85
Cake, Sweet Potato Surprise, '80 287
Candied Sweet Potatoes, '79 9, 251;
  '86 111; '88 207
Casserole, Pear-Sweet Potato, '86 280
Casserole, Sweet Potato, '79 289; '80 26;
  '85 256
Casserole, Sweet Potato-Banana, '86 276
Casserole, Sweet
  Potatoes-and-Berries, '84 231
Casserole, Sweet Potato-Rum, '84 231
Cheesecake, Sweet Potato, '80 287
Cheesecake, Yam, '81 224
Coconut-Orange Sweet Potatoes, '84 252
Croquettes, Sweet Potato, '81 223
Cups, Sunshine Sweet Potato, '82 195
Delight, Sweet Potato, '86 335; '87 83
Festive Sweet Potatoes, '80 244
Fried Sweet Potatoes, '83 226
Fried Sweet Potatoes, French-, '81 223
Fritters, Golden Sweet Potato, '79 9
Fritters, Sweet Potato, '88 44
Glazed Sweet Potatoes, '85 206
Glazed Sweet Potatoes, Apple-, '82 303
Glazed Sweet Potatoes, Apricot-, '81 295
Glazed Sweet Potatoes, Orange-, '81 223;
  '83 280
Glazed Sweet Potatoes, Tropical, '83 226
Gravy, Roast Duck with Sweet
  Potato-Eggplant, '83 90
Mashed Sweet Potatoes, '85 25
Muffins, Sweet Potato, '81 224; '85 6;
  '87 280
Muffins, Yam, '79 7
Orange-Baked Sweet Potatoes, '88 M294
Orange Cups, Sweet Potatoes in, '82 272
Orange Cups, Sweet
  Potato-Stuffed, '81 223
Orange Sweet Potatoes, '86 279
Pancakes, Sweet Potato, '87 280
Peaches, Sweet Potatoes and, '86 11
Pie, Louisiana Yam, '81 223
Pie, No-Crust Sweet Potato, '84 236
Pie, Old-Fashioned Sweet Potato, '79 9
Pie, Southern Sweet Potato
  Cream, '87 260
Pie, Sweet Potato, '79 207; '85 255, 275;
  '86 269
Pie, Sweet Potato Meringue, '81 126;
  '83 225
Pie, Sweet Potato-Orange, '88 207
Pie, Sweet Potato-Pecan, '83 90
Pie, Sweet Potato Pone, '80 288
Pudding, Sweet Potato, '79 244; '80 228;
  '86 52
Puffs, Peach Sweet Potato, '87 280
Puffs, Sweet Potato, '87 253
Puff, Sweet Potato, '85 235
Raspberry Sweet Potatoes, '87 280
Roll, Sweet Potato Log, '82 227
Salad, Fresh Sweet Potato, '86 226
Salad, Hawaiian Ham-Sweet Potato, '82 232
Sherry and Walnuts, Sweet Potatoes
  with, '86 286
Soufflé, Sweet Potato, '82 286; '86 121
Soup, Sweet Potato, '88 250

Stuffed Baked Sweet Potatoes, '79 207;
  '84 231
Stuffed Sweet Potatoes, '86 224
Stuffed Sweet Potatoes, Bacon-, '86 224
Stuffed Sweet Potatoes, Coconut-, '82 204
Stuffed Sweet Potatoes, Fluffy, '79 9
Stuffed with Apples, Sweet
  Potatoes, '82 228
Surprise, Holiday Sweet Potato, '84 254
Surprise, Sweet Potato, '81 267
Waffles, Sweet Potato, '88 208
Yam Rolls, Golden, '86 299
Yams, Cornwallis, '79 276

Pralines

Bananas, Praline, '84 313
Butterscotch Pralines, '81 253
Cake, Praline, '81 162
Cake, Praline Ice Cream, '80 84
Cake, Praline Pound, '82 88
Cheesecake, Praline, '83 270
Clusters, Dark Praline, '86 313
Coffee, Praline-Flavored, '87 69
Coffee Pralines, Plantation, '86 241
Compote, Warm Praline Fruit, '85 260
Cookies, Praline Shortbread, '88 242
Creamy Pralines, '80 198
Dark Pralines, '83 52
Delights, Spicy Praline, '84 299
Glaze, Praline, '82 196
Ham, Praline, '85 302
Ice Cream, Pralines and Cream, '82 184;
  '83 159
Maple-Pecan Pralines, '83 222
New Orleans-Style Pralines, '86 335
Pecan Pralines, Original, '81 11
Pie, Chocolate-Praline, '86 259
Pie, Pumpkin Praline, '80 244
Pralines, '79 272; '86 M288
Sauce, Bourbon Praline, '81 170
Sauce, Chocolate-Praline, '85 M295
Sauce, Peach-Praline, '85 161
Sauce, Praline, '83 25; '84 143
Sauce, Praline Ice Cream, '85 189
Sauce, Southern Praline Ice
  Cream, '86 M227
Southern Pralines, '79 M263
Texas-Size Pralines, '79 186
Toast, Orange Praline, '79 36
Torte, Chocolate Praline, '84 165

Pretzels

Brownies, Saucepan Pretzel, '85 171
Chocolate-Covered Pretzels, '82 295
Dressing, Pretzel, '86 280
Herb Pretzels with Lower Sodium
  Horseradish Mustard, '86 325
Homemade Pretzels, '84 159
Popcorn, Pretzel, '84 30
Soft Pretzels, '83 18
Soft Pretzels, Chewy, '87 159

Prunes

Bavarian, Prune, '86 223
Bread, Prune-Nut, '87 255
Cake and Sauce, Prune, '85 118
Cake, Prune, '85 223
Cake, Spicy Prune, '79 136
Muffins, Miniature Prune, '85 223
Muffins, Wheat Germ-Prune, '81 106
Pork Chops Stuffed with Prunes, '84 7
Pork Loin Roast, Prune-Stuffed, '80 29
Raspberry Prunes, '82 124
Spiced Prunes, Orange-, '85 224
Stuffed Prunes, '85 47
Tarts, Brandied Prune, '85 223

Puddings. *See also* Custards.

Apple-Nut Pudding with Hot Rum
  Sauce, '79 86
Applesauce-Graham Cracker
  Pudding, '81 34
Baked Christmas Pudding with Brandy
  Sauce, '88 279
Banana-Mallow Pudding, '86 139
Banana Pudding, '82 53; '84 94; '85 255;
  '88 16, 32
Banana Pudding, Almost, '88 174
Banana Pudding, Basic, '81 59
Banana Pudding, Delicious, '80 9
Banana Pudding, Surprise, '86 7
Biscuit Pudding, '79 86
Bread Pudding, Amish, '80 8
Bread Pudding, Apple-Raisin, '88 175
Bread Pudding, Apricot, '85 24
Bread Pudding, Blueberry, '88 154
Bread Pudding, Cheesy, '83 68
Bread Pudding, Chocolate, '80 8
Bread Pudding, French, '85 231
Bread Pudding, Old-Fashioned, '83 213;
  '88 175
Bread Pudding, Old-Fashioned
  Lemon, '88 95
Bread Pudding, Peachy, '88 175
Bread Pudding with Rum Sauce,
  Old-Fashioned, '88 32
Bread Pudding with Whiskey Sauce, '80 58
Brownie Pudding, '79 265; '80 295
Brown Sugar-Pecan Pudding, '86 M165
Cake, Carrot Pudding, '83 24
Cake, Lemon Pudding, '83 106
Cake Pudding, Chocolate, '81 99
Cake Pudding, Hot Fudge Sundae, '88 167
Cake Pudding, Wine, '79 230
Cheese Pudding, Baked, '86 78
Chocolate-Almond Pudding, '82 M142;
  '88 24
Chocolate Pudding, Creamy, '83 106
Chocolate-Rum Dessert, '81 247
Christmas Pudding, '79 230
Christmas Pudding, Flaming, '85 312
Corn-Cheese Pudding, '80 244
Corn Pudding, '79 276; '81 128; '86 192
Corn Pudding, Baked, '83 314
Corn Pudding, Creamy, '81 267
Corn Pudding, Easy, '83 280
Corn Pudding, Fresh, '80 157, 165
Cranberry Pudding, '84 306
Frozen Ozark Pudding, '88 127
Fruit Pudding Compote, Fresh, '86 151
Fudge Pudding, Hot, '81 208
Hansel Pudding, '80 9
Lemon Fluff Pudding, '85 304
Lemon Pudding, '79 86; '81 99

Lemon Pudding, Layered, '82 128
Mandarin-Almond Pudding, '85 M12
Orange Custard Pudding, '88 174
Orange Pudding, '81 85; '82 111; '83 153
Orange-Tapioca Crème, '82 M283
Peanut Butter Pudding, '85 95; '88 32
Persimmon Pudding, '79 206
Pineapple Pudding, '80 102
Plum Pudding, '79 281
Plum Pudding, Flamed, '84 276
Plum Pudding-Gelatin Mold, '86 300; '87 178
Plum Pudding, Light, '86 318
Plum Pudding, Old-Fashioned, '80 264
Potato Pudding, Sweet, '79 244; '80 228; '86 52
Pumpkin Pudding, Baked, '80 244
Raisin-Pumpkin Pudding, '84 315
Raisin-Rice Pudding, '87 46
Rice Pudding, Amaretto, '86 334
Rice Pudding, Brown, '85 77

Rice Pudding, Creamy, '81 51, 205
Rice Pudding, Fruited, '81 205; '86 95
Rice Pudding, Fudgy, '81 205
Rice Pudding, Old-Fashioned, '85 147
Rice Pudding, Velvety, '81 205
Rum Pudding with Raspberry Sauce, '82 288
Snowflake Pudding, '85 30
Snow White Pudding, '85 77
Squash Pudding, '82 277; '83 15
Steamed Date Pudding, '79 86
Steamed Holiday Pudding, '84 275
Steamed Mincemeat Pudding, '80 264
Tipsy Pudding, Parson's, '80 156
Vanilla Pudding, '88 32
Vanilla Pudding, Creamy, '83 227
Woodford Pudding, '79 86
Yorkshire Pudding, '80 252

Pumpkin
Baked Pumpkin, '82 217
Bars, Pumpkin, '80 40
Bars, Pumpkin Nut, '82 217
Bisque, Spicy Pumpkin, '86 67
Bread, Moist Pumpkin, '80 245
Bread, Orange-Pumpkin, '87 300
Bread, Pumpkin, '81 8
Bread, Pumpkin-Coconut, '87 255
Bread, Pumpkin-Nut, '83 294
Bread, Pumpkin-Pecan, '87 221
Bread with Cream Cheese and Preserves, Pumpkin, '84 264
Cake Bars, Pumpkin, '80 245
Cake, Pumpkin, '81 272
Cake, Pumpkin Date, '79 251
Cake, Pumpkin Kahlúa, '86 292
Cake, Pumpkin Layer, '80 245
Cake Squares, Orange-Pumpkin, '83 242
Calabaza Guisada con Puerco (Pumpkin Cooked with Pork), '80 193
Cheesecake, Pumpkin, '80 254; '85 280
Chiffon, Pumpkin, '82 216; '86 283; '88 260
Cooked Fresh Pumpkin, '88 M230
Cookies, Frosted Pumpkin-Walnut, '82 217
Cookies, Jack-O'-Lantern, '87 214
Cookies, Pumpkin Drop, '79 206
Cupcakes, Pumpkin, '85 121
Custard, Pumpkin, '88 279
Delight, Pumpkin-Orange, '86 321
Dessert, Frozen Pumpkin, '88 167
Dessert, Pumpkin Chiffon, '88 128
Empanadas, Pumpkin, '82 223
Flan, Pumpkin, '82 217
Loaf, Harvest Pumpkin, '85 232
Loaf, Pumpkin-Oatmeal, '81 49
Mold, Pumpkin, '82 311
Muffins, Nutty Pumpkin, '86 291
Muffins, Pumpkin, '79 206, 275; '81 272
Pancakes, Pumpkin, '80 228
Pie, Autumn Pumpkin, '87 213
Pie, Bourbon-Pecan Pumpkin, '87 264
Pie, Festive Pumpkin, '81 M269
Pie, Fluffy Pumpkin, '80 283
Pie in Spiced Nut Crust, Pumpkin, '87 295
Pie, Nutty Pumpkin, '82 67
Pie, Pumpkin Chiffon, '84 312
Pie, Pumpkin Ice Cream, '81 272
Pie, Pumpkin-Ice Cream, '87 243
Pie, Pumpkin-Pecan, '85 233, 282
Pie, Pumpkin Praline, '80 244
Pie, Quick Pumpkin, '88 M230
Pie, Rich Pumpkin, '86 292
Pie, Sour Cream-Pumpkin, '84 263
Pies, Spicy Pumpkin, '84 322
Pie Supreme, Pumpkin, '82 217
Pie, Traditional Pumpkin, '85 256
Pudding, Baked Pumpkin, '80 244
Pudding, Raisin-Pumpkin, '84 315
Roll, Pumpkin, '79 206
Rolls, Pumpkin, '87 254
Sauce, Pumpkin Seed, '88 246
Seeds, Toasted Pumpkin, '88 M230
Soup, Pumpkin, '79 48
Soup, Pumpkin-Tomato, '86 291
Tarts, No-Bake Pumpkin, '86 291
Waffles, Pumpkin-Nut, '86 96

Q

Quail
Baked Quail with Mushrooms, '81 259
Breasts, Southern Quail, '85 270
Currant Jelly Sauce, Quail with, '86 94
Fried Quail, '82 45
Fried Quail, Seasoned, '88 220
Fried Quail with Onion Gravy, '82 214
Gravy, Georgia Quail with, '87 240
Grilled Breakfast Quail, '88 220
Magnificent, Quail, '82 214
Marinated Quail, '80 221
Mushrooms, Quail with, '85 138
Orange Sauce in Potato Baskets, Quail with, '86 193
Plum Sauce, Quail with Red, '80 48
Superb, Quail, '81 303

Quiches
Asparagus-Tomato Quiche, '88 198
Bacon-Cheese Quiches, Miniature, '83 93
Bacon Quiche, '85 60
Benedict Quiche, '80 M107
Blue Cheese Quiche, '84 52
Broccoli Quiche, Easy, '82 34
Broccoli Quiche, Italian, '85 45
Broccoli-Rice Quiche, '81 228
Cauliflower Quiche, '83 86
Cheddar-Leek Quiche, '88 198
Cheese Pie, Mexican, '83 69
Cheese Quiches, Miniature, '80 150
Cheese-Vegetable Quiche, '81 228
Chicken Divan Quiche, '88 M125
Chile Pepper Quiche, '82 224
Chile Quiche, Green, '83 31
Clam Quiche, '83 215
Crab Quiche, '82 M122, 243
Crab Quiche, Almond-Topped, '79 127
Crab Quiche, Quick, '84 96
Crab Quiche, Sherried, '83 180
Crab Quiche, Simple, '85 207
Eggless Quiche, '87 220
Ham-and-Mushroom Quiche, '81 11
Ham-and-Vegetable Quiche, '84 326
Ham-Cheese Quiche, '79 26
Ham Quiche, '80 110
Ham Quiche, Cheesy, '79 127
Ham Quiche, Country, '87 287
Ham Quiche, Crustless, '84 235
Jalapeño-Corn Quiche, '85 122
Jalapeño Quiche, Cheesy, '84 31
Lorraine, Classic Quiche, '81 131
Lorraine, Mushroom-Quiche, '86 242
Lorraine, Peppery Quiche, '81 228
Lorraine, Perfect Quiche, '79 127
Lorraine, Quiche, '79 40; '80 M108
Mushroom Quiche, '80 222; '81 244
Noël, Quiche, '82 310
Olive Quiche Appetizers, '86 159
Onion Quiche, '83 121
Onion Quiche, Cheesy Green, '83 194; '84 42
Pastry, Microwaved Quiche, '81 M74; '82 M123
Pastry, Quiche, '80 M107
Pizza Quiche, '86 53
Potato Quiche, Crustless, '83 49
Salmon Quiche, '82 87; '87 38
Sausage-Apple Quiche, Crustless, '87 70
Sausage-Cheddar Quiche, '79 26
Sausage Quiche, Easy, '79 261
Sausage Quiche, Italian, '81 200
Sausage Quiche, Spicy, '80 M108
Shrimp Miniquiches, '87 146
Shrimp Quiche, '83 50
Spinach-Mushroom Quiche, '81 M74
Spinach Quiche, '81 44; '85 49
Spinach Quiche, Cheesy, '81 228
Spinach Quiche, Crustless, '84 235
Spinach Quiche, Greek, '86 10
Spinach Quichelets, '87 67
Spinach Quiches, Individual, '86 38
Spinach Quiches, Miniature, '82 38
Springtime Quiche, '83 122
Squares, Cheesy Hot Quiche, '79 124

Quiches (continued)

Squares, Quiche, **'84** 222
Squash-and-Green Chile Quiche, **'88** 143
Swiss-Zucchini Quiche, **'82** 49
Tarragon Cocktail Quiches, **'84** 127
Tasty Quiche, **'82** 264
Vegetable Quiche, **'87** M219
Zucchini Frittata, **'86** 103
Zucchini-Mushroom Quiche, **'79** 127
Zucchini Pie, Italian-Style, **'83** 43
Zucchini Quiche, Cheesy, **'83** 312
Zucchini-Sausage Quiche, **'83** 122

R

Raisins

Bread, Banana-Nut-Raisin, **'81** 59
Bread, Butternut-Raisin, **'79** 25
Bread, Caraway-Raisin Oat, **'86** 44
Bread, Cinnamon Raisin, **'80** 22
Bread, Curried Chicken Salad on
  Raisin, **'85** 96
Bread, Homemade Raisin, **'87** 300
Bread, Oatmeal Raisin, **'81** 14
Bread, Oatmeal-Raisin, **'83** 59
Bread, Raisin-Cranberry, **'81** 305; **'82** 36
Bread, Salt-Free Raisin Batter, **'86** 33
Buns, Rum-Raisin, **'80** 22
Butter, Raisin, **'81** 272
Cake, Spicy Raisin Coffee, **'88** 63
Cake, Spicy Raisin Layer, **'79** 230
Candy, Mixed Raisin, **'84** 111
Carrots, Orange-Raisin, **'80** 24
Cookies, Alltime Favorite Raisin, **'80** 24
Cookies, Frosted Oatmeal-Raisin, **'79** 290
Cookies, Nugget, **'79** 291
Cookies, Oatmeal-Raisin, **'87** 221
Cookies, Persimmon-Raisin, **'85** 232
Gingersnaps, Raisin, **'85** 324
Gravy, Currant, **'83** 276
Ham, Raisin, **'80** 124
Mix, Raisin-Nut Party, **'83** 60
Muffins, Breakfast Raisin, **'84** 59
Muffins, Carrot-and-Raisin, **'87** 24
Muffins, Raisin English, **'80** 75
Muffins, Raisin-Pecan Ginger, **'88** 9
Muffins, Whole Wheat Raisin, **'85** 207
Pie, Brandy Raisin-Apple, **'83** 192
Pie, Cranberry-Raisin, **'80** 283; **'85** 316
Pie, Peanut-Raisin, **'79** 85
Pie, Raisin, **'83** 220
Pie, Raisin-Pecan, **'87** 213
Pie, Rhubarb-Raisin, **'79** 112
Pie, Spiced Raisin, **'84** 148
Pudding, Apple-Raisin Bread, **'88** 175
Pudding, Raisin-Pumpkin, **'84** 315
Pudding, Raisin-Rice, **'87** 46
Pull-Aparts, Raisin Cinnamon, **'82** 205;
  '83 32
Rice with Curry, Raisin, **'85** 83

Rolls, Raisin Cinnamon, **'81** 107
Rollups, Sweet Raisin, **'86** 290
Salad, Carrot-Raisin, **'83** 117; **'84** 174;
  '87 10
Salad, Curried Apple-Raisin, **'80** 24
Sandwiches, Peanut-Cheese-Raisin, **'88** 140
Sauce, Baked Ham with
  Cranberry-Raisin, **'88** 244
Sauce, Caramel-Raisin, **'88** 127
Sauce, Ham with Raisin, **'82** M76
Sauce, Raisin, **'83** 59, 215; **'84** 91, 275;
  '87 127
Sauce, Raisin-Pineapple, **'82** 177
Sauce, Rum-Raisin, **'84** 7
Scones, Currant, **'84** 117
Scones, Lemon-Raisin, **'87** 69
Shake, Amazin' Raisin, **'86** 195
Spread, Peachy-Raisin, **'86** 326
Teacakes, Currant, **'80** 88

Raspberries

Appetizer, Orange-Berry, **'85** 81
Bars, Raspberry, **'82** 209; **'84** 212
Cake, Raspberry Coffee, **'83** 112
Chocolate Cups, Miniature, **'87** 132
Cobbler, Berry-Cherry, **'83** 270
Compote, Berry, **'81** 275
Compote, Berry-Peach, **'82** 133
Crêpes, Raspberry, **'87** 126
Crêpes Suzette, Raspberry, **'84** 84
Custard with Raspberries, Almond
  Creme, **'88** 174
Custard with Raspberries,
  Amaretto, **'86** 152
Dessert, Frozen Raspberry, **'84** 192
Dessert, Raspberry-Jellyroll, **'85** 95
Dessert, Raspberry Sauce, **'80** 147
Dream, Raspberry, **'83** 108
Dressing, Raspberry, **'87** 153
Granita, Raspberry Liqueur, **'88** 117
Ice Cream, Fresh Raspberry, **'86** 152
Ice Cream, Raspberry, **'80** 176
Jam, Raspberry Freezer, **'84** M181
Kir, Raspberry, **'86** 183
Mold, Raspberry Holiday, **'84** 253
Mounds, Raspberry Fruit, **'79** 35
Mousse, Raspberry, **'81** 34
Pie, Cran-Raspberry, **'87** 244
Potatoes, Raspberry Sweet, **'87** 280
Prunes, Raspberry, **'82** 124
Punch, Raspberry-Rosé, **'87** 242
Punch, Raspberry Sparkle, **'84** 57
Puree, Fruit Compote with
  Raspberry, **'88** 81
Salad, Frozen Raspberry, **'79** 287; **'80** 35
Salad, Raspberry, **'86** 286
Salad, Raspberry Ribbon, **'87** 236
Sauce, Crimson Raspberry, **'79** 91; **'85** 30
Sauce, Duck Breasts with
  Raspberry, **'87** 240
Sauce Flambé, Raspberry, **'84** 142
Sauce, Fresh Berries with Raspberry
  Custard, **'88** 163
Sauce, Melba, **'87** 77
Sauce, Peach-Berry, **'87** M165
Sauce, Poached Pears with
  Raspberry, **'87** 69; **'88** 223
Sauce, Raspberry, **'82** 289; **'83** 108;
  '84 73, 213; **'87** 69, 117, 183; **'88** 267
Sauce, Raspberry-Amaretto, **'88** 130
Sauce, Raspberry-Orange, **'88** 22
Sherbet, Raspberry, **'83** 162

Soufflé, Raspberry, **'86** 188
Soufflé, Raspberry-Topped, **'85** 317
Soup, Chilled Raspberry, **'81** 130
Strudel, Raspberry-Nut, **'83** 304
Topping, Raspberry, **'85** 317
Topping, Raspberry-Peach, **'87** 126

Trifle, Raspberry, **'88** 259
Vinegar, Raspberry-Lemon, **'87** 134

Relishes. *See* Pickles and Relishes.

Rhubarb

Ambrosia, Rhubarb, **'88** 93
Bavarian, Rhubarb-Strawberry, **'86** 140
Chutney, Rhubarb, **'87** 245
Cobbler, Rosy Strawberry-Rhubarb, **'79** 154
Cobbler, Strawberry-Rhubarb, **'88** 93
Mousse, Rhubarb, **'88** 93
Pie, Rhubarb-Peach, **'86** 140
Pie, Rhubarb-Raisin, **'79** 112
Salad, Rhubarb Congealed, **'86** 140
Sauce, Chilled Rhubarb, **'88** 94
Sauce, Pineapple-Rhubarb, **'88** 94
Squares, Rosy Rhubarb, **'79** 111
Whip, Rhubarb, **'79** 112

Rice

Almond Rice, **'81** 195; **'85** M112
Apple-Cinnamon Rice, **'86** 249
au Gratin, Rice, **'83** 129
au Gratin Supreme, Rice, **'86** 78
Bacon-Chive Rice, **'83** 129
Bake, Creole Sausage-and-Rice, **'88** 58
Bake, Egg and Rice, **'83** 119
Bake, Ham-Rice-Tomato, **'87** 78
Balls, Rice, **'81** 51
Basic Long-Grain Rice, **'83** M285
Basic Molding Rice, **'86** 221
Basic Quick-Cooking Rice, **'83** M285
Basic Rice, **'79** 64
Beans and Rice, Black, **'80** 222
Beans and Rice, Cajun Red, **'83** 26
Beans and Rice, Creole, **'80** 223
Beans and Rice, Red, **'80** 58; **'83** 89;
  '84 37; **'87** 45
Beans and Rice, South Texas, **'85** 252
Beans, and Rice, Texas Sausage, **'84** 296
Beef and Rice, Spiced, **'84** 285
Beef and Rice, Spicy, **'83** 231
Beef Rollups with Rice, Royal, **'79** 105
Beef Tips on Rice, **'85** 87
Black-Eyed Peas with Rice, **'83** 12
Black-Eyes and Rice, Creole, **'85** 6
Boudin, Old-Fashioned, **'85** 250
Braised Rice and Peas, **'79** 101
Broccoli with Rice, Holiday, **'87** 252
Brown Rice, **'82** 275

Brown Rice, Calico, '86 33
Brown Rice, Cornish Hens with, '82 275
Brown Rice Parmesan, '84 196
Brown Rice, Roast Chicken and, '83 268
Brown Rice, Spanish, '84 196
Brussels Sprouts and Rice, '79 288;
  '80 26
Cabbage Rolls, Stuffed, '88 18
Cacciatore, Quick Chicken-and-Rice, '88 38
Calico Rice, '85 83
Casserole, Broccoli-Rice, '81 101
Casserole, Brown Rice, '87 118
Casserole, Chicken and Rice, '80 260
Casserole, Chicken-Rice, '86 52
Casserole, Chili-Rice, '79 54
Casserole, Colorful Rice, '82 199
Casserole, Ham-and-Rice, '84 75
Casserole, Jalapeño Rice, '81 66
Casserole, Mexican Rice, '83 31
Casserole, Oriental Sausage and
  Rice, '82 M123
Casserole, Rice, '87 45
Casserole, Rice-and-Chicken, '87 154
Casserole, Sausage-Rice, '82 50; '83 75
Casserole, Shrimp and Rice, '79 228
Casserole, Spanish Rice, '79 192
Chantilly, Rice, '86 82
Chicken and Rice, Spicy, '88 200
Chicken-and-Rice Valencia, '85 113
Chicken-Flavored Rice, '84 M144
Chicken Livers and Rice Dish, '82 218
Chicken Livers with Rice, '80 200; '81 58;
  '84 292
Chicken over Rice, Cajun, '88 102
Chicken, Rice-Stuffed, '81 4
Chicken, Rice-Stuffed Roasted, '88 38
Chicken with Rice, Sherry, '81 97
Chiles, Rice and Green, '83 152
Chili-Cheesy Rice, '79 43
Chili with Rice, '82 11
Consommé Rice, '80 246
Cornish Hens, Rice-Stuffed, '82 302
Cream with Mandarin Oranges,
  Rice, '85 317
Cumin Rice, '85 83
Curried Beef and Rice, '88 164
Curried Rice and Shrimp, '83 231
Curried Rice, Quick, '86 81
Curried Rice with Almonds, '83 M285
Curried Rice with Pineapple, '79 142
Curry-Spiced Rice, '86 M226
Dinner, Mexican Beef-and-Rice, '88 199
Dirty Rice, '86 142
Dressing, Chicken and Rice, '79 288
Dressing, Chicken with
  Pecan-Rice, '85 M57
Dressing, Mexican Rice, '87 253
Dressing, Roast Turkey with
  Rice, '82 286
Fiesta Rice, '84 76
French Rice, '83 24
Fried Rice, '83 129; '84 197; '88 67
Fried Rice, Bacon, '80 115
Fried Rice, Easy, '84 76
Fried Rice, Egg, '79 252; '80 19
Fried Rice for Two, '81 31
Fried Rice Special, '80 56
Fried Rice, Turkey, '83 282
Fried Rice with Sausage, '83 12
Fruited Rice, Far East, '81 175
Ginger Rice, Fluffy, '83 102

Glorified Rice, '83 129
Golden Rice, '79 270
Green Rice Bake, '79 43
Green Rice, Celebrity, '81 207
Ham-Rice Toss, '82 40
Ham Rolls, Rice-Stuffed, '83 190
Ham with Rice, Curried, '80 111
Herbed Rice, '83 M285
Honey Rice, '85 83
Hopping John, Skillet, '79 10
Indian Rice, '79 64
Jalapeño Hot Rice, '80 126
Jalapeño Rice, '79 43
Lamb Curry with Rice, '80 83; '81 10
Lentil-and-Rice Supper, '84 202
Lime-Flavored Rice, '84 175
Lyonnaise, Rice, '83 151
Mango-Beef and Rice, '88 138
Meatballs Paprikash with Rice, '85 31
Medley, Rice, '79 270
Mélange, Rice, '87 240
Mexican Rice, '83 85; '85 147

Mexican Rice, Spicy, '88 149
Mix, Crunchy Rice, '85 327
Mix, Fruited Curry-Rice, '86 326
Mold, Chile-Rice, '86 221
Mold, Curried Rice, '85 36
Mold, Saffron Rice, '86 221
Noodles, Shredded Beef over Rice, '85 74
Nutted Rice, '85 269
Orange Rice, '79 43; '81 175; '82 200
Oriental Rice, '85 M12, 146
Oven Rice, '83 89
Paella, Chicken-Pork-Shrimp, '82 245
Paella, Garden, '82 245
Paella, Seafood, '82 245
Paella, Spanish, '85 26
Paella Valenciana, '82 246
Pancakes, Rice, '85 147
Parsleyed Rice, '83 M58
Parsley Rice, '84 197; '85 95
Parslied Rice, '87 167, 243
Parslied Rice, Creamy, '88 255
Peas and Rice, '88 97
Peas and Rice, Holiday, '86 328
Peas, Cajun, '88 3
Peas, Rice with Green, '87 45
Pecan Rice, '85 53
Peppered Rice, '82 4
Peppers, Beef-Stuffed, '85 146
Peppers, Rice-Stuffed, '80 65
Pepper Steak and Rice, '81 17
Peppers with Rice and Ham,
  Stuffed, '82 131

Pie, Tuna-Rice, '84 123
Pilaf, Browned Rice, '87 305
Pilaf, Chicken, '82 246
Pilaf, Fruit-and-Vegetable Rice, '84 196
Pilaf, Fruited Pork, '82 246
Pilaf Mold, Ham, '86 222
Pilaf, Near-Eastern, '82 246
Pilaf, Okra, '80 185; '82 126
Pilaf, Rice, '86 82; '87 229; '88 42
Pilaf, Rice-and-Lentil, '88 17
Pilaf, Savory, '83 93
Pilaf, Shrimp, '82 246
Pilaf, Turkey-Asparagus, '88 200
Pilaf, Turkey-Rice, '86 284
Pilaf, Turkish, '79 184
Pork Chops, Rice-Stuffed, '83 102
Pudding, Amaretto Rice, '86 334
Pudding, Brown Rice, '85 77
Pudding, Creamy Rice, '81 51, 205
Pudding, Fruited Rice, '81 205; '86 95
Pudding, Fudgy Rice, '81 205
Pudding, Old-Fashioned Rice, '85 147
Pudding, Raisin-Rice, '87 46
Pudding, Velvety Rice, '81 205
Quiche, Broccoli-Rice, '81 228
Raisin Rice with Curry, '85 83
Red Rice, Savannah, '80 119
Ring, Oregano Rice, '86 222
Ring, Rice-Carrot, '79 246
Ring, Shrimp Creole in a Rice, '86 222
Ring with Beets, Rice, '79 225
Risotto alla Milanese, '85 228
Rolls, Crunchy Cabbage-Rice, '85 32
Saffron Rice, '79 43
Saffron Rice Mold, '86 221
Salads
  Artichoke Hearts, Rice Salad
    with, '80 232
  Artichoke-Rice Salad, '80 178; '81 41;
    '85 81
  Bacon, Rice Salad with, '79 52
  Bean-and-Rice Salad,
    Marinated, '87 152
  Bean Salad, Rice-and-, '85 22
  Brown Rice-and-Vegetable
    Salad, '84 202
  Chicken-and-Rice Salad, Hot, '83 22
  Chicken-Rice Salad, '81 203
  Chicken-Rice Salad, Nutty, '83 157
  Chutneyed Rice Salad, '88 100
  Colorful Rice Salad, '81 253
  Confetti Rice Salad, '80 232
  Crunchy Rice Salad, '82 302
  Curried Rice Salad, '80 84;
    '85 147, 220
  Egg-Rice Salad, '84 18; '86 169
  Gazpacho-Rice Salad, Molded, '86 221
  Ham-and-Rice Salad, Mandarin, '87 145
  Hearty Rice Salad, '82 233
  Mandarin Rice Salad, '88 271
  Mushrooms, Rice Salad with
    Fresh, '80 231
  Paella Salad, '86 207
  Pea Salad, Rice-, '85 163
  Red Rice Salad, Charleston, '79 146
  Rice Salad, '79 74; '81 51
  Salmon-Rice Salad, '84 289
  Shrimp-and-Orange Rice Salad,
    Zesty, '87 155
  Shrimp and Rice Salad, '80 231;
    '82 207

Rice, Salads *(continued)*

  Shrimp-Rice Salad, Baked, **'83** 22
  Shrimp-Rice Salad, Tangy, **'84** 66
  Shrimp Salad, Rice-, **'79** 270
  Shrimp Salad, Rice-and-, **'83** 82
  Tuna-Rice Salad, **'87** 202
  Vegetable-Rice Salad, **'80** 148;
    '83 198; **'85** 87
  Vegetable Salad, Rice-and-, **'86** 42
  Zesty Rice Salad, **'81** 23
Sausage and Rice, Italian, **'86** 53
Seasoned Onion Rice, **'82** 166
Seasoned Rice, **'79** 244; **'83** 212
Shell, Rice-Cheese, **'82** 49
Shrimp and Sausage Rice, **'79** 64
Soufflé, Rice-Cheese, **'79** 270
Soup, Chicken-and-Rice, **'88** 236
Soup, Tomato-and-Rice, **'85** 24
Spanish Rice, **'81** 51; **'83** 209
Spanish Rice, Pork Chops and, **'83** 103;
  '85 293
Spanish Rice with Tofu, **'88** 26
Spanish-Style Rice, **'83** 152
Spicy Rice, **'83** 215; **'85** 256
Spinach Rice, **'85** 146
Squares, Creamed Chicken over Confetti
  Rice, **'81** 282; **'82** 31
Stew, Lentil-Rice, **'82** 232
Strata, Cheese-Rice, **'81** 176
Stuffing, Rice-and-Onion, **'88** 246
Timbales, Spinach-Rice, **'88** 271
Vegetables, Rice with, **'79** 64; **'85** 83
Waldorf Rice, **'84** 281
Wild Rice
  Almond Wild Rice, **'86** 50
  Belvedere, Wild Rice, **'86** 82
  Casserole, Chicken-Wild Rice, **'84** 241;
    '85 65
  Casserole, Duck and Wild
    Rice, **'79** 224
  Casserole, Oyster-and-Wild
    Rice, **'83** 34; **'84** 44
  Casserole, Sausage and Wild
    Rice, **'83** 196
  Casserole, Sausage-Wild Rice, **'84** 250
  Casserole, Veal and Wild Rice, **'79** 180
  Casserole, Wild Rice, **'82** 199
  Casserole, Wild Rice-Oyster, **'86** 256
  Chicken and Wild Rice, **'79** 248
  Chicken Rollups, **'88** 38
  Chicken, Wild Rice-Stuffed, **'79** 219
  Chicken-Wild Rice Supreme, **'79** 77
  Chicken with Wild Rice,
    Elegant, **'80** M76
  Cranberry-Pear Wild Rice, **'83** 279
  Creole, Wild Rice-and-Shrimp, **'84** 292
  Eggs with Wild Rice,
    Scrambled, **'80** 42
  Mushrooms, Wild Rice and, **'83** 278
  Popped Wild Rice, **'85** 65
  Pork Loin Stuffed with Wild
    Rice, **'84** 35
  Ring, Creamed Mushrooms in Wild
    Rice, **'80** 270
  Ring, Wild Rice, **'83** 253
  Salad, Crab and Wild Rice, **'79** 116
  Salad, Crab-Wild Rice, **'86** 207
  Salad, Springtime Wild Rice, **'88** 100
  Salad, Wild Rice, **'85** 65
  Salad, Wild Rice-Chicken, **'83** 146

Sausage and Wild Rice, **'85** 65
Sausage, Wild Rice and, **'86** 268
Stuffing, Cornish Hens with Wild
  Rice, **'79** 222; **'80** 64; **'82** 136
Yellow Rice, Black Beans with, **'82** 2
Yellow Rice with Water Chestnuts, **'85** 24

Rolls and Buns. *See also* Breads.
  Apple Pinwheel, Quick, **'85** 42
  Big-Batch Rolls, **'88** 289
  Blueberry Buns, Deluxe, **'81** 164
  Blueberry Pinwheels, **'82** 205
  Bolillos, **'88** 247
  Bran Rolls, **'85** 145
  Bran Yeast Rolls, **'87** 116
  Butter-and-Herb Rolls, **'86** 306
  Buttered Rum-Nut Rolls, **'86** 291
  Butterhorns, **'84** 267
  Buttermilk Rolls, Quick, **'83** 155
  Caramel Breakfast Rolls, **'79** 193
  Caramel-Nut Rolls, **'86** 312
  Caraway Puffs, **'82** 174
  Cheese Buns, Hurry-Up, **'81** 300
  Cheese Crescents, **'82** 18
  Cherry-Almond Rolls, **'84** M198
  Chocolate-Cinnamon Buns, **'85** 5
  Chocolate Sticky Buns, **'81** 300; **'82** 124
  Cinnamon Crisps, **'81** 113
  Cinnamon Rolls, **'79** 80; **'88** 290
  Cinnamon Rolls, Easy, **'85** 290
  Cinnamon Rolls, Glazed, **'86** 312
  Cinnamon Rolls, Old-Fashioned, **'86** 298
  Cinnamon Rolls, Spiral, **'82** 205; **'83** 32
  Cinnamon Sticky Buns, **'83** 244
  Cinnamon Twists, **'83** 53
  Cloverleaf Refrigerator Rolls, **'80** 256
  Cloverleaf Rolls, **'82** 18
  Cloverleaf Rolls, Light, **'83** 290
  Cornmeal Rolls, **'79** 60
  Cornmeal Yeast Rolls, **'86** 177
  Cottage Cheese Rolls, **'81** 78
  Cranberry-Pineapple Rolls, **'86** 275
  Cream Cheese Pinches, **'87** 85
  Crescent Rolls, **'84** 267
  Crescent Rolls, Butter-Rich, **'81** 211
  Crescent Rolls, Buttery, **'83** 180
  Crescent Rolls, Deep South, **'82** 309;
    '83 16
  Crescent Rolls, Easy, **'79** 60
  Crescent Rolls, French-Style, **'82** 288
  Crescents, Festive, **'80** 281
  Croissants, **'83** 54
  Cross Buns, Hot, **'81** 77
  Dinner Rolls, **'79** 251
  Dinner Rolls, Fancy, **'86** 299
  Dinner Rolls, How to Shape, **'83** 323
  Dinner Rolls, Italian, **'83** 254

Dinner Rolls, Italiano, **'85** 32
Dinner Rolls, Refrigerator, **'81** 78
Dough, Basic Roll, **'82** 17
Dough, Sweet Roll, **'79** 80
Fantan Rolls, French, **'80** 276
Finger Rolls, **'83** 254
Garlic Rolls, Easy, **'86** 234
Hard Rolls, **'86** 85, 306
Holiday Sparkle Rolls, **'83** 296
Honey Oatmeal Buns, **'83** 154
Honey Rolls, Super, **'80** 115
Honey Wheat Rolls, **'83** 278
Honey-Wheat Rolls, Dilled, **'83** 254
Icebox Rolls, **'80** 242
Jam Kolaches, **'85** 290
Jam Teasers, **'81** 8
Lemon Knots, Glazed, **'86** 290
Lemon Spirals, French, **'81** 94
Moravian Feast Buns, **'83** 295
Nutty Buns, **'86** 290
Onion Buns, Cheesy, **'85** 5
Onion-Cheese Buns, **'88** 218
Onion Rolls, Poppy Seed, **'81** 63
Orange Butter Rolls, **'82** 206; **'83** 33
Orange Rolls, **'80** 22; **'82** 17; **'88** 79
Orange Rolls, Frosted Hot, **'80** 257
Orange Rolls, Luscious, **'86** 298
Overnight Rolls, **'86** 233
Pan Rolls, **'88** 76
Parker House Refrigerator Rolls, **'82** 310;
  '83 17
Parkerhouse Rolls, Super, **'81** 78
Parmesan Rolls, **'79** 181
Pecan Rolls, **'81** 62
Pepperoni Rolls, Ground-, **'83** 244
Pineapple Buns, Easy, **'85** 14
Potato Rolls, **'81** 300
Potato Rolls, Feathery Light, **'81** 305;
  '82 36
Potato Rolls, Homemade, **'82** 252
Potato Rolls, Refrigerated, **'83** 254
Potato Rolls, Refrigerator, **'87** 15
Potato Rolls, Southern, **'86** 299
Potato Rolls, Super, **'85** 145
Potato Rolls, Supreme, **'82** 130
Potato Yeast Rolls, **'87** 53
Pull-Apart Buns, Easy, **'83** 100
Pumpkin Rolls, **'87** 254
Raisin Cinnamon Pull-Aparts, **'82** 205;
  '83 32
Raisin Cinnamon Rolls, **'81** 107
Raisin Rollups, Sweet, **'86** 290
Refrigerator Rolls, **'82** 287
Refrigerator Rolls, Buttermilk, **'81** 120;
  '82 22
Refrigerator Rolls, Low-Sodium, **'82** 67
Refrigerator Rolls, Party, **'79** 248
Refrigerator Rolls, Three-Day, **'86** 306
Reuben Buns, **'88** 298
Romano Sesame Rolls, **'87** 144
Rounds, Individual Bread, **'83** 159
Rum Buns, **'81** 299
Rum-Raisin Buns, **'80** 22
Rum Rolls, Easy, **'79** 287; **'80** 35
Saffron Rolls, **'83** 296
Sesame Buns, **'82** 17
Snack Buns, **'87** 279
Sour Cream Rolls, **'80** 71
Sour Cream Yeast Rolls, **'85** 259
Sourdough Hot Rolls, **'82** 201
Special Rolls, Extra-, **'88** 257

Spoon Rolls, '87 15
Sticky Buns, '80 23
Sweet Rolls, Mexican, '81 285
Sweet Rolls, Yummy, '80 281
Twists, Austrian, '80 45
Wheat Bread and Rolls, Hearty
    Whole, '79 92
Wheat Buns, Whole, '86 236
Wheat Feather Rolls, Shredded, '82 309;
    '83 16
Wheat Rolls, Easy Whole, '86 286; '87 74
Wheat Rolls, Light, '87 254
Wheat Rolls, Petite Whole, '85 146
Wheat Rolls, Whole, '79 275

Yam Rolls, Golden, '86 299
Yeast Rolls, Buttermilk, '79 59
Yeast Rolls, Easy, '81 78; '86 16
Yeast Rolls, Low-Sodium, '84 228
Yeast Rolls, Quick, '84 267
Yeast Rolls, Refrigerator, '81 296, 307;
    '82 309; '83 17, 118
Yeast Rolls, Speedy, '82 309; '83 17

Rutabagas
au Gratin, Rutabaga, '79 254
Bacon, Rutabaga with, '83 243
Boiled Rutabagas, '86 224
Buttered Rutabagas, '81 274
Creamy Rutabaga, '79 254
Glazed Rutabaga, '88 229
Mashed Rutabagas, '86 295
Simple Rutabaga, '83 243
Steamed Rutabagas, '81 274

S

Salad Dressings
Almond Salad Dressing, '81 37
Apple Dressing, '83 181
Artichoke Dressing, '84 126
Avocado Dressing, '80 15
Avocado Fruit Salad Dressing, '82 93
Bacon Dressing, Hot, '84 12
Barbecue Salad Dressing, '80 74
Basil Dressing, '88 24
Blender Dressing, '80 78
Blue Cheese Dressing, '79 69; '82 166;
    '86 233
Blue Cheese Dressing, Apple Salad
    with, '87 103
Blue Cheese Dressing, Creamy, '81 150
Blue Cheese Dressing, Special, '80 30
Blue Cheese Dressing, Tangy, '87 81
Blue Cheese Dressing, Zesty, '79 104
Blue Cheese Salad Dressing, '82 94
Blue Cheese Salad Dressing,
    Creamy, '86 123
Buttermilk Dressing, Down-Home, '84 114

Buttermilk Salad Dressing, '79 69
Caesar Salad Dressing, '82 94
Celery-Honey Dressing, '80 42
Celery Seed Dressing, '82 265
Celery Seed Salad Dressing, '82 94
Citrus Dressing, '85 92
Citrus Dressing, Fruit Salad with, '88 6
Coconut Dressing, '87 251
Coconut-Fruit Dressing, Tangy, '84 171
Creamy Dressing, '79 159; '83 81; '85 26
Creamy Salad Dressing, '83 181
Cucumber Dressing, '80 74
Cucumber-Mint Dressing, '87 153
Cucumber Salad Dressing, Creamy, '82 79
Curried Dressing, '84 115
Curry Dressing, '80 242; '82 78
Dairy Land Salad Dressing, '86 85
Date Dressing, '87 57
Delightful Salad Dressing, '83 181
Dill Dressing, '88 182
Dilly Dressing, '80 74
Egg Dressing, '86 79
French Dressing, Creamy, '81 60
French Dressing, Grapefruit, '80 101
French Dressing, Green Salad with
    Lemony, '85 67
French Dressing, Honey, '87 81
French Dressing, Miracle, '82 79
French Dressing, Onion-, '84 283
French Dressing, Piquant, '87 202; '88 43
French Dressing, Spicy, '81 150; '86 123
French Dressing, Sweet, '82 94
French Dressing, Tangy, '84 12
French Dressing, Tomato-Honey, '81 105
Fruit Dressing, Fluffy, '79 69
Fruit Dressing, Fresh, '87 134
Fruit Dressing, Marmalade-, '84 171
Fruit Dressing, Sweet-and-Sour, '84 125
Fruit Dressing, Whipped Cream, '79 270
Fruit Salad Dressing, '79 69
Fruit Salad Dressing, Creamy, '82 94
Fruit, Salad Dressing for, '86 40
Fruit Salad, Dressing for, '87 81
Fruit Salad Dressing, Red, '83 231
Garden Dew Dressing, '86 50
Garden Dressing, Spring, '85 157
Garlic Dressing, '79 269; '80 14
Garlic-Herb Salad Dressing, Creamy, '84 66
Garlic Salad Dressing, '86 123
Ginger Dressing, '82 194; '88 61
Ginger-Yogurt Dressing, '81 302
Grapefruit Salad Dressing, '84 262
Greek Goddess Dressing, '81 150
Herb Dressing, '80 122
Herbed Salad Dressing, '88 29
Herb-Mayonnaise Sauce, '85 73
Herb Salad Dressing, '86 40
Honey Dressing, '79 242; '83 146;
    '87 129
Honey-Lime Dressing, '83 139
Horseradish Dressing, '87 152
Italian-American Salad Dressing,
    Creamy, '79 69
Italian Dressing, '79 52; '85 261
Italian Dressing, Special, '79 190
Italian Dressing, Tomato, Onion, and
    Cucumber in, '81 83
Italian Salad Dressing, '80 82; '84 12
Lemon Cream Dressing, '82 170
Lemon Dressing, Chilled Broccoli
    with, '88 270

Lemon Dressing, Creamy, '88 M193
Lemon-Herb Salad Dressing, '82 67
Lemon-Pepper Dressing, '87 55
Lemon Salad Dressing, '79 8
Lemon-Yogurt Slaw or Salad
    Dressing, '88 54
Lime Dressing, '79 2; '83 120
Lime-Honey Fruit Salad Dressing, '87 81
Lime-Parsley Dressing, '85 131
Lime Sherbet Dressing, '80 221
Mayonnaise Dressing, '86 11
Mayonnaise Dressing, Herbed-, '86 119
Mayonnaise, Easy Homemade, '84 12
Mayonnaise, Homemade, '80 155
Mayonnaise, Hot Wine, '81 83
Mayonnaise, Parmesan, '86 79
Mayonnaise, Russian, '80 137
Mint Dressing, '80 183
Mint Dressing, Fresh, '84 126
Mustard Dressing, '80 112
Olive Oil Dressing, '84 266
Orange Blossom Dressing, '82 266
Orange-Coconut Dressing, '80 158
Orange Dressing, '81 141
Orange-Poppy Seed Dressing, '87 187
Orange-Yogurt Dressing, '85 304
Oregano Dressing, '86 141
Oregano-Vinaigrette Dressing, '79 113
Paprika Dressing, '86 191
Parmesan Dressing, '86 192
Pasta Salad Dressing, '86 121
Pear Dressing, '83 146
Pepper Dressing, '80 174

Pepper-Onion Salad Dressing,
    Green, '84 12
Peppery Salad Dressing, '79 69
Pesto Salad Dressing, '86 150
Pimiento Dressing, Lettuce Wedges
    with, '84 212
Pineapple Cream Dressing, '83 81
Pineapple Dressing, Fruit Salad
    with, '85 207
Pineapple-Poppy Seed Dressing, '85 55
Pineapple Salad Dressing, '81 36
Poppy Seed Dressing, '80 152; '81 63,
    252; '83 153, 316; '84 16; '86 123,
    305; '88 78
Poppy Seed Dressing, Blender, '79 176
Raspberry Dressing, '87 153
Rémoulade Dressing, '86 123
Romano Dressing, '80 174
Roquefort Dressing, '79 85; '80 74
Roquefort Dressing, Creamy, '84 12
Rosemary Dressing, '81 131
Rum Dressing, '80 139
Russian Dressing, '80 4
Russian Dressing, Spinach Salad
    with, '79 144

Salad Dressings (continued)

Russian Sour Cream Dressing, **'79** 55
Russian-Style Dressing, **'83** 181
Russian-Style Salad Dressing, **'86** 305
Sesame Seed Dressing, **'87** 81
Sherry Dressing, Cherry Salad
  with, **'79** 165
Sour Cream Dressing, **'82** 164;
  '86 331
Sour Cream Dressing Deluxe, Lettuce
  with, **'88** 48
Sour Cream Sauce, **'87** 233
Soy Dressing, **'86** 191
Soy-Sesame Dressing, **'87** 153
Spicy Dressing, **'80** 55
Spinach Salad Dressing, **'83** 181
Stay Trim Dressing, **'86** 40
Strawberry Dressing, Creamy, **'84** 161
Sweet-and-Sour Dressing, **'80** 247; **'84** 70,
  161; **'85** 163; **'87** 305
Sweet-Sour Dressing, **'80** 246
Tangy Dressing, **'83** 9
Tangy Red Dressing, **'86** 191
Tangy Salad Dressing, **'80** 146; **'84** 115
Thousand Island Dressing, **'80** 74; **'81** 104;
  '83 135; **'86** 123
Thousand Island Dressing, Special,
  '82 79
Tomato-Cream Cheese Dressing, Garden
  Salad with, **'79** 173
Tomato Salad Dressing, Fresh, **'83** 193
Tossed Salad Dressing, **'84** 115
Touchdown Salad Dressing, **'81** 197
Vinaigrette Dressing, **'79** 171; **'87** 138
Vinaigrette Dressing and
  Croutons, **'86** M288
Whipped Cream Salad Dressing, **'82** 145
Wine Dressing, Creamy, **'85** 20
Yogurt Dressing, **'85** 59, 215; **'88** 27
Yogurt Dressing, Sweet-Hot, **'86** 40
Yogurt Dressing, Turkey Waldorf Salad
  with, **'88** 53
Yogurt-Honey Poppy Seed
  Dressing, **'83** 177
Yogurt Salad Dressing, **'79** 69

Salads
Acini di Pepe Salad, **'83** 163
Alfalfa-Celery Salad, Overnight, **'82** 97
Ambrosia
  Anytime Ambrosia, **'86** 182
  Baked Ambrosia, **'83** 303
  Bowl, Ambrosia, **'80** 138; **'84** 313
  Brunch Ambrosia, **'83** 57
  Carrot-Ambrosia Salad, **'81** 252
  Carrot-Marshmallow Ambrosia, **'80** 5
  Chicken Salad Ambrosia, **'85** 216
  Citrus Ambrosia, **'82** 287

Fruit Ambrosia, Fresh, **'88** 184
Fruit Ambrosia, Mixed, **'83** 10
Honey Bee Ambrosia, **'83** 267
Layered Ambrosia, **'88** 304
Mold, Ambrosia, **'79** 241
Mold, Ambrosia Cream
  Cheese, **'79** 249
Old-Fashioned Ambrosia, **'80** 5
Orange Ambrosia Supreme, **'79** 37
Peach Ambrosia, **'83** 53
Pineapple-Orange Ambrosia, **'88** 252
Rhubarb Ambrosia, **'88** 93
Salad, Ambrosia, **'83** 231
Sherried Ambrosia, **'84** 324; **'86** 317
Tropical Ambrosia, **'79** 74
Antipasto, Easy, **'85** 114
Antipasto, Pasta, **'85** 286
Antipasto Salad, **'84** 66
Apple-Bran Salad, Lemony, **'86** 223
Apple-Carrot Salad, **'85** 22
Apple-Cream Salad, Frozen, **'82** 80
Apple-Nut Salad, **'80** 226
Apple-Raisin Salad, Curried, **'80** 24
Apple Salad, **'87** 233
Apple Salad, Cheesy, **'86** 301
Apple Salad, Crunchy, **'80** 138
Apple Salad, Double, **'84** 227
Apple Salad, Fresh, **'81** 207
Apple Salad, Spicy, **'85** 215
Apple Salad, Summer, **'80** 149
Apple Salad, Swiss-, **'84** 81
Apple Salad with Blue Cheese
  Dressing, **'87** 103
Apple Snow Salad, **'81** 224
Apple Toss, Sesame-, **'88** 21
Apple Wedges with Poppyseed
  Dressing, **'86** 131
Apricot Salad, Frosted, **'80** 248
Artichoke-Rice Salad, **'80** 178; **'81** 41;
  '85 81
Artichoke Salad, **'86** 333
Artichoke Salad, Marinated, **'83** 241
Artichokes Vinaigrette, **'88** 101
Artichokes with Orzo Salad, **'88** M193
Artichoke-Tomato Salad, **'82** 239
Asparagus-and-Egg Salad, **'86** 305
Asparagus-Artichoke Salad, **'85** 162
Asparagus-Horseradish Salad, **'87** 80
Asparagus, Marinated, **'83** 46; **'86** 92
Asparagus Salad Cups, **'83** 47
Asparagus Salad, Easy, **'88** 131
Asparagus Salad, Marinated, **'79** 20
Asparagus Salad Vinaigrette, **'88** 56
Asparagus Vinaigrette, **'80** 77
Asparagus Vinaigrette, Light, **'82** 50
Asparagus with Tarragon Marinade,
  '83 47
Asparagus with Yogurt Dressing, **'79** 66
Aspic
  Apple Aspic, Sunshine, **'81** 73
  Basic Aspic for Garnishing, **'84** 189
  Coating, White Aspic, **'85** 151
  Fish Aspic, **'84** 190
  Fish 'n Aspic, **'84** 190
  Grapefruit Aspic, **'80** 297; **'82** 112;
    '83 153
  Madeira Aspic, **'86** 65
  Orange-and-Carrot Aspic, **'86** 199
  Shrimp-Coleslaw Aspic, **'79** 88
  Shrimp-Cucumber Aspic, **'83** 108
  Sunshine Aspic, **'80** 103

Three-Layer Aspic, **'88** 120
Tomato-Artichoke Aspic, **'84** 320;
  '86 92
Tomato Aspic, Bloody Mary-, **'81** 77
Tomato Aspic, Chicken in, **'84** 190
Tomato Aspic, Chili Sauce, **'85** 252
Tomato Aspic, Herbed, **'81** 73
Tomato Aspic, Light, **'85** 83
Tomato Aspic, Ranch, **'83** 218
Tomato Aspic, Spicy, **'81** 40
Tomato Aspic, Tangy, **'83** 124
Tomato Aspic with Shrimp, **'79** 241
Tomato-Crab Aspic, **'85** 287
Two, Aspic for, **'83** 209
Vegetable Aspic, Cheesy, **'81** 73
Vegetable Aspic with Horseradish
  Dressing, Crisp, **'87** 152
Avocado Acapulco, **'83** 2
Avocado and Zucchini Salad,
  Creamy, **'79** 208
Avocado Garbanzo Salad, **'81** 33
Avocado-Grapefruit Salad, **'85** 26
Avocado-Melon Salad, **'82** 164
Avocado Salad, **'81** 195; **'82** 9; **'83** 69
Avocado Salad, Citrus-, **'82** 265
Avocado Salad, Spanish, **'87** 41
Avocados, Salmon-Stuffed, **'86** 74
Avocados, Shrimp-Filled, **'83** 2
Avocado with Crabmeat, **'86** 119

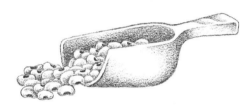

Bacon and Black-Eyed Salad, Hot, **'85** 7
Banana Salad, **'87** 80
Banana Salad, Frozen, **'82** 80, 132
Bananas, Nutty, **'79** 251
Bean
  Chilled Bean Salad, **'80** 178
  Cucumber-Bean Salad, **'83** 81
  Five-Bean Salad, Hot, **'81** 149
  Four-Bean Salad, **'79** 20; **'84** 82
  Full o' Beans Salad, **'81** 38
  Garbanzo Salad, **'82** 2
  Garbanzo Salad, Avocado-, **'81** 33
  Green Bean-and-Tomato Salad, **'86** 180
  Green Bean-Peanut Salad, **'86** 117
  Green Bean-Potato Salad, **'83** 80
  Green Bean Salad, **'87** 90
  Green Bean Salad, Cold, **'84** 106
  Green Bean Salad, Crispy, **'82** 239
  Green Bean Salad, Hot, **'86** 298;
    '87 176
  Green Bean Salad, Lettuce and, **'80** 79
  Green Bean Salad, Paprika-, **'86** 191
  Green Bean Salad, Pickled, **'82** 239
  Green Bean Salad, Speedy, **'84** 283
  Green Beans, Marinated, **'83** 145
  Green Beans Vinaigrette, **'83** 25
  Hacienda Salad, **'81** 67
  Kidney Bean-Salami Pasta
    Toss, **'85** 165
  Lima Beans, Chilly, **'81** 206

Lima Bean-Tomato Salad, '85 137
Marinated Bean-and-Rice
    Salad, '87 152
Marinated Bean Salad, '85 137, 296
Marinated Bean Salad,
    Crunchy, '84 197
Marinated Corn-Bean Salad, '87 9
Mexican Salad, '81 113
Mexican-Style Salad, '83 240
Mexican Tossed Salad, '81 280
Mixed Bean Salad, '83 217
Niçoise, Salad, '86 35
Overnight Fiesta Salad, '83 80
Pasta-Bean Salad, '86 169
Pinto Salad, '86 169
Pole Bean-Potato Salad, Hot, '79 74
Pork-'n'-Bean Salad, '87 83
Potato-Bean Salad, '82 301
Rice-and-Bean Salad, '85 22
Sandwiches, Bean Salad, '81 243
Saucy Bean Salad, '84 18
Six-Bean Salad, Colorful, '87 82
Southwest Salad, '81 113
Sprout Salad, Bean, '82 113
Sweet-and-Sour Bean Salad, '85 198;
    '86 147
Sweet-and-Sour Beans with
    Sprouts, '86 32
Beef-and-Broccoli Salad, '87 187
Beef-Cauliflower Salad, Corned, '83 16
Beef-Potato Salad, Corned, '85 213
Beef Salad, Gingered, '88 61
Beef Salad, Peking, '88 60
Beef Salad, Potato-Corned, '81 36
Beef Salad, Roast, '80 223; '81 56
Beef Salad, Tangy, '87 M218
Beef Salad, Vegetable-Corned, '80 148
Beef Salad, Zesty, '79 56
Beet Salad, Marinated, '83 216
Beets and Cauliflower, Chilled, '80 137
Berry Grapefruit Cup, '79 242
Blue Cheese-Pear-Apple Salad, '81 224
Blue Cheese Salad, '88 48
Boats, Salad, '80 93
Broccoli and Cauliflower Salad, '81 280
Broccoli and Cauliflower Salad,
    Creamy, '81 23
Broccoli and Cauliflower Toss,
    Crunchy, '83 25
Broccoli and Red Pepper Salad, '83 224
Broccoli-Cauliflower Pasta Salad, '88 269
Broccoli-Corn Salad, '87 24
Broccoli, Marinated, '81 40
Broccoli Medley, '81 206
Broccoli Salad, '82 24; '85 249
Broccoli Salad, Creamy, '79 143
Broccoli Salad, Crunchy, '83 39
Broccoli Salad, Curried, '86 225
Broccoli Salad, Fresh, '82 34; '87 103
Broccoli Salad, Marinated, '83 240
Broccoli Salad Supreme, '83 260
Brussels Sprouts Salad, '87 233
Cabbage and Fruit Salad, '79 286
Cabbage Salad, '87 120, 233
Cabbage Salad, Chinese, '81 271
Cabbage Salad, Garden, '81 210
Cabbage Salad, Nutty, '87 42
Cabbage Salad, Overnight, '79 83
Cabbage Salad, Tangy, '82 55
Cabbage, Sweet-Sour Red, '79 5
Cantaloupe-Cheese Salad, '88 184

Cantaloupe Cooler Salad, '79 176
Cantaloupe-Pecan Salad, '86 178
Cantaloupe Salad, '86 182
Carrot-and-Seed Salad, Fruity, '86 223
Carrot-and-Zucchini Salad, '83 240
Carrot-Fruit Toss, '82 235
Carrot-Raisin Salad, '83 117; '84 174;
    '87 10
Carrot Ring, Festive, '82 16
Carrot Salad, Favorite, '80 33
Carrot Salad, Shredded, '80 178
Carrot Salad, Simple, '82 101; '84 152
Carrot Salad, Sunshine, '82 132
Carrots, Creamy Marinated, '87 200
Carrot-Tangerine Salad, '83 316; '84 16
Cauliflower and Pea Salad, Savory, '81 280
Cauliflower-Broccoli Crunch, '88 216
Cauliflower-Broccoli Salad, '79 20
Cauliflower-Broccoli Toss, '82 54
Cauliflower-Broccoli Toss, Italian, '88 269
Cauliflower-Brussels Sprouts Salad, '83 240
Cauliflower-Olive Toss, '85 198; '86 147
Cauliflower Salad, '79 221; '80 83;
    '81 225; '84 291; '85 240, 279
Cauliflower Salad, Creamy, '82 102
Cauliflower Salad, Crunchy, '80 4; '82 75
Cauliflower Salad, Layered, '83 240
Cauliflower Salad, Marinated, '82 303;
    '84 232
Cauliflower Salad, Sweet-and-Sour, '81 2
Cauliflower-Vegetable Salad, '85 158
Celery-and-Cauliflower Salad, '83 39
Celery Salad, '79 70
Cheese-Banana Splits, Cottage, '87 56
Cheesy Italian Salad, '84 33
Chef Salad, Mexican, '85 84
Chef's Garden Salad, '83 146
Chef's Salad, '86 186
Chef's Salad Bowl, '84 66
Chef's Salad, Combination, '86 47
Chef's Salad, Vinaigrette, '81 9
Cherry-Orange Salad, '79 74; '82 56
Cherry Salad, Delicious Frozen, '81 252
Cherry Salad, Fresh, '83 120
Cherry Salad, Frozen, '79 126
Cherry Salad with Honey-Lime
    Dressing, '83 139
Cherry Salad with Sherry Dressing, '79 165
Chicken
    Almond Salad, Chicken-, '81 133
    Aloha Chicken Salad, '80 297
    Amandine, Chicken Salad, '81 37
    Ambrosia, Chicken Salad, '85 216
    Artichokes, Chicken Salad
        with, '86 186
    Aspic-Topped Chicken Salad, '88 88
    Avocado-Chicken Salad, '87 107
    Avocado Salad, Chicken-, '80 139
    Avocado Salad, Fruited
        Chicken, '82 101
    Avocado Salad Platter, Chicken-, '83 2
    Avocado Salad, Tossed Chicken-, '80 4
    Avocados, Chicken Salad in, '85 216
    Baked Chicken Salad, '86 297; '87 176
    BLT Chicken Salad, '87 144
    Celery Salad, Chicken-, '81 187
    Chicken Salad, '86 232, 261
    Chop Suey Salad, '81 37
    Chutney-Chicken Salad, '87 74
    Chutney Salad, Chicken, '82 108
    Coleslaw, Chicken, '84 2

Cream Puff Bowl, Chicken Salad
    in, '86 232
Crunchy Chicken Salad, '86 157, 207
Curried Chicken-and-Orange
    Salad, '87 144
Curried Chicken Salad, '79 219;
    '84 66; '85 96; '86 131
Curried Chicken Salad on Raisin
    Bread, '85 96
Curried Chicken Salad with
    Asparagus, '81 36
Fancy Chicken Salad, '79 55
Filling, Chicken Salad, '87 106
Fruit, Chicken Salad with, '82 171
Fruited Chicken Salad, '84 25, 290;
    '88 88
Fruited Chicken Salad in
    Avocados, '87 41
Fruit Salad, Chicken-, '82 79
Fruity Chicken Salad, '83 157
Grapes, Chicken Salad with, '86 117
Green Salad with Chicken,
    Mixed, '80 54

Hot Chicken Salad, '81 201; '83 196
Hot Chicken Salad, Country
    Club-Style, '86 10
Hot Chicken Salad, Crunchy, '80 138
Hot Chicken Salad Pinwheel, '80 139
Macadamia Chicken Salad, '80 138
Macaroni-Chicken Salad, '85 296;
    '86 302
Mandarin Chicken, Carousel, '79 88
Mango, Chicken Salad with, '86 215
Marinated Chicken-Grape Salad, '85 74
Mexican Chicken Salad, '85 84;
    '88 272
Nectarine Chicken Salad, '79 175
Old-Fashioned Chicken Salad, '83 79
Oriental Chicken Salad, '85 216;
    '88 271
Pasta-Chicken Salad, Tarragon, '87 155
Pasta Salad, Chicken, '88 89
Pea Salad, Chicken-, '83 218
Persian Chicken Salad, '81 12
Pineapple-Chicken Salad Pie, '80 138
Pineapple-Nut Chicken Salad, '83 80
Pocket, Chicken Salad in a, '88 139
Polynesian Chicken Salad, '88 272
Poulet Rémoulade, '87 144
Rice Salad, Chicken-, '81 203
Rice Salad, Hot Chicken-and-, '83 22
Rice Salad, Nutty Chicken-, '83 157
Sandwiches, Chicken-Salad
    Finger, '85 119
Southwestern Chicken Salad, '88 88

Salads, Chicken *(continued)*

Special Chicken Salad, **'85** 82;
  '87 183; **'88** M193
Spinach Tossed Salad,
  Chicken-and-, **'83** 157
Spread, Chicken Salad Party, **'88** M8
Stack-Up Salad, Chicken, **'83** 80
Summer Chicken Salad, **'83** 145
Super Chicken Salad, **'82** 174
Supreme, Chicken Salad, **'79** 107, 152
Tahitian Chicken Salad, **'84** 120
Tarts, Chicken Salad, **'84** 257
Tortellini Salad, Chicken, **'87** 288
Tropical Chicken Boats for
  Two, **'82** 186
Tropical Chicken Salad, **'85** 216
Twist, Chicken Salad with a, **'84** 221
Wild Rice-Chicken Salad, **'83** 146
Chili Salad, Spicy, **'86** 71
Citrus Salad, **'87** 103
Citrus Salad Bowl, **'86** 335; **'87** 83
Citrus Salad in Orange Cups, **'85** 47
Citrus Salad, Southern-Style, **'84** 262
Citrus Vinaigrette Salad, **'86** 192
Committee, Salad by, **'87** 288
Congealed
  Apple-Apricot Salad, **'88** 121
  Apple Cider Salad, **'83** 123
  Apple Cider Salad Mold, **'85** 54
  Apple Crunch Salad, **'84** 232; **'86** 331
  Apple Salad, Congealed, **'85** 252
  Apple Salad, Triple, **'88** 122
  Apricot Fruit Salad, **'82** 132
  Apricot Nectar Salad, **'83** 218; **'87** 236
  Apricot Salad, **'81** 251; **'83** 123
  Apricot Salad, Creamy, **'85** 263
  Asheville Salad, **'86** 199
  Asparagus-Cucumber Mold, **'85** 252
  Asparagus Mold, **'80** 104
  Asparagus Mousse Salad, **'86** 252
  Asparagus Salad, **'88** 121
  Asparagus Salad, Congealed, **'83** 260
  Asparagus Salad, Tart, **'81** 203
  Avocado Crunch Salad,
    Congealed, **'85** 26
  Avocado Salad, Congealed, **'84** 266
  Avocado Salads, Congealed, **'87** 42
  Bean Salad, Molded Green, **'85** 252
  Beef Salad, Corned, **'80** 104
  Beef Salad, Molded Corned, **'82** 86
  Beet-Nut Salad, **'79** 74
  Beet Salad Mold, **'82** 267
  Beet Salad, Pickled, **'83** 234
  Beet Salad, Tangy, **'86** 199
  Berry Salad, Layered, **'79** 173
  Broccoli Salad, Congealed, **'84** 124
  Cantaloupe, Southern
    Plantation, **'82** 179
  Carrot-Nut Salad, Creamy, **'86** 331
  Carrot Salad, **'82** 137
  Cauliflower-Lemon Salad, **'81** 23
  Cheese Molds, Snowcap, **'79** 242
  Cherry-Apple Salad, **'86** 31
  Cherry Cola Salad, **'80** 104
  Cherry-Salad, Best, **'82** 302
  Cherry Salad, Festive, **'84** 265
  Cherry Salad, Port Wine-, **'86** 11
  Cherry-Wine Salad, Elegant, **'82** 56
  Chicken-Cucumber Mold, **'80** 175
  Chicken Jewel Ring Salad, **'83** 282

Chicken-Pea Salad, **'83** 218
Chicken Salad Mold, **'83** 80; **'84** 163
Chile-Tomato Salad, Spicy, **'88** 121
Christmas Salad, **'88** 249
Christmas Snow Salad, **'82** 266
Citrus Mold, Sparkling, **'86** 331
Citrus Salad Mold, Golden, **'85** 303
Crabmeat-and-Asparagus, Congealed
  Salad with, **'84** 86
Cranberry Mold, **'79** 250
Cranberry Salad, Festive, **'81** 264, 296
Cranberry Salad, Holiday, **'82** 266, 288
Cranberry Salad, Jellied, **'83** 279;
  '85 281
Cranberry Salad, Layered, **'84** 322;
  '86 325
Cranberry Salad Ring, **'80** 247
Crème de Menthe Salad, **'82** 122
Creole Salad, **'79** 147
Cucumber Mold, Creamy, **'84** 164
Cucumber Mousse, **'88** 121
Cucumber-Pineapple Salad, **'84** 124
Cucumber Salad, Creamy, **'86** 147
Cucumber Salad Mold, **'82** 111;
  '83 81, 253
Eggnog Christmas Salad, **'86** 281
Egg Salad, Deviled, **'83** 124
Emerald Salad, **'81** 143
Emerald Salad, Snowy, **'87** 311
Fall Salad with Ginger
  Dressing, **'82** 194
Frosted Salad, Heavenly, **'79** 286
Fruit Salad, Cherry, **'87** 236

Fruit Salad, Sparkling, **'82** 266
Fruit Salad, Spiced Autumn, **'87** 228
Garden-Patch Salad Molds, **'86** 283
Garden Salad, Molded, **'86** 199
Gazpacho Salad Mold, **'87** 311
Gazpacho Salad, Molded, **'79** 159
Grape-Cantaloupe Mold,
  Double, **'79** 173
Grapefruit Congealed Salad, **'83** 190
Grapefruit Salad, **'83** 124; **'84** 325;
  '88 122
Grapefruit Salad, Congealed, **'84** 325;
  '85 279
Grape Salad Mold, **'83** 120
Green Spring Salad, **'83** 124
Ham Salad, Congealed, **'81** 36
Holiday Jewel Salad, **'81** 252
Horseradish Salad, **'85** 66
Layered Congealed Salad, **'81** 143
Layered Holiday Salad, **'81** 252
Layer Mold, Three-, **'82** 54
Lemon-Cheese Salad, **'85** 240
Lemon-Cranberry Congealed
  Salad, **'87** 311

Lemon-Cucumber Mold, **'87** 90
Lemon Mold, Cheesy, **'79** 241
Lemon-Onion Salad, **'85** 252
Lemon-Vegetable Congealed
  Salad, **'85** 22
Lime-Cheese Salad, Frosted, **'79** 286
Lime Sherbet Salad, **'80** 104
Mandarin Salad Molds, **'85** 54
Melon Ball Salad, Congealed, **'84** 125
Mincemeat Salad, Holiday, **'85** 263
Molds, Perfection, **'81** 153
Orange-Pear Salad, **'84** 164
Orange Salad, Creamy, **'84** 124
Orange Salad, Frosted, **'81** 154;
  '83 123
Orange Salad, Jeweled, **'83** 210
Orange Sherbet Salad, **'81** 154
Orange Surprise Salad, **'79** 12
Peach-Cranberry Ring, Spicy, **'85** 264
Peaches-and-Cream Salad, **'83** 108
Peach Frost, **'84** 164
Peach Party Salad, **'84** 290
Peach Salad, Pickled, **'80** 104; **'85** 264
Peachy Berry Cream Mold, **'83** 130
Pear-Lime Salad, **'84** 152
Pear Salad, Royal, **'84** 265
Pimiento Salad, Sunshine, **'84** 124
Pineapple-Buttermilk Salad, **'82** 80
Pineapple-Cucumber Congealed
  Salad, **'83** 118
Pineapple Daiquiri Salad, **'84** 232
Pineapple-Lime Salad, **'84** 320
Pineapple Mold, Minted, **'85** 240
Pineapple-Orange Congealed
  Salad, **'83** 218
Pineapple-Pear Delight, **'82** 54
Raspberry Fruit Mounds, **'79** 35
Raspberry Holiday Mold, **'84** 253
Raspberry Ribbon Salad, **'87** 236
Raspberry Salad, **'86** 286
Rhubarb Congealed Salad, **'86** 140
Roquefort Salad, Creamy, **'79** 73
Ruby-and-Emerald Salad, **'85** 79
Salmon Salad, Chilly, **'80** 104
Sangría Salad, **'86** 331
Shrimp Salad, **'84** 221
Strawberry Salad, Hidden
  Treasure, **'79** 11
Strawberry-Wine Salad Mold, **'83** 261
Sunshine Delight, **'86** 117
Tomato Mold, Tangy, **'79** 74
Tomato Ring, Tangy, **'84** 164
Tomato Salad, Frozen, **'84** 52
Tomato-Vegetable Ring, **'81** 302
Tuna-Cheese Mold, Creamy, **'81** 135
Tuna Ring, Creamy, **'80** 275
Tuna Salad, Congealed, **'84** 163
Tuna Salad, Creamy, **'82** 87, 208
Tuna Salad, Luncheon, **'81** 135
Vegetable Congealed Salad,
  Cheesy-, **'86** 199
Vegetable Relish Salad, **'82** 267
Vegetable Salad, Congealed, **'79** 276
Vegetable Salad, Congealed
  Fresh, **'82** 240
Waldorf Salad, Congealed, **'82** 80
Waldorf Salad, Molded, **'84** 326
Cornbread Salad, **'87** 172
Corn Salad, **'80** 247; **'81** 139; **'85** 236
Corn Salad, Chilled, **'79** 20
Corn Salad, Shoepeg, **'81** 23

Corn Salad, Tangy, '88 176
Corn Salad, Tasty, '84 289
Cottage Cheese Salad, Different, '85 328; '86 22
Cottage Cheese Salad in Tomatoes, '86 208
Cottage Cheese Salad, Out-of-This-World, '79 44
Cottage-Tomato Salad, '85 163
Crab and Wild Rice Salad, '79 116
Crab-Avocado Salad, '81 114
Crabmeat Luncheon Salad, '82 207
Crabmeat-Shrimp Pasta Salad, '86 208
Crab Mousse, '79 117
Crab Salad, Delightful, '87 145
Crab-Wild Rice Salad, '86 207
Cranberry-Cheese Ribbon Salad, '79 241
Cranberry Christmas Salad, '79 243
Cranberry Oriental, '79 126
Cranberry Salad, Tart, '79 286
Cranberry-Whipped Cream Salad, '83 261
Crawfish Salad, Dilled, '83 126
Crunchy-Creamy Salad, '88 100

Cucumber-Almond Salad, '86 147
Cucumber and Tomato Salad, Dilled, '81 153
Cucumber Cooler, Simple, '86 147
Cucumber Mousse, '79 11
Cucumber Salad, Dilled, '82 229
Cucumber Salad, Marinated, '82 111
Cucumbers and Artichokes, Marinated, '82 111
Cucumbers, Cool, '84 152
Cucumbers in Sour Cream, '79 52; '80 178
Cucumber-Vinaigrette Oriental, '85 198; '86 147
Cucumber-Yogurt Salad, '87 33
Curry Salad, Hot Indian, '83 23
Dude Ranch Salad, '80 15
Egg-Rice Salad, '84 18; '86 169
Egg Salad, Green Vegetable and, '79 191
Egg Salad Spread, Cottage-, '82 146
Escarole-and-Bacon Salad, '84 85
Extravaganza, Salad, '87 233
Fast-and-Easy Salad, '85 M328
Fruit. See also Salads/Congealed.
    Ambrosia, Mixed Fruit, '83 10
    Avocado Fruit Salad, '87 41
    Chef Salad, Fruited, '85 222
    Chef's Fruit Salad, '86 35
    Chilled Fruit with Dressing, '85 222

Citrus Dressing, Fruit Salad with, '88 6
Coconut Fruit Bowl, '83 111
Coconut Salad, Chunky Fruit-and-, '84 24
Colorful Fruit Salad, '82 113
Cottage Cheese-and-Fruit Salad, '86 16
Cottage-Fruit Split, '86 169
Creamy Fruit Salad, '84 265
Cups, Royal Fruit, '81 146
Cups with Pineapple Cream Dressing, Fruit, '83 81
Curried Fruit Salad, '85 107
Date Dressing, Fruit Salad with, '87 57
Delight, Fruit, '86 131
Dressed-Up Fruit, '82 5
Easy Fruit Salad, '80 221
Easy Patio Fruit Salad, '88 184
Festive Fruit Salad, '80 16
Fresh Fruit Bowl, Sparkling, '80 146
Fresh Fruit Cup with Mint Dressing, '80 183
Fresh Fruit Salad, '82 165
Fresh Fruit Salad with Celery-Honey Dressing, '80 42
Fresh Fruit Salad with Poppy-Seed Dressing, '80 137
Fresh Fruit with Lemon Sauce, '82 290
Frisky Fruit Salad, '85 46
Frozen Fruit Salad, '83 110
Frozen Fruit Salad, Dreamy, '79 126
Frozen Fruit Salad, Luscious, '81 204
Frozen Salad, Christmas Wreath, '79 241
Glazed Fruit Salad, '83 48; '84 290
Hawaiian Fruit Dish, '82 112
Heavenly Salad, '81 252
Holiday Fruit Salad, '87 236
Honeydew Fruit Boats, '81 147
Honeydew Fruit Bowl, '84 186
Honey Dressing, Fruit Salad with, '87 129
Honey Fruit Salad, '80 276
Hurry-Up Fruit Salad, '87 236
Jicama-Fruit Salad, '86 83
Layered Fruit Salad, '84 290
Lemonade Fruit Salad, '84 24
Lemon Freeze, Fruity, '82 145
Lettuce and Fruit Salad with Poppy Seed Dressing, '80 152
Main Dish Fruit Salad, '83 119
Marinated Fruit Bowl, '80 297
Marinated Fruit Deluxe, '81 146
Medley, Chilled Fruit, '84 60
Medley, Fruit Cup, '85 47
Mélange Delight, Fruit, '81 302
Melon Balls in Watermelon Sauce, '79 177
Melon-Citrus Mingle, '79 177
Melon Cocktail, Minted, '81 146
Melon Cooler, '81 146
Melon Mélange, '84 139
Melon Salad, Summertime, '82 101
Minted Fruit Medley, '80 182
Mint Sauce, Fruit Salad with, '88 M96
Mixed Fruit Cup, '87 233
Mixed Fruit Salad, Banana-, '79 270
Nut Salad, Cheesy Fruit-'n'-, '87 56
Old-Fashioned Fruit Salad, '82 80

Persimmon Fruit Salad, '79 206
Picks, Fruit on, '80 159
Pineapple Dressing, Fruit Salad with, '85 207
Pineapple-Fruit Salad, Icy, '87 9
Platter, Fruit Salad, '83 261
Poppy Seed Dressing, Fruit Salad with, '88 78
Quick-and-Easy Fruit Salad, '81 99
Refreshing Fruit Salad, '85 92
Rhapsody, Fruit, '80 158
Rum, Fruit Cup with, '83 55
Salad, Fruit, '83 209
Sherried Fruit Mélange, '80 158
Shrimp Salad, Fruited, '86 156
Sour Cream Fruit Salad, '80 138
Springtime Fruit Salad, '81 96
Summer Fruit Salad, '82 164
Summer Salad, Favorite, '80 158
Sunny Salad, '80 138
Sweet-and-Sour Fruit Salad, '80 13; '84 125

Tropical Fruit Salad with Fresh Mint Dressing, '84 126
Vanilla Fruit Cup, '80 183
Watermelon Fruit Basket, '84 161
Wine, Fruit in White, '81 48
Winter Fruit Delight, '80 243
Winter Fruit Salad, '80 248; '82 23
Wreath, Della Robbia Fruit, '87 294
Yogurt Fruit Salad, '81 114
Grapefruit-and-Shrimp Salad, '88 5
Grapefruit-Avocado Salad, '83 316; '84 16
Grapefruit Combo Salad, '80 50
Grapefruit-Cucumber Salad, '80 100
Grapefruit Winter Salad, '84 24
Greek Salad, '87 103
Green. See also Salads/Spinach.
    Bibb Salad, Tossed, '87 128
    Caesar Salad, '80 112; '86 80
    Caesar Salad, Easy, '87 116
    Caesar Salad, Flippo, '87 61
    California Green Salad, '81 84
    Chef's Salad. See Salads/Chef.
    Chinese Green Salad, '88 48
    Citrus Green Salad, '85 304
    Citrus Salad, Southern-Style, '84 262
    Combination Salad Bowl, '85 132

Salads, Green *(continued)*

Combo Salad Bowl, **'81** 9
Company's Coming Salad, **'79** 113
Cranberry-Topped Green
 Salad, **'87** 311
Crimson Greens, **'87** 153
Fenron Salad, **'79** 85
Garden Salad, **'85** 92
Garden Salad Centerpiece, **'83** 171
Garden Salad, Herbed, **'85** 328;
 '86 22
Garden Salad, Summer, **'87** 153
Garden Salad Toss, **'81** 9
Garden Salad with Rosemary Dressing,
 Fresh, **'81** 131
Grecian Green Salad, **'84** 266
Grecian Tossed Salad, **'79** 174
Hill Country Salad, **'81** 9
Lemony French Dressing, Green Salad
 with, **'85** 67
Lettuce, Cheesy Stuffed, **'79** 175
Lettuce, Confetti-Stuffed, **'87** 24
Lettuce, Delicate Garden, **'87** 62
Lettuce, Garden-Stuffed, **'83** 135

Lettuce Salad, French, **'84** 187
Lettuce Salad,
 Tennessee-Killed, **'88** 86
Lettuce Salad, Wilted, **'82** 302
Lettuce Salad, Wilted
 Bacon-and-, **'85** 69
Lettuce Wedges with Pimiento
 Dressing, **'84** 212
Lettuce, Wilted, **'86** 269
Lettuce with Sour Cream Dressing
 Deluxe, **'88** 48
Mixed Green Salad, Wilted, **'85** 69
Mixed Green Salad with
 Chicken, **'80** 54
Mixed Greens Salad, **'87** 62
Nutty Green Salad, **'87** 168
Oriental, Green Salad, **'85** 92
Romaine Salad, Tangy, **'80** 155
Salmagundi Salad, **'83** 146
Savory Green Salad, **'82** 74
Sensational Salad, **'84** 320
Sesame-Citrus Green Salad, **'86** 33
Shrimp, Green Salad with, **'88** 49
Simply Good Salad, **'85** 131
Soy Dressing, Green Salad
 with, **'86** 191
Spinach-Kiwifruit Salad, **'87** 305

Spring Salad, **'87** 62
Spring Salad, Mediterranean, **'80** 148
Spring Salad Wedges, **'87** 62
Summer Salad, Crisp, **'85** 92
Summertime Salad, **'79** 143; **'84** 195
Tangy Wilted Salad, **'85** 69
Tossed Mixed Green Salad, **'84** 126
Tossed Salad, Blue Cheese, **'84** 195
Tossed Salad, Boston, **'84** 85
Tossed Salad, Radish-Dressed, **'79** 104
Watercress-and-Mushroom
 Salad, **'88** 104
Guacamole Salad, **'80** 14; **'87** 181
Guacamole-Tomato Salad, **'81** 302
Ham-and-Apple Salad, **'88** 139
Ham-and-Cheese Salad, **'88** 138
Ham and Cheese Toss, **'79** 55
Ham and Macaroni Salad, **'79** 220
Ham-and-Rice Salad, Mandarin, **'87** 145
Ham 'n Egg Salad, **'81** 36
Ham-Noodle Salad, **'85** 249
Ham-Rice Toss, **'82** 40
Ham Salad, Crunchy Baked, **'83** 23
Ham Salad, Fruited, **'81** 36, 146
Ham Salad, Hearty, **'82** 40
Ham Salad Sandwich, Tangy, **'80** 272
Ham Salad, Spicy Italian, **'85** 74
Ham Salad Spread, **'87** 92
Ham-Sweet Potato Salad,
 Hawaiian, **'82** 232
Hearts of Palm Salad, **'81** 252
Hearts-of-Palm Salad, **'87** 138
Herb Salad, **'87** 90
Hominy-Bean Salad, **'88** 266
Honeydew Salad with Apricot Cream
 Dressing, **'84** 191
Ice Cream Salad, **'79** 126
Italian Salad, **'87** 145
Jicama-and-Orange Salad, **'88** 246
Jicama-Orange Salad, **'86** 83
Jicama Salad, **'87** 123
Layered Salad, **'86** 35, 79
Layered Salad, Cheesy, **'81** 37
Layered Salad Deluxe, **'81** 153
Layered Salad, Hearty, **'86** 79
Layered Salad, Majestic, **'86** 79
Layered Salad, Make-Ahead, **'81** 296
Layered Salad, Overnight, **'81** 188
Lobster and Orange Salad, **'82** 207
Macaroni-Cheese Salad, Dilled, **'86** 208
Macaroni-Crabmeat Salad, **'81** 153
Macaroni-Ham Salad, **'85** 218
Macaroni Salad, **'87** 92
Macaroni Salad, Barbecue, **'82** 276
Macaroni Salad, Confetti, **'82** 132; **'85** 297
Macaroni Salad, Crunchy, **'82** 24
Macaroni Salad for Two, **'81** 31
Macaroni Salad, Garden, **'84** 290
Macaroni Salad, Gourmet, **'81** 253
Macaroni Salad, Hearty, **'84** 90
Macaroni Salad, Pineapple, **'79** 220
Macaroni Salad, Refreshing, **'80** 177
Macaroni Salad, Spiral, **'82** 276
Macaroni Salad, Sweet-and-Sour, **'85** 166
Macaroni Salad, Taco, **'85** 165
Macaroni Salad Véronique, **'85** 164
Macaroni-Salmon Salad, **'82** 232
Macaroni Shell Salad, **'87** 38
Macaroni-Shrimp Salad, **'85** 121
Macaroni-Shrimp Salad, Festive, **'85** 165
Macaroni Toss, Corkscrew, **'83** 163

Macaroni-Tuna Salad, Whole
 Wheat, **'84** 193
Macaroni-Vegetable Salad, **'86** 209
Madras Salad, **'86** 82
Main-Dish Salad, **'86** 191
Mandarin, Salad, **'84** 231
Mandarin Spinach Salad, **'85** 163
Mango Salad, **'79** 137
Mango Salad, Fresh, **'84** 126
Marinated Salad, **'83** 170
Meal-in-One Salad, **'86** 43
Melon Balls, Minted, **'87** 162
Melon Salad with Dill Dressing, **'88** 182
Mexican Salad in a Shell, **'86** 4

Mexican Salad Supper, **'82** 9; **'83** 68
Middle Eastern Salad, **'87** 107
Minestrone Salad, **'79** 220
Mushroom-and-Pepper Salad, **'86** 68
Mushroom Salad, Fabulous, **'81** 190
Mushroom Salad, Marinated, **'88** 215
Mushroom-Zucchini Salad, **'85** 8
Noodle Salad, Ramen, **'88** 41
Olive Clubhouse Salad, **'81** 114
Olive Salad, Mexican, **'85** 84
Orange-and-Beet Salad, **'88** 43
Orange and Pineapple Salad,
 Mandarin, **'82** 266
Orange-Carrot Salad, **'80** 89; **'84** 325
Orange-Cauliflower Salad, **'82** 266
Orange-Cottage Cheese Salad, **'79** 44
Orange Cups, **'86** 92
Orange-Romaine Salad, **'84** 325; **'87** 239
Orange Salad Cups, **'85** 40
Orange Salad, Mandarin, **'81** 252; **'84** 161
Orange Salad, Quick, **'87** 80
Orange-Shrimp Salad, **'84** 197
Orange-Spinach Salad, **'83** 316; **'84** 16
Orange Walnut Salad, **'80** 246
Oriental Salad Bowl, **'87** 153
Paella Salad, **'86** 207
Party Freeze Salad, **'82** 145
Pasta-and-Shrimp Salad, **'83** 163
Pasta Platter, Cold, **'88** 42
Pasta Salad, **'84** 139; **'86** 120; **'87** 36
Pasta Salad, Crunchy, **'85** 166
Pasta Salad, Garden, **'86** 188
Pasta Salad, Main-Dish, **'82** 199
Pasta Salad, Overnight, **'82** 276
Pasta, Snappy, **'83** 164
Pea-and-Apple Salad, English, **'87** 24
Peaches in a Garden Nest, **'87** 154
Peach Pinwheel Salad, **'79** 11

Peach Salad, Frosted, **'82** 145
Peach Salad, Frozen, **'82** 54
Peach Salad, Georgia, **'80** 142
Peach Salad Supreme, Easy, **'79** 177
Peanut-Apple Salad, **'80** 5
Pear-and-Celery Salad, **'87** 56
Pear-and-Spinach Salad, Festive, **'85** 131
Pear Salad, Crunchy, **'83** 234; **'84** 244
Pea Salad, Black-Eyed, **'80** 112; **'86** 225; **'88** 92, 221
Pea Salad, Cheddar-, **'84** 82
Pea Salad, Creamy, **'80** 111
Pea Salad, English, **'81** 280
Pea Salad, Marinated, **'81** 204
Pea Salad, Marinated English, **'82** 54
Pea Salad, Mexi-, **'81** 7
Pea Salad, Overnight Black-Eyed, **'81** 280
Pea Salad, Special, **'83** 239
Pea Salad, Sugar Snap, **'86** 115
Pea Salad, Three, **'84** 290
Peas-and-Asparagus Salad, **'83** 141
Peas, Marinated Black-Eyed, **'82** 156
Pea Vinaigrette, Black-Eyed, **'86** 7
Pepper-Cheese Stacks, **'87** 80
Pepperoni-and-Broccoli Salad, **'83** 216
Pineapple Boat Aloha, **'80** 102
Pineapple Boats Ahoy, **'80** 148
Pineapple Boats, Fresh, **'83** 153
Pineapple-Celery Salad, **'85** 95
Pistachio-Pasta Salad, **'86** 141
Pita Salad Sandwiches, **'83** 134
Pizza, Salad, **'87** 182
Plentiful P's Salad, **'87** 12
Pork-and-Spinach Salad,
  Mandarin, **'88** M126
Potato
    Any Day Potato Salad, **'81** 154
    Asparagus-and-New Potato
      Salad, **'86** 69
    Bacon-Topped Potato Salad, **'85** 59
    Bean Salad, Potato-, **'82** 301
    Broccoli-Potato Salad, Hot, **'85** 23
    Chunky Potato Salad, **'81** M138
    Confetti Potato Salad, **'80** 5; **'88** 16
    Corned Beef-Potato Salad, **'85** 213
    Corned Beef Salad, Potato-, **'81** 36
    Cottage Cheese-Potato Salad,
      '79 147, 285
    Creamy Potato Salad, **'80** 178;
      '88 171
    Deluxe Potato Salad, **'80** 155
    Dill Potato Salad, **'85** 213
    Dill Potato Salad, Hot, **'79** 78
    Dutch Potato Salad, Hot, **'87** 176
    Fish-Potato Salad, Smoked, **'84** 233
    French-Style Potato Salad, **'88** 171
    Fruity Potato Salad, **'85** 214
    Garden Patch Potato Salad, **'84** 82
    German Potato Salad, **'82** 134, 239;
      '84 18
    German Potato Salad, Hot, **'79** 78
    German-Style Potato Salad, **'83** 23;
      '88 M194
    Grecian Potato Salad, **'82** 55
    Green Bean-Potato Salad, **'83** 80
    Ham-and-Egg Potato Salad, **'86** 84
    Ham and Potato Salad, **'80** 272
    Herbed Potato Salad, **'87** 171
    Hot Dutch Potato Salad, **'86** 297
    Hot Potato Salad, **'79** 78; **'81** 276;
      '86 10

Hot Potato Salad Supreme, **'79** 78
Layered Creamy Potato Salad, **'81** 23
Mustard Potato Salad, **'86** 302
New Potato Salad, **'84** 120, 139
Olive-Potato Salad, **'85** 114
Parmesan Potato Salad, Hot, **'79** 78
Parslied Potato Salad, **'85** 240
Pepper Cups, Potato Salad in, **'79** 78
Peppers, Potato Salad 'n', **'83** 135
Pickle-Potato Salad, Sweet, **'85** 213
Pole Bean-Potato Salad, Hot, **'79** 74
Salmon-Potato Salad, **'87** 285
Saucy Potato Salad, **'87** 123
Savory Potato Salad, **'80** 30
Sour Cream Potato Salad, **'79** 104;
  '80 79
Sour Cream-Potato Salad, **'84** 149
Spring Salad, Mediterranean, **'80** 148
Sweet and Sour Potato Salad, **'80** 152
Sweet Potato Salad, Fresh, **'86** 226
Tuna-Potato Salad, **'84** 289
Raspberry Salad, Frozen, **'79** 287; **'80** 35
Relish Salad, **'84** 121
Rice-and-Shrimp Salad, **'83** 82
Rice-and-Vegetable Salad, Brown, **'84** 202
Rice-Carrot Ring, **'79** 246
Rice-Pea Salad, **'85** 163
Rice Salad, **'79** 74; **'81** 51
Rice Salad, Charleston Red, **'79** 146
Rice Salad, Chutneyed, **'88** 100
Rice Salad, Colorful, **'81** 253
Rice Salad, Confetti, **'80** 232
Rice Salad, Crunchy, **'82** 302
Rice Salad, Curried, **'80** 84; **'85** 147, 220
Rice Salad, Hearty, **'82** 233
Rice Salad, Mandarin, **'88** 271
Rice Salad, Molded Gazpacho-, **'86** 221
Rice Salad, Springtime Wild, **'88** 100
Rice Salad, Vegetable-, **'80** 148; **'83** 198;
  '85 87
Rice Salad, Wild, **'85** 65
Rice Salad with Artichoke Hearts, **'80** 232
Rice Salad with Bacon, **'79** 52
Rice Salad with Fresh Mushrooms, **'80** 231
Rice Salad, Zesty, **'81** 23
Rice-Shrimp Salad, **'79** 270
Rolls, Hearty Salad, **'81** 206
Rolls, Picnic Salad, **'79** 127
Rotelle Salad, Crunchy, **'86** 209
Rotini Salad, **'88** 42
Salmon-and-Macaroni Salad, **'81** 114
Salmon-Pasta Salad, **'87** 9
Salmon-Rice Salad, **'84** 289
Salmon Salad, Crunchy, **'81** 148
Salmon Salad Shells, **'85** 286
Salmon Salad, Summertime, **'82** 207
Salmon-Spinach Salad, **'87** 145
Sauerkraut Salad, **'80** 178
Sauerkraut Salad, Crunchy, **'87** 9
Seafood Salad, Baked, **'86** 10
Seafood Salad, Hot, **'79** 117; **'80** 164
Seafood Salad, Polynesian, **'79** 57
Seafood Salad, Smoky, **'84** 46
Seashell Salad, **'86** 209
Shrimp and Avocado Salad, **'80** 266
Shrimp-and-Orange Rice Salad,
  Zesty, **'87** 155
Shrimp and Rice Salad, **'80** 231; **'82** 207
Shrimp Bowl, Mediterranean, **'80** 174
Shrimp-Egg Salad, Tossed, **'80** 4
Shrimp-Endive Salad, **'85** 73

Shrimp Macaroni Salad, **'79** 220
Shrimp-Macaroni Salad, **'85** 219
Shrimp Mousse, **'79** 57
Shrimp-Rice Salad, Baked, **'83** 22
Shrimp-Rice Salad, Tangy, **'84** 66
Shrimp Rotelle, **'85** 165
Shrimp Salad, **'81** 94; **'86** 186
Shrimp Salad, Avocado Stuffed
  with, **'82** 207
Shrimp Salad, Creamy, **'79** 56
Shrimp Salad Filling, **'87** 106
Shrimp Salad in Pastry, **'86** 105
Shrimp Salad, Layered, **'88** 100
Shrimp Salad, Marinated, **'85** 82
Shrimp Salad on the Half Shell, **'86** 73
Shrimp Salads, Individual, **'83** 146
Shrimp Salad, Super, **'81** 37
Shrimp Salad, Vegetable-, **'79** 190
Shrimp Vermicelli Salad, **'88** 139
Slaws
    Apple-Pineapple Slaw, **'79** 241
    Apple Slaw, Fresh, **'81** 63
    Bacon Coleslaw, **'83** 58
    Banana-Nut Slaw, **'86** 250
    Bean Slaw, Red, **'79** 247
    Cabbage-and-Apple Slaw, Red, **'87** 31
    Cabbage-Orange Slaw, **'79** 135
    Cabbage Slaw, Fresh, **'85** 139
    Chicken Coleslaw, **'84** 2
    Chili Coleslaw, **'80** 178
    Coleslaw, **'79** 152; **'82** 135
    Corn and Cabbage Slaw, **'79** 135

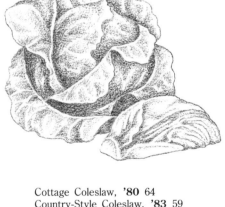

    Cottage Coleslaw, **'80** 64
    Country-Style Coleslaw, **'83** 59
    Creamy Coleslaw, **'83** 170
    Crunchy Coleslaw, **'86** 295
    Curried Coleslaw, **'85** 139
    Freezer Slaw, **'81** 279; **'82** 24;
      '83 154
    Frozen Coleslaw, **'82** 102
    Fruit Coleslaw, Three-, **'86** 250
    Fruited Coleslaw, **'83** 209; **'85** 139
    Grape-Poppy Seed Slaw, **'86** 225
    Grapes and Almonds, Coleslaw
      with, **'83** 59
    Guacamole Mexican Coleslaw, **'82** 302
    Ham Coleslaw, **'84** 195
    Hot-and-Creamy Dutch Slaw, **'87** 127
    Hot-and-Sour Chinese Slaw, **'85** 139
    Kentucky Coleslaw, **'81** 216
    Layered Coleslaw, **'86** 180
    Make-Ahead Coleslaw, **'81** 155

Salads, Slaws *(continued)*

Marinated Coleslaw, **'79** 135
Mexicali Coleslaw, **'84** 18
Old-Fashioned Coleslaw, **'80** 120;
 '82 225
Old-Fashioned Slaw, **'84** 149
Overnight Cabbage Slaw, **'81** 88;
 '82 7
Overnight Coleslaw, **'79** 135
Overnight Slaw, **'79** 5
Peach Slaw, Party, **'86** 250
Peanut Slaw, **'85** 139
Pear Slaw, Peanutty-, **'86** 250
Pineapple Slaw, Colorful, **'86** 250
Polka Dot Slaw, **'83** 59
Seafood Slaw, **'79** 56
Sour Cream Slaw, **'87** 10
Swedish Slaw, **'79** 135
Sweet and Crunchy Slaw, **'79** 104
Sweet-and-Sour Slaw, **'81** 237
Sweet Cabbage Slaw, **'79** 76
Tangy Coleslaw, **'83** 59
Tomatoes, Coleslaw with, **'80** 34
Vegetable Slaw, **'81** 280
Zesty Slaw, **'82** 127
Spaghetti Salad, **'82** 277; **'84** 205
Spinach and Bacon Salad, **'81** 143
Spinach and Mushroom Salad, **'80** 112
Spinach-and-Onion Salad Bowl, **'81** 157
Spinach-and-Orange Salad, **'86** 15
Spinach-Beet Salad, **'83** 227
Spinach-Blue Cheese Salad, **'82** 166
Spinach-Lamb Salad, **'85** 58
Spinach-Lettuce Salad, Layered, **'84** 266
Spinach, Pickled, **'81** 69
Spinach Salad, **'82** 102; **'86** 302; **'87** 62;
 '88 299
Spinach Salad, Combination, **'85** 327;
 '86 22
Spinach Salad, Creamy, **'83** 60
Spinach Salad, Crunchy, **'80** 147; **'81** 225
Spinach Salad, Curry, **'80** 242
Spinach Salad Delight, Fresh, **'80** 146
Spinach Salad, Festive, **'80** 247
Spinach Salad, French, **'79** 8
Spinach Salad, Fresh, **'82** 73; **'83** 240;
 '84 15, 77; **'86** 130
Spinach Salad, Green, **'79** 142
Spinach Salad, Layered, **'80** 5
Spinach Salad, Oriental, **'82** 23
Spinach Salad, Southern, **'80** 55
Spinach Salad, Special, **'80** 78
Spinach Salad, Springtime, **'81** 114
Spinach Salad, Supreme, **'79** 243
Spinach Salad, Sweet-Sour, **'85** M112
Spinach Salad, Wilted, **'81** M4
Spinach Salad with Citrus Dressing, **'88** 133
Spinach Salad with Creamy Dressing,
 Crisp, **'83** 81
Spinach Salad with Hot Bacon
 Dressing, **'82** 211
Spinach Salad with Orange
 Dressing, **'87** 187
Spinach Salad with Russian
 Dressing, **'79** 144
Spinach Salad, Zesty, **'79** 88
Spinach-Sprout Salad, Fresh, **'82** 281;
 '83 42
Spinach with Feta, Lemon, **'85** 190
Spinach with Spicy Dressing, Fresh, **'80** 55

Sprout Salad, Spanish, **'85** 327; **'86** 22
Steak Salad Cups, Pepper, **'86** 206
Strawberry Yogurt Salad, **'80** 232
Tabbouleh, **'85** 148
Taco Salad, **'79** 56; **'83** 145; **'84** 221;
 '85 84
Taco Salad Cups, **'85** M29
Taco Salad, Meatless, **'81** 204
Taco Salad, Spicy, **'87** 287
Tofu Salad, **'88** 27
Tomato-Avocado Salad, **'86** 74
Tomato-Basil Vinaigrette, **'87** 89
Tomato-Cucumber-Onion Salad, **'81** 239
Tomato-Cucumber Salad, **'86** 218
Tomatoes, Avocado-Stuffed, **'82** 101

Tomatoes, Cold Stuffed, **'80** 100
Tomatoes, Herbed, **'83** 173
Tomatoes, Marinated, **'85** 156, 163
Tomatoes, Marinated Salsa, **'82** 164
Tomatoes, Oregano, **'83** 145
Tomatoes Vinaigrette, **'84** 106
Tomato-Feta Salad, **'81** 246
Tomato Petal Salad, **'79** 88
Tomato Refresher, **'81** 94
Tomato Relish Salad, **'83** 111
Tomato Salad, Artichoke-Stuffed, **'82** 101
Tomato Salad, Cherry, **'87** 156
Tomato Salad, Crab-Stuffed, **'80** 148
Tomato Salad, Oriental-Stuffed, **'82** 101
Tomato Salad, Vidalia-, **'84** 65
Tomato Slices, Marinated, **'83** 193
Tomato Slices with Lemon
 Dressing, **'87** 167
Tomato Treat, Summer, **'79** 143
Tossed Salad with Parmesan
 Dressing, **'86** 192
Tropical Salad, **'85** 91
Tuna
 Cannellini Bean Salad,
  Tuna-and-, **'86** 143
 Cheese-Sauced Tuna Salad, **'87** M124
 Chef Salad, Tuna, **'82** 78
 Company Tuna Salad, **'87** 201
 Confetti Salad, **'80** 4
 Crunchy Tuna Salad, **'87** 201
 Curried Tuna Salad, **'86** 208
 Curried Tuna Salad with
  Grapes, **'87** 201
 Egg Salad, Tuna-, **'81** 135
 Favorite Tuna Salad, **'82** 208
 Flavorful Tuna Salad, **'81** 37
 Greens and Tuna Salad, Fresh, **'80** 55
 Layered Tuna Salad, **'84** 221
 Macaroni Salad, Tuna, **'83** 44
 Macaroni Salad, Tuna-, **'83** 145;
  '84 66

Potato Salad, Tuna-, **'84** 289
Rice Salad, Tuna-, **'87** 202
Rolls, Hot Tuna Salad, **'84** 281
Swiss Tuna Salad, **'86** 186
Taco Salad, Tuna-, **'87** 145
Tomatoes, Tuna-Mac in, **'87** 188
Whole Wheat Macaroni-Tuna
 Salad, **'84** 193
Turkey-and-Pepper Stir-Fry Salad,
 Chilled, **'88** 140
Turkey-Apple Salad, **'88** 123
Turkey-Carrot Salad, **'86** 283
Turkey-Fruit Salad, **'79** 56
Turkey Fruit Salad, **'83** 233; **'84** 244
Turkey Macaroni Salad, **'83** 282
Turkey Salad Bake, **'79** 253
Turkey Salad, Curried, **'88** 140
Turkey Salad, Fruitful, **'84** 197
Turkey Salad, Holiday, **'84** 320
Turkey Salad, Hot, **'86** 10, 297; **'87** 176
Turkey Salad, Layered, **'86** 332
Turkey Salad Pita Sandwiches, **'87** 202;
 '88 43
Turkey Salad, Polynesian, **'87** 285
Turkey Salad with Hot Bacon
 Dressing, **'87** 285
Turkey Salad with Sautéed
 Walnuts, **'86** 117
Turkey Waldorf Salad with Yogurt
 Dressing, **'88** 53
Turkey-Zucchini Salad, **'85** 74
Turnip Salad, **'85** 235
Vegetable. *See also* Salads/Congealed.
 Antipasto, Vegetable, **'85** 263
 Boats, Salad, **'80** 93
 Calico Salad, **'82** 35
 Cauliflower-Pea Salad, **'87** 231
 Chinese Salad, **'80** 4
 Composée, Salad, **'79** 171
 Creamy Vegetable Salad, **'79** 47
 Creole Salad, **'79** 147
 Crunchy Vegetable Salad, **'79** 11;
  '80 217; **'83** 216
 Different Vegetable Salad, **'82** 143
 Easy Vegetable Salad, **'83** 316; **'84** 16
 Garden Marinade, **'81** 23
 Garden Medley Salad, **'80** 122
 Garden Salad, **'87** 62
 Garden Salad Bowl, **'82** 239
 Garden Salad with Tomato-Cream
  Cheese Dressing, **'79** 173
 Greek Salad, Garden, **'86** 173
 Green-and-White Vegetable
  Salad, **'79** 286
 Green Vegetable Salad,
  Overnight, **'80** 5
 Italian Vegetable Salad, **'81** 253;
  '82 19
 Luncheon Salad, **'84** 232
 Marinade, Fresh Vegetable, **'83** 209
 Marinade, Garden, **'81** 23
 Marinade, Medley, **'79** 20
 Marinade, Tossed Vegetable, **'84** 266
 Marinated Combo Salad, **'82** 267
 Marinated Garden Vegetables,
  '87 252
 Marinated Salad,
  Eight-Vegetable, **'80** 218
 Marinated Summer Salad, **'81** 153
 Marinated Vegetable-Bacon
  Bowl, **'79** 191

Marinated Vegetable Patch
  Salad, '84 232
Marinated Vegetables, '79 146;
  '81 239; '85 67; '88 4, 170
Marinated Vegetable Salad, '79 106,
  143; '81 280; '82 163; '83 260;
  '84 13; '87 243
Marinated Vegetable Salad,
  Crispy, '84 193
Marinated Vegetable Salad,
  Fresh, '86 173
Marinated Vegetables,
  Sweet-and-Sour, '83 266
Marinated Vegetables, Zesty, '82 272
Marinate, Fresh Vegetable, '80 33;
  '81 230
Meal-in-One Salad, '82 232
Medley Salad, Vegetable, '88 86
Mexican Salad, '81 36, 113
Minted Vegetable Salad, '88 23
Mixed Vegetable Salad, '80 115;
  '81 302; '82 239; '83 317; '84 16;
  '86 136
Next-Day Vegetable Salad, '83 81
Oriental Salad, Make-Ahead, '82 163
Oriental Vegetable Salad, '84 290
Party Vegetable Salad, '86 79
Rainbow Vegetable Salad, '83 111
Refrigerated Vegetable Salad, '84 120
Rice-and-Vegetable Salad, '86 42
Rolls, Vegetable Salad, '82 278
Senator's Salad, '79 191
Seven-Layer Vegetable Salad, '79 88
Spring Vegetable Salad, '88 48
Swedish Vegetable Salad, '82 23
Sweet-and-Sour Vegetable
  Salad, '81 25
Tangy Vegetable Toss, '79 144
Tarragon-Vegetable Salad, '85 288
Variety Salad, '79 113
Vinaigrette Salad,
  Vegetable-Chicken, '86 135
Vinaigrette, Vegetables, '82 225, 290
Walnuts, Vegetable Salad with, '86 118
Winter Vegetable Salad, '86 42
Vermicelli Vinaigrette Salad, '82 189
Waldorf Salad, Creamy, '87 311

Waldorf Salad, Deluxe, '83 81
Waldorf Salad, Frozen, '79 126; '82 145
Waldorf Salad, Jiffy, '88 100
Waldorf Salad, Old-Fashioned, '81 295
Waldorf Salad, Overnight, '81 309
Watercress Salad, '79 144

Watercress-Tomato Salad, '85 132
Watermelon Salad with Celery Nut
  Dressing, '80 182
Watermelon Sparkle, '84 191
Yogurt-Cucumber Salad, '82 122
Ziti-Cheddar Salad, '85 165
Zucchini Chef's Salad, '83 143
Zucchini, Marinated, '80 33
Zucchini Salad, '82 104; '87 103
Zucchini Salad, Marinated, '82 164

Salmon
Avocados, Salmon-Stuffed, '86 74
Ball, Salmon, '80 149; '86 262
Ball, Smoky Salmon Cheese, '82 247
Barbecued Salmon, '81 181
Carbonara, Salmon, '83 43
Casserole, Salmon, '81 22
Chilled Salmon with Dill Sauce, '84 285
Croquettes, Baked Salmon, '81 22
Florentine, Salmon, '83 43
Kabobs, Salmon, '81 182
Loaf, Easy Salmon, '80 4
Loaf with Cucumber-Dill Sauce,
  Salmon, '86 5
Log, Salmon, '81 22
Mousse, Irresistible Salmon, '79 284
Mousse, Salmon, '83 79
Mousse, Salmon Dill, '81 21
Patties, Open-Faced Salmon, '87 M218
Patties with Sauce, Salmon, '88 164
Poached Salmon, '83 35
Potatoes, Salmon-Topped, '84 124
Quiche, Salmon, '82 87; '87 38
Roll, Salmon Party, '83 127
Salad, Chilly Salmon, '80 104
Salad, Crunchy Salmon, '81 148
Salad, Macaroni-Salmon, '82 232
Salad, Salmon-and-Macaroni, '81 114
Salad, Salmon-Pasta, '87 9
Salad, Salmon-Potato, '87 285
Salad, Salmon-Rice, '84 289
Salad, Salmon-Spinach, '87 145
Salad Shells, Salmon, '85 286
Salad, Summertime Salmon, '82 207
Scalloped Salmon, '81 273
Smoked Salmon, Drizzled, '88 91
Soufflé, Fresh Salmon, '81 182
Spread, Salmon, '81 149
Spread, Salmon-and-Horseradish, '87 146
Spread, Smoked Salmon, '84 324
Steaks, Baked Salmon, '85 54
Steaks, Glazed Salmon, '86 256
Steaks, Marinated Salmon, '87 6
Steaks, Oven-Fried Salmon, '81 181
Steaks with Dill Sauce, Salmon, '85 164
Steaks with Tarragon Butter,
  Salmon, '87 155
Terrine, Layered
  Salmon-and-Spinach, '84 132
Turnovers, Salmon-Spinach, '83 44

Sandwiches
Alfalfa Pocket Bread Sandwiches, '82 282;
  '83 41
Apple-Cinnamon Breakfast
  Sandwiches, '85 298
Apple Sandwiches, '79 164; '80 130
Asparagus-and-Ham Melt
  Sandwiches, '88 M96
Asparagus Grill Sandwiches, '79 164;
  '80 130
Asparagus Spear Sandwiches, '84 165

Avocado, Bacon, and Cheese
  Sandwiches, '87 279
Avocado-Crabmeat Sandwiches, '83 2
Bacon, Cheese, and Tomato
  Sandwiches, '84 14
Bacon-Cheese Sandwiches, Grilled, '83 242
Bacon Sandwiches, Open-Faced
  Cheesy, '80 78
Bagels, Meal-in-One, '88 159
Basket of Sandwiches, Bread, '86 126
Bean Salad Sandwiches, '81 243
Beef and Pork Tenderloin
  Sandwiches, '80 175
Beef-Eater Sandwiches, '86 72
Beef Pocket Sandwich, Saucy, '80 92
Beef Salad Pocket Sandwiches, '83 267
Beef Sandwiches, Barbecued, '81 25;
  '82 31; '83 34
Beef Sandwiches, Grilled Corned, '87 54
Beef Slice, French, '79 125

BLT's, Cheesy, '85 92
Breakfast Sandwiches, '80 52; '82 M123
Brown Bread-Cream Cheese
  Sandwiches, '87 M6
Bunwiches, '80 92
Calzone, '85 94
Cheeseburger Biscuits, '79 194
Cheese-Ham Sandwiches, Creamy
  Blue, '87 279
Cheese Sandwiches, Grilled, '82 M172
Cheese Sandwiches, Hot French, '82 3
Chef's Salad, '86 186
Chicken-Almond Pocket
  Sandwiches, '81 240; '83 69
Chicken-and-Cheese Sandwiches,
  Toasted, '85 242
Chicken Club Sandwiches, '86 160
Chicken in a Sandwich, Marinated, '86 185
Chicken-Salad Finger Sandwiches, '85 119
Chicken Salad in a Pocket, '88 139
Chicken Salad on Raisin Bread,
  Curried, '85 96
Chicken Salad with Artichokes, '86 186
Chicken Sandwich, Crispy, '81 114
Chicken Sandwiches, Baked, '79 164;
  '80 130; '84 165
Chicken Sandwiches, Cheesy, '82 190
Chicken Sandwiches, Hot, '83 291
Chicken Sandwiches, Marinated, '86 M45
Chicken Sandwiches, Puffed, '82 35
Chicken Spread, Tasty, '84 193
Chick-Wiches, Saucy, '81 25; '82 31;
  '83 34

Sandwiches *(continued)*

Club Sandwiches, Tangy, '80 93
Club Sandwich, South Seas, '84 282
Confetti Sandwiches, '79 236
Corned Beef and Cheese Sandwich, '79 214
Corned Beef Sandwiches, '83 291; '85 242
Corned Beef Sandwiches,
  Barbecued, '83 130
Crab-and-Cheese Sandwiches, Hot, '87 279
Crabmeat Sandwiches, '84 285
Crabmeat Sandwiches, Deluxe, '81 M74
Crab Sandwiches, Open-Faced, '87 106
Crab Sandwiches, Puffy, '83 291
Crab Tomato Sandwiches,
  Open-Face, '81 29
Cucumber Pinwheel Sandwiches, '85 120
Cucumber Sandwiches, '88 159
Cucumber Sandwiches, Dainty, '81 119
Deviled Delight, '83 130
Eggplant Sandwiches, Baked, '82 230
Egg Sandwiches, Open-Face, '83 292;
  '84 78; '86 160
Egg Sandwiches, Open-Faced
  Cheesy, '86 67

Eggsclusive Sandwiches, '79 164; '80 130
Eggs-Tra Special Sandwiches, '81 240;
  '83 69
English Muffin Delight, '82 45
Frankfurter Sandwiches, '84 M11
Garden Sandwiches, Open-Faced, '87 105
Garden, The, '83 134
Grilled Sandwiches, Tasty, '84 30
Grinder Sandwich, '85 299
Guacamole Sandwiches, '82 9; '83 68
Guacamole Subs, '84 293
Gumbo Joes, '88 158
Ham-and-Cheese Pita Sandwiches, '87 202
Ham-and-Cheese Rolls, '82 3
Ham-and-Cheese Sandwiches, Hot, '85 299
Ham and Cheese Sandwich, Tex Mex, '86 4
Ham and Eggs à la Swiss, '88 158
Ham and Swiss in the Pocket, '83 31
Ham-and-Swiss Sandwiches, Tangy, '85 164
Ham-and-Turkey Specials, Cheesy, '84 14
Ham Hideaways, '81 29
Ham Hot Rods, '86 136
Ham Loaves, Country, '86 255
Ham Salad Sandwich, Tangy, '80 272
Ham Sandwiches, Baked, '81 29

Ham Sandwiches, Hot, '79 214
Ham Sandwiches, Open-Face, '82 40;
  '85 8
Ham Sandwiches, Virginia, '80 155
Heroes, Neptune, '84 281
Hot Brown Sandwiches, '80 M202
Lamb Pockets with Dilled Cucumber
  Topping, '87 104
Loaf, Big Wheel, '84 281
Meal-in-One Sandwiches, '80 218
Monte Cristo Sandwiches, '83 134
Muffaletta-Style Po-Boys, '83 230
Muffin Stacks, Mushroom-Topped, '80 271
Mushroom Sandwiches, Toasted, '87 281
Omelet Sandwich, '86 95
Open-Faced Sandwiches, '79 214
Open-Face Sandwiches, '84 13
Orange Blossom Special, '88 158
Oyster-and-Bacon Poor Boys, '87 40
Oyster Submarine Sandwich, '80 92
Peanut Butter-and-Jelly Sandwiches,
  Christmas Tree, '85 319
Peanut Butter Breakfast Sandwich, '82 55
Peanut-Cheese-Raisin Sandwiches, '88 140
Pimiento Cheese Sandwiches, '82 278
Pita Salad Sandwiches, '83 134
Pita Sandwiches, '84 139
Pita Sandwiches, Bavarian, '83 31
Pita Sandwiches, Denver, '86 M12
Pita Sandwiches, Dried Beef, '86 160
Pita Sandwiches, Ham-and-Cheese, '88 44
Pita Sandwiches, Hot, '83 217; '87 M6
Pita Sandwiches, Turkey Salad, '88 43
Pita Sandwiches, Vegetarian, '84 193
Pitas, Curried Beef, '85 220
Pitas, Spinach-Walnut, '88 43
Pitas, Taco, '83 31
Pizza Sandwiches, Open-Face, '82 3;
  '83 85; '84 M198; '85 22
Pizza Sandwich, Giant, '80 93
Pocket Sandwiches, Hearty, '80 93
Pockets, Oriental Stuffed, '79 14
Pork Sandwiches, Party, '88 M273
Rarebit, Tangy Welsh, '88 159
Rarebit, Uptown Welsh, '87 279
Reuben Sandwiches, '80 M201
Reuben Sandwiches, Broiled, '81 240;
  '83 69
Reuben Sandwiches, Crispy, '85 299
Reuben Sandwiches, Grilled, '81 206
Salad Boats, '80 93
Salad Rolls, Hearty, '81 206
Salami Sandwiches, Open-Faced, '87 279
Sausage and Pepper Loaves, Italian, '83 11
Sausage-Cheese Loaves, '88 235
Sausage Sandwiches with Mustard
  Sauce, '84 250
Sausage Sandwich, Italian, '80 92
Sausage Sloppy Joes, Italian, '86 160
Seafood Hot Brown, '88 158
Shrimp-Cheese Sandwiches, '85 242
Shrimp Destin, '82 29
Shrimp Salad, '86 186
Sloppy Joe Pocket Sandwiches, '81 200
Snack Buns, '87 279
Snackwiches, '88 172
Spinach-Oyster Loaves, '84 213
Spinach Sandwiches, Fresh, '85 59
Spinach-Walnut Pitas, '87 202
Sprout Sandwiches, Polynesian, '85 51
Stacking Sandwiches, '86 127

Steaks, Greek Pocket, '81 262
Steak Stroganoff Sandwiches, '85 110
Stromboli, '88 272
Submarine Sandwiches, Superb, '84 250
Tea Sandwiches, Gingered, '84 116
Tempting Twosome, '81 240; '83 69
Tofu-Veggie Sandwiches, Open-Face, '86 5
Tomatoes with Cheese Sauce over
  Toast, '88 159
Tuna Burgers, Zippy, '81 135
Tuna Cheesies, '82 191
Tuna Club Sandwiches, '83 134
Tuna-in-a-Pita Pocket, '87 202
Tuna Melts, Tempting, '88 158
Tuna Pockets, '88 139
Tuna Salad Rolls, Hot, '84 281
Tuna Salad, Swiss, '86 186
Tuna Sandwiches, French Toasted, '80 275
Tuna Sandwiches, Hot, '85 299; '86 M194
Tuna Waffle-Wich, Hot, '88 272
Turkey-Cheese Puffs, '87 301
Turkey-Mozzarella Rounds, '82 3
Turkey Open-Facers, '82 190
Turkey Salad Pita Sandwiches, '87 202
Vegetable Garden Heroes, '84 14

Vegetable Pockets, '85 215
Vegetable Puff Sandwich, '85 51
Vegetable Salad Rolls, '82 278
Vegetarian Melt, Open-Faced, '87 106
Vidalia Sandwiches on Salt-Rising
  Bread, '79 145
Wake-Up Sandwiches, '84 58
Wreath, Festive Sandwich, '86 333
Yummy Sandwiches, '81 229
Zucchini Sandwiches, Open-Faced, '88 159

Sauces. *See also* Desserts/Sauces.
Anchovy-Garlic Sauce over
  Vermicelli, '86 158
Apple-Horseradish Sauce, '82 229
Apricot Sauce, '87 172
Apricot-Sauced Pork Chops, '85 22
Avocado Sauce, '80 198; '83 200
Barbecue
  Beer Barbecue Sauce, '84 173
  Bourbon Barbecue Sauce, '85 90
  Dressed-Up Barbecue Sauce, '84 173
  Eastern-Style Barbecue Sauce, '88 145
  Easy Barbecue Sauce, '79 90; '82 178
  Mustard Barbecue Sauce, '84 173
  Oven Barbecue Sauce, '82 233
  Paprika Barbecue Sauce, '79 90
  Peanut Butter Barbecue
    Sauce, '81 233
  Piquant Barbecue Sauce, '79 159
  Sauce, Barbecue, '84 172; '86 153;
    '88 218
  Savory Barbecue Sauce, '86 153
  Special Barbecue Sauce, '82 177
  Tomato Barbecue Sauce,
    Fresh, '84 172
  Western-Style Barbecue Sauce, '88 145

Basil Sauce, Asparagus with, '86 33
Bean Sauce, Pork-and-Onions with, '85 76
Béarnaise Sauce, '83 138; '85 37;
  '86 193
Béarnaise Sauce, Blender, '81 90
Béarnaise Sauce, Classic, '86 244
Béarnaise Sauce, Quick, '82 84
Béchamel Sauce, '80 190; '83 277;
  '84 M239; '87 286
Blueberry Sauce, '80 144; '86 248
Bordelaise Sauce, '83 138, 262
Bouillon Sauce, '80 8
Brandy-Butter Sauce, '79 230
Brandy Sauce, Carrots in, '83 86
Brandy Sauce, Lemony-Butter Steak
  with, '85 78
Buttermilk Sauce, '84 6
Butter Sauce, '86 268
Butter Sauce, Vegetable, '86 174
Catsup Sauce, '81 228
Catsup Topping, '81 170
Champagne Sauce, Chicken Breasts
  with, '86 49
Cheese
    Brussels Sprouts with Cheese
      Sauce, '79 246
    Cottage Cheese Sauce, '87 232
    Cream Sauce, Cheesy, '82 79
    Easy Cheese Sauce, '79 22
    Garlic-Cheese Sauce, '84 M70
    Lemony Cheese Sauce, '84 183
    Monterey Jack Sauce, '84 293
    Mornay Sauce, '80 120; '81 90;
      '83 138; '84 295
    Mushroom-Cheese Sauce, '83 190;
      '86 48
    Parmesan Cheese Sauce, '79 165;
      '80 162; '85 143
    Rich Cheese Sauce, '81 89
    Sauce, Cheese, '79 M156; '81 43, 44,
      225; '82 M123; '83 49, 138, 188;
      '84 57; '85 92; '86 241;
      '88 78, 272
    Swiss Cheese Sauce, '79 35; '87 289;
      '88 135
    Swiss Sauce, '83 M195
    Swiss Sauce, Creamy, '80 M53
    Topper, Vegetable-Cheese
      Potato, '86 6
    Turnips in Cheese Sauce, '84 229
    Vegetable-Cheese Sauce, '85 M152
Cherry Sauce, '83 276; '84 91
Cherry Sauce, Elegant, '79 M156
Cherry Sauce, Roast Ducklings
  with, '86 312
Cherry Sauce, Royal, '85 224; '86 83
Cherry Sauce, Spicy, '83 244
Chervil Sauce, '83 128
Chicken Sauce, Creamy, '81 91
Chile Cream, Ancho, '87 121
Chile Sauce, Ancho, '87 122
Chile Sauce, Green, '82 220
Chili Meat Sauce, '83 4
Chili Sauce, '81 175
Chili Sauce, Chunky, '85 188
Chili Sauce, Red, '85 245
Chili Sauce, Spicy, '87 127
Chive Sauce, Steamed Broccoli with
  Tangy, '83 101
Cider Sauce, '87 224
Cilantro Cream, '87 121

Citrus Sauce, Stuffed Flounder Rolls
  with, '85 180
Clam Sauce, Linguine with, '88 90
Clam Sauce, Vermicelli and Sprouts with
  Red, '86 143
Cocktail Sauce, '87 128
Cocktail Sauce, Boiled Shrimp with, '79 151
Cocktail Sauce, French Fried Zucchini
  with, '86 146
Cocktail Sauce, Spicy, '83 258
Cranberry-Apricot Sauce, Fresh, '87 243

Cranberry Juice Sauce, '85 224; '86 83
Cranberry-Raisin Sauce, Baked Ham
  with, '88 244
Cranberry Sauce, Baked, '88 257
Cranberry Sauce, Cornish Hens
  with, '79 180
Cranberry Sauce, Fresh, '79 283; '84 275
Cranberry Sauce, Tart, '83 261
Cranberry Wine Sauce, '83 276
Cream Sauce, '85 291
Cream Sauce, Brandied, '82 70
Cream Sauce, Peppery, '88 206
Cream Sauce, Sherried, '84 210; '85 M152
Cream Sauce, Shrimp in, '84 M286
Cream Sauce, Spicy, '82 45
Cream-Wine Sauce, Potatoes in, '86 18
Creamy Sauce, '79 41
Creolaise Sauce, '83 91, 262
Cucumber-Dill Sauce, '86 5
Cucumber Sauce, '82 111; '84 M286
Currant Jelly Sauce, Quail with, '86 94
Currant Sauce, '87 240
Curry Sauce, '79 M156; '83 138; '84 M71
Devonshire Cream, Mock, '81 288
Devonshire Sauce, Processor, '87 58
Dill Sauce, '84 M70, 107; '85 39; '88 162
Dill Sauce, Chilled Salmon with, '84 285
Dill Sauce, Creamy, '79 M156
Dill Sauce, Salmon Steaks with, '85 164
Egg Foo Yong Sauce, '86 232
Enchilada Sauce, '81 194
Enchilada Sauce, Red Chile, '85 245
Foo Yong Sauce, '80 223
French Sauce, Broccoli with, '81 295
Fruit Sauce, '81 177
Garlic Buerre Blanc Sauce, '88 222
Garlic Sauce, Stir-Fried Pork in, '84 141
Grape Sauce, White, '80 38
Green Sauce, Herbed, '86 244
Ham-and-Mushroom Sauce, Steak
  with, '83 109
Heather Sauce, '84 182
Herb Butter Sauce, Corn with, '79 150
Herb-Mayonnaise Sauce, '85 73
Herb Sauce, Green, '83 36
Hollandaise Sauce, '80 M107, M268;
  '81 90; '83 137; '85 295; '86 94;
  '87 195; '88 58, M177, 222

Hollandaise Sauce, Blender, '79 39;
  '82 84, 234
Hollandaise Sauce, Broccoli
  with, '79 244, 276
Hollandaise Sauce, Broccoli with
  Mock, '82 272
Hollandaise Sauce, Classic, '88 53
Hollandaise Sauce, Mock, '85 49
Hollandaise-Shrimp Sauce, Flounder
  with, '86 234
Hollandaise, Tangy, '85 148
Honey-Butter Sauce, '85 18
Honey-Lemon Mustard Sauce, '84 275
Honey-Lime Sauce, '82 85
Honey-Mustard Sauce, '85 13
Horseradish-Mustard Sauce,
  Creamy, '88 M177
Horseradish Sauce, '84 190; '85 224;
  '86 83; '87 127; '88 207, M273
Horseradish Sauce and Curried Bananas,
  Fillets with, '85 230
Horseradish Sauce, Broccoli with, '81 2;
  '83 206; '84 33
Horseradish Sour Cream, '86 244
Hot Sauce, '79 185; '83 74
Hot Sauce, San Antonio, '84 291
Italian Sauce, '80 63
Italian Sauce, Quick, '82 230
Italian-Style Sauce, '83 250
Jalapeño Sauce, '80 193
Jezebel Sauce, '81 29; '82 55
Lemon-Butter Sauce, '84 252
Lemon-Celery Sauce, Baked Fillets
  in, '84 91
Lemon Garlic Sauce, Shrimp in, '83 67
Lemon Meunière Sauce, '88 222
Lemon Parsley Sauce, '81 106
Lemon Sauce, '82 290
Lemon Sauce, Asparagus with, '86 62
Lemon Sauce, Chicken Scaloppine
  with, '86 156
Mandarin-Almond Cream Sauce, '84 183
Mandarin Sauce, '84 60
Marinade, '86 153
Marinade, Sweet-and-Sour, '86 113
Marinade, Tangy Beef, '86 113
Marinade, Tangy Light, '82 178
Marinade, Teriyaki, '86 114
Marinara Sauce, '82 178
Meat Sauce, Italian, '83 193
Meunière Sauce, '80 57
Mexican Sauce, '80 198
Microwaving Sauces, '84 M70
Mimosa, Sauce, '88 288
Mint Sauce, '84 107; '88 M96
Mushroom-Dill Sauce, '80 271
Mushroom Sauce, '81 90, 200; '82 46;
  '83 71, 205, 212; '84 M70; '85 40;
  '86 198; '87 36, 186, 284
Mushroom Sauce Supreme on
  Vermicelli, '86 158
Mushroom-Wine Sauce, '84 84; '86 24
Mustard Cream Sauce, '88 61
Mustard-Hollandaise Sauce, Mock, '87 269
Mustard Sauce, '80 222, 283; '83 21, 321;
  '84 M70; '86 185; '87 22
Mustard Sauce, Creamy, '80 272; '86 257;
  '87 232
Mustard Sauce, Extra-Special, '79 82
Mustard Sauce, Hamburger Steaks
  with, '84 230

Sauces *(continued)*

Mustard Sauce, Light, **'82** 178
Mustard Sauce, Mild, **'85** 224; **'86** 84
Mustard Sauce, Sausage Sandwiches with, **'84** 250
Mustard Sauce, Scallops with, **'84** 163
Mustard Sauce, Smoked Sausages with, **'81** 56
Mustard Sauce, Sweet, **'85** 12
Mustard-Sour Cream Sauce, **'81** 68
Mustard-Vinaigrette Sauce, **'84** 174
Natillas Sauce, **'83** 179
Olive-Butter Sauce, Broccoli with, **'83** 118
Onion Cream Sauce, **'87** 232
Onion-Mushroom Sauce, **'85** 224; **'86** 84
Onion-Parsley Sauce, **'85** 148
Onion Sauce, **'82** 72; **'87** 248
Onion Sauce, Brussels Sprouts in, **'81** 308
Orange-Almond Sauce, Chicken in, **'79** 219; **'80** 13
Orange Butter Sauce, Asparagus with, **'85** 43
Orange Liqueur Sauce, **'86** 142
Orange Sauce, **'82** 47; **'83** 10, 277; **'84** M286
Orange Sauce, Asparagus with, **'83** 46
Orange Sauce, Brussels Sprouts in, **'86** 55
Orange Sauce, Celery in, **'79** 70
Orange Sauce, Chicken Breasts with, **'79** 77
Orange Sauce, Lobster Tails with Spiced, **'86** 155
Pancake Sauce, Cinnamon-Pecan-Honey, **'88** 46
Parsley-Chive Sauce, **'84** 212
Parsley-Garlic Sauce, **'83** 138; **'84** M70
Parsley Sauce, **'82** 248; **'86** 108
Peach-Blueberry Pancake Sauce, **'82** 177
Peach-Blueberry Sauce, **'81** 170
Peach Sauce, Creamy Fresh, **'79** 177
Peanut Hot Sauce, **'86** 305
Pea Sauce, Green, **'83** 22
Pepper-Onion Sauce, **'84** 125
Pesto, **'80** 242
Pesto, Fresh, **'86** 150
Pesto, Garlic, **'84** 108
Pesto, Tomatoes, **'86** 150
Pico de Gallo, **'79** 185; **'86** 19
Pineapple-Curry Sauce, **'79** 252
Pineapple-Rhubarb Sauce, **'88** 94
Pineapple Sauce, **'84** 236
Pizza Sauce, **'84** 33; **'85** 285
Plum Sauce, **'80** 249; **'82** 40; **'88** 152
Plum Sauce, Chinese, **'82** 237
Plum Sauce, Gingered, **'87** 175
Plum Sauce, Red, **'80** 49
Plum Sauce, Spicy, **'86** 11
Port Wine Sauce, **'84** 252
Pumpkin Seed Sauce, **'88** 246
Raisin-Pineapple Sauce, **'82** 177
Raisin Sauce, **'83** 59, 215; **'84** 91, 275; **'87** 127
Raisin Sauce, Ham with, **'82** M76
Rancheros Sauce, **'88** 148
Rémoulade Sauce, **'80** 58; **'81** 89; **'82** 178
Rhubarb Sauce, Chilled, **'88** 94
Rum Sauce, Mango-Spiced, **'86** 215
Salsa, **'87** 217; **'88** 147
Salsa, Chunky, **'86** 130
Salsa Cruda, **'88** 148

Salsa, Pepper, **'88** 26
Salsa with Homemade Tostados, Hot Chile, **'88** 115
Savory Sauce, **'84** 196
Seafood
  Clam Sauce, Linguine with, **'84** 124
  Clam Sauce, Pasta with, **'84** 291
  Clam Sauce, Vermicelli with, **'85** 295
  Clam Sauce with Linguine, **'84** 9
  Crab and Shrimp Sauce Piquante, **'83** 92
  Crab Marinara Sauce, Quick, **'85** M151
  Delight, Seafood Sauce, **'82** 91
  Linguine with Seafood Sauce, **'83** 232
  Sauce, Seafood, **'79** 3; **'82** 84; **'83** 36; **'86** 304
  Shrimp Sauce, Broccoli and Cauliflower with, **'84** 248
  Shrimp Sauce, Flounder Fillets in, **'83** 227
  Stone Crab Mustard Sauce, **'80** 3
  Stone Crab Sauce, Tangy, **'80** 3
Sesame Sauce, Vegetables with, **'83** 112
Sherry Sauce, **'87** 96
Shrimp-and-Almond Sauce, **'87** 282
Shrimp Sauce, **'87** 138, 232
Sour Cream-Dill Sauce, Mushrooms in, **'84** 215
Sour Cream-Horseradish Sauce, **'88** 4
Sour Cream, Mock, **'83** 71, 205
Sour Cream Sauce, **'82** 68; **'84** 132; **'87** 233
Sour Cream Sauce, Broccoli with, **'87** 127
Soy Sauce, Grilled Trout with Ginger and, **'85** 228
Spaghetti Sauce, Beer, **'85** 13
Spaghetti Sauce, Herbed, **'85** 13
Spaghetti Sauce, Thick, **'84** 118
Spaghetti Sauce, Turkey, **'85** 13
Spicy Sauce, **'84** 77
Spinach Sauce, Fettuccine with, **'84** 329
Strawberry-Banana Sauce, **'81** 41
Sunshine Sauce, **'87** 96
Sweet-and-Sour Sauce, **'80** 20; **'85** 12, 34; **'86** 240

Taco Sauce, **'82** M283
Tarragon Sauce, **'83** 56; **'84** 190; **'87** 229
Tarragon-Tomato Sauce, **'84** 131
Tartar Sauce, **'79** 184; **'81** 134; **'82** 135; **'86** 233
Tartar Sauce, Bold-and-Spicy, **'86** 180
Tartar Sauce, Creamy, **'80** 164
Tartar Sauce, Quick, **'87** 128
Tempura Sauce, Basic, **'81** 68

Tomato-Cream Sauce, Linguine with, **'86** 158
Tomato Sauce, **'85** 193, 244; **'87** 249; **'88** 116
Tomato Sauce, Fish in, **'85** 75
Tomato Sauce for Spaghetti, Italian, **'81** 134
Tomato Sauce, Fresh, **'83** 224; **'87** 171
Tomato Sauce, Herbed, **'86** 277
Tomato Sauce, Herbed Fresh, **'85** M151
Tomato Sauce, Italian, **'82** M68
Tomato Sauce, Italian-Style, **'87** 182
Tomato Sauce, Refrigerator, **'85** 188
Tomato Sauce, Seasoned, **'83** 150
Tomato Sauce, Spicy, **'84** 294; **'88** 19
Tomato Sauce, Vermicelli with, **'83** 164
Tomato Sauce with Green Chiles, **'81** 196
Vegetable Sauce, Greek Fish with, **'82** 72
Vegetable Sauce, Pasta with, **'83** 163
Velouté Sauce, **'84** 22
Walnut Sauce, Spaghetti with Parsley and, **'80** 30
Whiskey Sauce, **'80** 58
White Sauce, **'82** 269; **'83** 138, 245; **'87** 166
White Sauce, Asparagus, **'80** 147
White Sauce, Basic, **'79** M156; **'81** 89
White Sauce, Low-Calorie, Medium, **'87** 26
White Sauce, Thick, **'82** 42
Wine Sauce, Beef Cubes in, **'79** 264
Wine Sauce, Broccoli with, **'84** 187
Wine Sauce, Chicken in, **'80** 8
Wine Sauce, Marsala, **'81** 77
Wine Sauce, Mushrooms with, **'85** 292
Wine Sauce, Red Snapper in, **'85** 138
Wine Sauce, Skillet Steak in Red, **'85** 21
Wine Sauce, Veal and Carrots in, **'86** M139
Wine Sauce, White, **'84** 132
Yogurt-Horseradish Sauce, **'85** 66
Yogurt Sauce, Lamb Meatballs with, **'85** 132
Zippy Sauce, **'86** 44
Zucchini Sauce, Spaghetti with, **'81** 38

Sauerkraut
Beany Kraut and Franks, **'79** 64
Bratwurst and Sauerkraut, **'84** 250
Homemade Sauerkraut, **'81** 216
Meatballs, Sauerkraut, **'86** 257
Pork Chops and Sauerkraut, **'88** 98
Relish, Sauerkraut, **'85** 136
Salad, Crunchy Sauerkraut, **'87** 9
Salad, Sauerkraut, **'80** 178
Sausage and Kraut, **'83** 11

Sausage
Appetizers, Party Rye, **'86** 262
Bake, Creole Sausage-and-Rice, **'88** 58
Baked Peaches and Sausage, **'82** 50
Baked Zucchini and Sausages, **'80** 300
Bake, Eggplant-Sausage, **'85** 221
Bake, Hominy-Sausage, **'88** 51
Bake, Sausage-Cheese, **'88** 58
Bake, Sausage Egg, **'81** 225
Bake, Sausage-Noodle, **'81** 92
Bake, Smoked Sausage-Egg, **'85** 248
Balls in Cheese Pastry, Sausage, **'80** 248
Balls, Venison Sausage, **'80** 42
Barbecued Sausage, **'86** 153
Basic Sausage, **'88** 104
Beans, and Rice, Texas Sausage, **'84** 296
Biscuit Bites, Sausage, **'84** 95
Biscuits, Cheesy Sausage, **'80** 78

Biscuits, Southern Sausage and, '82 43
Biscuits with Sausage, Angel
    Heart, '87 156
Boudin, Old-Fashioned, '85 250
Bratwurst and Sauerkraut, '84 250
Bratwurst Dinner, Krause's Café, '87 238
Breakfast Dish, Sausage-Apricot, '82 10
Brunch for a Bunch, '88 57
Burgers, Sausage, '83 212
Burritos, Breakfast, '84 57
Cabbage, Italian Stuffed, '84 294
Cabbage Rolls, Hot-and-Spicy, '84 249

Cabbage, Sausage-Sauced, '81 271
Cabbage, Stuffed, '84 282
Calzone, '85 94
Casserole, Brunch, '82 124
Casserole, Cheesy Sausage, '82 124
Casserole, Country Sausage, '79 192
Casserole, Crunchy Sausage, '81 288
Casserole, Easy Sausage, '87 M189
Casserole, Eggplant-Sausage, '84 215
Casserole, Grits-Sausage, '84 75; '86 241
Casserole, Ground Beef and
    Sausage, '80 260
Casserole, Hawaiian Sausage, '85 42
Casserole, Oriental Sausage and
    Rice, '82 M123
Casserole, Sausage, '81 112; '82 12
Casserole, Sausage and Broccoli, '80 33
Casserole, Sausage and Noodle, '82 123
Casserole, Sausage and Wild Rice, '83 196
Casserole, Sausage Breakfast, '81 270
Casserole, Sausage-Chile Rellenos, '88 52
Casserole, Sausage-Egg, '86 M12
Casserole, Sausage Jambalaya, '82 M203
Casserole, Sausage-Mushroom
    Breakfast, '86 95
Casserole, Sausage-Potato, '86 217
Casserole, Sausage-Rice, '82 50; '83 75
Casserole, Sausage-Wild Rice, '84 250
Casserole, Spanish Rice, '79 192
Casserole, Swiss Sausage, '80 209
Chicken Rolls Élégante, '80 210
Chile con Queso Supreme, '80 265
Chili, Beefy Sausage, '82 11
Chili, Company, '82 311

Chili con Carne, Beef and Sausage, '83 284
Chili con Queso Dip, '86 81
Chili, Sausage-Beef, '86 232
Chili, Texas-Style, '82 311; '83 30
Chorizo and Egg Tortillas, '81 193
Chorizo (Spicy Spanish Sausage), '81 193
Chorizo Substitute, '87 238
Chowder, Sausage-Bean, '83 20
Cocktail Sausages, Saucy, '87 173
Country Sausage, '88 104
Country Sausage, Spiced, '88 104
Crêpes, Cheesy Sausage, '82 240; '83 71
Crêpes, Sausage, '88 295
Crêpes, Sausage-Filled, '79 39
Dinner, Beefy Sausage, '80 M9
Dinner, Sausage-Vegetable, '84 250
Dip, Braunschweiger-and-Beer, '85 69
Dressing, Cajun, '82 307
Dressing, Cornbread-and-Sausage, '83 213
Dressing, Cornbread-Sausage, '82 307;
    '85 280
Dressing, Harvest Sausage, '88 254
Dressing, Sausage, '86 280
Dressing, Turkey with
    Sausage-Cornbread, '83 287
Eggplant Parmesan, '86 53
Eggplant, Sausage Stuffed, '81 204
Eggs, Scotch, '79 261; '83 289
Filling, Omelet with Sausage, '81 43
Garlic Sausage, '88 104
Grits and Sausage, Country, '83 54
Grits, Sausage, '86 92
Gumbo, Dove and Sausage, '81 199
Gumbo, Duck, Oyster, and
    Sausage, '79 226
Gumbo Ya Ya, '87 210
Homemade Sausage, Spicy, '84 320
Hominy-Sausage Skillet, '81 29
Italian Meat Sauce, '83 193
Italian Sauce with Noodles, '84 250
Italian Sausage, '88 104
Italian Sausage and Pepper Loaves, '83 11
Italian Sausage and Peppers, '84 9
Italian Sausage and Rice, '86 53
Italian Sausage Brunch, '88 57
Italian Sausage Quiche, '81 200
Italian Sausage Sandwich, '80 92
Italian Sausage Sloppy Joes, '86 160
Italian Sausage Soup, '84 235
Italian Sausage Soup with Tortellini, '88 46
Italian Sausage-Stuffed Mushrooms, '83 127
Italian Sausage Supper, '88 164
Italian Sausage-Zucchini Soup, '84 4
Jambalaya, Chicken-and-Sausage, '88 200
Jambalaya, Creole, '81 51
Jambalaya de Covington, '87 211
Jambalaya, Northshore, '87 45
Jambalaya, Oven, '84 44
Jambalaya, Sausage, '80 210; '84 249
Kielbasa and Cabbage, '85 67
Kielbasa, Cabbage, '87 42
Kraut, Sausage and, '83 11
Lasagna Rollups, Sausage-, '80 236
Lasagna, Sausage, '83 288
Lasagna Sausage Pinwheels, '79 6
Loaf, Hawaiian Ham, '79 71
Loaf, Skillet Liver, '81 11
Loaves, Sausage-Cheese, '88 235
Log, Phyllo Sausage, '84 294
Log, Stuffed Beef, '79 71
Main Dish, Sausage-Eggplant, '80 211

Manicotti, Saucy Stuffed, '83 288
Meatballs and Sausage, Spicy, '79 163
Meatballs, Chestnut, '79 110
Meatballs, Sweet-and-Sour, '82 247
Meat Loaf, Mozzarella-Layered, '79 71
Mexican Luncheon, '87 192
Muffins, Sausage, '88 52
Muffins, Sausage-Cheese, '86 213
Mushrooms, Sausage-Stuffed, '80 248
Omelet, Puffy Sausage, '80 M268
Onions, Baked Stuffed, '83 135
Pasta with Broccoli and Sausage, '87 109
Pasta with Sausage and Mixed
    Vegetables, '84 249
Patties, Apples on Sausage, '82 120
Peas Mexicano, Black-Eyed, '79 10
Peas with Sausage, Black-Eyed, '86 7
Pepperoni-and-Broccoli Salad, '83 216
Pepperoni and Cheese Loaf, '82 32
Pepperoni Biscuits, '84 95
Pepperoni Pasta, '83 105
Pepperoni Rolls, Ground-, '83 244
Pepperoni-Squash Toss, '84 127
Pie, Breakfast, '86 242
Pie, Cornbread-Sausage-Apple, '87 171
Pintos and Sausage, Hearty, '88 296

Pinwheels, Sausage, '80 209
Pizza, Breakfast, '85 44; '88 288
Pizza, Double Cheesy
    Beef-and-Sausage, '86 77
Pizza Luncheon Pie, Deep-Dish, '80 286
Pizza Peppers, '83 135
Pizza Pie, Link-Sausage, '85 33
Pizza Sandwich, Giant, '80 93
Pizza Snacks, Tasty Little, '79 248
Pizza, Speedy, '81 214
Pizza, Spicy Sausage-Pepperoni, '83 226
Pizza, Thick 'n' Crusty Pepperoni, '85 244
Polish Sausage, Cabbage with, '83 104
Pork Sausage, '81 55
Pork Sausage Ring, '80 49
Potatoes, Mexican-Topped, '83 3
Quiche, Crustless Sausage-Apple, '87 70
Quiche, Easy Sausage, '79 261
Quiche, Pizza, '86 53
Quiche, Sausage-Cheddar, '79 26
Quiche, Spicy Sausage, '80 M108
Quiche, Zucchini-Sausage, '83 122
Rice, Shrimp and Sausage, '79 64
Rice with Sausage, Fried, '83 12
Rolls with Sweet-and-Sour Sauce,
    Sausage, '83 74

Sausage *(continued)*

Rollups, Pancake-Sausage, **'83** 246; **'84** 42
Rollups, Sausage-Bacon, **'88** 51
Salami-Corn Casserole, **'80** 209
Salami Sandwiches, Open-Faced, **'87** 279
Sandwiches, Breakfast, **'80** 52
Sandwiches with Mustard Sauce,
  Sausage, **'84** 250
Skillet Dinner, Sausage, **'83** 29
Skillet Express, Sausage, **'83** 117
Skillet, Mexican-Style, **'83** 12
Skillet Supper, Sausage, **'85** 293
Smoked Sausage, **'86** 154
Smoked Sausage, Chicken Gumbo
  with, **'81** 199
Smoked Sausage, Jambalaya, **'79** 42
Smoked Sausage Stew, **'82** 231
Smoked Sausages with Mustard
  Sauce, **'81** 56
Soup, Sausage and Okra, **'80** 209
Soup, Sausage-Bean, **'85** 88
Soup, Sausage-Potato, **'80** 25
Soup, Spicy Sausage-Bean, **'83** 229
Spaghetti Dinner, Sausage, **'79** 194
Spaghetti, Italian, **'81** 38
Spaghetti, Italian Zucchini, **'85** 2
Spaghetti, Real Italian, **'81** 233
Spaghetti, Sausage, **'83** 160
Spicy Sausage, Dieters', **'85** 49
Squares, Chile-Sausage, **'86** 297
Squares, Sausage-Onion, **'83** 112
Squash, Harvest, **'80** 214

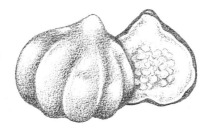

Squash, Sausage-Stuffed Acorn, **'81** 231;
  '83 296; **'84** 285
Squash, Sausage-Stuffed Turban, **'80** 214
Squash with Sausage, Acorn, **'85** 9
Stew, Venison Sausage, **'87** 238
Stir-Fry, Sausage, **'82** 236
Stir-Fry Sausage and Vegetables, **'86** 213;
  '87 82
Strata, Sausage, **'83** 243; **'84** 101
Stuffing, Crown Roast of Pork with
  Cranberry-Sausage, **'88** 49
Supper, Sausage-Bean, **'86** 52
Surprise, Sausage, **'83** 245; **'84** 42
Sweet-and-Sour Sausage, **'88** 296
Tacos, Breakfast, **'80** 43
Taquitos, Breakfast, **'87** 237
Tarts, Sausage 'n' Cheese, **'88** 51
Tomatoes, Sausage-Stuffed, **'80** 47
Tortillas, Egg-and-Sausage, **'83** 246; **'84** 42
Turnovers, Sausage-Cheese, **'88** 231
Vegetables and Sausage, Spicy, **'80** 82
Venison-Vegetable Bake, **'87** 304
Waffles, Sausage, **'83** 50

Wild Rice and Sausage, **'86** 268
Wild Rice, Sausage and, **'85** 65
Zucchini and Sausage, Sautéed, **'83** 289

Scallops
Appetizer, Scallop, **'86** 155
Appetizers, Flaky Scallop, **'86** 327
Artichokes Stuffed with Shrimp and
  Scallops, **'84** 174
Broiled Scallops with Tartar Sauce, **'80** 164
Broth with Black Beans and Cilantro,
  Southwestern Scallop, **'87** 123
Casserole, Scallop, **'79** 228
Ceviche (Marinated Raw Fish), **'82** 220
Cheese Scallops, Chip and, **'80** 301
Coquilles Saint Cyrano, **'86** 90
Creamy Scallops and Mushrooms, **'83** 144
Crêpes, Coquilles St. Jacques, **'83** 13
Fresh Scallops and Pasta, **'83** 164
Grilled Scallops, Marinated, **'84** 171
Kabobs, Grilled Scallop, **'83** 101
Kabobs, Scallop-Bacon, **'81** 111
Kabobs, Sea Scallop, **'82** 162
Mornay, Scallops, **'80** 164
Mustard Sauce, Scallops with, **'84** 163
Provençal, Scallops, **'85** 66
Salad, Hot Seafood, **'80** 164
Sautéed Scallops with Cranberry
  Relish, **'83** 144
Sauté, Scallop, **'88** 28
Sauté, Shrimp-and-Scallop, **'85** 103
Savannah, Scallops, **'79** 145
Sherried Scallops, **'83** 281
Supreme, Seafood, **'82** 284
Tostada, Grilled Scallops, **'87** 120
Vegetables, Bay Scallops with, **'84** 233
Vegetables, Scallops en Brochette
  with, **'80** 163
Vermicelli, Scallop-Vegetable, **'87** 143
Véronique, Scallops, **'83** 144

Seafood. *See also* specific types and Fish.
Appetizer, Layered Seafood, **'88** 2
Bisque, Seafood, **'86** 66
Boil, Low Country Seafood, **'80** 119
Bouillabaisse, Florida, **'79** 158
Brochette, Seafood, **'87** 96
Broiled Shellfish, Quick, **'79** 228
Casserole, Seafood, **'87** 109
Chowder, Seafood, **'85** 9
Chowder, Southern Seafood, **'83** 20
Delight, Seafood, **'86** 208
Dip, Hot Artichoke-Seafood, **'80** 241
Dip, Hot Artichoke Seafood, **'85** M212
Dip, Hot Cheesy Seafood, **'84** 221
Dip, Seafood, **'79** 3
Eggplant, Seafood Stuffed, **'79** 187
Gumbo, Champion Seafood, **'86** 293
Gumbo, Chicken-Ham-Seafood, **'81** 6
Gumbo, Creole, **'86** 228
Gumbo, Creole Seafood, **'82** 278
Gumbo, Ham and Seafood, **'81** 199
Gumbo, Light Seafood-Okra, **'86** 155
Gumbo, Quick Creole, **'82** 87
Gumbo, Seafood, **'79** 198, 286; **'80** 34;
  '81 5; **'83** 90; **'84** 87, 92; **'87** 210
Gumbo with Whole Crabs, Seafood, **'85** 2
Hot Brown, Seafood, **'88** 158
Imperials, Individual Seafood, **'84** 162
Jambalaya, Three-Seafood, **'82** 126
Linguine, Seafood, **'79** 227
Mayonnaise, Seafood with Dill, **'86** 234
Mold, Chilled Seafood, **'86** 70

Mornay, Seafood, **'83** 67
Paella, Chicken-Seafood, **'88** 68
Paella, Party, **'88** M189
Paella, Seafood, **'82** 245
Papillote, Ocean, **'84** M287
Pie, Hot Seafood, **'80** 32
Salad, Baked Seafood, **'86** 10
Salad, Hot Seafood, **'79** 117; **'80** 164
Salad, Paella, **'86** 207
Salad, Polynesian Seafood, **'79** 57
Salad, Seaside, **'86** 183
Salad, Smoky Seafood, **'84** 46
Sauce Delight, Seafood, **'82** 91
Sauce, Linguine with Seafood, **'83** 232
Sauce, Seafood, **'79** 3; **'82** 48; **'86** 304
Sautéed Seafood Platter, **'83** 89
Scallops, Bacon-Wrapped, **'87** 94
Seasoning Blend, Fish-and-Seafood, **'88** 28
Slaw, Seafood, **'79** 56
Spread, Seafood, **'86** M58; **'87** 146
Spread, Seafood Sandwich, **'82** 87
Stew, Seafood, **'84** 280
Supreme, Seafood, **'82** 284
Tartlets, Seafood, **'87** 247
Tempura, Basic, **'81** 68
Tempura, Cornmeal, **'81** 68

Seasonings
Blend, Seasoning, **'82** 296
Fish-and-Seafood Seasoning Blend, **'88** 28
Meat Seasoning Blend, **'88** 29
Poultry Seasoning Blend, **'88** 28
Salt, Gourmet Seasoning, **'82** 297
Vegetable Seasoning Blend, **'88** 29

Sherbets. *See* Ice Creams and Sherbets.

Shrimp
Appetizer, Layered Seafood, **'88** 2
Appetizer, Shrimp-Pineapple, **'85** 80
Ariosto, Shrimp and Chicken, **'79** 31
Artichokes, Shrimp-Stuffed, **'84** 67; **'87** 55
Artichokes Stuffed with Shrimp and
  Scallops, **'84** 174
Aspic, Shrimp-Coleslaw, **'79** 88
Aspic, Shrimp-Cucumber, **'83** 108
Aspic with Shrimp, Tomato, **'79** 241
au Gratin, Shrimp, **'85** 79
Avocados, Shrimp-Filled, **'83** 2
Baked Shrimp, **'87** 35
Ball, Shrimp-Cheese, **'85** 208
Barbecued Shrimp, **'82** 74; **'84** 93
Barbecued Shrimp, Cajun, **'87** 95
Bayou, Shrimp, **'88** 261
Bisque, Shrimp-Cucumber, **'79** 172
Bisque, Shrimp-Vegetable, **'82** 313; **'83** 66
Bisque, Tomato-Shrimp, **'86** 66
Boats, Shrimp, **'79** 57
Boiled Shrimp, **'79** 3
Boiled Shrimp, Ray Kidd's, **'84** 87
Boiled Shrimp, Special, **'83** 36
Boiled Shrimp, Spicy, **'83** 320; **'84** 289
Boiled Shrimp with Cocktail Sauce, **'79** 151
Boil, Low Country Seafood, **'80** 119

Broiled Shrimp, Beer-, '87 142
Broiled Shrimp, Garlic-, '83 193
Broiled Shrimp, Lemon-Garlic, '82 29;
  '86 182
Broiled Shrimp Supreme, '79 3
Canapés, Shrimp, '84 116
Cashew Shrimp Supreme, '83 29
Casserole, Chayotes and Shrimp, '80 230
Casserole, Crab-and-Shrimp, '84 71
Casserole, Shrimp, '85 240
Casserole, Shrimp and Rice, '79 228
Catfish, Crown Room's
  Shrimp-Stuffed, '84 182
Cheese Ball, Curried Shrimp, '86 135
Cheese, Shrimp with Herbed
  Jalapeño, '87 112
Chicken Breasts, Stuffed, '88 50
Chowder, Shrimp and Corn, '79 199
Chow Mein, Shrimp, '82 30
Cocktail, Shrimp, '87 173
Coconut-Beer Shrimp, '85 230
Combo, Snow Pea-Shrimp, '79 57
Cream Sauce, Shrimp in, '84 M286
Creole in a Rice Ring, Shrimp, '86 222
Creole, Shrimp, '86 256; '87 18
Creole, Special Shrimp, '87 172
Creole, Spicy Shrimp, '79 181
Creole, Wild Rice-and-Shrimp, '84 292
Curried Rice and Shrimp, '83 231
Curried Shrimp, '84 110
Curried Shrimp, Quick, '84 M198
Curried Shrimp, West Indian, '79 227
Curry, Charleston-Style Shrimp, '84 109
Curry, Shrimp Malai, '84 110
Curry, Sour Cream and Shrimp, '81 10
Curry, Sour Cream Shrimp, '80 83
de Jonghe, Shrimp, '79 228
Delight, English Muffin, '82 45
Delight, Shrimp, '79 192
Destin, Shrimp, '82 29
Dijonnaise, Shrimp, '87 91
Dilled Sauced Shrimp, '86 88
Dilled Shrimp, '88 150
Dip, Hot Cheesy Seafood, '84 221
Dip, Hot Shrimp, '87 190
Dippers, Shrimp, '84 324
Dip, Quick Shrimp, '79 153
Dip, Shrimp, '86 84; '88 M261
Dip, Zesty Shrimp, '80 150
Egg Foo Yong, '80 19; '86 232
Egg Foo Yong, Shrimp, '83 22
Egg Rolls, '86 81
Eggrolls, Shrimp and Pork, '82 240; '83 18
Eggs, Saucy Shrimp-Curried, '84 143
Eggs, Shrimp and Crab Scrambled, '79 261
Élégante, Shrimp, '83 48
en Papillote, Shrimp with
  Asparagus, '86 145
Étouffée, Shrimp, '79 4
Filling, Shrimp Salad, '87 106
Fish with Shrimp, Veracruz, '86 130
Flounder Stuffed with Shrimp, '88 51
Fondue, Shrimp, '86 244
French Shrimp, '80 85
Fresh Shrimp, Preparing, '82 127
Fried Shrimp, French-, '79 4
Fried Shrimp, Golden, '82 29
Fried Shrimp, Puffy, '79 4
Fried Shrimp with Apricot Sauce, '87 172
Garlic-Buttered Shrimp, '86 M226
Garlic Shrimp, '79 268; '80 14

Grilled Shrimp, '85 103
Gumbo, Crab and Shrimp, '81 200
Gumbo, Quick Shrimp, '86 71
Gumbo, Seafood, '87 210
Gumbo, Shrimp, '81 199
Jalapeños, Shrimp-Stuffed, '88 115
Jambalaya, Creole, '81 51; '87 210
Jambalaya, Good Luck, '87 11
Jambalaya, Oven, '84 44
Jambalaya, Sausage, '80 210
Kabobs, Marinated Shrimp, '84 276;
  '85 158
Kabobs, Shrimp, '80 150, 184
Kabobs, Steak-and-Shrimp, '80 184
Lamb Chops with Shrimp, '88 58
Lemon Butter, Shrimp in, '84 163
Lemon Garlic Sauce, Shrimp in, '83 67
Lemon Shrimp, Luscious, '88 150
Manale, Shrimp, '86 268
Marinara, Shrimp, '84 233
Marinated and Grilled Shrimp, '87 141
Marinated Shrimp, Grilled, '87 173
Marinated Shrimp, Icy, '84 215
Marinated Shrimp, Zesty, '87 173
Mediterranean Shrimp Bowl, '80 174
Medley, Eggplant-Shrimp, '79 188
Melba, Shrimp, '84 86
Miniquiches, Shrimp, '87 146
Mold, Shrimp, '87 94
Mornay, Seafood, '83 67
Mousse, Shrimp, '79 57; '87 196, 251
Mushrooms, Shrimp-Stuffed, '80 M135
Omelet, Shrimp-and-Cheddar, '84 57
Paella, Chicken-Pork-Shrimp, '82 245
Paella, Chicken-Seafood, '88 68
Paella, Party, '88 M189
Paella, Spanish, '85 26
Paella Valenciana, '82 246

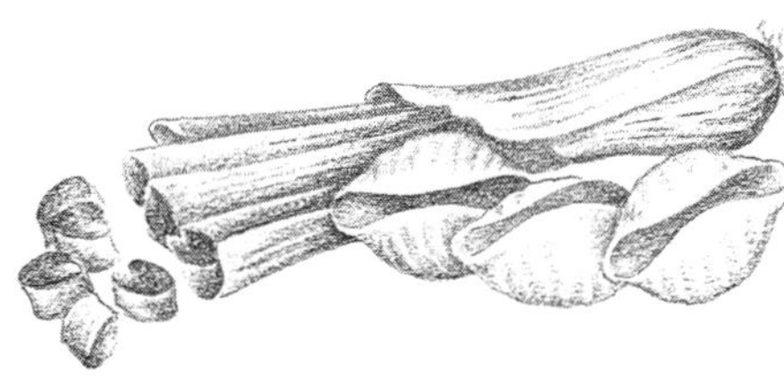

Pasta Medley, Shrimp-, '88 302
Pasta with Shrimp-Mushroom Italienne,
  Green, '79 170
Pâté with Dill Sauce, Shrimp, '85 39
Peas, Shrimp with Snow, '85 75
Peppers, Shrimp-Stuffed, '80 162;
  '86 131, 197
Pickled Shrimp, '79 3
Pickled Shrimp, New Orleans, '79 145
Pickle, Shrimp-in-a-, '86 326
Pie, Hot Seafood, '80 32
Pilaf, Shrimp, '82 246
Polynesian Shrimp, '79 3
Potatoes, Creamy Shrimp-Stuffed, '80 36
Potatoes, Shrimp-Sauced, '81 M61
Puffs, Gouda-Shrimp, '79 234
Puff, Shrimp-Crab, '79 57
Puffs, Luncheon Shrimp, '85 72
Quiche, Shrimp, '83 50
Rémoulade, Shrimp, '83 173
Rice, Shrimp and Sausage, '79 64
Rock Shrimp Conga, '80 2

Rock Shrimp Tails, Batter-Fried, '80 2
Rock Shrimp Tails, Broiled, '80 3
Rock Shrimp Tails, Sweet-and-Sour, '80 3
Rollups, Shrimp-Stuffed, '82 234
Rotelle, Shrimp, '85 165
Sailor Shrimp for Two, '82 276
Salad, Avocado Stuffed with
  Shrimp, '82 207
Salad, Baked Shrimp-Rice, '83 22
Salad, Crabmeat-Shrimp Pasta, '86 208
Salad, Creamy Shrimp, '79 56
Salad, Festive Macaroni-Shrimp, '85 165
Salad, Fruited Shrimp, '86 156
Salad, Grapefruit-and-Shrimp, '88 5
Salad in Pastry, Shrimp, '86 105
Salad, Layered Shrimp, '88 100
Salad, Macaroni-Shrimp, '85 121
Salad, Marinated Shrimp, '85 82
Salad on the Half Shell, Shrimp, '86 73
Salad, Orange-Shrimp, '84 197
Salad, Pasta-and-Shrimp, '83 163
Salad, Rice-and-Shrimp, '83 82
Salad, Rice-Shrimp, '79 270
Salad, Shrimp, '81 94; '84 221; '86 186
Salad, Shrimp and Avocado, '80 266
Salad, Shrimp and Rice, '80 231; '82 207
Salad, Shrimp-Endive, '85 73
Salad, Shrimp Macaroni, '79 220
Salad, Shrimp-Macaroni, '85 219
Salad, Shrimp Vermicelli, '88 139
Salad, Shrimp-Walnut, '86 182
Salads, Individual Shrimp, '83 146
Salad, Super Shrimp, '81 37
Salad, Tangy Shrimp-Rice, '84 66
Salad, Tossed Shrimp-Egg, '80 4
Salad, Vegetable-Shrimp, '79 190
Salad with Shrimp, Green, '88 49
Salad, Zesty Shrimp-and-Orange
  Rice, '87 155
Sandwiches, Shrimp-Cheese, '85 242
Sauce, Broccoli and Cauliflower with
  Shrimp, '84 248
Sauce, Flounder Fillets in Shrimp, '83 227
Sauce, Flounder with
  Hollandaise-Shrimp, '86 234
Sauce, Oysters in Shrimp, '87 40
Sauce Piquante, Crab and Shrimp, '83 92
Sauce, Shrimp, '87 138, 232
Sauce, Shrimp-and-Almond, '87 282
Sautéed Seafood Platter, '83 89
Sautéed Shrimp, '79 3
Sauté, Shrimp-and-Grouper, '87 91
Sauté, Shrimp-and-Scallop, '85 103
Scampi, Easy, '84 291
Scampi, Orange, '85 303
Scampi, Quick, '88 301
Scampi, Shrimp, '84 230
Shells, Creamy Shrimp, '79 4
Sirloin Supreme, Shrimp and, '81 131
Skillet, Quick Shrimp, '87 50
Soup, Shrimp-and-Corn, '84 88
Soup, Shrimp-Mushroom, '85 87
Spaghetti with Black Olives, Shrimp, '85 13
Spread, Chunky Shrimp, '85 300; '86 18
Spread, Curried Shrimp, '87 158
Spread, Shrimp, '81 306; '85 135; '87 111
Spread, Shrimp-Cucumber, '79 81
Spread, Tempting Shrimp, '79 57
Squash, Shrimp-Stuffed Yellow, '84 194
Steak and Shrimp, '88 123
Stew and Grits, Shrimp, '80 118

Shrimp *(continued)*

Stewed Shrimp with Dumplings, **'79** 31
Stew over Grits, Shrimp, **'88** 126
Stew, Shrimp, **'83** 4
Stir-Fry Shrimp and Vegetables, **'87** 91
Stroganoff, Oven-Baked Shrimp, **'81** 297
Stroganoff, Shrimp, **'79** 81
Stuffed Shrimp Bundles, Crab-, **'81** 176
Stuffed Shrimp, Crab-, **'84** 259
Stuffed Shrimp, Parmesan-, **'85** 103
Supreme, Seafood, **'82** 284
Sweet-and-Sour Shrimp, **'83** 278
Sweet-and-Sour Shrimp and
    Chicken, **'87** 267; **'88** 103
Szechuan Shrimp, **'86** 173
Tart, Shrimp, **'87** 70
Toast, Shrimp, **'86** 91
Tree, Shrimp, **'83** 320; **'84** 288; **'85** 318
Vegetables, Shrimp and, **'82** 6
Vermicelli, Shrimp and Feta Cheese
    on, **'87** 108

Soufflés

Apricot Soufflé, Baked, **'88** 267
Asparagus Soufflé, **'79** 66; **'83** 265
Banana Daiquiri Soufflé, **'84** 317
Blintz Soufflé, **'88** 155
Brandy Alexander Soufflé, **'82** 173;
    '83 M114
Broccoli Soufflé, **'81** 24
Broccoli Soufflé, Golden, **'84** 283
Butternut Soufflé, **'83** 266
Carrot Soufflé, **'79** 73; **'83** 265
Cauliflower Soufflé, **'82** 76
Cheese Soufflé, **'79** 72, 261
Cheese Soufflé, Cream, **'88** 11
Cheese Soufflé for Two, **'81** 226
Cheese Soufflé, Three-Egg, **'87** 234
Chicken-Chestnut Soufflé, **'79** 107
Chocolate Mint Soufflé, **'81** 16
Chocolate Soufflé, **'84** 317
Chocolate Soufflé, Light, **'83** 278
Coconut Soufflé, **'79** 73; **'85** 212
Corn-and-Cheese Soufflé, **'88** 122
Crab Soufflé Spread, **'85** 4
Cranberry-Topped Holiday Soufflé, **'84** 306
Cups, Hot Soufflé, **'85** 284
Daiquiri Soufflé, Elegant, **'80** 69
Devonshire Soufflé, Chilled, **'88** 279
Egg Soufflé Casserole, **'83** 55
Egg Soufflés, Little, **'83** 57
Frozen Soufflés, Individual, **'80** 52
Grand Marnier Soufflé, **'79** 281
Grasshopper Soufflé, **'81** 248; **'86** 188
Grits Soufflé, **'80** 30
Grits Soufflé, Mexican, **'79** 55
Individual Soufflés, **'80** 190
Kahlúa Soufflé, **'82** 173
Lemon-Lime Soufflé, Cold, **'84** 24
Lemon Sauce Soufflés, Quick, **'88** 43
Lemon Soufflé, **'82** 170, 223
Lemon Soufflé, Tart, **'85** 82
Lemon Soufflé with Raspberry-Amaretto
    Sauce, Frozen, **'88** 130
Mushroom Soufflés, **'87** 282
Onion Soufflé, **'79** 247
Orange Dessert Soufflé, **'83** 206
Orange Soufflé, Chilled, **'84** 317; **'86** 189
Orange Soufflé, Frozen, **'79** 211
Parsnip Soufflé, Golden, **'83** 266
Pineapple Dessert Soufflé, **'80** 153

Potatoes, Soufflé, **'84** 295; **'85** 196
Potato Soufflé, Sweet, **'82** 286; **'86** 121
Raspberry Soufflé, **'86** 188
Raspberry-Topped Soufflé, **'85** 317
Rice-Cheese Soufflé, **'79** 270
Salmon Soufflé, Fresh, **'81** 182
Sour Cream Soufflé, **'80** 43
Spinach Soufflé, **'79** 73; **'81** 304; **'84** 78;
    '85 248; **'86** 108
Spinach Soufflé, Cheesy, **'81** 53
Spinach Soufflé Deluxe, **'79** 8
Spinach Soufflé Roll, **'80** 215
Squash Soufflé, Cheesy, **'82** 146
Turkey Soufflé, **'80** 271
Turnip Soufflé, **'79** 254
Vanilla Soufflé, Frozen, **'79** 230; **'82** 173
Zucchini-and-Corn Soufflé, **'83** 265
Zucchini Soufflé, **'79** 157

Soups. *See also* Chili, Chowders, Gumbos,
    Stews.
Almond Soup, **'79** 48
Artichoke Soup, Cream of, **'82** 232
Asparagus Soup, **'84** 67
Asparagus Soup, Cream of, **'84** 111
Avocado-Banana-Yogurt Soup, **'80** 78
Avocado-Mushroom Soup, Creamy, **'85** 25
Avocado Soup, **'88** 160
Avocado Soup, Chilled, **'81** 34; **'87** 37
Avocado Soup, Creamy, **'79** 107
Avocado Soup, Sherried, **'84** 181
Bacon-Beer Cheese Soup, **'87** M7
Bean and Bacon Soup, **'83** 26
Bean-and-Barley Soup, Hearty, **'86** 304
Bean Pot, White, **'86** 194
Bean Soup, **'80** 25
Bean Soup, Black, **'88** 30, 266
Bean Soup, Capitol Hill, **'80** 222
Bean Soup, Chunky Navy, **'83** 291
Bean Soup, Cream of Green, **'84** 111
Bean Soup, Drunken, **'87** 283
Bean Soup, Ham-and-, **'84** 4
Bean Soup, Leafy, **'86** 223
Bean Soup, Navy, **'84** 280
Bean Soup, Sausage-, **'85** 88
Bean Soup, Savory Navy, **'87** 282
Bean Soup, Spicy Sausage-, **'83** 229
Bean Soup, White, **'83** 229
Beer-Cheese Soup, **'84** 246
Bisque, Brisk Mushroom, **'81** 190
Bisque, Clam, **'86** 228
Bisque, Crab, **'88** 251
Bisque, Crab-and-Corn, **'87** 137

Bisque, Oyster, **'83** 252
Bisque, Seafood, **'86** 66
Bisque, Shrimp-Cucumber, **'79** 172
Bisque, Shrimp-Vegetable, **'82** 313; **'83** 66
Bisque, Spicy Pumpkin, **'86** 67
Bisque, Spinach-Potato, **'86** 66
Bisque, Squash, **'84** 280
Bisque, Tomato-Shrimp, **'86** 66
Bisque, Tuna, **'79** 76
Black-Eyed Soup, Beefy, **'85** 6
Borscht, Ruby Red, **'83** 176
Bouillabaisse, Florida, **'79** 158
Bouillon, Redfish Court, **'83** 290; **'84** 93
Bouillon, Tomato, **'83** 8
Broccoli Soup, **'86** 161, M194; **'87** 288
Broccoli Soup, Cheesy-, **'86** 258
Broccoli Soup, Creamed, **'85** 24
Broccoli Soup, Cream of, **'79** 130; **'80** 188,
    M225; **'82** 314; **'83** 66; **'86** 259
Broccoli Soup, Cream-of-, **'88** 56
Broccoli Soup, Creamy, **'81** 75; **'82** 13;
    '83 99
Broccoli Soup, Easy, **'81** 307
Broccoli Soup, Hot, **'81** 235; **'83** 44
Broccoli Soup, Mock Cream of, **'85** 288
Broccoli-Swiss Soup, **'86** 6
Broth, Savory Vegetable, **'81** 230
Butternut-and-Apple Soup,
    Creamed, **'88** 228
Cabbage Soup, **'83** 291; **'85** 88
Cantaloupe Soup, **'83** 120; **'88** 160
Cantaloupe Soup, Chilled, **'81** 156
Cantaloupe Soup, Fresh, **'84** 190
Carrot-Leek Soup, **'86** 34
Carrot-Orange Soup, **'79** 172
Carrot Soup, **'80** 88
Carrot Soup, Cheesy, **'81** 262
Carrot Soup, Cream of, **'81** 307; **'88** 46
Carrot Soup, Curried, **'82** 157
Carrot Soup, Savory, **'84** 107
Cauliflower and Caraway Soup, **'82** 264
Cauliflower and Watercress Soup, Cream
    of, **'83** 126
Cauliflower Soup, Cream of, **'87** M7;
    '88 12
Cauliflower Soup, Creamy, **'82** 76
Cauliflower Soup, Fresh, **'84** 279
Celery Soup, Burnet-, **'84** 107
Celery Soup, Cream of, **'79** 71
Celery Soup, Light Cream-of-, **'82** 279
Cheese Soup, Bacon-Topped, **'80** M224
Cheese Soup, Cream of, **'83** 99
Cheese Soup, Hearty, **'84** 4
Cheese Soup, Monterey Jack, **'81** 112;
    '85 M211
Cheese Velvet Soup, **'80** 74
Cheesy Anytime Soup, **'81** 307; **'82** 314;
    '83 66
Chicken-and-Rice Soup, **'88** 236
Chicken Enchilada Soup, **'86** 22
Chicken, Ham, and Oyster Soup, **'79** 198
Chicken Noodle Soup, **'80** 264
Chicken-Noodle Soup, Chunky, **'88** 12
Chicken Soup, **'81** 98
Chicken Soup, Cream of, **'85** 243
Chicken Soup, Curried, **'86** 34
Chicken Soup, Homemade, **'82** 34
Chicken Soup, Mexican, **'84** 234
Chicken Soup, Quick, **'86** M72
Chicken-Vegetable Soup, **'88** 18
Chill-Chaser Soup, **'87** 282

Clam Florentine Soup, '85 23
Consommé aux Champignons, '79 48
Corned Beef Soup, '83 16
Corn Soup, '80 56; '85 243; '87 156
Corn Soup, Favorite, '85 155
Corn Soup, Grilled, '87 121
Crabmeat Soup, '84 123
Crab Soup, Cream of, '88 302
Crab Soup, Creamy, '80 M224
Crab Soup, Elegant, '80 188
Crab Soup, Quick, '84 279
Crab Soup, Steamboat's Cream of, '81 127
Crab Soup with Marigold, She-, '79 32
Cucumber Soup, Chilled, '79 144
Cucumber Soup, Cold, '79 130; '81 130
Cucumber Soup, Cold Minted, '86 34
Cucumber Soup, Cream of, '81 98
Cucumber Soup, Creamy, '80 171
Cucumber-Yogurt Soup, '82 157; '83 205
Curried Soup, '81 130
Dill Soup, Cold, '84 107
Egg Drop Soup, '83 21; '86 16
Egg-Drop Soup, '85 M12
Egg Flower Soup, '81 307; '82 313;
   '83 65
Eggplant Supper Soup, '85 221
Fire Water, '80 188
French Market Soup, '85 277
Fruit Soup, '87 98
Fruit Soup, Chilled Fresh, '88 160
Fruit Soup, Cold Fresh, '87 157
Fruit Soup Dessert, '79 172
Fruit Soup, Dried, '79 23
Fruit Soup, Swedish, '82 313; '83 65
Garden Soup, '85 241
Gazpacho, '79 172; '80 266; '81 98;
   '82 73; '84 112; '85 164
Gazpacho, Blender, '85 93
Gazpacho, Chilled, '84 138
Gazpacho, Cool, '83 140
Gazpacho, Saucy, '82 157
Gazpacho, Spring, '81 112
Gazpacho, Summer, '84 181
Green Pepper Soup, '88 250
Guadalajara Soup, '88 30
Hamburger Soup, '80 263
Ham Soup, Hearty, '82 4
Harvest Soup, '79 101
Homemade Soup, '79 198
Hot-and-Sour Soup, '83 68
Jambalaya, '84 282
Jambalaya, Creole, '81 51; '87 210
Jambalaya de Covington, '87 211
Jambalaya, Good Luck, '87 11
Jambalaya, Oven, '84 44
Jambalaya, Sausage, '80 210; '84 249
Jambalaya, Smoked Sausage, '79 42
Jambalaya, Three-Seafood, '82 126
Jambalaya, Tuna, '83 44
Lemon Soup, '85 94
Lentil Soup, '83 292; '86 304
Lentil Soup, Beefy, '87 282
Lime Soup, '88 31
Melon Soup, '80 182
Melon Soup, Swirled, '87 162
Minestrone, '82 4
Minestrone Soup, '84 202; '86 144
Mix, French Market Soup, '85 277
Mushroom-Onion Soup, '80 25
Mushroom Soup, '82 286; '86 M73
Mushroom Soup, Chunky, '88 12

Mushroom Soup, Cream of, '84 5;
   '85 93, 261
Mushroom Soup, Creamy, '79 243;
   '81 307
Mushroom Soup, Curried, '84 M89
Mushroom Soup, Elegant, '83 99
Mushroom Soup, Fresh, '81 109
Mushroom Soup, Shrimp-, '85 87
Okra Soup, Charleston, '87 156
Onion-Beef Soup, French, '87 54
Onion-Cheese Soup, '87 81
Onion Soup, Classic, '84 65
Onion Soup, Creamed Green, '83 82
Onion Soup, Double-Cheese, '85 227
Onion Soup, Double Cheese-Topped, '79 49
Onion Soup, Easy, '85 226
Onion Soup, French, '79 49; '80 188;
   '83 126; '85 226; '86 M212
Onion Soup, Green, '84 112
Onion Soup, Oven-Browned, '79 49
Onion Soup, Rich, '85 226
Onion Soup, Shortcut French, '85 M328
Onion Soup, Superb, '81 86
Onion Soup, Toasty French, '81 306
Oyster-and-Mushroom Soup, '87 39
Oyster-Cheese Soup, '84 213
Oyster Soup, '79 228; '83 211
Peach-Plum Soup, '87 157
Peach Soup, '83 120, 180
Peanut Butter Soup, Cream of, '84 29
Peanut Soup, '87 184
Peanut Soup, Chilled, '79 130
Peanut Soup, Creamy, '79 50
Pea Soup, Chilled, '84 181
Pea Soup, Country-Style, '86 267
Pea Soup Élégante, '79 53
Pea Soup, Fresh, '86 181
Pea Soup, Peppery, '82 271
Pea Soup, Spring, '88 M96
Plum Soup, '85 107
Plum Soup, Chilled Purple, '79 162
Potato-Bacon Soup, '84 M38
Potato-Beet Soup, '88 156
Potato-Carrot Soup, '88 297
Potato-Cucumber Soup, Cold, '88 160
Potato Potage, Subtle, '80 78
Potato Soup, '82 278; '83 292
Potato Soup, Asparagus-, '85 23
Potato Soup, Celery-and-, '84 279
Potato Soup, Chilled Cucumber-, '85 93
Potato Soup, Cream of, '80 M224; '82 21
Potato Soup, Creamy, '81 19, 98; '84 112
Potato Soup, Golden Cream of, '86 302
Potato Soup, Holiday, '79 236
Potato Soup, Leek-and-, '84 112
Potato Soup, Sausage-, '80 25
Potato Soup, Special, '82 3
Potato Soup, Sweet, '88 250
Potato Soup, Three-, '86 16
Pot-of-Gold Soup, '86 259
Pumpkin Soup, '79 48
Pumpkin-Tomato Soup, '86 291
Raspberry Soup, Chilled, '81 130
Sausage and Okra Soup, '80 209
Sausage Soup, Italian, '84 235
Sausage Soup with Tortellini, Italian, '88 46
Sausage-Zucchini Soup, Italian, '84 4
Scallop Broth with Black Beans and Cilantro,
   Southwestern, '87 123
Shrimp-and-Corn Soup, '84 88
Sopa de Lima, '79 211

Southwest Soup, '86 255
Spinach Soup, Cream of, '82 38
Spinach Soup, Hot Cream of, '84 29
Spinach Soup, Oriental, '83 151
Split Pea and Frankfurter Soup, '79 64
Split Pea Soup, '88 235
Squash Soup, Cold Cream of, '81 130
Squash Soup, Cream of, '81 246
Squash Soup, Perky, '85 20

Squash Soup, Summer, '83 99; '84 193;
   '85 136
Strawberry-Banana Soup, '86 181
Strawberry Soup, '88 160
Strawberry Soup, Cold, '82 157
Strawberry Soup Supreme, '81 M144
Tomato-and-Rice Soup, '85 24
Tomato-Celery Soup, '83 M58
Tomato Consommé, '88 250
Tomato Cream Soup, Refreshing, '79 172
Tomato Juice Soup, Hot, '86 302
Tomato Potage, '79 250
Tomato Soup, '81 236; '83 44
Tomato Soup, Appetizer, '86 258
Tomato Soup, Chilled, '82 155
Tomato Soup, Cold, '88 160
Tomato Soup, Creamy, '83 267; '86 258
Tomato Soup, Easy, '84 14
Tomato Soup, Fresh, '83 140
Tomato Soup, Iced, '79 170
Tomato Soup Plus, '88 170
Tomato Soup, Sour Cream-Topped, '80 246
Tomato Soup, Summer, '79 130
Tomato Soup with Parmesan Cheese, Cream
   of, '86 161
Tomato-Vegetable Soup, '81 M177; '86 9
Tortilla Soup, '88 31, 245
Turkey Carcass Soup, '86 284
Turkey Soup, Curried, '86 332
Turkey-Vegetable Soup, '84 4; '88 264
Turnip Soup, Creamy, '84 279
Turtle Soup au Sherry, '80 56
Vegetable-Bean Soup, '83 317
Vegetable-Beef Soup, '88 296
Vegetable-Beef Soup, Hearty, '84 102
Vegetable-Beef Soup, Spicy, '88 11
Vegetable-Burger Soup, '82 6
Vegetable-Cheese Soup, Creamy, '81 244
Vegetable Cheese Soup, Creamy, '83 230
Vegetable Soup, '80 128; '84 148;
   '85 106; '86 187; '87 83, 123; '88 266
Vegetable Soup, Beefy, '79 113; '84 M38
Vegetable Soup, Cheesy, '80 73
Vegetable Soup, Clear, '79 130
Vegetable Soup, Cold Garden, '84 197
Vegetable Soup, Garden, '83 140; '86 160
Vegetable Soup, Hearty, '80 26
Vegetable Soup, Leek-, '86 304
Vegetable Soup, Light, '84 280
Vegetable Soup, Marvelous, '82 3
Vegetable Soup Mix, '84 148
Vegetable Soup, Old-Fashioned, '86 304

Soups *(continued)*

Vegetable Soup, Quick, '79 190;
  '85 24, 32
Vegetable Soup, Quick Beefy, '80 25
Vegetable Soup, Spicy, '79 198
Venison Soup, '82 216
Vichyssoise, '86 181
Vichyssoise, Velvety Roquefort, '83 223
Watercress-and-Leek Soup, '86 161
Watercress Soup, '79 82; '88 104
Yogurt Fruit Soup, '86 176
Zucchini Soup, '82 104; '84 181; '86 181
Zucchini Soup, Chilled, '87 90
Zucchini Soup, Cold, '85 265
Zucchini Soup, Cream of, '83 99
Zucchini Soup, Creamy, '83 140

Spaghetti

Bacon Spaghetti, '86 213; '87 82
Carbonara, Salmon, '83 43
Carbonara, Spaghetti, '85 34; '87 167
Carbonara, Spaghetti alla, '81 38
Casserole, Asparagus-Spaghetti, '80 77
Casserole, Chicken-Spaghetti, '84 15
Casserole, Spaghetti, '84 241
Casserole, Spaghetti and Beef, '79 129
Cheese Spaghetti, Three-, '83 105
Chicken Spaghetti, '83 105; '87 221
Chili-Spaghetti, Herbed, '84 222
Crawfish Spaghetti, '85 104
Easy Spaghetti, '83 M317; '84 72
Etcetera, Spaghetti, '83 105
Ham Spaghetti Skillet, '83 283
Herbal Dressing, Spaghetti with, '86 158
Hot Dog and Spaghetti Skillet, '83 144

Italian Spaghetti, '81 38
Italian Spaghetti, Real, '81 233
Meatballs, Spaghetti-and-Herb, '84 75
Meatballs, Spaghetti with, '81 38
Meaty Spaghetti, '82 19
Mushrooms, Spicy Spaghetti with, '85 2
Parmesan Noodles, Cheesy, '83 M7
Parsley and Walnut Sauce, Spaghetti
  with, '80 30
Parsley, Spaghetti with, '80 236
Pea Spaghetti, Black-Eyed, '81 7
Pepperoni Pasta, '83 105
Pepperoni Spaghetti, Quick, '88 40
Pie, Spaghetti, '81 M32
Pizzazz, Spaghetti with, '80 85
Pork Spaghetti Bake, '81 11
Pot Roast with Spaghetti, '80 59
Salad, Spaghetti, '82 277; '84 205
Sauce, Beer Spaghetti, '85 13
Sauce for Spaghetti, Italian
  Tomato, '81 134

Sauce, Herbed Spaghetti, '85 13
Sauce, Pasta with Vegetable, '83 163
Sauce, Spaghetti with Zucchini, '81 38
Sauce, Thick Spaghetti, '84 118
Sauce, Turkey Spaghetti, '85 13
Sausage Spaghetti, '83 160
Sausage Spaghetti Dinner, '79 194
Shrimp Spaghetti with Black Olives, '85 13
Tetrazzini, Chicken, '79 268; '80 75;
  '83 288
Tetrazzini, Ham, '82 77; '84 241
Tetrazzini, Herbed Turkey, '86 47
Thick-and-Spicy Spaghetti, '83 287
Veal and Peppers, Spaghetti with, '81 201;
  '82 14
Veal Spaghetti, '84 276
Vegetables, Spaghetti with, '85 67
Vegetables with Spaghetti, Fresh, '86 257
Vegetables with Spaghetti, Sautéed, '81 89
Zucchini Spaghetti, '83 160
Zucchini Spaghetti, Italian, '85 2

Spice

Balls, Decorative Ribbon-Spice, '84 325

Spinach

Baked Spinach, Gourmet, '82 180
Bake, Spinach-Cheese, '88 10
Bake, Spinach-Ricotta, '88 97
Bisque, Spinach-Potato, '86 66
Bread, Spinach, '83 121; '87 144
Cannelloni, '85 60
Casserole, Cheesy Spinach, '81 263
Casserole, Cottage
  Cheese-and-Spinach, '84 77
Casserole, Creamy Crab and Spinach, '80 3
Casserole, Creamy Spinach, '86 111
Casserole, Oyster-and-Spinach, '83 34;
  '84 44
Casserole, Spinach, '79 265
Casserole, Spinach and Artichoke, '81 103
Casserole, Spinach and Beef, '79 192
Casserole, Spinach-and-Celery, '84 294
Casserole, Spinach and Egg, '82 270
Casserole, Spinach-Artichoke, '88 252
Casserole, Spinach-Beef-Macaroni, '83 313
Casserole, Spinach-Cheese, '83 216
Casserole, Spinach-Parmesan, '82 281;
  '83 32
Casserole, Turkey-Spinach, '84 71
Cheesy Topped Spinach, '84 85
Chicken Breasts, Fried
  Spinach-Stuffed, '88 206
Chicken Rolls, Spinach-Stuffed, '86 248
Chinese Spinach, '79 179; '82 39
Chinese Spinach Sauté, '83 208
con Queso, Easy Spinach, '88 101
Creamed Spinach, '81 54; '86 110
Creamed Spinach with Noodles, '84 29
Creamy Spinach, '85 289
Crêpes, Spinach-Ricotta, '81 52
Cups, Cottage Cheese-Spinach, '87 190
Delight, Spinach, '84 M144
Dip, Cheesy Spinach, '82 59
Dip, Creamy Spinach, '88 132
Dip, Hot Spinach, '80 249
Dip in Cabbage, Spinach, '82 155
Dip, Spinach, '80 86; '86 159; '87 25, 214
Dressing, Spinach Salad, '83 181
Enchiladas, Spinach, '83 60; '84 14
Fettuccine and Spinach, '88 90
Fettuccine, Easy Chicken with
  Spinach, '88 89

Fettuccine, Fresh Spinach, '83 60
Fettuccini, Spinach, '82 179
Filling, Spinach, '79 34
Filling, Spinach-Mushroom, '80 215
Filling, Spinach-Ricotta, '81 53
Florentine, Baked Eggs, '86 M12
Florentine, Cheesy Trout, '85 53
Florentine Crêpe Pie, '79 34
Florentine, Crêpes, '80 190
Florentine, Eggs, '79 39; '83 56
Florentine, Fish, '86 35
Florentine in Parchment, Fish, '87 22
Florentine, Jumbo Seashells, '79 6
Florentine, Lasagna, '88 196
Florentine, Salmon, '83 43
Florentine, Stuffed Mushrooms, '82 270
Florentine-Style Eggs, '82 38
Florentine, Turkey, '88 264
Florentine with Mushroom Sauce,
  Chicken, '87 250
Frittata, Spinach, '81 53
Garden, The, '83 134
Lasagna, Cheesy Spinach, '80 32; '83 204
Lasagna, Spinach, '79 25; '81 243
Lemon Spinach, Creamy, '82 302
Loaves, Spinach-Oyster, '84 213
Madeleine in Chafing Dish, Spinach, '85 319
Manicotti, Spinach, '82 199
Manicotti, Spinach-Stuffed, '88 255
Mushrooms, Spinach-Stuffed, '86 81;
  '88 131, M261

Mushrooms, Spinach with, '80 19
Nests, Baked Eggs in Spinach, '82 70
Noodles, Chicken and Spinach, '82 19
Omelet, Spinach-Cheese, '83 119
Parmesan Spinach, Savory, '85 68
Pasta Bites, Pesto-Cheese, '87 251
Pasta Verde, '84 201
Pasta with Shrimp-Mushroom Italienne,
  Green, '79 170
Pâté with Spinach and Cream,
  Pork, '83 224
Peppers, Spinach-Stuffed, '82 180
Pesto, Orange Roughy with
  Spinach, '88 M192
Phyllo Triangles, Spinach-Filled, '84 52
Phyllo Triangles, Spinach-Ricotta, '88 212
Pie, Greek Spinach '85 59
Pie, Spinach, '82 191; '88 56
Pie, Spinach-Pasta, '85 286
Pitas, Spinach-Walnut, '87 202; '88 43
Puffs, Cheese-and-Spinach, '87 246
Puff, Spinach-Cheese, '84 96
Quiche, Cheesy Spinach, '81 228
Quiche, Crustless Spinach, '84 235
Quiche, Greek Spinach, '86 10
Quichelets, Spinach, '87 67

Quiches, Individual Spinach, '86 38
Quiches, Miniature Spinach, '82 38
Quiche, Spinach, '81 44; '85 49
Quiche, Spinach-Mushroom, '81 M74
Rice Bake, Green, '79 43
Rice, Spinach, '85 146
Ring au Fromage, Spinach, '79 8
Rolls, Spinach-Ham, '88 78
Rollups, Chicken and Spinach, '80 90;
    '82 M68
Roll-Ups, Ham and Spinach, '81 143
Rollups, Spinach-and-Ham, '86 84
Salads
    Bacon Dressing, Spinach Salad with
        Hot, '82 211
    Bacon Salad, Spinach and, '81 143
    Beet Salad, Spinach-, '83 227
    Blue Cheese Salad, Spinach-, '82 166
    Chicken-and-Spinach Tossed
        Salad, '83 157
    Citrus Dressing, Spinach Salad
        with, '88 133
    Combination Spinach Salad, '85 327;
        '86 22
    Creamy Spinach Salad, '83 60
    Crisp Spinach Salad with Creamy
        Dressing, '83 81
    Crunchy Spinach Salad, '80 147;
        '81 225
    Curry Spinach Salad, '80 242
    Festive Spinach Salad, '80 247
    French Spinach Salad, '79 8
    Fresh Spinach Salad, '82 73; '83 240;
        '84 15, 77; '86 130
    Fresh Spinach Salad Delight, '80 146
    Fresh Spinach with Spicy
        Dressing, '80 55
    Garden Salad Toss, '81 9
    Green Spinach Salad, '79 142
    Kiwifruit Salad, Spinach-, '87 305
    Lamb Salad, Spinach-, '85 58
    Layered Salad, Make-Ahead, '81 206
    Layered Spinach-Lettuce Salad, '84 266
    Layered Spinach Salad, '80 5
    Lemon Spinach with Feta, '85 190
    Mandarin Spinach Salad, '85 163
    Mushroom Salad, Spinach and, '80 112
    Onion Salad Bowl,
        Spinach-and-, '81 157
    Orange Dressing, Spinach Salad
        with, '87 187
    Orange Salad, Spinach-and-, '86 15
    Orange-Spinach Salad, '83 316; '84 16
    Oriental Spinach Salad, '82 23
    Pickled Spinach, '81 69
    Pork-and-Spinach Salad,
        Mandarin, '88 M126
    Russian Dressing, Spinach Salad
        with, '79 144
    Salmon-Spinach Salad, '87 145
    Southern Spinach Salad, '80 55
    Special Spinach Salad, '80 78
    Spinach Salad, '82 102; '86 302;
        '87 62; '88 299
    Springtime Spinach Salad, '81 114
    Sprout Salad, Fresh Spinach-, '82 281;
        '83 42
    Supreme, Spinach Salad, '79 243
    Sweet-Sour Spinach Salad, '85 M112
    Twist, Spinach-Mustard, '86 209
    Vinaigrette Spinach, '79 8

    Wilted Spinach Salad, '81 M4
    Zesty Spinach Salad, '79 88
Sandwiches, Fresh Spinach, '85 59
Sauce, Fettuccine with Spinach, '84 329
Sauce, Herbed Green, '86 244
Scalloped Spinach with Cheese, '79 8
Shells, Spinach-Stuffed, '85 60; '87 20
Soufflé, Cheesy Spinach, '81 53
Soufflé Deluxe, Spinach, '79 8
Soufflé Roll, Spinach, '80 215
Soufflé, Spinach, '79 73; '81 304; '84 78;
    '85 248; '86 108
Soup, Cream of Spinach, '82 38
Soup, Hot Cream of Spinach, '84 29
Soup, Oriental Spinach, '83 151
Spanakópita, '86 58
Spread, Savory Spinach, '82 180
Spread, Spinach, '88 132
Squares, Spinach, '88 131
Squash, Spinach-Stuffed, '82 4
Stir-Fry Spinach, '81 182
Supreme, Layered Spinach, '82 38
Supreme, Spinach, '84 77
Surprise, Spinach, '82 42
Tart Milan, '87 70
Tarts, Spinach, '82 249
Terrine, Layered
    Salmon-and-Spinach, '84 132
Timbales, Spinach, '84 29
Timbales, Spinach-Rice, '88 271
Tomatoes, Spinach-Stuffed Baked, '86 14
Tomatoes, Spinach-Topped, '88 265
Tortellini with Tomato Sauce,
    Spinach, '88 302
Triangles, Phyllo-Spinach, '87 53
Turnovers, Salmon-Spinach, '83 44
Wontons, Spinach, '83 74
Zucchini Boats with Spinach, '82 252

Spreads. *See also* Appetizers/Spreads.
Almond Cheese Spread, '87 292
Aloha Spread, '83 93
Antipasto Spread, '81 25
Apricot Brie Spread, '86 275
Apricot-Cream Cheese Spread, '87 158
Artichoke-Crab Spread, Hot, '85 81
Artichoke Hearts with Caviar, '79 142
Artichoke Spread, Hot, '79 110
Beef Spread, Hot, '83 50
Braunschweiger-Onion Spread, '79 82
Bread Spread, Party, '82 161
Broccamoli Curry Spread, '88 55
Caraway Spread, '85 276
Cheese, Herbed, '88 152
Cheese-Horseradish Spread, '84 222
Cheese-Olive Spread, '79 82
Cheese-Olive Spread, Cream, '82 35
Cheese Spread, '86 135

Cheese Spread, Apricot-Cream, '82 161
Cheese Spread, Bacon-, '83 241
Cheese Spread, Beer, '81 69
Cheese Spread, Beer-, '85 69
Cheese Spread, Caviar-Cream, '84 256
Cheese Spread, Chile, '86 297
Cheese Spread, Confetti, '84 256
Cheese Spread, Cottage, '87 107
Cheese Spread, Creamy Sweet, '79 264
Cheese Spread, Cucumber and
    Cream, '82 140
Cheese Spread, Deviled Cream, '81 235
Cheese Spread, Fruit and, '81 245
Cheese Spread, Garlic Pimiento, '79 58
Cheese Spread, German, '79 82
Cheese Spread, Hawaiian, '87 158
Cheese Spread, Herb-Cream, '83 24
Cheese Spread, Herbed, '87 247
Cheese Spread, Jalapeño-, '82 248
Cheese Spread, Low-Calorie
    Pimiento, '85 215
Cheese Spread, Pimiento, '82 35; '83 93;
    '86 127
Cheese Spread, Pineapple-Cream, '82 35
Cheese Spread, Tipsy, '80 150
Cheese Spread, Tomato-, '81 157
Cheese Spread, Zesty, '82 140
Cheese Spread, Zippy, '85 4
Cheesy Beer Spread, '87 196
Chicken Salad Party Spread, '88 M8
Chicken Spread, Festive, '87 158
Chicken Spread, Low-Fat, '82 290
Chicken Spread, Tasty, '84 193
Chocolate Cheese Spread, '87 292
Corned Beef Spread, '87 196
Crabmeat Spread, '79 81
Crabmeat Spread, Layered, '83 127
Crab Soufflé Spread, '85 4
Crab Spread, Baked, '80 86
Crab Spread, Superb, '81 255
Cucumber Spread, '79 295; '80 31
Date Spread, Breakfast, '84 7
Date-Walnut Spread, '87 292
Deviled Delight, '83 130
Edam-Sherry Spread, '84 257
Eggplant Spread, '86 278
Egg Salad Spread, '86 127
Egg Salad Spread, Cottage-, '82 146
Egg, Sour Cream, and Caviar
    Spread, '85 279
Fruit-and-Cheese Spread, Nutty, '87 246
Fruit Spread, '85 135
Fruit Spread, Sugarless, '84 60
Garden Spread, '86 135
Garlic Spread, '85 111
Gruyère-Apple Spread, '81 160
Ham-and-Egg Spread, '79 59
Ham and Pimiento Spread, '80 285; '81 56
Ham Spread, '86 126
Ham Spread, Cold, '82 248
Ham Spread, Country, '87 8
Ham Spread, Deviled, '79 81
Ham Spread, Hawaiian, '87 106
Honey-Nut Spread, '87 157
Honey Spread, '81 229
Italian Spread, '85 135
Liver Spread, Sherried, '80 86
Mushroom Spread, Hot, '81 190
Mustard Spread, '86 105
Olive Spread, Creamy, '81 290
Olive Spread, Tomatoes with, '85 114

Spreads *(continued)*

Orange Cheese Spread, **'87** 292
Orange Toast Topper, **'79** 36
Pineapple-Cheese Spread, **'86** 126
Pineapple Sandwich Spread, **'84** 166
Radish Spread, Fresh, **'84** 166
Raisin Spread, Peachy-, **'86** 326
Salad Dressing Spread, **'82** 140
Salmon-and-Horseradish Spread, **'87** 146
Salmon Spread, **'81** 149
Salmon Spread, Smoked, **'84** 324
Sandwich Spread, Benedictine, **'80** 299
Sandwich Spread, Chunky, **'82** 140
Sandwich Spread, Home-Style, **'80** 179
Seafood Sandwich Spread, **'82** 87
Seafood Spread, **'86** M58; **'87** 146
Shrimp-Cucumber Spread, **'79** 81
Shrimp Spread, **'81** 306; **'85** 135;
   '87 111
Shrimp Spread, Chunky, **'85** 300
Shrimp Spread, Curried, **'87** 158
Shrimp Spread, Tempting, **'79** 57
Sombrero Spread, **'87** 111
Spinach Spread, **'88** 132
Spinach Spread, Savory, **'82** 180
Strawberry Spread, Light, **'85** 55
Sweet 'n' Sour Spread, **'86** 184
Tomato-Cheese Spread, Fiery, **'87** 196
Trout Spread, Smoked, **'84** 47
Tuna Spread, **'83** 174
Turkey Party Spread, **'83** 282
Vegetable-Egg Spread, **'87** 106
Vegetable Party Spread, **'84** 166
Vegetable Sandwich Spread, **'83** 174;
   '85 135
Watercress Spread, **'88** 103
Sprouts
Beans with Sprouts,
   Sweet-and-Sour, **'86** 32
Beef and Bean Sprouts, **'82** 281; **'83** 42
Meat Loaf, Sprout, **'85** 51
Omelet, Potato-Sprout, **'79** 128
Omelet, Rising Sun, **'82** 281
Patties, Ham-Sprout, **'85** 51
Salad, Bean Sprout, **'82** 113
Salad, Fresh Spinach-Sprout, **'82** 281;
   '83 42
Salad, Spanish Sprout, **'85** 327; **'86** 22
Sandwiches, Alfalfa Pocket Bread, **'82** 282;
   '83 41
Sandwiches, Polynesian Sprout, **'85** 51
Squash. *See also* Zucchini.
Acorn
   Apple-and-Pecan-Filled Squash, **'88** 228
   Bake, Acorn Squash, **'83** 280
   Baked Acorn Squash, **'81** 24
   Bake, Squash, **'82** 107
   Bread, Squash, **'79** 210
   Custard-Filled Acorn Squash, **'86** 334
   Delight, Acorn Squash, **'81** 267
   Deluxe Acorn Squash, **'80** 215
   Filled Acorn Squash,
      Cranberry-, **'81** M231
   Fruited Acorn Squash, **'85** 235
   Molasses and Pecans, Acorn Squash
      with, **'85** 205
   Nutmeg, Acorn Squash with, **'85** 267
   Rings, Easy Glazed Acorn, **'81** M231
   Rings, Glazed Acorn, **'80** 214
   Sausage, Acorn Squash with, **'85** 9

Sherried Acorn Squash, **'85** 9
Stuffed Acorn Squash, **'82** 277; **'83** 15
Stuffed Acorn Squash, Apple-, **'83** 296;
   '84 285
Stuffed Acorn Squash, Fruit-, **'81** 295
Stuffed Acorn Squash, Ham-, **'81** 239;
   '83 66
Stuffed Acorn Squash,
   Pineapple-, **'84** 255
Stuffed Acorn Squash, Sausage-,
   '81 M231; **'83** 296; **'84** 285
Stuffed Baked Squash, **'85** 206
Stuffed Squash, Apple-, **'85** 206
Stuffed Squash,
   Maple-Flavored, **'85** 205
Butternut
   Bake, Butternut-Orange, **'86** 295
   Baked Butternut Squash, **'85** 205
   Bake, Squash and Apple, **'79** 210
   Bisque, Squash, **'84** 280
   Bread, Butternut-Raisin, **'79** 25
   Bread, Squash, **'79** 210
   Casserole, Butternut, **'83** 280
   Casserole, Butternut Squash, **'79** 210
   Casserole, Squash and Apple, **'79** 209
   Casserole, Sweet Butternut, **'83** 256
   Harvest Squash, **'80** 214
   Pie, Butternut Squash, **'80** 40;
      '87 212
   Pie, Butternut Squash Chiffon, **'83** 296;
      '84 285
   Pie, Spicy Butternut Squash, **'80** 296
   Pie, Spicy Squash, **'85** 9
   Pudding, Squash, **'82** 277; **'83** 15
   Puff, Butternut Squash, **'85** 205
   Ring, Butternut Squash, **'81** M232
   Sauté, Savory Butternut, **'85** 205
   Skillet Butternut and Bacon, **'85** 9
   Soufflé, Butternut, **'83** 266
   Soup, Creamed
      Butternut-and-Apple, **'88** 228
   Stuffed Butternut Squash,
      Apple-, **'81** 232
   Sunshine Squash, **'85** 205
   Whipped Squash, Tasty, **'82** 277;
      '83 15
Cajun Squash, **'88** 142
Casserole, Squash, **'87** 163
Casserole, Two-Squash, **'79** 101
Chile Squash, **'84** 77
Dressing, Turkey with Squash, **'87** 248
Hubbard Squash, Tart, **'80** 214
Medley, Carrot-Lima-Squash, **'80** 123
Medley, Fresh Squash, **'81** M165
Medley, Sautéed Vegetable, **'83** 101
Medley, Squash, **'81** 139; **'84** 128
Pattypan Squash, Stuffed, **'82** 103;
   '85 136; **'88** 142
Pattypan-Zucchini Skillet, **'82** 103
Pickles, Squash, **'87** 150
Pie, Mock Coconut, **'86** 200
Puff, Golden Squash, **'82** 288
Rosemary, Summer Squash
   with, **'88** 143
Sauté, Squash, **'82** 67
Scallop, Green-and-Gold, **'81** 159
Skillet Squash, **'82** 195
Spaghetti Squash Lasagna, **'84** 127
Spaghetti Squash Pie, **'80** 186
Spaghetti Squash, Sautéed Vegetables
   with, **'84** 128

Spaghetti Squash with Meat
   Sauce, **'88** M180
Stir-Fried Squash Medley, **'80** 123
Stir-Fry, Squash, **'80** 184
Stir-Fry, Two-Squash, **'86** 174
Tomatoes, Squash-Stuffed, **'82** 102
Tomato Squash, **'86** 111
Toss, Pepperoni-Squash, **'84** 127
Turban Squash, Glazed, **'81** 24
Turban Squash, Sausage-Stuffed, **'80** 214
Turban Squash, Stuffed Turks, **'88** 228
Yellow
   à l'Orange, Squash, **'85** 230
   Bacon-Flavored Squash, **'82** 158
   Bake, Cheddar-Squash, **'84** M113, 128
   Bake, Cheesy Squash, **'80** 183
   Beans, and Tomatoes, Squash, **'83** 148
   Bread, Spicy Squash, **'83** 121
   Bread, Yellow Squash, **'84** 140
   Buttered Summer Squash, **'81** 84
   Cake, Squash, **'86** 200
   Casserole, Baked Squash, **'83** 149
   Casserole, Blender Squash, **'81** 212
   Casserole, Cheesy Squash, **'79** 123;
      '82 M21
   Casserole, Company Squash, **'81** 183
   Casserole, Crunchy Squash, **'84** 293

   Casserole, Fresh Squash, **'82** 204
   Casserole, Jiffy Squash, **'81** M144
   Casserole, Squash and Egg, **'80** 146
   Casserole, Squash-Carrot, **'81** 157
   Casserole, Summer Squash,
      '81 102, 184
   Casserole, Yellow Squash, **'79** 179;
      '85 135; **'88** 166
   Casserole, Zippy Squash, **'80** 183
   Country Club Squash, **'79** 158;
      '88 M16
   Croquettes, Squash, **'79** 157; **'83** 148;
      '88 142
   Dressing, Squash, **'83** 315; **'86** 280
   Fiesta Squash, **'82** 102
   Fried Yellow Squash, **'86** 211
   Grilled Squash and Onion, **'79** 150
   Grilled Vegetables, **'84** 172
   Marinated Cucumbers and
      Squash, **'86** 146
   Medley, Summer Garden, **'84** 158
   Mexican Squash, **'82** 103
   Muffins, Yellow Squash, **'81** 163
   Pats, Squash, **'80** 298; **'81** 25
   Patties, Squash, **'79** 158
   Patties, Summer Squash, **'81** 184
   Pickles, Squash, **'81** 174
   Plantation Squash, **'79** 225
   Posh Squash, **'81** 159
   Puffs, Yellow Squash, **'82** 103

Puppies, Squash, '83 170
Quiche, Squash-and-Green
    Chile, '88 143
Rings, Asparagus in Squash, '87 68
Skillet Summer Squash, '82 96
Soufflé, Cheesy Squash, '82 146
Soup, Cold Cream of Squash, '81 130
Soup, Cream of Squash, '81 246
Soup, Perky Squash, '85 20
Soup, Summer Squash, '83 99;
    '85 136
Stir-Fried Squash Medley, '80 123
Stuffed Squash, Beef-, '83 134
Stuffed Squash Boats,
    Parmesan-, '79 156
Stuffed Squash, Cheesy, '82 134
Stuffed Squash, Sausage-, '81 183
Stuffed Squash, Spinach-, '82 4
Stuffed Squash, Vegetable-, '84 104
Stuffed Squash with Green
    Chiles, '83 148
Stuffed Yellow Squash,
    Garden-, '84 106
Stuffed Yellow Squash, Italian, '86 111
Stuffed Yellow Squash,
    Mushroom-, '84 154
Stuffed Yellow Squash,
    Shrimp-, '84 194
Stuffed Yellow Squash with Cheese
    Sauce, '80 162
Summer Squash, '80 127; '85 105
Toss, Crisp
    Squash-and-Pepper, '87 M152
Toss, Simple Squash, '85 M142
Vegetable-Herb Trio, '83 172
Stews. See also Chili, Gumbos, Soups.
Bean Pot, White, '86 194
Beef-and-Onion Stew, '87 18
Beef and Vegetable Stew,
    Sweet-and-Sour, '85 87
Beef Stew, '86 51
Beef Stew, Burgundy, '88 234
Beef Stew, Company, '83 85
Beef Stew, Oven, '79 222; '80 64
Beef Stew, Quick, '86 302
Beef Stew, Spicy, '86 228
Beef Stew with Dumplings, '84 3
Beef Stew with Parsley Dumplings, '81 76;
    '82 13; '85 M246
Brown Stew, '85 239
Brunswick Stew, '80 264
Brunswick Stew, Aunt Willette's, '85 320
Brunswick Stew, Bama, '87 4
Brunswick Stew, Blakely, '87 4
Brunswick Stew, Sonny Frye's, '87 4
Burgoo, Five-Meat, '87 3
Burgoo, Harry Young's, '87 3
Burgoo, Kentucky, '88 235
Burgoo, Old-Fashioned, '87 3
Burgundy Stew with Drop
    Dumplings, '83 125
Catfish Stew, Cajun-Style, '88 12
Chicken Stew and Dumplings, '84 4
Chicken Stew, Brunswick, '87 4
Fish-and-Vegetable Stew, '87 220
Fisherman's Stew, '81 98
Hamburger Oven Stew, '84 4
Hungarian Stew with Noodles, '80 263
Hunter's Stew, '85 270
Lamb Stew, '79 293; '88 58
Lamb Stew-in-a-Loaf, '85 37

Lentil-Rice Stew, '82 232
Meatball Stew, '79 198
Mexican Stew, '82 231
Mexican Stew Olé, '86 296
Okra Stew, Old-Fashioned, '84 158
Oyster Stew, '80 221
Oyster Stew, Company, '80 297
Oyster Stew, Golden, '86 132
Oyster Stew, Holiday, '85 264
Pollo en Pipián, Mexican, '88 31
Sausage Stew, Smoked, '82 231
Seafood Stew, '84 280
Shrimp Creole, Spicy, '79 181
Shrimp Creole, Wild Rice-and-, '84 292
Shrimp Stew, '83 4
Shrimp Stew and Grits, '80 118
Shrimp Stew over Grits, '88 126
Turkey Stew, Hearty, '79 252
Vegetable Stew, Mixed, '84 13
Venison Sausage Stew, '87 238
Venison Stew, '86 294
Venison Stew with Potato
    Dumplings, '87 304
White Wine Stew, '82 228
Strawberries
Banana-Berry Flip, '88 215
Bars, Strawberry, '81 301
Bavarian, Rhubarb-Strawberry, '86 140
Beets, Strawberry-Glazed, '83 234
Brandied Orange Juice, Strawberries
    with, '82 160
Bread, Strawberry, '81 250; '83 140;
    '84 49
Bread, Strawberry Jam, '79 216
Bread, Strawberry-Nut, '79 24
Butter, Strawberry, '79 36; '81 286
Cake Roll, Strawberries 'n Cream
    Sponge, '81 95
Cake Roll, Strawberry, '79 49; '83 129;
    '84 305; '85 172
Cake, Strawberry Coffee, '85 46
Cake, Strawberry Cream, '86 61
Cake, Strawberry Crunch, '79 288; '80 35
Cake, Strawberry Delight, '85 30
Cake, Strawberry Meringue, '86 240
Cake with Strawberries and Chocolate
    Glaze, White, '87 76
Cheesecake, Almost Strawberry, '86 32
Cheesecake, Pear-Berry, '82 M141
Cherry-Berry on a Cloud, '79 94
Christmas Strawberries, '87 293
Cobbler, Rosy Strawberry-Rhubarb, '79 154
Cobbler, Strawberry-Rhubarb, '88 93
Combo, Strawberry-Chocolate, '85 96
Cooler, Strawberry, '83 56; '84 51
Cooler, Strawberry-Mint, '84 57
Cream Puffs, Strawberry, '81 95
Cream Puffs, Strawberry-Lemon, '87 75
Cream, Strawberries and, '82 100
Cream, Strawberries 'n Lemon, '85 120
Cream, Strawberries with Chocolate, '85 81
Cream, Strawberries with French, '83 191
Cream, Strawberries with
    Strawberry, '84 108
Cream, Strawberry, '88 153
Cream with Fresh Strawberries,
    Almond, '87 93
Crêpes, Nutritious Brunch, '80 44
Crêpes, Strawberry Dessert, '83 122
Crêpes with Fruit Filling, '81 96
Daiquiri, Strawberry, '81 156

Delight, Frozen Strawberry, '82 112, 174
Delight, Strawberry, '81 85
Delight, Strawberry Cheese, '79 50
Delight, Strawberry Yogurt, '85 77
Dessert, Chilled Strawberry, '84 164
Dessert, Glazed Strawberry, '84 33
Dessert, Honeydew-Berry, '83 120
Dessert, Strawberry, '83 123
Dessert, Strawberry-Cream
    Cheese, '83 123
Dessert, Strawberry-Lemon, '86 162
Dressing, Creamy Strawberry, '84 161
Float, Strawberry-Banana, '87 160
Fried Strawberries, Deep-, '84 109
Frost, Banana-Strawberry, '87 199
Frost, Strawberry, '81 279; '82 24;
    '83 154
Glaze, Strawberry, '80 35; '83 142
Ice Cream Crêpes, Strawberry, '87 290;
    '88 135
Ice Cream, Homemade Strawberry, '84 184
Ice Cream, Old-Fashioned
    Strawberry, '79 94
Ice Cream Roll, Strawberry, '84 105
Ice Cream, Straw-Ba-Nut, '80 177
Ice Cream, Strawberry, '80 177
Ice Cream, Strawberry-Banana-Nut, '88 203

Ice Cream Torte,
    Chocolate-Strawberry, '79 7
Ice Cream, Very Strawberry, '81 155
Ice, Strawberry, '84 175; '85 108
Ice, Strawberry-Orange, '86 196
Jamaica, Strawberries, '85 161
Jam, Christmas, '88 288
Jam, Strawberry Freezer, '84 M182
Jellyroll, Easy, '82 176
Jelly, Strawberry, '81 147
Juliet, Strawberries, '84 82
Lemonade, Strawberry, '80 160
Marmalade, Strawberry-Pineapple, '85 130
Marsala, Strawberries, '88 171
Melon, Berry-Filled, '86 93
Meringues, Strawberry, '84 188
Milkshake, Fresh Strawberry, '82 113
Mimosa, Sparkling Strawberry, '88 169
Mousse, Fresh Strawberry, '82 72
Mousse, Strawberry, '81 95
Mousse, Strawberry-Lemon, '82 128
Napoleons, Strawberry, '81 126
Nests, Strawberry Coconut, '88 136
Pancakes, Strawberry, '84 219
Parfait, Crunchy
    Strawberry-Yogurt, '79 124
Parfaits, Frosty Strawberry, '85 213
Parfaits, Strawberry-Lemon, '84 198
Parfait, Strawberry, '79 99
Parfait, Surprise Strawberry, '86 151
Pie, Chilled Strawberry, '82 112
Pie, Glazed Strawberry, '82 M142
Pie, Heavenly Chocolate-Berry, '85 102

Strawberries *(continued)*

Pie, Lemon-Strawberry, **'88** 127
Pie, Strawberry Angel, **'88** 136
Pie, Strawberry-Banana Glazed, **'81** 181
Pie, Strawberry-Glaze, **'81** 141
Pie, Strawberry Yogurt, **'80** 232
Pie, Strawberry-Yogurt, **'85** 122; **'86** 124
Pizza, Kiwi-Berry, **'86** 198; **'87** 55
Pizza, Strawberry, **'79** 94
Popsicles, Smoothie Strawberry, **'82** 112
Preserves Deluxe, Strawberry, **'82** 150
Preserves, Freezer Strawberry, **'82** 112
Preserves, Strawberry, **'79** 120; **'81** 96
Puff, Strawberry, **'82** 5
Punch, Creamy Strawberry, **'86** 195
Punch, Strawberry-Lemonade, **'85** 116
Raspberry Custard Sauce, Fresh Berries
  with, **'88** 163
Ring, Strawberry-Cheese, **'86** 14
Roll, Heavenly Strawberry, **'82** 176
Roll, Strawberry, **'82** 120
Romanoff, Strawberries, **'84** 108; **'88** 95
Ruby Strawberries, **'82** 100
Sabayon, Strawberries, **'79** 94
Salad, Hidden Treasure Strawberry, **'79** 11
Salad Mold, Strawberry-Wine, **'83** 261
Salad, Strawberry Yogurt, **'80** 232
Sangría, Teaberry, **'87** 147
Sauce, Amaretto-Strawberry, **'87** M165
Sauce, Berry, **'87** 290; **'88** 135
Sauce, Brandied Strawberry, **'88** 196
Sauce, Fresh Strawberry, **'82** 177
Sauce, Melon Wedges with Berry, **'86** 178
Sauce, Peaches with Strawberry, **'85** 8
Sauce, Strawberry, **'84** 144; **'87** 93, 198
Sauce, Strawberry-Banana, **'81** 41
Sauce with Crunchy Topping,
  Strawberry, **'81** 170
Sauce with Dumplings, Strawberry, **'84** 314
Shake, Strawberry-Orange
  Breakfast, **'87** 186
Shake, Strawberry-Pineapple, **'84** 166
Shake, Strawberry-Yogurt, **'87** 199
Sherbet, Strawberry, **'82** 112, 160
Shortcake, A Favorite Strawberry, **'88** 136
Shortcake, Elegant Strawberry, **'88** 37
Shortcake Jubilee, Strawberry, **'88** 209
Shortcake Shells, Strawberry, **'88** 196
Shortcake Squares, Strawberry, **'86** 124
Shortcake, Strawberry, **'81** 96; **'83** 122
Skewered Pineapple and
  Strawberries, **'84** 251
Slurp, Strawberry, **'81** 96
Slush, Strawberry-Orange, **'83** 172
Smoothie, Strawberry, **'86** 183
Smoothie, Strawberry-Banana, **'81** 59
Smoothie, Tropical, **'81** 50
Soda, Old-Fashioned Strawberry, **'79** 149
Soda, Strawberry, **'84** 115
Sorbet, Strawberry, **'88** 117
Sorbet, Strawberry-Champagne, **'83** 162
Soup, Cold Strawberry, **'82** 157
Soup, Strawberry, **'88** 160
Soup, Strawberry-Banana, **'86** 181
Soup Supreme, Strawberry, **'81** M144
Spread, Light Strawberry, **'85** 55
Squares, Strawberry Shortcake, **'85** 122
Stuffed Strawberries with Walnuts, **'85** 122;
  '86 124
Sundaes, Hot Strawberry, **'81** M5

Supreme, Banana-Berry, **'81** 205
Swirl, Strawberry, **'84** 108
Tarts, Strawberry, **'80** 70
Tart, Strawberry, **'84** 138
Tea, Strawberry, **'88** 248
Topping, Strawberry, **'86** 32
Topping, Strawberry-Banana, **'87** 125
Torte, Strawberry Meringue, **'88** 136
Trifle, Easy Strawberry, **'88** 201
Zabaglione, Strawberries, **'81** 95

Stroganoff

Beef Burgundy Stroganoff, **'85** 31
Beef Stroganoff, **'79** 163; **'81** 179
Beef Stroganoff, Ground, **'84** 71
Beef Stroganoff, Light, **'86** 36
Chicken Livers Stroganoff, **'80** 200; **'81** 57
Chicken Livers Supreme, **'81** 298
Crab Stroganoff, **'79** 116
Hamburger Stroganoff, **'82** 108, 110
Hamburger Stroganoff, Easy, **'79** 208
Ham Stroganoff, **'82** 40
Liver Stroganoff, **'79** 54
Meatballs, European Veal, **'85** 30
Meatballs Paprikash with Rice, **'85** 31
Meatball Stroganoff, **'81** 297
Mushroom-Meatball Stroganoff, **'85** 85
Mushroom Stroganoff, **'81** 298
Quickie Stroganoff, **'81** 200
Shrimp Stroganoff, **'79** 81
Shrimp Stroganoff, Oven-Baked, **'81** 297
Sirloin Stroganoff, **'81** 297
Steak Stroganoff Sandwiches, **'85** 110
Steak Stroganoff with Parslied
  Noodles, **'85** 31
Tofu, Stroganoff, **'84** 202
Veal Stroganoff, **'79** 108

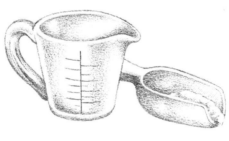

Stuffings and Dressings

Apple-Crumb Stuffing, **'81** 234; **'82** 26;
  '83 39
Cajun Dressing, **'82** 307
Chicken and Dressing, Baked, **'79** 296
Cornbread-and-Sausage Dressing, **'83** 213
Cornbread-Biscuit Dressing, **'79** 296
Cornbread Dressing, **'86** 286; **'88** 254
Cornbread Dressing, Fruited, **'80** 262
Cornbread Dressing,
  Herb-Seasoned, **'83** 315
Cornbread Dressing, Kentucky, **'86** 281
Cornbread Dressing,
  Old-Fashioned, **'84** 321
Cornbread Dressing, Sage-, **'84** 283
Cornbread Dressing, Savory, **'88** 303
Cornbread Dressing, Texas, **'82** 243
Cornbread Dressing, Turkey with
  Sausage-, **'83** 287
Cornbread-Sage Dressing, **'80** 262
Cornbread-Sausage Dressing, **'82** 307;
  '85 280

Corn Dressing Balls, Zesty, **'82** 307
Crabmeat Stuffing, Chicken Breasts
  with, **'85** 302
Cranberry-Sausage Stuffing, Crown Roast
  of Pork with, **'88** 49
Fruit-and-Pecan Dressing, **'84** 252
Fruit Dressing, Baked, **'87** 253
Low-Sodium Stuffing, **'82** 66
Oyster Bread Dressing, **'82** 251
Oyster Dressing, **'79** 250
Oyster Stuffing, Roast Turkey
  with, **'80** 251
Peanut Dressing, Roast Turkey
  with, **'79** 283
Pecan-Rice Dressing, Chicken
  with, **'85** M57
Pecan-Sage Dressing, **'80** 262
Pecan Stuffing, **'79** 292; **'80** 32
Pecan Stuffing, Wild Duck with, **'85** 269
Pretzel Dressing, **'86** 280
Rice-and-Onion Stuffing, **'88** 246
Rice Dressing, Chicken and, **'79** 288
Rice Dressing, Mexican, **'87** 253
Rice Dressing, Roast Turkey with, **'82** 286
Sausage Dressing, **'86** 280
Sausage Dressing, Harvest, **'88** 254
Seasoned Dressing, Stuffed Turkey Breast
  with, **'83** 320; **'84** 128
Squash Dressing, **'83** 315; **'86** 280
Squash Dressing, Turkey with, **'87** 248
Turkey and Dressing, Easy, **'79** 296
Turkey-and-Dressing Pie, **'84** 326
Turkey Dressing, **'85** 298
Whole Wheat-Mushroom Dressing, **'84** 283
Wild Rice Stuffing, Cornish Hens
  with, **'79** 222; **'80** 64; **'82** 136
Zucchini Dressing, **'86** 282

Sweet-and-Sour

Beans and Carrots, Sweet-and-Sour
  Green, **'83** 6
Beans, Sweet-and-Sour, **'87** 197
Beans, Sweet-and-Sour Green, **'79** 184;
  '81 158; **'82** 90
Beans with Sprouts,
  Sweet-and-Sour, **'86** 32
Beets, Sweet-and-Sour, **'81** 167; **'82** 22
Cabbage, Sweet-and-Sour, **'86** 295;
  '87 189
Cabbage, Sweet-Sour Red, **'79** 5
Carrots, Sweet-and-Sour, **'82** 137
Chicken, Sweet-and-Sour, **'79** 106;
  '86 217, 240
Chicken, Sweet-and-Sour Lemon, **'84** 93
Dressing, Sweet-and-Sour, **'80** 247; **'84** 70,
  161; **'85** 163; **'87** 305
Dressing, Sweet-and-Sour Fruit, **'84** 125
Dressing, Sweet-Sour, **'80** 246
Fish, Sweet-and-Sour, **'80** M54
Ham, Sweet-and-Sour Glazed, **'88** M15
Ham, Sweet-Sour Glazed, **'83** 311
Kale, Sweet-and-Sour, **'80** 298
Liver, Sweet-and-Sour, **'81** 277
Marinade, Sweet-and-Sour, **'86** 113;
  '87 115
Meatballs, Sweet-and-Sour, **'82** 233, 247;
  '86 240
Meatballs, Sweet-and-Sour Party, **'79** 233
Peas, Sweet-and-Sour, **'88** 3
Peas, Sweet-and-Sour Black-Eyed, **'85** 290
Pork Chops, Sweet-and-Sour, **'83** 160
Pork, Pineapple Sweet-and-Sour, **'82** 120

Pork, Sweet-and-Sour, **'79** 42; **'80** 72,
227; **'81** 26, 104, 111; **'82** 12; **'84** 218;
'85 34, 194; **'86** 241
Potatoes, Sweet-and-Sour-Topped, **'83** 4
Pot Roast, Sweet-and-Sour, **'83** 8
Riblets, Sweet-and-Sour, **'85** 276
Salad, Sweet-and-Sour Bean, **'85** 198;
'86 147
Salad, Sweet-and-Sour Cauliflower, **'81** 2
Salad, Sweet-and-Sour Fruit, **'80** 13;
'84 125
Salad, Sweet-and-Sour Macaroni,
'85 166
Salad, Sweet and Sour Potato, **'80** 152
Salad, Sweet-and-Sour Vegetable, **'81** 25
Salad, Sweet-Sour Spinach, **'85** M112
Sauce, Sausage Rolls with
Sweet-and-Sour, **'83** 74
Sauce, Sweet-and-Sour, **'80** 20; **'85** 12, 34;
'86 240
Sauce, Sweet-and-Sour Pineapple, **'85** 66

Sausage, Sweet-and-Sour, **'88** 296
Shrimp and Chicken,
Sweet-and-Sour, **'87** 267; **'88** 103
Shrimp, Sweet-and-Sour, **'83** 278
Shrimp Tails, Sweet-and-Sour Rock, **'80** 3
Slaw, Sweet-and-Sour, **'81** 237
Spareribs, Sweet-and-Sour, **'83** 21
Spread, Sweet 'n' Sour, **'86** 184
Steaks, Sweet-and-Sour Marinated, **'83** 110
Stew, Sweet-and-Sour Beef and
Vegetable, **'85** 87
Turkey, Sweet-and-Sour, **'79** 252
Turnips, Sweet-and-Sour, **'81** 274
Vegetables, Sweet-and-Sour
Marinated, **'83** 266

Swiss Chard
Buttered Chard, **'83** 36
Tomatoes, Swiss Chard with, **'83** 36

Syrups
Almond Syrup, **'82** 47
Anise Sugar Syrup, **'86** 248
Apple Syrup, Spiced, **'79** 114
Apricot Fruit Syrup, **'82** 10
Caramel Syrup, **'82** 43
Cherry-Lemonade Syrup, **'86** 214
Citrus Syrup, Sweet, **'86** 270
Fruit Syrup, **'86** 176
Kirsch Syrup, **'80** 280
Maple-Honey-Cinnamon Syrup, **'85** 19
Maple-Nut Syrup, **'80** 228
Maple Syrup, **'81** 120; **'82** 23
Maple Syrup, Homemade, **'79** 114
Orange Syrup, **'80** 228
Pecan Syrup, Chunky, **'85** 278

T

Tacos
al Carbón, Tacos, **'86** 19
al Carbon, Tailgate Tacos, **'79** 185
Appetizer, Layered Taco, **'84** 206
Bake, Taco Beef-Noodle, **'81** 141
Basic Tacos, **'83** 199
Breakfast Tacos, **'80** 43
Casserole, Taco, **'80** 33
Corn Chip Tacos, **'81** 67
Jiffy Tacos, **'83** M318
Lentil Tacos, **'88** 197
Lobster Taco with Yellow Tomato Salsa and
Jicama Salad, Warm, **'87** 122
Microwave Tacos, **'88** M213
Navajo Tacos, **'84** 246
Peppers, Taco, **'81** 86
Pie, Crescent Taco, **'80** 80
Pie, Double-Crust Taco, **'88** 272
Pies, Individual Taco, **'82** M282
Pie, Taco, **'88** 256
Pitas, Taco, **'83** 31
Salad Cups, Taco, **'85** M29
Salad, Meatless Taco, **'81** 204
Salad, Spicy Taco, **'87** 287
Salad, Taco, **'79** 56; **'83** 145; **'85** 84
Salad, Taco Macaroni, **'85** 165
Salad, Tuna-Taco, **'87** 145
Sauce, Taco, **'82** M283
Tacos, **'80** 196

Tamales
Bake, Cornbread Tamale, **'79** 163
Chicken Tamales, **'88** 151
Hot Tamales, **'83** 51
Meatballs, Tamale, **'80** 194
Miniature Tamales, **'85** 154
Pie, Chili-Tamale, **'82** 9; **'83** 68
Sweet Tamales, **'83** 52
Tamales, **'80** 195

Tea
Almond-Lemonade Tea, **'86** 229
Almond Tea, **'85** 43; **'86** 329
Apple-Cinnamon Tea, Hot, **'87** 57
Apricot Tea, Hot Spiced, **'88** 248
Brew, Quilter's, **'85** 43
Citrus Tea, Hot, **'83** 275
Citrus Tea, Iced, **'85** 162
Cranberry-Apple Tea, **'88** 169
Cubes, Frozen Tea, **'85** 161
Fruit Tea, Christmas, **'83** 275
Fruit Tea, Hot Spiced, **'87** 242
Ginger Tea, **'81** 100
Granita, Mint Tea, **'88** 117
Grape Juice Tea, White, **'87** 57
Grape Tea, Spiced, **'79** 174
Hawaiian Tea, **'87** 57
Honey Tea, **'81** 105
Iced Tea, Bubbly, **'81** 168
Johnny Appleseed Tea, **'85** 23
Lemon-Mint Tea, **'85** 162
Lemon Tea, **'82** 156
Minted Tea, **'86** 101; **'88** 163
Mint Tea, **'87** 107
Mint Tea, Frosted, **'84** 161
Mint Tea, Fruited, **'88** 79
Mint Tea, Iced, **'83** 170
Mix, Deluxe Spiced Tea, **'88** 257
Mix, Friendship Tea, **'83** 283
Mix, Spiced Tea, **'86** 32

Punch, Apple-Tea, **'85** 82
Punch, Bourbon-Tea, **'87** 57
Punch, Citrus-Tea, **'85** 116
Punch, Spiked Tea, **'86** 101
Sangría, Teaberry, **'87** 147
Spiced Tea Cooler, **'83** 55
Spiced Tea, Hot, **'83** 244
Strawberry Tea, **'88** 248
Summer Tea, **'85** 162
Summertime Tea, **'81** 167
Sun Tea, Southern, **'81** 168
Yaupon Tea, **'79** 31

Tempura
Basic Tempura, **'81** 68
Chicken Tempura Delight, **'85** 66
Cornmeal Tempura, **'81** 68
Sauce, Basic Tempura, **'81** 68
Sauce, Mustard-Sour Cream, **'81** 68
Vegetable Tempura, **'79** 112

Terrines
Black Bean Terrine with Goat
Cheese, **'87** 120
Chicken Terrine Ring, **'84** 132
Chicken-Vegetable Terrine, **'84** 131
Pork Terrine, Jeweled, **'84** 130
Salmon-and-Spinach Terrine,
Layered, **'84** 132
Vegetable-Chicken Terrine, **'83** 224

Timbales
Cheesy Mexicali Appetizer, **'82** 108
Chicken Chutney Salad, **'82** 108
Grits Timbales, **'88** 223
Hamburger Stroganoff, **'82** 108
Peach Almond Cream, **'82** 108
Shells, Timbale, **'82** 108
Spinach-Rice Timbales, **'88** 271
Spinach Timbales, **'84** 29

Tofu
Dip, Tofu, **'86** 109
Drink, Tofruitti Breakfast, **'88** 26
Lasagna, Tofu, **'83** 312
Rice with Tofu, Spanish, **'88** 26
Salad, Tofu, **'88** 27
Sandwiches, Open-Face Tofu-Veggie, **'86** 5
Stroganoff Tofu, **'84** 202

Tomatoes
Aspic, Bloody Mary-Tomato, **'81** 77
Aspic, Chicken in Tomato, **'84** 190
Aspic, Chili Sauce Tomato, **'85** 252
Aspic, Herbed Tomato, **'81** 73
Aspic, Light Tomato, **'85** 83
Aspic, Ranch Tomato, **'83** 218
Aspic, Spicy Tomato, **'81** 40
Aspic, Tangy Tomato, **'83** 124
Aspic, Tomato-Artichoke, **'84** 320; **'86** 92
Aspic, Tomato-Crab, **'85** 287
Aspic with Shrimp, Tomato, **'79** 241
au Gratin, Zucchini and Tomato, **'82** 208
Bake, Chicken-Tomato, **'83** 35
Baked Cheddar Tomatoes, **'85** 43
Baked Tangy Tomatoes, **'81** 168
Baked Tomatoes, **'83** 53; **'87** 197
Baked Tomatoes, Spinach-Stuffed, **'86** 14
Baked Tomatoes with Corn, **'80** 161
Baked Tomato Halves, Zippy, **'81** 182
Bake, Ham-Rice-Tomato, **'87** 78
Bake, Okra-Tomato, **'80** 298; **'81** 26
Bake, Potato-Tomato, **'86** 17
Bake, Tomato-and-Artichoke Heart, **'85** 81
Bake, Zucchini and Tomato, **'82** 158
Beans and Tomatoes, Basil, **'83** 172

Tomatoes (*continued*)

Beans with Tomatoes, Green, '85 137
Beef Saltillo (Beef with Tomatillos), '82 219
Biscuits, Tomato, '86 72
Bisque, Tomato-Shrimp, '86 66
Bites, Tomato, '84 80
Bouillon, Tomato, '83 8
Bowl, Tomato, '81 69
Bread, Herbed Tomato-Cheese, '88 143
Broiled Tomatoes, '80 152
Broiled Tomatoes, Quick, '79 153
Broiled Tomatoes, Romano, '80 42
Broiled Tomatoes with Dill Sauce, '80 161
Broiled Tomatoes with Mushroom
   Sauce, '81 103
Broil, Tomato-English Pea, '83 192
Buffet Tomatoes, '82 180
Butter, Tomato, '86 128
Cabbage and Tomatoes, '83 104
Cabbage and Tomatoes, Tasty, '86 72
Cacciatore, Chicken, '86 42
Canning Tomatoes, '80 128; '85 106
Casserole, Corn and Tomato, '81 127
Casserole, Corn-and-Tomato, '84 145
Casserole, Eggplant-and-Tomato, '83 187
Casserole, Saucy Potato-Tomato, '79 46
Casserole, Scalloped Tomato, '88 144
Casserole, Zucchini-and-Tomato, '88 265
Catsup, Spicy Tomato, '83 182
Cheese Herbed-Topped Tomatoes, '86 108
Cheese Sauce over Toast, Tomatoes
   with, '88 159
Cheese-Topped Tomatoes, '81 160
Cheesy Puff-Top Tomatoes, '86 187

Cherry Tomatoes, Cheesy, '83 135
Cherry Tomatoes, Crab-Stuffed, '82 289;
   '88 78
Cherry Tomatoes,
   Cucumber-Stuffed, '88 262
Cherry Tomatoes, Green Beans
   with, '86 177
Cherry Tomatoes, Herbed, '82 128
Cherry Tomatoes in Brown Butter
   Sauce, '81 168
Cherry Tomatoes, Stuffed, '84 160;
   '88 95, 212
Cherry Tomatoes with Rum, '83 192
Chicken, Tomato-Baked, '81 281; '82 30
Chowder, Tomato-Clam, '84 251
Chutney, Tomato-Apple, '84 180
Cocktail, Tomato, '83 M203
Cocktail, Tomato-Clam, '87 252
Cocktail, Tomato Juice, '79 212; '83 230
Cocktail, Tomato-Orange Juice, '83 169
Cocktail, Zesty Tomato Juice, '83 289
Coleslaw with Tomatoes, '80 34
Consommé, Tomato, '88 250
Creole-Style Tomatoes-and-Corn, '84 142
Cucumber on Tomatoes, Dilled, '84 142
Cups, Turkey-Tomato, '84 119
Delights, Tomato, '81 140

Delight, Tomato-Pea, '84 196
Dressing, Fresh Tomato Salad, '83 193
Dressing, Garden Salad with Tomato-Cream
   Cheese, '79 173
Dressing, Tomato-Honey French, '81 105
Dumplings, Tomato, '88 144
Eggs Benedict, Bacon-and-Tomato, '87 195
Fire-and-Ice Tomatoes, '87 92
Fried Herb Tomatoes, '88 144
Fried Red Tomatoes, '81 102
Fried Ripe Tomatoes, '81 168
Fried Ripe Tomatoes with Gravy, '82 180
Fried Tomatoes with Bacon, Saucy, '81 210
Fried Tomatoes with Gravy, '86 211
Green Tomatoes, Fried, '79 123; '80 178;
   '81 210; '85 214
Green Tomatoes, Herb-Baked, '85 214
Green Tomatoes, Italian-Sauced, '85 214
Green Tomatoes, Okra and, '79 160
Green Tomatoes, Oven-Fried, '82 107
Green Tomato Jam, '79 121
Green Tomato Pie, '79 195
Grilled Tomatoes, '85 158
Grilled Tomatoes, Cheesy, '79 150
Herbed Tomatoes, '81 102; '82 49;
   '83 173
Italian Dressing, Tomato, Onion, and
   Cucumber in, '81 83
Italiano, Tomatoes, '88 29
Juice, Homemade Tomato, '81 50
Juice, Spicy Tomato, '85 189
Lemon Dressing, Tomato Slices
   with, '87 167
Lima and Tomato Combo, Hot, '83 219
Marinade, Bright Tomato, '88 176
Marinated Salsa Tomatoes, '82 164
Marinated Tomatoes, '85 156, 163
Marinated Tomato Slices, '82 134; '83 193
Medley, Okra-Corn-Tomato, '81 159
Medley, Tomato, '81 159
Mold, Tangy Tomato, '79 74
Muffins, Tomato Corn, '81 137
Mustard, Green Beans and Tomatoes
   with, '87 83
Mustard Tomatoes, Zippy, '86 M226
Okra and Tomatoes, '80 185; '81 139
Okra and Tomatoes, Fresh, '81 M165;
   '87 89
Okra-Tomato Combo, '83 157
Okra, Tomatoes and, '86 170; '87 164
Okra, Tomatoes with, '85 106
Olive Spread, Tomatoes with, '85 114
Oregano Tomatoes, '83 145
Parmesan Tomatoes, '80 161
Pasta Toss, Tomato-Olive, '86 209
Peas and Tomatoes, Basil Snow, '88 M185
Peas and Tomatoes, Snow, '83 111
Pesto, Tomatoes, '86 150
Pickles, Green Tomato, '87 134
Pie, Tomato, '88 198
Potage, Tomato, '79 250
Primavera, Tomato-Pasta, '86 209
Provençal, Tomatoes, '82 181
Puffs, Tomato Cheese, '81 48
Puree, Seasoned Tomato, '83 182
Quiche, Asparagus-Tomato, '88 198
Ratatouille, '84 105, 243; '85 92
Ratatouille-Bran Stuffed Eggplant, '86 44
Ratatouille, Eggplant-Zucchini, '81 205
Ratatouille, Niçoise, '81 22
Ratatouille, Quick-and-Easy, '80 212

Ratatouille-Stuffed Eggplant, '83 187
Refresher, Tomato, '81 94; '83 318
Relish, Black Bean-Tomatillo, '87 121
Relish, Easy Tomato, '80 126
Relish, End-of-the-Garden, '80 179
Relish, Tomato, '85 188
Ring, Tangy Tomato, '84 164
Ring, Tomato-Vegetable, '81 302
Rose, Tomato, '82 51; '85 338

Rotelle, Chicken and Tomato
   with, '87 108
Salad, Artichoke-Stuffed Tomato, '82 101
Salad, Artichoke-Tomato, '82 239
Salad, Cherry Tomato, '87 156
Salad, Cottage-Tomato, '85 163
Salad, Crab-Stuffed Tomato, '80 148
Salad, Dilled Cucumber and
   Tomato, '81 153
Salad, Frozen Tomato, '84 52
Salad, Guacamole-Tomato, '81 302
Salad in Tomatoes, Cottage
   Cheese, '86 208
Salad, Lima Bean-Tomato, '85 137
Salad, Marinated, '83 170
Salad, Oriental-Stuffed Tomato, '82 101
Salad, Ruby-and-Emerald, '85 79
Salad, Spicy Chile-Tomato, '88 121
Salad, Tomato-Avocado, '86 74
Salad, Tomato-Cucumber, '86 218
Salad, Tomato-Cucumber-Onion, '81 239
Salad, Tomato-Feta, '81 246
Salad, Tomato Petal, '79 88
Salad, Tomato Relish, '83 111
Salad, Vidalia-Tomato, '84 65
Salad, Watercress-Tomato, '85 132
Salsa, '88 147
Salsa, Chunky, '86 130
Salsa, Tomato, '87 120
Salsa, Yellow Tomato, '87 122
Sandwiches, Bacon, Cheese, and
   Tomato, '84 14
Sandwiches, Open-Face Crab
   Tomato, '81 29
Sauce, Asparagus with Tomato, '83 46
Sauce, Chunky Chili, '85 188
Sauce, Fish in Tomato, '85 75
Sauce for Spaghetti, Italian
   Tomato, '81 134
Sauce, Fresh Tomato, '83 224; '87 171
Sauce, Hamburgers with Tomato, '81 73
Sauce, Herbed Fresh Tomato, '85 M151
Sauce, Italian-Style Tomato, '87 182
Sauce, Italian Tomato, '82 M68
Sauce, Linguine with
   Tomato-Cream, '86 158
Sauce, Quick Crab Marinara, '85 M151
Sauce, Rancheros, '88 148
Sauce, Refrigerator Tomato, '85 188
Sauce, Seasoned Tomato, '83 150

Sauce, Spicy Tomato, '84 294; '88 19
Sauce, Spinach Tortellini with
  Tomato, '88 302
Sauce, Tarragon-Tomato, '84 131
Sauce, Tomato, '85 193, 244; '87 249;
  '88 116
Sauce, Turkey Patties in
  Vegetable-Tomato, '87 18
Sauce, Vermicelli with Tomato, '83 164
Sauce with Green Chiles, Tomato, '81 196
Sauté, Tomato-Pepper, '84 142
Scalloped Tomatoes, '84 142
Scalloped Tomato Slices, '81 168
Sesame Tomatoes, '84 142
Skillet, Cabbage-and-Tomato, '86 110
Skillet Tomatoes, '81 108
Soup, Appetizer Tomato, '86 258
Soup, Chilled Tomato, '82 155
Soup, Cold Tomato, '88 160
Soup, Creamy Tomato, '83 267; '86 258
Soup, Easy Tomato, '84 14
Soup, Fresh Tomato, '83 140
Soup, Hot Tomato Juice, '86 302
Soup, Iced Tomato, '79 170
Soup Plus, Tomato, '88 170
Soup, Pumpkin-Tomato, '86 291
Soup, Refreshing Tomato Cream, '79 172
Soup, Sour Cream-Topped Tomato,
  '80 246
Soup, Summer Tomato, '79 130
Soup, Tomato, '81 236; '83 44
Soup, Tomato-and-Rice, '85 24
Soup, Tomato-Celery, '83 M58
Soup, Tomato-Vegetable, '81 M177; '86 9
Soup with Parmesan Cheese, Cream of
  Tomato, '86 161
Spicy Tomato Sipper, '86 229
Spinach-Topped Tomatoes, '88 265
Spread, Fiery Tomato-Cheese, '87 196
Spread, Home-Style Sandwich, '80 179
Spread, Tomato-Cheese, '81 157
Squash, Beans, and Tomatoes, '83 148
Squash, Tomato, '86 111
Stack-Ups, Jiffy Tomato, '80 161
Stewed Tomatoes, '83 182
Stir-Fry, Tomato-Zucchini, '80 158
Stir-Fry, Zucchini-and-Tomato, '85 108
Strata, Tomato-Cheese, '81 209
Stuffed Eggs-and-Tomato Slices, '84 152
Stuffed Tomatoes, '83 252
Stuffed Tomatoes, Avocado-, '82 101
Stuffed Tomatoes, Bacon-and-Egg-,
  '80 162
Stuffed Tomatoes, Baked, '88 162
Stuffed Tomatoes, Bean-, '84 34
Stuffed Tomatoes, Broccoli-, '83 136
Stuffed Tomatoes, Cheesy, '80 161
Stuffed Tomatoes, Cold, '80 100
Stuffed Tomatoes, Corn-, '82 270
Stuffed Tomatoes, Easy, '82 264
Stuffed Tomatoes, Maque Chou, '87 89
Stuffed Tomatoes, Mushroom-, '86 218
Stuffed Tomatoes, Sausage-, '80 47
Stuffed Tomatoes, Squash-, '82 102
Stuffed Tomato with Tuna Pasta, '88 54
Swiss Chard with Tomatoes, '83 36
Treat, Summer Tomato, '79 143
Tuna-Mac in Tomatoes, '87 188
Venison and Tomatoes, '85 270
Vinaigrette, Tomato-Basil, '87 89
Vinaigrette, Tomatoes, '84 106

Tortillas. *See also* Burritos, Enchiladas,
  Tacos.
Appetizers, Tex-Mex Tortilla, '86 297
Bake, Cheesy Beef-and-Bean, '82 89
Bake, Chicken Tortilla, '82 89
Buñuelos, '80 199
Buñuelos, King-Size, '86 5
Casserole, Chicken Tortilla, '81 166
Casserole, El Dorado, '81 140
Casserole, Mexican Chicken, '82 143
Chalupas, Bean, '83 313
Chalupas, Chicken, '79 185
Chalupas, Chicken-Olive, '81 227
Chalupas, Texas Turkey, '80 196
Cheesy Tortillas, '81 62
Chicken Acapulco, '84 32
Chicken-Tortilla Stack, Cheesy, '86 3
Chilaquiles, '82 220
Chilaquiles con Pollo, '81 66
Chimichangas, '86 114
Chimichangas, Pineapple Dessert, '86 4
Chorizo and Egg Tortillas, '81 193
Dippers, Rolled Tortilla, '86 4
Egg-and-Sausage Tortillas, '83 246; '84 42
Eggs Sonora, '80 196
Fajitas, '84 233
Fajitas, Favorite, '86 114
Flautas, '83 199
Flour Tortillas, '81 303
Flour Tortillas, Never-Fail, '80 198
Picadillo, '84 118
Pie, Mexican Cheese, '82 9; '83 69
Pie, Montezuma Tortilla, '83 199
Pie, Tortilla, '85 M211
Salad in a Shell, Mexican, '86 4
Sandwiches, Guacamole, '82 9; '83 68
Sandwich, Tex-Mex Ham-and-Cheese, '86 4
Soup, Tortilla, '88 31, 245
Tostada Compuestas, '81 194
Tostadas, Crispy, '83 2
Tostadas, Super, '83 199

Tuna
Baked Tuna and Peas in Wine
  Sauce, '83 196
Bake, Shoestring Potato Tuna, '82 211
Ball, Tuna-Pecan, '87 94
Barbecued Tuna, '80 275
Bisque, Tuna, '79 76
Boats, Cucumber Tuna, '83 136
Burgers, Zippy Tuna, '81 135
Casserole, Biscuit-Topped Tuna, '79 113
Casserole, Easy Tuna, '82 M203
Casserole, Nippy Tuna, '84 241
Casserole, Tangy Tuna-Broccoli, '83 75
Casserole, Tuna, '82 119
Casserole, Tuna Vegetable, '81 135
Casserole with Cheese Swirls,
  Tuna, '88 256
Cheesies, Tuna, '82 191
Croquettes, Tuna-Egg, '80 275
Croquettes with Parsley
  Sauce, Tuna, '86 108
Dip, Low-Cal Tuna, '87 25
Dip, Tuna-Curry, '84 31
Eggs, Tuna-Stuffed, '83 83
Jambalaya, Tuna, '83 44
Lasagna, Tuna, '83 44; '84 123
Macaroni Treat, Tuna-, '82 131
Melts, Tempting Tuna, '88 158
Mold, Creamy Tuna-Cheese, '81 135
Mound, Tuna, '80 276

Mousse, Tuna, '80 275
Pasta, Stuffed Tomato with Tuna, '88 54
Pie, Tuna-Rice, '84 123
Pie with Cheese Roll Crust, Tuna, '80 286
Pita Pocket, Tuna-in-a-, '87 202
Pockets, Tuna, '88 139
Potatoes, Tuna-Stuffed, '79 210
Ring, Creamy Tuna, '80 275
Salad, Cheese-Sauced Tuna, '87 M124
Salad, Company Tuna, '87 201
Salad, Confetti, '80 4
Salad, Congealed Tuna, '84 163
Salad, Creamy Tuna, '82 87, 208
Salad, Crunchy Tuna, '87 201
Salad, Curried Tuna, '86 208
Salad, Favorite Tuna, '82 208
Salad, Flavorful Tuna, '81 37
Salad, Fresh Greens and Tuna, '80 55
Salad, Layered Tuna, '84 221
Salad, Luncheon Tuna, '81 135
Salad, Meal-in-One, '82 232
Salad Rolls, Hot Tuna, '84 281
Salad, Swiss Tuna, '86 186
Salad, Tuna-and-Cannellini Bean, '86 143
Salad, Tuna Chef, '82 78
Salad, Tuna-Egg, '81 135

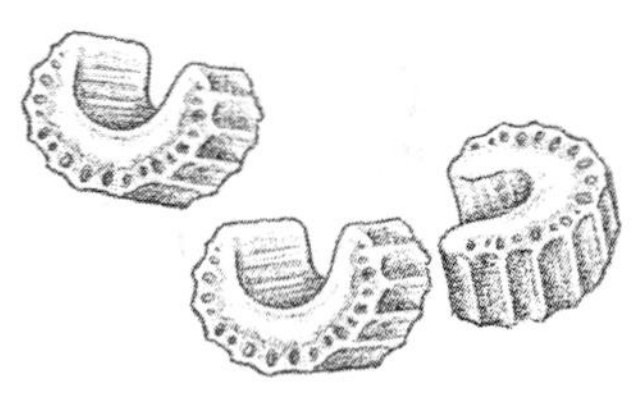

Salad, Tuna Macaroni, '83 44, 145
Salad, Tuna-Macaroni, '84 66
Salad, Tuna-Potato, '84 289
Salad, Tuna-Rice, '87 202
Salad, Tuna-Taco, '87 145
Salad, Whole Wheat
  Macaroni-Tuna, '84 193
Salad with Grapes, Curried Tuna, '87 201
Sandwiches, French Toasted Tuna, '80 275
Sandwiches, Hot Tuna, '85 299; '86 M194
Sandwiches, Tuna Club, '83 134
Spread, Tuna, '83 174
Tomatoes, Tuna-Mac in, '87 188
Waffle-Wich, Hot Tuna, '88 272

Turkey
Baked Turkey, Cider, '83 263
Bake, Layered Ham and Turkey, '79 252
Braised Turkey Breast, '84 260
Breast, Herb Butter-Basted
  Turkey, '86 285
Buffet Turkey, '80 29
Cabbage Rolls, Stuffed, '88 18
Casserole, Golden Turkey, '80 271
Casserole, Stuffed Turkey, '88 246
Casserole, Turkey, '84 327
Casserole, Turkey-and-Broccoli, '86 332
Casserole, Turkey-Asparagus, '86 284
Casserole, Turkey-Olive, '87 268
Casserole, Turkey-Spinach, '84 71
Casserole, Turkey-Swiss, '86 283
Chalupas, Texas Turkey, '80 196
Chili Topping, '84 246
Chili, Turkey-Bean, '88 M213

Turkey *(continued)*

Chowder, Turkey, **'85** 10
Chowder, Turkey-Corn, **'81** 98
Creamed Turkey, Southern, **'80** 272
Crêpes, Elegant Turkey, **'83** 282
Cups, Turkey-Tomato, **'84** 119
Cutlets with Pepper Salsa, Spicy
  Turkey, **'88** 26
Divan, Turkey, **'82** 268
Dressing, Easy Turkey and, **'79** 296
Dressing, Turkey, **'85** 298
Fast-and-Savory Turkey, **'87** 306
Florentine, Turkey, **'88** 264
Galantine of Turkey, **'85** 150
Gumbo, Turkey, **'82** 268; **'85** 258
Ham-and-Turkey Specials, Cheesy, **'84** 14
Indian Turkey, **'85** 302
Jambalaya de Covington, **'87** 211
Kabobs, Turkey-and-Fruit, **'88** 140
Lasagna, Lean, **'86** 37
Lasagna, Turkey, **'83** 239
Loaf, Cranberry-Glazed Turkey, **'86** 171
Loaf, Ground Turkey, **'86** 171
Open-Facers, Turkey, **'82** 190
Oriental Turkey, **'82** 268
Parmesan, Turkey, **'82** 268
Parmigiana, Turkey, **'87** 193
Patties in Vegetable-Tomato Sauce,
  Turkey, **'87** 18
Patties, Stuffed Ground Turkey, **'86** 171
Pie, Broccoli-and-Turkey Pasta, **'88** 269
Pie, Crumb-Crust Curried Turkey, **'86** 265
Pie, Golden Turkey, **'79** 253
Pie, Lattice-Topped Turkey, **'81** 277; **'82** 7
Pie, Potato-Topped Turkey, **'86** 265
Pie, Turkey, **'80** 285
Pie, Turkey-and-Dressing, **'84** 326
Pie, Turkey-and-Oyster, **'82** 267
Pie, Turkey-Cheese, **'88** 264
Pie, Turkey Pot, **'86** 265
Pilaf, Turkey-Asparagus, **'88** 200
Pilaf, Turkey-Rice, **'86** 284
Puffs, Turkey-Cheese, **'87** 301
Rice, Turkey Fried, **'83** 282
Roast Turkey, **'79** 250; **'80** 262; **'86** 47;
  '88 253
Roast Turkey Breast and Gravy, **'88** 303
Roast Turkey Breast with Special
  Gravy, **'86** 282
Roast Turkey, How to, **'83** 286
Roast Turkey with Oyster Stuffing, **'80** 251
Roast Turkey with Peanut
  Dressing, **'79** 283
Roast Turkey with Rice Dressing, **'82** 286
Rollups, Turkey, **'86** 198
Rounds, Turkey-Mozzarella, **'82** 3
Salad Bake, Turkey, **'79** 253
Salad, Chilled Turkey-and-Pepper
  Stir-Fry, **'88** 140
Salad, Curried Turkey, **'88** 140
Salad, Fruitful Turkey, **'84** 197
Salad, Holiday Turkey, **'84** 320
Salad, Hot Turkey, **'86** 10, 297; **'87** 176
Salad, Layered Turkey, **'86** 332
Salad, Meal-in-One, **'86** 43
Salad Pita Sandwiches, Turkey, **'87** 202;
  '88 43
Salad, Polynesian Turkey, **'87** 285
Salad, Turkey-Apple, **'88** 123
Salad, Turkey-Carrot, **'86** 283

Salad, Turkey-Fruit, **'79** 56
Salad, Turkey Fruit, **'83** 233; **'84** 244
Salad, Turkey Macaroni, **'83** 282
Salad, Turkey-Zucchini, **'85** 74
Salad with Hot Bacon Dressing,
  Turkey, **'87** 285
Salad with Sautéed Walnuts,
  Turkey, **'86** 117
Salad with Yogurt Dressing, Turkey
  Waldorf, **'88** 53
Sandwiches, Hot Brown, **'80** M202
Sandwiches, Meal-in-One, **'80** 218
Sandwiches, Monte Cristo, **'83** 134
Sandwiches, Open-Faced, **'79** 214
Sauce, Turkey Spaghetti, **'85** 13
Sausage-Cornbread Dressing, Turkey
  with, **'83** 287
Schnitzel, Turkey, **'84** 230
Skillet, Oriental Turkey-Orange, **'86** 284
Smoked Turkey, **'79** 293; **'84** 160;
  '85 258
Smoked Turkey Breast, **'88** 169
Soufflé, Turkey, **'80** 271
Soup, Curried Turkey, **'86** 332
Soup, Turkey Carcass, **'86** 284
Soup, Turkey-Vegetable, **'84** 4; **'88** 264
Spread, Turkey Party, **'83** 282
Squash Dressing, Turkey with, **'87** 248
Stew, Hearty Turkey, **'79** 252
Stuffed Turkey Breast, **'87** 270
Stuffed Turkey Breast with Seasoned
  Dressing, **'83** 320; **'84** 128
Sweet-and-Sour Turkey, **'79** 252
Tetrazzini, Herbed Turkey, **'86** 47

Turnips

au Gratin, Turnip, **'79** 289
au Gratin, Turnips, **'84** 229; **'88** 229
Boiled Turnips, **'83** 242
Casserole, Baked Turnip, **'82** 274
Casserole, Turnip, **'83** 242; **'84** 229
Cheese Sauce, Turnips in, **'84** 229
Cooked Turnips, Creamy, **'86** 224
Fried Turnips, Shoestring, **'81** 274
Gingered Turnips, **'82** 274
Glazed Turnips, **'81** 274
Greens and Ham Hock, Southern
  Turnip, **'80** 119
Greens, Old-Fashioned Turnip, **'85** 255
Greens with Turnips, Turnip, **'84** 230
Hash Brown Turnips, **'79** 254
Julienne, Turnips and Carrots, **'86** 295
Onions, Turnips and, **'83** 242
Parsleyed Turnips and Carrots, **'79** 253
Party Turnips, **'84** 230
Potatoes, Turnips and, **'79** 254
Saucy Turnips, **'85** 289

Scalloped Potatoes and Turnips, **'85** 235
Scalloped Turnips, **'79** 254
Soufflé, Turnip, **'79** 254
Soup, Creamy Turnip, **'84** 279
Southern Turnips, **'87** 190
Supreme, Turnip, **'79** 254
Sweet-and-Sour Turnips, **'81** 274

Turtle

Fried Cooter (Soft-Shell Turtle), **'80** 99
Soup au Sherry, Turtle, **'80** 56

V

Vanilla

Cake, Vanilla Chiffon, **'79** 266
Cookies, Vanilla Slice-and-Bake, **'85** 171
Cream, Vanilla, **'81** 248; **'83** M115
Crescents, Vanilla, **'82** 307
Cupcakes, Golden Vanilla, **'85** 121
Custard, Baked Vanilla, **'82** 129
Dessert, Glorified Vanilla Sherry, **'81** 85
Extract, Home-Brewed Vanilla, **'83** 228
Extract, Homemade Vanilla, **'83** 228
Frosting, Vanilla, **'84** 36; **'85** 236
Frosting, Vanilla-Rum, **'85** 324
Frosty, French Vanilla, **'79** 148
Fruit Cup, Vanilla, **'80** 183
Glaze, Vanilla, **'85** M89
Helado, Caramel-Vanilla (Caramel-Vanilla
  Ice Cream), **'81** 67
Ice Cream, Basic Vanilla, **'88** 202
Ice Cream, Country Vanilla, **'82** 143
Ice Cream Spectacular, Vanilla, **'82** 166
Ice Cream, Vanilla, **'80** 176; **'86** 129
Pie, Fruit-Topped Vanilla Cream, **'84** 49
Pudding, Creamy Vanilla, **'83** 227
Pudding, Vanilla, **'88** 32
Sauce, Almond-Vanilla Custard, **'88** M177
Soufflé, Frozen Vanilla, **'79** 230; **'82** 173

Veal

Amelio, Veal, **'86** 142
au Madeira, Veal, **'81** 131
Birds, Veal, **'84** 260
Burgoo, Five-Meat, **'87** 3
Casserole, Veal and Wild Rice, **'79** 180
Casserole, Veal Cutlet, **'79** 109
Chops, Apple Veal, **'87** 220
Chops Mediterranean, Veal, **'79** 108
Company Veal and Carrots, **'85** 22
Cordon Bleu, Veal, **'87** 219
Delight, Veal, **'79** 109
Herbed Veal and Onions, **'79** 108
Herbed Veal with Wine, **'86** 193
Italian Style, Veal, **'82** M68
Lemon Veal Piccata, **'86** 118
Lemon Veal with Artichoke Hearts, **'87** 219
Meatballs, European Veal, **'85** 30
Meat Loaf, Italian, **'79** 187
Meat Loaf, Savory, **'87** 216
Meat Loaf, Triple, **'79** 186
New Orleans Veal with Crabmeat, **'86** 94
Paprika, Veal, **'88** 113
Parmigiana, Veal, **'81** 227
Peppercorns, Veal with Green, **'87** 220
Picante, Veal, **'87** 31
Picatta with Capers, Veal, **'87** 142
Roast, Best Baked Veal, **'87** 219
Sauce, Noodles with Veal, **'80** 236

Savory Veal, **'83** 281
Scallopini à la Marsala, Veal, **'79** 109
Scallopini Marsala, Veal, **'85** 295
Scallopini, Veal, **'83** 8, 125
Scaloppine of Veal al Sorriso, **'79** 85
Schnitzel, Swiss, **'80** 189
Skillet Veal, **'83** 200
Spaghetti, Veal, **'84** 276
Spaghetti with Veal and Peppers, **'81** 201;
  '82 14
Steak, Veal, **'82** 276
Stroganoff, Veal, **'79** 108
Supreme, Veal, **'85** 109
Swirls, Veal-and-Smithfield Ham, **'86** 253
Wine Sauce, Veal and Carrots in, **'81** 31;
  '86 M139

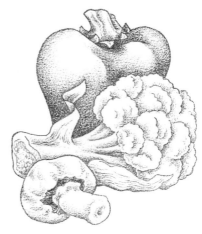

Vegetables. *See also* specific types and
  Canning.

à la Grill, Vegetables, **'88** 130
Antipasto, Vegetable, **'85** 263
Appetizer, Tarragon Vegetable, **'83** 277
Aspic, Cheesy Vegetable, **'81** 73
Beef and Vegetables, Company, **'88** 234
Beef and Vegetables in a Noodle
  Ring, **'85** 285
Beef and Vegetables, Savory, **'79** 163
Beef with Chinese Vegetables, **'81** 211
Blanching Chart, Microwave, **'80** M181
Bread, Breakaway Vegetable, **'82** 74
Bread, Herb-Vegetable-Cheese, **'88** 172
Burgers, Beef-and-Vegetable, **'84** 125
Burritos, Vegetable, **'80** 197
Burritos with Avocado Sauce,
  Vegetable, **'83** 200
Buttermilk Sauce, Vegetables with, **'84** 6
Casserole, Beef and Vegetable Chow
  Mein, **'83** 313
Casserole, Beefy Vegetable, **'79** 248
Casserole, Cheesy Vegetable, **'81** 103
Casserole, Fresh Vegetable, **'82** 225
Casserole, Garden, **'82** 168; **'88** 122
Casserole, Mixed Vegetable, **'83** 208, 256;
  '86 327
Casserole, Mixed-Vegetable, **'87** 154
Casserole, Tuna Vegetable, **'81** 135
Casserole, Vegetable-and-Ham, **'84** 91
Casserole, Veggies, **'88** 123
Chicken and Dumplings with
  Vegetables, **'85** M56
Chicken-and-Vegetable Platter, **'88** M52
Chicken and Vegetables, **'88** 165

Chicken and Vegetables, Almond, **'86** 21
Chicken and Vegetables, Chinese, **'81** 212
Chicken and Vegetables, Lemon, **'88** 118
Chicken and Vegetables, Roast, **'81** 3
Chicken and Vegetables, Walnut, **'85** 194
Chili, Vegetarian, **'84** 280, 327
Chowder, Hearty Vegetable, **'88** 56
Cocktail, Fresh Vegetable, **'82** 165
Creamed Spring Vegetables, **'87** 127
Crêpes, Chicken-Vegetable, **'83** 70
Crêpes, Vegetable-Filled Bran, **'86** 44
Croutons, Vegetable-Flavored, **'84** 148
Dilled Vegetable Sticks, **'88** 179
Dip, Creamy Vegetable, **'83** 180
Dip, Cucumber-Cheese Vegetable, **'83** 128
Dip, Fresh Vegetable, **'80** 249
Dip, Starburst Vegetable, **'82** 248
Dip, Tangy Vegetable, **'87** 196
Dip, Vegetable, **'79** 52; **'82** 161
Dip, Vegetable Garden, **'85** 215
Dip, Zippy Vegetable, **'84** 256
Egg Rolls, Vegetarian, **'86** 148
en Papillote, Chicken and
  Vegetables, **'86** 145
Fennel, Braised, **'88** 46
Fettuccine, Vegetable, **'83** 312
Fish Rolls, Vegetable-Filled, **'86** M251
Flounder Rolls, Vegetable-Stuffed, **'87** 6
Flounder-Vegetable Medley, **'85** 217
Freezing Chart, Vegetable, **'85** 185
Fresh Vegetable Party Tray, **'82** 122
Fresh Vegetable Potpourri, **'79** 208
Fresh Vegetables, Parsley-Dill Dip
  with, **'85** 79
Fried Vegetables, Skillet-, **'88** 156
Garden Combo, **'86** 172
Garden Harvest, **'85** M142
Garden Surprise, **'83** 112
Garnishes, **'82** 280; **'85** 338, 339
Grilled Vegetables, **'84** 172
Grouper with Confetti
  Vegetables, **'88** M189
Ham-and-Vegetables, Skillet, **'84** 90
Herbed-Smoked Vegetables, **'85** 145
Heroes, Vegetable Garden, **'84** 14
Juice Delight, Vegetable, **'84** 58
Julienne Vegetables with Walnuts, **'86** M251
Kabobs, Fresh Vegetable, **'81** 158
Kabobs, Marinated Vegetable, **'83** M195
Kabobs, Tangy Marinated
  Vegetable, **'88** 142
Kabobs, Vegetable, **'87** 116
Lamb with Vegetables, Fillets of, **'85** 36
Lasagna, Cheesy Vegetable, **'79** 84
Lasagna, Colorful Vegetable, **'87** 19
Lasagna, Garden, **'83** 119
Lasagna, Vegetable, **'84** 201
Liver with Vegetables, Calf's, **'85** 219
Loaf, Beef-Vegetable, **'79** 164
Loaf, Pureed Vegetable-Cheese, **'85** 297
Marinade, Fresh Vegetable, **'83** 209
Marinated Vegetable Medley, **'85** 319
Marinated Vegetables, **'79** 146; **'81** 239;
  '85 67; **'86** 286
Marinated Vegetables,
  Sweet-and-Sour, **'83** 266
Marinated Vegetables, Zesty, **'82** 272
Marinated Vegetable Toss, **'82** 113
Meat Loaf, Vegetable, **'85** M29
Medley, Baked Vegetable, **'81** 75
Medley Bake, Vegetable, **'81** 268

Medley, Chinese Vegetable, **'84** 33
Medley, Crunchy Vegetable, **'84** 254
Medley, Fresh Vegetable, **'85** 155
Medley, Green Vegetable, **'79** 287; **'80** 34
Medley, Italian Vegetable, **'88** 143
Medley, Mixed Vegetable, **'82** 126
Medley, Sautéed Vegetable, **'83** 101
Medley, Skillet Vegetable, **'81** 134
Medley, Spring Vegetable, **'86** 115
Medley, Summer Garden, **'84** 158
Medley, Summer Vegetable, **'83** 208
Medley, Vegetable, **'79** 102; **'83** 112;
  '86 327
Microwaving Fresh Vegetables, **'82** M138
Minestrone, **'82** 4

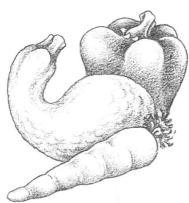

Mixed Vegetables, **'83** M195
Mixed Vegetables, Pasta with Sausage
  and, **'84** 249
Mushroom Caps, Vegetable, **'81** 246
Omelet, Beefy Vegetable, **'83** 188
Omelet, Cheddar-Vegetable, **'83** 205
Omelet, Cheesy Vegetable, **'85** 49
Omelet, Fresh Vegetable, **'84** 211
Omelet, Golden Vegetable, **'82** 123
Omelet Primavera, **'87** 71
Omelet, Puffy Vegetable, **'83** 188
Omelet, Vegetarian, **'84** 114
Open-Faced Vegetarian Melt, **'87** 106
Oriental Vegetables, **'84** 26; **'85** 108
Oriental Vegetables, Beef with, **'84** 140
Paella, Garden, **'82** 245
Paella, Spanish, **'85** 26
Pancakes, Vegetable, **'88** 297
Pasta and Garden Vegetables, **'87** 192
Pasta, Garden, **'82** 199
Pasta Primavera, **'85** 86
Pasta Primavera, Almost, **'86** 38
Pâté, Vegetable-Chicken, **'86** 66
Pepper Cups, Hot Vegetable, **'88** M188
Pie, Chicken-Vegetable Pot, **'81** 281;
  '82 30
Pies, Vegetable-Beef, **'80** 286
Pizza, Deep-Dish Vegetarian, **'85** 243
Platter, Vegetable, **'88** M187
Pockets, Vegetable, **'85** 215
Pork Chops and Garden Vegetables, **'88** 297
Pork Chops, Skillet Vegetable, **'85** 179
Pork Combo, Vegetable-, **'85** 113
Pork with Vegetables, Medaillions
  of, **'88** 223
Potatoes, Vegetable-Topped
  Stuffed, **'85** 235
Pot Roast Medley, Vegetable-, **'83** 319

Vegetables *(continued)*

Pot Roast with Vegetables, '80 59;
  '81 M208
Pot Roast with Vegetables,
  Marinated, '88 M52
Quiche, Cheese-Vegetable, '81 228
Quiche, Ham-and-Vegetable, '84 326
Quiche, Vegetable, '87 M219
Ratatouille, '84 105, 243; '85 92
Ratatouille-Bran Stuffed Eggplant, '86 44
Ratatouille, Eggplant-Zucchini, '81 205
Ratatouille Niçoise, '81 22
Ratatouille Pie, '88 198
Ratatouille, Quick-and-Easy, '80 212
Ratatouille Supreme, '86 172

Relish, Eight-Vegetable, '84 179
Relish, Garden, '83 259
Relish Tree, Christmas, '84 257
Rice Pilaf, Fruit-and-Vegetable, '84 196
Rice with Vegetables, '79 64; '85 83
Ring, Tomato-Vegetable, '81 302
Salads
  Aspic with Horseradish Dressing,
    Crisp Vegetable, '87 152
  Boats, Salad, '80 93
  Calico Salad, '82 35
  Cauliflower-Vegetable Salad, '85 158
  Chinese Salad, '80 4
  Composée, Salad, '79 171
  Congealed Fresh Vegetable
    Salad, '82 240
  Congealed Salad,
    Cheesy-Vegetable, '86 199
  Congealed Vegetable Salad, '79 276
  Corned Beef Salad,
    Vegetable-, '80 148
  Creamy Vegetable Salad, '79 47
  Creole Salad, '79 147
  Crunchy Vegetable Salad, '79 11;
    '80 217; '83 216
  Different Vegetable Salad, '82 143
  Easy Vegetable Salad, '83 316;
    '84 16
  Garden Medley Salad, '80 122
  Garden Salad, '87 62
  Garden Salad Bowl, '82 239
  Greek Salad, Garden, '86 173
  Green-and-White Vegetable
    Salad, '79 286
  Green Vegetable and Egg
    Salad, '79 191
  Green Vegetable Salad,
    Overnight, '80 5
  Italian Vegetable Salad, '81 253;
    '82 19
  Lemon-Vegetable Congealed
    Salad, '85 22
  Luncheon Salad, '84 232

Macaroni-Vegetable Salad, '86 209
Marinade, Garden, '81 23
Marinade, Medley, '79 20
Marinade, Tossed Vegetable, '84 266
Marinated Combo Salad, '82 267
Marinated Garden Vegetables, '87 252
Marinated Salad,
  Eight-Vegetable, '80 218
Marinated Summer Salad, '81 153
Marinated Vegetable-Bacon
  Bowl, '79 191
Marinated Vegetable Patch
  Salad, '84 232
Marinated Vegetables, '88 4, 170
Marinated Vegetable Salad, '79 106,
  143; '81 280; '82 163; '83 260;
  '84 13; '87 243
Marinated Vegetable Salad,
  Crispy, '84 193
Marinated Vegetable Salad,
  Fresh, '86 173
Marinate, Fresh Vegetable, '80 33;
  '81 230
Meal-in-One Salad, '82 232
Medley Salad, Vegetable, '88 86
Mexican Salad, '81 113
Minted Vegetable Salad, '88 23
Mixed Vegetable Salad, '80 115;
  '81 302; '82 239; '83 317; '84 16;
  '86 136
Next-Day Vegetable Salad, '83 81
Oriental Salad, Make-Ahead, '82 163
Oriental Vegetable Salad, '84 290
Rainbow Vegetable Salad, '83 111
Refrigerated Vegetable Salad, '84 120
Relish Salad, Vegetable, '82 267
Rice-and-Vegetable Salad, '86 42
Rice-and-Vegetable Salad,
  Brown, '84 202
Rice Salad, Vegetable-, '80 148;
  '83 198; '85 87
Rolls, Vegetable Salad, '82 278
Senator's Salad, '79 191
Seven-Layer Vegetable Salad, '79 88
Shrimp Salad, Vegetable-, '79 190
Slaw, Vegetable, '81 280
Spring Vegetable Salad, '88 48
Summertime Salad, '79 143
Swedish Vegetable Salad, '82 23
Sweet-and-Sour Vegetable
  Salad, '81 25
Tangy Vegetable Toss, '79 144
Tarragon-Vegetable Salad, '85 288
Variety Salad, '79 113
Vinaigrette Salad,
  Vegetable-Chicken, '86 135
Vinaigrette, Vegetables, '82 225, 290
Walnuts, Vegetable Salad with,
  '86 118
Winter Vegetable Salad, '86 42
Sandwiches, Open-Face Tofu-Veggie, '86 5
Sandwiches, Vegetarian Pita, '84 193
Sandwich, Vegetable Puff, '85 51
Sauce, Greek Fish with Vegetable, '82 72
Sauce, Pasta with Vegetable, '83 163
Sauce, Turkey Patties in
  Vegetable-Tomato, '87 18
Sauce, Vegetable Butter, '86 174
Sauce, Vegetable-Cheese, '85 M152
Sausage Vegetable Dinner, '84 250
Sautéed Vegetables with Spaghetti, '81 89

Sautéed Vegetables with Spaghetti
  Squash, '84 128
Sauté, Garden, '87 90
Sautéing Fresh Vegetables, '82 138
Scalloped Mixed Vegetables, '83 5
Scallops en Brochette with
  Vegetables, '80 163
Scallops with Vegetables, Bay, '84 233
Seasoning Blend, Vegetable, '88 29
Sesame Sauce, Vegetables with, '83 112
Shrimp and Vegetables, '82 6
Skillet, Vegetable-Beef, '86 172

Soups
  Bean Soup, Vegetable-, '83 317
  Beef Soup, Hearty Vegetable-, '84 102
  Beef Soup, Spicy Vegetable-, '88 11
  Beef Soup, Vegetable-, '88 296
  Beefy Vegetable Soup, '79 113;
    '84 M38
  Beefy Vegetable Soup, Quick, '80 25
  Burger Soup, Vegetable-, '82 6
  Cheese Soup, Creamy
    Vegetable-, '81 244
  Cheese Soup, Creamy
    Vegetable, '83 230
  Cheesy Vegetable Chowder, '80 25;
    '83 20
  Cheesy Vegetable Soup, '80 73
  Chicken-Vegetable Soup, '88 18
  Clear Vegetable Soup, '79 130
  Garden Soup, '85 241
  Garden Vegetable Soup, '83 140;
    '86 160
  Garden Vegetable Soup, Cold, '84 197
  Gazpacho, '84 112; '85 164
  Gazpacho, Chilled, '84 138
  Gazpacho, Cool, '83 140
  Gazpacho, Spring, '81 112
  Gazpacho, Summer, '84 181
  Harvest Chowder, '83 317
  Harvest Soup, '79 101
  Hearty Vegetable Soup, '80 26
  Homemade Soup, '79 198
  Leek-Vegetable Soup, '86 304
  Light Vegetable Soup, '84 280
  Marvelous Vegetable Soup, '82 3
  Mix, Vegetable Soup, '84 148
  Old-Fashioned Vegetable Soup, '86 304
  Quick Vegetable Soup, '79 190;
    '85 24, 32
  Savory Vegetable Broth, '81 230
  Shrimp-Vegetable Bisque, '82 313;
    '83 66
  Spicy Vegetable Soup, '79 198
  Tomato-Vegetable Soup, '81 177;
    '86 9

Turkey-Vegetable Soup, '84 4;
  '88 264
  Vegetable Soup, '80 128; '84 148;
  '85 106; '86 187; '87 83, 123;
  '88 266
Spaghetti, Fresh Vegetables with, '86 257
Spaghetti with Vegetables, '85 67
Spicy Vegetables and Sausage, '80 82
Spread, Garden, '86 135
Spread, Vegetable-Egg, '87 106
Spread, Vegetable Party, '84 166
Spread, Vegetable Sandwich, '83 174;
  '85 135
Squash, Vegetable-Stuffed, '84 104
Steak with Vegetables, Skewered, '81 124
Steak with Vegetables, Swiss, '81 273
Steamed and Minted Garden Toss, '83 173
Steamed Dinner, Easy, '83 M314
Steamed Vegetable Medley, '86 50
Steamed Vegetables with Mustard
  Sauce, '83 208
Steaming Fresh Vegetables, '82 138, 183
Stew, Fish-and-Vegetable, '87 220
Stew, Mixed Vegetable, '84 13
Stew, Sweet-and-Sour Beef and
  Vegetable, '85 87

Stir-Fried Beef and Vegetables, '88 301
Stir-Fried Vegetables, '79 217; '83 193
Stir-Fried Vegetables with Curry, '87 51
Stir-Fry, Almond-Vegetable, '86 222
Stir-Fry, Beef-and-Vegetable, '81 211;
  '87 22
Stir-Fry Beef-and-Vegetables, '84 141
Stir-Fry, Chicken and Vegetable, '82 237
Stir-Fry Chicken-and-Vegetables, '86 68
Stir-Fry Chicken and Vegetables, '86 249
Stir-Fry, Chicken-Vegetable, '83 151;
  '84 13, 141
Stir-Frying Fresh Vegetables, '82 138
Stir-Fry Medley, '88 156
Stir-Fry, Mixed Vegetable, '79 268; '80 14
Stir-Fry Sausage and Vegetables, '86 213;
  '87 82
Stir-Fry Shrimp and Vegetables, '87 91
Stir-Fry, Steak-and-Vegetable, '84 8
Stir-Fry, Three-Vegetable, '86 174
Stir-Fry, Vegetable, '79 214; '82 M172,
  208; '84 104
Stir-Fry, Vegetable Medley, '85 109
Stir-Fry Vegetables with Chicken, '84 195
Succotash, '85 106
Succotash, Easy, '80 165

Succotash, Summer, '86 170
Supper, Vegetarian, '86 222
Tempura, Basic, '81 68
Tempura, Cornmeal, '81 68
Tempura, Vegetable, '79 112
Terrine, Chicken-Vegetable, '84 131
Terrine, Vegetable-Chicken, '83 224
Topper, Vegetable-Cheese Potato, '86 6
Topping, Vegetable, '79 79
Torte, Layered Vegetable, '84 52
Trio, Vegetable-Herb, '83 172
Turnovers, Vegetable, '86 24
Venison-Vegetable Bake, '87 304
Vermicelli, Scallop-Vegetable, '87 143
Vermouth, Chicken and
  Vegetables, '87 M37
Wine-Soaked Vegetables, Baked Chicken
  with, '84 277

Venison
Appetizers, Venison Tenderloin, '88 249
Bake, Venison-Vegetable, '87 304
Balls, Venison Sausage, '80 42
Burgers, Venison, '87 304
Chili, Double-Meat, '79 269; '80 12
Chili, Venison, '82 216; '86 3; '87 304
Fried Venison, Country-, '81 233
Kabobs, Venison, '82 215; '88 249
Roast, Venison, '82 226
Roast with Red Wine Gravy,
  Venison, '85 270
Soup, Venison, '82 216
Steak, Country-Fried Venison, '83 262
Steaks, Country-Style Venison, '82 215
Steaks, Grilled Venison, '82 215
Stew, Venison, '86 294
Stew, Venison Sausage, '87 238
Stew with Potato Dumplings,
  Venison, '87 304
Tomatoes, Venison and, '85 270

Vinegars
Dill-and-Chive Vinegar, '84 300
Garlic-Basil Vinegar, '85 124
Herb Vinegar, Five-, '85 124
Herb Vinegar, Homemade, '79 100
Herb Vinegar, Mixed, '84 107
Lemon-Mint Vinegar, '85 124
Oregano-Lemon Vinegar, Spicy, '85 124
Raspberry-Lemon Vinegar, '87 134
Tarragon-Dill Vinegar, '85 124
Tarragon Vinegar, '84 107

W

Waffles
Banana-Ginger Waffles, '86 96
Chicken-Pecan Waffles, Southern, '82 231
Chocolate Waffles with Strawberry
  Cream, '88 153
Cornbread Waffles, '79 265
Cornmeal Waffles, '85 201
Crunchy Brunch Waffles, '81 41
French Toast, Waffled, '82 47
French Waffles, '86 138
Ham Waffles, '80 44
Oatmeal-Nut Waffles, '83 96
Pecan Waffles, '87 225
Potato Waffles, Sweet, '88 208
Pumpkin-Nut Waffles, '86 96

Quick Bread Mix, '81 90
Quick Mix Waffles, '86 9
Refrigerator Waffles, Best Ever, '87 225
Sausage Waffles, '83 50
Sorghum-Ginger Waffles, '85 239

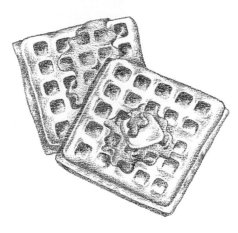

Southern Waffles, '87 225
Tuna Waffle-Wich, Hot, '88 272
Waffles, '81 90
Walnut Waffles, Crunchy, '85 48
Whole Wheat Dessert Waffle, '79 92
Whole Wheat Waffles, '84 228

Walnuts
Bonbons, Coconut-Black Walnut, '82 307
Bread, Apple-Nut, '79 12
Bread, Applesauce-Honey Nut, '87 300
Bread, Apricot-Nut, '79 24
Bread, Carrot-Walnut, '88 284
Bread, Cherry Nut, '81 306; '82 36
Bread, Chocolate Date-Nut, '81 284
Bread, Cinnamon-Nut Bubble, '80 22
Bread, Cranberry-Orange Nut, '80 288
Bread, Date-Nut, '85 306
Bread, Fresh Apple-Nut, '87 256
Bread, Wine-Date Nut, '82 253
Brie, Walnut-Fried, '86 244
Brownies, Walnut-Cream Cheese, '84 240
Burgers, Nutty, '87 185
Cake, Apple-Nut, '87 76
Cake, Black Walnut, '80 253; '84 316
Cake, Cranberry-Nut Coffee, '81 250
Cake, Orange Nut, '80 70
Cake, Orange-Nut Butter, '80 254
Cakes, Mini-Mincemeat Nut, '88 257
Cake, Sour Cream-Walnut Coffee, '79 209
Candied Nuts, '81 261
Carrots with Walnuts, Julienne, '84 188
Cheese, Nutty Date Dessert, '87 299
Chicken and Vegetables, Walnut, '85 194
Chicken Breasts, Walnut-Stuffed, '85 293
Chicken, Deep-Fried Walnut, '87 175
Chicken, Walnut, '85 126
Chocolate-Nut Chews, '81 92
Cobbler, Apple-Walnut, '79 154; '81 248
Cookies, Apple-Nut, '80 228
Cookies, Frosted Pumpkin-Walnut, '82 217
Cookies, Nutty Oatmeal, '81 130
Cookies, Walnut, '81 301
Cupcakes, Apple-Nut, '82 279
Cups, Chocolate-Walnut, '85 213
Filling, Honey-Walnut, '80 21
Fried Walnuts, Chinese, '81 254

Walnuts *(continued)*

Frosting, Nutty Coconut, **'86** 8
Fudge, Nutty White, **'81** 253
Honey-Walnut Swirl, **'80** 21
Loaf, Apricot-Nut, **'81** 8
Loaf, Blue Ribbon Date-Walnut, **'80** 15
Meatballs, Mock, **'81** 243
Mousse, Coffee-Nut, **'86** 319
Muffins, Carrot-Date-Nut, **'86** 262
Muffins, Nutty Pumpkin, **'86** 291
Pie, Walnut-Cranberry, **'87** 259
Pitas, Spinach-Walnut, **'87** 202; **'88** 43
Salad, Orange Walnut, **'80** 246
Salad, Shrimp-Walnut, **'86** 182
Salad with Walnuts, Vegetable, **'86** 118
Sauce, Apricot-Walnut Hard, **'88** 153
Sauce, Spaghetti with Parsley and
  Walnut, **'80** 30
Sautéed Walnuts, Turkey Salad
  with, **'86** 117
Sherry-Orange Nuts, **'86** M289
Slaw, Nutty Apple, **'88** 216
Spread, Date-Walnut, **'87** 292
Spread, Nutty Fruit-and-Cheese, **'87** 246
Strawberries with Walnuts,
  Stuffed, **'85** 122; **'86** 124
Sweet Potatoes with Sherry and
  Walnuts, **'86** 286
Syrup, Maple-Nut, **'80** 228
Topping, Nutty, **'86** 16
Twists, Fruit-Nut, **'82** 253

Vegetables with Walnuts,
  Julienne, **'86** M251
Waffles, Crunchy Walnut, **'85** 48
Zucchini with Walnuts, **'84** 213
Watermelon. *See* Melons.
Wheat Germ
Biscuits, Wheat Germ, **'86** 261
Bread, Banana Wheat, **'81** 14
Crackers, Oatmeal-Wheat Germ, **'84** 236
Crisps, Sesame Wheat, **'81** 106
Muffins, Carrot-Wheat, **'88** 9
Muffins, Wheat Germ-Prune, **'81** 106
Pancakes, Wheat Germ, **'86** 242
Pancakes, Wheat Germ-Banana, **'79** 114
Squares, Spicy Wheat Germ, **'80** 44
Wild Rice. *See* Rice/Wild Rice.
Wok Cooking
Asparagus and Mushrooms, **'85** 108
Asparagus, Stir-Fried, **'87** 52
Bean Medley, Green, **'85** 108
Beans, Stir-Fried Green, **'85** 148
Beef and Broccoli, Stir-Fry, **'79** 47
Beef and Pea Pods, Stir-Fry, **'80** 19
Beef and Snow Peas, Oriental, **'79** 105
Beef and Snow Peas, Stir-Fry, **'83** 22
Beef and Snow Pea Stir-Fry, **'82** 98
Beef and Vegetables, Stir-Fried, **'88** 301
Beef-and-Vegetables, Stir-Fry, **'84** 141

Beef-and-Vegetable Stir-Fry, **'81** 211;
  '87 22
Beef, Chinese-Style, **'87** 50
Beef, Mongolian, **'85** 2, 75
Beef, Oriental, **'85** 20
Beef over Rice Noodles, Shredded, **'85** 74
Beef Stew, **'86** 51
Beef, Stir-Fried, **'84** 26
Beef Stir-Fry, Chinese, **'83** 151
Beef with Chinese Vegetables, **'81** 211
Beef with Oriental Vegetables, **'84** 140
Bok Choy-Broccoli Stir-Fry, **'84** 2
Broccoli and Beef, Stir-Fry, **'83** 110
Broccoli, Jade-Green, **'80** 12
Broccoli, Stir-Fried, **'83** 227
Broccoli, Stir-Fry, **'80** 19
Broccoli with Sesame, **'80** 13
Broccoli with Sesame Seeds, **'82** 34
Brussels Sprouts Stir-Fry, **'81** 308
Cabbage, Lemon-Butter, **'88** 156
Cabbage, Stir-Fried, **'81** 75, 271; **'85** 109
Catfish Stir, **'84** 184
Cheese Wontons with Hot Sauce, **'83** 74
Chicken à l'Orange, Stir-Fry, **'83** 82
Chicken and Vegetables, Almond, **'86** 21
Chicken and Vegetables, Chinese, **'81** 212
Chicken-and-Vegetables, Stir-Fry, **'86** 68
Chicken and Vegetable Stir-Fry, **'82** 237
Chicken and Vegetables, Walnut, **'85** 194
Chicken, Braised Bourbon, **'86** 51
Chicken-Broccoli Stir-Fry, **'82** 33
Chicken, Cashew, **'79** 255; **'83** 21
Chicken Curry, Stir-Fried, **'87** 51
Chicken-in-a-Garden, **'80** 18
Chicken in Soy and Wine, **'84** 26
Chicken, Lemon, **'86** 173
Chicken, Princess, **'86** 122
Chicken Stir-Fry, Kyoto Orange-, **'87** 96
Chicken Stir-Fry, Orange-, **'84** 68
Chicken, Stir-Fry Vegetables with, **'84** 195
Chicken, Sweet-and-Sour, **'86** 240
Chicken, Szechwan, **'83** 85
Chicken Tempura Delight, **'85** 66
Chicken-Vegetable Stir-Fry, **'83** 151;
  '84 13, 141
Chicken, Walnut, **'85** 126
Chicken with Cashews, **'79** 207
Chicken with Cashews, Szechwan, **'81** 212
Chicken with Peanuts, Oriental, **'82** 236
Chicken with Pineapple, Oriental, **'86** 42
Chicken with Plum Sauce, **'82** 236
Chicken, Zesty Stir-Fried, **'83** 82
Chicken-Zucchini Stir-Fry, **'84** 50
Chinese-Style Dinner, **'84** 26
Egg Rolls, **'86** 81
Eggrolls, Shrimp and Pork, **'82** 240; **'83** 18
Egg Rolls, Vegetarian, **'86** 148
Ham and Zucchini Stir-Fry, **'79** 47
Ham Stir-Fry, Easy, **'86** 332
Meatballs, Sweet-and-Sour, **'86** 240
Medley, Stir-Fry, **'88** 156
Mushrooms with Bacon, Stir-Fried, **'80** 123
Pear Fritters, Ol' Timey, **'86** 51
Peas and Peppers, Stir-Fried, **'87** 51
Pork-and-Onions with Bean Sauce, **'85** 76
Pork, Hot-and-Spicy, **'81** 228
Pork in Garlic Sauce, Stir-Fried, **'84** 141
Pork Oriental, **'81** 212
Pork, Stir-Fried, **'87** 51
Pork, Sweet-and-Sour, **'79** 42; **'80** 227;
  '81 26; **'85** 34, 194

Pork Tenderloin, Curried, **'86** 76
Potato Pudding, Sweet, **'86** 52
Potato-Snow Pea Stir-Fry, **'86** 173
Rice, Easy Fried, **'84** 76
Rice, Egg Fried, **'80** 19
Rice Special, Fried, **'80** 56
Rice with Sausage, Fried, **'83** 12
Sausage Rolls with Sweet-and-Sour
  Sauce, **'83** 74
Sausage Stir-Fry, **'82** 236
Shrimp and Sirloin Supreme, **'81** 131
Shrimp and Vegetables, Stir-Fry, **'87** 91
Shrimp Skillet, Quick, **'87** 50
Shrimp, Szechuan, **'86** 173
Shrimp with Snow Peas, **'85** 75
Spinach, Chinese, **'79** 179
Spinach, Stir-Fry, **'81** 182
Spinach with Mushrooms, **'80** 19
Spinach Wontons, **'83** 74
Squash Medley, **'84** 128
Squash Medley, Stir-Fried, **'80** 123
Squash Stir-Fry, **'80** 184
Squash Stir-Fry, Two-, **'86** 174
Steak, Chinese Pepper, **'82** 236
Steak, Fast-and-Easy Stir-Fried, **'87** 50
Steak, Pepper Stir-Fry, **'81** 240
Steak Sukiyaki, Flank, **'88** 233
Sugar Flips, **'83** 74
Teriyaki Stir-Fry, **'83** 110
Tomato-Zucchini Stir-Fry, **'80** 158
Vegetable Medley, Chinese, **'84** 33
Vegetable Medley Stir-Fry, **'85** 109
Vegetables, Oriental, **'84** 26; **'85** 108
Vegetables, Skillet-Fried, **'88** 156
Vegetables, Stir-Fried, **'79** 217; **'83** 193
Vegetable Stir-Fry, **'82** 208; **'84** 104
Vegetable Stir-Fry, Mixed, **'79** 268; **'80** 14
Vegetable Stir-Fry, Three-, **'86** 174
Vegetables with Curry, Stir-Fried, **'87** 51
Wontons, Tex-Mex, **'87** 196
Zucchini-and-Tomato Stir-Fry, **'85** 108
Zucchini, Italian-Style, **'80** 123
Zucchini Pesto, **'84** 194
Zucchini Toss, Stir-Fry, **'88** 156
Wontons
Cheese Wontons with Hot Sauce, **'83** 74
Fried Wontons, Crispy, **'83** 21
Fruit-Filled Wontons, **'85** 287
Nibbles, Wonton, **'85** 287
Preparation Techniques, **'83** 74
Sausage Rolls with Sweet-and-Sour
  Sauce, **'83** 74
Spinach Wontons, **'83** 74
Sugar Flips, **'83** 74
Tex-Mex Wontons, **'87** 196

Y

Yogurt
Bars, Lemon Yogurt Wheat, **'79** 93
Cake, Yogurt Pound, **'84** 10
Chicken, Grilled Yogurt-Lemon, **'81** 111
Dip, Curry, **'85** 132
Dip, Fruited Yogurt, **'84** 171
Dip, Yogurt Herring, **'80** 232
Dressing, Asparagus with Yogurt, **'79** 66
Dressing, Ginger-Yogurt, **'81** 302
Dressing, Orange-Yogurt, **'85** 304

Dressing, Sweet-Hot Yogurt, '86 40
Dressing, Turkey Waldorf Salad with
    Yogurt, '88 53
Dressing, Yogurt, '85 59, 215; '88 27
Dressing, Yogurt-Honey Poppy
    Seed, '83 177
Dressing, Yogurt Salad, '79 69
Ice, Apricot Yogurt, '81 177
Ice, Peach-Yogurt, '84 83
Lemon-Chiffon Frozen Yogurt, '85 54
Muffins, Yogurt, '88 55
Nectarines Royale, '85 132
Omelet, Yogurt-Avocado, '81 33
Pancakes, Orange-Yogurt, '87 225
Parfait, Crunchy
    Strawberry-Yogurt, '79 124
Pie, Strawberry Yogurt, '80 232
Pie, Strawberry-Yogurt, '85 122; '86 124
Pie, Yogurt-Apricot, '85 132
Pie, Yogurt-Cheese, '82 121
Potatoes, Yogurt-Stuffed, '88 24
Salad, Crème de Menthe, '82 122
Salad, Cucumber-Yogurt, '87 33
Salad, Strawberry Yogurt, '80 232
Salad, Yogurt-Cucumber, '82 122
Salad, Yogurt Fruit, '81 114
Sauce, Lamb Meatballs with
    Yogurt, '85 132
Sauce, Yogurt-Horseradish, '85 66
Shake, Strawberry-Yogurt, '87 199
Slaw or Salad Dressing,
    Lemon-Yogurt, '88 54
Smoothie, Fruited Honey-Yogurt, '88 231
Snack, Yogurt, '88 55
Soup, Avocado-Banana-Yogurt, '80 78
Soup, Cucumber-Yogurt, '82 157; '83 205
Soup, Yogurt Fruit, '86 176
Strawberry Yogurt Delight, '85 77
Topping, Yogurt-Cheese, '88 55
Vanilla Frozen Yogurt, '87 125

Z

Zucchini
au Gratin, Potatoes-and-Zucchini, '84 5
au Gratin, Zucchini and Tomato, '82 208
Bake, Corn-Zucchini, '79 178
Baked Zucchini, '83 209
Baked Zucchini and Sausages, '80 300
Baked Zucchini Fans, '87 243
Bake, Squash, '82 107
Bake, Zucchini and Tomato, '82 158
Bake, Zucchini-Beef, '86 146
Bars, Zucchini, '85 77
Beans with Zucchini, Green, '84 128
Bites, Crab-Zucchini, '84 M216
Boats with Spinach, Zucchini, '82 252
Boats, Zucchini, '85 M143
Bread, Banana-Zucchini, '85 326
Bread, Spiced Zucchini, '79 161; '86 162
Bread, Spicy Zucchini, '81 305; '82 36
Bread, Zucchini, '85 111; '86 93
Bread, Zucchini-Apple, '87 255
Bread, Zucchini-Carrot, '83 190
Broiled Zucchini, Quick-and-Easy, '86 169
Buttered Zucchini and Carrots, '83 252
Cajun Squash, '88 142
Cake, Chocolate-Zucchini, '85 156

Cake, Zucchini, '79 24
Calabaza Guisada con Puerco (Pumpkin
    Cooked with Pork), '80 193
Calabaza Mexicana (Mexican
    Squash), '81 196
Carrots and Zucchini, '84 262
Carrots, Zucchini with Baby, '88 24
Casserole, Carrot and Zucchini, '83 256
Casserole, Cheese-Egg-Zucchini, '84 114
Casserole, Cheesy Zucchini, '82 168;
    '84 145
Casserole, Italian Zucchini, '85 59
Casserole, Zucchini, '79 157; '87 154
Casserole, Zucchini-and-Tomato, '88 265
Casserole, Zucchini-Egg, '84 M113
Casserole, Zucchini-Jack, '85 296
Caviar, Zucchini, '88 212
Combo, Zucchini-Corn, '86 218
Corn and Zucchini, '83 190
Corn, Zucchini and, '86 177
Crêpes, Zucchini, '79 157
Delight, Zucchini-Basil, '85 267
Dilled Fresh Zucchini, '81 174
Dilled Zucchini and Corn, '83 173
Dressing, Zucchini, '86 282
Easy Zucchini, '87 167
Eggplant and Squash, '83 187
Eggplant and Zucchini,
    Italian-Style, '79 289; '80 26
Eggplant and Zucchini, Sautéed, '82 96
Fans, Baked Zucchini, '88 246
Fried Zucchini, Oven-, '86 211
Fried Zucchini Strips, '81 184
Fried Zucchini with Cocktail Sauce,
    French, '86 146
Fries, Zucchini French, '82 78
Frittata, Zucchini, '86 103

Fritters, Cheesy Zucchini, '88 44
Fritters, Zucchini, '81 163
Fruitcake, Zucchini, '88 284
Fry, Zucchini, '81 102
Herbed Zucchini, '84 104
Hors d'Oeuvres, Zucchini, '80 151
Italiano, Zucchini, '81 183
Italian Squash, '79 158
Italian-Style Zucchini, '80 123
Italian Zucchini, '83 M147
Lasagna, Garden, '83 119
Lasagna, Zucchini, '85 194
Manicotti, Zucchini, '84 194
Marinated Zucchini, '80 33
Medley, Zucchini-and-Corn, '80 298; '81 25
Mexican Squash, '83 31
Mexican Style, Zucchini, '80 184
Muffins, Zucchini, '83 121; '86 146
Omelet, Zucchini, '81 99

Parmesan, Zucchini, '81 108; '82 103
Parmesan Zucchini, '81 234
Pecans, Zucchini with, '87 31
Pesto, Zucchini, '84 194
Pie, Cheesy Zucchini, '82 103
Pie, Italian-Style Zucchini, '83 43
Pie, Zucchini-Ham-Cheese, '80 272
Pizzas, Zucchini, '88 212
Pollo con Calabacita (Mexican Chicken with
    Zucchini), '82 219
Provençal, Zucchini, '86 146
Quiche, Cheesy Zucchini, '83 312
Quiche, Swiss-Zucchini, '82 49
Quiche, Zucchini-Mushroom, '79 127
Quiche, Zucchini-Sausage, '83 122
Ratatouille, '84 105, 243; '85 92
Ratatouille, Eggplant-Zucchini, '81 205
Ratatouille Niçoise, '81 22
Ratatouille, Quick-and-Easy, '80 212
Ratatouille-Stuffed Eggplant, '83 187
Relish, Zucchini, '87 200
Rosemary, Summer Squash with, '88 143
Salad, Carrot-and-Zucchini, '83 240
Salad, Creamy Avocado and
    Zucchini, '79 208
Salad, Marinated Zucchini, '82 164
Salad, Mushroom-Zucchini, '85 8
Salad, Turkey-Zucchini, '85 74
Salad, Zucchini, '82 104; '87 103
Salad, Zucchini Chef's, '83 143
Sandwiches, Open-Faced Zucchini, '88 159
Sauce, Spaghetti with Zucchini, '81 38
Sautéed Zucchini, '83 86
Sautéed Zucchini and Sausage, '83 289
Sauté, Zucchini, '81 183; '84 35
Scallop, Green-and-Gold, '81 159
Scramble, Zucchini-Basil, '87 34
Skillet, Pattypan-Zucchini, '82 103
Skillet, Squash, '82 195
Skillet, Zippy Zucchini, '82 158
Soufflé, Zucchini, '79 157
Soufflé, Zucchini-and-Corn, '83 265
Soup, Chilled Zucchini, '87 90
Soup, Cold Zucchini, '85 265
Soup, Cream of Zucchini, '83 99
Soup, Creamy Zucchini, '83 140
Soup, Italian Sausage-Zucchini, '84 4
Soup, Summer Squash, '84 193
Soup, Zucchini, '82 104; '84 181; '86 181
South-of-the-Border Zucchini, '85 135
Spaghetti, Italian Zucchini, '85 2
Spaghetti, Zucchini, '83 160
Squares, Zucchini, '82 103
Stir-Fried Squash Medley, '80 123
Stir-Fry, Chicken-Zucchini, '84 50
Stir-Fry, Ham and Zucchini, '79 47
Stir-Fry, Squash, '80 184
Stir-Fry, Tomato-Zucchini, '80 158
Stir-Fry, Two-Squash, '86 174
Stir-Fry, Zucchini-and-Tomato, '85 108
Stir-Fry Zucchini Toss, '88 156
Stuffed Zucchini, '86 54, 187
Stuffed Zucchini, Beef-, '86 M139
Stuffed Zucchini, Ham and Cheese, '79 157
Stuffed Zucchini, Italian, '84 119
Stuffed Zucchini Main Dish, '79 215
Stuffed Zucchini, Savory, '80 161
Stuffed Zucchini Supreme, '83 136
Stuffing, Haddock Fillets with
    Zucchini, '88 M191
Walnuts, Zucchini with, '84 213

Favorite Recipes

Record your favorite recipes below for quick and handy reference.

Appetizers	Source/Page	Remarks

Beverages	Source/Page	Remarks

Breads	Source/Page	Remarks

Desserts	Source/Page	Remarks

Eggs and Cheese   Source/Page   Remarks

_____

_____

_____

_____

_____

_____

_____

_____

_____

_____

_____

_____

_____

_____

_____

_____

_____

Meats   Source/Page   Remarks

_____

_____

_____

_____

_____

_____

_____

_____

_____

_____

_____

_____

_____

_____

_____

_____

Pasta	Source/Page	Remarks

Salads	Source/Page	Remarks

Soups and Stews   Source/Page   Remarks

Vegetables and Side Dishes   Source/Page   Remarks